Can you determine correct radical? — NO → Can you count the total number of strokes in the kanji?

YES

Locate kanji in Radical Chart (endpaper) or Radical Index (p. 835).

YES

Locate kanji in Stroke Index (p. 885).

Turn to page as indicated in Radical Index.

Turn to page as indicated in Stroke Index.

END

END

KODANSHA'S ESSENTIAL
KANJI DICTIONARY

KODANSHA'S ESSENTIAL KANJI DICTIONARY

A compact character dictionary
for students and professionals

KODANSHA INTERNATIONAL
Tokyo · New York · London

Previously published by Kodansha International Ltd. under the title *Kodansha's Compact Kanji Guide*.

Distributed in the United States by Kodansha America, Inc., and in the United Kingdom and continental Europe by Kodansha Europe Ltd.

Published by Kodansha International Ltd., 17-14, Otowa 1-chome, Bunkyo-ku, Tokyo 112-8652 and Kodansha America, Inc.

ISBN-13: 978-4-7700-2891-4
ISBN-10: 4-7700-2891-1

Original edition, 1991
First edition, 2002
12 11 10 09 08 07 06 05   12 11 10 9 8 7 6 5

www.kodansha-intl.com

CONTENTS

Publisher's Note   ix

Introduction to the Japanese Writing System   xiii

User's Manual   xxiii

THE JŌYŌ KANJI   1

Radical Index   835

ON/KUN Index   853

Stroke Index   885

KODANSHA'S ESSENTIAL
KANJI DICTIONARY

PUBLISHER'S NOTE

Kodansha's Essential Kanji Dictionary is an up-to-date dictionary of Jōyō Kanji, the 1,945 most commonly used characters in modern Japanese writing. It aims to be as comprehensive as possible within self-imposed limits, but at the same time to be portable and handy. Maximum priority has been given to ease of access: first, by listing the characters according to their most familiar, traditional radicals; and secondly, by providing three types of indices to facilitate the often time-consuming task of locating the desired character. Definitions of individual characters and kanji compounds are given in clear, straightforward English. Distinctions are made between noun and verb forms of character compounds for utmost precision.

In the realm of kanji compounds, particular attention has been paid to combinations that appear frequently in contemporary newspapers, magazines, and other forms of mass media, but which are sometimes neglected in Japanese-English dictionaries. Thus, the *Essential Kanji Dictionary* does not confine itself to the standard selection of compounds. It chooses, rather, to include any kanji combination that is likely to be a problem for the student of modern Japanese.

The *Essential Kanji Dictionary* devotes considerable space to the language of the business world—financial terms, business jargon, special business senses of ordinary words, and many standard business abbreviations. Some 2,000 kanji compounds of immediate use to the businessperson studying Japanese are set off for ready reference. It is hoped that this sampling will provide a foundation for further study and the eventual mastery of this sphere of written Japanese.

In the compilation of the *Essential Kanji Dictionary*, numerous domestic Japanese and Japanese-English character dictionaries were consulted, the most important of which are listed below. Meanings given for characters and compounds follow modern domestic and Japanese-English practice.

Nelson, Andrew Nathaniel. *The Modern Reader's Japanese-English Character Dictionary.* Second revised edition. Tokyo: Charles E. Tuttle Company, 1974.

Nishio Minoru et al. *Iwanami Kokugo Jiten.* Tokyo: Iwanami Shoten, 1986.

Onoue Kanehide et al. *Ōbunsha Shōgaku Kanji Saishin Jiten.* Tokyo: Obunsha, 1990.

Ōmura Hama et al. *Sanseidō Shōgaku Kanwa Jiten.* Tokyo: Sanseido, 1989.

Masuda, Koh et al. *Kenkyusha's New Japanese-English Dictionary.* Fourth edition. Tokyo: Kenkyusha, 1974.

Spann, M., and W. Hadamitzky. *Japanese Character Dictionary: With Compound Lookup via any Kanji.* Tokyo: Nichigai Associates, 1989.

Suzuki Shūji et al. *Kadokawa Saishin Kanwa Jiten.* Tokyo: Kadokawa Shoten, 1990.

Umesao Tadao et al. *Nihongo Daijiten.* Tokyo: Kodansha, 1989.

Yamaguchi Akiho et al. *Iwanami Kango Jiten.* Tokyo: Iwanami Shoten, 1987.

Global Management Group. *Shin Bijinesu Eigo Daijiten.* Tokyo: PMC, 1990.

Kodansha's Essential Kanji Dictionary has been previously published as *Kodansha's Compact Kanji Guide*. The compilation of the *Guide* was a collaborative effort, and the publisher wishes to thank the many people who took part in the project, in particular Yvette Flower, whose invaluable advice and energetic, dependable work were a great factor in bringing the book into being. Special thanks are also owed to Kaoru Ichikawa of AJALT, who rigorously reviewed the choice of entries for relevance and accuracy. The publisher is likewise heavily indebted to Stefan Kaiser of the Institute of Literature and Linguistics, University of Tsukuba, who kindly undertook the task of writing the introduction to the Japanese writing system. A heartfelt thank-you is due Yukie Seki, Yoshie Hamano, and Megumi Shimonoto, whose efforts were indispensable to the completion of the book. Appreciation is also extended to Laura Holland for her timely assistance. The publisher is grateful to the Toppan Printing Company for developing the computer program that expedited the typesetting of the dictionary.

INTRODUCTION TO THE JAPANESE WRITING SYSTEM

Stefan Kaiser

1. A Mixed Writing System

Japanese is written with a combination of kanji (Chinese characters) and two sets of phonetic syllabaries or *kana*, known as *hiragana* and *katakana*. Apart from a few exceptions, such as children's books (written in *hiragana*), Japanese Braille (*hiragana* based), and telegrams (traditionally written in *katakana*), these components are rarely used independently in running text.

Kanji, *hiragana*, and *katakana* are therefore not three separate writing systems but rather three different but complementary scripts used in conjunction within the Japanese writing system. They can be broadly defined as follows: (1) Kanji. Used for elements that carry meaning (or content), such as proper and common nouns, and the stem part of verbs and adjectives. (2) *Katakana* (the angular *kana* script). Used in a similar way to that of italics in English: namely, for foreign words and names (other than those that have been rendered into kanji), certain scientific and technical terms (such as names of species), and for emphasis of a particular word or phrase in a sentence. (3) *Hiragana* (the cursive *kana* script). Used for functional elements expressing grammatical relations (case particles, conjunctions, etc.) and inflectional endings.

In sum, kanji and *katakana* can be grouped together as expressing content units (often compared to building blocks), whereas *hiragana* is used to hold units (blocks) together within sentences like mortar.

この自動車はデザインがたいへん優れている。
"The design of this car is quite outstanding."

Here, the noun *jidōsha* "car" and the stem of the verb *sugureru* "be outstanding" are written in kanji; the foreign word *dezain* "design" is written in *katakana*; and grammatical elements such as the determiner *kono* "this," the adverb of degree *taihen* "quite," the topic and subject particles *wa* and *ga*, and the inflectional ending *-te iru* are written in *hiragana*. (For an explanation of *hiragana* usage for the penultimate syllable *re* in vowel-stem verbs, see section 4, below.)

2. The Function of Kanji in Running Japanese Text

As Japanese does not mark word boundaries in text, the use of visually distinct kanji (and *katakana*) within the basic *hiragana* script itself functions as an indicator of a word boundary. As kanji are used for content words, a typical unit of meaning begins with a kanji and ends with *hiragana* (particles or inflectional endings etc.).

3. Readings

As the term "Chinese characters" implies, kanji were originally imported from China, along with Buddhism (in its Chinese form) and Chinese culture, accompanied by a large number of Chinese loanwords pertaining to these areas. A kanji therefore entered Japan accompanied by its Chinese pronunciation, in a form adapted to the Japanese sound system; this is called its ON (音) reading. Later, Japanese readings developed for many kanji by using them to express a Japanese word of equivalent or related meaning. This is called the KUN (訓) reading. Thus, the Chinese word for "child" acquired the KUN reading こ ("child" in native Japanese) in addition to its ON reading シ. Sometimes several Japanese words became attached to one kanji, as in the following example which has a total of two ON and eight KUN readings:

上
ジョウ・ショウ
うえ・うわ・かみ・あ（げる）・あ（がる）・の（ぼる）・の（ぼせる）・の（ぼす）

There are some kanji that have more than one ON reading. This is because readings entered Japan from China in three major waves, at different times and from different areas in China, or in other cases, such as 楽, because the kanji had more than one meaning attached to it in the original Chinese. 楽 has two ON readings: pronounced ガク, it means "music"; pronounced ラク, "easy, happy."

Kanji with multiple readings, however, are infrequent: of the 1,945 Jōyō Kanji, about two-thirds have either only a single ON reading or one ON and one KUN reading.

4. The Use of *Okurigana*

Most verbs and adjectives have their (unchanging) stems written in kanji, and their (changing) inflectional endings written in *hiragana*.

VERBS
consonant-stem: 読む・読んだ・読めば
vowel-stem: 起きる・起きた・起きれば
　　　　　　食べる・食べた・食べれば

ADJECTIVES
-i: 早い・早かった・早ければ
-shii: 新しい・新しかった・新しければ

This use of *hiragana* is referred to as *okurigana*, which literally means "*kana* suffix." There are a number of conventions to be observed when using *okurigana*, whose main function, as alluded to above, is to show the inflectional ending of a verb or adjective. The following points should also be noted: *okurigana* does not always show the inflectional ending clearly (*yom-u*, for example, would be a better analysis of a consonant-stem verb than *yo-mu*). Likewise, vowel-stem verbs and -*shii* adjectives follow a stylistic convention whereby the penultimate syllable, though not being strictly a part of the inflectional ending, is written as *okurigana*. Further examples of adjectives whose penultimate syllables conventionally appear in the *kana* script are 大きい and 小さい.

5. Readings: Single Elements and Compounds (熟語 *Jukugo*)

- ON or KUN?

Kanji are used to write either Chinese loanwords (漢語 *kango*) or native Japanese words (和語 *wago*). There is a marked difference between their usage in that, while *kango* are usually found as compounds comprising two or more single elements, *wago* most commonly consist of a single kanji.

When used in *kango*, therefore, kanji typically represent what we may call "the building blocks of word formation," whereas *wago* free-words are commonly expressed by one kanji (although it is not uncommon to find *wago* compounds in written Japanese). To illustrate this point with an example given earlier, the kanji for "child" can only be used alone in its *wago* form, as in the following sentence:

この子は大きい子だ。
"This child is a big child."

Used in *kango*, however, it can only be used in compounds.

子孫 シソン "descendant"
子宮 シキュウ "uterus"
子音 シオン "vowel"
母子 ボシ "mother and child"
分子 ブンシ "element; molecule"

This use of kanji proved invaluable during the introduction of Western technology in the nineteenth century, when in both China and Japan a great many new terms had to be coined in order to convey new ideas and technology. Take, for instance, the element 圧 アツ "pressing down; pressure."

圧縮 アッシュク "compression"
圧搾 アッサク "constriction"
圧力 アツリョク "pressure"
気圧 キアツ "atmospheric pressure"
血圧 ケツアツ "blood pressure"
高圧 コウアツ "high pressure"
水圧 スイアツ "water/hydraulic pressure"

Thus, given the fact that a compound can be either a *kango* or *wago* combination, the learner of Japanese often has trouble deciding the correct reading of a kanji in running text (is it ON or is it KUN?). Unfortunately, there is no foolproof way to determine the right reading, but some statistical tendencies do help in forming a number of ground rules.

Ground Rule 1

Groups of kanji do not generally mix in their readings; i.e., they are read as either ON or KUN.

ON: 教育学概論 キョウイクガクガイロン　制度化 セイドカ
KUN: 安値 やすね　閏年 うるうどし

Ground Rule 2

A kanji that is part of a compound is almost always read in its ON reading.

音楽 オンガク　政治改革 セイジカイカク

Ground Rule 3

If a compound contains *okurigana*, it normally has a KUN reading.

乗り換える のりかえる　引き渡す ひきわたす

Ground Rule 4

A kanji that stands alone is normally read in its KUN reading.

この子は大きい子だ。

Although there are exceptions to these rules, they can nevertheless serve as useful guidelines to the beginner while he or she learns to determine how a kanji is read from experience.

• *Ateji*

One area of kanji usage whose unpredictable nature makes it particularly difficult for the learner is *ateji*. *Ateji* are kanji that are used to represent Japanese sounds regardless of their meaning or, conversely, meanings regardless of their sounds.

乙女 オトめ "maiden," where the first part of the Japanese word is similar in sound to the kanji's ON reading (オツ).

意気地なし イクジなし "spineless," where the first and third syllables represent ON readings, and the second, an approximation of the kanji's KUN reading.

Sometimes kanji with auspicious meanings are chosen for *ateji*; this is particularly common in the case of personal names.

美千代 Michiyo ("beauty" + "one thousand" + "generations")

Ateji include cases where a compound made from two kanji elements is equated with a Japanese word of equal or similar meaning.

悪戯 いたずら "mischief"
悪阻 つわり "morning sickness"

6. How Many Kanji Does One Need?

The Japan Industrial Standard (JIS) kanji codes of 1978 (rev. 1983) list well over 6,000 kanji, a number that may be regarded as the upper level of kanji usage in Japan. In newspapers and magazines, the total number used has been counted at approximately 3,300 or so. In contrast, the Jōyō Kanji number only 1,945. How useful is this number for reading Japanese?

Because the more frequent kanji are encountered over and over again, one can in fact achieve a great deal with a limited number of kanji; thus, the most frequent 500 cover about eighty percent of newspaper kanji; that figure increases to ninety-four percent if you know the top 1,000 kanji.

7. Kanji Composition

The majority (about two-thirds) of Jōyō Kanji are "phonetic compounds"; these are made up from a "radical" indicating the field of meaning to which the kanji belongs, and a "phonetic," which gives an indication of the ON reading. These two elements are arranged in a variety of combinations (the shaded section is the radical; examples are at right).

河・何、待・持

教・政、次・歌

花・茶、字・家

貿・貸、煮・熱

厚・原、病・痛

円・同、開・閉

 速・通、延・建

 区・医

術・街

回・因

The remainder can be divided into simple kanji and non-phonetic compounds. Simple kanji are typically stylized drawings of objects.

山	川	木	口
"mountain"	"river"	"tree"	"mouth"

There is a correlation between the frequency of use of a kanji and its complexity in terms of number of strokes. Simply put, the kanji with the fewest strokes are the most frequently used. The implications of this fact are that a significant proportion of simple kanji (which give no phonetic clues and need to be memorized on the basis of their shape) are composed of a limited number of strokes and do not, for that reason, put an undue strain on the learner's memory. Furthermore, they are encountered so often that they are easily retained.

Non-phonetic compounds consist of two or four simple kanji put together to indicate a new idea.

roof + pig = house 家
tree + tree = woods 林
tree + tree + tree = forest 森

8. Phonetic Compounds and Kanji Learning Strategy

The proportion of phonetic compounds in which the phonetic indicator gives a perfect indication of the kanji's ON reading is almost fifty-eight percent (a), while a partly reliable indication is achieved in nearly thirty-three percent (b); just under ten percent of cases provide no useful indication (c).

a) 寺 ジ　持 ジ
b) 古 コ　苦 ク
c) 十 ジュウ　針 シン

It is, therefore, quite possible to make an "educated guess" about the ON reading of an unknown kanji (and the field of meaning to which it belongs).

Apart from its use in guesswork, the phonetic indicator can also be used as a tool in the memorization process that is inevitably associated with kanji learning. An efficient way of committing new kanji to memory is to relate the phonetic indicator to known elements with the same or similar ON readings, keeping in separate drawers identical or similar elements with different ON.

9. Kanji Made in Japan: *Kokuji*

A number of kanji have been made up by the Japanese on the Chinese model. The composition of these kanji is mostly of the non-phonetic compound variety, such as 畑 はたけ (burning + field = dry field), and 峠 とうげ (mountain + high/low = mountain pass), and therefore tend not to have an ON reading. However, some have both ON and KUN, like 働 ドウ はたら・く, and some even have ON readings only, such as 塀 ヘイ and 錠 ジョウ. Although not part of the Jōyō Kanji list, there are many more such characters, of which a good number are names of indigenous fish and vegetation.

10. Kanji and Writing Styles

Finally, a word should be said about the stylistic dimension of kanji in general and Jōyō Kanji in particular. The use of kanji in a text can be regarded as a broad indicator of technical content, as they typically express Sino-Japanese vocabulary. This explains why kanji are used liberally in scientific articles etc. but only sparingly in poetry.

Insofar as the Jōyō Kanji are concerned, the media and even many academic periodicals tend, by and large, to abide by the official list. Literature, on the other hand, is quite a different story, making good use of *ateji* and other kanji not officially recognized. Some authors even go out of their way to dot their texts with rare and abstruse kanji, employing their multifunctional nature (variant readings etc.) as stylistic devices.

USER'S MANUAL

This section offers you a few tips on how to use *Kodansha's Essential Kanji Dictionary*—how to get the information you need as efficiently as possible. It is organized into the following sections: (1) keywords, (2) the organization of the book, (3) how to look up the characters, (4) how to look up the compounds, (5) sample entries with explanatory notes, and (6) abbreviations.

1. Keywords

This section sets out to explain the meaning of the following keywords and how they are used throughout this dictionary: kanji, radical, stroke number, stroke order, ON reading, KUN reading, *jukugo*, and *gojūon-jun*.

Kanji 漢字

"Kanji" (literally "Han letters") is the term used by the Japanese for the ideographs borrowed from China. They are ideographs in the sense that each character symbolizes a single idea and, by extension, represents the sound associated with that idea. Characters are used alongside the native phonetic syllabaries, *hiragana* and *katakana*, to express meaning as opposed to indicating the grammatical form of a word or phrase.

Radical 部首

A "radical" (*bushu*) is that part of a character that indicates the field of meaning to which the kanji belongs. It may appear at the left- or right-hand side of a kanji, at the top or bottom, or it may be an enclosure. Alternatively, as in the case of simple kanji, the character itself may be a radical. Chinese characters have been classified according to their radicals for nearly three centuries, and like most domestic character dictionaries for Japanese consumption, *Kodansha's Essential Kanji Dictionary* orders kanji by radical. It is therefore quite important for the student of written

Japanese to be able to identify a radical both promptly and correctly.

Some radicals have variants. A variant is an abbreviated form of a radical, usually with a lower stroke count. A complete list of the radicals and their variants, arranged strictly by stroke count, has been collected together in the Radical Chart printed inside the back cover of the book. In contrast to the Radical Chart, both the Radical Index and the running column of radicals in the margin of the body of the book list variants according to the number of strokes of their parent radical, not the abbreviated number of strokes of the variant itself. For example, the variant 扌, which has three strokes, is listed under its parent radical 手, which has four.

Stroke Number 画数

"Stroke number" (*kakusū*) is the term that refers to the total number of strokes that make up a single character. The kanji listed in *Kodansha's Essential Kanji Dictionary* contain between 1 and 23 strokes. Over two-thirds of these have a stroke number of between 9 and 12 strokes. As kanji are often listed according to their stroke number, we have appended an index that classifies the Jōyō Kanji by the total number of strokes. In addition, within each radical section all characters have been put in stroke-number order.

Stroke Order 書き順

The strokes of a Chinese character are written in a set sequence, known as "stroke order" (*kakijun*). It is essential to learn the correct stroke order if you wish to write kanji. The stroke order for all 1,945 Jōyō Kanji is shown at the head of each entry.

ON Reading 音読み

Nearly all kanji entered Japan accompanied by a Chinese pronunciation in a form adapted to the Japanese sound system; this is called an ON reading (*on-yomi*). All ON readings are shown in *katakana*.

KUN Reading 訓読み

Kanji acquired further readings used to express native Japanese words of equivalent or related meaning, often called KUN readings (*kun-yomi*). In order to distinguish between ON and KUN readings, all KUN readings are given here in *hiragana*.

Jukugo　熟語

Two or more kanji can be combined in the form of a compound to make new words. These compounds are known as *jukugo*. Here the term *jukugo* refers to those compounds where all the kanji are read with their ON reading.

Gojūon-jun　五十音順

Gojūon-jun refers to the standard order of the two Japanese phonetic syllabaries. Literally it means the "order of the fifty sounds" and is reproduced below for both *hiragana* and *katakana*. Japanese words appearing in *Kodansha's Essential Kanji Dictionary* are generally listed according to the *gojūon-jun* standard.

Hiragana

あ	か	さ	た	な	は	ま	や	ら	わ	ん
い	き	し	ち	に	ひ	み		り		
う	く	す	つ	ぬ	ふ	む	ゆ	る		
え	け	せ	て	ね	へ	め		れ		
お	こ	そ	と	の	ほ	も	よ	ろ	を	

Katakana

ア	カ	サ	タ	ナ	ハ	マ	ヤ	ラ	ワ	ン
イ	キ	シ	チ	ニ	ヒ	ミ		リ		
ウ	ク	ス	ツ	ヌ	フ	ム	ユ	ル		
エ	ケ	セ	テ	ネ	ヘ	メ		レ		
オ	コ	ソ	ト	ノ	ホ	モ	ヨ	ロ	ヲ	

Note: The tables are read from top to bottom, left to right: i.e., *a, i, u, e, o, ka, ki, ku*, etc.

2. About the Organization of the Book

This section deals with the structure and organization of *Kodansha's Essential Kanji Dictionary*.

Jōyō Kanji

In 1946 the Japanese Ministry of Education (known today as the Ministry of Science, Education, and Culture) issued a list of 1,945 "Common Use Characters" (Jōyō Kanji) in an attempt to simplify the written language, with the recommendation that publishers and writers confine themselves to these characters. Today nearly all newspapers and major periodicals have adopted this official list, making the Jōyō Kanji the single most relevant list of characters for the student of written Japanese. Accordingly, each of the 1,945 Jōyō Kanji is explained in a separate entry in this dictionary.

Arrangement of Characters

As mentioned above, it is most convenient to arrange kanji according to their radicals, and in fact most character dictionaries, both for native Japanese speakers and foreign learners as well, are structured in this way. All entry characters in *Kodansha's Essential Kanji Dictionary* are listed by their traditionally attributed radical. Thus the 1,945 Jōyō Kanji are divided into 218 radical sections. The radical sections themselves are arranged by stroke number, the first radical being of a single stroke and the final radical containing fourteen strokes. Within each radical section, the kanji are also arranged by their stroke number, a character of a lower stroke number coming before one of a higher stroke number.

Compounds

It is possible in most cases to combine two or more characters together and make a compound. *Kodansha's Essential Kanji Dictionary* lists a generous selection of commonly used compounds for each entry character where compounds exist. However, such compounds are listed only when the entry character is the first kanji in the compound. Within each entry there are three categories of compounds.

a) *Jukugo* Group, where the entry character is read in its ON reading

b) KUN Group, where the entry character is read in its KUN reading

c) Business Group, where the compound is a business word

Compounds within each category are arranged in *gojūon-jun* order.

3. How to Look Up the Characters

There are three ways to look up characters in *Kodansha's Essential Kanji Dictionary*: by radical, by ON/KUN reading, and by stroke number.

Radical

Perhaps the quickest way to find a kanji is by using the Radical Chart printed inside the back cover. The Radical Chart is a table showing the radicals and their variants in stroke-number order and indicating the page on which each radical section begins. Looking up a character in this way depends on your skill at being able to identify a radical correctly (see "Kanji Composition," p. xviii). The procedure for looking up a character in this way is as follows: (a) determine the radical; (b) count the number of strokes contained in the radical; (c) locate the radical in the Radical Chart; (d) go to the page number as indicated in the chart; (e) and, last of all, find the character within its radical section.

There will be occasions when you will waste a lot of time looking for a character in the wrong radical section. This sometimes happens because the character in question has two or more possible radicals. In such cases, use of the Radical Index is recommended. This is a very useful index. Not only does it show all the characters that belong to a particular radical section, but it also lists those characters whose radicals are easily mistaken. Take the character 頭 "head," for instance. It contains two possible radicals: the radical 豆 "bean" and the radical 頁 "page." Unless you know that the correct radical for 頭 is 豆, then you will not be able to find the character by using just the Radical Chart. However, 頭 is listed under both radicals in the Radical Index. Consequently, unless you are absolutely sure of a kanji's correct radical, you should first check in the Radical Index.

ON/KUN Reading

If you know either the ON or KUN reading of a Chinese character, then it may be quicker to go to the ON/KUN Index. Here the regular ON/KUN readings, as established by the Japanese Ministry of Science, Education, and Culture, are listed in *gojūon-jun* order, together with the kanji number. As elsewhere in the book, ON reading are shown in *katakana* and KUN readings in *hiragana*.

Stroke Number

When you have problems determining the correct radical and don't know the ON or KUN reading of a kanji, you should refer to the Stroke Index. Here the characters are classified according to their stoke number. You simply count the number of strokes contained in the character, and then look it up in the corresponding list in the Stroke Index.

The various ways of looking up characters are summarized in the diagram printed inside the front cover.

4. How to Look Up the Compounds

Once you have learned how to look up characters, finding a compound is a relatively easy task. The first thing to remember is that all compounds in *Kodansha's Essential Kanji Dictionary* are listed under the character that is the initial kanji in the compound. For example, the compound 洗濯 "washing; laundry," is listed under the character 洗, not the character 濯. The second thing to have in mind is that, where applicable, there are three separate compound groups:

a) *Jukugo* Group (clue: first kanji is read with its ON reading)
b) KUN Group (clue: first kanji is read with its KUN reading)
c) Business Group (clue: compound is a business word or word used in a business context)

Take, for example, the compound 断言 ダンゲン "assertion; affirmation; declaration." This compound will be found under the entry for the character 断. When you go to this entry you will find that there are two compound groups—the *jukugo* and KUN groups. In this case, however, the first kanji is used with its ON reading and will therefore be located in the *jukugo* group, marked by the symbol .

Again, take the compound 旅人 たびびと "traveler; wayfarer; pilgrim," which is listed under the entry for 旅. Here, the first kanji is read in KUN and so it can be found in the KUN group, marked with the symbol .

Finally, how about 普通銀行 フツウギンコウ "ordinary bank," which is listed under the entry for the first character of the compound 普. As the word is obviously a business word, it is located in the Business Group with the symbol .

5. Sample Entries with Explanatory Notes

This section deals with the typography used throughout *Kodansha's Essential Kanji Dictionary*.

Radical Section Header

① This digit represents the radical or variant's stroke number.
② Radical or variant.
③ Traditional Japanese name of radical or variant.
④ Given English name of radical or variant.

Character Entry

① Kanji number. This is the number that is used to identify

the character in each of the indices that have been appended at the back of the book.

② Kanji box. An enlarged example of the entry character in a
box.

③ Stroke number. The total number of strokes contained in
the entry character.

④ Stroke order. The order of strokes when writing the entry
character.

ON Reading

① ON reading symbol—the character for ON 音 in a black
box.

② Entry character illustrated in standard type.

③ Regular ON reading.

④ Meaning attached to the regular ON reading.

⑤ Irregular ON reading.

⑥ Meaning attached to the irregular ON reading.

Compounds (*Jukugo*)

Compounds are listed as shown above in *gojūon-jun* order. The
compound can be made into a verb by adding the verb *suru* "to
do" when a verb form (indicated by the abbreviations *v* or *vt*) is
included in the definition.

① *Jukugo* symbol—the character for *juku* 熟 in a black box.

② Compound.

③ Regular reading of compound.

④ Definition/explanation of the meaning and usage of the compound.

KUN Reading and KUN Compounds

① KUN reading symbol—the character for KUN 訓 in a black box.
② Entry character.
③ Regular KUN reading.
④ Meaning attached to this KUN reading.
⑤ Regular KUN compound.
⑥ Symbol to indicate irregular reading.

Business Words

A brief selection of commonly used business words appears at the end of many entries in this dictionary.
① Business word symbol—the yen sign in a black box.
② Business compounds.
③ Regular readings.
④ Definitions/explanations of meaning and usage.

6. Abbreviations

adj.	adjective
bas.	baseball
bio.	biology
Bud.	Buddhist
chem.	chemistry
clas.	classical
col.	colloquial
derog.	derogatory
fig.	figurative(ly)
hist.	historical
hon.	honorific
hum.	humble
math.	mathematics
med.	medicine
n.	noun
phy.	physics
v.	verb
vi.	intransitive verb
vt.	transitive verb

THE JŌYŌ KANJI

1

① 一

一
丶
ノ
乙
亅

音	一	イチ	one; equal; the first; whole
		イツ	one; entirely
熟	一因	イチイン	one cause among many; a single factor
	一員	イチイン	a member of a group; one member
	一円	イチエン	the whole area; all over; one yen
	一応	イチオウ	tentatively; provisionally; anyhow; once; in outline; for the time being
	一月	イチガツ	January
	一丸	イチガン	one lump
	一群	イチグン	one group
	一芸	イチゲイ	one art; one of the arts
	一合目	イチゴウめ	arbitrary tenth of the height of a mountain; beginning of a mountain climb
	一言	イチゴン	(one) word/phrase; utterance
	一次	イチジ	the first *math*. linear
	一時	イチジ	for a time; (at) one time; once; one o'clock
	一日	イチジツ	one/some day; first day of the month
	一日千秋	イチジツセンシュウ	feel as if a day were so many years; waiting impatiently
	一巡	イチジュン	once around —*vi*. go once around; go round the block
	一助	イチジョ	aid; some help
	一条	イチジョウ	one line; one of a series of articles in a document; an event
	一場	イチジョウ	one scene/place
	一族	イチゾク	one's whole family; one's kinsmen
	一存	イチゾン	one's own will/opinion
	一代	イチダイ	one life/dynasty; one/first generation
	一大事	イチダイジ	serious matter/affair
	一団	イチダン	body; group; crowd of people
	一段落	イチダンラク	pause; one pause for the present —*vi*. pause; suspend
	一同	イチドウ	all present; all persons concerned; everybody
	一読	イチドク	a reading —*v*. read over; read through once
	一日	イチニチ	some day; all day; one day
	一任	イチニン	delegation; trust —*v*. leave a matter to a person; entrust

1

一｜、ノ乙しﾘ

一人前	イチニンまえ	grown-up; adult; one adult portion (of food)
一年	イチネン	one year
一念	イチネン	zeal; enthusiasm; concentration
一部	イチブ	one part/section/book
一部始終	イチブシジュウ	the whole story from beginning to end; all the details
一望	イチボウ	one view —*v.* look out; take in the view
一望千里	イチボウセンリ	a fine view of a boundless plain; a clear view in the distance
一味	イチミ	the same group/party; a single flavor
一名	イチメイ	one person; another name; alias
一命	イチメイ	(one) life
一面	イチメン	one side
一網打尽	イチモウダジン	catching a lot of fish in the same net
一文	イチモン	old Japanese coin; one tenth of a sen; tiny sum of money
一門	イチモン	whole family; one clan
一問一答	イチモンイットウ	question and answer —*vi.* give an immediate answer to each question
一夜	イチヤ	one night; some night; single night
一躍	イチヤク	at a bound —*vi.* raise (to the top) in one go
一様	イチヨウ	even; equality
一覧	イチラン	a look; a glance —*v.* look over; take a look; glance through
一理	イチリ	some truth; a truth
一利一害	イチリイチガイ	advantages and disadvantages
一律	イチリツ	equality; monotony; uniformity
一流	イチリュウ	first or highest in a group; unique; first class
一両日	イチリョウジツ	a day or two
一輪	イチリン	one flower/wheel; the next full moon
一例	イチレイ	an example
一連	イチレン	series; ream
一路	イチロ	road; straight
一割	イチワリ	ten percent
一家	イッカ	family; master; an authority
一画	イッカク	a stroke in writing; building lot
一括	イッカツ	summary —*v.* do all at once; complete at one time
一貫	イッカン	consistency —*v.* run through
一喜一憂	イッキイチユウ	joy and sorrow —*vi.* swing from joy to sorrow
一級	イッキュウ	first/top class; first rate
一挙一動	イッキョイチドウ	one's every action
一挙両得	イッキョリョウトク	kill two birds with one stone

2

一計	イッケイ	plan; idea
一見	イッケン	(one) glance —*v*. have a look; glance; take a quick look
一件	イッケン	affair; matter; item
一考	イッコウ	consideration —*v*. consider
一行	イッコウ	one event; party; group
一刻	イッコク	moment; instant
一切	イッサイ	all; entire; whole
一策	イッサク	plan; idea
一昨日	イッサクジツ	the day before yesterday
一式	イッシキ	complete set
一首	イッシュ	one poem
一種	イッシュ	one kind/type
一周	イッシュウ	a round; one lap —*v*. go round
一蹴	イッシュウ	refusal —*v*. refuse
一瞬	イッシュン	instant; moment
一緒	イッショ	all in one; together; with; at the same time; in the lump; same
一笑	イッショウ	laugh —*v*. laugh at
一生	イッショウ	one's (whole) life
一生懸命 (一所懸命)	イッショウ ケンメイ (イッショケンメイ)	with all one's might; the hardest one can try
一身	イッシン	oneself; one's whole body
一身上	イッシンジョウ	personal; private
一新	イッシン	renewal —*v*. renew; change completely
一進一退	イッシンイッタイ	advance and retreat; ebb and flow
一心不乱	イッシンフラン	heart and soul; concentration
一睡	イッスイ	wink of sleep; nap
一世	イッセ	one existence (past, present, or future)
一世	イッセイ	a life; era; the first monarch in line of succession; first generation of immigrants
一斉	イッセイ	equal; all together
一席	イッセキ	meeting; sitting; first place
一石二鳥	イッセキニチョウ	kill two birds with one stone
一節	イッセツ	one paragraph/phrase
一説	イッセツ	another opinion/view; one opinion; one way of looking at things
一線	イッセン	a line; the front line
一掃	イッソウ	a clean sweep —*v*. dispel; eradicate
一層	イッソウ	even more; all the more
一体	イッタイ	one body; a style; a form; (who/what) on earth?
一帯	イッタイ	tract of land; whole area

1

一隊	イッタイ	company of soldiers
一旦	イッタン	once
一端	イッタン	one end; a part; outline
一致	イッチ	agreement; unity; accord —*vi.* be in agreement; be united
一致団結	イッチダンケツ	cooperation —*v.* unite (in doing); cooperate
一朝一夕	イッチョウ イッセキ	brief space of time
一長一短	イッチョウ イッタン	merits and demerits
一張羅	イッチョウラ	one's Sunday best
一直線	イッチョクセン	straight line
一対	イッツイ	pair
一手	イッテ	move in go or *shōgi*; monopoly
一定	イッテイ	fixed; definite; certain —*v.* fix; set; settle; define
一滴	イッテキ	drop of liquid
一転	イッテン	change; complete change —*vi.* make a complete change
一等	イットウ	first place/prize/class
一時	イットキ	short time
一派	イッパ	school of thought
一般	イッパン	ordinary; general
一般的	イッパンテキ	general; ordinary
一筆	イッピツ	one uninterrupted stroke of a pen; brief note
一服	イップク	dose of medicine; puff of a cigarette; rest —*v.* have/take a rest
一幅	イップク	scroll
一片	イッペン	piece; fragment of a thin object
一辺	イッペン	one side
一辺倒	イッペントウ	loyal support; unquestioning devotion
一変	イッペン	(complete) change —*v.* change (completely)
一歩	イッポ	step; footstep
一方	イッポウ	one side/part; on one hand
一方的	イッポウテキ	one-sided; unilateral
一本気	イッポンギ	single-minded
一本調子	イッポンチョウシ	a monotone; monotony

訓

一つ	ひとつ	one
一	ひと	(prefix) one; single
一雨	ひとあめ	shower; rainfall
一息	ひといき	breath; rest; breather
一重	ひとえ	single; onefold
一際	ひときわ	in general; one time (long ago)
一癖	ひとくせ	peculiarity; idiosyncrasy

4

一粒種	ひとつぶだね	one's only child
一昔	ひとむかし	decade
一休み	ひとやすみ	brief rest; breather; break —*vi*. take a rest; take a breather
※一日	ついたち	first day (of the month); 1st
Ⓨ 一任業務	イチニンギョウム	discretionary business
一般会計	イッパンカイケイ	General Account
一般事業債	イッパンジギョウサイ	general corporate bonds

音	七	シチ	seven
熟	七月	シチガツ	July
	七五三	シチゴサン	(celebration of) a child's third, fifth, and seventh years
	七五調	シチゴチョウ	the seven-and-five-syllable meter in Japanese poetry
	七転八倒	シチテンバットウ	writhing in agony/pain —*vi*. writhe in agony/pain
	七福神	シチフクジン	Seven Gods of Good Fortune
	七面鳥	シチメンチョウ	turkey
訓	七	なな	seven
	七つ	ななつ	seven
	七日	なのか	seventh day (of the month); 7th
	※七夕	たなばた	the seventh day of the seventh month of the lunar calendar
	※七夕祭	たなばたまつり	Star Festival; Tanabata Matsuri

音	丁	チョウ	leaf; page; block; even number
		テイ	youth; servant; the fourth of the ten calendar signs; polite
熟	丁度	チョウド	exactly; just; right; quite
	丁場	チョウば	the distance between stages
	丁半	チョウハン	odd and even numbers
	丁字	テイジ	T
	丁字形	テイジケイ	T-shaped
	丁字路	テイジロ	T junction
	丁重	テイチョウ	polite; courteous; civil; respectful; reverent

丁寧　　テイネイ　　polite; courteous; careful; scrupulous; thorough
丁寧語　テイネイゴ　polite respect language

訓 ※丁　ひのと　　*hinoto* (fourth sign of the lunar calendar)

下 ④ 一 丁 下

音 下　カ　under; lower part; descend;
　　　　　below; lower; go down; fall

　　　ゲ　below; lower part; be inferior; lower

熟 下位　カイ　lower rank; subordinate position
下院　カイン　Lower House
下記　カキ　the following; undermentioned; below
下級　カキュウ　lower class/grade
下弦　カゲン　waning moon; last phase of the moon
下降　カコウ　descent; fall; drop —*vi.* descend; fall; drop; decline
下層　カソウ　lower classes
下等　カトウ　low grade; meanness; inferiority
下半身　カハンシン　lower half of the body
下部　カブ　lower part
下流　カリュウ　lower part of a river; downstream
下界　ゲカイ　the earth; here below
下戸　ゲコ　teetotaler; nondrinker
下校　ゲコウ　leaving school for the day; coming home from school —*vi.* leave school for the day; come home from school
下剤　ゲザイ　*med.* laxative; purgative
下山　ゲザン　descent of a mountain —*vi.* climb down a mountain
下車　ゲシャ　alighting —*vi.* alight from a train, car, bus
下宿　ゲシュク　lodgings; boarding house —*vi.* lodge; board; take up lodgings
下旬　ゲジュン　the last ten days of a month; the last third of a month
下水　ゲスイ　sewage; sewer; drainage
下船　ゲセン　disembarkation; going ashore —*vi.* leave a ship; go ashore
下足　ゲソク　footwear
下駄　ゲタ　*geta* (wooden clogs)
下段　ゲダン　lowest step; lower berth
下馬評　ゲバヒョウ　common talk; gossip; rumor
下品　ゲヒン　coarse; rude; vulgar
下落　ゲラク　fall; decline; drop; deterioration —*v.* fall; decline; drop; deteriorate

下痢	ゲリ	diarrhea; loose bowels —*vi.* suffer from diarrhea; pass fluid stools
下劣	ゲレツ	meanness; baseness; vulgarity

訓

下	した	low; inferior to; below; under; young
下絵	したえ	rough sketch; undersketch; design
下書き	したがき	rough draft
下着	したぎ	underwear; undergarments
下心	したごころ	ulterior motive
下地	したヂ	groundwork; preparations; first coat (of paint/lacquer); aptitude
下調べ	したしらべ	preliminary inquiry; preparations
下積み	したづみ	goods at the bottom of a pile; lowest social classes; the lowest
下手	したて (したで)	inferiority; downwards
下火	したび	fire that has burnt out; decline
下町	したまち	*shitamachi* (traditional working-class neighborhood)
下見	したみ	preliminary examination; clapboard; narrow board thicker at one edge than the other used for sliding
下役	したヤク	petty official; underling
下りる	おりる	*vi.* come down; get off/down/out
下ろす	おろす	*vt.* take down; grate; put down
下す	くだす	*vt.* let down; subdue; give; issue; pass; have loose bowels
下る	くだる	*vi.* descend; go down; pass
下り	くだり	descent; going down; away from the center of town
下さる	くださる	*vt.* **hon.** give; receive; oblige; favor with
下がる	さがる	*vi.* come down; leave; hang down; fall
下げる	さげる	*vt.* take down; lower; hang
下	しも	low; lower part; the governed; lower classes; lower half of the body
下座	しもザ	lower seat
下々	しもじも	the masses; lower classes
下手	しもて	downwards; right side of a stage; actor's right
下	もと	under; base
※下手	へた	unskillful; poor at

¥

下げ足	さげあし	downward trend
下げ屋	さげや	lower (in a quotation)
下請け	したうけ	subcontract; subcontracting
下支え	したざさえ	support
下値	したね	lower price
下放れ	したばなれ	down gap

5

三　一　二　三 ③

音	三	サン	three
熟	三角	サンカク	triangle
	三角関係	サンカクカンケイ	eternal triangle; love triangle
	三角形	サンカクケイ	triangle
	三角州	サンカクス	delta
	三月	サンガツ	March
	三脚	サンキャク	tripod
	三権	サンケン	three branches of government
	三原色	サンゲンショク	three primary colors
	三次元	サンジゲン	three-dimensional (3-D)
	三段跳び	サンダンとび	triple jump; hop, step, and jump
	三拍子	サンビョウシ	triple time; three-part time
	三方	サンポウ	three directions/sides; small wooden stand
	三面記事	サンメンキジ	city news; police news
	※三味線	シャミセン	*shamisen* (three-string Japanese mandolin)
訓	三つ	みっつ	three
	三	み	three
	三日	みっか	third day (of the month); 3rd
	三日月	みかづき	new/crescent moon
	三つ	みつ	three

6

上　｜　ト　上 ③

音	上	ジョウ （ショウ）	upper part; good; first; rise; get on
熟	上位	ジョウイ	superior/higher rank
	上映	ジョウエイ	movie screening/showing —*v.* screen; show/put on a movie
	上演	ジョウエン	performance; presentation —*v.* perform; present
	上官	ジョウカン	senior officer; superior
	上記	ジョウキ	the above; the above-mentioned
	上気	ジョウキ	blushing; rush of blood to the cheeks —*vi.* have a rush of blood to the head; blush; go red in the cheeks
	上機嫌	ジョウキゲン	good humor/mood
	上級	ジョウキュウ	upper grade; upper; higher; senior

上京	ジョウキョウ	going to Tokyo —*vi.* come up to Tokyo
上下	ジョウゲ	vertical; up and down; top and bottom; fluctuation; social standing —*v.* go up and down; rise and fall; fluctuate
上下関係	ジョウゲカンケイ	social standing
上下動	ジョウゲドウ	up-and-down movement; vertical earthquake
上限	ジョウゲン	upper limit; maximum
上弦	ジョウゲン	moon in its first quarter
上戸	ジョウゴ	heavy drinker
上告	ジョウコク	final appeal —*vi.* make a final appeal
上司	ジョウシ	one's superior/boss
上質	ジョウシツ	fine/choice quality
上述	ジョウジュツ	the above; the above-mentioned
上首尾	ジョウシュビ	great success
上旬	ジョウジュン	first ten days of the month; beginning/first part of the month
上昇	ジョウショウ	rise; ascension —*vi.* rise; go up; ascend
上々	ジョウジョウ	excellent; the very best
上申	ジョウシン	report —*v.* report to one's superiors
上申書	ジョウシンショ	written report
上水	ジョウスイ	water supply; tap/city water
上水道	ジョウスイドウ	water works
上席	ジョウセキ	seniority; upper rank
上訴	ジョウソ	appeal —*v.* appeal to a higher court
上奏	ジョウソウ	report —*v.* report to the emperor
上層	ジョウソウ	upper class/layer/stratum/air
上体	ジョウタイ	upper part of the body
上代	ジョウダイ	in old/ancient times
上達	ジョウタツ	advancement; progress; improvement —*vi.* make progress; advance; improve; become proficient
上段	ジョウダン	upper section/deck/berth
上程	ジョウテイ	lay before/introduce/present to the Diet
上出来	ジョウでき	good work; well-made; well-done
上等	ジョウトウ	fine/top quality; excellent
上人	ショウニン	saint; holy priest
上半身	ジョウハンシン	upper half of the body
上品	ジョウヒン	elegant; refined; in good taste
上部	ジョウブ	upper part; top
上物	ジョウもの	choice/high quality goods
上陸	ジョウリク	landing; disembarkation —*vi.* land; make a landing; go on shore
上流	ジョウリュウ	upper reaches of a river; upstream; upper classes

訓	上がり	あがり	rise; income; returns; proceeds
	上がる	あがる	*vi.* rise; go up; come in; enter; be promoted; (rain) stops *hon.* eat
	上げる	あげる	*v.* raise; lift; invite; send; give; be promoted; vomit
	上	うえ	top; upper part; above; over; on; upon; older; senior; better
	上	うわ	(prefix) upper; up-
	上書き	うわがき	address
	上着	うわぎ	coat; jacket
	上手	うわて	upper part/course
	上の空	うわのそら	absentmindedly
	上辺	うわべ	surface; outward; seeming
	上回る	うわまわる	*vi.* exceed; be better; surpass
	上向き	うわむき	upward; looking up
	上目使い	うわめづかい	upturned eyes/glance
	上役	うわヤク	one's superior
	上	かみ	up a river; upstream
	上方	かみがた	Kyoto and vicinity; the Kyoto-Osaka area
	上座	かみザ	front seat; seat of honor; top of the class
	上手	かみて	upper part/course; right hand side of the stage
	上せる	のぼせる	*vt.* put in; put on record *vi.* feel dizzy; get upset
	上り	のぼり	ascent; going up; toward the center of town
	上る	のぼる	*vi.* climb; go up; reach; amount to
	※上手	じょうず	skillful; clever; good; expert
¥	上ザヤ	うわザヤ	higher in quotation
	上値	うわね	higher price
	上乗せ	うわのせ	rise in price
	上放れ	うわばなれ	up gap
	上屋	うわや	shed
	上寄る	うわよる	open higher
	上院	ジョウイン	Upper House
	上場	ジョウジョウ	listed —*v.* list; be listed at a stock market
	上場株	ジョウジョウかぶ	listed stock
	上場企業	ジョウジョウキギョウ	listed company
	上場基準	ジョウジョウキジュン	initial listing requirement
	上場銘柄	ジョウジョウメイがら	listed issue
	上伸	ジョウシン	(share prices) jump; rise; upward turn

一｜、ノ乙しｊ

7 丈 ③ 一 ナ 丈

音	丈	ジョウ	length
熟	丈夫	ジョウブ	strong; robust; solid; durable; health
訓	丈	たけ	height; length; size

8 万 ③ 一 フ 万

音	万	バン	countless; myriad; all
		マン	ten thousand; myriad
熟	万感	バンカン	flood of emotions; various emotions
	万古	バンコ	perpetuity; eternity
	万国	バンコク	all nations
	万歳	バンザイ	Hurrah!
	万策	バンサク	every means; all possible ways
	万事	バンジ	everything; all
	万障	バンショウ	all obstacles; various problems/business
	万象	バンショウ	the universe; all things; everything
	万全	バンゼン	perfect; sure
	万難	バンナン	innumerable difficulties; all obstacles
	万人	バンニン	all people; everybody
	万能	バンノウ	almighty; omnipotent; all-around; all-purpose
	万般	バンパン	all; everything
	万物	バンブツ	all things; all creation
	万民	バンミン	all the people; nation
	万有	バンユウ	all things; all creation; universal
	万有引力	バンユウインリョク	universal gravitation
	万一	マンイチ	by any chance; should happen to
	万華鏡	マンゲキョウ	kaleidoscope
	万年	マンネン	eternity; perpetuity; ten thousand years
	万年筆	マンネンヒツ	fountain-pen
	万引き	マンびき	shoplifting; shoplifter
	万病	マンビョウ	all kinds of diseases; all diseases
	万力	マンリキ	vise
訓	※万	よろず	ten thousand; all sorts of; everything

9 与 ③ ｜ 与 与

音	与	ヨ	give; join
訓	与える	あたえる	*vt*. give; bestow; cause
	※与する	くみする	*vi*. take part in; side with
¥	与信業務	ヨシンギョウム	credit business
	与党	ヨトウ	the Government; the Administration; party in power
	与野党	ヨヤトウ	governing and opposition parties

10 不 ④ 一 フ 不 不

音	不	フ	not
		ブ	
熟	不安	フアン	uneasy; uncertain; insecure; suspenseful; fearful; nervous
	不安定	フアンテイ	instability; lack of stability
	不案内	フアンナイ	ignorance; unfamiliarity
	不意	フイ	suddenly; unexpectedly
	不運	フウン	misfortune
	不穏	フオン	disorder; disquiet; unrest
	不可	フカ	bad; wrong; improper; impossible
	不可解	フカカイ	mysterious; beyond comprehension; inscrutable
	不可欠	フカケツ	indispensable; essential; vital
	不可抗力	フカコウリョク	beyond human control; unpreventable
	不可思議	フカシギ	strange; mysterious
	不可侵	フカシン	inviolable; sacred; nonaggressive
	不可分	フカブン	inseparable; indivisible; undetachable
	不快	フカイ	unpleasant; rotten; disagreeable; offensive; sickness
	不快指数	フカイシスウ	discomfort index
	不覚	フカク	negligent; improvident; unprepared; unexpected
	不恰好	ブカッコウ	unshapely; ill-fitting; awkward
	不規則	フキソク	irregular; unsystematic
	不吉	フキツ	unlucky; inauspicious; ominous
	不気味	ブキミ	weird; eerie; ominous; uncanny
	不朽	フキュウ	immortal; eternal; undying
	不急	フキュウ	nonurgent; not pressing

不興	フキョウ	displeasure; ill humor; disgrace
不義理	フギリ	ingratitude; dishonesty; injustice
不器量	ブキリョウ	plain; ugly; homely
不謹慎	フキンシン	imprudent; indiscreet; immodest; rash
不具	フグ	*derog.* deformed; malformed; crippled
不遇	フグウ	underestimated; unrecognized (talent/ability); misfortune; bad luck; ill fate
不屈	フクツ	inflexible; invincible; inexhaustible; indomitable
不景気	フケイキ	depression (esp. economic)
不経済	フケイザイ	uneconomical; wasteful; extravagant; expensive
不潔	フケツ	dirty; smutty; unclean; impure
不言実行	フゲンジッコウ	work before talk; action before words
不孝	フコウ	undutiful; disobedient; impious; thankless; ungrateful
不幸	フコウ	unhappy; unfortunate; unlucky; death of a close relative
不合格	フゴウカク	failure; disqualification
不合理	フゴウリ	irrational; illogical; unreasonable; preposterous
不心得	フこころえ	indiscreet; imprudent; unwise
不在	フザイ	absence; being away
不在投票	フザイトウヒョウ	absentee voting
不作	フサク	poor crop; bad harvest
不作法	ブサホウ	bad manners/form; rudeness
不治	フジ	incurable; malignant (disease)
不時	フジ	emergency; unexpectedness; sudden
不思議	フシギ	mysterious; wonderful; marvelous; strange; uncanny
不自然	フシゼン	unnatural; artificial
不時着	フジチャク	forced/emergency landing
不実	フジツ	unfaithful; insincere; cold-hearted; untruth; falsehood
不始末	フシマツ	mismanagement; misconduct; malpractise; improvidence
不死身	フジみ	immortal; invincible; indomitable
不自由	フジユウ	inconvenient; uncomfortable —*vi.* be troubled by
不純	フジュン	impure; foul; mixed
不順	フジュン	changeable; unsettled; unfavorable; irregular
不詳	フショウ	unknown; unidentified
不浄	フジョウ	uncleaniness; dirtiness; impurity; menstruation; feces; urine
不祥事	フショウジ	scandal
不承不承	フショウブショウ	unwillingly; reluctantly; grudgingly
不信	フシン	distrust; mistrust; disbelief; insincerity; fidelity

不信任	フシンニン	lack of confidence
不振	フシン	dull; inactive; slack; stagnate; depressed
不審	フシン	suspicion; doubt; distrust
不随	フズイ	paralysis; palsy
不正	フセイ	injustice; unfairness; wrong; illegality
不世出	フセイシュツ	rare
不成績	フセイセキ	poor results; bad record; underachievement
不摂生	フセッセイ	neglect of health; unwholesome living
不全	フゼン	imperfect; incomplete
不戦勝	フセンショウ	unearned win; win by default
不相応	フソウオウ	unsuitable; unfit; inappropriate; unbecoming
不足	フソク	lack; insufficiency; shortage; need; want; discontent; dissatisfaction —*vi.* lack; be short of; be discontented
不測	フソク	unforeseen; unexpected
不断	フダン	ceaseless; incessant; continual; usually; habitually
不調	フチョウ	bad condition; rupture; failure; fiasco
不通	フツウ	interruption; suspension (of traffic); unreliable; hard to understand; unclear
不都合	フツゴウ	inconvenient; inexpedient
不定	フテイ	indefinite; uncertain; unsettled; unfixed
不定期	フテイキ	irregular (time period)
不体裁	フテイサイ	unseemly; unsightly; indecent; improper
不敵	フテキ	brave; daring; intrepid; fearless
不出来	フでき	poor work; failure; bungle
不適合	フテキゴウ	incongruent
不手際	フてぎわ	clumsy; awkward; inept
不徹底	フテッテイ	inconclusive; inconsistent; weak
不当	フトウ	injustice; wrongfulness; impropriety; unreasonableness
不同	フドウ	unequal; uneven; irregular; dissimilar
不動	フドウ	immovability; immobility; firmness; stability
不統一	フトウイツ	disorganized; disunited; divided; chaotic
不徳	フトク	vice; immorality; delinquency
不慣れ	フなれ	inexperience
不人情	フニンジョウ	unkind; unfeeling; inhuman; cold-hearted
不燃	フネン	incombustible; fireproof
不能	フノウ	inability; impotence
不敗	フハイ	invincible; undefeated; unbeatable
不発	フハツ	misfire; backfire
不備	フビ	deficiency; imperfection; inadequacy; lack; defect
不評	フヒョウ	unpopular; disreputable

不平等	フビョウドウ	unequal; unfair
不服	フフク	dissatisfaction; discontentment; disagreement; objection; protest
不平	フヘイ	complaint; grievance; discontent; displeasure
不変	フヘン	unchangeable; invariable; constant
不便	フベン	inconvenient
不法	フホウ	unlawful; illegal; unjust
不本意	フホンイ	reluctant; unwilling
不満	フマン	discontent; dissatisfaction; displeasure
不眠	フミン	insomnia; loss of sleep
不眠不休	フミンフキュウ	without resting/sleeping; devotedly
不向き	フむき	unsuitable; unfit; ill-fitting
不明	フメイ	unknown; obscure; unclear; vague; ambiguous
不名誉	フメイヨ	dishonor; disgrace; discredit; infamy; shame
不滅	フメツ	immortality
不毛	フモウ	unproductive; sterile; infertile; barren (land, projects, etc.)
不問	フモン	ignore; disregard
不夜城	フヤジョウ	nightless quarter; city that never sleeps
不要	フヨウ	unnecessary; useless; needless
不用	フヨウ	useless; unnecessary
不用意	フヨウイ	unprepared; not organized
不用心	ブヨウジン	careless; imprudent; insecure; unsafe
不養生	フヨウジョウ	neglect of one's health
不利	フリ	disadvantage
不慮	フリョ	unexpected; unforeseen
不良	フリョウ	badness; inferiority; deliquency
不漁	フリョウ	poor catch (of fish)
不老不死	フロウフシ	eternal youth; immortality
不和	フワ	discord; trouble; differences; disharmony
¥ 不況	フキョウ	depression; slump; recession
不均衡	フキンコウ	imbalance; unbalance
不動産	フドウサン	real estate; realty
不良債権	フリョウサイケン	bad debts
不渡り手形	フわたりてがた	dishonored notes (bill)

11

且 ⑤　　丨 冂 月 月 且

| 音 | 且 | （ショ） | moreover; besides |
| 訓 | 且つ | かつ | also; moreover; besides |

15

12

丘 ⑤　　ノ　ィ　セ　斤　丘

音	丘	キュウ	hill; mound
熟	丘陵	キュウリョウ	hill; hillock
訓	丘	おか	hill

13

世 ⑤　　一　十　卅　廿　世

音	世	セ	world; life
		セイ	
熟	世紀	セイキ	century
	世界	セカイ	world; earth; circle; sphere
	世界的	セカイテキ	worldwide; international
	世間	セケン	the world; people; the public; circle of acquaintances
	世間体	セケンテイ	decency; appearances
	世間話	セケンばなし	chat; small talk
	世襲	セシュウ	hereditary; descent —v. inherit
	世情	セジョウ	worldly matters; the ways of the world
	世相	セソウ	social conditions/aspects
	世俗	セゾク	worldly things
	世帯	セタイ	household
	世代	セダイ	generation
	世論	セロン（よロン）	public opinion; consensus of opinion
	世話	セワ	aid; help; assistance; service; care; trouble; everyday life —v. help; assist; serve; care
	お世辞	おセジ	compliment
訓	世	よ	society; times; life
	世の中	よのなか	in the world/society; at large

14

丙 ⑤　　一　丆　丙　丙　丙

音	丙	ヘイ	third in a series; C
訓	※丙	ひのえ	*hinoe* (third sign of lunar calendar)

両 ⑥ 一 厂 厅 丙 両 両

音 両	リョウ	both; two; *ryō* (old Japanese coin); (counter for cars, carriages, rolling stock)	
熟 両院	リョウイン	both houses (of parliament/congress); upper and lower houses	
両替	リョウがえ	money exchange —*v.* exchange money	
両極	リョウキョク	the two poles; both extremities	
両軍	リョウグン	two armies	
両日	リョウジツ	both/two days	
両者	リョウシャ	both people	
両親	リョウシン	parents	
両性	リョウセイ	both sexes; male and female	
両生類	リョウセイルイ	amphibia (animal)	
両端	リョウタン	both ends/edges; sitting on the fence	
両断	リョウダン	divided into two —*v.* cut in two	
両刀	リョウトウ	two swords	
両得	リョウトク	double profit	
両人	リョウニン	two/both people	
両刃	リョウば	double-edged	
両方	リョウホウ	both	
両面	リョウメン	both faces/sides	
両雄	リョウユウ	two great men	
両用	リョウヨウ	serving a double purpose	
両様	リョウヨウ	two/both ways	
両翼	リョウヨク	both wings/flanks	
両立	リョウリツ	coexistence; compatibility —*vi.* coexist; be compatible	
両輪	リョウリン	two wheels	

1 │	ぼう	rod; stick; line

16

中 ④ 丶 𠃌 口 中

音 中	チュウ	center; middle; medium; mediocrity; average
熟 中央	チュウオウ	center; middle; heart

中華	チュウカ	China; Chinese (food, etc.)
中核	チュウカク	core; kernel; nucleus
中学生	チュウガクセイ	junior high school student
中学校	チュウガッコウ	junior high/middle school
中型	チュウがた	medium-size
中間	チュウカン	middle; midway
中期	チュウキ	middle period
中級	チュウキュウ	medium grade
中近東	チュウキントウ	The Near and Middle East
中位	チュウくらい	medium size; middling; moderate; passable
中継	チュウケイ	relay; broadcast —*v.* relay; broadcast
中堅	チュウケン	backbone; nucleus; main body; center; people forming the backbone
中古	チュウコ	the middle ages; second hand; old
中古車	チュウコシャ	used/second hand car
中国	チュウゴク	China
中腰	チュウごし	half-sitting posture
中座	チュウザ	leaving in the middle of a meeting —*vi.* leave before the meeting is over
中産階級	チュウサンカイキュウ	the middle class
中止	チュウシ	discontinuance; interruption; suspension; stoppage —*v.* discontinue; interrupt; suspend; stop
中旬	チュウジュン	middle ten days of a month
中傷	チュウショウ	slander; libel; malicious gossip —*v.* slander; libel
中心	チュウシン	center; middle; heart; balance
中枢	チュウスウ	pivot; hub; nucleus
中世	チュウセイ	Middle Ages
中性	チュウセイ	neuter
中性子	チュウセイシ	*phy.* neutron
中絶	チュウゼツ	abortion; interruption; suspension; intermission; stoppage —*v.* interrupt; suspend; stop; abort
中退	チュウタイ	dropping out of school
中段	チュウダン	middle of the stairs; middle berth
中断	チュウダン	interruption; discontinuance; suspension —*v.* interrupt; discontinue; suspend
中途	チュウト	halfway; midway; mid-course
中途半端	チュウトハンパ	undone; not complete; unfinished
中東	チュウトウ	Middle East
中道	チュウドウ	halfway; middle of the road
中毒	チュウドク	poisoning; toxication; intoxication —*v.* be poisoned
中二階	チュウニカイ	mezzanine floor

中肉中背	チュウニク チュウぜい	medium height and build; middle-sized person
中日	チュウニチ	equinox; China and Japan
中年	チュウネン	middle age; middle-aged person
中盤	チュウバン	middle stage/phase
中腹	チュウフク	heart of the mountain
中米	チュウベイ	Central America
中庸	チュウヨウ	moderation; mean; middle
中立	チュウリツ	neutrality; neutral; independent —*vi.* be neutral/independent
中立国	チュウリツコク	neutral power/country
中流	チュウリュウ	midstream; middle class
中和	チュウワ	neutralization; counteraction —*v.* neutralize; counteract
お中元	おチュウゲン	*ochūgen* (midyear gift)

訓 | 中 | なか | interior; middle; inside; contents; among; mean |
中入り	なかいり	recess; intermission; interval
中頃	なかごろ	middle
中身	なかみ	interior; contents; substance
中休み	なかやすみ	rest; recess; break
中指	なかゆび	middle finger

¥ | 中央銀行 | チュウオウ ギンコウ | central bank |
中央集権	チュウオウ シュウケン	centralization of government
中間決済	チュウカン ケッサイ	semi-annual settlement
中間配当	チュウカン ハイトウ	interim dividend
中堅株	チュウケン かぶ	middle-priced stock
中堅企業	チュウケン キギョウ	medium-sized enterprize
中小企業	チョウショウ キギョウ	small and medium-sized enterprises

---

1 ヽ てん dot; point

17
丸 ③ ノ 九 丸

音 丸 ガン ball; round

1

一丨、丿乙乚丨

熟	丸薬	ガンヤク	pill
訓	丸	まる	ball; circle; whole; castle tower
	丸い	まるい	round; globular; spherical
	丸暗記	まるアンキ	memorize everything just as it is
	丸木舟	まるきぶね	canoe
	丸損	まるゾン	complete loss
	丸太	まるタ	log
	丸出し	まるだし	exposed; uncovered
	丸裸	まるはだか	stark naked
	丸々	まるまる	completely; entirely; wholly
	丸見え	まるみえ	fully exposed to view; in plain sight
	丸め込む	まるめこむ	*vt.* cajole; coax; wheedle
	丸める	まるめる	*vt.* round; shave; make round; make a circle

18

丹 ④ ） 刀 丹 丹 丹

音	丹	タン	red; red lead; cinnabar
熟	丹精	タンセイ	exertion; efforts; labor; work; sincerity —*vi.* exert oneself; apply oneself; work sincerely
	丹前	タンゼン	padded kimono
	丹念	タンネン	elaborate; diligent; careful; laborious

19

主 ⑤ 、 二 亠 主 主

音	主	シュ	master; lord; the Lord; first concern; chief; main; principle
		（ス）	master
熟	主位	シュイ	position of leadership; central position
	主因	シュイン	primary/main cause; main factor
	主演	シュエン	star of a movie or a play
	主客	シュカク （シュキャク）	host and guest; primary and subordinate
	主観	シュカン	subjectivity
	主観的	シュカンテキ	subjective
	主管	シュカン	supervision; superintendence —*v.* supervise; have charge of
	主眼	シュガン	main point; principal objective
	主義	シュギ	principle; doctrine; belief

20

主君	シュクン	one's lord/master
主計	シュケイ	accountant; accounting
主権	シュケン	sovereignty
主権在民	シュケンザイミン	sovereignty rests with the people
主権者	シュケンシャ	sovereign; supreme ruler
主語	シュゴ	*gram.* subject
主査	シュサ	chief examiner/investigator
主宰	シュサイ	superintendence; presidency —*v.* supervise; preside over
主宰者	シュサイシャ	leader; chairman
主催	シュサイ	sponsorship; promotion —*v.* sponsor; be promoted
主旨	シュシ	purport; main point
主事	シュジ	director; superintendent
主治医	シュジイ	family doctor; attending physician
主従	シュジュウ	master and servant; employer and employee
主将	シュショウ	captain; supreme commander; commander-in-chief
主唱	シュショウ	advocacy —*v.* advocate
主食	シュショク	staple/principal food
主審	シュシン	chief umpire; referee
主人	シュジン	one's husband; head of the family; owner; proprietor
主人公	シュジンコウ	hero; heroine; protagonist
主席	シュセキ	the Chairman (as used in China—Chairman Mao, etc.)
主体	シュタイ	main constituent; subject
主題	シュダイ	theme; subject
主張	シュチョウ	assertion; insistence; emphasis; advocacy —*v.* assert; insist; emphasize; advocate; lay stress on
主導	シュドウ	leadership
主任	シュニン	chief; head; manager
主犯	シュハン	principal offender; ring leader
主筆	シュヒツ	editor-in-chief; chief editor
主賓	シュヒン	guest of honor
主婦	シュフ	housewife
主部	シュブ	main part; subject
主役	シュヤク	leading part; starring role; star
主要	シュヨウ	principal; chief; main
主流	シュリュウ	main current/stream
主力	シュリョク	main force
訓 主	おも	chief; principal; leading
主	ぬし	master; owner

21

1 丿　の at the top; *no* (katakana)

20

久　｜　ノ ク 久 ③

音	久	キュウ （ク）	long; long-standing
熟	久遠	クオン	eternity
訓	久しい	ひさしい	long; long-continued; long time
	久し振り	ひさしぶり	for the first time in a long while; long time no see

---

21

及　｜　ノ 乃 及 ③

音	及	キュウ	catch up with; come level with; reach; attain; amount to; expand; reach; range; extend; spread; diffuse; in addition; together with; including; and
熟	及第	キュウダイ	examination pass —*vi.* pass an examination; make the grade
	及落	キュウラク	examination result; passing and failing
訓	及び	および	and; as well as
	及ぶ	およぶ	*vi.* reach; attain to; amount to; come up to (standard); match; equal; be a match for
	及ぼす	およぼす	*vt.* exercise (influence upon); cause (harm)

22

屯　｜　一 ヒ 口 屯 ④

音	屯	トン	station
熟	屯田兵	トンデンヘイ	colonial troops; colonial soldier

23

乏　｜　一 イ 乏 乏 ④

音	乏	ボウ	scanty; meager; scarce
訓	乏しい	とぼしい	scanty; meager; scarce

乘⑨　一　二　三　千　手　毛　乖　垂　乗

音	乗	ジョウ	get on; ride; multiply
熟	乗じる	ジョウじる	v. take advantage of (weakness, darkness, etc.); multiply
	乗員	ジョウイン	crew; crew member
	乗客	ジョウキャク	passenger
	乗降	ジョウコウ	getting on and off —vi. get on and off
	乗算	ジョウサン	**math**. multiplication
	乗車	ジョウシャ	taking a train/taxi —vi. take a train/taxi
	乗車賃	ジョウシャチン	fare; busfare; trainfare
	乗除	ジョウジョ	multiplication and division —v. multiply and divide
	乗数	ジョウスウ	**math**. multiplier
	乗船	ジョウセン	boarding ship; embarkation —vi. get on; board; embark
	乗馬	ジョウバ	riding; horseback riding —vi. ride/mount a horse
	乗法	ジョウホウ	**math**. multiplication
	乗務員	ジョウムイン	train crew; crew member
訓	乗る	のる	vi. get/step onto; take; board; mount; ride
	乗せる	のせる	vt. help a person get on; give a person a lift; take someone in
	乗り合い	のりあい	riding together; fellow passenger partnership
	乗り入れる	のりいれる	v. ride; drive into
	乗り換える	のりかえる	vi. transfer/change/switch (trains, buses, etc.)
	乗り気	のりキ	interest; enthusiasm
	乗り切る	のりきる	vi. ride out; weather; survive
	乗組員	のりくみイン	crew
	乗り越える	のりこえる	vt. climb over; overcome
	乗り越す	のりこす	vt. go past one's destination
	乗り捨てる	のりすてる	v. get out of a vehicle
	乗り手	のりて	rider; passenger
	乗り場	のりば	stop; place to get on
	乗り物	のりもの	vehicle; vessel; aircraft; ride (at an amusement park)
¥	乗っ取り	のっとり	buyout; takeover
	乗換え	のりかえ	carrying-over; continuation; refunding
	乗換取引	のりかえとりひき	swap; changeover

1 乙 おつ second

25

乙 ① 乙

| 音 | 乙 | オツ | grade B; the second in a series |
| 熟 | ※乙女 | おとめ | maiden; girl; virgin |

26

九 ② ノ 九

音	九	キュウ	nine
		ク	nine
熟	九官鳥	キュウカンチョウ	myna bird; hill myna
	九死	キュウシ	narrowly escape death
	九月	クガツ	September
	九九	クク	*math.* multiplication table
訓	九つ	ここのつ	nine
	九日	ここのか	ninth day (of the month); 9th

27

乾 ⑪ 一 十 十 古 古 直 直 卓 卓 軋 乾

音	乾	カン	dry
熟	乾季	カンキ	dry season
	乾性	カンセイ	dryness
	乾燥	カンソウ	dryness; aridity —*v.* dry; dehydrate; become dry/parched
	乾電池	カンデンチ	dry cell/battery
	乾杯	カンパイ	toast; cheers —*vi.* drink a toast
	乾物	カンブツ	dried goods/foods
	乾布摩擦	カンプマサツ	having a rubdown with a dry towel
訓	乾く	かわく	*vi.* dry up; run dry; be parched
	乾かす	かわかす	*vt.* dry; dessicate; weather
	※乾す	ほす	*vt.* dry; dry up; drink up

28 乱 ⑦

ー ニ チ 手 舌 舌 乱

音	乱	ラン	disorder; riot; rebellion
熟	乱交	ランコウ	orgy
	乱雑	ランザツ	disorder; confusion
	乱視	ランシ	astigmatism
	乱射	ランシャ	random shooting —*vi.* fire/shoot at random
	乱心	ランシン	derangement; insanity —*vi.* become mentally deranged/insane
	乱世	ランセ	tumultuous times
	乱戦	ランセン	confused/free-for-all fight
	乱造	ランゾウ	overproduction; careless manufacture —*v.* overproduce
	乱丁	ランチョウ	mixed-up collation
	乱闘	ラントウ	free-for-all fight —*vi.* have a free-for-all fight
	乱読	ランドク	indiscriminate reading —*v.* read indiscriminately
	乱入	ランニュウ	intrusion; trespassing (in large numbers) —*vi.* intrude/trespass (in large numbers)
	乱売	ランバイ	dumping/selling at a loss —*v.* dump/sell at a loss
	乱筆	ランピツ	hasty writing; scrawl
	乱暴	ランボウ	violence; rough; reckless —*vi.* be violent/rough/reckless
	乱脈	ランミャク	confusion; chaos
	乱用	ランヨウ	abuse; misuse; misappropriation —*v.* abuse; misuse; missappropriate
	乱立	ランリツ	profusion —*vi.* profuse; flood
訓	乱れる	みだれる	*vi.* be in disorder; be confused/disorganized
	乱す	みだす	*vt.* put in disorder
¥	乱高下	ランコウゲ	violent fluctuations; jumps and slumps —*v.* fluctuate violently

29 乳 ⑧

ー く く 牟 母 孚 孚 乳

音	乳	ニュウ	milk
熟	乳液	ニュウエキ	milky liquid

乳化	ニュウカ	emulsification —*vt.* emulsify
乳牛	ニュウギュウ	cow in milk; dairy cow
乳剤	ニュウザイ	emulsion
乳酸	ニュウサン	lactic acid
乳酸菌	ニュウサンキン	lactic acid bacilli
乳歯	ニュウシ	milk tooth
乳児	ニュウジ	baby; infant; suckling
乳製品	ニュウセイヒン	dairy product
乳頭	ニュウトウ	nipple; teat
乳糖	ニュウトウ	milk sugar; lactose
乳白色	ニュウハクショク	milky white
乳鉢	ニュウバチ	mortar
乳幼児	ニュウヨウジ	infants

訓

乳	ちち	mother's milk; breast
乳	ち	milk
乳首	ちくび	nipple; teat
乳飲み子	ちのみご	unweaned baby; suckling child
乳房	ちぶさ	breasts; udder
※乳母	うば	nurse; wet nurse; nanny

---

1 亅　はねぼう　feathered stick; hook; barb

30

事 ⑧　一 一 㐅 㐅 㐅 写 写 亖 事

音　事　ジ　matter; work
　　　　（ズ）

熟

事業	ジギョウ	work; undertaking; business; enterprise
事件	ジケン	event; happening; incident; matter; affair
事故	ジコ	accident; mishap; hitch; incident
事後	ジゴ	after the event/fact
事後承諾	ジゴショウダク	*ex post facto* approval
事項	ジコウ	matters; facts; data
事実	ジジツ	fact; the truth; actually; really; as a matter of fact
事実無根	ジジツムコン	groundless; false; unfounded
事象	ジショウ	matter; aspect; phase
事情	ジジョウ	reasons; circumstances; the situation; the case; conditions

事前	ジゼン	beforehand; in advance
事前調査	ジゼンチョウサ	feasibility study
事態	ジタイ	situation; state of affairs
事大主義	ジダイシュギ	submission to power; toadyism
事典	ジテン	encyclopedia
事物	ジブツ	things
事変	ジヘン	incident; disturbance
事務	ジム	office/clerical work; business
事務員	ジムイン	clerk
事務所	ジムショ	office
事務的	ジムテキ	clerical; businesslike
事由	ジユウ	reason; cause
事例	ジレイ	precedent; case; example

訓

事	こと	thing; matter; incident; circumstances; work
事柄	ことがら	matter; affair; circumstances
事毎	ことごと	everything; always

¥

事業家	ジギョウカ	entrepreneur; businessman
事業債	ジギョウサイ	industrial bond
事業税	ジギョウゼイ	business tax
事業年度	ジギョウネンド	business year
事業費	ジギョウヒ	business expenses

2

2 二 に two

31
二 ① ② 一 二

音	二	ニ	two; twice; again; next; (prefix) bi-
熟	二回	ニカイ	twice; two times; again
	二階	ニカイ	second floor; upstairs
	二月	ニガツ	February
	二級	ニキュウ	second-class
	二元	ニゲン	duality
	二号	ニゴウ	number two; concubine; mistress
	二言	ニゴン	duplicity; double-dealing; say something twice
	二次	ニジ	second (time)
	二次試験	ニジシケン	secondary examination
	二次的	ニジテキ	secondary
	二重	ニジュウ	duplicated; double
	二重人格	ニジュウジンカク	dual personality
	二乗	ニジョウ	*math.* square of a number —*v.* square (a number)
	二世	ニセイ	second generation; second generation of Japanese immigrants
	二足	ニソク	two legs/feet/pairs
	二束三文	ニソクサンモン	dirt-cheap
	二兎	ニト	two hares/rabbits
	二度	ニド	twice; two times
	二等	ニトウ	second-class/rate
	二等分	ニトウブン	bisection —*v.* bisect
	二の次	ニのつぎ	secondary importance
	二の舞	ニのまい	same mistake
	二倍	ニバイ	double; twice; two-fold; as much again
	二番	ニバン	second; number two; runner-up
	二百十日	ニヒャクとうか	210th day; first day of spring
	二部	ニブ	two parts/copies
	二分	ニブン	division into two parts; bisection —*v.* divide into two parts; halve; bisect
	二枚	ニマイ	two leaves/sheets
	二枚舌	ニマイじた	double-tongued; duplicity; equivocation
	二毛作	ニモウサク	two crops a year; double cropping
	二流	ニリュウ	second-rate

28

| 二輪 | ニリン | two wheels/flowers |
| 二輪車 | ニリンシャ | two-wheeled vehicle; bicycle |

訓

二つ	ふたつ	two
二	ふた	(prefix) two; bi-; double
二重	ふたえ	fold; two-layered; double
二心	ふたごころ	duplicity; double-dealing; treachery
二葉	ふたば	seed leaf; bud; sprout
二股	ふたまた	fork; branch; parting
※二十	はたち	twenty years old
※二十歳	はたち	twenty years old
※二十日	はつか	twentieth day (of the month); 20th
※二人	ふたり	two people; couple; we two; you two
※二日	ふつか	second day (of the month); 2nd

32

五 ④ 　一 丆 五 五

音

| 五 | ゴ | five |

熟

五月	ゴガツ	May
五感	ゴカン	the five senses
五色	ゴシキ	the five colors (blue, red, yellow, white, and black)
五十音図	ゴジュウオンズ	*gram*. systematic table of the fifty sounds of the Japanese language
五体満足	ゴタイマンゾク	person who is without any physical defect
五分	ゴブ	five percent; half
五分五分	ゴブゴブ	fifty-fifty
五輪大会	ゴリンタイカイ	Olympic games

訓

五つ	いつつ	five
五	いつ	five
※五月晴れ	さつきばれ	clearing up/clear sky (in May); lull in the early summer rain
※五月雨	さみだれ	early summer rain

33

互 ④ 　一 丆 互 互

音

| 互 | ゴ | each other; mutual |

熟

| 互角 | ゴカク | equality; equal; balanced |
| 互助 | ゴジョ | mutual aid/help —*vi*. aid/help mutually |

互選	ゴセン	election by mutual vote —*v.* elect by mutual vote
訓 互い	たがい	each other; mutual
互い違い	たがいちがい	alternately

34
井 ④　一 二 ⺕ 井

音 井	セイ（ショウ）	well
訓 井	い	well
井戸	いど	well

35
亜 ⑦　一 ⺀ 一口 一口 一甲 亜 亜

音 亜	ア	(prefix) sub-; Asia
熟 亜鉛	アエン	zinc
亜種	アシュ	subspecies
亜熱帯	アネッタイ	subtropical zones
亜流	アリュウ	follower; adherent; epigone

36
来 ⑦　一 ⺀ 丆 口 ⊏ 平 来 来

音 来	ライ	come; next; since
熟 来意	ライイ	purpose of one's visit
来客	ライキャク	visitor; caller
来月	ライゲツ	next month
来校	ライコウ	coming to school —*vi.* come to school
来航	ライコウ	arrival of ships/by ships —*vi.* arrive by ship
来襲	ライシュウ	attack; invasion; raid —*vi.* attack; invade; raid
来週	ライシュウ	next week
来春	ライシュン	next spring
来場	ライジョウ	attendance —*vi.* attend; be in attendance
来信	ライシン	received letter
来診	ライシン	doctor's visit; house call —*vi.* make a house call
来世	ライセ	afterlife; next world

来朝	ライチョウ	*clas.* visit/arrival in Japan —*v.* visit/arrive in Japan	
来店	ライテン	visit to a store/shop —*vi.* visit a store/shop	
来日	ライニチ	coming to Japan —*vi.* come to Japan	
来年	ライネン	next year	
来賓	ライヒン	guest; visitor	
来訪	ライホウ	visit; call —*vi.* come visiting/calling	
訓 来る	くる	come	
来る	きたる	*vi.* come; be forth coming	
来す	きたす	*vt.* cause/bring about (unpleasant circumstamces)	

---

2 亠 なべぶた kettle lid

37

音 亡	ボウ (モウ)	dead	
熟 亡君	ボウクン	one's deceased lord	
亡兄	ボウケイ	one's late elder brother	
亡国	ボウコク	ruined country; destruction/ruination (of a country)	
亡妻	ボウサイ	one's late wife	
亡失	ボウシツ	loss —*v.* lose; be lost	
亡夫	ボウフ	one's late husband	
亡父	ボウフ	one's late father	
亡母	ボウボ	one's late mother	
亡命	ボウメイ	escaping one's native country for political reasons; defecting —*vi.* flee one's country; defect	
亡命者	ボウメイシャ	exile; émigré; refugee; defector	
亡霊	ボウレイ	ghost; soul of a dead person	
亡者	モウジャ	ghost; the dead	
訓 亡びる	ほろびる	*vi.* perish; come to ruin	
亡ぼす	ほろぼす	*vt.* destroy; bring to ruin	
亡い	ない	the late/deceased	
亡き	なき	the late/deceased	
亡骸	なきがら	corpse; dead body	
亡くなる	なくなる	*vi.* die; pass away	

交 ⑥　　ヽ 亠 产 六 亦 交

二 亠 人 亼 イ 儿 入 八 冂 冖 冫 几 凵 刀 刂 力 勹 匕 匸 十 卜 卩 巳 厂 厶 又 ノ マ

音	交	コウ	intercourse; exchange; cross; mix
熟	交易	コウエキ	trade; commerce; barter —*v.* trade; exchange; barter
	交換	コウカン	exchange; interchange; give and take; substitution —*v.* exchange; reciprocate; substitute
	交互	コウゴ	alternation; interaction
	交差	コウサ	crossing; point of intersection —*v.* cross; intersect
	交差点	コウサテン	crossing; intersection; junction
	交際	コウサイ	intercourse; association; society; company; fellowship —*vi.* associate/fraternize with; keep company with
	交錯	コウサク	mixture; blending; complexity; intricacy —*vi.* mingle with; be complicated/intricate
	交渉	コウショウ	negotiation; bargaining; relationship —*vi.* negotiate; bargain; discuss; have a relationship
	交戦	コウセン	war; hostilities; combat; action —*vi.* fight; engage in hostilities/combat
	交替	コウタイ	relief; change; shift —*vi.* take turns; alternate; rotate; relieve
	交通	コウツウ	traffic; communication; transportation; navigation
	交通機関	コウツウキカン	transit system
	交通費	コウツウヒ	traveling expenses; fare
	交配	コウハイ	crossbreeding; hybridization; crossfertilization —*v.* hybridize; cross; crossbreed; interbreed
	交番	コウバン	police box
	交付	コウフ	delivery; grant; transfer; service —*v.* deliver; grant; transfer; service
	交友	コウユウ	friend; aquaintance
	交遊	コウユウ	companionship; friendship —*vi.* associate with; keep company with
	交流	コウリュウ	alternating current (AC); interchange
訓	交わす	かわす	*vt.* exchange; cross; intersect
	交う	かう	(suffix) cross; intersect
	交ざる	まざる	*vi.* mix; mingle; blend
	交える	まじえる	*vt.* mix; cross; exchange
	交じる	まじる	*vi.* be mixed/mingled/blended; mix; mingle; join

| 交わる | まじわる | *vi.* associate with; keep company with; cross; intersect; join |
| 交ぜる | まぜる | *vt.* blend; mix; include |

39 京 ⑧

`, 一 亠 亠 亠 亨 亨 京`

音 京	キョウ	capital; metropolis; Kyoto; Tokyo; ten quadrillion
	ケイ	
熟 京風	キョウフウ	Kyoto-style (food)
訓 京	みやこ	capital; metropolis

40 享 ⑧

`, 一 亠 亠 亠 亨 享 享`

音 享	キョウ	receive; accept; possess; enjoy
熟 享受	キョウジュ	enjoyment of artistic beauty —*v.* enjoy; have; be given
享年	キョウネン	age when one dies; length of one's life
享楽	キョウラク	enjoyment —*v.* enjoy
享楽主義	キョウラクシュギ	epicurism; hedonism

41 亭 ⑨

`, 一 亠 亠 亠 亨 亭 亭 亭`

| 音 亭 | テイ | inn; restaurant; arbor |
| 熟 亭主 | テイシュ | master; host; landlord; innkeeper; one's husband |

2 人 ひと man

42 人 ②

`ノ 人`

| 音 人 | ジン | man |
| | ニン | man; character |

33

人為	ジンイ	act of man
人為的	ジンイテキ	artificial
人員	ジンイン	number of persons; staff; personnel
人家	ジンカ	house; dwelling
人格	ジンカク	personality; character
人格化	ジンカクカ	personification —v. personify
人絹	ジンケン	rayon; artificial silk
人権	ジンケン	human rights
人権宣言	ジンケンセンゲン	Declaration of Human Rights
人件費	ジンケンヒ	personnel expenses
人後	ジンゴ	next person
人工	ジンコウ	artificial; man-made
人工衛星	ジンコウエイセイ	artificial satelite
人工栄養	ジンコウエイヨウ	bottle feeding
人工呼吸	ジンコウコキュウ	artificial respiration; mouth-to-mouth resuscitation —vi. give mouth-to-mouth resuscitation
人工受精	ジンコウジュセイ	artificial insemination —vi. be artificially inseminated
人工知能	ジンコウチノウ	artificial intelligence
人工的	ジンコウテキ	artificial; man-made
人口	ジンコウ	population
人口密度	ジンコウミツド	population density
人災	ジンサイ	disaster caused by human error
人材	ジンザイ	talent; ability
人士	ジンシ	man of good breeding; gentleman
人事	ジンジ	personnel affairs
人事不省	ジンジフセイ	unconscious; fainting; coma
人種	ジンシュ	race; ethnic group
人種差別	ジンシュサベツ	racial discrimination —vi. discriminate on the basis of race
人種的偏見	ジンシュテキヘンケン	racial prejudice
人心	ジンシン	the people's mind; public feeling
人生	ジンセイ	life
人生観	ジンセイカン	view of life; outlook on life
人跡	ジンセキ	human traces
人跡未踏	ジンセキミトウ	unexplored; untrodden
人選	ジンセン	selection of a suitable person —vi. select a suitable person
人造	ジンゾウ	artificial; manmade; imitation; synthetic
人造繊維	ジンゾウセンイ	synthetic fiber
人造人間	ジンゾウニンゲン	robot
人造皮革	ジンゾウヒカク	artificial leather

人体	ジンタイ	human body
人知	ジンチ	human intelligence/knowledge/understanding
人畜	ジンチク	man and beast; human or animal
人的	ジンテキ	human
人道	ジンドウ	humanity
人道主義	ジンドウシュギ	humanitarianism
人道的	ジンドウテキ	humane
人頭税	ジントウゼイ	poll tax
人徳	ジントク	natural virtue
人品	ジンピン	character; personality; appearance
人物	ジンブツ	character; person; figure
人物画	ジンブツガ	portrait
人物画家	ジンブツガカ	portrait painter
人文	ジンブン	humanity; civilization; culture
	ジンモン	
人文科学	ジンブンカガク	the humanities
人望	ジンボウ	popularity
人民	ジンミン	the people/citizens
人名	ジンメイ	person's name
人命	ジンメイ	human life; people's lives
人力車	ジンリキシャ	rickshaw
人力	ジンリョク	human power/strength
人類	ジンルイ	human race; mankind; humanity
人類学	ジンルイガク	anthropology
人気	ニンキ	popularity
人気歌手	ニンキカシュ	pop singer/idol
人気作家	ニンキサッカ	popular writer
人魚	ニンギョ	mermaid
人形	ニンギョウ	doll; puppet
人間	ニンゲン	man; human being; mankind
人間衛星	ニンゲンエイセイ	manned satellite
人間関係	ニンゲンカンケイ	human relations
人間国宝	ニンゲンコクホウ	living national treasure
人間性	ニンゲンセイ	humanity
人間味	ニンゲンミ	warm-hearted
人称	ニンショウ	*gram.* grammatical person
人情	ニンジョウ	humaneness; human feelings
人参	ニンジン	carrot
人数	ニンズウ	number of persons
人相	ニンソウ	looks; physiognomy
人足	ニンソク	*derog.* laborer; navvy
人夫	ニンプ	*derog.* laborer; navvy

二十人・人ヘイ儿入八冂冖冫几凵刀刂力勹匕匚十卜卩巳厶又了ケマ

2

訓	人	ひと	man; person; people
	人影	ひとかげ	figure; form; shadow
	人柄	ひとがら	person; character; type/kind/sort (of person)
	人気	ひとけ	sign/presense of people
	人事	ひとごと	other people's affairs
	人殺し	ひとごろし	murder —v. murder
	人里	ひとざと	village; human dwellings
	人質	ひとジチ	hostage
	人手	ひとで	help; hand
	人出	ひとで	crowds; crowded
	人並み	ひとなみ	ordinary; commonplace; average
	人波	ひとなみ	surging crowd
	人々	ひとびと	people; each person
	人前	ひとまえ	in public; in the prescence of others
	人任せ	ひとまかせ	leaving (work) to someone else
	人見知り	ひとみしり	bashful/shy (in front of strangers)
	人目	ひとめ	notice; attention
¥	人為相場	ジンイソウバ	artificial price; manipulated quotation
	人員整理	ジンインセイリ	personnel cut/reduction
	人件費	ジンケンヒ	personnel expenses; labor cost
	人材銀行	ジンザイギンコウ	talent bank
	人気株	ニンキかぶ	active stock

43

以 ⑤ 　丶 𠄌 𠄎 𠄐 以

音	以	イ	by; since; with
熟	以遠	イエン	beyond; farther
	以下	イカ	less than; below; not more than
	以外	イガイ	except; outside of; excluding; besides
	以後	イゴ	after this; from now on; hereafter; henceforth; since
	以降	イコウ	from that time; from now on
	以上	イジョウ	not less than; or more; and over; more than
	以心伝心	イシンデンシン	communion of mind with mind; telepathy; empathy
	以前	イゼン	formerly; before
	以内	イナイ	within; less than; not more than
	以来	イライ	since then; from that time on; ever since
訓	以て	もって	by means of
	以ての外	もってのほか	outrageous; preposterous; scandalous

44

介 ④ ノ ヘ 介 介

音	介	カイ	mediate; interpose
熟	介する	カイする	*vt.* help; support; aid
	介在	カイザイ	interposition —*vi.* interpose; lie between
	介入	カイニュウ	intervention —*vi.* intervene
	介抱	カイホウ	nursing; care —*v.* nurse/care for

45

今 ④ ノ ヘ 스 今

音	今	キン	present
		コン	now; this time
熟	今回	コンカイ	lately; this time
	今月	コンゲツ	this month
	今後	コンゴ	after this; henceforth; hereafter
	今昔	コンジャク	past and present
	今週	コンシュウ	this week
	今度	コンド	this/next time
	今日	コンニチ	today
	今晩	コンバン	this evening
訓	今	いま	now
	※今日	きょう	today
	※今朝	けさ	this morning
	※今年	ことし	this year

46

令 ⑤ ノ ヘ 스 今 令

音	令	レイ	rule; order; command (honorific prefix)
熟	令室	レイシツ	*hon.* your wife
	令状	レイジョウ	warrant; writ
	令嬢	レイジョウ	*hon.* your daughter
	令息	レイソク	*hon.* your son

令夫人　　レイフジン　　*hon*. Mrs.; Lady; Madam; your wife

二　一人　へ　イ　几　入　八　冂　冖　丷　几　凵　刀　刂　力　勹　匕　匚　十　卜　卩　卩　厂　厶　又　了　ク　マ

音	会	エ	meet; memorial service
		カイ	meet; meeting; society
熟	会釈	エシャク	bow; greeting —*vi*. bow; greet
	会得	エトク	comprehension; understanding —*v*. comprehend; understand
	会員	カイイン	member; membership
	会館	カイカン	hall; assembly hall
	会議	カイギ	conference; meeting —*vi*. have a conference/meeting
	会合	カイゴウ	meeting; gathering; assembly —*vi*. meet; gather; assemble
	会社	カイシャ	company; corporation
	会食	カイショク	dining together —*vi*. dine together
	会則	カイソク	rules of an association
	会談	カイダン	talk; conference; conversation —*vi*. talk together; have a conference
	会報	カイホウ	bulletin; report
	会話	カイワ	conversation; talk —*vi*. converse; talk
訓	会う	あう	*vi*. meet
¥	会期	カイキ	session/period (of a meeting)
	会計	カイケイ	accounts; finance; bill; accounting —*v*. settle accounts; pay bills
	会計監査	カイケイカンサ	accounting audit
	会計帳簿	カイケイチョウボ	book of accounts
	会計年度	カイケイネンド	fiscal year
	会社法	カイシャホウ	company law
	会頭	カイトウ	president (of a society, etc.)

音	企	キ	plan; plot
熟	企画	キカク	plan; planning —*v*. plan
	企図	キト	plan; project; design; attempt —*v*. plan; design; attempt
訓	企て	くわだて	plan; scheme; project

企てる	くわだてる	*vt*. plan; scheme; design; attempt; try; undertake
¥ 企業	キギョウ	enterprise

49

全 ⑥　ノ 入 入 仝 全 全

音	全	ゼン	all; complete
熟	全域	ゼンイキ	the whole area
	全員	ゼンイン	all the members; the whole staff/crew
	全快	ゼンカイ	full recovery —*vi*. recover fully
	全壊	ゼンカイ	complete destruction —*vi*. be completely destroyed
	全額	ゼンガク	sum total
	全権	ゼンケン	full authority
	全校	ゼンコウ	whole school; all the schools
	全国	ゼンコク	the whole country; nationwide; national
	全集	ゼンシュウ	complete/collected works
	全書	ゼンショ	complete book; compendium
	全焼	ゼンショウ	total destruction by fire —*vi*. be totally destroyed by fire
	全勝	ゼンショウ	complete victory —*vi*. win a complete victory
	全身	ゼンシン	the whole body
	全盛	ゼンセイ	prime; height of prosperity
	全盛期	ゼンセイキ	one's prime period
	全然	ゼンゼン	utterly; entirely; not at all
	全速力	ゼンソクリョク	full speed; top speed
	全体	ゼンタイ	the whole; in all
	全治	ゼンチ	complete cure —*vi*. fully recover; heal completely
	全長	ゼンチョウ	overall length
	全土	ゼンド	the whole country
	全能	ゼンノウ	omnipotent; all powerful
	全敗	ゼンパイ	complete defeat —*vi*. be/defeated completely
	全廃	ゼンパイ	total abolition —*v*. be totally abolished
	全般	ゼンパン	whole; general; overall
	全部	ゼンブ	all; whole; entirely
	全文	ゼンブン	full text; whole sentence
	全貌	ゼンボウ	the whole thing
	全滅	ゼンメツ	annihilation; extermination; destruction —*v*. annihilate; exterminate; destroy
	全面的	ゼンメンテキ	full; general

二亠人へイ儿入八冂冖冫几凵刀刂力勹匕匸十卜卩巳厂厶又了冫マ

	全訳	ゼンヤク	complete/unabridged translation —*v.* make a complete and unabridged translation
	全容	ゼンヨウ	full story/picture
	全力	ゼンリョク	all one's power; one's every effort; full capacity
訓	全うする	まっとうする	*vt.* accomplish; fulfil
	全く	まったく	entirely; completely; truly; indeed

50

余 ⑦　ノ　人　ム　全　会　余　余

音	余	ヨ	remainder; the rest; other; more than; myself; I
熟	余韻	ヨイン	trailing note; reverberation; aftertaste
	余暇	ヨカ	leisure; spare time
	余技	ヨギ	hobby; avocation
	余儀なく	ヨギなく	unavoidable; obliged to
	余興	ヨキョウ	entertainment; side show
	余計	ヨケイ	unnecessary; more than enough; extra; uncalled for
	余罪	ヨザイ	other crimes
	余剰	ヨジョウ	surplus
	余震	ヨシン	aftershock (of an earthquake)
	余人	ヨジン	other people; others
	余生	ヨセイ	the rest of one's life
	余勢	ヨセイ	surplus energy
	余談	ヨダン	digression
	余地	ヨチ	room; place; margin; scope
	余熱	ヨネツ	lingering summer heat
	余念	ヨネン	thinking of other matters
	余波	ヨハ	after/secondary effects; consequences
	余白	ヨハク	blank; space; margin
	余病	ヨビョウ	complications; secondary disease
	余分	ヨブン	extra; excess
	余程	ヨほど	very; much; to a great degree
	余命	ヨメイ	the rest of one's life
	余裕	ヨユウ	surplus; leeway; room; margin
	余力	ヨリョク	remaining strength; surplus energy
訓	余る	あまる	*vi.* remain; be more than enough; exceed
	余り	あまり	remainder; surplus; more than; very; as a result of

| 余す | あます | *vt.* leave; save |
| ¥ 余財 | ヨザイ | spare cash; surplus assets |

51

舎 ⑧　ノ 人 ハ 스 仐 全 佘 舎 舎

音	舎	シャ	inn; building
熟	舎監	シャカン	dormitory superintendent
	舎兄	シャケイ	*hum.* my elder brother
	舎弟	シャテイ	*hum.* my younger brother
	舎利	シャリ	*Bud.* one's remains/ashes; rice (in sushi bar)

52

倉 ⑩　ノ 人 ハ 今 今 仐 仒 佥 倉 倉

音	倉	ソウ	warehouse; storehouse
熟	倉庫	ソウコ	warehouse
訓	倉	くら	warehouse; storehouse
	倉敷	くらしき	storage place
	倉主	くらぬし	warehouse owner
¥	倉敷料	くらしきリョウ	storage fee
	倉荷証券	くらにショウケン	warehouse claim check

53

傘 ⑫　ノ 人 ハ 人 夅 夅 夅 夅 夅 夅 夲 傘

音	傘	サン	umbrella
熟	傘下	サンカ	under the umbrella; affiliated; subsidary
訓	傘	かさ	umbrella

54

舗 ⑮　入 人 牟 全 舎 舎 舎 舘 舘 銬 舗 舗

音	舗	ホ	shop; store
熟	舗装	ホソウ	pavement; paving —*v.* pave (a road, street, etc.)
	舗道	ホドウ	pavement; paved street

二十人入イ几入八冂冖冫几凵刀刂力勹匕匚十卜卩㔾厂厶又了ク㔾

2 イ　にんべん　man to the left

55

化④　ノ　イ　イ′　化

音	化	カ	transform; change
		ケ	die; civilize; change
熟	化学	カガク	chemistry
	化学肥料	カガクヒリョウ	chemical fertilizer
	化学兵器	カガクヘイキ	chemical weapons
	化合	カゴウ	*chem*. chemical combination; compound —*vi*. combine to make a compound out of two or more elements
	化成	カセイ	transformation —*vi*. transform
	化石	カセキ	fossil
	化繊	カセン	synthetic fiber
	化膿	カノウ	*med*. festering; suppuration; discharge of pus —*vi*. fester; suppurate; generate pus
	化粧	ケショウ	cosmetic makeup; toiletries —*v*. make up; put on make up
	化粧室	ケショウシツ	toilet; lavatory
	化粧品	ケショウヒン	makeup; cosmetics
	化身	ケシン	incarnation/manifestation of a god or buddha; reincarnation
訓	化ける	ばける	*vi*. transform; disguise oneself
	化かす	ばかす	*vt*. bewitch; enchant; deceive
	化けの皮	ばけのかわ	disguise
	化け物	ばけもの	apparition; goblin; monster

56

仁④　ノ　イ　イ一　仁

音	仁	ジン	compassion
		（ニ）	
熟	仁愛	ジンアイ	benevolence
	仁義	ジンギ	humanity and justice; duty; respect
	仁慈	ジンジ	benevolence; mercy
	仁術	ジンジュツ	benevolent act; caring profession; art of healing
	仁徳	ジントク	benevolence
	仁王	ニオウ	the two Deva kings

仏 ④ ノ イ 仏 仏

音	仏	フツ	France; French
		ブツ	Buddha; Buddhism
熟	仏閣	ブッカク	Buddhist temple
	仏教	ブッキョウ	Buddhism
	仏具	ブツグ	Buddhist altar articles
	仏寺	ブツジ	Buddhist temple
	仏事	ブツジ	Buddhist memorial service
	仏式	ブッシキ	Buddhist rite
	仏舎利	ブッシャリ	Buddha's ashes
	仏心	ブッシン	Buddha's heart/character
	仏前	ブツゼン	before/in front of Buddha/the tablet of the deceased; Buddhist altar offerings
	仏像	ブツゾウ	Buddhist image
	仏陀	ブツダ	Buddha
	仏壇	ブツダン	household Buddhist altar
	仏頂面	ブッチョウづら	sour face; pout; scowl
	仏典	ブッテン	Buddhist scripture/literature
	仏殿	ブツデン	Buddhist temple
	仏道	ブツドウ	Buddhism
	仏法	ブッポウ	Buddhism
	仏法僧	ブッポウソウ	Buddha, doctrine, and priesthood; broad-billed roller; Japanese scops owl
	仏間	ブツマ	Buddhist altar room
	仏滅	ブツメツ	Buddha's death *fig.* unlucky day (on the Japanese calendar)
	仏門	ブツモン	Buddhism; Buddhist priesthood
	※仏蘭西	フランス	France
訓	仏	ほとけ	Buddha; Buddhist image; the dead
	仏心	ほとけごころ	merciful; kindhearted (like Buddha)
	仏様	ほとけさま	Buddha; dead person

58

仕 ⑤ ノ イ 仁 仕 仕

音	仕	シ	serve; work; to do
		ジ	
熟	仕上げる	しあげる	*vt.* finish; complete

二 亠 人 ∧ イ 几 入 八 冂 冖 冫 几 凵 刀 刂 力 勹 匕 匸 十 卜 卩 㔾 厂 厶 又 マ ㇉

仕打ち	シうち	treatment; behavior; action; conduct
仕送り	シおくり	allowance; remittance —v. send/remit money; make an allowance
仕返し	シかえし	revenge; retaliation —vi. avenge oneself; retaliate
仕掛ける	シかける	vt. start; begin; set up; prepare; challenge
仕官	シカン	government service —vi. enter government service
仕切り	シきり	dividing line; boundary; partition
仕草	シぐさ	behavior; acting; gestures
仕事	シごと	occupation; work; job; business
仕込む	シこむ	vt. train; teach; stock up
仕立て	シたて	tailoring
仕立てる	シたてる	vt. sew; tailor; prepare; train
仕舞う	シまう	vt. put away; put back; close; close down; finish

訓 仕える　つかえる　vi. serve; work under; be clogged/blocked

¥ 仕入れ　シいれ　purchase; stocking

仕掛かり品	シかかりヒン	work in process
仕切り	シきり	transaction on dealer's basis
仕組み	シくみ	set up; structure; mechanism
仕手	シて	speculator
仕手株	シてかぶ	speculative leaders

59

仙 ⑤　ノ イ 仁 仙 仙

音 仙　セン　hermit; wizard

熟 仙人　センニン　hermit; wizard

60

他 ⑤　ノ イ 化 仲 他

音 他	タ	other; another; outside; different
熟 他意	タイ	another intention; ulterior motive; secret purpose
他界	タカイ	death; demise; the other world; another world —vi. die; pass away
他国	タコク	strange land; foreign country; another province
他言	タゴン	disclosure —v. divulge; reveal; let out; disclose
他殺	タサツ	murder; homicide; manslaughter

他薦	タセン	recommendation by another person —*v*. be recommended by another person
他人	タニン	another person; others; unrelated person; outsider; third party; stranger
他方	タホウ	the other hand/side; another side/place
他面	タメン	the other/another side
他力本願	タリキホンガン	salvation through faith in the Amida Buddha
訓 他	ほか	other; another
¥ 他人資本	タニンシホン	borrowed capital

61

代⑤　ノ　イ　仁　代　代

音 代	タイ	
	ダイ	substitution; proxy; reign; era
熟 代案	ダイアン	alternative plan
代議員	ダイギイン	representative; delegate
代議士	ダイギシ	congressman; dietman; member of Parliament
代償	ダイショウ	compensation; indemnification —*v*. compensate; indemnify
代数	ダイスウ	*math*. algebra
代打	ダイダ	*bas*. pinch hitter —*vi*. pinch hit
代々	ダイダイ	from generation to generation
代読	ダイドク	reading by proxy —*v*. read by proxy; read on behalf of someone else
代筆	ダイヒツ	writing by proxy —*v*. write on behalf of someone else
代表	ダイヒョウ	representative; delegation; deputation —*v*. represent; be representative of; stand/act for
代表的	ダイヒョウテキ	representative; typical
代弁	ダイベン	speaking by proxy; agency; commission; payment by proxy —*v*. speak/pay by proxy
代名詞	ダイメイシ	*gram*. pronoun
代役	ダイヤク	substitution; substitute; understudy
代用	ダイヨウ	substitution —*v*. substitute
代理	ダイリ	representation; agency; proxy —*v*. act for; represent; deputy
訓 代える	かえる	*vt*. change; alter; convert; renew; reform
代わる	かわる	*vi*. take the place of; replace; be substituted
代わり	かわり	substitute; deputy; alternative; compensation
代	よ	the world; society; age; era; rule; reign
¥ 代価	ダイカ	price; cost

二 亠 人 ⼈ イ 儿 入 八 冂 ⼍ 冫 几 凵 刀 刂 力 勹 匕 匚 十 卜 卩 㔾 厂 ム 又 了 ク マ

代金	ダイキン	price; cost; charge; bill; fee
代行	ダイコウ	proxy —*v.* carry out as proxy; act for another
代表者	ダイヒョウシャ	representative; delegate
代表団	ダイヒョウダン	delegation
代理店	ダイリテン	agency; agent

62 付 ⑤ ノ イ 亻 付 付

音	付	フ	attach
熟	付する	フする	*vt.* add; attach; wear; apply; use; refer to
	付加	フカ	addition; annexation; supplement; appendix —*v.* add; annex; supplement; append
	付記	フキ	written addition; additional/supplementary (written) remark —*v.* add in writing; append
	付近	フキン	neighborhood; vicinity; environs
	付随	フズイ	annex; accompanied —*vi.* be annexed; accompany; go with; follow; attend
	付箋	フセン	memo tag; slip
	付属	フゾク	belonging to; adjunctive; incidental; subsidiary; branch school —*vi.* be attached/belong to
	付着	フチャク	adherence; sticking; adhesion; cohesion —*vi.* adhere to; stick; attach
	付与	フヨ	grant; bestowal; allowance —*v.* give; grant; allow; bestow
	付録	フロク	supplement in a book/magazine; appendix
	付和雷同	フワライドウ	blind following —*vi.* follow blindly/suit
訓	付く	つく	*vi.* stick; adhere; touch; reach; come; set; be dyed/colored; be decided
	付き合う	つきあう	*vi.* accompany; socialize; go out together
	付き添う	つきそう	*vi.* accompany; be with
	付ける	つける	*vt.* add; attach; append; fix; put on; wear; apply; use; add; join; attend to; name; light a fire; load
¥	付随業務	フズイギョウム	appended business

63 仮 ⑥ ノ イ 亻 仔 仮 仮

音	仮	カ	temporary; provisional; forgive
		（ケ）	false; feigned

熟	仮死	カシ	*med.* suspended animation; asphyxia; temporary suspension of the vital functions
	仮借	カシャク	pardoning; leniency; forgiveness; borrowing —*v.* pardon; be lenient; borrow; forgive
	仮称	カショウ	tentative/provisional name —*v.* give (something) a provisional name
	仮性	カセイ	(prefix) false; psuedo-
	仮設	カセツ	temporary construction —*v.* put up a temporary construction; construct temporarily
	仮説	カセツ	hypothesis
	仮装	カソウ	disguise; fancy clothes —*vi.* disguise oneself; wear fancy clothes
	仮定	カテイ	supposition; assumption; presumption —*v.* suppose; assume; presume
	仮名	カな	*kana* (Japanese syllabary)
	仮眠	カミン	doze; nap —*vi.* take a nap; have forty winks
	仮名	カメイ	pseudonym; assumed name; alias
	仮面	カメン	mask
	仮病	ケビョウ	feigned illness
訓	仮	かり	temporary
¥	仮受金	かりうけキン	suspense receipt
	仮需要	かりジュヨウ	credit/loan demand; emergency/speculative demand
	仮払金	かりばらいキン	temporary payment

64

休 ⑥ ノ イ 仁 什 休 休

音	休	キュウ	resting; taking a break; giving up; quitting
熟	休暇	キュウカ	holiday; holidays; vacation
	休会	キュウカイ	adjournment; recess —*vi.* adjourn
	休学	キュウガク	temporary absence from school —*vi.* be absent from school for a time
	休火山	キュウカザン	dormant volcano
	休刊	キュウカン	suspension/discontinuation of publication —*vi.* suspend publication
	休憩	キュウケイ	rest; break; time off —*vi.* rest; have a break
	休校	キュウコウ	closing down of school —*vi.* close; be closed
	休講	キュウコウ	cancelling a lecture —*vi.* cancel a lecture
	休止	キュウシ	pause; standstill; suspension; stoppage —*v.* cease; pause; suspend; stop
	休日	キュウジツ	holiday; day off
	休診	キュウシン	No Surgery Today —*vi.* close a doctor's surgery (for the day)

二二人へイ儿入八冂冖冫几凵刀刂力勹匕匚十卜卩巴厂厶又了〻マ

休戦	キュウセン	armistice; truce; ceasefire —*vi.* conclude an armistice; cease firing
休息	キュウソク	rest; repose; relaxation; respite —*vi.* rest; take a rest; relax
休養	キュウヨウ	rest; relaxation; recuperation —*vi.* rest; take a rest; recuperate
訓 休み	やすみ	rest; respite; break; repose; holiday
休む	やすむ	*vi.* rest from; stop; suspend; be absent
¥ 休業	キュウギョウ	shutdown; closure of business operation —*vi.* close a business
休職	キュウショク	temporary retirement —*vi.* retire from work for a short time

65
仰 ⑥ ノ イ イ 化 仞 仰

音 仰	ギョウ (コウ)	look up; respect; revere
熟 仰角	ギョウカク	elevation *math.* angle of elevation
仰天	ギョウテン	astonishment —*vi.* be astounded
訓 仰ぐ	あおぐ	*v.* look up; respect; ask for; depend on; drink
仰向け	あおむけ	turning to face upward
仰せ	おおせ	*hon.* what you say

66
件 ⑥ ノ イ イ 仆 件 件

音 件	ケン	matter; case (counter for cases)
熟 件数	ケンスウ	number of cases
訓 ※件	くだり	clause; paragraph
※件の	くだんの	the same; the said; in question

67
仲 ⑥ ノ イ 什 化 们 仲

音 仲	チュウ	relations; relationships; terms
熟 仲介	チュウカイ	intermediation; mediation; agency —*v.* mediate; intercede
仲裁	チュウサイ	arbitration; mediation; intervention; intercession —*v.* arbitrate; mediate; intervene; interceed

訓	仲	なか	relations; relationship; terms
	仲居	なかい	parlormaid; waitress
	仲買	なかがい	broking; brokerage
	仲買人	なかがいニン	broker; middleman; agent
	仲違い	なかたがい	quarrel; discord; dissension —*vi.* quarrel; get into a dispute
	仲立ち	なかだち	mediation; matchmaking —*v.* mediate; matchmake
	仲直り	なかなおり	reconciliation; peacemaking; restoration of friendship —*vi.* reconcile; make up; make the peace
	仲間	なかま	company; party; set; circle; friends
	仲良し	なかよし	intimacy; familiar terms; intimate friend
	※仲人	なこうど	go-between; marriage broker; matchmaker

68

伝 ⑥ ノ イ イ 仁 伝 伝

音	伝	デン	convey; transmit; communicate; legend; tradition; life; biography
熟	伝記	デンキ	biography; life
	伝言	デンゴン	message —*v.* leave word; give/send a message
	伝言板	デンゴンバン	message board
	伝授	デンジュ	initiation; instruction —*v.* initiate; instruct
	伝承	デンショウ	oral tradition; transmission; handing down —*v.* hand down; transmit by word of mouth
	伝心	デンシン	mutual understanding of mutual thoughts
	伝説	デンセツ	legend; tradition
	伝染	デンセン	contagion; infection; communication of disease —*vi.* be contagious/infectious/infective
	伝染病	デンセンビョウ	contagious disease
	伝送	デンソウ	transmission —*v.* transmit
	伝達	デンタツ	transmission; conveyance; communication; propagation —*v.* transmit; convey; communicate; deliver; notify
	伝統	デントウ	tradition; conversion
	伝統的	デントウテキ	traditional; conventional
	伝道	デンドウ	missionary work; evangelism —*vi.* evangelize; engage in missionary work
	伝導	デンドウ	conduction; transmission —*v.* conduct; transmit
	伝播	デンパ	dissemination; circulation; propagation; diffusion —*vi.* be propagated/disseminated/circulated
	伝票	デンピョウ	chit; slip; ticket
	伝聞	デンブン	rumor; hearsay; report —*v.* hear from others;

二一人ヘイ几入八冂一冫几凵刀刂力勹匕匚十卜卩巳厂厶又了勹マ

			be informed; learn by hearsay
	伝来	デンライ	introduction; transmission —*vi.* be transmitted/handed down/introduced
	伝令	デンレイ	message
訓	伝える	つたえる	*vt.* convey; report; deliver; communicate; transmit; teach
	伝わる	つたわる	*vi.* be handed down/transmitted/conveyed/introduced
	伝う	つたう	*vi.* go along
	伝え	つたえ	legend
	伝わり	つたわり	propagation
	伝	つて	intermediary; introducer; medium

69

任 ⑥ ノ イ イ 仁 仟 任

音	任	ニン	trust, duty
熟	任じる	ニンじる	appoint; nominate; assume; profess; pose
	任意	ニンイ	option; pleasure; discretion
	任官	ニンカン	appointment; installation; commission —*vi.* be appointed/installed/commissioned
	任期	ニンキ	term/period of office
	任地	ニンチ	place of one's appointment; one's post
	任務	ニンム	duty; office; task; function; mission
	任命	ニンメイ	appointment; nomination; designation; commission —*v.* appoint; nominate; designate; commission
	任免	ニンメン	appointment and dismissal; hiring and firing —*v.* appoint and dismiss
	任用	ニンヨウ	employment; appointment —*v.* employ; appoint
訓	任せる	まかせる	*vt.* entrust; delegate; commission
	任す	まかす	*vt.* entrust; delegate; commission
¥	任意積立金	ニンイ つみたてキン	voluntary reserve

70

伐 ⑥ ノ イ 伀 代 伐 伐

音	伐	バツ	subjugate; cut
熟	伐採	バッサイ	lumbering; felling —*v.* lumber; fell
	伐木	バッボク	logging —*vi.* fell trees

二 亠 人 ヘ イ 儿 入 八 冂 冖 冫 几 凵 刀 刂 力 勹 匕 匚 十 卜 卩 卪 厂 厶 又 了 亅 マ

71 伏 ⑥ ノ イ 亻 仆 伏 伏

音	伏	フク	bend down
熟	伏線	フクセン	foreshadowing; precautionary measures
	伏兵	フクヘイ	ambush
	伏流	フクリュウ	undercurrent
訓	伏す	ふす	bend down; prostrate oneself be bed-ridden; lie down; hide
	伏せる	ふせる	turn downward; cover; lay; conceal
	伏して	ふして	bowing down; respectfully
	伏し目	ふしめ	downcast expression

72 位 ⑦ ノ イ 亻 什 竹 竹 位 位

音	位	イ	rank; position; grade
熟	位相	イソウ	*math.* topology *phy.* phase
	位置	イチ	position; situation; location —*vi.* be positioned/situated/located
	位牌	イハイ	Buddhist mortuary tablet
訓	位	くらい	grade; rank; dignity; the throne; about; approximately
	位する	くらいする	*vi.* rank; be ranked/located/placed

73 何 ⑦ ノ イ 亻 仃 何 何 何

音	何	カ	what
訓	何	なに	what; anything else
		（なん）	what
	何事	なにごと	what; everything; whatever
	何者	なにもの	who; what
	何十	なんジュウ	(how) many; tens of
	何度	なんド	how many degrees; how many times; how often
	何人	なんニン	how many (people)
	何分	なにぶん	please, at any rate; somewhat
	何故	なにゆえ	why

二十 人 入 ヘ
• イ 几 入 八 冂 宀
丷 几 凵 刀 刂 力 勹 匕 匸 十 卜 卩 㔾 厂 ム 又 了 マ

74

佐 ⑦
ノ イ 仁 件 佐 佐 佐

音	佐	サ	assist; help; aid; colonel
熟	佐官	サカン	field officer; captain; commander

75

作 ⑦
ノ イ 仁 仁 竹 竹 作 作

音	作	サ	working
		サク	make; work; harvest
熟	作業	サギョウ	work; operations —*vi.* work; operate
	作業員	サギョウイン	worker
	作業時間	サギョウジカン	working hours
	作為	サクイ	deliberate; intentional; contrived
	作意	サクイ	intentional; deliberate
	作柄	サクがら	crops
	作詞	サクシ	lyrical writing —*v.* write lyrics
	作詩	サクシ	poetry composition —*vi.* write poetry/verse
	作者	サクシャ	author; writer; poet
	作図	サクズ	drawing figures; construction of diagrams —*v.* draw a diagram; construct a shape
	作製	サクセイ	manufacture; production —*v.* manufacture; production
	作成	サクセイ	preparation; drawing up —*v.* make; prepare; draw up
	作戦	サクセン	tactics; operations; action; strategy
	作品	サクヒン	work (of art, literature, etc.)
	作風	サクフウ	literary style; style
	作文	サクブン	composition; essay
	作物	サクモツ	crops; farm produce
	作家	サッカ	novelist; writer; author
	作曲	サッキョク	musical composition —*v.* compose/write music
	作曲家	サッキョクカ	composer
	作法	サホウ	manners; etiquette
	作用	サヨウ	action; effect —*vi.* act on
訓	作る	つくる	*vt.* make; manufacture; grow; till; form; establish; cook
	作り	つくり	composition; workmanship
	作り出す	つくりだす	*vt.* make; manufacture

76

伺 ⑦ ノ イ 亻 门 佰 伺 伺

音	伺	シ	visit
熟	伺候	シコウ	waiting upon a person; presenting oneself to a superior —*vi.* wait upon a person; present oneself to a superior
訓	伺う	うかがう	*vt. hon.* ask; visit

77

似 ⑦ ノ イ 亻 们 仯 似 似

音	似	ジ	resemble
訓	似合う	にあう	*vi.* go well with; look good with
	似顔絵	にがおえ	portrait
	似る	にる	*vi.* resemble; look like

78

住 ⑦ ノ イ 亻 广 住 住 住

音	住	ジュウ	live
熟	住居	ジュウキョ	residence; house; home
	住所	ジュウショ	address
	住職	ジュウショク	chief priest (of a Buddhist temple)
	住宅	ジュウタク	house; residence
	住人	ジュウニン	inhabitant; resident
	住民	ジュウミン	inhabitant; resident
訓	住む	すむ	*vi.* live; dwell; be resident
	住まい	すまい	house; residence; home
	住まう	すまう	*vi.* live; dwell; be resident

79

伸 ⑦ ノ イ 亻 们 伃 伸 伸

音	伸	シン	extend; stretch; grow
熟	伸縮	シンシュク	expansion and contraction; elasticity —*v.* be elastic

53

二 十 人 ∧ イ 儿 入 八 冂 宀 ⺀ 几 凵 刀 刂 力 勹 ヒ 匚 十 卜 卩 已 厂 ム 又 了 ⺈ マ

伸縮自在	シンシュクジザイ	elastic
伸長	シンチョウ	elongation; lengthing —v. elongate; lengthen
伸張	シンチョウ	extension; expansion —v. extend; expand

訓

伸びる	のびる	*vi*. grow; get long; slacken; improve; increase
伸び	のび	increase; growth
伸び伸び	のびのび	free and easy; carefree —*vi*. be free and easy; be carefree
伸び率	のびリツ	rate of growth/increase
伸ばす	のばす	*vt*. make long; grow; extend; straight; stretch; develop; expand

80

体 ⑦ ノ イ 仁 什 付 休 体

音

体	タイ	body; style; form; substance; center
	テイ	appearance

熟

体位	タイイ	physique; posture; body position
体育	タイイク	physical education/training
体温	タイオン	temperature; body temperature/heat
体温計	タイオンケイ	thermometer
体格	タイカク	physique; constitution; frame
体形	タイケイ	form; figure
体系	タイケイ	system; organization; scheme
体験	タイケン	experience; personal experience —v. have an experience; experience; undergo
体質	タイシツ	one's physical constitution
体臭	タイシュウ	body odor
体重	タイジュウ	(body) weight
体制	タイセイ	structure; system; organization; order; the Establishment
体勢	タイセイ	posture; stance
体積	タイセキ	volume; capacity
体操	タイソウ	gymnastics; physical exercises; calisthenics —*vi*. practice gymnastics/calisthenics
体得	タイトク	realization; experience; comprehension; mastering —v. realize; learn; comprehend; master
体内	タイナイ	inside the body
体罰	タイバツ	corporal punishment
体面	タイメン	honor; dignity; prestige; reputation; appearances
体力	タイリョク	physical strength; stamina
体裁	テイサイ	appearance; decency; form; style

訓 体　　　からだ　　　body

81 但 ⑦ ノ イ 亻 们 佃 但 但

音	但	タン	however
訓	但し	ただし	but; however; on condition that; provided that
	但し書	ただしがき	proviso; provisory clause

82 低 ⑦ ノ イ 亻 仁 作 低 低

音	低	テイ	low
熟	低圧	テイアツ	low pressure/tension/voltage
	低位	テイイ	low position/rank/degree
	低音	テイオン	low voice; bass; low pitched sound
	低温	テイオン	low temperature
	低下	テイカ	lowering; fall; decline; drop; dip; depreciation; deterioration —*v.* fall; drop; dip; decline; lower; depreciate; deteriorate
	低額	テイガク	small amount
	低気圧	テイキアツ	low atmospheric pressure
	低級	テイキュウ	low grade/class
	低空	テイクウ	low altitude
	低血圧	テイケツアツ	*med.* low blood pressure
	低減	テイゲン	fall; depreciation; reduction; decrease
	低質	テイシツ	low quality
	低速	テイソク	low speed
	低俗	テイゾク	vulgar
	低地	テイチ	low-lying land; lowlands; flats
	低調	テイチョウ	dull; weak; inactive; bearish
	低能	テイノウ	weak intellect; low intelligence; feeble mindedness
	低木	テイボク	shrub
	低迷	テイメイ	overhanging; threatening; floundering —*v.* overhang; threaten; flounder
	低落	テイラク	fall; depreciation; slump —*v.* fall; depreciate; decline; go down
	低率	テイリツ	low rate/ratio
訓	低い	ひくい	low; short; humble; mean
	低まる	ひくまる	*vi.* sink; become lower

二 亠 人 ヘ イ 几 入 八 冂 冖 丶 几 凵 刀 刂 力 勹 匕 匚 十 卜 卩 卪 厂 厶 又 了 ク マ

二 | 人 へ イ 儿 入 八 冂 冖 冫 几 凵 刀 刂 力 勹 匕 匚 十 卜 卩 巳 厂 厶 又 了 夂 マ

	低める	ひくめる	*vt*. lower; make low; bring down
¥	低位株	テイイかぶ	low-priced stock
	低価法	テイカホウ	valuation on lowest of original cost or current market principle
	低賃金	テイチンギン	low wages
	低利	テイリ	low rate of interest

83

伯 ⑦ ノ イ イ´ 化 伯 伯 伯

音	伯	ハク	uncle and aunt; count; earl
熟	伯爵	ハクシャク	count; earl
	伯仲	ハクチュウ	equal; matching; even; on par —*vi*. be equal; match; be even/on par
訓	※伯父	おじ	one's uncle
	※伯母	おば	one's aunt

84

伴 ⑦ ノ イ 伫 伫 伴 伴 伴

音	伴	ハン	company
		バン	
熟	伴奏	バンソウ	musical accompaniment —*vi*. play an accompaniment; accompany a person
	伴侶	ハンリョ	partner; companion; associate
訓	伴う	ともなう	*v*. accompany; go/take/be with; involve; entail

85

依 ⑧ ノ イ 什 伫 汴 佐 佐 依

音	依	イ	rely on; as before
		（エ）	
熟	依嘱	イショク	commission; appointment —*v*. appoint
	依然	イゼン	as before; still; as ever
	依存	イゾン	dependence; reliance —*vi*. depend; rely on; trust
	依託	イタク	trust; reliance —*v*. entrust; rely on
	依頼	イライ	request; solicitation —*v*. request; solicit; entrust; depend; rely on

依頼状	イライジョウ	letter of request; written request
依怙地	エコジ	obstinacy; stubborness; spitefulness; selfishness
依怙ひいき	エコひいき	partial; unfair —*v.* be partial to; show favoritism to
訓 依る	よる	*vi.* depend/rely on

86

価 ⑧

ノ イ 仁 仃 仁 価 価 価

音	価	カ	price; value
熟	価値	カチ	value; worth
訓	価	あたい	price; value —*vi.* price; put a price on; value; praise
¥	価格	カカク	price; value; cost

87

佳 ⑧

ノ イ 仁 仆 仕 住 佳 佳

音	佳	カ	excellence; beautiful
熟	佳境	カキョウ	most interesting part; climax
	佳作	カサク	fine piece of work
	佳人	カジン	beautiful woman
訓	※佳い	よい	fine; beautiful; excellent

88

供 ⑧

ノ イ 仁 仁 件 供 供 供

音	供	キョウ (ク)	offer; submit; serve (a meal); supply
熟	供する	キョウする	*vt.* offer; submit; serve (a meal); supply
	供給	キョウキュウ	supply; service —*v.* supply; provide; furnish; serve
	供述	キョウジュツ	testimony; statement; deposition; confession —*v.* testify; state; confess (to a fact)
	供物	クモツ	offering (to ancestors)
	供養	クヨウ	memorial service —*v.* hold a memorial service
訓	供える	そなえる	*vt.* offer (to a god); make an offering
	供	とも	attendant; servant retinue
¥	供託	キョウタク	security deposit —*v.* to make a security deposit

二 亠 人 へ イ 几 入 八 冂 冖 冫 几 凵 刀 刂 力 勹 匕 匚 十 卜 卩 卪 厶 又 了 勹 マ

二十人入イ儿入八冂冖〉几凵刀刂力勹匕匚十卜卩巳厂厶又了ク丶

89 使 ⑧ ノ イ イ 仁 仁 伊 伊 使

音	使	シ	use; messenger
熟	使者	シシャ	messenger; envoy
	使節	シセツ	envoy; delegate; delegation; mission (to a foreign country)
	使徒	シト	apostle; disciple
	使命	シメイ	mission
	使用	シヨウ	use —*v.* use; make use of; employ
	使用人	シヨウニン	person who works under his/her master; employee; servant
訓	使う	つかう	*vt.* use; handle; employ
	使い	つかい	errand; messenger
	使い方	つかいかた	usage; how to use
	使い込む	つかいこむ	*vt.* embezzle; defalcate; appropriate (money) for one's own use
	使い捨て	つかいすて	disposable
	使い手	つかいて	user; consumer
	使い道	つかいみち	way of using

90 侍 ⑧ ノ イ イ 仕 侍 侍 侍 侍

音	侍	ジ	wait on
熟	侍する	ジする	*vi.* attend on (a lord); wait on (a lady)
	侍者	ジシャ	servant to a lord
	侍従	ジジュウ	chamberlain; lord-in-waiting
	侍女	ジジョ	lady's maid; lady-in-waiting
訓	侍	さむらい	samurai; warrior
	※侍る	はべる	*vi.* attend; wait on; serve *clas.* be

91 侮 ⑧ ノ イ イ 仁 �ケ 侮 侮 侮

音	侮	ブ	despise
熟	侮辱	ブジョク	insult; affront —*v.* insult
	侮蔑	ブベツ	contempt; scorn —*v.* contempt; scorn; slight

| 訓 | 侮る | あなどる | despise; look down on |

92 併⑧　ノ イ 亻 亽 伫 伫 併 併

音	併	ヘイ	put together
熟	併合	ヘイゴウ	annexation; amalgamation; merge —*v.* annexe; amalgamate; merge
	併殺	ヘイサツ	***bas.*** double play —*v.* ***bas.*** make a double play
	併置	ヘイチ	putting two things in the same place —*v.* put two or more things in the same place; construct two or more things simultaneously
	併発	ヘイハツ	concurrence —*v.* occur simultaneously
	併有	ヘイユウ	combining/owning two or more things together —*v.* combine/own two or more things together
	併用	ヘイヨウ	joint-use; combined-use —*v.* use together/in combination
訓	併せる	あわせる	put together; combine; merge

93 例⑧　ノ イ 亻 伃 伤 例 例 例

音	例	レイ	example; precedent; practice
熟	例会	レイカイ	regular meeting
	例外	レイガイ	exception
	例証	レイショウ	example; illustration —*v.* show by example; illustrate
	例題	レイダイ	exercise; example
	例年	レイネン	every year; normal/average year
	例文	レイブン	example sentence (in a dictionary, etc.)
訓	例えば	たとえば	for example
	例話	たとえばなし	verbal example
	例える	たとえる	*vt.* show by example; illustrate
	※例	ためし	instance; example; precedent

94 係⑨　ノ イ 亻 伛 係 係 係 係 係

| 音 | 係 | ケイ | connection; involve; concern; affect |

熟	係争	ケイソウ	dispute; conflict; conflaglation; litigation —*vi.* dispute; be in conflict
訓	係	かかり	the person in charge/responsible
	係る	かかる	*vi.* affect; engender; modify
	係わり	かかわり	involvement; connection
	係わる	かかわる	*vi.* have to do with; be involved with

95 侯 ⑨ ノ 亻 亻 亻 亻 侁 侯 侯

音	侯	コウ	feudal lord; marquis
熟	侯爵	コウシャク	marquis; marquess

96 俊 ⑨ ノ 亻 亻 亻 亻 俨 俊 俊 俊

音	俊	シュン	excel
熟	俊英	シュンエイ	distinguished person
	俊才	シュンサイ	man of talent; genius
	俊足	シュンソク	swift-footed; fast
	俊敏	シュンビン	alert and agile

97 信 ⑨ ノ 亻 亻 亻 佇 佇 信 信 信

音	信	シン	fidelity; trust; letter
熟	信じる	シンじる	*vt.* believe; trust; have faith in
	信義	シンギ	faith; loyalty; honor
	信教	シンキョウ	religious belief; religion
	信仰	シンコウ	faith; belief —*v.* have faith in; believe in
	信号	シンゴウ	signal; traffic lights
	信実	シンジツ	sincerity
	信者	シンジャ	believer in a religion
	信書	シンショ	correspondence; letter
	信条	シンジョウ	belief; creed; principle
	信賞必罰	シンショウ ヒツバツ	certain penalty and certain reward
	信心	シンジン	faith; belief; piety —*v.* believe; worship
	信託	シンタク	trust

信徒	シント	adherent; believer
信任	シンニン	confidence; trust —*v*. place confidence in; trust
信念	シンネン	belief; faith; conviction
信服	シンプク	self-conviction —*vi*. convince oneself; be convinced
信望	シンボウ	confidence; popularity
信奉	シンポウ	belief; faith —*v*. believe; have faith in; espouse
信奉者	シンポウシャ	devotee; follower; adherent
信用	シンヨウ	confidence; trust; faith; reliance; reputation —*v*. believe; trust; have faith in; have confidence in; be reliable/reputable
信頼	シンライ	reliance; confidence; trust —*v*. trust; rely on; depend on
¥ 信託銀行	シンタクギンコウ	trust bank
信販 (信用販売)	シンパン （シンヨウ ハンバイ）	sale on credit
信用金庫	シンヨウキンコ	credit association; cooperative bank
信用組合	シンヨウくみあい	credit association
信用状	シンヨウジョウ	letter of credit
信用創造	シンヨウソウゾウ	credit creation
信用取引	シンヨウとりひき	margin transaction

98
侵⑨ ノ イ イ⁻ 仴 侵 侵 侵 侵 侵

音	侵	シン	invade
熟	侵害	シンガイ	infringement; invasion —*v*. infringe; encroach; invade; violate
	侵攻	シンコウ	invasion —*v*. invade
	侵食	シンショク	erosion; corrosion —*vt*. erode; corrode
	侵入	シンニュウ	invasion; incursion; raid; intrusion —*vi*. invade; incur; raid; intrude; trespass; march into
	侵入軍	シンニュウグン	invading army
	侵入者	シンニュウシャ	invader; trespasser; intruder
	侵犯	シンパン	invasion; violation; infringement —*v*. invade; violate; infringe
	侵略	シンリャク	aggression; invasion —*v*. invade; act aggressively
	侵略国	シンリャクコク	aggressor nation
	侵略者	シンリャクシャ	invader
	侵略的	シンリャクテキ	aggressive
訓	侵す	おかす	*vt*. invade; violate; infringe; encroach

二十人入イ儿入八冂冖丷几凵刀刂力勹匕匚十卜卩巳厂厶又了ク マ

99

促 ⑨ ノ イ 亿 亿 伊 仔 仔 伊 促

音	促	ソク	urge; promote; prompt
熟	促音	ソクオン	assimilated sound
	促進	ソクシン	promotion; encouragement —v. promote; encourage
	促成	ソクセイ	growth promotion —v. prompt growth
訓	促す	うながす	vt. urge; promote; prompt

100

俗 ⑨ ノ イ 亿 亿 佟 佟 俗 俗

音	俗	ゾク	custom; manners; worldliness; laymen; vulgarity
熟	俗悪	ゾクアク	vulgar; coarse
	俗語	ゾクゴ	slang; colloquial language
	俗字	ゾクジ	popular form of a Chinese character
	俗事	ゾクジ	worldly affairs
	俗称	ゾクショウ	common/popular name
	俗人	ゾクジン	layman; worldly minded person
	俗世間	ゾクセケン	this world; secular society
	俗説	ゾクセツ	common saying; folklore
	俗評	ゾクヒョウ	popular opinion
	俗物	ゾクブツ	worldly-minded person; person of vulgar tastes
	俗名	ゾクミョウ	secular name
	俗名	ゾクメイ	popular/common name
	俗話	ゾクワ	gossip
	俗化	ゾッカ	vulgarization; popularization —v. vulgarize; popularize

101

便 ⑨ ノ イ 厂 忉 佰 佰 佰 便 便

音	便	ビン	mail; transport; flight; opportunity
		ベン	convenience; facilities; excrement; feces
熟	便乗	ビンジョウ	getting in a car or on a boat (with someone); taking advantate of —vi. get in a car (with someone); take advantage of

62

便箋	ビンセン	letter paper
便意	ベンイ	urge to go to the toilet; call of nature
便益	ベンエキ	convenience; benefit; advantage
便器	ベンキ	toilet; urinal
便宜	ベンギ	convenience; expedience
便宜上	ベンギジョウ	for convenience
便宜的	ベンギテキ	convenient; expedient
便所	ベンジョ	toilet; lavatory
便通	ベンツウ	bowel movement
便秘	ベンピ	constipation
便法	ベンポウ	convenient/easy way
便覧	ベンラン （ビンラン）	handbook; manual
便利	ベンリ	convenient; handy
便利屋	ベンリヤ	handyman
訓 便り	たより	news; tidings

102
保 ⑨   ノ イ イ イ イ イ 伊 伊 保

音	保	ホ	keep; preserve; maintain
熟	保安	ホアン	maintenance of public peace and security
	保育	ホイク	childcare; —v. bring up/raise a child
	保育園	ホイクエン	nursery (school)
	保育所	ホイクジョ	nursery (school)
	保温	ホオン	keeping warm; heat maintenance —vi. keep warm
	保管	ホカン	custody; deposit; storage —v. keep in custody; store
	保菌者	ホキンシャ	carrier (of a disease)
	保険	ホケン	insurance; assurance
	保健	ホケン	health preservation; hygiene
	保健所	ホケンジョ	health center
	保護	ホゴ	protection; shelter —v. protect; shelter
	保護国	ホゴコク	protectorate
	保護者	ホゴシャ	guardian; protector
	保護色	ホゴショク	protective coloration
	保持	ホジ	maintenance; preservation —v. maintain; preserve; keep (a memory, etc.)
	保持者	ホジシャ	(record) holder
	保釈	ホシャク	bail —v. bail
	保守	ホシュ	conservation —v. conserve; preserve; maintain

二 イ 人 へ イ 儿 入 八 冂 冖 冫 几 凵 刀 刂 力 勹 匕 匚 十 卜 卩 巳 厂 厶 又 マ 九 マ

保守的	ホシュテキ	conservative
保守党	ホシュトウ	conservative party
保証	ホショウ	guarantee —*v.* guarantee; promise
保障	ホショウ	guarantee; security —*v.* guarantee; assure
保身	ホシン	self-protection
保全	ホゼン	preservation —*v.* preserve; conserve
保存	ホゾン	preservation —*v.* preserve; conserve
保母	ホボ	kindergarten teacher
保有	ホユウ	possession; ownership —*v.* possess; own; hold; maintain
保有者	ホユウシャ	owner; holder
保養	ホヨウ	recreation; recuperation; health preservation —*vi.* recreate; recuperate
保養所	ホヨウジョ	sanatorium; rest home
保養地	ホヨウチ	health resort
保留	ホリュウ	reservation; putting on hold —*v.* reserve; defer
訓 保つ	たもつ	*vt.* keep; preserve; maintain
¥ 保険会社	ホケンガイシャ	insurance company
保険金	ホケンキン	insurance money
保険つなぎ	ホケンつなぎ	short sale against the box
保険料	ホケンリョウ	insurance premium
保護預かり	ホゴあずかり	safety deposit
保護主義	ホゴシュギ	protectionism
保護貿易	ホゴボウエキ	protectionistic trade
保証金	ホショウキン	security deposit; key money
保証人	ホショウニン	guarantor

103

倹 ⑩ ノ イ イ 伫 伀 伀 佥 佥 倹 倹

音 倹	ケン	economize; be thrift; frugal
熟 倹約	ケンヤク	economy; thrift; frugality —*v.* economize; be thrifty/frugal

104

個 10 4 ノ イ 们 们 佃 佣 佣 個 個 個

音 個	コ	piece (counter for small objects)
熟 個々	ココ	separately; individually

個人	コジン	individual
個人差	コジンサ	difference among individuals
個人主義	コジンシュギ	individualism
個人的	コジンテキ	individually; personally; privately
個数	コスウ	number of items
個性	コセイ	personality; individuality; originality
個展	コテン	personal exhibition; one-man show
個別	コベツ	individually; separately; one by one
¥ 個人株主	コジンかぶぬし	individual stockholder

105

候 ⑩ 　ノ　イ　individual strokes: 亻 亻 仁 伖 仭 伒 侯 候

音	候	コウ	attend; season
熟	候補	コウホ	candidacy
	候補者	コウホシャ	candidate; applicant
訓	候	そうろう	*vi. clas.* be; exist

106

借 ⑩ 　ノ　イ　individual strokes: 亻 仁 仁 佧 併 併 借 借

音	借	シャク	borrow
訓	借りる	かりる	*vt.* borrow; have a loan; get into debt
	借り	かり	debt; loan
	借り倒す	かりたおす	*vt.* fail to pay a debt; bilk
	借り主	かりぬし	borrower
¥	借り入れ金	かりいれキン	loan (of money); borrowed money; debt
	借方勘定	カリカタ カンジョウ	debtor account
	借財	シャクザイ	debts *vt.* borrow money
	借地	シャクチ	leased/rented land
	借間	シャクま	rented room
	借家	シャクヤ	rented house
	借家人	シャクヤニン	tenant
	借用	シャクヨウ	borrowing —*v.* borrow
	借用証書	シャクヨウ ショウショ	loan bond; certificate of loan
	借料	シャクリョウ	rental fee; rent
	借款	シャッカン	loan (an overseas loan)
	借金	シャッキン	debt —*vi.* borrow money; get into debt

二 亠 人 へ イ 儿 入 八 冂 冖 冫 几 凵 刀 刂 力 勹 匕 匚 十 卜 卩 卩 厂 厶 又 了 ク マ

2

二
亠
人
亻
・
入
八
冂
冖
冫
几
凵
刀
刂
力
勹
匕
匸
十
卜
卩
巴
厂
厶
又
了
ク
マ

107 修 ⑩ ノ イ 仆 什 仆 仲 修 修 修 修

音	修	シュウ（シュ）	learn; repair
熟	修業	シュウギョウ	studying; learning —*v.* study; learn
	修士	シュウシ	master's degree
	修飾	シュウショク	decoration; ornamentation *gram.* modification —*v.* decorate; ornament *gram.* modify
	修繕	シュウゼン	repair —*v.* repair; mend; fix
	修築	シュウチク	building repairs —*v.* make repairs to a building
	修道院	シュウドウイン	monastery; abbey; religious house
	修道士	シュウドウシ	monk; friar
	修得	シュウトク	acquisition of skills —*v.* acquire; learn; master
	修理	シュウリ	repair; mending —*v.* repair; mend; fix
	修了	シュウリョウ	completion of a course —*v.* complete; finish
	修練	シュウレン	training; practice —*v.* train; practice; rehearse
	修行	シュギョウ	training; religious training —*v.* practice asceticism
訓	修まる	おさまる	*vi.* conduct oneself well
	修める	おさめる	*vt.* study; master; behave oneself
¥	修正	シュウセイ	amendment; revision; correcting —*v.* amend; revise; correct
	修復	シュウフク	restoration —*v.* restore; repair

108 値 ⑩ ノ イ 仁 什 併 佔 佔 佔 値 値

音	値	チ	value; price; cost
訓	値する	あたいする	*vi.* be worth; be worthy; deserve; merit
	値	あたい	price; cost; value; worth; merit
	値	ね	price; cost; figure; value
	値打ち	ねうち	price; value
	値段	ねダン	price; cost
¥	値上がり	ねあがり	rise in price; rising prices
	値上げ	ねあげ	rise in price —*v.* raise prices
	値動き	ねうごき	price fluctuation
	値を崩す	ねをくずす	lower prices
	値がさ株	ねがさかぶ	high-priced stocks

66

値切る	ねぎる	*vt*. beat down the price; haggle
値崩れ	ねくずれ	(sudden/sharp) drop in price (caused by oversupply)
値頃	ねごろ	reasonable/moderate price
値下げ	ねさげ	reduction in price; price decrease —*v*. lower prices
値ざや	ねざや	margin; spread
値幅制限	ねはばセイゲン	restriction of price range
値引き	ねびき	discount; price reduction —*v*. reduce prices

109

倒 ⑩ ノ イ イ 亻 仁 侄 侄 侄 倒 倒

音	倒	トウ	fall down; upside down
熟	倒壊	トウカイ	collapse; destruction —*vi*. collapse; be destroyed
	倒置	トウチ	turning upside down —*v*. turn upside down
	倒置法	トウチホウ	*gram*. inversion
	倒立	トウリツ	handstand —*vi*. do a handstand
訓	倒す	たおす	*vt*. bring/throw down; beat; defeat
	倒れる	たおれる	*vi*. fall; collapse; topple; break down; be ruined; go to ruin
¥	倒産	トウサン	bankruptcy; insolvency —*vi*. become bankrupt/insolvent

110

俳 ⑩ ノ イ 亻 什 付 付 倅 俳 俳 俳

音	俳	ハイ	performer; haiku poetry
熟	俳諧	ハイカイ	comic linked verse
	俳句	ハイク	haiku poem
	俳号	ハイゴウ	haiku poet's pen name
	俳人	ハイジン	haiku poet
	俳壇	ハイダン	the haiku world/poets
	俳優	ハイユウ	actor; actress

111

倍 ⑩ ノ イ イ 亻 仁 产 伫 倅 倅 倍 倍

| 音 | 倍 | バイ | times |

二イ人ヘイ几入八冂亠ㇽ几凵刀刂力勹匕匚十卜卩㔾厂厶又了ク マ

熟	倍加	バイカ	doubling; great/marked increase —v. double; increase twofold; add much to
	倍額	バイガク	double the price
	倍数	バイスウ	**math.** multiple
	倍増	バイゾウ	redoubling; double —v. redouble; double
	倍率	バイリツ	magnification

112

俵⑩　ノ　イ　イ－　イ⁺　イ⁺　佳　俵　俵　俵

| 音 | 俵 | ヒョウ | straw bag (counter for sacks) |
| 訓 | 俵 | たわら | straw bag |

113

倣⑩　ノ　イ　イ′　イ′　仿　仿　仿′　仿′　仿′　倣

| 音 | 倣 | ホウ | imitate; follow; emulate |
| 訓 | 倣う | ならう | **vt.** imitate; follow; emulate |

114

俸⑩　ノ　イ　イ－　イ－　仁　伫　俵　俵　俵　俸

音	俸	ホウ	pay; salary
熟	俸給	ホウキュウ	salary; pay; wages
	俸禄	ホウロク	stipend; pay; salary

115

倫⑩　ノ　イ　イ′　价　价　价　伶　伶　倫　倫

| 音 | 倫 | リン | ethics; sequence |
| 熟 | 倫理 | リンリ | ethics; morals |

116

偽⑪　ノ　イ　イ′　伊　伊　伊　偽　偽　偽　偽

| 音 | 偽 | ギ | falsify; deceive |

熟	偽証	ギショウ	false evidence; perjury —*v*. bear false witness; commit perjury
	偽善	ギゼン	hypocrisy
	偽善的	ギゼンテキ	hypocritical
	偽造	ギゾウ	forgery; fabrication —*v*. forge; fabricate
	偽名	ギメイ	false name
訓	偽る	いつわる	*vt*. lie; deceive; feign; pretend
	偽	にせ	imitation; counterfeit; phony
	偽物	にせもの	imitation; counterfeit

117

偶 ⑪ ノ イ イ´ イ⺈ イㅋ イㅋ イㄹ 侣 偶 偶 偶

音	偶	グウ	surprise; unexpected
熟	偶数	グウスウ	*math*. even number
	偶然	グウゼン	by chance; accidentally
	偶像	グウゾウ	image; statue
	偶発	グウハツ	accidental occurrence —*vi*. occur accidently
¥	偶発債務	グウハツサイム	contingent/accidental liability

118

健 ⑪ ノ イ イ⺇ イㅋ イ⺕ イㅌ 信 倬 倢 健 健

音	健	ケン	health
熟	健脚	ケンキャク	good walker
	健康	ケンコウ	health
	健康的	ケンコウテキ	healthy
	健康保健	ケンコウホケン	health insurance
	健在	ケンザイ	in good health ; alive and well
	健全	ケンゼン	healthy; normal; sound; wholesome
	健闘	ケントウ	good fight —*v*. put up a good fight
	健忘症	ケンボウショウ	forgetfulness; amnesia
訓	健やか	すこやか	healthy; fit; well

119

側 ⑪ ノ イ イ⺆ 仈 佀 侃 伹 俱 俱 側

| 音 | 側 | ソク | side |

二亻人ヘイ儿入八冂冖冫几凵刀刂力勹匕匸十卜卩巳厂厶又了ケマ

熟	側線	ソクセン	siding; sidetrack; side lines
	側面	ソクメン	side; flank
	側近	ソッキン	close associate
訓	側	かわ	side

120

停 ⑪　ノ イ イ 亻 亠 亠 亠 亠 亠 停 停

音	停	テイ	stop
熟	停学	テイガク	suspension from school
	停止	テイシ	suspension; stoppage; stay; prohibition; temporary ban; standstill; stop; halt; deadlock; stalemate; interruption; cessation —*v.* suspend; stop; prohibit; cease; come to an end
	停車	テイシャ	stop; stoppage —*vi.* stop; come to a halt
	停戦	テイセン	truce; ceasefire; armistice —*v.* cease fire; stop fighting
	停滞	テイタイ	stagnation; retention; congestion; falling into arrears —*v.* be stagnant; stagnate; congest; be sluggish; fall into arrears
	停電	テイデン	power failure/cut —*v.* have a power cut
	停泊	テイハク	anchorage; anchoring; mooring —*v.* anchor; lie; berth; moor
	停留	テイリュウ	stoppage; stop —*v.* stop; halt
	停留所	テイリュウジョ	stop; stand; station; depot
訓	停まる	とまる	*vi.* stop; cease; be stopped/suspended
	停める	とめる	*vt.* stop; suspend
¥	停職	テイショク	suspension from office

121

偵 ⑪　ノ イ イ′ 亻ˊ 亻ˊ 佔 佔 偵 偵 偵

音	偵	テイ	spy
熟	偵察	テイサツ	reconnaissance; scouting —*v.* scout; patrol

122

偏 ⑪　ノ イ 亻 亻 亻 伊 伊 偏 偏 偏 偏

音	偏	ヘン	lean toward; be biased; left-hand side of a *kanji*

熟	偏する	ヘンする	*vi.* lean toward; be biased
	偏愛	ヘンアイ	partiality; favoritism —*v.* favor
	偏狭	ヘンキョウ	narrow-minded; intolerant
	偏屈	ヘンクツ	obstinate; bigoted; narrow-minded
	偏見	ヘンケン	prejudice; biased view
	偏向	ヘンコウ	bias; leanings; deviations; tendency
	偏差	ヘンサ	bias/deviation (in statistics, etc)
	偏差値	ヘンサチ	deviation (value)
	偏在	ヘンザイ	uneven distribution —*vi.* be unevenly distributed
	偏執	ヘンシュウ	bigotry; obstinacy
	偏食	ヘンショク	unbalanced diet —*vi.* have an unbalanced diet
	偏人	ヘンジン	eccentric person
	偏頭痛	ヘンズツウ	migraine headache
	偏重	ヘンチョウ	overemphasis —*v.* overemphasize
	偏平	ヘンペイ	flat; level; even
	偏平足	ヘンペイソク	flat feet
	偏流	ヘンリュウ	drift; drifting
訓	偏る	かたよる	*vi.* lean toward; be biased
	偏り	かたより	inclination; deviation; polarization
	※偏に	ひとえに	earnestly; humbly; solely

123 偉 ⑫ ノ イ イ' イ⼧ 伫 伟 俨 偉 偉 偉 偉 偉

音	偉	イ	great; grand; famous; eminent; lofty; distinguished
熟	偉業	イギョウ	great work/achievement/feat
	偉丈夫	イジョウフ	prodigy; hero; great man
	偉人	イジン	great man/mind; hero
	偉大	イダイ	greatness; grandeur; might; eminence; distinction
訓	偉い	えらい	great; grand; mighty; celebrated; heroic; serious

124 備 ⑫ ノ イ 亻 㐭 㐭 傗 僃 僃 備 備 備 備

音	備	ビ	provide; furnish; preparation
熟	備考	ビコウ	note; remarks
	備蓄	ビチク	emergency savings —*vt.* save for an emergency

71

二 亠 人 ヘ イ 儿 入 八 冂 冖 冫 几 凵 刀 刂 力 勹 匕 匚 十 卜 卩 卩 厂 厶 又 了 亅 マ

2

二十人へイ几入八冂冖丷几凵刀刂力勹匕匚十卜卩巴厂厶又了ク亠マ

	備品	ビヒン	fixture; equipment; kit
	備忘録	ビボウロク	memorandum; notebook
訓	備える	そなえる	*vt.* provide; possess; equip
	備え	そなえ	provision; preparations; preparedness; equipment
	備え付ける	そなえつける	*vt.* provide; furnish; equip; fit; outfit
	備わる	そなわる	*vi.* be furnished/provided/equipped

125

傍 ⑫ ノ イ イ´ 亻´ 亻´ 亻´ 亻´ 俕 俕 傍 傍

音	傍	ボウ	side
熟	傍観	ボウカン	looking on; spectating —*v.* look on; spectate
	傍系	ボウケイ	collateral family line; affiliated; subsidiary
	傍若無人	ボウジャクブジン	impudent; arrogant; insolent
	傍受	ボウジュ	intercepting/monitoring/tapping (radio signals, etc.) —*v.* intercept/monitor/tap (radio signals, etc.)
	傍証	ボウショウ	circumstantial evidence —*vt.* prove circumstantially
	傍線	ボウセン	sideline; underline (for emphasis, etc.)
	傍聴	ボウチョウ	attendance at the proceeding (at a court, meeting, etc.) —*v.* attend the proceedings (at a court, meeting, etc.)
	傍聴席	ボウチョウセキ	visitors' gallery (in a court)
訓	傍ら	かたわら	side

126

傾 ⑬ ノ イ 亻 化 化 化 俌 傾 傾 傾 傾 傾

音	傾	ケイ	incline; slope; slant; tend; devote; concentrate
熟	傾向	ケイコウ	tendency; trend; propensity; inclination
	傾斜	ケイシャ	inclination; slope —*v.* incline; slope; slant
	傾注	ケイチュウ	devotion —*vt.* devote oneself to
	傾聴	ケイチョウ	listening closely/intently —*v.* listen closely/intently
	傾倒	ケイトウ	devotion; concentration —*vi.* devote oneself to; concentrate on
訓	傾く	かたむく	*vi.* tilt; lean; lurch; tip; slop; slant; decline
	傾ける	かたむける	*vt.* tilt; lean; be ruined; devote; concentrate
	傾き	かたむき	inclination; slope; slant; tendency; trend

127

傑 ⑬ ノ イ イ イ' イ' イ'' イ'' イ'' 俏 俏 傑

音	傑	ケツ	great
熟	傑作	ケッサク	masterpiece
	傑出	ケッシュツ	excellence; prominence —*vi.* excel at; be prominent in; stand out; shine

128

催 ⑬ ノ イ イ' イ'' イ'' イ'' イ'' イ'' 催 催 催

音	催	サイ	urge; encourage; hold
熟	催告	サイコク	demand; appeal —*vt.* demand; appeal
	催促	サイソク	demand; urge; request —*v.* demand; press; urge; request
	催眠	サイミン	hypnosis
	催眠剤	サイミンザイ	sleeping pill
	催眠術	サイミンジュツ	hypnotism
	催涙	サイルイ	*med.* lachrymal
訓	催し	もよおし	meeting; function; is sponsored by; under the auspices of
	催す	もよおす	*v.* hold (a party); feel (sleepy, chilly, etc.)

129

債 ⑬ ノ イ イ' イ' イ' 伫 倩 倩 債 債 債 債

音	債	サイ	debt; duty; obligation
¥	債権	サイケン	credit; claim; obligatory right
	債権国	サイケンコク	creditor nation
	債権者	サイケンシャ	creditor
	債権所有者	サイケンショユウシャ	bond holder
	債権取引所	サイケンとりひきジョ	bond market
	債権発行	サイケンハッコウ	loan issue; flotation; issuance
	債券	サイケン	(loan) bond; debenture
	債務	サイム	debt; liabilities; obligation
	債務国	サイムコク	debtor nation
	債務者	サイムシャ	debtor

二 亠 人 へ イ 儿 入 八 冂 冖 冫 几 凵 刀 刂 力 勹 匕 匚 十 卜 卩 已 厂 厶 又 了 ヽ マ

二十人ヘイ儿入八冂冖冫几凵刀刂力勹匕匚十卜卩巳厂厶又了ク マ

130
傷 ⑬　ノ　イ　イ　イ　イ　作　作　倬　倬　傷　傷　傷

音	傷	ショウ	wound; injure; damage
熟	傷害	ショウガイ	injury
	傷害保険	ショウガイホケン	accident insurance
	傷心	ショウシン	broken heart; heartbreak; grief; sorrow
	傷病	ショウビョウ	injuries and illness
訓	傷む	いたむ	*v.* be damaged/hurt/bruised/spoilt
	傷める	いためる	*vt.* damage; hurt; spoil
	傷	きず	injury; wound; cut; flaw; defect
	傷跡	きずあと	scar
	傷口	きずぐち	wound; sore
	傷付く	きずつく	*vi.* be hurt/injured/damaged
	傷付ける	きずつける	*vt.* wound; injure; bruise; scratch; crack
	傷物	きずもの	defective article

131
僧 ⑬　ノ　イ　イ　イ　イ　伫　伫　僧　僧　僧　僧

音	僧	ソウ	priest; monk
熟	僧庵	ソウアン	monk's cell; hermitage
	僧院	ソウイン	monastery; temple
	僧正	ソウジョウ	high priest; bishop
	僧俗	ソウゾク	clergy and laity
	僧尼	ソウニ	monks and nuns
	僧兵	ソウヘイ	monk soldier
	僧侶	ソウリョ	priest; monk; bonze

132
働 ⑬　ノ　イ　イ　イ　イ　仟　信　俥　俥　偅　働　働

音	働	ドウ	work
訓	働く	はたらく	*vi.* work
	働き	はたらき	work; labor; achievements; function; effect; workings
	働き口	はたらきぐち	job; position
	働き者	はたらきもの	hard worker

133
像 ⑭ イ イ′ イ″ イ‴ 俨 俨 侮 侭 像 像 像

| 音 | 像 | ゾウ | image |

134
僕 ⑭ イ イ′ イ″ イ‴ イ‴ 俨 俨 伴 僢 僕 僕

音	僕	ボク	manservant; I; me (male)
	僕婢	ボクヒ	male and female servants
訓	※僕	しもべ	manservant

135
僚 ⑭ イ 仁 伊 伏 伏 伙 佟 倅 倅 倅 僚 僚

音	僚	リョウ	colleague; official
	僚機	リョウキ	consort plane
	僚船	リョウセン	consort ship
熟	僚友	リョウユウ	colleague; co-worker

136
億 ⑮ イ イ′ イ″ イ‴ イ‴ 俨 佗 倅 倅 億 億

音	億	オク	one-hundred million; 100,000,000
熟	億万長者	オクマンチョウジャ	billionaire; multimillionaire
	億劫	オックウ	bothersome; troublesome

137
儀 ⑮ イ イ″ 伊 伊 佯 佯 佯 佯 佯 儀 儀 儀

音	儀	ギ	rule; ceremony
熟	儀式	ギシキ	ceremony; function
	儀礼	ギレイ	etiquette; courtesy
	儀礼的	ギレイテキ	formal

138

儒 ⑯ イ イ 伫 伔 伒 伒 傝 傝 儒 儒 儒 儒

音	儒	ジュ	Confucianism
熟	儒学	ジュガク	Confucianism
	儒教	ジュキョウ	Confucianism

139

償 ⑰ イ イ´ イ゙ イ゙ イ゙ 俨 償 償 償 償 償 償

音	償	ショウ	compensate
訓	償う	つぐなう	*vt.* compensate; recompense; make up for; atone
¥	償還	ショウカン	repayment; refund; redemption —*v.* repay; refund; pay back
	償却	ショウキャク	repayment; refund; depreciation; redemption; amortization —*v.* repay; refund; depreciate; redeem

140

優 ⑰ イ イ イ゙ 俨 俋 俋 侽 侽 優 優 優 優

音	優	ユウ	superior; gentle; actor
熟	優位	ユウイ	high position
	優越	ユウエツ	superiority; supremacy —*vi.* be superior to
	優越感	ユウエツカン	superiority complex
	優雅	ユウガ	elegance; grace; refinement
	優遇	ユウグウ	kind treatment; hospitality —*v.* treat someone well
	優秀	ユウシュウ	excellent; superior
	優柔不断	ユウジュウフダン	irresolute; indecisive
	優勝	ユウショウ	championship; victory —*v.* win
	優勢	ユウセイ	predominance; superiority
	優先	ユウセン	preference; superiority —*vi.* be prior to; have preference to
	優先的	ユウセンテキ	preferential
	優待	ユウタイ	generous/preferential treatment —*v.* treat generously; receive hospitality
	優等	ユウトウ	excellent; superior
	優美	ユウビ	graceful; elegant

| 優良 | ユウリョウ | excellent; superior |
| 優劣 | ユウレツ | superiority and inferiority; relative merits |

訓 優れる　すぐれる　*vi.* excel; surpass
優しい　やさしい　graceful; gentle; kind
※優る　まさる　*vi.* excel; surpass

¥ 優先株　ユウセンかぶ　preferred stock
優良株　ユウリョウかぶ　blue chip

---

2 儿　ひとあし　legs

141
元 ④　一 二 テ 元

音 元	ガン	
	ゲン	the origin; background; cause
熟 元日	ガンジツ	New Year's Day
元祖	ガンソ	originator; founder; ancestor; forerunner
元旦	ガンタン	New Year's Day
元年	ガンネン	first year of an imperial era
元来	ガンライ	originally; essentially; by nature
元気	ゲンキ	healthy; happy; jolly; cheerful
元首	ゲンシュ	head of state
元帥	ゲンスイ	general of the army; field marshal
元素	ゲンソ	*chem.* element
元服	ゲンプク	coming of age day for boys —*v.* celebrate one's coming of age
元老	ゲンロウ	elder statesman
訓 元	もと	origin; originally; background; cause; former; ex-
元帳	もとチョウ	ledger
元通り	もとどおり	former; as it used to be
元々	もともと	originally; from the outset; by nature
¥ 元金	ガンキン	principal; capital
元本	ガンポン	capital; principal
元利	ガンリ	principal and interest
元手	もとで	capital; funds; assets
元値	もとね	the cost; cost price

二
十
人
ヘ
イ
儿
入
八
冂
冖
冫
几
凵
刀
刂
力
勹
匕
匚
十
卜
卩
㔾
厂
厶
又
了
ク
マ

142

兄 ⑤ ` ㇑ 口 口 尸 兄

音	兄	ケイ	elder brother; elder brother of one's spouse
		（キョウ）	elder brother
熟	兄弟	キョウダイ	brother(s); brothers and sisters
	兄弟姉妹	ケイテイシマイ	brothers and sisters
訓	兄	あに	one's elder brother
	兄弟子	あにでし	senior fellow disciple/pupil
	兄嫁	あによめ	wife of one's elder brother
	※お兄さん	おにいさん	your elder brother; another person's elder brother

143

光 ⑥ ` ㇑ ㇒ ⺌ 业 半 光

音	光	コウ	light; shine; brilliance; time
熟	光陰	コウイン	time; Father Time
	光栄	コウエイ	honor; glory; privilege
	光化学	コウカガク	photochemistry
	光学	コウガク	optics; optical science
	光学器械	コウガクキカイ	optical instrument
	光輝	コウキ	brilliance
	光景	コウケイ	scene; sight; spectacle; scenery; view
	光源	コウゲン	*phy.* light source
	光合成	コウゴウセイ	photosynthesis
	光線	コウセン	light; ray/beam of light
	光沢	コウタク	gloss; luster; brilliance; glaze; polish
	光度	コウド	*phy.* luminous intensity; light intensity; brightness; luminosity
	光年	コウネン	light-year
	光波	コウハ	*phy.* light waves
	光明	コウミョウ	hope; light; bright future
訓	光	ひかり	light; ray; beam; lumisary; influence; power
	光る	ひかる	*vi.* shine; be bright/brilliant; illuminate; glitter
¥	光熱費	コウネツヒ	light and fuel costs; utilities
	光ディスク	ひかりディスク	optical disc
	光ファイバー	ひかりファイバー	optical fiber
	光メモリー	ひかりメモリー	optoelectronic memory

充 ⑥ 　 丶 一 亠 云 产 充

音	充	ジュウ	allot; overflow; be full
熟	充血	ジュウケツ	*med.* congestion —*vi.* congest; be congested with blood
	充実	ジュウジツ	full; substantial —*vi.* live a full life; live life to the full
	充実感	ジュウジツカン	sense of fulfillment
	充足	ジュウソク	contentment —*v.* satisfy; be contented; make content
	充電	ジュウデン	battery charging; electricity storage —*v.* charge a battery; store electricity
	充当	ジュウトウ	appropriation —*v.* allot
	充分	ジュウブン	plenty of; enough; entirely; really
	充満	ジュウマン	fullness; completeness —*vi.* be full of; be filled
訓	充てる	あてる	*vt.* assign; use; allot

145

先 ⑥ 　 丿 ᅩ 屮 生 牛 先

音	先	セン	future; priority; precedence
熟	先覚者	センカクシャ	pioneer (in a particular field)
	先客	センキャク	previous visitor/customer
	先駆者	センクシャ	forerunner/pioneer (in a particular field)
	先月	センゲツ	last month
	先見	センケン	foresight
	先賢	センケン	wise men of old; ancient sage
	先刻	センコク	while ago; already
	先史時代	センシジダイ	prehistoric times
	先日	センジツ	the other day
	先週	センシュウ	last week
	先人	センジン	ancestor; predecessor
	先陣	センジン	vanguard; advanced guard
	先進国	センシンコク	advanced/developed nation
	先生	センセイ	teacher; master; doctor
	先祖	センゾ	ancestor
	先代	センダイ	predecessor; previous age/generation
	先達	センダツ	pioneer (in a field); leader; guide
	先端	センタン	tip; point; end; the latest; advanced

2

二十人ヘイ儿入八冂冖丶几凵刀刂力勹匕匚十卜卩㔾厶又了ケマ

先着	センチャク	first arrival
先手	センテ	first move; initiative
先天的	センテンテキ	inborn; congenital; hereditary
先途	セント	destruction; end of the road
先頭	セントウ	head; lead
先導	センドウ	guidance; leadership —v. guide; lead
先入観	センニュウカン	prejudice; preconception; preoccupation
先年	センネン	former years; a few years ago
先輩	センパイ	superior; senior; older graduate
先発	センパツ	starting in advance —vi. start in advance; go ahead
先般	センパン	some time ago; the other day
先方	センポウ	the other part; the other member/partner
先約	センヤク	previous engagement
先例	センレイ	precedent

訓
先	さき	tip; point; end; lead; the future; recent
先立つ	さきだつ	vi. coming forward; precede; die before (someone)
先細り	さきぼそり	gradual decline —vi. decline gradually
先回り	さきまわり	vi. beat (a person) to it
※先ず	まず	first; nearly; anyway; well

¥
先入れ 先出し法	さきいれ さきだしホウ	first-in-first-out method
先高	さきだか	higher quotations for future months
先払い	さきばらい	advance payment; payment on delivery
先物	さきもの	futures
先物買い	さきものがい	purchase of futures; forward buying
先物取引	さきものとりひき	futures transaction
先安	さきやす	lower quotations for future months
先駆株	センクかぶ	forerunner
先行投資	センコウトウシ	prior investment

146

兆 ⑥ ノ ノ ノ 儿 北 兆

音	兆	チョウ	sign; indication; sympton; omen; trillion; 1,000,000,000
熟	兆候	チョウコウ	sign; indication; omen; symptom
訓	兆し	きざし	signs; symptoms; indication; sprouting; germination
	兆す	きざす	vi. show signs of; indicate; show symptons; sprout; germinate

80

二 亠 人 亻 儿 入 八 冂 冖 冫 几 凵 刀 刂 力 勹 匕 匚 十 卜 卩 巳 厂 厶 又 了 勹 マ

147

克 ⑦ 一 十 市 古 古 声 克

音	克	コク	overcome; conquer
熟	克服	コクフク	conquest; subjugation; overcoming —v. conquer; subjugate; overcome
	克明	コクメイ	fidelity; diligence; conscientiousness
	克己	コッキ	self-denial; self-control; self-restraint

148

児 ⑦ ｜ ｜｜ ｜冂 ｜日 ｜日 ｜尸 児

音	児	ジ	infant; child
		（ニ）	infant
熟	児童	ジドウ	child; elementary school pupil
	児童憲章	ジドウケンショウ	The Children's Charter
	児童文学	ジドウブンガク	children's literature

149

免 ⑧ ⺈ ⺈ ⺈ 免 免 免 免 免

音	免	メン	exemption; permission; dismissal
熟	免疫	メンエキ	*med*. immunity (from disease, etc.)
	免許	メンキョ	license; permission
	免罪	メンザイ	acquittal; pardon —*vt*. acquit
	免除	メンジョ	exemption; immunity —v. be exempt
	免状	メンジョウ	license; diploma
	免職	メンショク	discharge/dismissal (from a job) —v. discharge; dismiss; fire
	免責	メンセキ	exemption from responsibility —v. exempt (somebody) from responsibility
	免訴	メンソ	dismissal of a court case
訓	免れる	まぬがれる （まぬかれる）	*vt*. escape; be saved; avoid; evade
¥	免許証	メンキョショウ	license; certificate; permit
	免許制	メンキョセイ	licensing system
	免税	メンゼイ	tax exemption —v. make (a product, etc.) exempt from tax
	免責	メンセキ	insurance deductible

81

二一人ヘイ儿入八冂冖冫几凵刀刂力勹匕匚十卜卩巳厂厶又了⺅マ

2 入 いる enter

150

入 ② ノ 入

音	入	ニュウ	enter
熟	入院	ニュウイン	hospitalization; admittance into a hospital —*vi.* be hospitalized; go into hospital
	入営	ニュウエイ	enrollment/enlistment (in the army) —*vi.* enlist/enroll/volunteer (for the army)
	入会	ニュウカイ	admission/entrance/enrollment (into a club) —*vi.* register/join a club; become a club member)
	入閣	ニュウカク	entry into the Cabinet —*vi.* enter the Cabinet
	入学	ニュウガク	entrance into a school; matriculation —*vi.* enter/be admitted into a school; matriculate
	入居	ニュウキョ	occupancy —*vi.* move (into a flat, house, etc.)
	入居者	ニュウキョシャ	tenant
	入金	ニュウキン	receipt of money —*vi.* receive money; make a part payment
	入港	ニュウコウ	arrival in port —*vi.* enter/make port
	入国	ニュウコク	entry into a country; immigration —*vi.* gain entry into a country
	入社	ニュウシャ	joining a company —*vi.* join a company; become a member of a company
	入手	ニュウシュ	receipt; aquisition; procurement —*v.* procure; obtain; come by
	入所	ニュウショ	entrance; admission (to a training school, laboratory, prison, etc.) —*vi.* enter; be admitted; be put into prison
	入賞	ニュウショウ	winning a prize —*vi.* win a prize
	入場	ニュウジョウ	entrance; admission; admittance; —*vi.* enter; get in; be admitted
	入植	ニュウショク	immigration; settlement —*vi.* immigrate; settle
	入信	ニュウシン	religious conversion —*vi.* be converted; come to believe
	入籍	ニュウセキ	entry into the family register —*v.* have one's name put into the family register
	入選	ニュウセン	winning —*vi.* be accepted/selected
	入隊	ニュウタイ	joining the army; enlistment; enrollment —*vi.* join; enlist
	入団	ニュウダン	joining an organization; enlistment —*vi.* join an organization; enlist
	入湯	ニュウトウ	taking a hot bath —*vi.* take/have a bath

入念	ニュウネン	careful
入梅	ニュウバイ	beginning of the rainy season
入費	ニュウヒ	expenditure; expenses
入部	ニュウブ	admission into a club —*vi.* enter/be admitted into a club
入門	ニュウモン	becoming a disciple; learner's book —*vi.* become a pupil
入門書	ニュウモンショ	guide; primer; manual; introduction
入用	ニュウヨウ	need; want; demand; necessity
入浴	ニュウヨク	bath; bathing —*vi.* take a bath; bathe
入力	ニュウリョク	input —*v.* input

訓

入れる	いれる	*vt.* put in; insert; employ; make tea
入れ替える	いれかえる	*vt.* replace; substitute
入れ知恵	いれヂエ	idea put into one's head
入れ歯	いれば	false tooth/teeth
入れ物	いれもの	receptable; container
入る	いる	*v.* go/come in; set; sink; begin; attain; crack
入口	いりぐち	entrance
入る	はいる	*vi.* enter; come in; break in; join; begin

¥

入荷	ニュウカ	receipt of goods —*v.* receive (goods)
入札	ニュウサツ	tender; bid; bidding —*vi.* tender; offer tender; make a bid
入超	ニュウチョウ	excess of imports; adverse balance of trade

---

2 八 は eight

151

八 ② ノ 八

音 八	ハチ	eight
熟 八月	ハチガツ	August
八十八夜	ハチジュウハチヤ	eighty-eighth day from the beginning of spring
八幡	ハチマン	Hachiman (the god of war)
八頭身	ハットウシン	well-proportioned figure
八方	ハッポウ	every side; all around
八方美人	ハッポウビジン	everybody's friend
訓 八	や	eight
八重	やえ	eightfold
八重歯	やえば	double/extra tooth

二 十 人 へ イ 儿 入 八 冂 冖 冫 几 凵 刀 刂 力 勹 匕 匸 十 卜 卩 㔾 厂 厶 又 了 ク マ

八つ	やつ	eight
八つ	やっつ	eight
※八日	ようか	eighth day (of the month); 8th
※八百屋	やおや	greengrocer

152

公 ④　ノ 八 公 公

音 公	コウ (ク)	the public; duke

熟		
公卿	クギョウ	court noble
公家	クゲ	court noble
公安	コウアン	public peace
公園	コウエン	park
公演	コウエン	public performance —*vi*. perform in public
公海	コウカイ	open sea; international waters
公開	コウカイ	open to the public —*v*. be open to the public
公害	コウガイ	pollution
公休日	コウキュウび	legal/public holiday
公共	コウキョウ	the public
公告	コウコク	public notice —*v*. give notice to the public
公算	コウサン	probability
公私	コウシ	public and private matters
公使	コウシ	vice-ambassador
公式	コウシキ	***math***. formula
公衆	コウシュウ	the public
公衆衛生	コウシュウエイセイ	public health
公称	コウショウ	nominal; public/official name —*vi*. name publicly/officially
公職	コウショク	public office
公正	コウセイ	justice
公選	コウセン	election by popular vote —*v*. elect by popular vote
公然	コウゼン	open; public; not secret
公聴会	コウチョウカイ	public hearing
公道	コウドウ	public road
公認	コウニン	official recognition; authorized —*v*. recognize officially
公判	コウハン	public/open trial
公費	コウヒ	public expenses
公表	コウヒョウ	public announcement —*v*. announce publicly

公布	コウフ	promulgation; proclaimation —*v.* promulgate; proclaim
公平	コウヘイ	fairness
公報	コウホウ	official gazette —*v.* keep an official gazette
公民	コウミン	citizen
公民館	コウミンカン	community center
公務	コウム	public duties
公務員	コウムイン	civil servant
公明正大	コウメイセイダイ	fairness; fair and square; just and right
公用	コウヨウ	official business
公立	コウリツ	public foundation/institution

訓 公　おおやけ　the public

¥

公営	コウエイ	public management
公益	コウエキ	public interest
公開価格	コウカイカカク	price of introduced stock
公開株	コウカイかぶ	introduced stock
公開市場	コウカイシジョウ	open market
公共団体	コウキョウダンタイ	public body
公共料金	コウキョウリョウキン	public utilities charge
公庫	コウコ	People's Finance Corporation; finance/loan corporation
公債	コウサイ	public loan/bond
公社	コウシャ	public corporation
公社債	コウシャサイ	public corporate bonds and debentures
公団	コウダン	public corporation
公定価格	コウテイカカク	official price
公定歩合	コウテイブアイ	official discount rate
公認会計士	コウニンカイケイシ	certified public accountant
公募	コウボ	public subscription/offer/placement —*v.* offer (shares) for public subscription
公募債	コウボサイ	public issue
公明党	コウメイトウ	Komeito (the *clean and fair* government party)

153
六 ④ 　 ' 亠 六 六

音 六　ロク　six
　　　（リク）

熟 六合　リクゴウ　universe; cosmos

二
十
人
へ
イ
儿
入
八
冂
宀
冫
几
凵
刀
刂
力
勹
匕
匚
十
卜
卩
巴
厂
厶
又
了
ヌ
マ

六書	リクショ	the six styles of Chinese characters
六月	ロクガツ	June
六三制	ロクサンセイ	6-3 educational system (six years of elementary school and three years of junior high school)
六角形	ロッカクケイ	*math*. hexagon
六法全書	ロッポウゼンショ	Compendium of Laws; the statute books

訓
六つ	むっつ	six
六	む	six
六つ	むつ	six
※六日	むいカ	the sixth day (of a month); 6th

154 共 ⑥

一 十 艹 共 共 共

音
| 共 | キョウ | together; common; joint; (prefix) co- |

熟
共栄	キョウエイ	mutual prosperity —*vi*. prosper
共演	キョウエン	costar —*vi*. costar
共学	キョウガク	coeducation
共感	キョウカン	sympathy —*vi*. feel sympathy
共催	キョウサイ	joint sponsorship —*v*. sponsor jointly
共済組合	キョウサイくみあい	benefit society
共産主義	キョウサンシュギ	Communism
共存	キョウゾン	coexistence —*vi*. coexist
共通	キョウツウ	common —*vi*. commune; be common
共通語	キョウツウゴ	common language
共同	キョウドウ	cooperation; union —*vi*. cooperate; collaborate
共同募金	キョウドウボキン	community chest
共犯	キョウハン	complicity
共謀	キョウボウ	collusion; conspiracy —*v*. collude; conspire
共鳴	キョウメイ	resonance; agreement; sympathy —*vi*. agree; sympathize
共有	キョウユウ	common ownership —*v*. own communally
共用	キョウヨウ	common use —*v*. use communally
共和国	キョウワコク	republic

訓
| 共 | とも | together; common; joint; co- |

¥
共産党	キョウサントウ	Communist Party
共通農業政策	キョウツウノウギョウセイサク	Common Agricultural Policy (C.A.P.)
共同請負	キョウドウうけおい	joint venture

共同経営	キョウドウ ケイエイ	cooperative management
共同資本	キョウドウシホン	joint capital
共同出資者	キョウドウ シュッシシャ	partner
共有資産	キョウユウシサン	common property
共和党	キョウワトウ	Republican Party (US)

155

 兵 ⑦   ノ ／ 斤 斤 丘 乒 兵

音	兵	ヘイ	soldier; weapon; warfare
		ヒョウ	
熟	兵糧	ヒョウロウ	provisions for troops
	兵員	ヘイイン	military strength; numerical strength of an army
	兵営	ヘイエイ	barracks
	兵役	ヘイエキ	military service
	兵器	ヘイキ	arms; weapon
	兵士	ヘイシ	soldier
	兵舎	ヘイシャ	barracks
	兵隊	ヘイタイ	troops; soldier
	兵法	ヘイホウ (ヒョウホウ)	military tactics; strategy
	兵力	ヘイリョク	military force; troop strength

156

 具 ⑧   丨 冂 月 目 目 且 具 具

音	具	グ	equipment; tool; utensil; detail
熟	具合	グアイ	condition; circumstances
	具体案	グタイアン	definite/concrete plan
	具体化	グタイカ	embodiment; materialization —v. embody; manifest
	具体的	グタイテキ	concrete; definite; tangible

157

 典 ⑧   丨 冂 冊 冊 曲 曲 典 典

| 音 | 典 | テン | book; model; ceremony; celebration; code |

二亠人へイ儿入八冂
● ハ冂冖冫几凵刀刂力勹
● 匕匚匸十卜卩㔾厂厶又了ク
マ

熟	典雅	テンガ	refinement; elegance
	典拠	テンキョ	authority
	典型	テンケイ	model; type; pattern
	典型的	テンケイテキ	typical; representative; model; ideal
	典礼	テンレイ	ceremony

158

興 ⑯ ⟍ ⟋ ⼂ ⼓ ⼚ 印 仴 𦥑 𦥒 𦥓 舆 興 興

音	興	キョウ	interest
		コウ	spring up
熟	興じる	キョウじる	*vi*. amuse oneself; have fun; make merry
	興醒める	キョウざめる	*vi*. spoil the fun; damper (a person's) enthusiasm
	興味	キョウミ	interest
	興行	コウギョウ	public entertainment; entertainment industry; performance —*v*. give a performance; produce; show; exhibit
	興廃	コウハイ	rise and fall; fate; destiny
	興奮	コウフン	excitement; stimulation —*vi*. be excited/aroused/stimulated
	興亡	コウボウ	rise and fall; ups and downs; existence; destiny
	興隆	コウリュウ	rise; prosperity —*vi*. rise; flourish; prosper; thrive; grow
訓	興す	おこす	*vt*. revive; resuscitate
	興る	おこる	*vi*. rise; flourish; be prosperous
¥	興業	コウギョウ	industrial enterprise; promotion of industry
	興業銀行	コウギョウ ギンコウ	industrial bank

2 冂 どうがまえ upside-down box

159

円 ④ ⼃ 冂 冂 円

音	円	エン	round; circle; yen (unit of currency)
熟	円滑	エンカツ	even and uninterrupted; smooth
	円形	エンケイ	circular; round
	円周	エンシュウ	circumference

円周率	エンシュウリツ	**math.** pi; π
円熟	エンジュク	maturity; mellowness
		—**vi.** be matured/well-rounded
円陣	エンジン	circle of people
円柱	エンチュウ	column; pillar
円筒	エントウ	cylinder
円盤	エンバン	disk; discus; flying saucer
円舞曲	エンブキョク	waltz (music)
円満	エンマン	harmony; peaceful; perfect; well-roundedness
訓 円い	まるい	round; circular; spherical; globular
¥ 円相場	エンソウバ	exchange rate of the yen
円高	エンだか	appreciation of the yen
円建て	エンだて	yen-based
円建て外債	エンだてガイサイ	yen-denominated foreign bond
円安	エンやす	depreciation of the yen

160

内 ④ 丨 冂 内 内

二 亠 人 ⼈ イ 儿 入 八 冂 ⼍ 冫 几 凵 刀 刂 力 勹 匕 匚 十 卜 卩 巳 厂 厶 又 了 ⼌ マ

音 内	ナイ	inside
	（ダイ）	
熟 内裏	ダイリ	imperial palace
内意	ナイイ	secret intention; private opinion
内縁	ナイエン	common-law marriage
内科	ナイカ	internal medicine
内海	ナイカイ	inland sea
内外	ナイガイ	inside and outside; interior and exterior; some; about
内角	ナイカク	**math.** interior angle
内閣	ナイカク	Cabinet; administration
内規	ナイキ	bylaw; customary rules
内勤	ナイキン	office duty; indoor service; desk work
		—**vi.** work in an office
内外科	ナイゲカ	internal medicine and surgery
内向	ナイコウ	introversion
内向的	ナイコウテキ	introverted; unsociable
内妻	ナイサイ	common-law wife
内在	ナイザイ	immanence; indwelling; inherence
		—**vi.** be immanent; indwell; inhere
内在的	ナイザイテキ	immanent; indwelling; inherent; intrinsic
内耳	ナイジ	**med.** internal ear; labyrinth
内実	ナイジツ	facts; truth

内出血	ナイシュッケツ	*med*. internal bleeding; internal hemorrhage —*vi*. *med*. bleed internally
内緒	ナイショ	secret; private; confidential
内助	ナイジョ	wife's help; internal assistance —*v*. help one's husband; get inside help
内情	ナイジョウ	internal conditions; inside affairs
内職	ナイショク	side job —*vi*. do another job on the side; moonlight
内心	ナイシン	one's heart/real intention; inner center
内申	ナイシン	unofficial report —*v*. make an unofficial report
内診	ナイシン	*med*. internal examination —*v*. *med*. examine internally; make an internal examination
内申書	ナイシンショ	report on a pupil; secret school report
内政	ナイセイ	internal/domestic affairs
内省	ナイセイ	reflection; introspection; inward-looking; self-examination —*v*. introspect; reflect on oneself
内省的	ナイセイテキ	introspective; reflective; indrawn
内戦	ナイセン	civil war
内線	ナイセン	interior wiring; (telephone) extension
内蔵	ナイゾウ	built-in; containing —*v*. contain; have built-in
内臓	ナイゾウ	internal organs
内諾	ナイダク	informal consent —*v*. give informal consent
内談	ナイダン	private talk; personal conversation —*vi*. have a private talk/word
内地	ナイチ	inland; the interior; back country
内通	ナイツウ	secret communication/understanding; treachery; betrayal —*vi*. collude; conspire; betray
内定	ナイテイ	informal/tentative decision —*v*. decide tentatively; make an informal decision
内偵	ナイテイ	scouting; reconnaissance —*v*. scout; make private inquiries
内的	ナイテキ	inner; internal; intrinsic
内々	ナイナイ	private; secret; confidential
内燃機関	ナイネンキカン	internal-combustion engine
内部	ナイブ	interior; inner part; inside
内服	ナイフク	*med*. internal use (of medicine) —*v*. take (medicine) internally
内服薬	ナイフクヤク	internal medicine; medicine for internal use
内紛	ナイフン	internal trouble; srtife; storm in a teacup
内分	ナイブン	*math*. interior division —*v*. *math*. divide internally
内聞	ナイブン	secret; secrecy; privacy
内分泌	ナイブンピツ	*med*. incretion; internal secretion
内包	ナイホウ	connotation; comprehension —*v*. connote; contain; involve

内密	ナイミツ	secret; private; confidential; backdoor; under-the-table
内務	ナイム	home/domestic affairs
内面	ナイメン	inside; interior
内約	ナイヤク	private contract; tacit agreement —*v*. make a private agreement; have a tacit understanding
内憂	ナイユウ	domestic/internal troubles
内容	ナイヨウ	contents; substance; details; depth
内乱	ナイラン	civil war; insurrection; rebellion
内覧	ナイラン	preview; preliminary inspection —*v*. preview; give a preliminary inspection
内陸	ナイリク	inland

訓
内	うち	inside; interior; house; within
内気	うちキ	reserved; shy; timid
内金	うちキン	money paid on account; deposit; down payment
内幕	うちマク	inside; inner workings
内輪	うちわ	inside; family circle; moderate; conservative
内訳	うちわけ	items; details; breakdown; classification

¥
内閣官房長官	ナイカクカンボウチョウカン	chief cabinet secretary
内需	ナイジュ	domestic demand (requirements)
内政	ナイセイ	domestic (internal) affairs (politics)
内務省	ナイムショウ	Ministry of Home Affairs

161

冊 ⑤ 丨 冂 冊 冊 冊

音 冊	サク	
	サツ	book; volume (counter for books)
熟 冊子	サッシ	book; booklet; pamphlet

162

再 ⑥ 一 厂 冂 币 再 再

音 再	サイ (サ)	again; repeat; second; (prefix) re-
熟 再演	サイエン	repeat/second performance —*v*. perform again; give a second performance
再会	サイカイ	reunion; meeting again —*vi*. meet again
再開	サイカイ	reopening; resumption —*v*. reopen; resume

二
ト
人
へ
イ
儿
入
八
冂
•冖
冫
几
凵
刀
刂
力
勹
匕
匚
十
卜
卩
厂
厶
又
了
ク
マ

再刊	サイカン	republication; reissue —v. republish; reissue
再起	サイキ	comeback; recovery —vi. make a comeback; recover; resume
再挙	サイキョ	second attempt; comeback
再建	サイケン	reconstruction; rebuilding —v. reconstruct; rebuild
再現	サイゲン	reappearance; reproduction; reincarnation —v. reappear; reproduce; reincarnate
再検討	サイケントウ	reexamination; reconsideration; review; reppraisal —v. reexamine; reconsider; review; reppraise
再考	サイコウ	reconsideration; second thought; reflection —v. reconsider; reflect; think over again
再婚	サイコン	second marriage; remarriage —vi. remarry
再々	サイサイ	often; repeatedly; over and over
再三再四	サイサンサイシ	repeatedly; time and time again
再出発	サイシュッパツ	restart; fresh start
再審	サイシン	retrial; review —v. retry; review
再生	サイセイ	regeneration; restoration; recycle —v. come to life again; recycle; regenerate; playback a recording
再生産	サイセイサン	reproduction —v. reproduce
再製	サイセイ	recycling —v. remanufacture; remake; recycle
再選	サイセン	reelection —v. reelect
再度	サイド	second time; twice; again
再読	サイドク	second reading —v. reread; read a book again
再入国	サイニュウコク	reentery (into a country) —vi. reenter (a country)
再入国許可	サイニュウコク キョカ	reentry permit
再任	サイニン	reappointment; reinstatement —vi. reappoint; reinstate
再認識	サイニンシキ	recognizing anew —v. recognize anew; realize
再燃	サイネン	recurrence; revival —vi. recur; revive; be revived
再発	サイハツ	recurrence; relapse —vi. recur; come back
再発見	サイハッケン	rediscovery
再版	サイハン	reprint; second impression —v. reprint; print a second edition
再犯	サイハン	second offense —v. recidivate
再放送	サイホウソウ	repeat of a program; rebroadcast; rerun —v. repeat; show a rerun
再来	サイライ	second coming —vi. come again
訓 再び	ふたたび	again; once more
¥ 再販価格	サイハンカカク	resale price
再販制度	サイハンセイド	resale system

二十人へイ几入八冂冖冫几凵刀刂力勹匕匚十卜卩㔾厂厶又了勹マ

163

冖 ⟨④⟩　丶　冖　冖　冗

音	冗	ジョウ	waste
熟	冗員	ジョウイン	superfluous staff
	冗談	ジョウダン	joke
	冗長	ジョウチョウ	wordiness; verbosity; long-winded
	冗費	ジョウヒ	unnecessary expenses; wasteful spending; squandering
	冗漫	ジョウマン	verbose

164

写 ⟨⑤⟩　丶　冖　写　写　写

音	写	シャ	copy; film; photograph
熟	写実	シャジツ	realism
	写実的	シャジツテキ	realistic
	写植	シャショク	photocomposition; phototypesetting
	写真	シャシン	photograph; photo
	写真家	シャシンカ	photographer; cameraman
	写生	シャセイ	sketch; sketching
	写本	シャホン	written copy; manuscript
訓	写す	うつす	*vt*. copy; reproduce; take a photo
	写る	うつる	*vi*. be taken (a photo); come out; appear; be projected on a screen

165

冠 ⟨⑨⟩　丶　冖　冖　冖　冖　冠　冠　冠　冠

音	冠	カン	crown; coronet
熟	冠婚葬祭	カンコンソウサイ	coming of age, marriage, funeral, and ancestor worship; ceremonial occasions
	冠詞	カンシ	*gram*. article
	冠水	カンスイ	submergence; flooding —*vi*. be covered with water; be flooded
訓	冠	かんむり	crown; top part of a Chinese character

93

2 冫 にすい ice

---

166 冷 ⑦

丶 冫 冫 仒 冷 冷 冷

音	冷	レイ	cold
熟	冷害	レイガイ	cold-weather damage
	冷気	レイキ	cold; chill; cold weather
	冷却	レイキャク	cooling —*v.* cool off/down; cool
	冷遇	レイグウ	cold reception/treatment —*v.* treat/receive coldly
	冷血	レイケツ	coldhearted; cold-blooded
	冷血動物	レイケツドウブツ	cold-blooded animal
	冷酷	レイコク	cruel; callous
	冷笑	レイショウ	sneer; scornful laugh —*v.* sneer; laugh scornfully
	冷水	レイスイ	cold/ice water
	冷静	レイセイ	calm; cool
	冷戦	レイセン	cold war
	冷蔵	レイゾウ	cold storage; refrigeration —*v.* keep in cold storage; refrigerate
	冷蔵庫	レイゾウコ	refrigerator
	冷淡	レイタン	cold; coldhearted; indifferent; apathetic
	冷凍	レイトウ	refrigeration; freezing; frozen —*v.* refrigerate; freeze
	冷凍機	レイトウキ	freezer
	冷房	レイボウ	air conditioning
訓	冷たい	つめたい	cold
	冷える	ひえる	*vi.* get cold
	冷	ひや	cold water/saké/rice
	冷やかす	ひやかす	*vt.* tease; banter
	冷やす	ひやす	*vt.* cool; refrigerate
	冷や奴	ひややっこ	chilled tofu
	冷ます	さます	*vt.* let cool
	冷める	さめる	*vi.* get cold; cool down

---

167 准 ⑩

丶 冫 冫 仴 仴 汁 汁 准 准 准

音	准	ジュン	apply correspondingly

熟 准将　ジュンショウ　brigadier-general

168

凍⑩ 　丶　冫　厂　厂　沪　沪　沪　凍　凍　凍

音 凍　　　トウ　　　　freeze
熟 凍結　　トウケツ　　freezing —v. freeze; freeze up; be frozen
　　凍死　　トウシ　　　death from cold —vi. freeze to death
　　凍傷　　トウショウ　frostbite
訓 凍る　　こおる　　　v. freeze; be frozen
　　凍える　こごえる　　vi. be frozen/chilled/numbed
¥ 凍結株　トウケツかぶ frozen stock

169

凝⑯ 　冫　冫　泞　浐　渙　渙　渙　渙　凝　凝　凝　凝

音 凝　　　ギョウ　　　　grow stiff; congelation; clot; concentrate
熟 凝結　　ギョウケツ　　congelation; solidification; freezing
　　　　　　　　　　　　　—vi. congeal; solidify; freeze
　　凝固　　ギョウコ　　　congelation; solidification; freezing
　　　　　　　　　　　　　—vi. congeal; solidify; freeze
　　凝視　　ギョウシ　　　steady gaze; stare; fixation —v. gaze; stare
　　凝縮　　ギョウシュク condensation —v. condense
訓 凝らす　こらす　　　　vt. concentrate
　　凝る　　こる　　　　　vi. grow stiff; clot; refine; devote oneself to

---

2 几 つくえ　table

170

凡③ 　丿　几　凡

音 凡　　　ボン　　　　common; ordinary; mediocre
　　　　　（ハン）
熟 凡例　　ハンレイ　　introductory notes
　　凡才　　ボンサイ　　mediocre talent
　　凡作　　ボンサク　　mediocre work (novel, etc.)
　　凡人　　ボンジン　　ordinary person

二一人ヘイ儿入八冂冖冫几凵刀刂力勹匕匚十卜卩巳厂ム又了ケマ

凡俗	ボンゾク	mediocre; common; vulgar; ordinary person
凡庸	ボンヨウ	mediocre; commonplace; banal
訓 ※凡そ	およそ	approximately; generally
※凡て	すべて	all

171

風 ⑨ ）几几凡凡凧凨風風風

音 風	フウ	wind; air; look; appearance; fashion; style; type
	（フ）	
熟 風圧	フウアツ	wind pressure
風雨	フウウ	wind and rain; rainstorm
風雲	フウウン	winds and clouds; times of change
風雲児	フウウンジ	adventurer; soldier of fortune
風化	フウカ	weathering —*vi.* weather
風雅	フウガ	elegant; refined; tasteful
風害	フウガイ	storm damage; gale damage
風格	フウカク	personality; character; style
風変わり	フウがわり	eccentric; peculiar
風紀	フウキ	public morals
風景	フウケイ	scenery; landscape; view
風月	フウゲツ	wind and moon; the beauty of nature
風光	フウコウ	scenery; natural beauty
風采	フウサイ	appearance; bearing
風刺	フウシ	satire —*v.* satirize
風車	フウシャ	windmill
風習	フウシュウ	customs; manners; ways
風疹	フウシン	*med.* German measles; rubella
風水害	フウスイガイ	storm and flood damage
風雪	フウセツ	blizzard; snow storm
風説	フウセツ	rumor
風船	フウセン	balloon
風速	フウソク	wind velocity
風速計	フウソクケイ	anemometer
風俗	フウゾク	customs; manners; morals
風俗営業	フウゾク エイギョウ	disreputable businesses (hostess clubs, massage parlors, etc.)
風潮	フウチョウ	tide; trend of the times; social climate
風体	フウテイ	appearance; looks; attitude
風土	フウド	climate; topography; natural features

風土病	フウドビョウ	endemic disease
風波	フウハ	wind and waves; storm; rough seas; fight; disagreement
風媒花	フウバイカ	wind-pollinated flower
風評	フウヒョウ	rumor
風物	フウブツ	scenery; nature; natural objects; seasonal scenery
風物詩	フウブツシ	nature poem; poem about a season
風聞	フウブン	rumor; report
風貌	フウボウ	looks; features
風味	フウミ	taste; flavor
風来坊	フウライボウ	wanderer; vagabond
風流	フウリュウ	elegant; refined
風力	フウリョク	wind force
風鈴	フウリン	wind chime
風浪	フウロウ	heavy seas
風情	フゼイ	taste; appearance; air
風呂	フロ	bath
風呂桶	フロオケ	bathtub
風呂敷	フロしき	wrapping cloth
風呂場	フロば	bathroom

訓

風	（かざ）	(prefix) wind
風足	かざあし	wind velocity
風上	かざかみ	windward
風下	かざしも	leeward
風見	かざみ	weathercock; weather vane
風向き	かざむき	wind direction *fig.* situation; condition; (bad) temper
風	かぜ	wind
風当たり	かぜあたり	force of the wind; criticism; opposition
※風邪	かぜ	a cold

---

2 凵 うけばこ open box

172

凵④ ノ メ 凵 凵

音 凶 キョウ ill fortune; poor workmanship; violence; injury

熟 凶悪 キョウアク terrible; evil
凶器 キョウキ murder weapon

二一人へイ儿入八冂冖冫几凵刀刂力勹匕匚十卜卩巳厂厶又了⺈⺕

凶行	キョウコウ	terrible happening (murder or assault)
凶作	キョウサク	poor harvest
凶報	キョウホウ	bad news; sad tidings
凶暴	キョウボウ	violence

173

凹 ⟍ 乚 冚 凹 凹 ⑤

音	凹	オウ	hollow; concave
熟	凹凸	オウトツ	unevenness; ruggedness; irregularity
訓	凹み	へこみ	hollow; dent
	凹む	へこむ	*vi.* sink; collapse; hollow out; cave in

174

出 丨 屮 屮 出 出 ⑤

音	出	シュツ (スイ)	go/put out; exit
熟	出演	シュツエン	stage/TV appearance —*vi.* appear on the stage/TV
	出火	シュッカ	outbreak of fire; fire —*vi.* break out in flames; catch fire
	出荷	シュッカ	shipment; shipping —*v.* ship; forward
	出願	シュツガン	application —*v.* apply
	出金	シュッキン	contribution; expenses; investment —*vi.* pay; contribute; invest
	出家	シュッケ	Buddhist priest —*vi.* become a priest; renounce the world
	出血	シュッケツ	bleeding —*vi.* bleed
	出欠	シュッケツ	attendance
	出現	シュツゲン	appearance; emergence —*vi.* appear; emerge; come into existence
	出航	シュッコウ	departure —*vi.* sail; leave; fly; take off
	出港	シュッコウ	departure from a port —*vi.* leave from a port
	出国	シュッコク	leaving a country —*vi.* leave/get out of a country
	出札	シュッサツ	ticket issue —*vi.* issue a ticket
	出産	シュッサン	childbirth —*v.* give birth to
	出所	シュッショ	source; release from prison —*vi.* be released from prison
	出生	シュッセイ (シュッショウ)	birth —*vi.* give birth

出生地	シュッセイチ	birthplace
出生率	シュッセイリツ	birth rate
出場	シュツジョウ	participation —*vi*. participate; take part
出色	シュッショク	eminent; outstanding; remarkable; excellent
出身	シュッシン	one's hometown
出陣	シュツジン	going to battle/the front —*vi*. go to battle/the front
出世	シュッセ	success in life; promotion —*vi*. rise; be promoted
出席	シュッセキ	presence; attendance —*vi*. be present; attend
出題	シュツダイ	question setting —*vt*. set test questions
出張	シュッチョウ	business trip —*vi*. take a business trip
出廷	シュッテイ	court appearance —*vi*. appear in court
出典	シュッテン	source (of a quote, etc.)
出頭	シュットウ	appearance; presentation —*vi*. appear; present oneself
出動	シュツドウ	dispatch —*vi*. dispatch; call in; alert
出馬	シュツバ	in person —*vi*. run for; go in person
出発	シュッパツ	start; departure —*vi*. depart; leave
出帆	シュッパン	sailing for —*vi*. sail for
出版	シュッパン	publication; publishing —*v*. publish
出品	シュッピン	exhibition; exhibit —*v*. exhibit; enter; be on display
出兵	シュッペイ	troop dispatchment —*vt*. dispatch troops
出没	シュツボツ	appearance and disappearance; coming and going —*vi*. frequent; be haunted by
出漁	シュツリョウ	fishing (on a boat) —*vi*. go out fishing (on a boat)
出力	シュツリョク	output

訓

出す	だす	*vt*. let out; show; hold out
出る	でる	*vi*. go out; start; leave; rise; appear; protrude
出会う	であう	*vi*. meet; run into; encounter
出足	であし	start; initial charge (in sumo)
出掛ける	でかける	*vi*. go out; leave
出来事	できごと	happening; affair; incident; event
出来物	できもの	swelling; tumor
出来る	できる	*vi*. be finished/ready/made from; come into being; can; be possible

¥

出資	シュッシ	investment —*vi*. invest; provide capital
出超	シュッチョウ	excess of exports
出費	シュッピ	expenses; expenditure
出納	スイトウ	receipts and disbursements
出来高	できだか	volume
出来値	できね	actual price

二 亠 人 へ イ 儿 入 八 冂 冖 冫 几 凵 刀 刂 力 勹 匕 匚 十 卜 卩 巴 厂 厶 又 了 勹 マ

二 亠 人 ヘ イ 几 入 八 冂 冖 冫 几 凵 刀 刂 力 勹 匕 匸 十 卜 卩 巴 厂 ム 又 了 ク マ

175

凸 ⑤ 　 一 丿 凸 凸 凸

音	凸	トツ	convex
熟	凸版	トッパン	relief printing; letter press
	凸レンズ	トツレンズ	convex lens

176

画 ⑧ 　 一 冂 冂 币 币 両 画 画

音	画	ガ	picture; painting
		カク	stroke in calligraphy; division; plan
熟	画家	ガカ	painter; artist
	画一的	カクイツテキ	uniform; uniformized
	画策	カクサク	plan; scheme —*v.* plan; scheme
	画数	カクスウ	number of strokes (in a Chinese character)
	画然	カクゼン	distinct; clear cut
	画材	ガザイ	painting materials
	画商	ガショウ	picture/art dealer
	画像	ガゾウ	portrait
	画題	ガダイ	title/subject of a painting
	画期的	カッキテキ	epoch-making
	画伯	ガハク	great/master painter
	画風	ガフウ	style of painting
	画面	ガメン	picture; (television) screen
	画用紙	ガヨウシ	drawing paper
	画廊	ガロウ	art gallery
訓	画	え	picture; painting

2 刀 かたな knife; sword

177

刀 ② 　 フ 刀

音	刀	トウ	sword
熟	刀剣	トウケン	swords

刀工	トウコウ	swordmaker; swordsmith
刀匠	トウショウ	swordsmith
刀身	トウシン	sword blade
刀自	トジ	Madame; lady; matron; mistress
訓 刀	かたな	sword; blade; knife

178

刃 ③ フ 刀 刃

音 刃	ジン	edge
	（ニン）	
熟 刃傷	ニンジョウ	bloodshed
訓 刃	は	blade
刃向かう	はむかう	*vi*. oppose; resist
刃物	はもの	cutlery; knives and forks
刃渡り	はわたり	length of a blade; walking on swords

179

切 ④ 一 七 七刀 切

音 切	セツ	cut
	（サイ）	all
熟 切開	セッカイ	incision **med**. section; operation —*v*. make an incision; carry out a surgical operation
切実	セツジツ	pressing; acute; keen; urgent; earnest
切除	セツジョ	cutting off; removal **med**. excision —*v*. cut off; remove **med**. excise
切々	セツセツ	ardent; earnest; sincere
切断	セツダン	cutting; section; amputation —*v*. cut; sever; amputate
切ない	セツない	melancholic
切に	セツに	desperately; very much
切迫	セッパク	imminence —*vi*. draw near; impend; be imminent; become acute
切腹	セップク	hara-kiri; suicide by disembowelment —*vi*. commit hara-kiri; disembowel oneself
切望	セツボウ	earnest desire; yearning —*v*. desire earnestly; yearn for
訓 切る	きる	*v*. cut; give up; finish
切れる	きれる	*vi*. break; cut well; be sharp
切り上げる	きりあげる	*vt*. stop doing something

二 亠 人 へ イ 几 入 八 冂 ⌐ 冫 几 凵 刀 刂 力 勹 匕 匚 十 卜 卩 㔾 厂 ム 又 了 ク マ

二一人へイ几入八冂冖冫几凵刀刂力勹匕匚十卜卩㔾厂厶又了ケ マ

切り替える	きりかえる	*vt*. change
切手	きって	postage stamp
切符	きっプ	ticket
¥ 切り上げ	きりあげ	revolution; upward valuation
切り替える	きりかえる	*vt*. convert; review
切り詰める	きりつめる	*vt*. cut down; economize

180

分④ ノ 八 分 分

音	分	ブ	rate; percentage; one percent; thickness; *bu* (unit of length, approx. 3.03 cm)
		フン	minute (of time or arc); *fun* (unit of weight, approx. 375 mg)
		ブン	dividing; portion
熟	分化	ブンカ	specialization; differentiation —*vi*. specialize; differentiate
	分解	ブンカイ	resolution; decomposition; dissection —*v*. be resolved; decompose; dissect; fall apart; take apart
	分割	ブンカツ	division; partition —*v*. divide; partition
	分岐	ブンキ	divergence —*vi*. diverge; branch off
	分岐点	ブンキテン	turning point; junction; crossroads
	分業	ブンギョウ	division of labor —*v*. divide an operation into separate tasks
	分極化	ブンキョクカ	polarization —*vi*. polarize
	分家	ブンケ	branch family —*vi*. move out and set up a branch family
	分権	ブンケン	decentralization of power/authority
	分光	ブンコウ	*phy*. spectrum —*v*. separate a ray of light into a spectrum
	分校	ブンコウ	branch school
	分際	ブンザイ	one's status/position
	分冊	ブンサツ	division of a book into separate volumes; volume —*v*. divide into separate volumes
	分散	ブンサン	dispersion —*vi*. disperse; be dispersed; break up
	分詞	ブンシ	*gram*. participle
	分子	ブンシ	*chem*. molecule *math*. numerator *n*. elements; function
	分室	ブンシツ	branch office; partitioned room
	分宿	ブンシュク	separate hotels, etc. —*vi*. stay at separate hotels, etc.
	分掌	ブンショウ	division of a job into separate tasks —*v*. divide a job into separate tasks

分乗	ブンジョウ	separate cars/buses —*vi.* ride in separate cars /buses
分身	ブンシン	child; branch(of a family/organization)
分水	ブンスイ	diversion/shedding of water; diverted water —*vi.* divert/shed water
分水界	ブンスイカイ	watershed; (continental) divide
分水嶺	ブンスイレイ	watershed; (continental) divide
分数	ブンスウ	*math.* fraction
分析	ブンセキ	analysis —*v.* analyse; assay
分節	ブンセツ	decomposition; division; articulation —*v.* break something down into its constituent parts; divide a sentence into clauses; articulate (each syllable)
分隊	ブンタイ	squad; division; detachment
分担	ブンタン	division; share; assignment —*v.* divide; share; assign; allot
分団	ブンダン	branch; chapter; group
分銅	ブンドウ	balance weight
分度器	ブンドキ	protractor
分納	ブンノウ	installment —*v.* pay in installments
分派	ブンパ	branch; faction; sect; denomination; separation; division —*vi.* branch out into factions/sects; separate; divide
分売	ブンバイ	separate sales —*v.* sell separately; break up and sell
分配	ブンパイ	distribution; division; share —*v.* distribute; divide; share
分泌	ブンピ（ツ）	*med.* secretion —*v.* secrete
分筆	ブンピツ	subdivision (of a lot) —*vi.* subdivide land
分布	ブンプ	distribution —*v.* distribute
分別	フンベツ	discretion; good sense —*v.* be discrete
分別	ブンベツ	classification —*v.* classify; sort; separate
分娩	ブンベン	childbirth —*v.* give birth to
分母	ブンボ	*math.* denominator
分野	ブンヤ	field; sphere; realm
分与	ブンヨ	distribution; allocation; apportionment —*v.* distribute; allocate; apportion
分離	ブンリ	separation; segregation; selectivity —*v.* separate; segregate; select
分立	ブンリツ	separation; independence —*v.* separate; make independent; act separately/independently
分流	ブンリュウ	tributary; branch
分留	ブンリュウ	fractional distillation —*v.* carry out fractional distillation
分量	ブンリョウ	quantity; amount; dose
分類	ブンルイ	classification —*v.* classify; sort; break down

二 亠 人 ヘ イ 儿 入 八 冂 冖 冫 几 凵 刀 刂 力 勹 匕 匸 十 卜 卩 卪 厂 ム 又 了 ク マ

2

二亠人へイ几入八冂冖冫几凵刀刂力勹匕匚十卜卩㔾厂厶又了久マ

	分裂	ブンレツ	division; split; schism; segmentation —*vi*. split; break up; segment
訓	分ける	わける	*vi*. divide into; separate; classify; share
	分け合う	わけあう	*vt*. share
	分け前	わけまえ	one's share; cut
	分け目	わけめ	part; parting
	分かる	わかる	*vi*. understand; see; appreciate; know; find out; recognize
	分らず屋	わからずや	obstinate person; blockhead
	分かれる	わかれる	*vi*. branch off; separate; be divided; disperse; break up
	分かれ道	わかれみち	branch/forked road
	分かれ目	わかれめ	turning point; dividing line
	分かつ	わかつ	*vt*. share; know; divide; separate
¥	分割払い	ブンカツばらい	installment; easy payment; hire purchase
	分散投資	ブンサントウシ	diversified investment
	分譲	ブンジョウ	sale (of land) in lots/parcels —*v*. sell off (land) in lots/parcels

181

 初 ⑦   丶 ラ ラ ネ ネ 初 初

音	初	ショ	beginning
熟	初夏	ショカ	early summer; beginning of summer
	初回	ショカイ	the first time; the beginning
	初刊	ショカン	first publication
	初期	ショキ	early days; first stages
	初級	ショキュウ	beginner's class
	初産	ショサン（ういザン）	first birth
	初志	ショシ	original intention/purpose
	初秋	ショシュウ	early fall/autumn
	初春	ショシュン	early spring; beginning of spring
	初旬	ショジュン	first ten days of a month
	初心	ショシン	original intention; immaturity; inexperience
	初心者	ショシンシャ	beginner; novice
	初診	ショシン	first medical examination
	初代	ショダイ	first generation; the first
	初対面	ショタイメン	first meeting
	初潮	ショチョウ	*med*. one's first menstruation
	初冬	ショトウ	early winter; beginning of winter
	初等	ショトウ	elementary

初七日	ショなのか	seventh day from a person's death
初日	ショニチ	first day; the start
初版	ショハン	first edition
初犯	ショハン	first offense
初歩	ショホ	the first step; rudiments; elements
初夜	ショヤ	wedding night
初老	ショロウ	middle-aged; elderly

初め	はじめ	beginning; outset
初めて	はじめて	for the first time
初	はつ	first
初恋	はつこい	first love
初荷	はつに	first cargo of the New Year
初耳	はつみみ	news heard for the first time
初詣	はつもうで	first shrine visit of the year
初物	はつもの	first product of the season
初雪	はつゆき	first snowfall of the year
初夢	はつゆめ	one's dream on the second day of the New Year
初める	そめる	*vt.* start; begin
※初々しい	ういういしい	innocent; naive
※初子	ういご	one's first child
※初陣	ういじん	one's first military campaign; first competition
¥ 初任給	ショニンキュウ	starting salary

182

⑧ 券 　 、 䒑 䒑 䒑 䒑 券 券 券

音 券	ケン	ticket

---

2 刂 りっとう standing sword

183

刈 ④ 　 ノ メ 刈 刈

音 刈	ガイ	mow; cut
訓 刈る	かる	mow; cut
刈り入れる	かりいれる	*vt.* harvest; collect; reap
刈り込む	かりこむ	*vt.* cut; clip; trim; crop

二 亠 人 へ イ 几 入 八 冂 冖 冫 几 凵 刀 刂 力 勹 匕 匚 十 卜 卩 卪 厂 厶 又 了 勹 マ

184

刊 ⑤　一 二 干 刊 刊

音	刊	カン	publish
熟	刊行	カンコウ	publication —*vt.* publish; issue; bring out
訓	刊む	きざむ	*vt.* engrave; chisel; carve

185

刑 ⑥　一 二 干 开 刑 刑

音	刑	ケイ	punishment; penal; penalty
熟	刑期	ケイキ	prison term/sentence
	刑死	ケイシ	death penalty; execution —*vi.* be executed
	刑事	ケイジ	police detective
	刑事裁判所	ケイジ サイバンショ	criminal court
	刑事犯	ケイジハン	criminal offense
	刑場	ケイジョウ	execution site
	刑罰	ケイバツ	penalty; punishment
	刑法	ケイホウ	criminal law; the penal code
	刑務所	ケイムショ	jail; prison

186

列 ⑥　一 ア 歹 歹 列 列

音	列	レツ	line; row; queue
熟	列する	レッする	*v.* line up; queue
	列記	レッキ	written list; enumeration —*v.* list; enumerate
	列挙	レッキョ	list; enumeration —*v.* list; enumerate
	列強	レッキョウ	treaty/world powers
	列国	レッコク	nations; the powers
	列車	レッシャ	train
	列席	レッセキ	attendance; presence —*vi.* attend; be present
	列伝	レツデン	biographies
	列島	レットウ	chain of islands; archipelago
訓	列なる	つらなる	*vi.* lie in a row
	列ねる	つらねる	*vt.* put/lie in a row

判 ⑦ 　 丶 　ヽ 　ソ 　ン 　ニ 　半 　半 　判

音	判	ハン バン	judge; decide; seal; stamp; format
熟	判決	ハンケツ	judgment; judicial decision —*v.* judge; pass judgment
	判事	ハンジ	judge; justice
	判然	ハンゼン	clear; evident
	判断	ハンダン	judgment; decision; conclusion; divination —*v.* judge; make judgment; decide; conclude
	判定	ハンテイ	judgment; decision; adjudication —*v.* judge; decide; adjudicate
	判読	ハンドク	interpretation; reading; decipherment (of unclear writing) —*v.* interpret; read; decipher (unclear writing)
	判別	ハンベツ	discrimination; distinction —*v.* distinguish; discriminate
	判明	ハンメイ	clear; confirmed —*vi.* become clear; be ascertained/confirmed
	判例	ハンレイ	precedent; leading case
訓	※判る	わかる	*vi.* understand; become clear/evident

別 ⑦ 　 丶 　口 　口 　号 　另 　別 　別

音	別	ベツ	different; separate; another; special; parting; farewell
熟	別格	ベッカク	special; exceptional
	別館	ベッカン	annex; separate building
	別記	ベッキ	stated elsewhere —*v.* be stated elsewhere
	別居	ベッキョ	(legal) separation (of a married couple); living apart —*vi.* live separately; be separated
	別口	ベツくち	different kind/item
	別個	ベッコ	separate; different
	別冊	ベッサツ	separate volume; supplement
	別紙	ベッシ	attached sheet; enclosure
	別辞	ベツジ	parting words; farewell speech
	別室	ベッシツ	separate/special room
	別種	ベッシュ	another/different kind
	別称	ベッショウ	another name; alias; pseudonym
	別状	ベツジョウ	something unusual/different

別人	ベツジン	another/different person
別世界	ベッセカイ	another world
別席	ベッセキ	different/special seat; different/special room
別送	ベッソウ	by separate mail; under separate cover —*v*. send by separate mail
別荘	ベッソウ	villa; country residence
別宅	ベッタク	second home/residence
別段	ベツダン	special; particular
別邸	ベッテイ	villa; separate residence
別天地	ベッテンチ	another world
別途	ベット	different method; separatedly
別納	ベツノウ	payment made at different time or in a different way —*v*. pay at a different time; pay in a different way
別嬪	ベッピン	*col*. beautiful woman
別便	ベツビン	by separate mail
別封	ベップウ	by separate cover —*v*. send by separate cover
別々	ベツベツ	separate; individual
別法	ベッポウ	different way/method
別棟	ベツむね	separate/different building; annex
別名	ベツメイ	another name (used in biology when referring to the different names used for the same animal or plant)
別物	ベツもの	something else; exception; special case
別離	ベツリ	parting; separation
訓 別ける	わける	*vt*. divide; separate; distinguish
別れ道	わかれみち	forked road; crossroads
別れ目	わかれめ	turning point; junction
別れる	わかれる	*vi*. part company with; leave; separate; get divorced; diverge
別け隔て	わけへだて	making distinctions; discriminating
別つ	わかつ	*vt*. divide; separate; distinguish

189

 利 ⑦ 一 二 千 禾 禾 利 利

音	利	リ	profit; advantage; interest
熟	利する	リする	*v*. profit; benefit; do (a person) good
	利害	リガイ	advantages and disadvantages; interests
	利器	リキ	sharp-edged/useful tool; convenience
	利権	リケン	rights; interests; concession
	利己	リコ	egoism; self-interest

利己主義	リコシュギ	egoism; selfishness
利口	リコウ	smart; clever; bright
利点	リテン	advantage; point in favor
利得	リトク	profit; benefit; gain
利尿	リニョウ	urination
利発	リハツ	cleverness; intelligence
利用	リヨウ	utilization; application —v. utilize; apply; make use of
訓 利く	きく	vi. take effect; work
利かす	きかす	vt. make effective; use; exercise
利腕	ききうで	one hand more skillful than other
¥ 利上げ	りあげ	increase in the interest rate
利益	リエキ	profit; gain; returns
利益準備金	リエキジュンビキン	legal retained earnings
利益準備金積立額	リエキジュンビキンつみたてガク	provision of legal retained surplus
利食い	りぐい	profit taking (cashing); realizing; reselling at a profit
利ざや	りざや	margin of profit
利子	リシ	interest
利潤	リジュン	profit
利殖	リショク	moneymaking —v. make money
利息	リソク	interest (on a loan)
利払い	りばらい	interest payment
利回り	りまわり	return; yield; profit
利用者	リヨウシャ	user
利率	リリツ	rate of interest

190

 刻 ⑧　　丶 亠 ナ ㇖ 亥 亥 刻 刻

音 刻	コク	carve
熟 刻一刻	コクイッコク	gradually; moment by moment
刻印	コクイン	carved seal —v. impress a seal
刻限	コクゲン	fixed/appointed time
刻々	コクコク	every moment; moment by moment; gradually
刻苦	コック	hard work; arduous labor —vi. work hard; be arduous
訓 刻む	きざむ	vt. carve; engrave; sculpt

109

二十人へイ几入八冂冖冫几凵刀刂力勹匕匚十卜卩巴厂厶又了クマ

191

刷 ⑧ 　コ コ ア ア 月 吊 刷 刷

音	刷	サツ	print; reform
熟	刷新	サッシン	reform —*v*. reform
訓	刷る	する	***vt***. print

192

刺 ⑧ 　一 ㄈ 戸 市 束 束 剌 刺

音	刺	シ	stab; pierce; stick
熟	刺客	シカク	assassin
	刺激	シゲキ	stimulus; stimulation; incentive —*v*. stimulate; irritate; spur
	刺殺	シサツ	death by stabbing —*v*. stab to death; put out; ***bas***. put out
	刺繍	シシュウ	embroidery —*v*. embroider
	刺青	シセイ	tattoo —*v*. tattoo
訓	刺す	さす	***vt***. pierce; stab; prick; bite; sting; sew; stick
	刺さる	ささる	***vi***. stick; get stuck
	刺し身	さしみ	*sashimi* (Japanese dish of thinly-sliced raw fish)

193

制 ⑧ 　丿 ㇗ 乍 乍 与 朱 制 制

音	制	セイ	regulation; control
熟	制する	セイする	***vt***. control; command; dominate
	制圧	セイアツ	control —*v*. gain control; suppress
	制海権	セイカイケン	maritime control
	制癌剤	セイガンザイ	anticancer drug
	制球	セイキュウ	***bas***. ball control —*vi*. have ball control
	制御	セイギョ	control —*v*. control
	制御装置	セイギョソウチ	control system/device
	制空権	セイクウケン	air superiority
	制限	セイゲン	limit; restriction; limitation —*v*. limit; restrict; control
	制裁	セイサイ	punishment; sanction; penalty —*v*. punish; sanction; penalize

制裁金	セイサイキン	penalty; fine
制作	セイサク	work; production —*v.* produce; make
制作者	セイサクシャ	producer
制止	セイシ	check; control; restrain —*v.* control; restrain; hold back; check
制定	セイテイ	enactment; establishment —*v.* enact; establish; create
制度	セイド	system; institution; organization
制度化	セイドカ	systematization; organization —*v.* systematize; organize
制動	セイドウ	brake; braking —*v.* brake
制動機	セイドウキ	brake
制覇	セイハ	supremacy; championship; conquest —*vi.* conquer; dominate; win
制服	セイフク	uniform
制帽	セイボウ	regulation/school cap
制約	セイヤク	restriction; limitation; condition —*v.* restrict; limit
制令	セイレイ	regulations

194

 一 乛 亙 亙 至 至 到 到

⑧

音	到	トウ	reach
熟	到達	トウタツ	arrival; attainment —*vi.* arrive; reach; attain; touch
	到着	トウチャク	arrival —*vi.* arrive at; reach
	到底 (〜ない)	トウテイ (〜ない)	not possibly; not at all; by no means; hardly
	到頭	トウトウ	at last; finally
	到来	トウライ	arrival; advent; influx —*vi.* come; arrive; occur

195

 ⼃ ⼂ ⺌ 𠂆 片 肖 肖 肖' 削

⑨

音	削	サク	shave; sharpen; delete; erase
熟	削減	サクゲン	reduction; cut; cutback; curtailment —*v.* reduce; cut; curtail
	削除	サクジョ	elimination; deletion —*v.* eliminate; delete; cross out
訓	削る	けずる	*vt.* shave; scrape; sharpen; remove; delete; erase; cut

196

前 ⑨ 、 ＾ ＾ 广 广 市 首 首 前 前

音	前	ゼン	before; fornt
熟	前衛	ゼンエイ	vanguard; advance guard; avant-guarde
	前回	ゼンカイ	last time
	前科者	ゼンカもの	person's criminal record
	前記	ゼンキ	above-mentioned
	前期	ゼンキ	first term; preceeding period
	前言	ゼンゲン	one's previous remarks
	前後	ゼンゴ	about; approximately; order; sequence; front and back —*vi.* reverse order
	前座	ゼンザ	minor performer; opening performance
	前菜	ゼンサイ	hors d'oeuvres
	前史	ゼンシ	prehistory
	前日	ゼンジツ	previous day; day before
	前者	ゼンシャ	the former
	前述	ゼンジュツ	the above-mentioned —*vi.* mention above
	前身	ゼンシン	one's form in a previous existence; previous form; former position
	前進	ゼンシン	advance; drive; progress —*vi.* advance; drive forward; progress
	前世	ゼンセ	previous existence
	前線	ゼンセン	front lines; the front; front (meteorology)
	前奏	ゼンソウ	prelude (in music)
	前奏曲	ゼンソウキョク	prelude; overture
	前代	ゼンダイ	previous generation; former ages
	前代未聞	ゼンダイミモン	news heard for the first time
	前兆	ゼンチョウ	omen; portent; sign
	前提	ゼンテイ	premise; prerequiste
	前途	ゼント	one's future prospects; the road ahead
	前任	ゼンニン	former official; previous job
	前年	ゼンネン	preceeding year; last year
	前半	ゼンハン	first half
	前文	ゼンブン	preamble; the above statement
	前面	ゼンメン	front
	前夜	ゼンヤ	last night; previous night
	前夜祭	ゼンヤサイ	celebration held on the eve of an anniversary or event
	前略	ゼンリャク	first part omitted (salutation in letter)
	前例	ゼンレイ	precedent

前歴	ゼンレキ	one's past record

訓 前　　まえ　　before; front

前売り	まえうり	advance sale —*vi.* sell in advance
前置き	まえおき	introductory remark; preliminary —*vi.* make introductory remarks
前払い	まえばらい	advance payment —*v.* pay in advance

¥ 前期繰越
利益金　ゼンキくりこし
リエキキン　retained earnings brought forward

前期損益
修正　ゼンキソンエキ
シュウセイ　prior period adjustments

前渡金	ゼントキン	advance payments
前年同期	ゼンネンドウキ	corresponding period the previous year
前場	ゼンば	morning session
前受金	まえうけキン	advances received
前受収益	まえうけ シュウエキ	deferred income
前払費用	まえばらいヒヨウ	prepaid expenses
前引け	まえびけ	closing of the morning session

197

則 ⑨　丨 冂 冃 月 目 目 貝 貝 則

音 則　ソク　rule

198

剣 ⑩　丿 丿 𠂉 仌 仒 合 争 佥 剣 剣

音 剣　ケン　sword

熟
剣士	ケンシ	fencer; swordsman
剣術	ケンジュツ	fencing; swordsmanship
剣道	ケンドウ	kendo (Japanese fencing)
剣法	ケンポウ	art of fencing; swordsmanship

訓 剣　つるぎ　sword

199

剛 ⑩　丨 冂 冂 門 門 岡 岡 剛 剛

音 剛　ゴウ　firm; hard; solid; brave; strong

熟 剛健　ゴウケン　sturdiness; fortitude; robustness

二エ人ヘイ几入八冂冖冫几凵刀刂力勹匕匚十卜卩阝厂厶又了ク冫

200 剤 ⑩
丶 亠 ナ 文 产 产 斉 斉 斉 剤

| 音 | 剤 | ザイ | medicinal preparation |

201 剖 ⑩
丶 亠 ナ 立 音 音 音 剖 剖

| 音 | 剖 | ボウ | divide; cut |

202 剰 ⑪
一 二 三 三 丰 垂 乗 乗 乗 乗 剰

音	剰	ジョウ	extra; surplus
熟	剰余	ジョウヨ	surplus; remainder; balance; residue
¥	剰余金	ジョウヨキン	retained earnings

203 副 ⑪
一 厂 戸 戸 戸 冨 畐 畐 畐 副 副

音	副	フク	accompany; vice-; deputy; assistant
熟	副官	フクカン	adjutant; aide
	副業	フクギョウ	side job
	副作用	フクサヨウ	*med.* ill/side effect
	副産物	フクサンブツ	byproduct
	副詞	フクシ	*gram.* adverb
	副次的	フクジテキ	secondary
	副収入	フクシュウニュウ	additional/side income
	副賞	フクショウ	extra/supplementary prize
	副将	フクショウ	second-in-command; vice-captain
	副食	フクショク	side dish (to be eaten with rice)
	副葬品	フクソウヒン	articles buried with the dead
	副題	フクダイ	subtitle; subheading
	副読本	フクドクホン	supplementary reader
	副本	フクホン	duplicate; copy (of a written work)
訓	※副う	そう	*vi.* accompany

| ¥ | 副会長 | フクカイチョウ | vice-chairman |
| | 副社長 | フクシャチョウ | (company) vice-president |

204

割 ⑫

、 ` 宀 宀 中 宀 宀 宀 害 害 害 割

音	割	カツ	divide; cut
熟	割愛	カツアイ	omission —*v*. omit; part with
	割拠	カッキョ	holding one's own ground —*vi*. hold one's own ground
	割腹	カップク	*hara-kiri* (self-disembowelment) —*vi*. disembowel oneself
	割礼	カツレイ	circumcision
訓	割る	わる	*vt*. break; divide; split; water; allot
	割	わり	rate; one tenth; ten percent; division
	割り当てる	わりあてる	*vt*. assign; allot; distribute
	割り切る	わりきる	*vt*. divide; leave no doubt; give a clear-cut solution (for a problem)
	割れる	われる	*vi*. break; be divisible; crack; be torn
	割く	さく	*vt*. tear; sever; estrange; spare
¥	割賦	カップ	installment
	割合	わりあい	ratio; proportion
	割り当て	わりあて	allotment; allocation
	割高	わりだか	comparatively high price
	割引き	わりびき	discount
	割引債	わりびきサイ	discount bond
	割引手形	わりびきてがた	discounted notes
	割引料	わりびきりょう	discount charge
	割り引く	わりびく	*vt*. discount; give a discount; reduce
	割安	わりやす	comparatively low price
	～割れ	～われ	(suffix) below the level

205

創 ⑫

ノ 𠆢 𠂊 今 今 今 戶 戶 倉 倉 倉 創

音	創	ソウ	create; originate; make; wound; injury
熟	創案	ソウアン	original idea —*v*. come up with an original idea
	創意	ソウイ	originality; inventiveness
	創痍	ソウイ	wound

二 亠 人 へ イ 几 入 八 冂 宀 ソ 几 凵 刀 刂 • 力 勹 ヒ 匚 十 卜 卩 卩 厂 ム 又 了 ク マ

創刊	ソウカン	first edition —v. start/launch a magazine
創業	ソウギョウ	inauguration; establishment —v. found; establish
創建	ソウケン	foundation; establishment —v. found; establish
創作	ソウサク	creation; work —v. create; write a novel/story
創始	ソウシ	origination; creation —v. originate; create; found
創世	ソウセイ	creation of the world
創世記	ソウセイキ	Genesis
創設	ソウセツ	foundation; establishment —v. found; establish
創造	ソウゾウ	creation —v. create
創立	ソウリツ	foundation; establishment

206

 ⑮　　ヽ　ト　ト　广　庐　庐　庐　虍　虜　虜　豦　劇

音	劇	ゲキ	play; drama; the theater; acute; sharp
熟	劇化	ゲキカ	dramatization —vi. dramatize
	劇画	ゲキガ	comics with a realistic narrative
	劇作家	ゲキサッカ	dramatist
	劇場	ゲキジョウ	theater; play house
	劇団	ゲキダン	troupe; theatrical company
	劇中劇	ゲキチュウゲキ	play within a play
	劇的	ゲキテキ	dramatic; dramatically
	劇毒	ゲキドク	deadly poison
	劇薬	ゲキヤク	powerful drug

---

2 力　ちから　strength; power

207

 ②　　フ　カ

音	力	リキ	strength; force; power
		リョク	strength; force; power
熟	力演	リキエン	superb performance —vi. give a superb performance
	力学	リキガク	dynamics; mechanics
	力作	リキサク	great work; masterpiece
	力士	リキシ	sumo wrestler

116

力説	リキセツ	emphasis; stress —v. emphasize; stress
力走	リキソウ	sprinting; fast running —vi. run as fast as one can; sprint
力点	リキテン	fulcrum; emphasis
力む	リキむ	vi. exert one's strength; strain; bear down
力量	リキリョウ	ability; capacity; physical strength
訓 力	ちから	force; power; strength
力一杯	ちからイッパイ	with full force; with all one's might
力仕事	ちからシごと	physical labor
力添え	ちからぞえ	aid; help; assistance —vi. aid; help; assist
力試し	ちからだめし	trial of one's strength; test of one's ability
力づける	ちからづける	vt. encourage; cheer up
力持ち	ちからもち	man of great (physical) strength

208

加 ⑤　フ　カ　カ　加　加

音 加	カ	add; increase; join; participate; Canada; California
熟 加害	カガイ	assault; violence
加害者	カガイシャ	assailant
加減	カゲン	addition and subtraction; degree; extent; adjustment —v. allow for; make allowances for; adjust; moderate
加護	カゴ	divine protection —v. receive divine protection
加算	カサン	math. addition —v. add; include
加重	カジュウ	weighted (average) —vt. add weight/intensity
加勢	カセイ	help; aid; support; assistance —vi. help; aid; support; assist
加速	カソク	acceleration —v. accelerate
加速度	カソクド	acceleration rate
加担	カタン	support; help; assistance; participation —v. support; help; assist; participate
加入	カニュウ	joining; admission; entry; affiliation —vi. join; enter; affiliate
加入者	カニュウシャ	member; subscriber
加熱	カネツ	heating —v. heat up
加筆	カヒツ	correction; revision (of an essay, a painting, etc.) —v. correct; revise
加法	カホウ	math. addition
加味	カミ	flavoring; seasoning —v. flavor; season
加盟	カメイ	affiliation; participation —vi. join; affiliate; participate

訓	加える	くわえる	*vt*. add; increase; include
	加わる	くわわる	*vi*. join; participate; take part
¥	加工	カコウ	industrial process; processing; manufacturing; treatment —*v*. process; work; treat
	加工品	カコウヒン	finished article; processed goods
	加重平均	カジュウヘイキン	weighted average/mean
	加重平均利回り	カジュウヘイキンりまわり	compound yield based a weighted average

209

功 ⑤   一 丁 工 功 功

音	功	コウ (ク)	exploit; achievement; merit
熟	功徳	クドク	act of charity; blessings
	功罪	コウザイ	merits and demerits; pros and cons
	功績	コウセキ	meritorious deed; services; merits; achievement
	功名	コウミョウ	great exploit; distinguished services
	功名心	コウミョウシン	ambition; aspiration; love of fame
	功利的	コウリテキ	utilitarian; matter of fact
	功労	コウロウ	merits; service; exploit
	功労者	コウロウシャ	person of distinguished service

210

劣 ⑥   ⼃ ⼩ ⼩ 少 劣 劣

音	劣	レツ	inferior
熟	劣悪	レツアク	poor; inferior; coarse
	劣勢	レッセイ	numerical inferiority
	劣性	レッセイ	(racial, sexual, etc.) inferiority
	劣等	レットウ	inferiority
	劣等感	レットウカン	inferiority complex
訓	劣る	おとる	*vi*. be inferior to

211

助 ⑦   丨 冂 月 月 且 助 助

| 音 | 助 | ジョ | help |

118

熟	助演	ジョエン	supporting performance/role —*v.* play a supporting role
	助教授	ジョキョウジュ	assistant professor
	助言	ジョゲン	advice; counsel —*vi.* advise; counsel
	助詞	ジョシ	*gram.* particle
	助手	ジョシュ	helper; assistant
	助成	ジョセイ	aid; help with research or an enterprise —*v.* help; aid; assist
	助勢	ジョセイ	aid; support —*vi.* back; help
	助走	ジョソウ	run-up; approach run —*vi.* run up; make an approach run
	助長	ジョチョウ	promotion; encouragement —*v.* promote; encourage
	助動詞	ジョドウシ	*gram.* auxiliary verb
	助命	ジョメイ	sparing a person's life —*v.* spare a person's life
	助役	ジョヤク	assistant stationmaster; deputy mayor
	助力	ジョリョク	aid; help assistance; cooperation; support
訓	助	すけ	help; aid; assistance
	助太刀	すけだち	help; assistance; support
	助っ人	すけっと	helper; assistant
	助平	すけべイ	lechery; lewdness
	助かる	たすかる	*vi.* be helped/saved/rescued
	助ける	たすける	*vt.* help; assist; rescue; save

212

 努 ⑦ 　く　タ　女　奴　奴　努　努

音	努	ド	effort; endeavor
熟	努力	ドリョク	effort; endeavor; exertion; labor; strain; industry —*vi.* endeavor; do one's best; strive; make efforts
訓	努める	つとめる	*vt.* endeavor; make efforts; strive; apply oneself; try hard

213

励 ⑦ 　一　厂　厂　厉　厉　励　励

音	励	レイ	encouragement; diligence
熟	励行	レイコウ	strict enforcement —*v.* enforce strictly
訓	励ます	はげます	*vt.* encourage; urge
	励む	はげむ	*vi.* be diligent

二 亠 人 ハ イ 儿 入 八 冂 冖 冫 几 凵 刀 刂 ● 力 勹 匕 匚 十 卜 卩 巴 厂 厶 又 了 勹 マ

214

労 ⑦

丶 〃 �"〃 ⺍ 兴 学 労

音	労	ロウ	work; labor; toil
熟	労役	ロウエキ	labor; work; toil
	労苦	ロウク	labor; pains; toil
	労作	ロウサク	laborious work; toil; labor
	労賃	ロウチン	labor cost
	労働	ロウドウ	labor; work; toil —*vi*. labor; work; toil
	労働者	ロウドウシャ	laborer; worker
	労働力	ロウドウリョク	labor; manpower; workforce
	労務者	ロウムシャ	worker; laborer
	労力	ロウリョク	labor; effort; trouble
訓	労る	いたわる	*vt*. sympathize with; be kind to; treat well; *vi*. get sick/ill
¥	労使	ロウシ	labor and management
	労資	ロウシ	capital and labor
	労働組合	ロウドウくみあい	labor union
	労働集約的農業	ロウドウシュウヤクテキノウギョウ	labor-intensive industry
	労働省	ロウドウショウ	Ministry of Labor
	労働人口	ロウドウジンコウ	working population
	労働大臣	ロウドウダイジン	minister of labor
	労働費	ロウドウヒ	labor cost

215

劾 ⑧

丶 一 亠 玄 亥 亥 刻 劾

音	劾	ガイ	impeach; investigate

216

効 ⑧

丶 一 亠 六 亠 交 効 効

音	効	コウ	effect; efficacy; efficiency
熟	効果	コウカ	effect; effectiveness; efficiency
	効果的	コウカテキ	effective; effectual; successful
	効能	コウノウ	efficacy; effect; virtue; benefit; effectiveness
	効用	コウヨウ	effect; use; usefulness; utility; benefit

	効率	コウリツ	utility factor; efficiency
	効力	コウリョク	effect; efficacy; value; validity; force
訓	効き目	ききめ	effect; virtue; efficacy
	効く	きく	*vi.* be effective; work; act

217

勅 ⑨ 一 厂 厅 日 巿 束 束 軪 勅

音	勅	チョク	imperial edict
熟	勅語	チョクゴ	imperial rescript
	勅使	チョクシ	imperial envoy
	勅旨	チョクシ	imperial mandate
	勅令	チョクレイ	imperial decree

218

勇 ⑨ フ マ 丙 丙 甬 甬 面 勇 勇

音	勇	ユウ	courage; bravery; heroism
熟	勇敢	ユウカン	heroism; gallantry; bravery
	勇気	ユウキ	courage; bravery; valor; nerve; audacity
	勇士	ユウシ	brave man; hero
	勇姿	ユウシ	brave/gallant figure
	勇者	ユウシャ	brave man; hero; man of valor
	勇将	ユウショウ	brave general; great soldier
	勇壮	ユウソウ	bravery; heroism
	勇退	ユウタイ	voluntary retirement —*v.* retire voluntarily; bow out
	勇断	ユウダン	resolute decision
	勇猛	ユウモウ	valor; daring; bravery
	勇躍	ユウヤク	high spirits —*vi.* be in high spirits; take heart
訓	勇ましい	いさましい	courageous; valiant
	勇む	いさむ	*vi.* cheer up; be in high spirits

219

勉 ⑩ ノ ク ケ 务 务 务 免 免 免 勉

| 音 | 勉 | ベン | diligence |
| 熟 | 勉学 | ベンガク | diligent study —*v.* study hard |

121

二 亠 人 ヘ イ 儿 入 八 冂 冖 丷 几 凵 刀 刂 • 力 勹 匕 匚 十 卜 卩 卪 厂 厶 又 了 冫 マ

	勉強	ベンキョウ	studying; diligence *col.* selling cheap —*v.* study; be diligent *col.* sell cheaply
	勉励	ベンレイ	diligence; industriousness —*vi.* be diligent/industrious; work hard
訓	※勉める	つとめる	make efforts; work hard; be diligent

220

勘 ⑪　一　十　廿　廿　甘　其　其　其　甚　勘　勘

音	勘	カン	think; intuition; ponder
熟	勘定	カンジョウ	counting; computation; accounts; payment of bills —*v.* count; reckon; calculate; compute
	勘違い	カンちがい	misunderstanding —*vi.* misunderstand; mistake; guess wrong
	勘当	カンドウ	disowning; disinheritance; renunciation —*v.* disown; disinherit; renounce
	勘弁	カンベン	pardon; forgiveness; permission; excuse —*v.* pardon; forgive; permit; excuse

221

動 ⑪　一　ニ　亍　亓　亓　盲　重　重　重　動　動

音	動	ドウ	movement; motion
熟	動じる	ドウじる	*vi.* be upset/perturbed/confused
	動員	ドウイン	mobilization —*v.* mobilize; set in motion
	動悸	ドウキ	palpitation (of the heart)
	動機	ドウキ	motive; inducement; incentive
	動議	ドウギ	motion (of a meeting)
	動向	ドウコウ	trend; tendency; movement
	動作	ドウサ	movement; motion; action
	動詞	ドウシ	*gram.* verb
	動静	ドウセイ	movements; state of things; conditions
	動的	ドウテキ	dynamic; kinetic
	動転	ドウテン	fright —*vi.* be frightened
	動物	ドウブツ	animal; beast
	動物園	ドウブツエン	zoo; zoological gardens
	動脈	ドウミャク	artery
	動揺	ドウヨウ	shaking; trembling; restlessness; unrest —*vi.* shake; tremble; be restless/disturbed
	動乱	ドウラン	disturbance; upheaval; agitation; commotion; riot
	動力	ドウリョク	power; dynamic force; moment

訓	動かす	うごかす	**vt**. move; stir; put in motion; inspire; touch; impress
	動く	うごく	**vi**. move; stir; budge; shake; work; operate; be moved/touched
¥	動産	ドウサン	movable assets

222

務⑪ 　マ マ ヲ 予 矛 矛 矛 矛 矛 務 務

音	務	ム	serve; work
訓	務め	つとめ	work; responsibility
	務める	つとめる	**vt**. work; serve

223

勤⑫ 一 十 廿 廿 甘 苫 芾 革 革 堇 勤 勤

音	勤	キン	work; hold a post; exert oneself; endeavor; be diligent; try hard
		ゴン	
熟	勤勉	キンベン	diligence; industry; hard work
	勤労	キンロウ	labor; work; service; industry
訓	勤まる	つとまる	**vi**. be fit for; be equal to
	勤める	つとめる	**vt**. serve; work; hold a position; be diligent
	勤め先	つとめさき	one's place of work; the office
¥	勤続	キンゾク	continuance in office
	勤務	キンム	service; duty —**vi**. serve; work
	勤務先	キンムサキ	one's workplace
	勤務時間	キンムジカン	working/office hours
	勤労者	キンロウシャ	worker; laborer

224

勝⑫) 刀 月 月 月 月゛ 月- 朋- 胖 朕 勝 勝

音	勝	ショウ	win; excel
熟	勝因	ショウイン	the cause of victory
	勝運	ショウウン	one's winning luck
	勝機	ショウキ	winning opportunity/chance
	勝算	ショウサン	chance of success; prospects; odds; chances
	勝者	ショウシャ	winner; victor

二　人　ヘ　イ　几　入　八　冂　＾　冫　几　凵　刀　刂　力　勹　匕　匚　十　卜　卩　巴　厂　厶　又　了　ク　マ

	勝敗	ショウハイ	victory or defeat; win or lose; the outcome
	勝負	ショウブ	match; game; contest —*vi.* play; have a game; have a match
	勝利	ショウリ	victory; triumph
訓	勝つ	かつ	*vi.* win; beat; defeat
	勝ち気	かちき	unyielding spirit
	勝ち抜く	かちぬく	*vi.* win; advance to the next round
	勝ち目	かちめ	chances of winning
	勝る	まさる	*vi.* excel; be superior to

225

募 ⑫　一　十　艹　艹　莒　莒　莒　草　莫　莫　募　募

音	募	ボ	appeal; invite; raise; grow intense
熟	募金	ボキン	fund raising —*vi.* raise money
	募集	ボシュウ	recruitment; solicitation —*v.* recruit; solicit
訓	募る	つのる	*v.* appeal; invite (donations); raise (funds); grow intense; deteriorate (illness, etc.)
¥	募集 (債権)	ボシュウ (サイケン)	flotation; subscription

226

勧 ⑬　ノ　ヶ　ヶ　ヶ　午　牟　秊　秊　隼　隹　釗　勧

音	勧	カン	advise; urge; encourage
熟	勧業	カンギョウ	encouragement of industry
	勧告	カンコク	advice; counsel; recommendation —*v.* advise; consel; recommend
	勧誘	カンユウ	solicitation; persuasion; inducement —*v.* solicit; canvass; persuade; induce
訓	勧める	すすめる	*vt.* advise; encourage; urge

227

勢 ⑬　一　十　土　夫　去　奉　坴　坴丿　埶　埶　勢　勢

音	勢	セイ	power; force; energy; vigor
熟	勢揃い	セイぞろい	array; full line up
	勢力	セイリョク	influence; force
訓	勢い	いきおい	force; energy; vigor

2 勹　つつみがまえ　wrapping

228

勹 ③ 　ノ　勹

| 音 | 勺 | シャク | *shaku* (unit of capacity, approx. 818 ml) |

229

勾 ④ 　ノ　勹　匀　匁

| 訓 | 匁 | もんめ | *monme* (unit of weight, approx. 3.75g) |

230

包 ⑤ 　ノ　勹　勹　勺　包

音	包	ホウ	wrap; cover; envelop; conceal
熟	包囲	ホウイ	siege; surrounding (the enemy) —*v.* besiege; surround (the enemy)
	包括	ホウカツ	included —*v.* include
	包括的	ホウカツテキ	inclusive; comprehensive
	包含	ホウガン	including —*v.* include; contain; imply
	包茎	ホウケイ	foreskin; uncircumsized penis
	包装	ホウソウ	packing; packaging; wrapping —*v.* pack; package; wrap
	包蔵	ホウゾウ	concealment —*vt.* contain; imply; hold
	包帯	ホウタイ	bandage; dressing
	包丁	ホウチョウ	kitchen knife; cooking knife
	包皮	ホウヒ	outer skin; foreskin
	包容	ホウヨウ	tolerance; implication; comprehension —*v.* tolerate; comprehend imply
	包容力	ホウヨウリョク	capacity; tolerance; broad-mindedness
訓	包み紙	つつみがみ	wrapping paper
	包み込む	つつみこむ	*vt.* wrap up
	包む	つつむ	*vt.* wrap; cover; envelop; conceal

二十人ヘイ儿入八冂冖冫几凵刀刂力勹 • ヒ匚十卜卩巴厂厶又了ク マ

2 匕　ひ spoon; hi (katakana)

231
北 ⑤　一　ナ　키　키ト　北

音	北	ホク	north
熟	北緯	ホクイ	north latitude
	北欧	ホクオウ	Northern Europe
	北上	ホクジョウ	going north —*vi.* go north
	北端	ホクタン	northern extremity/tip
	北天	ホクテン	northern sky
	北斗七星	ホクトシチセイ	Big Dipper
	北部	ホクブ	north; northern part
	北米	ホクベイ	North America
	北辺	ホクヘン	northern regions/extremes
	北洋	ホクヨウ	northern sea
	北海道	ホッカイドウ	Hokkaido
	北極	ホッキョク	North Pole
	北極熊	ホッキョクぐま	polar bear
	北極圏	ホッキョクケン	Arctic Circle
	北極星	ホッキョクセイ	North Star; Polaris
	北氷洋	ホッピョウヨウ	Arctic Ocean
	北方	ホッポウ	north; northward; northern
訓	北	きた	north
	北回帰線	きたカイキセン	Tropic of Cancer
	北風	きたかぜ	north wind
	北大西洋	きたタイセイヨウ	North Atlantic
	北朝鮮	きたチョウセン	North Korea
	北半球	きたハンキュウ	Northern Hemisphere
	北向き	きたむき	facing north

232
旨 ⑥　一　匕　匕　匕ヒ　匕目　旨

音	旨	シ	effect; principle
訓	旨	むね	effect; principle; meaning; gist; main points
※	旨い	うまい	delicious; tasty; good

126

はこがまえ　box on side

233

区 ④ 一 フ 又 区

音	区	ク	divide; punctuate; partition; borough; ward; diverse
熟	区域	クイキ	the limits; boundary; domain
	区画	クカク	division; demarcation —v. divide; demarcate
	区間	クカン	section between two points; territory
	区分	クブン	division; demarcation —v. divide; demarcate
	区別	クベツ	distinguishing; discrimination —v. distinguish; discriminate
	区民	クミン	ward/borough citizens
	区役所	クヤクショ	ward office
	区立	クリツ	funded/run and organized by the ward/borough

234

匹 ④ 一 ア 兀 匹

音	匹	ヒツ	same kind; comparable; man of low birth
熟	匹敵	ヒッテキ	match; equal; rival —vi. match; equal; rival; compare with
訓	匹	ひき	(counter for birds, animals, fish, insects); *hiki* (unit of length for measuring cloth, approx. 21.8 m)

235

巨 ⑤ 丨 厂 厂 戶 巨

音	巨	キョ	huge; enormous; immense
熟	巨額	キョガク	very large sum of money; fortune
	巨視的	キョシテキ	macroscopic
	巨匠	キョショウ	person renowned for his craft; master craftsman
	巨人	キョジン	giant; Titan; Goliath; person who is particularly big; person with special powers
	巨体	キョタイ	very large body; gigantic figure
	巨大	キョダイ	huge; gigantic; enormous; mega-
	巨頭	キョトウ	leading figure; bigwig; big shot

2

二 亠 人 宀 イ 儿 入 八 冂 冖 冫 几 凵 刀 刂 力 勹 ヒ 匚 十 卜 卩 卩 厂 厶 又 マ ク マ

巨費	キョヒ	large outlay; great cost
巨万	キョマン	millions; extremely numerous
¥ 巨大企業	キョダイキギョウ	big business; business giant
巨大国	キョダイコク	superpower

236

匠 ⑥ 一 ア ア 戸 斤 匠

音 匠	ショウ	craftsman
訓 ※匠	たくみ	skillful; clever

237

医 ⑦ 一 ア 歹 歹 歹 矢 医

音 医	イ	heal; cure; doctor; medicine
熟 医院	イイン	physician's office; doctor's surgery
医学	イガク	medical science; medicine
医師	イシ	doctor; physician
医務	イム	medical affairs
医薬品	イヤクヒン	medicine; drugs
医療	イリョウ	medical treatment/care

238

匿 ⑩ 一 一 干 干 芋 芋 芋 若 若 匿

音 匿	トク	hide
熟 匿名	トクメイ	anonymity; alias

2 十 じゅう ten; cross

239

十 ② 一 十

音 十	ジュウ	ten
熟 十一月	ジュウイチガツ	November

128

十月	ジュウガツ	October
十五夜	ジュウゴヤ	full-moon night
十字	ジュウジ	cross
十字架	ジュウジカ	cross; Holy Cross
十字軍	ジュウジグン	Crusaders
十字路	ジュウジロ	crossroads
十二月	ジュウニガツ	December
十二支	ジュウニシ	twelve signs of the Chinese/Japanese zodiac
十二分	ジュウニブン	more than enough
十人十色	ジュウニンといろ	everyone to his own taste; to each his own
十人並	ジュウニンなみ	average; ordinary
十年一日	ジュウネンイチジツ	without any change over a long period
十八番	ジュウハチバン	what one is best at
十分	ジュウブン	enough; plenty
十中八九	ジュッチュウハック	almost

訓 十	と	ten
十	とお	ten
十日	とおか	tenth day (of the month); 10th
※十八番	おはこ	what one is best at

240

千 ③   一 ニ 千

音 千	セン	thousand
熟 千金	センキン	lot of money
千差万別	センサバンベツ	infinite variety; various kinds
千秋楽	センシュウラク	the last day of a play, sumo, etc.
千里眼	センリガン	clairvoyance
訓 千	ち	one thousand

241

午 ④   ノ 广 ニ 午

音 午	ゴ	noon
熟 午後	ゴゴ	afternoon; p.m.
午睡	ゴスイ	nap —*vi*. take a nap
午前	ゴゼン	morning; a.m.
訓 ※午	うま	the horse (seventh sign of the Chinese zodiac)

二
亠
人
ヘ
イ
儿
入
八
冂
冖
冫
几
凵
刀
刂
力
勹
匕
匚
•
十
卜
卩
卩
厂
厶
又
了
ク
マ

242

升 ④

ノ ナ チ 升

| 音 | 升 | ショウ | *shō* (unit of capacity, approx. 1.8 ℓ) |
| 訓 | 升 | ます | measure; box |

243

半 ⑤

、 ゞ ゛ ⸏ 半

音	半	ハン	half
熟	半永久的	ハンエイキュウテキ	semipermanent
	半円	ハンエン	semicircle; half-circle
	半音	ハンオン	semitone; halftone
	半開	ハンカイ	half open; partly open; semi-civilized
	半額	ハンガク	half the sum; half price
	半期	ハンキ	half year; half term
	半旗	ハンキ	flag at half-mast
	半休	ハンキュウ	half-holiday
	半球	ハンキュウ	hemisphere
	半径	ハンケイ	*math.* radius
	半月	ハンゲツ	half moon; half-month
	半減	ハンゲン	reduction by half —*v.* reduce by half; halve; take off half
	半紙	ハンシ	common Japanese paper
	半死半生	ハンシハンショウ	more dead than alive; all but dead; half dead
	半周	ハンシュウ	semicircle —*vi.* go half way around a circuit, etc.
	半熟	ハンジュク	half-boiled; half-done; half-ripe
	半身	ハンシン	half the body
	半身不随	ハンシンフズイ	*med.* paralysis of one lateral half of the body
	半信半疑	ハンシハンギ	incredulous; half in doubt; dubious
	半数	ハンスウ	half the number (of objects)
	半生	ハンセイ	half one's life; half a lifetime
	半世紀	ハンセイキ	half a century
	半袖	ハンそで	half-length sleeves; short sleeves
	半田	ハンだ	solder; pewter
	半濁音	ハンダクオン	semi-voiced sound
	半濁点	ハンダクテン	semi-voiced sound sign
	半月	ハンつき	half a month; half-month

半纏	ハンテン	*hanten* (half-length Japanese style coat)
半島	ハントウ	peninsula
半時	ハンとき	about an hour; short time; short while; half an hour
半年	ハンとし	half a year; half year
半日	ハンニチ	half a day; half day
半値	ハンね	half price
半端	ハンパ	odd thing; fragment
半白	ハンパク	salt and pepper hair
半々	ハンハン	half and half; fifty-fifty
半分	ハンブン	half
半面	ハンメン	one side; half; profile
半裸	ハンラ	half naked; topless
訓 半ば	なかば	half; semi-; middle; center; in part; partially
¥ 半導体	ハンドウタイ	semiconductor

244

協 ⑧ 一 十 ナ ナワ ナカ ナカ 拘 協 協

音 協	キョウ	cooperation; group; organization
熟 協会	キョウカイ	association; league; society
協議	キョウギ	conference; council; consultation —*v.* confer; consult; deliberate
協賛	キョウサン	support; cooperation —*v.* support; cooperate
協商	キョウショウ	entente —*vi.* reach agreement
協奏曲	キョウソウキョク	concerto
協調	キョウチョウ	cooperation; harmony; conciliation —*v.* cooperate; act in union/harmony/concert
協定	キョウテイ	agreement; convention; pact —*v.* agree upon; arrange; make an agreement
協同	キョウドウ	cooperation; collaboration; union —*v.* cooperate with; collaborate; work together
協約	キョウヤク	agreement; convention; pact
協力	キョウリョク	cooperation; collaboration; working together —*vi.* cooperate; work together; collaborate
協和	キョウワ	harmony —*vi.* be in harmony
¥ 協業化	キョウギョウカ	grouping into a cooperative
協調融資	キョウチョウユウシ	joint financing; participation loan
協調融資国	キョウチョウユウシコク	syndication group
協同組合	キョウドウくみあい	cooperative association

二十人へイ几入八冂冖冫几凵刀刂力勹匕匸十卜卩巳厂厶又了勹マ

245

卒 ⑧ 　 丶 亠 广 六 存 卒 卒 卒

音	卒	ソツ	soldier; private; sudden; come to an end; die; graduate
熟	卒業	ソツギョウ	graduation —v. graduate
	卒中	ソッチュウ	*med.* apoplexy; cerebral stroke
	卒倒	ソットウ	swooning —v. swoon

246

卓 ⑧ 　 丶 卜 広 占 占 卢 卣 卓

音	卓	タク	desk; table; excellence; eminence
熟	卓越	タクエツ	excellence; superiority; eminence —vi. excel; surpass; be distinguished; transcend
	卓上	タクジョウ	desk top; on top of a desk
	卓抜	タクバツ	excellent —vi. excell in
	卓球	タッキュウ	table tennis; ping-pong
	卓見	タッケン	farsightedness

247

南 ⑨ 　 一 十 广 内 内 肉 南 南 南

音	南	ナン	south
熟	南緯	ナンイ	south latitude
	南下	ナンカ	going south —vi. go down south
	南極	ナンキョク	South Pole
	南極圏	ナンキョクケン	Antarctic Circle
	南船北馬	ナンセンホクバ	constant traveling; being on the move
	南端	ナンタン	southern extremity/tip
	南中	ナンチュウ	southing; culmination —vi. go south; cross the meridian; culminate
	南蛮	ナンバン	southern barbarians; cayenne pepper
	南氷洋	ナンピョウヨウ	Antarctic Ocean
	南米	ナンベイ	South America
	南洋	ナンヨウ	South Seas
訓	南	みなみ	south
	南回帰線	みなみカイキセン	Tropic of Capricorn
	南十字星	みなみジュウジセイ	Southern Cross
	南半球	みなみハンキュウ	Southern Hemisphere

卑 ⑨ ノ ⼃ ⼧ 卢 甴 由 甶 鱼 卑

音	卑	ヒ	humble; base; ignoble; vulgar
熟	卑怯	ヒキョウ	cowardice; meanness; unfairness
	卑怯者	ヒキョウもの	coward
	卑近	ヒキン	common; ordinary
	卑屈	ヒクツ	mean; inferior; poor
	卑下	ヒゲ	humble; humility; self-abasement —*v.* humble oneself
	卑語	ヒゴ	vulgar word/expression
	卑俗	ヒゾク	vulgar; coarse
	卑劣	ヒレツ	mean; unfair; contemptible; sneaky
	卑猥	ヒワイ	indecency; obscenity; coarseness
訓	卑しい	いやしい	mean; humble
	卑しむ	いやしむ	*vt.* despise; condemn; disdain; scorn; look down on
	卑しめる	いやしめる	*vt.* despise; condemn; disdain; scorn; look down on

博 ⑫ ノ ⼀ ⼗ ⼗ ⼴ 博 博 恒 博 博 博 博 博

音	博	ハク	broad; doctor; professor
		（バク）	gambling
熟	博する	ハクする	*vt.* gain/win (reputation); win/enjoy (credit/confidence)
	博愛	ハクアイ	philantropy; charity; benevelonce; humanity
	博学	ハクガク	erudition; extensive learning; wide knowledge
	博士	ハクシ(ハカセ)	doctor; professor
	博士号	ハクシゴウ（ハカセゴウ）	doctorate
	博識	ハクシキ	wide knowledge; erudition
	博徒	バクト	professional gambler
	博物	ハクブツ	extensive knowlege; natural sciences (term used in prewar Japanese schools)
	博物館	ハクブツカン	museum
	博覧	ハクラン	wide reading; extensive knowledge —*vi.* be widely read; have extensive knowledge
	博覧会	ハクランカイ	fair; exhibition; exposition
※	博打	バクチ	gambling; gaming; speculation; venture

2 卜　ぼく　divination; to (katakana)

250

占 ⑤　丶　ト　卜　占　占

音	占	セン	occupy; hold
熟	占拠	センキョ	occupation —v. occupy
	占星術	センセイジュツ	astrology
	占有	センユウ	occupancy; exclusive possession —v. occupy/possess exclusively
	占領	センリョウ	occupation; capture —v. occupy; capture
訓	占う	うらなう	vt. divine; tell fortunes
	占師	うらないシ	fortune teller
	占める	しめる	vt. occupy

2 卩　わりふ／ふしづくり　joint; seal

251

印 ⑥　丿　亻　F　E　印　印

音	印	イン	stamp; printing; seal
	印鑑	インカン	official personal seal
	印刷	インサツ	printing —v. print
	印紙	インシ	revenue stamp
	印字	インジ	printing —v. print
	印象	インショウ	impression
	印象的	インショウテキ	impressive; memorable
	印税	インゼイ	royalty (on a book)
訓	印	しるし	sign; proof; signal
	印す	しるす	vt. mark; inscribe

252

却 ⑦　一　十　土　去　去　却　却

音	却	キャク	retreat; recede; repulse; repel; avoid

| 熟 | 却下 | キャッカ | rejection; dismissal; turndown —*v.* reject; dismiss; turn down |

253

即 ⁷ ⼁ ⼁ ヨ ⺼ ⺝ 卽 即

音	即	ソク	at once; immediate; as is; on the spot
熟	即位	ソクイ	accession to the throne; coronation —*v.* ascend/accede to the throne
	即応	ソクオウ	conformity —*v.* conform; adapt; meet
	即座	ソクザ	prompt; on the spot
	即死	ソクシ	instantaneous death —*v.* die instantly
	即時	ソクジ	instantly; immediately; on the spot
	即日	ソクジツ	on the same day
	即製	ソクセイ	on-the-spot manufacture
	即席	ソクセキ	impromptu; instant; extemporaneous
	即断	ソクダン	prompt decision —*v.* make a prompt decision
	即答	ソクトウ	ready answer —*v.* give a ready answer
	即納	ソクノウ	immediate payment/delivery
	即決	ソッケツ	prompt decision —*v.* make a prompt decision
	即発	ソクハツ	immediate departure
	即効	ソッコウ	immediate effect
	即刻	ソッコク	instantly; immediately; at once
訓	*即ち	すなわち	namely; i.e.
	*即く	つく	*vi.* ascend; succeed to
¥	即売	ソクバイ	spot sale —*v.* make a spot sale
	即金	ソッキン	payment in cash

254

卵 ⁷ ⼂ ⼃ ⼃ ⼇ ⼇⼁ ⼇⼃ 卵

音	卵	ラン	egg
熟	卵黄	ランオウ	yolk
	卵殻	ランカク	eggshell
	卵管	ランカン	*med.* fallopian tube
	卵子	ランシ	*med.* ovum; egg cell
	卵生	ランセイ	*med.* oviparity
	卵巣	ランソウ	*med.* ovary
	卵白	ランパク	white of an egg; albumin
訓	卵	たまご	spawn; egg

二十人入イ入八冂冖冫几凵刀刂力勹匕匚十卜卩巴厶又了ク乛

二十人へイ儿入八冂冖冫几凵刀刂力勹匕匚十卜卩巳厂厶又了々マ

255

卸 ⑨ 　ノ ト ⼇ 午 午 年 钅 釕 卸

訓	卸	おろし	wholesale
	卸す	おろす	wholesale; sell by wholesale
¥	卸売	おろしうり	wholesale
	卸値	おろしね	wholesale price

---

2 巳 わりふ／ふしづくり crooked seal

256

危 ⑥ 　ノ ク ⼑ 产 产 危

音	危	キ	dangerous; hurt
熟	危害	キガイ	harm; injury
	危機	キキ	crisis; emergency
	危機一髪	キキイッパツ	imminent danger; close shave
	危惧	キグ	fear; misgivings; apprehensions —*v.* feel misgivings; be apprehensive
	危険	キケン	danger; hazard; risk
	危篤	キトク	critical condition
訓	危ない	あぶない	dangerous; doubtful; risky
	危うい	あやうい	dangerous; critical; hazardous; risky
	危ぶむ	あやぶむ	*vi.* fear; be apprehensive/afraid

---

2 厂 がんだれ cliff

257

厄 ④ 　一 厂 万 厄

音	厄	ヤク	misfortune; disaster
熟	厄年	ヤクどし	unlucky/bad year
	厄払い	ヤクばらい	exorcism —*vi.* exorcize; drive away evil
	厄日	ヤクび	unlucky/evil day
	厄介	ヤッカイ	troublesome; burdensome; help; care

258

厚 ⑨ 一 厂 厂 厃 戸 匣 匣 厚 厚

音	厚	コウ	thick; kind; tender
熟	厚意	コウイ	favor; kind intentions; kindness
	厚顔	コウガン	impudence; shamelessness
	厚情	コウジョウ	kindness
訓	厚い	あつい	thick; heavy; bulky; kind; cordial; tender; warm; deep
	厚着	あつぎ	thick/warm clothes —*vi.* be thick/warmly dressed
	厚化粧	あつゲショウ	heavy/thick makeup
	厚手	あつで	thick; bulky
¥	厚相 （厚生大臣）	コウショウ （コウセイ ダイジン）	minister of health and welfare
	厚生	コウセイ	public welfare
	厚生省	コウセイショウ	Ministry of Welfare

259

厘 ⑨ 一 厂 厂 厍 戸 匣 匣 厘 厘

音	厘	リン	*rin* (former unit of currency, 1/1000 yen); *rin* (unit of lengh, approx. 0.3 mm; unit of weight, approx. 375 mg)
熟	厘毛	リンモウ	insignificant amount of money; a little

260

原 ⑩ 一 厂 厂 厃 原 原 盾 原 原 原

音	原	ゲン	plain; field; source; origin; crude
熟	原案	ゲンアン	original bill/plan
	原因	ゲンイン	cause; factor
	原画	ゲンガ	original picture
	原形	ゲンケイ	original form
	原型	ゲンケイ	model; prototype; archetype
	原語	ゲンゴ	original language; the original
	原稿	ゲンコウ	manuscript; draft; notes
	原稿用紙	ゲンコウヨウシ	manuscript paper; Japanese writing pad
	原告	ゲンコク	prosecutor; plaintiff; complainant

二
十
人
へ
イ
儿
入
八
冂
亠
丷
几
凵
刀
刂
力
勹
匕
匸
十
卜
卩
巴
•
厂
厶
又
了
ク
マ

原材料	ゲンザイリョウ	raw materials
原作	ゲンサク	original story; the original; the book
原産	ゲンサン	country of origin; native
原始	ゲンシ	genesis; primitive; primeval
原始時代	ゲンシジダイ	primitive age
原始人	ゲンシジン	primitive man
原始的	ゲンシテキ	primitive; primeval
原子	ゲンシ	atom
原子核	ゲンシカク	atomic nucleus
原子爆弾	ゲンシバクダン	atomic/nuclear bomb
原子力	ゲンシリョク	atomic energy; nuclear power
原子力発電所	ゲンシリョクハツデンショ	nuclear power plant
原子炉	ゲンシロ	nuclear reactor
原紙	ゲンシ	stencil paper; stencil
原住民	ゲンジュウミン	natives; aborigines
原書	ゲンショ	original book; the original; in the original
原色	ゲンショク	primary color
原図	ゲンズ	original drawing/plan/map
原寸	ゲンスン	actual size; life-size; full-size
原生動物	ゲンセイドウブツ	*bio.* protozoa
原生林	ゲンセイリン	primeval forest
原則	ゲンソク	general/fundamental rule; principle
原典	ゲンテン	original text
原点	ゲンテン	starting point; origin
原動力	ゲンドウリョク	motivating power; driving force
原爆	ゲンバク	A-bomb; atomic bomb
原爆症	ゲンバクショウ	radiation sickness
原文	ゲンブン	original text; the original
原簿	ゲンボ	ledger
原木	ゲンボク	raw lumber
原野	ゲンヤ	wilderness; field; plain
原油	ゲンユ	crude oil; petroleum
原理	ゲンリ	principle
原料	ゲンリョウ	raw materials
訓 原	はら	plain; field
¥ 原価	ゲンカ	cost; cost price; cost of production; prime cost
原価計算	ゲンカケイサン	cost accounting; costing
原価主義	ゲンカシュギ	cost principle

2 ム む *mu* (katakana)

261

去 ⑤ 一 十 土 去 去

音	去	キョ	depart; go away; leave; the past; remove; clear away
		コ	
熟	去就	キョシュウ	one's course of action
	去勢	キョセイ	emasculation —*vt*. emasculate
	去年	キョネン	last year
	去来	キョライ	coming and going; recurrence —*vi*. recur
訓	去る	さる	*vi*. take off; remove; eliminate; take away; get rid of; divorce; leave; depart from; pass; elapse; be over

262

弁 ⑤ 厶 厸 厼 弁 弁

音	弁	ベン	speech; dialect; valve; petal; distinguish between; braid; bind
熟	弁じる	ベンじる	*vi*. speak; talk; debate; discriminate; pledge; vow; solve; finish; arrange
	弁解	ベンカイ	explanation; justification; defense; excuse; apology —*v*. explain; justify; excuse; apologize
	弁護	ベンゴ	defense; pleading for —*v*. defend; plead for
	弁護士	ベンゴシ	lawyer; attorney
	弁護団	ベンゴダン	the defense counsel (composed of several attorneys-at-law)
	弁護人	ベンゴニン	counsel; defender; lawyer
	弁才	ベンサイ	oratorical talents; eloquence
	弁済	ベンサイ	compensation; settlement; return of a borrowed item —*vi*. compensate; settle; return
	弁士	ベンシ	speaker; orator; silent movie narrator
	弁償	ベンショウ	compensation; indemnification —*v*. compensate; indemnify
	弁証法	ベンショウホウ	logical argumentation; dialectic
	弁舌	ベンゼツ	speech; eloquence
	弁天	ベンテン	Sarasvati (Indian goddess of music, eloquence, wisdom, and wealth)
	弁当	ベントウ	(box) lunch; packed lunch

二十人ヘイ儿入八冂宀儿凵刀刂力勹匕匚十卜卩巴厂厶又了ケ マ

弁別	ベンベツ	discrimination; distinction —*v.* discriminate; distinguish	
弁膜	ベンマク	*med.* valve (in internal organs)	
弁務官	ベンムカン	commissioner (in colony/commonwealth country)	
弁明	ベンメイ	explanation; justification —*vi.* explain; justify	
弁理	ベンリ	management; dealing	
弁理士	ベンリシ	patent attorney (lawyer, agent)	
弁論	ベンロン	argument; debate —*vi.* argue; debate	

263

参 ⑧ ㇉ ㇁ 厽 夅 矣 矣 参 参

音	参	サン	visit; go; worship join; assemble
熟	参じる	サンじる	*vi.* go; visit
	参加	サンカ	participation —*vi.* participate in; take part; enter
	参賀	サンガ	congratulatory visit to the imperial palace —*vi.* visit the imperial palace to express congratulations
	参会	サンカイ	attendance at a meeting —*vi.* attend a meeting
	参画	サンカク	participation in planning
	参観	サンカン	visit; observation —*v.* visit; observe
	参議院	サンギイン	House of Councilors; Upper House
	参詣	サンケイ	visit to a temple or a shrine —*vi.* visit a temple or a shrine
	参考	サンコウ	reference; consultation
	参考書	サンコウショ	reference book
	参考人	サンコウニン	witness
	参酌	サンシャク	selection —*vt.* select; choose
	参集	サンシュウ	gathering; collecting —*vi.* gather; collect
	参照	サンショウ	reference; consultation; comparison —*v.* refer; consult; compare
	参上	サンジョウ	*hum.* visit —*vi. hum.* visit; go to see
	参政権	サンセイケン	suffrage; right to vote; franchise
	参戦	サンセン	participation in a war —*vi.* enter a war
	参道	サンドウ	approach/path leading to a shrine
	参拝	サンパイ	worship at a shrine or temple —*vi.* go and worship at a shrine or temple
	参謀	サンボウ	staff officer
	参謀本部	サンボウホンブ	General Staff Office
	参列者	サンレツシャ	attendant; one of those present
訓	参る	まいる	*hum. vi.* come; go; visit; worship

2 又 また again

264

又 フ 又 ②

音	又	（ユウ）	another; again
訓	又	また	again; also; moreover
	又貸し	またがし	subletting; subleasing —v. sublet; sublease
	又聞き	またぎき	indirect information; hearsay —v. hear secondhand; learn by hearsay

265

収 丨 屮 収 収 ④

音	収	シュウ	receive payment; harvest; store; keep
熟	収穫	シュウカク	harvest; crop —v. harvest; reap
	収拾	シュウシュウ	control; reinstating order —v. put under control; settle
	収集	シュウシュウ	collection; collecting —v. collect; gather; amass
	収縮	シュウシュク	shrinkage; contraction —v. shrink; contract
	収束	シュウソク	conclusion; convergence —v. gather and bundle; conclude; converge
	収納	シュウノウ	receipt of payment/goods —v. receive payment/goods
	収納家具	シュウノウカグ	cabinet
	収納庫	シュウノウコ	shed; closet
	収容	シュウヨウ	accommodation of people/things in a place —v. accommodate; send
	収容所	シュウヨウジョ	concentration camp
	収録	シュウロク	record; recording —v. record music/pictures (on magnetic tape, etc.)
	収賄	シュウワイ	accepting/taking of bribes (accept/take bribes)
訓	収まる	おさまる	vi. hold; contain; settle down
	収める	おさめる	vt. put away/back; include; obtain; pay a bill
¥	収益	シュウエキ	earnings; profit; proceeds
	収益金	シュウエキキン	earnings; profit; proceeds
	収益力	シュウエキリョク	earning power
	収支	シュウシ	income and expenditure; earnings and expenses
	収支一覧表	シュウシイチランヒョウ	balance sheet

二一人ヘイ几入八冂亠冫几凵刀刂力勹匕匚十卜卩巳厂厶又了ク マ

収支決算	シュウシケッサン	settlement of accounts	
収税	シュウゼイ	tax collection; taxation —*v.* collect taxes	
収入	シュウニュウ	income; earnings; means; revenue; proceeds	
収入印紙	シュウニュウインシ	revenue stamp; fiscal stamp	
収納伝票	シュウノウデンピョウ	receipt	

266

双 ④ フ ヌ 双 双

音	双	ソウ	pair; both
熟	双眼鏡	ソウガンキョウ	binoculars
	双曲線	ソウキョクセン	**math**. hyperbola
	双肩	ソウケン	one's shoulders
	双子葉植物	ソウシヨウショクブツ	**bio**. dicotyledons
	双書	ソウショ	series (of books, etc.)
	双生児	ソウセイジ	twins
	双方	ソウホウ	both parties/sides
訓	双	ふた	pair; both
	双子	ふたご	twins; twin

267

反 ④ 一 厂 厅 反

音	反	ハン	return; disobey
		（タン）	dry goods; drapery
		（ホン）	
熟	反する	ハンする	*vi.* be opposed/contrary to; go against
	反物	タンもの	dry goods; drapery
	反意語	ハンイゴ	**gram**. antonym
	反映	ハンエイ	reflection; influence —*v.* reflect; be reflected; influence
	反感	ハンカン	ill feeling; antipathy; adverse sentiment
	反旗	ハンキ	standard of revolt; banner of rebellion
	反逆	ハンギャク	treason; treachery; insurrection; rebellion; mutiny —*vi.* turn traitor; rebel; revolt
	反共	ハンキョウ	anti-communist
	反響	ハンキョウ	echo; reverberation; repurcussions; influence —*vi.* echo; resound; reverberate
	反撃	ハンゲキ	counterattack; counteroffensive —*vi.* make a counteroffensive; counterattack; strike back

142

反語	ハンゴ	rhetorical question; irony
反抗	ハンコウ	resistance; insubordination; opposition; disobedience —*vi.* oppose; resist; offer resitance to; disobey
反抗的	ハンコウテキ	rebellious; defiant; antagonistic; hostile
反作用	ハンサヨウ	*phy.* reaction; counterreaction
反射	ハンシャ	reflection; reflex —*v.* reflect
反証	ハンショウ	counterevidence; proof to the contrary; disproof —*v.* disprove; prove to the contrary
反省	ハンセイ	reflection; self-examination; introspection; reconsideration —*v.* examine oneself; reflect; introspect; reconsider
反戦	ハンセン	antiwar
反則	ハンソク	foul; irregularity; violation of rules
反対	ハンタイ	opposition; resistance; contrast; reverse; inverse —*vi.* oppose; resist; contrast
反転	ハンテン	turning over; reversal —*v.* turn around; be reversed
反動	ハンドウ	reaction; counteraction
反応	ハンノウ	reaction; response; effect —*vi.* react/respond to; act upon
反発	ハンパツ	repulsion; opposition; resistance; rebellion —*v.* repel; repulse; oppose; resist; rebel
反比例	ハンピレイ	inverse proportion —*vi.* be inversely proportionate
反復	ハンプク	repetition —*v.* repeat; do over again
反面	ハンメン	other side; reverse
反目	ハンモク	antagonism; variance; hostility; enmity; feud —*vi.* be at odds; feud with
反乱	ハンラン	rebellion; revolt; insurrection —*vi.* rebel; revolt; rise up
反論	ハンロン	refutation; counterargument —*v.* refute
訓 反らす	そらす	*vt.* bend; warp; curve
反る	そる	*vi.* warp; be warped/curved
¥ 反対売買	ハンタイバイバイ	cross trade
反騰	ハントウ	sharp rally
反発	ハンパツ	rally; rebound
反落	ハンラク	reactionary fall (in stock price)

268

友 ④ 一 ナ 方 友

音 友	ユウ	friend
熟 友愛	ユウアイ	friendship; brotherly love

二ナ人ヘイ几入八冂宀ソ几凵刀刂力勹匕匚十卜卩巳厂厶又了ク丶マ

友軍	ユウグン	friendly troops; allied army
友好	ユウコウ	friendship; amity
友情	ユウジョウ	friendship; fellowship
友人	ユウジン	friend

訓

| 友 | とも | friend |
| 友達 | ともだち | friend |

269

取 ⑧ 一 丁 下 Ｆ 耳 耳 取 取

音 取 シュ　take

熟

取材	シュザイ	data collection; gathering material —*vi.* collect data; gather material
取材記者	シュザイキシャ	reporter
取捨	シュシャ	choice; selection
取捨選択	シュシャセンタク	choice of adoption or rejection
取得	シュトク	acquisition —*v.* acquire

訓

取る	とる	*vt.* take; remove; gather; get
取り敢えず	とりあえず	first of all; in the meantime; for the time being
取り上げる	とりあげる	*vt.* pick up; take up; adopt; take away; deliver a baby
取り扱う	とりあつかう	*vt.* handle; treat; deal
取り入る	とりいる	*vi.* ingratiate oneself; curry favor; flatter
取り入れる	とりいれる	*vt.* take in; harvest; introduce; accept; adopt
取り柄	とりえ	redeeming feature; strong point
取り替える	とりかえる	*vt.* exchange; change; renew; replace
取り組む	とりくむ	*vi.* wrestle; tackle
取り消す	とりけす	*vt.* cancel; withdraw; retract
取り込む	とりこむ	*vt.* take in; pocket; embezzle; be busy
取り下げる	とりさげる	*vt.* withdraw
取り締まる	とりしまる	*vt.* control; regulate; supervise
取り次ぎ	とりつぎ	intermediation; agency
取り付ける	とりつける	*vt.* install; fit; be equipped
取り外す	とりはずす	*vt.* take down; remove; detach; dismantle

¥

取り扱い	とりあつかい	handling; treatment; transaction
取り崩し	とりくずし	disposition; liquidation
取り組み	とりくみ	drawing of bill; technical position; open interest
取締役	とりしまりヤク	director
取締役会	とりしまりヤクカイ	board of directors

取引	とりひき	business; dealings
取引所	とりひきジョ	exchange; stock exchange
取引先	とりひきさき	customer; client; business connection
取り止め	とりやめ	cancellation

270 受 ⑧ 一 ⌒ ⌒ ⌒ ⍉ ⍉ 严 严 受

音	受	ジュ	accept
熟	受益	ジュエキ	in receipt of benefits —*vi.* receive benefits
	受給	ジュキュウ	in receipt of salary/pension —*vt.* receive a salary/pension
	受刑	ジュケイ	under sentence —*vi.* serve a prison sentence
	受刑者	ジュケイシャ	convict
	受験	ジュケン	examination —*v.* sit an examination
	受講	ジュコウ	lecture attendance —*v.* attend a lecture
	受賞	ジュショウ	receiving a prize; prize winning —*v.* receive a prize; win a prize; be awarded a prize
	受賞作品	ジュショウサクヒン	prize-winning novel or work
	受信	ジュシン	reception of telecommunications —*v.* receive
	受信人	ジュシンニン	addressee
	受精	ジュセイ	*bio.* fertilization; pollination —*vi.* be fertilized/pollinated
	受像	ジュゾウ	on T.V. —*v.* receive a picture/image
	受胎	ジュタイ	conception —*vi.* conceive (a child)
	受諾	ジュダク	acceptance; consent —*v.* accept; agree to
	受注	ジュチュウ	acceptance of an order —*v.* accept/receive an order
	受動的	ジュドウテキ	passive
	受難	ジュナン	sufferings; ordeals; Passion of Christ
	受粉	ジュフン	pollination —*vi.* pollinate
	受理	ジュリ	acceptance of forms, papers, etc. —*v.* accept; receive
	受話器	ジュワキ	telephone receiver
訓	受かる	うかる	*vi.* pass an examination
	受け入れる	うけいれる	*vt.* receive; accept
	受け売り	うけうり	retailing; borrowing; parrot learning
	受け皿	うけざら	saucer
	受け継ぐ	うけつぐ	*vt.* inherit; succeed to (one's father's business); take over (a task)
	受付	うけつけ	information; reception
	受け付ける	うけつける	*vt.* accept; receive

2

二 亠 人 亻 へ イ 儿 入 八 冂 ⼍ 冫 几 凵 刀 刂 力 勹 匕 匸 十 卜 卩 ⼓ 厂 ム 又 了 ⼓ マ

受け取る	うけとる	receive
受身	**うけみ**	defensive fall; break-fall; negative; passive; *gram*. passive voice
受け持つ	うけもつ	*vt*. take charge of; be in charge of
受ける	うける	*vt*. be given; receive; get; obtain; suffer; accept
¥ 受け取り	うけとり	receipt
受取手形	うけとりてがた	bill receivable
受取配当金	うけとりハイトウキン	dividends earned
受取利息	うけとりりそく	interest received
受取利息割引料	うけとりリソクわりびきりょう	interest and discounts earned
受け渡し	うけわたし	delivery
受益者	ジュエキシャ	beneficiary
受領証	ジュリョウショウ	receipt; proof of payment
受託銀行	ジュタクギンコウ	trustee bank
受納	ジュノウ	acceptance of money or goods —*v*. accept
受領	ジュリョウ	receipt; acceptance —*v*. receive; accept

271
叔 ⑧ ⼀ ⼅ 上 ⺀ ⺀ ⺀ 叔 叔

音 叔	シュク	uncle
訓 ※叔父	おじ	one's uncle
※叔母	おば	one's aunt

272
叙 ⑨ ノ 𠆢 𠂉 ⺈ ⼿ � 余 𣂪 叙

音 叙	ジョ	preface; state
熟 叙する	ジョする	*vt*. confer (a rank on a person); describe; narrate
叙勲	ジョクン	decoration; medal —*v*. decorate; confer a decoration
叙景	ジョケイ	descriptions of scenery
叙事詩	ジョジシ	epic poem
叙述	ジョジュツ	description; narration —*v*. describe; narrate
叙情	ジョジョウ	lyricism
叙情詩	ジョジョウシ	lyric poetry

2 了　りょう　finish; end

273

了 ⁻了
②

音	了	リョウ	complete; finish; understand
熟	了解	リョウカイ	Roger!; understanding; comprehension —*v.* understand; comprehend
	了見	リョウケン	idea; forgiveness; intention; discretion —*vi.* forgive; intend; be discreet
	了承	リョウショウ	acknowledgment; understanding —*v.* acknowledge; understand

2 　ク　く　*ku* (katakana)

274

争　
⑥

音	争	ソウ	conflict; dispute; argue
熟	争議	ソウギ	dispute; strife; conflict
	争奪	ソウダツ	scrambling/contending for —*v.* scramble/contend for
	争乱	ソウラン	rioting; disturbance
訓	争う	あらそう	*vt.* compete; dispute; argue

2 　マ　ま　*ma* (katakana)

275

予　
④

音	予	ヨ	previously; beforehand myself; I
熟	予価	ヨカ	intended price; overcharge
	予覚	ヨカク	premonition; hunch —*v.* have a hunch
	予感	ヨカン	premonition; hunch —*v.* have a premonition/ hunch

147

二 十 人 へ イ 儿 入 八 冂 丶 丷 几 凵 刀 刂 力 勹 匕 匚 十 卜 卩 㔾 厂 厶 又 了 ㄑ マ •

予期	ヨキ	anticipation; expectation —v. anticipate; expect
予見	ヨケン	forecast; foreknowledge —v. foresee; foreknow
予言	ヨゲン	prediction —v. predict
予行	ヨコウ	rehearsal —v. rehearse
予告	ヨコク	advance notice; preview —v. notify beforehand
予習	ヨシュウ	lesson preparation —v. prepare lessons
予選	ヨセン	preliminary selection/screening; championship
予想	ヨソウ	expectation; anticipation; conjecture —v. expect; anticipate; conjecture; imagine; guess
予測	ヨソク	forecast; estimate; prediction —v. forecast; estimate; predict
予断	ヨダン	prediction; guess —v. predict; guess
予知	ヨチ	foreknowledge —v. foresee; foretell; predict
予定	ヨテイ	plan; prearrangement; expectation —v. make a plan; prearrange
予備	ヨビ	in reserve; spare; preliminary; preparatory
予備校	ヨビコウ	preparatory school
予備知識	ヨビチシキ	preliminary/background knowledge
予報	ヨホウ	forecast; prediction —v. forecast; predict
予防	ヨボウ	prevention; protection —v. prevent; protect
予防接種	ヨボウセッシュ	*med.* inoculation
予約	ヨヤク	reservations; booking; advance order; subscription; appointment —v. make a reservation; book previously
訓 ＊予め	あらかじめ	previously; in advance
＊予て	かねて	previously; already
¥ 予算	ヨサン	budget; estimate
予算案	ヨサンアン	draft budget; bill of budget
予備会議	ヨビカイギ	preliminary negotiation

276

口 丶 冂 口
③

音	口	ク	
		コウ	mouth; speak; entrance
熟	口調	クチョウ	tone of voice
	口伝	クデン	oral instruction; by word of mouth —*v.* instruct/tell orally
	口外	コウガイ	uttering; telling —*v.* utter; tell; let out
	口腔外科	コウクウゲカ	*med.* oral surgery
	口径	コウケイ	diameter; aperture; caliber
	口語	コウゴ	*gram.* spoken colloquial language
	口語体	コウゴタイ	*gram.* colloquial style
	口座	コウザ	bank account
	口実	コウジツ	excuse
	口上	コウジョウ	statement; prologue
	口頭	コウトウ	orally
	口頭試問	コウトウシモン	oral test
	口答	コウトウ	oral answer/reply —*v.* answer orally
	口論	コウロン	quarrel —*v.* quarrel; row
訓	口	くち	mouth; entrance
	口当たり	くちあたり	taste
	口絵	くちえ	frontispiece
	口金	くちがね	bottle cap; top (of a jar, etc.); metal clasp (on a handbag)
	口癖	くちぐせ	one's favorite phrase; pet saying
	口車	くちぐるま	coaxing; flattering; honeyed words
	口答え	くちごたえ	back talk; retort —*vi.* talk back
	口先	くちさき	glib talk
	口添え	くちぞえ	good offices; recommendation —*vi.* put in a good word on one's behalf; recommend
	口出し	くちだし	poking one's nose —*vi.* meddle/chip in
	口止め	くちどめ	muzzle; hush money —*vi.* muzzle
	口走る	くちばしる	*vt.* let/blurt out
	口火	くちび	fuse (on a stick of dynamite, etc.)
	口振り	くちぶり	the way of one's talking
	口下手	くちべた	poor in expressing oneself; poor talker
	口約束	くちやくそく	verbal promise; one's word

3

右⑤ ノ ナ オ 右 右

音	右	ウ	
		ユウ	right; right hand
熟	右往左往	ウオウサオウ	in all directions —*vi*. go right and left; go this way and that way
	右折	ウセツ	turn right —*vi*. make a right turn
	右党	ウトウ	right-wing party
	右派	ウハ	the right; rightists
	右方	ウホウ	the right; the right side
	右翼	ウヨク	right-wing; right field/flank
訓	右	みぎ	right; right-hand
	右利き	みぎきき	right-handed
	右巻き	みぎまき	clockwise
	右回り	みぎまわり	clockwise

古⑤ 一 十 十 古 古

音	古	コ	old; ancient; antique; classic
熟	古稀	コキ	seventy years old
	古語	コゴ	archaic word
	古今	ココン	ancient and modern times; all ages
	古参	コサン	seniority; old-timer
	古式	コシキ	ancient rite; traditional ritual
	古人	コジン	the ancients; men of old
	古跡	コセキ	historic remains/place
	古代	コダイ	ancient times; antiquity
	古典	コテン	classics; classical literature
	古都	コト	ancient capital/city
	古風	コフウ	antique; old-fashioned; archaic; classic
	古墳	コフン	ancient tomb; old burial mound
	古文	コブン	ancient writings; classics
	古米	コマイ	old rice; rice stored from a previous year's harvest
	古来	コライ	from ancient times; time-honored
	古老	コロウ	old man; elderly person
訓	古い	ふるい	old

古傷	ふるきず	old wound; (a person's) misdeeds/scandals
古臭い	ふるくさい	antiquated; old-fashioned; hackneyed
古す	ふるす	(suffix) used; worn out
古巣	ふるす	old nest
古めかしい	ふるめかしい	old; old-fashioned
※古	いにしえ	ancient times; old days

279

召 ⑤   コ　カ　ア　召　召

音	召	ショウ	summon
熟	召喚	ショウカン	summons; subpoena —*v.* summon; serve a summons
	召還	ショウカン	recall —*v.* recall
	召集	ショウシュウ	summons; call; call-up; conscription; the draft —*v.* summon; call; call-up; conscript; draft
	召集令状	ショウシュウ レイジョウ	call-up/draft papers
	召書	ショウショ	summons
	召状	ショウジョウ	summons
	召致	ショウチ	summons —*v.* summon; call
訓	召す	めす	*vt.* call; summon
	召し上がる	めしあがる	*vt. hon.* eat; drink; partake
	召使	めしつかい	servant; maid

280

台 ⑤   ム　ム　ム　台　台

音	台	タイ	
		ダイ	stately mansion; stand; basis; (counter for vehicles, machines, etc.)
熟	台紙	ダイシ	pasteboard
	台地	ダイチ	plateau
	台帳	ダイチョウ	ledger; register; script
	台所	ダイどころ	kitchen
	台無し	ダイなし	ruined; spoiled; coming to nothing
	台風	タイフウ	typhoon
	台本	ダイホン	script; scenario; screenplay
訓	※台詞	せりふ	script; lines

口 ●
口
土
士
夕
大
女
子
宀
寸
小
⺌
⺍
尢
尸
山
川
工
己
巾
干
幺
广
廴
廾
弋
弓
彐
彡
彳
⻌
阝
⺍
忄
扌
氵
犭

3

口口土士夂夕大女子宀寸小丷⺍尢尸山川工己巾干幺广廴廾弋弓ヨ彡彳⺍⻌阝音忄扌犭氵

281

各 ⑥　　ノ　ク　夂　各　各

音	各	カク	each; every
熟	各位	カクイ	every one; all the members concerned
	各自	カクジ	each person; everyone
	各人各様	カクジンカクヨウ	in all their respective ways
訓	各（各々）	おのおの	each; every one

282

吉 ⑥　　一　十　士　吉　吉　吉

音	吉	キチ	good; fortunate; lucky; auspicious
		キツ	lucky; good luck
熟	吉日	キチニチ （キチジツ） （キツジツ）	lucky/auspicious day
	吉凶	キッキョウ	good or ill luck; fortune
	吉報	キッポウ	good news/tidings
訓	※吉い	よい	good; fortunate; auspicious

283

后 ⑥　　一　厂　厂　斤　后　后

音	后	コウ	empress; emperor's wife
熟	后妃	コウヒ	queen consort; empress; queen
訓	※后	きさき	empress; queen; consort

284

合 ⑥　　ノ　人　人　合　合　合

音	合	ガッ ゴウ （カッ）	combine; join; union; fit; match
熟	合作	ガッサク	joint work/production; collaboration —v. collaborate; produce jointly
	合衆国	ガッシュウコク	United States

合宿	ガッシュク	communal lodgings —*vi*. lodge together; be billeted together	**3**
合唱	ガッショウ	chorus; ensemble —*v*. sing together/in chorus	
合掌	ガッショウ	prayer —*vi*. join one's hands in prayer	
合奏	ガッソウ	concert; ensemble —*v*. play in concert	
合致	ガッチ	agreement; coincidence; concurrence —*vi*. correspond to; be in agreement; concur	
合点	ガッテン (ガテン)	understanding; comprehension —*vi*. understand; comprehend; grasp the meaning	
合羽	カッパ	raincoat; mackintosh	
合併	ガッペイ	combination; union; amalgamation; merger; coalition —*v*. combine; unite; amalgamate; merge	
合意	ゴウイ	mutual consent/agreement; concurrence —*vi*. come to mutual agreement; concur	
合一	ゴウイツ	unity; union; oneness —*v*. unite; be united; act as one	
合格	ゴウカク	success in an examination; passing an examination —*vi*. pass an examination	
合議	ゴウギ	conference; consultation; counsel —*v*. confer; consult; hold a conference	
合金	ゴウキン	alloy; compound metal	
合計	ゴウケイ	total; aggregate —*v*. add up; total	
合成	ゴウセイ	composition; synthesis —*v*. compose; compound; synthesize	
合同	ゴウドウ	union; combination; amalgamation; merger; fusion —*v*. combine; unite; amalgamate; incorporate; merge	
合板	ゴウバン	plywood; veneer board	
合理化	ゴウリカ	rationalization —*v*. rationalize	
合理的	ゴウリテキ	rational; logical; reasonable	
合流	ゴウリュウ	confluence; conflux; linking; union —*vi*. join; link; unite	

訓

合鍵	あいかぎ	duplicate key; master key; passkey	
合う	あう	*vi*. fit; suit; agree; be agreeable; be right; be correct	
合図	あいズ	signal; sign; alarm	
合わす	あわす	*vt*. expose/subject to	
合わせる	あわせる	*vt*. expose/subject to	

285

名 ⑥ ノ ク タ タ 名 名

音 名　ミョウ

　　　　メイ　　　name; fame; reputation

153

熟

名字	ミョウジ	surname
名代	ミョウダイ	proxy; deputy; representative
名案	メイアン	good idea
名医	メイイ	famous doctor; skilled physician
名園	メイエン	famous garden
名家	メイカ	distinguished family; celebrity
名菓	メイカ	famous cake
名歌	メイカ	famous/excellent poem or song
名画	メイガ	famous picture; masterpiece
名義	メイギ	official name; moral duty
名曲	メイキョク	famous music
名句	メイク	famous haiku; well-put phrase
名月	メイゲツ	harvest moon
名言	メイゲン	wise saying; apt remark
名工	メイコウ	master craftsman
名作	メイサク	literary masterpiece
名産	メイサン	noted product/speciality of a particular area
名山	メイザン	famous mountain
名士	メイシ	prominent figure; celebrity
名刺	メイシ	calling/business card
名詞	メイシ	*gram.* noun
名実	メイジツ	in name and fact
名手	メイシュ	expert
名酒	メイシュ	famous/renowned saké
名所	メイショ	place of interest
名将	メイショウ	famous general/military commander
名称	メイショウ	name
名勝	メイショウ	scenic spot
名匠	メイショウ	master craftsman
名人	メイジン	master; expert; virtuoso
名声	メイセイ	fame; reputation
名僧	メイソウ	eminent priest
名著	メイチョ	famous work; great book
名店街	メイテンガイ	street of famous shops
名刀	メイトウ	fine sword; famed blade
名馬	メイバ	fine horse
名物	メイブツ	noted product of a particular area; standout
名文	メイブン	excellent composition; fine prose
名分	メイブン	moral duty; justice
名目	メイモク	name; pretext; nominal; ostensible
名門	メイモン	famous family; prestigious school
名訳	メイヤク	excellent/famous translation

●口口土士夂夕大女子宀寸小⺌⺍尢尸山川工己巾干幺广廴廾弋弓彐彡彳艹辶阝阝丷忄扌氵

| 名優 | メイユウ | famous actor; star |
| 名誉 | メイヨ | honor; glory; fame; prestige |

訓 名 な name; fame; reputation

名	な	name; fame; reputation
名残	なごり	traces; remains; vestiges
名指す	なざす	*vt*. name; call by a name
名代	なだい	fame
名高い	なだかい	famous; renowned
名付ける	なづける	*vt*. name; call; entitle
名無し	ななし	nameless; anonymous; unknown
名主	なぬし	*hist*. village headman (Edo period)
名札	なふだ	name plate/tag
名前	なまえ	name

¥ 名義 メイギ stock transfer

| 名義書き換え | メイギかきかえ | stock transfer |
| 名目賃金 | メイモクチンギン | nominal wages |

---

286 含 ⑦ ノ 人 人 今 今 含 含

音 含	ガン	hold; include
熟 含蓄	ガンチク	implication; significance; suggestiveness
含有	ガンユウ	containment; holding —*v*. contain; have; hold
訓 含む	ふくむ	*vt*. contain; keep in one's mouth
含める	ふくめる	*vt*. include
¥ 含み益	ふくみえき	hidden/off-record profit
含み資産	ふくみシサン	hidden/off-record assets
含み損	ふくみゾン	hidden/off-record loss

---

287 君 ⑦ フ ⴺ ⴺ 尹 尹 君 君

音 君	クン	you; lord; splendid person; (suffix) attached to the names of young men
熟 君子	クンシ	gentleman; man of virture
君主	クンシュ	monarch
君主国	クンシュコク	monarchy
君臨	クンリン	reigning —*vi*. reign
訓 君	きみ	you (used among friends, by teachers to students, by seniors to juniors, etc.)

155

288

告 ⑦ 　 ノ ← ⺧ 生 牛 告 告

音	告	コク	tell; announce; inform
熟	告示	コクジ	notification; notice; bulletin —v. notify; proclaim; announce
	告訴	コクソ	complaint; accusation; legal action —v. accuse; charge; complain
	告知	コクチ	notice; announcement —v. notify; announce
	告白	コクハク	confession; avowal; admission —v. confess; admit; declare
	告発	コクハツ	prosecution; indictment; accusation —v. prosecute; indict; accuse; charge
	告別	コクベツ	leave-taking; parting —vi. take leave of; bid farewell
訓	告げる	つげる	vt. notice; inform; proclaim
	告げ口	つげぐち	telling tales —vi. tell tales; rat on
	お告げ	おつげ	announcement

289

否 ⑦ 　 一 ア オ 不 丕 否 否

音	否	ヒ	no; negative; refuse; decline
熟	否決	ヒケツ	rejection; voting against —v. reject; vote against
	否定	ヒテイ	denial; negation —v. deny; negate
	否定的	ヒテイテキ	negative; contradictory
	否認	ヒニン	denial; repudiation —v. deny; repudiate
訓	否	いな	no
	否や	いなや	as soon as; no sooner than; yes or no; objection; if; whether
	否	いや	no; nay; yes; well
	否々	いやいや	grudgingly; by no means
	否応なし	いやオウなし	whether one likes it or not

290

唇 ⑩ 　 一 厂 厂 戶 厔 辰 辰 辰 唇 唇

音	唇	シン	lip
訓	唇	くちびる	lip

156

291 哲 ⑩

一 十 才 才 扩 扩 折 折 哲 哲

音	哲	テツ	sage; philosophy
熟	哲学	テツガク	philosophy
	哲人	テツジン	philosopher
訓	※哲い	さとい	clever; intelligent

292 唐 ⑩

' 亠 广 庐 庐 序 唐 唐 唐 唐

音	唐	トウ	China
熟	唐突	トウトツ	abruptly; in an abrupt way
訓	唐	から	(former name) China; Cathay
	唐紙	からかみ	sliding screen
	唐草模様	からくさモヨウ	arabesque pattern

293 啓 ⑪

一 ㇕ ㇕ 戸 戸 戸 所 啟 啟 啓 啓

音	啓	ケイ	enlighten; state; say
熟	啓具	ケイグ	(closing phrase in a letter)
	啓示	ケイジ	revelation —v. reveal
	啓上	ケイジョウ	Dear Sir/Madam (opening phrase of a letter)
	啓発	ケイハツ	enlightenment —v. enlighten; illuminate; educate
	啓蒙	ケイモウ	enlightenment —v. enlighten; illuminate; educate

294 喜 ⑫

一 十 士 古 吉 吉 声 吉 壴 壴 喜 喜

音	喜	キ	gladness; joy; happiness
熟	喜歌劇	キカゲキ	comic opera; musical comedy
	喜劇	キゲキ	comedy
	喜寿	キジュ	one's seventy-seventh birthday
	喜色	キショク	countenance; mood; humor; feelings; happy expression

口口土士夂夕大女子宀寸小⺌⺍尢戸山川工己巾干幺广廴廾弋弓⺕彡彳艹⻌阝阝⺍忄扌氵

	喜怒哀楽	キドアイラク	joy and anger; emotion; feelings
訓	喜び	よろこび	joy; happiness
	喜ぶ	よろこぶ	*vi*. rejoice; be glad/happy

295

善 ⑫ ` ` ⺍ ⺌ ⺍ 羊 羊 羊 羔 善 善 善

音	善	ゼン	good
熟	善悪	ゼンアク	good and evil
	善意	ゼンイ	good faith; well-intentioned; good will
	善行	ゼンコウ	good conduct/deed
	善後策	ゼンゴサク	remedial measures
	善処	ゼンショ	appropriate action —*vi*. take appropriate action
	善戦	ゼンセン	good fight —*vi*. put up a good fight
	善男善女	ゼンナンゼンニョ	devout men and women
	善導	ゼンドウ	edification —*vt*. edify
	善人	ゼンニン	good man/people
	善良	ゼンリョウ	good; good-natured; virtuous
訓	善い	よい	right; fine; good

296

吸 ⑥ ` 口 口 吖 吸 吸

音	吸	キュウ	inhale; suck; smoke
熟	吸引	キュウイン	absorption; suction —*v*. absorb; suck
	吸気	キュウキ	air supply; ventilation
	吸血鬼	キュウケツキ	vampire
	吸湿性	キュウシツセイ	**chem**. hygroscopicity
	吸収	キュウシュウ	absorption; imbibition —*v*. absorb; imbibe
	吸着	キュウチャク	absorption —*vi*. absorb
	吸入	キュウニュウ	inhalation —*v*. breathe in; inhale
	吸盤	キュウバン	sucker; cupule
訓	吸う	すう	*vt*. breathe in; inhale; imbibe; smoke
	吸い上げる	すいあげる	*vt*. suck/pump up
	吸い殻	すいがら	cigarette end; butt
	吸い込む	すいこむ	*vt*. inhale; breathe in; imbibe
	吸い出す	すいだす	*vt*. suck out; aspirate
	吸い付く	すいつく	*vi*. stick/cling to; adhere
	吸い物	すいもの	*suimono* (Japanese clear soup)

297 叫 ⑥　㇉ ㄸ ㄸ ㄸ 叫 叫

音	叫	キョウ	shout; scream
熟	叫喚	キョウカン	shout; cry; shriek; scream
訓	叫ぶ	さけぶ	*vi.* shout; scream; call out
	叫び声	さけびごえ	shout; cry; exclamation; yell; clamor; shriek; scream; wail

298 吐 ⑥　㇉ ㄸ ㄸ ㄸ 吐 吐

音	吐	ト	vomit; spit out; emit; express
熟	吐息	トイキ	sigh; gasp : sharp intake of breath
	吐血	トケツ	vomiting of blood *med.* hemoptysis; stomach hemorrhage —*vi.* vomit/cough up blood; suffer a stomach hemorrhage
訓	吐く	はく	*vt.* vomit; spew; spit out; throw up; belch; emit; express; confess

299 吟 ⑦　㇉ ㄸ ㄸ ㄸ 叭 吟 吟

音	吟	ギン	reciting/writing poetry
熟	吟じる	ギンじる	*vt.* recite/write poetry
	吟詠	ギンエイ	singing; recital —*v.* sing; give a recital
	吟味	ギンミ	close examination; inquiring; scrutiny —*v.* examine; inquire; scrutinize

300 吹 ⑦　㇉ ㄸ ㄸ ㄸ 吵 吵 吹

音	吹	スイ	blow
熟	吹奏楽	スイソウガク	wind music
訓	吹く	ふく	*v.* blow; breathe; play a musical instrument
	吹聴	ふいチョウ	spreading; publicizing; boasting; advertising —*v.* spread; make public/known; boast; advertise
	※吹雪	ふぶき	snowstorm

3

口口土士夂夕大女子宀寸小⺌⺍尢尸山川工己巾干幺广廴廾弋弓彐彡彳艹辶阝阝⺌扌犭氵

301

呼 ⑧ 　 ＼ ⏋ 口 口' 叮' 叮' 吖 呼

音	呼	コ	call; expire; exhale; breathe out
熟	呼応	コオウ	shouting; agreement; correlation —v. shout to each other; agree; go together; correlate; act in concert
	呼気	コキ	expiration; exhalation
	呼吸	コキュウ	breathing; respiration —v. breathe
	呼吸器	コキュウキ	*med.* respiratory organs
	呼称	コショウ	given name —v. call/give somebody a name
訓	呼ぶ	よぶ	*vt.* call; ring for; invite; name
	呼び子	よびこ	whistle
	呼び声	よびごえ	call; cries
	呼び捨て	よびすて	calling a person by name without any honorific title
	呼び出す	よびだす	*vt.* ask to come; call up; summon
	呼び水	よびみず	priming water (for a pump)
	呼鈴	よびリン	bell; doorbell

302

味 ⑧ 　 ＼ 口 口 口⁻ 叮 吁 味 味

音	味	ミ	taste; flavor
熟	味覚	ミカク	taste; sense of taste
	味方	ミかた	friend; ally; supporter
	味噌汁	ミソしる	miso soup
	味読	ミドク	read with appreciation
訓	味	あじ	taste; flavor
	味気ない	あじケない	dull; wearisome; dreary; wretched
	味付け	あじつけ	seasoning; salting —v. season; salt
	味わう	あじわう	*vt.* taste; experience; relish; appreciate

303

咲 ⑨ 　 ＼ 口 口 口' 口'' 咗 咩 咲

訓	咲く	さく	*vi.* bloom; blossom
	咲き乱れる	さきみだれる	*vi.* be in full bloom

160

304

唆 ⑩ 　 丶 丶 丶 丶 丶 丶 丶 丶 丶 丶

| 音 | 唆 | サ | suggest; coax; incite |
| 熟 | 唆す | そそのかす | *vt*. tempt; incite; coax; suggest |

305

喝 ⑪ 　 丶 丶 丶 丶 丶 丶 丶 丶 丶 丶 丶

音	喝	カツ	cheers; shout
熟	喝采	カッサイ	applause; cheers —*v*. applaud; cheer
	喝破	カッパ	declaration; proclamation —*v*. declare; proclaim

306

唱 ⑪ 　 丶 丶 丶 丶 丶 丶 丶 丶 丶 丶 丶

音	唱	ショウ	recite; sing; advocate
熟	唱歌	ショウカ	singing; songs
	唱和	ショウワ	chorus —*vi*. sing in chorus/unison
訓	唱える	となえる	*vt*. recite; chant; advocate; urge; preach

307

唯 ⑪ 　 丶 丶 丶 丶 丶 丶 丶 丶 丶 丶 丶

音	唯	ユイ (イ)	only; solely; merely
熟	唯一	ユイイツ	only; sole
	唯我独尊	ユイガドクソン	self-conceit; vain glory
	唯心論	ユイシンロン	idealism; spiritualism
	唯美主義	ユイビシュギ	estheticism
	唯物論	ユイブツロン	materialism
	唯物史観	ユイブツシカン	materialist historical perspective
	唯名論	ユイメイロン	nominalism
訓	※唯	ただ	solely; only; merely
	※唯今	ただいま	right now; just now; I'm back (said by person returning home)

口口土士夂夕大女子宀寸小⺌⺍尢尸山川工已巾干幺广廴廾弋弓彐彡彳艹辶阝阝丷忄扌犭氵

308

喚 ⑫

丶 口 口 口' 口ツ 吖 吶 吶 唤 唤 喚 喚

音	喚	カン	cry; scream
熟	喚起	カンキ	awakening —v. awaken; arouse; evoke
	喚声	カンセイ	loud cry
	喚問	カンモン	summons —v. summon
訓	※喚ぶ	よぶ	vt. call; summon

309

喫 ⑫

丶 口 口 口 口ᵗ 吽 哇 唡 唡 唡 喫 喫

音	喫	キツ	eat; drink; smoke
熟	喫煙	キツエン	smoking —vi. smoke; have a smoke
	喫茶店	キッサテン	coffee house/shop; café

310

嘆 ⑬

丶 口 口 口⁻ 口ザ 口ザ 咕 哞 嘆 嘆 嘆 嘆

音	嘆	タン	grieve; lament; deplore; sigh
熟	嘆願	タンガン	entreaty; appeal; petition; suit —v. entreat; appeal; petition; sue
	嘆声	タンセイ	sigh; lamentation
	嘆息	タンソク	sigh; lamentation; grief; deploration —vi. sigh; lament; grieve
訓	嘆く	なげく	v. sigh; grieve; lament; deplore
	嘆き	なげき	grief; sorrow; lamentation
	嘆かわしい	なげかわしい	sad; wretched; lamentable; regrettable; deplorable

311

嘱 ⑮

口 口⁻ 口⁻ 呎 呎 呎 喝 喝 喝 嘱 嘱 嘱

音	嘱	ショク	request; expect
熟	嘱託	ショクタク	entrust; commission; contract —v. entrust; employ temporarily
	嘱望	ショクボウ	promising; hopeful —v. pin one's hopes on; be promising

噴 ⑮ 口 ロー ロ⁺ 吐 吐 吐 噅 啫 噎 噴 噴

音	噴	フン	emit; spout; spew forth
熟	噴煙	フンエン	thick smoke (from a volcano, etc.)
	噴火	フンカ	(volcanic) eruption —*vi.* erupt
	噴火口	フンカコウ	crater (of a volcano)
	噴火山	フンカザン	active volcano
	噴射	フンシャ	jet; spray; injection —*v.* shoot out/spray (water)
	噴出	フンシュツ	eruption; gushing; spouting —*v.* spew/gush/spurt out
	噴水	フンスイ	fountain; jet of water
	噴霧器	フンムキ	sprayer; vaporizer
	噴門	フンモン	*med.* esophageal orifice
訓	噴く	ふく	gush; emit; spew forth

嚇 ⑰ 口 ロー ロ⁺ 吐 吘 啈 啈 嚇 嚇 嚇 嚇 嚇

音	嚇	カク	threaten; intimidate
熟	嚇努	カクド	fury; rage —*vi.* become furious; get angry

可 ⑤ 一 丆 冂 可 可

音	可	カ	possible; can; permit; good
熟	可動	カドウ	movable; mobile
	可燃性	カネンセイ	inflammability; combustibility
	可燃物	カネンブツ	inflammable/combustible substance
	可能	カノウ	possible
	可能性	カノウセイ	possibility
	可否	カヒ	right or wrong; pro and con; for and against
	可憐	カレン	pretty; cute; coy
	可愛い	カワイい	cute; pretty; dear; darling; charming
	可哀相	カワイソウ	poor; pitiable; pathetic; pitiful
訓	※可い	よい	good; fine; nice

口口土士夕夕大女子宀寸小⺌⺍尢尸山川工己巾干幺广廴廾弋弓彐彡彳艹辶阝⻖业忄扌氵

口口土士夂夕大女子宀寸小⺌⺍尢尸山川工己巾干幺广廴廾弋弓ヨ彡彳⺾⻌阝⺖⺌忄扌犭氵

¥	可決	カケツ	passage (of a bill); approval; adoption (of a recommendation) —*v.* pass a bill; carry a motion
	可処分所得	カショブンショトク	disposable income; dispensible earnings

315

句 ⑤ ノ ク ⼓ 句 句

音	句	ク	phrase; part of a sentence; haiku poem
熟	句会	クカイ	haiku gathering; meeting for the purpose of reading haiku
	句集	クシュウ	haiku anthology
	句点	クテン	period; full stop
	句読点	クトウテン	punctuation marks

316

号 ⑤ 丶 ⼝ ⼝ 号 号

音	号	ゴウ	shout; cry; name; sign; title; order; command
熟	号外	ゴウガイ	extra/special edition (of a newspaper, magazine, periodical, etc.)
	号泣	ゴウキュウ	wailing; lamentation; moaning; weeping —*vi.* wail; lament; moan; weep bitterly
	号数	ゴウスウ	number (of editions)
	号砲	ゴウホウ	signal/watch gun
	号令	ゴウレイ	order; command —*vi.* order; command; give an order

317

史 ⑤ 丿 ⼝ ⼝ 史 史

音	史	シ	history
熟	史家	シカ	historian
	史学	シガク	history; historical studies
	史実	シジツ	historical fact
	史書	シショ	historical writing
	史上	シジョウ	in history; historical
	史跡	シセキ	historic place/site
	史料	シリョウ	historical records
	史論	シロン	historical thesis

司 ⑤ 　コ　フ　司　司　司

音	司	シ	official; officer; control; manage
熟	司会	シカイ	presiding; taking the chair —*v.* preside; take the chair
	司会者	シカイシャ	master of ceremonies (MC); chairman
	司祭	シサイ	Roman Catholic priest
	司書	シショ	librarian
	司法	シホウ	the judiciary
	司法官	シホウカン	judicial officer; judges and prosecutors
	司法行政	シホウギョウセイ	judicial administration; the judiciary
	司法権	シホウケン	right to justice
	司令	シレイ	command; commander —*v.* command
	司令部	シレイブ	military headquarters
訓	※司る	つかさどる	*vt.* manage; look after; control; take charge

向 ⑥ 　′　𝆑　向　向　向　向

音	向	コウ	face; front; opposite; the other side
熟	向学心	コウガクシン	love of learning; desire to learn
	向上	コウジョウ	improvement; elevation; rise —*vi.* rise; be elevated; become higher; improve; advance
訓	向かう	むかう	*vi.* face; front; look at; be opposite; meet; confront; approach
	向き	むき	direction; quarter; exposure; aspect
	向く	むく	*vi.* turn; look to; face; point; tend; suit
	向ける	むける	*vt.* turn; face; direct; point; aim; send; address; refer
	向こう	むこう	the other side; beyond; one's destination; the other party

同 ⑥ 　丨　冂　冂　同　同　同

音	同	ドウ	same; similar
熟	同意	ドウイ	same meaning/opinion; agreement; consent —*vi.* agree with; consent to; approve
	同意語	ドウイゴ	*gram.* synonym

口口土士夂夕大女子宀寸小ㇱ⺍尢尸山川工己巾干幺广廴廾弋弓彐彡彳艹辶⻏⻏亠忄扌犭冫

同一	ドウイツ	identity; sameness; oneness; equality; indiscrimination
同一視	ドウイツシ	*vt.* regard A in the same light as B; look at things indiscriminately
同音語	ドウオンゴ	*gram.* homophone
同化	ドウカ	adaptation; assimilation —*v.* adapt; assimilate
同格	ドウカク	same rank; equal footing; equality
同額	ドウガク	equal sum/amount (of money)
同感	ドウカン	same sentiment; sympathy; empathy; agreement; concurrence
同期	ドウキ	same period/class; synchronism
同義	ドウギ	synonymy; same meaning
同義語	ドウギゴ	*gram.* synonym
同居	ドウキョ	living together —*vi.* live together
同郷	ドウキョウ	same province/village
同業	ドウギョウ	same trade/business
同権	ドウケン	equal rights
同行	ドウコウ	going/traveling together —*vi.* go/travel together
同好	ドウコウ	same tastes; liking the same thing
同士	ドウシ	fellow; companion
同志	ドウシ	same mind; congenial spirit; like-minded person
同乗	ドウジョウ	riding together; sharing a carriage —*vi.* ride together; share a carriage
同乗者	ドウジョウシャ	fellow passenger
同情	ドウジョウ	sympathy; compassion; fellow feeling —*vi.* sympathize; be sympathetic; have compassion
同人	ドウジン	same person; coterie; clique; fraternity; club
同姓	ドウセイ	of the same surname
同性	ドウセイ	same sex
同性愛	ドウセイアイ	homosexuality
同席	ドウセキ	sitting with/together —*vi.* sit with
同然	ドウゼン	same
同窓	ドウソウ	alumnus
同調	ドウチョウ	alignment; conformity —*vi.* align oneself; conform; follow suit; fall into line
同等	ドウトウ	equality; parity
同伴	ドウハン	company; companion —*v.* accompany; go with
同封	ドウフウ	enclosure (in a letter) —*v.* enclose (in a letter)
同胞	ドウホウ	brethren; brothers and sisters; citizens of a country
同盟	ドウメイ	alliance; league; union; confederation —*v.* ally with; form an alliance/union
同様	ドウヨウ	same; similar; identical
同僚	ドウリョウ	colleague

同類	ドウルイ	same kind/class
訓 同じ	おなじ	same

321

吏 ⑥　一　一　一　一　吏　吏

音	吏	リ	official
熟	吏員	リイン	official

322

呉 ⑦　丶　口　口　呂　呂　吳　呉

音	呉	ゴ	Wu dynasty; be given
熟	呉音	ゴオン	Wu pronunciation of Chinese characters
	呉服	ゴフク	kimono fabrics; drapery and haberdashery
	呉服屋	ゴフクや	shop selling kimono fabrics
訓	呉れる	くれる	*vt.* give

323

呈 ⑦　丶　口　口　呈　早　呈　呈

音	呈	テイ	present
熟	呈示	テイジ	presentation —*v.* present; idicate; bring up; suggest; come up with
	呈上	テイジョウ	presentation —*v.* present

324

周 ⑧　丿　冂　冂　冃　冃　冃　周　周

音	周	シュウ	round; surround; Zhou/Chou dynasty
熟	周囲	シュウイ	circumference; girth; periphery; surroundings; the environment
	周回	シュウカイ	lap; going around —*v.* go around
	周忌	シュウキ	anniversary of a person's death
	周期	シュウキ	period; cycle
	周航	シュウコウ	sailing around; circumnavigation —*vi.* sail around; circumnavigate
	周旋	シュウセン	agency; brokerage —*v.* act as an agent; broker

口口土士夕夕大女子宀寸小ㅛㅛ尤尸山川工己巾干幺广廴廾弋弓ヨ彡彳艹辶阝阝爿忄扌犭氵

口口土士夂夕大女子宀寸小⺌⺍尢尸山川工己巾干幺广廴廾弋弓彐彡彳艹辶阝阝䒑忄扌犭氵

周知	シュウチ	well-known; widely-known
周到	シュウトウ	careful; scrupulous; meticulous
周年	シュウネン	(suffix) whole year; anniversary
周波	シュウハ	cycle; frequency
周波数	シュウハスウ	frequency
周辺	シュウヘン	outskirts; around; environs
周遊	シュウユウ	tour; excursion

訓
| 周り | まわり | surroundings; neighborhood; environment; those around one |

¥
| 周旋業 | シュウセンギョウ | brokerage |
| 周旋業者 | シュウセンギョウシャ | broker; agency |

325

 ⑧　ノ 人 ⼊ 合 合 命 命 命

音
| 命 | ミョウ | |
| | メイ | life; destiny; fate order; command |

熟
命じる	メイじる	order; command
命運	メイウン	fate
命数	メイスウ	one's natural life span; destiny
命題	メイダイ	proposition
命中	メイチュウ	hit —*vi.* hit (the target)
命日	メイニチ	anniversary of a death
命脈	メイミャク	life
命名	メイメイ	naming; christening; calling —*vi.* name; christen; call
命令	メイレイ	order; command —*v.* order; command

訓
命	いのち	life
命懸け	いのちがけ	desperate; risking one's life
命知らず	いのちしらず	recklessness; daredevil
命取り	いのちとり	fatal
命拾い	いのちびろい	narrow escape from death
※命	みこと	lord; prince

326

 ⑧　ノ ニ 千 チ 禾 禾 和 和

音
| 和 | ワ | peace; harmony; Japan |
| | （オ） | |

熟
| 和尚 | オショウ | chief priest of a Buddhist temple |

和英	ワエイ	Japanese and English languages; Japan and England
和音	ワオン	chord (in music)
和歌	ワカ	*tanka* (31-syllable poem)
和解	ワカイ	amicable settlement; compromise; reconciliation —*vi*. be reconciled; settle one's differences
和菓子	ワガシ	Japanese cakes
和気	ワキ	harmony; peacefulness; calm (sea, wind, etc.)
和議	ワギ	peace talks; settlement (to avoid declaring bankcruptcy)
和合	ワゴウ	harmony; concord; concord of husband and wife —*vi*. be in harmony/concord
和裁	ワサイ	Japanese dress-making; sewing kimono
和紙	ワシ	*washi* (Japanese paper)
和室	ワシツ	Japanese-style room
和食	ワショク	Japanese cuisine
和声	ワセイ	harmony (in music)
和製	ワセイ	made in Japan
和装	ワソウ	Japanese dress
和風	ワフウ	Japanese style
和服	ワフク	kimono; Japanese clothes
和文	ワブン	something written in Japanese; Japanese writing (especially *kana*)
和平	ワヘイ	peace
和睦	ワボク	reconciliation; rapport; peace —*vi*. be reconciled; make peace
和訳	ワヤク	translation into Japanese —*v*. translate into Japanese
和洋	ワヨウ	Japanese and Western
和様	ワヨウ	Japanese style
訓 和む	なごむ	*v*. become calm; calm down *vt*. calm down; moderate
和やか	なごやか	peaceful; calm
和らぐ	やわらぐ	*vi*. soften; become soft/gentle/peaceful *vt*. soften; moderate
和らげる	やわらげる	*vt*. soften; lessen; relieve; pacify; moderate; modify
※和える	あえる	*vt*. dress food (with mayonnaise, etc.)

327

哀 ⑨ `　亠　宀　宀　亠　声　亨　亨　哀

音 哀	アイ	pity; pathos; regret; sadness; sorrow

3

口 口 土 士 夂 夕 大 女 子 宀 寸 小 ⺌ ⺌ 尢 尸 山 川 工 已 巾 干 幺 广 廴 廾 弋 弓 彐 彡 彳 艹 辶 阝 阝 ⺮ 忄 扌 氵

熟	哀願	アイガン	earnest request; entreaty; appeal; petition —*v.* make an earnest request; entreat; implore; appeal; petition
	哀愁	アイシュウ	sadness; sorrow; grief; pathos
	哀調	アイチョウ	mournful melody
	哀悼	アイトウ	mourning; grief; lamentation —*v.* mourn; grieve; lament
訓	哀れ	あわれ	pity; pathos; sorrow; misery
	哀れむ	あわれむ	*vt.* pity; feel compassion/sympathy
	哀しい	かなしい	sad; sorrowful; pathetic; pitiful

328

品 ⑨　丶 冂 口 丬 吊 吊 品 品 品

音	品	ヒン	article; refinement
熟	品	ヒン	elegance; grace; refinement; dignity; article; piece; item; course
	品位	ヒンイ	dignity; nobility; grade; carat
	品格	ヒンカク	dignity; nobility
	品行	ヒンコウ	conduct; behavior; actions
	品行方正	ヒンコウホウセイ	well-mannered; exemplary conduct
	品詞	ヒンシ	*gram.* part of speech
	品質	ヒンシツ	quality
	品種	ヒンシュ	kind; variety; type; grade; breed
	品性	ヒンセイ	character
	品評会	ヒンピョウカイ	competitive show/exhibition; fair
	品目	ヒンモク	item; list of articles
訓	品	しな	article; goods; wares; quality; personality
	品書き	しながき	catalog; menu
	品切れ	しなぎれ	out of stock; sold out
	品物	しなもの	article; thing; goods; wares; stuff; stock
¥	品薄	しなうす	shortage of goods/stock/supply
	品薄株	しなうすかぶ	rare stock; narrow market securities
	品揃え	しなぞろえ	assembling; assortment
	品質管理	ヒンシツカンリ	quality control

329

員 ⑩　丶 冂 口 尸 月 月 冒 冒 員 員

音	員	イン	member; staff
熟	員数	インズウ	the number of persons or things

商⑪ 　 ′ 宀 亠 立 产 产 产 产 商 商 商

音	商	ショウ	trade; merchant; business; commerce
熟	商科	ショウカ	commercial department; department of business and commerce
	商魂	ショウコン	commercial spirit
	商船	ショウセン	merchant ship/marine
	商店	ショウテン	store; shop
	商店街	ショウテンガイ	shopping center/mall
	商人	ショウニン	merchant; tradesman; dealer
訓	商う	あきなう	*vt.* sell; deal; trade
¥	商い	あきない	trade; business
	商会	ショウカイ	company; firm
	商況	ショウキョウ	business trends; market situation
	商業	ショウギョウ	commerce; trade; business
	商業化	ショウギョウカ	commercialization —*v.* commercialize
	商業界	ショウギョウカイ	business circles; commercial world
	商業銀行	ショウギョウギンコウ	commercial bank
	商業手形	ショウギョウてがた	commercial paper (CP)
	商権	ショウケン	commercial rights
	商号	ショウゴウ	trade/shop name
	商工会議所	ショウコウカイギショ	Chamber of Commerce and Industry
	商工組合中央金庫	ショウコウくみあいチュウオウキンコ	Central Cooperative Bank for Commerce and Industry
	商事	ショウジ	business affairs
	商社	ショウシャ	trading company
	商習慣	ショウシュウカン	business practices
	商戦	ショウセン	sales battle; selling competition
	商談	ショウダン	business discussion/negotiations —*vi.* talk business
	商取引	ショウとりひき	business transaction
	商売	ショウバイ	trade; business; commerce; occupation —*v.* trade; do business
	商標	ショウヒョウ	trademark; brand
	商品	ショウヒン	commodity; merchandise; goods
	商法	ショウホウ	commercial law
	商用	ショウヨウ	business; business call/use

口
口
土
士
夂
夕
大
女
子
宀
寸
小
ツ
ツ
尢
尸
山
川
工
己
巾
干
幺
广
廴
廾
弋
弓
ヨ
彡
彳
艹
辶
阝
丷
忄
扌
氵
冫

・口口土士夕夕大女子宀寸小⺌⺍尢尸山川工己巾干幺广廴廾弋弓ヨ彡彳艹辶阝阝⺀忄扌犭氵

331

問 ⑪ ｜ 冂 冂 冃 尸 尸' 門 門 門 門 問 問

音	問	モン	question; problem
熟	問罪	モンザイ	accusation; indictment —*vi*. accuse; indict
	問責	モンセキ	censure; reprimand —*v*. censure; reprimand
	問題	モンダイ	question; problem; issue
	問答	モンドウ	questions and answers —*v*. question and answer
訓	問う	とう	*vt*. inquire; ask; care about; accuse
	問い	とい	question; inquiry
	問い合わせる	といあわせる	*vt*. inquire; ask about
	※問屋	とんや	wholesale dealer

332

喪 ⑫ 一 十 十 古 吉 吉 吉 吉 車 車 喪 喪 喪

音	喪	ソウ	mourning; loss
熟	喪失	ソウシツ	loss —*v*. lose
訓	喪	も	mourning; loss
	喪章	もショウ	mourning badge/band
	喪中	もチュウ	period of mourning
	喪服	もフク	mourning clothes

333

嗣 ⑬ 丶 丶 口 口 尸 尸 咼 咼 嗣 嗣 嗣

音	嗣	シ	heir
熟	嗣子	シシ	heir

334

器 ⑮ 丶 口 口 吅 吅 吅 哭 哭 器 器 器

音	器	キ	receptacle; vessel; organ
熟	器械	キカイ	instrument; appliance
	器械体操	キカイタイソウ	gymnastics
	器楽	キガク	instrumental music

172

器官	キカン	*med.* body organ
器具	キグ	implement; appliance; apparatus
器材	キザイ	materials; tools and materials
器物	キブツ	utensil; vessel; container
器用	キヨウ	skillfulness; dexterity
器量	キリョウ	countenance; talent; ability
訓 器	うつわ	vessel; container; utensil; capacity

---

3 □　くにがまえ　box

335
四⑤　丨 冂 冂 四 四

音	四	シ	four
熟	四角	シカク	square
	四角四面	シカクシメン	stiff; serious; stuffy; prim
	四月	シガツ	April
	四季	シキ	the four seasons
	四苦八苦	シクハック	struggling —*vi.* struggle; sweat blood
	四散	シサン	dispersion; scatter —*vi.* disperse; scatter
	四肢	シシ	limbs; arms and legs; fins
	四捨五入	シシャゴニュウ	*math.* rounding off —*v.* round off
	四分五裂	シブゴレツ	in disarray/chaos
	四方	シホウ	in all directions
	四六時中	シロクジチュウ	day and night; twenty-four hours a day *fig.* always; often
訓	四	よん	four
	四	よ	four
	四	よつ	four
	四日	よっか	fourth day (of the month); 4th
	四	よっつ	four
	四隅	よすみ	four corners

336
囚⑤　丨 冂 冂 囚 囚

音	囚	シュウ	capture; prisoner
熟	囚人	シュウジン	prisoner; convict

口 •
口 •
土
士
夂
夕
大
女
子
宀
寸
小
⺌
⺍
尢
尸
山
川
工
己
巾
干
幺
广
廾
弋
弓
彐
彡
彳
艹
辶
阝
⺍
忄
扌
犭
氵

口口土士夕夕大女子宀寸小⺌⺍尢尸山川工己巾干幺广廴廾弋弓ヨ彡彳艹阝阝丬忄扌犭氵

337

因 ⑥ 一 冂 冂 𠃜 因 因

音	因	イン	cause
熟	因果	インガ	cause and effect; retribution; karma; fate
	因果応報	インガオウホウ	reward in accordance with deed; law of cause and effect
	因襲	インシュウ	conventions
	因縁	インネン	fate; origin; karma; pretext
訓	因る	よる	*vi.* be caused by; be due to
	＊因む	ちなむ	*vi.* be related/connected
	＊因みに	ちなみに	by the way

338

回 ⑥ 一 冂 冂 冋 回 回

音	回	カイ	pass; turn; go round; circumference
		（エ）	turn round; service
熟	回帰線	カイキセン	the tropics
	回教	カイキョウ	Islam
	回顧	カイコ	recollection; retrospection — *v.* look back on; recollect; retrospect
	回収	カイシュウ	withdrawal; collection; recovery — *v.* withdraw from circulation; recover; collect
	回診	カイシン	doctor's round of visits — *vi.* make house calls; visit one's patients
	回数	カイスウ	frequency; common occurence
	回数券	カイスウケン	coupon (commutation) ticket
	回送	カイソウ	forwarding; transportation — *v.* forward; send on; transport
	回想	カイソウ	retrospection; reminiscence; recollection — *v.* retrospect; recollect
	回虫	カイチュウ	*med.* roundworm; intestinal worm
	回転	カイテン	rotation — *vi.* revolve; rotate; turn around
	回答	カイトウ	reply; answer; response — *vi.* reply; answer; respond
	回避	カイヒ	evasion; avoidance — *v.* evade; dodge; avoid
	回復	カイフク	restoration; recovery — *v.* restore; recover
	回復期	カイフクキ	convalescence
	回覧	カイラン	circulation — *v.* circulate; send around
	回路	カイロ	electric circuit

174

訓	回る	まわる	*vi.* go around; pass; spread
	回す	まわす	*vt.* turn; pass; revolve
	回り	まわり	circumference; surroundings; by way of
	回り道	まわりみち	making a detour

339

団 ⑥   ⼁ ⼌ ⺆ ⽤ 団 団

音	団	ダン	body; group; corps; organization; association
		（トン）	
熟	団員	ダンイン	group member
	団結	ダンケツ	unity; union; solidarity; combination —*vi.* unite; be united; stand together; combine
	団子	ダンゴ	dumpling
	団体	ダンタイ	party; company; group; body; organization; association
	団地	ダンチ	housing development; public housing complex
	団長	ダンチョウ	leader; head of a group
	団欒	ダンラン	happy circle/family; sitting in a circle —*vi.* sit in a circle

340

囲 ⑦   ⼁ ⼌ ⺆ ⺆ ⺆ 用 囲

音	囲	イ	surround; enclose
熟	囲碁	イゴ	game of go
	囲炉裏	イロリ	Japanese-style open hearth
訓	囲む	かこむ	*vt.* enclose; surround; encircle
	囲う	かこう	*vt.* enclose; fence
	囲い	かこい	enclosure; fence
	囲み	かこみ	surrounding the enemy; enclosure

341

困 ⑦   ⼁ ⼌ ⺆ 用 困 困 困

音	困	コン	suffer; distress
熟	困窮	コンキュウ	poverty; need; want; destitution —*vi.* be poor; be destitute
	困苦	コンク	hardships; adversity; trials; suffering
	困難	コンナン	difficulty; hurdle; trouble; distress

175

3

口
口 •
土
士
夂
夕
大
女
子
宀
寸
小
⺌
⺍
尢
尸
山
川
工
己
巾
干
幺
广
廴
廾
弋
弓
ヨ
彡
彳
艹
⻌
阝
阝
亠
忄
扌
犭
氵

3 　訓 困る　　こまる　　　*vi.* suffer; be in trouble; have a problem

口口土士夂夕大女子宀寸小⺌⺍尢尸山川工己巾干幺广廴廾弋弓ヨ彡彳艹辶阝阝丷忄扌犭氵

342

図 ⑦ 　｜ 冂 冂 冈 冈 図 図

音　図　　ズ　　　　drawing; picture; plan; figure
　　　　　ト　　　　plan
熟　図案　ズアン　　design; device; sketch; plan
　　図画　ズガ　　　drawing; sketching
　　図解　ズカイ　　illustration; explanatory diagram —*v.* illustrate; explain with diagrams
　　図鑑　ズカン　　picture book
　　図形　ズケイ　　figure; device; diagram
　　図示　ズシ　　　illustration; graphic representation —*v.* illustrate; represent graphically
　　図式　ズシキ　　diagram; graph; chart; figure
　　図版　ズハン　　figure; illustration; plate
　　図板　ズバン　　drafting/drawing board
　　図表　ズヒョウ　diagram; chart; graph
　　図譜　ズフ　　　picture book
　　図法　ズホウ　　drawing; draftmanship
　　図面　ズメン　　drawing; sketch; map
　　図書　トショ　　books
　　図書館　トショカン　library
訓　図る　はかる　　*vt.* plan; devise; contrive; design; plot

343

固 ⑧ 　｜ 冂 冂 円 円 円 固 固

音　固　　コ　　　　hard; solid; obstinate
熟　固形　コケイ　　solid body; solid
　　固持　コジ　　　persistence —*v.* be persistent; hold to; stand by; stick to
　　固辞　コジ　　　categorical refusal —*v.* categorically refuse; refuse flatly
　　固執　コシツ　　persistence; insistence —*v.* persist; stick/cling to; insist on
　　固守　コシュ　　adherence; persistence; insistence —*v.* adhere to; persist in; insist on
　　固体　コタイ　　solid; solid matter
　　固定　コテイ　　fixed; settled —*v.* fix; settle

| 固有 | コユウ | peculiar; characteristic; indigenous; particular |
| 固有名詞 | コユウメイシ | *gram.* proper noun |

訓

固い	かたい	hard; tough; tight; firm; strict; obstinate; rigid
固まる	かたまる	*vi.* harden; become stiff; congeal; coagulate; thicken
固める	かためる	*vt.* make hard; strengthen; fortify; solidify

¥

固定金利	コテイキンリ	fixed rate of interest
固定資産	コテイシサン	fixed assets
固定資産売却益	コテイシサンバイキャクエキ	profits on disposal of fixed assets
固定資産売却損	コテイシサンバイキャクソン	losses on disposal of fixed assets
固定負債	コテイフサイ	fixed liabilities

344

国 ⑧ 丨 冂 冂 冂 用 国 国 国

音

| 国 | コク | state; country; nation; province |

熟

国営	コクエイ	state/government management
国外	コクガイ	outside the country
国学	コクガク	study of classical Japanese literature, history, and thought (late Edo period)
国技	コクギ	national sport
国語	コクゴ	one's mother tongue; the Japanese language
国際	コクサイ	international
国際化	コクサイカ	internationalization —*v.* internationalize
国際的	コクサイテキ	international; universal; cosmopolitan
国際連合	コクサイレンゴウ	United Nations
国策	コクサク	national policy
国産	コクサン	domestic production
国史	コクシ	national history
国字	コクジ	Japanese script; *kanji* invented in Japan
国事	コクジ	affairs of state; national affairs
国情	コクジョウ	conditions of a country; state of affairs
国是	コクゼ	national/government policy
国政	コクセイ	national administration; government
国勢	コクセイ	state of a country
国勢調査	コクセイチョウサ	census
国籍	コクセキ	nationality; citizenship
国葬	コクソウ	state funeral
国体	コクタイ	polity; national structure

口口 •
土
士
夂
夕
大
女
子
宀
寸
小
⺍
⺌
尢
尸
山
川
工
已
巾
干
幺
广
爻
廾
弋
弓
彐
彡
彳
艹
辶
阝
阝
⺍
忄
扌
氵

177

口
•口
土
士
夂
夕
大
女
子
宀
寸
小
⺌
⺍
尢
尸
山
川
工
己
巾
干
幺
广
廴
廾
弋
弓
彐
彡
彳
艹
辶
阝
⻏
丷
忄
扌
犭
氵

国土	コクド	country; territory; realm; domain
国道	コクドウ	national road/highway
国内	コクナイ	internal; domestic
国費	コクヒ	national expenditure
国賓	コクヒン	state/national guest
国文学	コクブンガク	Japanese literature
国宝	コクホウ	national treasure
国防	コクボウ	national defense
国民	コクミン	nation; people; nationality
国民性	コクミンセイ	national character
国務	コクム	affairs of state; state affairs
国立	コクリツ	national
国力	コクリョク	national power/resourses
国家	コッカ	state; nation; country
国家主義	コッカシュギ	nationalism
国家的	コッカテキ	national; state
国歌	コッカ	national anthem
国花	コッカ	national flower
国会	コッカイ	Diet; national assembly; congress; parliament
国旗	コッキ	national flag
国境	コッキョウ	border; frontier
国交	コッコウ	diplomatic relations
訓 国	くに	state; nation; country; province
国柄	くにがら	national character
¥ 国営化	コクエイカ	nationalization —*v.* nationalize
国債	コクサイ	government/national bond
国際収支	コクサイシュウシ	balance of international payments
国際通貨基金	コクサイツウカキキン	International Monetary Fund (IMF)
国税	コクゼイ	national/direct taxes
国民総生産	コクミンソウセイサン	gross national product (GNP)
国務大臣	コクムダイジン	minister of state
国有	コクユウ	state ownership —*v.* be owned by the state

345

圏 ⑫ 丨 冂 冂 冃 冃 罒 圂 罖 圂 圈 圈 圈

音 圏	ケン	circle; sphere; range; zone
熟 圏外	ケンガイ	out of the sphere/range
圏内	ケンナイ	within the sphere/range

346

園 ⑬ 丨 冂 冂 冃 冃 冏 周 胃 夁 園 園 園

音	園	エン	garden; park
熟	園芸	エンゲイ	gardening; horticulture; floriculture
	園児	エンジ	kindergarten pupils
	園長	エンチョウ	head zookeeper; head of a kindergarten
	園遊会	エンユウカイ	garden party
訓	園	その	garden

---

3 土 つち／つちへん earth

347

土 ③ 一 十 土

音	土	ト	
		ド	soil; earth; dirt
熟	土方	ドかた	construction worker; navvy
	土管	ドカン	earthen pipe
	土器	ドキ	earthenware; crockery
	土下座	ドゲザ	prostrating oneself; paying obeisance —*vi*. prostrate oneself; apologize; show respect; pay obeisance
	土建	ドケン	civil engineering and construction
	土工	ドコウ	construction worker; navvy
	土左衛門	ドザエモン	drowned person
	土質	ドシツ	soil quality
	土砂	ドシャ	earth and sand
	土砂降り	ドシャぶり	pouring/heavy rain
	土壌	ドジョウ	soil; earth
	土人	ドジン	native; aboriginal
	土製	ドセイ	earthen; made of clay
	土星	ドセイ	the planet Saturn
	土葬	ドソウ	interment; burial
	土蔵	ドゾウ	warehouse; storehouse
	土足	ドソク	with one's shoes on
	土台	ドダイ	foundation; groundwork; base; basis; cornerstone

口 口 土 士 夂 夕 大 女 子 宀 寸 小 ⺌ 尢 尸 山 川 工 己 巾 幺 广 廴 廾 弋 弓 彐 彡 彳 艹 辶 阝 阝 䒑 忄 扌 氵

口口土士夂夕大女子宀寸小⺌⺍尢尸山川工己巾干幺广廴廾弋弓彐彡彳艹辶阝阝⺥忄扌氵

	土壇場	ドタンバ	place of execution; scaffold; last moment of life
	土地	トチ	earth; land
	土着	ドチャク	native; aboriginal; indigenous
	土手	ドて	embankment; dike
	土鍋	ドなべ	earthenware pot; casserole
	土俵	ドヒョウ	sandbag; ring for sumo wrestling
	土木	ドボク	engineering/public works
	土間	ドマ	unfloored part of the house; earthen floored room; pit in a theater
	土民	ドミン	natives; aborigines
	土用	ドヨウ	dog days; midsummer; hottest period of summer
	土曜日	ドヨウび	Saturday
訓	土	つち	Mother Earth; earth; soil; ground; clay
	土煙	つちけむり	cloud of dust
	土踏まず	つちふまず	arch of the foot
	土埃	つちぼこり	dust
	※土産	みやげ	souvenir

348

圧 ⑤ 一 厂 厂 圧 圧

音	圧	アツ	pressure; press down
熟	圧する	アッする	*vt*. press; press down; oppress
	圧搾	アッサク	compression; pressure; pressing —*v*. reduce in size or volume as if by squeezing; compress; press hard
	圧死	アッシ	death from crushing —*v*. be crushed to death; be suffocated
	圧縮	アッシュク	compression; constriction; condensation —*v*. compress; constrict; make compact; condense
	圧勝	アッショウ	landslide win; sweeping victory —*vi*. defeat decisively; win a landslide victory
	圧倒	アットウ	overpowering; overcoming —*v*. overwhelm; overpower; overcome
	圧倒的	アットウテキ	overwhelming; overpowering
	圧迫	アッパク	unjust exercize of power; oppression; suppression —*v*. oppress; be oppressive; suppress
	圧力	アツリョク	pressure; stress
¥	圧縮記帳	アッシュクキチョウ	reduced-value entry (of acquired property)
	圧力団体	アツリョクダンタイ	pressure group

在 ⑥　一 ナ ナ 存 存 在

音	在	ザイ	be
熟	在外	ザイガイ	being abroad/overseas
	在学	ザイガク	enrolled —*vi.* be in school; be a student at; be enrolled at
	在勤	ザイキン	while working —*vi.* be working; be at work
	在庫	ザイコ	stock; inventory
	在住	ザイジュウ	living; in residence —*vi.* live; be in residence at
	在住者	ザイジュウシャ	resident
	在職	ザイショク	in the office; at work —*vi.* be in office
	在籍	ザイセキ	registered; enrolled; on the roll —*vi.* be registered; be enrolled; be on the roll
	在宅	ザイタク	at home —*vi.* be at home
	在来	ザイライ	usual; common; conventionally
	在留	ザイリュウ	in residence —*vi.* reside; live
	在留邦人	ザイリュウホウジン	Japanese residents abroad
訓	在る	ある	*vi.* be; exist; live; be situated; be located
¥	在外資産	ザイガイシサン	overseas assets
	在外投資	ザイガイトウシ	overseas investments
	在庫一掃	ザイコイッソウ	stock clearance
	在庫過剰	ザイコカジョウ	overstocking
	在庫管理	ザイコカンリ	stock control; inventory management
	在庫表	ザイコヒョウ	stock list; inventory

垂 ⑧　一 二 三 亖 垂 垂 垂 垂

音	垂	スイ	droop; hang down
熟	垂訓	スイクン	teaching; instruction
	垂線	スイセン	perpendicular (line)
	垂涎	スイゼン	envy; covetness —*vi.* envy; covet
	垂直	スイチョク	perpendicular; vertical; plumb; sheer; at right angles
	垂範	スイハン	example —*vi.* set an example
訓	垂らす	たらす	*vt.* hang down; suspend; slouch
	垂れる	たれる	*v.* hang down; droop; drop; drip

3

口口土士夂夕大女子宀寸小ㅛ⼩尢尸山川工己巾干幺广廴廾弋弓ヨ彡彳⾉辶阝阝丬忄扌犭氵

| 垂氷 | たるひ | icicle |
| 垂水 | たるみ | waterfall |

351

執 ⑪ 一 十 土 ￢ ㄎ 幸 幸 幸 幹 執 執

音	執	シツ	execute; perform; carry out; do
		シュウ	stick to; attachment; tenacity
熟	執権	シッケン	regent; regency
	執行	シッコウ	execution (of a deed, etc.) —*v.* execute; carry out
	執行委員	シッコウイイン	executive committee
	執行人	シッコウニン	executor; executioner
	執行猶予	シッコウユウヨ	suspended sentence; probation
	執事	シツジ	butler; steward; majordomo
	執政	シッセイ	administration; governing; government
	執達吏	シッタツリ	bailiff
	執刀	シットウ	operation —*vi.* operate; perform an operation
	執筆	シッピツ	writing —*v.* write
	執務	シツム	work —*vi.* attend to one's business
	執拗	シツヨウ	obstinacy; persistence; tenacity
	執心	シュウシン	attachment; infatuation —*vi.* be attached; be infatuated
	執着	シュウチャク	deep attachment; tenacity —*vi.* be attached; stick to; insist
	執念	シュウネン	devotion; tenacity; persistence
訓	執る	とる	*vt.* do; handle; execute; write; command; defend

352

報 ⑫ 一 十 土 ㄎ ㄎ 幸 幸 幸 幸 幹 報 報

音	報	ホウ	news; report; reward
熟	報じる	ホウじる	*v.* repay; requite; report; inform
	報恩	ホウオン	showing gratitude; repaying a kindness
	報国	ホウコク	service to one's country
	報告	ホウコク	report —*v.* report; make a report
	報告書	ホウコクショ	(written) report/statement
	報酬	ホウシュウ	pay; remuneration; salary
	報奨	ホウショウ	compensation; bonus; reward —*v.* compensate; reward; remunerate

182

報償	ホウショウ	compensation; reward; remuneration —*vi*. be compensated/rewarded/remunerated	**3**
報知	ホウチ	information; news; intelligence —*v*. inform; make known; announce	
報道	ホウドウ	reporting; news coverage —*v*. report; inform; make known	
報道陣	ホウドウジン	press corps	
報徳	ホウトク	showing gratitude; repaying a kindness	
報復	ホウフク	revenge; vengence —*vi*. take revenge; revenge oneself	
訓 報いる	むくいる	*vt*. reward; repay; retaliate; avenge oneself	

353

 型 ⑨   一 二 チ 开 刑 刑 刑 型 型

音	型	ケイ	pattern; model; shape; form
訓	型	かた	model; pattern; mold; shape; form
	型紙	かたがみ	paper pattern
	型通り	かたどおり	in due/correct form; formal; formulaic (speech)
	型破り	かたやぶり	unconventional; unusual; break with tradition
	型	がた	(suffix) -type; -model

354

 基 ⑪   一 十 廿 卄 甘 其 其 其 基 基 基

音	基	キ	foundation; radical
熟	基金	キキン	fund; endowment
	基準	キジュン	standard; criterion
	基数	キスウ	*math*. cardinal numbers
	基礎	キソ	foundation; basics
	基地	キチ	(military) base
	基調	キチョウ	keynote; underlying tone/theme
	基点	キテン	*math*. cardinal/reference point
	基盤	キバン	base; basis
	基本	キホン	basis; foundation
	基本的	キホンテキ	basically; fundamentally
訓	基	もと	basis; base
	基	もとい	basis; foundation
	基づく	もとづく	*vi*. be based on; originate; be due to
¥	基軸通貨	キジクツウカ	key currency

口口土士夕大女子宀寸小ㇴ尢尸山川工己巾干幺广廴廾弋弓彐彡彳艹辶阝阝丷忄扌犭氵

3

口
口
土
士
夂
夕
大
女
子
宀
寸
小
⺌
⺍
尤
尸
山
川
工
己
巾
干
幺
广
廴
廾
弋
弓
彐
彡
彳
艹
辶
阝
阝
丷
忄
扌
犭
氵

355

堂 ⑪　　ⅠⅠⅠ ⅠⅠ ⅠⅠ ⅠⅠ ⅠⅠ 冖 尚 尚 営 営 堂

音	堂	ドウ	palace; temple
熟	堂宇	ドウウ	temple eaves; temple
	堂塔	ドウトウ	temple buildings
	堂々	ドウドウ	stately; imposing; dignified
	堂々巡り	ドウドウめぐり	going round and round in circles

356

 堅 ⑫　　Ⅰ Γ Γ ⴺ ⴺ ⴺ 臣 臤 臤 堅 堅 堅

音	堅	ケン	hard; solid; robust; strong; firm
熟	堅固	ケンゴ	firm; strong
	堅持	ケンジ	perseverance; maintenance —*v.* hold fast; stick to; maintain
	堅実	ケンジツ	steady; sound; reliable; stable; steady
	堅調	ケンチョウ	sturdy; solid
訓	堅い	かたい	hard; tough; stiff; firm; strict; strong
	堅苦しい	かたくるしい	unrelaxed; formal

357

堕 ⑫　　ⴺ ⴺ 阝 阝 阡 阽 防 陏 陏 陏 陏 堕

音	堕	ダ	fall; idle
熟	堕胎	ダタイ	abortion —*vi.* have an abortion; be aborted
	堕落	ダラク	depravity; corruption; degradation; delinquency; decadence —*vi.* become depraved; degenerate; fall into decadence

358

 塁 ⑫　　Ⅰ 冂 田 田 田 田 甲 畀 畀 畀 塁 塁

音	塁	ルイ	fort; base (in baseball)
熟	塁手	ルイシュ	*bas.* baseman
	塁審	ルイシン	*bas.* base umpire
	塁打	ルイダ	*bas.* base hit; single

塑 ⑬ 　 丶　ヽ　ヾ　ᅩ　ᅩ　ヰ　ヰ　朔　朔　朔　塑　塑

音	塑	ソ	molding; plastic
熟	塑像	ソゾウ	plastic image; clay figure
	塑造	ソゾウ	modeling; molding

塗 ⑬ 　 丶　丶　冫　シ　氵　氵　沙　沙　涂　涂　塗　塗

音	塗	ト	paint
	塗擦	トサツ	smearing and rubbing; inunction
熟	塗装	トソウ	coating; painting —*v.* coat with paint
	塗炭	トタン	misery; filth
	塗布	トフ	application (of paint, etc.) —*v.* apply (paint, etc.)
	塗抹	トマツ	—*vt.* coat with; paint over
	塗料	トリョウ	paints; paints and varnish; coating
訓	塗る	ぬる	*vt.* paint; gild
	塗り立て	ぬりたて	freshly painted

墓 ⑬ 　 一　サ　ガ　サ　甘　昔　莒　苷　莫　莫　墓　墓

音	墓	ボ	tomb; grave
熟	墓穴	ボケツ	grave
	墓参	ボサン	visiting a grave —*vi.* visit a grave
	墓所	ボショ	graveyard; cemetery
	墓前	ボゼン	before the grave; in front of a grave
	墓地	ボチ	graveyard; cemetery
	墓碑	ボヒ	tombstone; grave stone; headstone
	墓碑銘	ボヒメイ	epitaph (on a headstone)
	墓標	ボヒョウ	grave post
訓	墓	はか	tomb; grave
	墓石	はかいし	gravestone; headstone
	墓場	はかば	graveyard; cemetery
	墓守	はかもり	gravekeeper
	お墓参り	おはかまいり	visiting a grave —*vi.* visit a grave

3

口口土士夂夕大女子宀寸小㞢⺌尢尸山川工己巾干幺广廴廾弋弓彐彡彳艹辶阝阝丷忄扌犭氵

362

塾 ⑭ ` 亠 亠 亠 古 亯 亨 享 訇 孰 孰 塾

音	塾	ジュク	private/cram school
熟	塾生	ジュクセイ	student of a private school; person studying at a cram school

363

墨 ⑭ ` 冂 冂 日 甲 甲 里 里 黒 黒 墨 墨

音	墨	ボク	India ink; ink stick; Mexico; Sumida River
熟	墨画	ボクガ	*sumie* (India ink drawing)
	墨守	ボクシュ	strict adherence (to tradition, etc.) —*v.* show strict adherence (to tradition, etc.)
	墨汁	ボクジュウ	India ink
訓	墨	すみ	*sumi* (India ink; ink stick)
	墨色	すみいろ	shade of India ink
	墨絵	すみえ	*sumie* (India ink drawing)
	お墨付き	おすみつき	recommendation from a superior/famous person

364

墜 ⑮ ' ⻖ ⻖ ⻖ ⻖ ⻖ 陊 陊 隊 隊 隊 墜

音	墜	ツイ	fall
熟	墜死	ツイシ	death by falling —*vi.* fall to death
	墜落	ツイラク	(plane) crash; fall —*vi.* fall; drop; crash

365

墾 ⑯ ⺍ ⺌ 夕 豸 豸 豸 豸 豸 豹 豹 貇 墾

音	墾	コン	clear land

366

壁 ⑯ ⺄ ⼂ 尸 尸 居 居 居 居 居 辟 辟 壁

音	壁	ヘキ	wall

186

熟	壁画	ヘキガ	fresco; mural
訓	壁	かべ	wall
	壁掛け	かべかけ	tapestry; wall hanging
	壁紙	かべがみ	wallpaper
	壁際	かべぎわ	by/near the wall
	壁新聞	かべシンブン	wall newspaper/poster

367

地 ⑥   一 十 土 圵 圠 地

音	地	ジ	earth; ground; soil; land; spot; place; district; region
		チ	
熟	地上げ	ジあげ	forcing a landowner to sell his land against his will (through violence)
	地金	ジがね	metal; ore; one's true character/colors
	地声	ジごえ	one's natural voice
	地獄	ジゴク	hell
	地所	ジショ	land; ground; piece of land
	地震	ジシン	earthquake
	地震帯	ジシンタイ	earthquake zone/belt
	地蔵	ジゾウ	Jizō (Buddhist guardian deity of children)
	地鎮祭	ジチンサイ	Shintō ceremony of purifying a building site
	地主	ジぬし	landlord; landowner
	地盤	ジバン	ground; base; foundation; sphere of influence; constituency
	地味	ジミ	plain; simple; quiet; sober; conservative
	地道	ジみち	the honest way; beaten track
	地面	ジメン	ground; earth's surface
	地元	ジもと	local
	地元民	ジもとミン	local people; people of the district
	地位	チイ	position; status; standing; place
	地域	チイキ	area; region; zone
	地下	チカ	underground
	地階	チカイ	basement; cellar
	地殻	チカク	earth's crust
	地下資源	チカシゲン	underground resources
	地下水	チカスイ	ground water
	地下鉄	チカテツ	subway; the underground
	地下道	チカドウ	underpass
	地球	チキュウ	earth; globe

口口土士夕夕大女子宀寸小⺌⺍尢尸山川工己巾幺广廴廾弋弓ヨ彡彳艹辶阝阝丷忄扌氵犭

187

口口土士夂夕大女子宀寸小⺌⺍尤尸山川工己巾干幺广廴廾弋弓彐彡彳忄扌犭⺿阝⻏⻌⻖

地球儀	チキュウギ	globe (model of the earth)
地区	チク	area; disrict; region; zone
地形	チケイ	topography
地軸	チジク	earth's axis
地質	チシツ	geology; geological features
地上	チジョウ	on the ground; on earth
地図	チズ	map; atlas; chart; plan
地勢	チセイ	topography; geographical features; physical aspect
地層	チソウ	layer; stratum
地帯	チタイ	zone; area; region; belt
地点	チテン	spot; point; place; position
地熱	チネツ	terrestrial heat
地表	チヒョウ	earth's surface
地平線	チヘイセン	horizon; skyline
地方	チホウ	district; region; area; locality
地方化	チホウカ	localization —*v.* localize
地方裁判所	チホウサイバンショ	district court
地方自治	チホウジチ	local autonomy; self-government; home rule
地方色	チホウショク	local color
地方新聞	チホウシンブン	local newspaper
地方税	チホウゼイ	local taxes
地方分権	チホウブンケン	decentralization of power
地理	チリ	geography; geographical features; topography

訓 地 / つち / earth; soil; dirt; ground

¥ 地価 / チカ / land price/value

地方銀行	チホウギンコウ	regional/local bank
地方公共団体	チホウコウキョウダンタイ	local (prefectural, etc.) government
地方債	チホウサイ	municipal/local bonds
地方自治体	チホウジチタイ	local (prefectural, etc.) government
地方取引	チホウトリヒキ	regional stock exchange

368

均 ⑦　一 十 土 圡 圴 均 均

音 均 / キン / equal; identical; the same

熟
均一	キンイツ	uniformity; equality
均衡	キンコウ	equilibrium; balance
均質	キンシツ	homogeneity
均整	キンセイ	symmetry

均斉	キンセイ	symmetry
均等	キントウ	equality; uniformity; evenness —*v.* be equal/uniform/even
均分	キンブン	equal division —*v.* divide equally
¥ 均一料金	キンイツリョウキン	flat rate
均衡予算	キンコウヨサン	balanced budget

369
坑 ⑦
一　十　土　圵　圹　圹　坑

音	坑	コウ	pit; mine
熟	坑道	コウドウ	level; gallery; shaft; pit; tunnel
	坑夫	コウフ	miner; pit worker

370
坂 ⑦
一　十　土　圵　圹　坂　坂

音	坂	ハン	slope
訓	坂	さか	slope
	坂道	さかみち	sloping road; slope

371
坊 ⑦
一　十　土　圵　圹　坊　坊

音	坊	ボウ（ボッ）	priest's residence; Buddhist priest
熟	坊主	ボウズ	Buddhist priest; bonze; shaven head; boy; rascal
	坊や	ボウや	little boy
	坊ちゃん	ボッちゃん	(your) boy/son; young master

372
坪 ⑧
一　十　土　圵　圹　圹　坪　坪

| 音 | 坪 | （ヘイ） | *hei* (unit of area, approx. 3.3㎡) |
| 訓 | 坪 | つぼ | *tsubo* (unit of area, approx. 3.3㎡) |

口口土士夂夕大女子宀寸小⺌⺍尢尸山川工己巾干幺广廴廾弋弓彐彡彳艹辶阝阝䒑忄扌犭氵

口口土士夂夕大女子宀寸小⺌⺍尢尸山川工己巾干幺广廴廾弋弓ヨ彑彡彳艹辶阝阝⺍忄扌犭氵

373

垣 ⑨ 一 十 土 圹 垣 坥 垣 垣 垣

音	垣	（エン）	fence
訓	垣	かき	fence
	垣根	かきね	fence; hedge

374

城 ⑨ 一 十 土 圹 圹 坊 城 城 城

音	城	ジョウ	castle
	城下町	ジョウカまち	castle town
	城主	ジョウシュ	feudal lord; lord of a castle
	城跡	ジョウセキ （しろあと）	castle ruins
訓	城	しろ	castle; fort

375

埋 ⑩ 一 十 土 圹 圹 坰 坦 坤 埋 埋

音	埋	マイ	bury; fill up
熟	埋設	マイセツ	installing; laying —v. install; lay
	埋葬	マイソウ	burial; interment —v. bury; inter
	埋蔵	マイゾウ	buried stores; underground reserve —v. store underground
	埋没	マイボツ	buried; obscure —vi. lie buried; be buried; fall into obscurity
訓	埋まる	うまる	vi. be buried/filled up
	埋める	うめる	vt. bury; fill up
	埋め合わせる	うめあわせる	vt. make up with; compensate
	埋め立てる	うめたてる	vt. reclaim (land from the sea); fill in/up
	埋もれる	うもれる	vi. be buried

376

域 ⑪ 一 十 土 圡 圤 圹 垣 垣 域 域 域

| 音 | 域 | イキ | district; region; boundary; scope |

190

| 熟 | 域外 | イキガイ | outside the region/scope |
| | 域内 | イキナイ | within the region/scope |

377

培 ⑪　　一　十　土　土'　圹　圹　垃　垃　培　培　培

音	培	バイ	cultivate
熟	培養	バイヨウ	cultivation; nurture; culture of bacteria —*v*. cultivate; nurture; culture; breed; raise;
訓	培う	つちかう	*vt*. cultivate; nurture; breed; raise; grow

378

堀 ⑪　　一　十　土　圹　圹　炉　圻　堀　堀　堀　堀

| 訓 | 堀 | ほり | moat; ditch; canal |
| | 堀割 | ほりわり | canal; waterway; ditch |

379

堪 ⑫　　一　十　土　圹　圹　坩　坩　垪　堪　堪　堪　堪

音	堪	カン	endure; bear
		（タン）	
熟	堪忍	カンニン	patience; forbearance —*vi*. be patient; have patience; put up with
	堪忍袋	カンニンぶくろ	controlling one's anger
	堪能	タンノウ	skill; proficiency; satisfaction —*vi*. be satisfied; be fed up with; have enough of
訓	堪える	たえる	*vi*. endure; bear; put up with; be up to; be able to

380

場 ⑫　　一　十　土　圹　圹　圯　坦　坦　垾　場　場　場

音	場	ジョウ	place; scene
熟	場外	ジョウガイ	outside of the grounds/premises
	場内	ジョウナイ	in the hall/grounds
訓	場	ば	place; spot; room; space; scene; field
	場合	ばあい	situation; circumstances; conditions; case; occasion
	場数	ばかず	experience

口口土士夂夕大女子宀寸小⺌⺍尢尸山川工己巾干幺广廴廾弋弓彐彡彳艹辶阝⻖亠忄扌犭氵

191

口口土士夕夕大女子宀寸小ニニ尢尸山川工己巾干幺广廴廾弋弓彐彡彳艹辶阝丬忄扌犭氵

場所	ばショ	place; spot; site; location; room; space
場末	ばすえ	the suburbs/outskirts; off the beaten track
場違い	ばちがい	not the place; out of place
場面	ばメン	scene; sight
¥ 場外株式	ジョウガイかぶシキ	unlisted/over-the-counter stock
場外市場	ジョウガイシジョウ	over-the-counter market
場外取り引き	ジョウガイとりひき	over-the-counter transaction
場立ち	ばだち	floor representative

381

塚 ⑫ 一 十 土 土 圵 圹 圹 圹 坿 坿 塚 塚 塚

| 音 | 塚 | （チョウ） | mound |
| 訓 | 塚 | つか | mound; hillock; tumulus |

382

堤 ⑫ 一 十 土 圤 圳 圬 坦 坦 埠 埠 堤

音	堤	テイ	bank
熟	堤防	テイボウ	bank; embankment
訓	堤	つつみ	bank; embankment; dike

383

塔 ⑫ 一 十 土 圹 圹 圹 圹 圤 垯 塔 塔 塔

| 音 | 塔 | トウ | tower |
| 熟 | 塔婆 | トウバ | pagoda; stupa |

384

塀 ⑫ 一 十 土 圹 圹 圹 坭 坭 堀 堀 塀 塀

| 音 | 塀 | ヘイ | wall; fence |

385

塩 ⑬ 一 十 土 圵 圹 圹 垆 垆 垆 塩 塩 塩

音	塩	エン	salt
熟	塩化	エンカ	***chem***. chloridation; saltification —***vi. chem***. chloridate; saltify
	塩酸	エンサン	***chem***. hydrochloric acid
	塩水	エンスイ （しおみず）	salt water; brine
	塩素	エンソ	***chem***. chlorine
	塩田	エンデン	salt field/farm
	塩分	エンブン	saltiness; amount of salt; salt content
訓	塩	しお	salt
	塩辛い	しおからい	salty; briny

386

塊 ⑬ 一 十 土 圵 圹 圹 坤 坤 坤 塊 塊 塊

音	塊	カイ	clod; lump
熟	塊状	カイジョウ	massive
訓	塊	かたまり	lump; group

387

境 ⑭ 土 圵 圹 圹 圹 垆 垆 培 培 垆 境 境

音	境	キョウ （ケイ）	barrier; border; place; fortune; chance; fate; circumstances
熟	境界	キョウカイ	boundary; border; frontier
	境遇	キョウグウ	one's lot; circumstances; station in life
	境地	キョウチ	state; stage
	境内	ケイダイ	precincts; grounds; compound
訓	境	さかい	border; boundary; frontier

388

増 ⑭ 土 圵 圹 圹 圹 坤 坤 増 増 増 増 増

音	増	ゾウ	increase

口口土士夂夕大女子宀寸小⺌⺍尢尸山川工己巾干幺广廴廾弋弓ヨ彡彳艹辶阝阝亠冫扌犭氵

•

熟	増員	ゾウイン	personnel increase —*v.* increase the staff
	増加	ゾウカ	increase; addition; rise; growth —*v.* increase; add; rise; grow
	増額	ゾウガク	increase —*v.* increase; raise
	増刊	ゾウカン	special edition; extra number —*v.* publish a special edition
	増強	ゾウキョウ	reinforcement —*v.* reinforce; augment; beef up
	増結	ゾウケツ	additional cars/carriages —*v.* add cars/carriages (to a train)
	増減	ゾウゲン	increase and decrease —*v.* increase of decrease; vary (in quantity)
	増刷	ゾウサツ	reprinting; additional printing —*v.* reprint; print additional copies
	増殖	ゾウショク	increase; multiplication; propagation —*v.* increase; multiply; propagate
	増進	ゾウシン	improvement; increase —*v.* improve; increase; further
	増水	ゾウスイ	rising/swelling (of a river); flooding —*v.* swell; rise; flood
	増設	ゾウセツ	extension —*v.* build on; extend; establish; install more
	増大	ゾウダイ	increase; enlargement —*v.* increase; enlarge
	増築	ゾウチク	extension —*v.* build on; extend; enlarge
	増長	ゾウチョウ	*v.* grow presumptuous/impudent
	増発	ゾウハツ	extra train; extra issue (of bonds) —*v.* put on an extra train; issue extra (bonds)
	増兵	ゾウヘイ	reinforcements —*v.* reinforce
	増補	ゾウホ	enlargement; supplement —*v.* enlarge; supplement
訓	増える	ふえる	*vi.* increase; rise; raise
	増やす	ふやす	*vi.* increase; rise; raise
	増す	ます	*vi.* increase; rise; raise
¥	増益	ゾウエキ	profit increase
	増産	ゾウサン	expansion/increase in production —*v.* expand/increase production
	増資	ゾウシ	increase of capital stock —*v.* increase capital stock
	増収	ゾウシュウ	increased revenue/income/yield —*v.* increase revenue/income/yield
	増税	ゾウゼイ	tax increase —*v.* increase/raise taxes

389

墳 ⑮ 土 圫 圫 圹 圹 圹 圹 坊 埻 墳 墳 墳 墳

| 音 | 墳 | フン | (burial) mound; tomb |
| 熟 | 墳墓 | フンボ | grave; tomb |

390

壊 ⑯　士　圹　圹　圹　圹　坤　坤　埣　埣　壞　壞　壊

音	壊	カイ	destroy; crumble; break
熟	壊血病	カイケツビョウ	*med.* scurvy
	壊滅	カイメツ	destruction; annihilation; demolition —*v.* destroy; annihilate; demolish; waste
訓	壊す	こわす	*vt.* break; destroy; demolish; tear down
	壊れる	こわれる	*vi.* break; be broken
	※壊る	やぶる	*vt.* tear; rip; break; beat

391

壌 ⑯　士　圹　圹　圹　圹　坤　埣　壌　壤　壤　壤

音	壌	ジョウ	soil
熟	壌土	ジョウド	fertile soil
訓	※壌	つち	soil; earth; ground

392

壇 ⑯　士　圹　圹　圹　圹　埼　埼　壇　壇　壇　壇

音	壇	ダン (タン)	platform; raised floor; stage
熟	壇上	ダンジョウ	*v.* mount on a platform/stage

3　士　さむらい　samurai; gentleman

393

士 ③　一　十　士

音	士	シ	samurai; warrior; man; gentleman
熟	士官	シカン	military officer
	士気	シキ	morale
	士族	シゾク	samurai family; descendant of a samurai
	士農工商	シノウコウショウ	*hist.* the military, agricultural, industrial and mercantile classes of feudal Japan (Edo period)

口口土士夂夕大女子宀寸小丷丷尢尸山川工己巾干幺广廴廾弋弓彐彡彳艹辶阝丷忄扌犭

394

壮 ⑥　丶　丬　丬　爿　壯　壮

音	壮	ソウ	manhood; strength; prosperity
熟	壮快	ソウカイ	stirring; exhilarating; thrilling
	壮観	ソウカン	grand sight; awe-inspiring view
	壮健	ソウケン	healthy
	壮者	ソウシャ	man in his prime
	壮絶	ソウゼツ	sublime; magnificent
	壮大	ソウダイ	grand; magnificent; splendid
	壮年	ソウネン	prime of manhood
	壮麗	ソウレイ	splendor; glory
	壮烈	ソウレツ	heroic; brave

395

壱 ⑦　一　十　士　声　声　声　壱

| 音 | 壱 | イチ | one (used on Japanese currency and official documents) |
| 熟 | 壱万円 | イチマンエン | ten thousand yen |

396

声 ⑦　一　十　士　声　声　声　声

音	声	セイ	voice; reputation
		(ショウ)	
熟	声域	セイイキ	voice range; register
	声援	セイエン	cheering; encouragement; support —*v.* cheer; encourage; support
	声楽	セイガク	vocal music; singing
	声楽家	セイガクカ	vocalist
	声帯	セイタイ	vocal chords
	声望	セイボウ	popularity; fame; reputation
	声明	セイメイ	declaration; proclamation —*v.* declare; proclaim
	声明書	セイメイショ	statement; public/official statement
	声優	セイユウ	actor/actress specializing in dubbing films
	声量	セイリョウ	volume
訓	声	こえ	voice

声	こわ	(prefix) voice; vocal
声高	こわだか	loud voice
声音	こわね	tone of voice

売⑦ 一 十 士 声 声 声 売

音	売	バイ	sell
熟	売却	バイキャク	sale; disposal by sale —v. sell; sell off
	売国奴	バイコクド	traitor
	売春	バイシュン	prostitution; harloty; streetwalking —vi. prostitute; walk the streets; sell oneself for money
	売春婦	バイシュンフ	prostitute; street girl
	売店	バイテン	stand; stall; booth
	売買	バイバイ	buying and selling; trade; dealing; transaction —v. buy and sell; trade/deal in; market; handle
	売名	バイメイ	self-advertisement
	売約	バイヤク	sales contract
訓	売る	うる	vt. sell; deal offer; deceive
	売り	うり	sale; selling;
	売り切れ	うりきれ	being sold out; exhausted supplies; sold out
	売り込む	うりこむ	vt. sell; find a new market and sell; advertize oneself
	売り出す	うりだす	vt. offer for sale; become popular
	売り主	うりぬし	seller; vendor
	売り場	うりば	counter; shop; store
	売れる	うれる	vi. sell; be in demand; be well know/popular
	売れ口	うれくち	market; outlet; one's place of employment
	売れっ子	うれっこ	popular singer/actor
	売れ行き	うれゆき	market; sale; demand
¥	売上げ	うりあげ	proceeds; takings
	売上原価	うりあげゲンカ	cost of sales/goods sold
	売上総利益	うりあげ ソウリエキ	gross profit
	売上高	うりあげだか	sales
	売掛金	うりかけキン	accounts receivable
	売気配	うりケハイ	asked quotation
	売越し	うりこし	selling a balance
	売出し	うりだし	secondary offering
	売叩き	うりたたき	bear raid; gunning for a stock

口口土士夂夕大女子宀寸小⺌⺍尢戸山川工己巾干幺广廴廾弋弓彐彡彳艹辶阝⺍忄扌犭氵

口口土士夂夕大女子宀寸小⺌⺍尢尸山川工己巾干幺广廴廾弋弓彐彡彳⺌辶阝阝艹忄扌氵犭

売りつなぎ	うりつなぎ	hedge-selling; short selling (against the box)
売り場	うりば	counter; best time to sell
売価	バイカ	selling/labeled price

---

3 夂 ふゆがしら／なつあし winter

398

処 ⑤ ノ ク 夂 処 処

音	処	ショ	place; deal with
熟	処する	ショする	*vi.* face; conduct; deal with; manage
	処刑	ショケイ	execution —*v.* execute
	処子	ショシ	virgin; innocent child
	処女	ショジョ	virgin
	処女作	ショジョサク	maiden work
	処世訓	ショセイクン	the secret of getting along in the world
	処断	ショダン	ruling; judgment
	処置	ショチ	treatment; disposal; measures —*v.* dispose; deal with; take measures; treat
	処罰	ショバツ	punishment; penalty —*v.* punish; penalize
	処分	ショブン	disposal; punishment; measure —*v.* dispose of; deal with; punish
	処方	ショホウ	*med.* prescription —*v.* prescribe
	処理	ショリ	management —*v.* deal with; handle

399

冬 ⑤ ノ ク 夂 冬 冬

音	冬	トウ	winter
熟	冬季	トウキ	winter
	冬期	トウキ	wintertime
	冬至	トウジ	winter solstice
	冬眠	トウミン	hibernation —*vi.* hibernate
訓	冬	ふゆ	winter
	冬ごもり	ふゆごもり	winter confinement; wintering —*vi.* stay indoors for the winter
	冬物	ふゆもの	winter clothing/wear
	冬休み	ふゆやすみ	winter vacation

400

麦 ⑦　一　十　キ　圭　丰　麦　麦

音	麦	バク	barley; wheat
熟	麦芽	バクガ	malt; germ wheat; barley
訓	麦	むぎ	wheat; barley; oats; rye

401

変 ⑨　丶　亠　广　亣　亣　亦　亦　変　変

音	変	ヘン	change; strange; mishap; accident; flat (in music)
熟	変じる	ヘンじる	v. change; alter; renew
	変圧器	ヘンアツキ	transformer (voltage)
	変移	ヘンイ	change; alteration —v. change; alter
	変異	ヘンイ	change; fluctuation; variation; mishap —vi. change; fluctuation; be different
	変化	ヘンカ	change; transformation —vi. change; transform
	変革	ヘンカク	reformation; change; revolution —v. reform; change; be revolutionized
	変換	ヘンカン	change; conversion **math**. transformation —v. change; convert
	変化	ヘンゲ	goblin; apparition; god that has taken on human form
	変形	ヘンケイ	transformation; modification; deformation —v. transform; modify; deform
	変幻自在	ヘンゲンジザイ	ever-changing; changeable; unexpected; free
	変更	ヘンコウ	change; alteration; amendment —v. change; alter; amend
	変死	ヘンシ	unnatural death (by accident, murder, suicide, etc.) —vi. die an unnatural death
	変事	ヘンジ	mishap; accident; incident
	変質	ヘンシツ	deterioration; degeneration —vi. be degenerate
	変質者	ヘンシツシャ	pervert; deviant
	変種	ヘンシュ	variety; strain
	変色	ヘンショク	discoloration; change of color —v. change the color; discolor
	変身	ヘンシン	metamorphosis; transformation —vi. metamorphose; transform
	変心	ヘンシン	change of mind/heart; fickleness —vi. change one's mind; be fickle
	変人	ヘンジン	odd person; eccentric
	変数	ヘンスウ	**math**. variable

口 口 土 士 夂 夕 大 女 子 宀 寸 小 ⺌ ⺍ 尢 尸 山 川 工 已 巾 干 幺 广 廴 廾 弋 弓 彐 彡 彳 艹 辶 阝 阝 丷 忄 扌 氵

口口土士夂夕大女子宀寸小⺌⺍尢尸山川工己巾干幺广廴廾弋弓彐彡彳⺌辶阝阝⺍忄扌氵犭

変成	ヘンセイ	metamorphosis; change of shape/form —*v.* change shape/form
変節	ヘンセツ	change of seasons; apostasy
変遷	ヘンセン	changes; vicissitudes —*vi.* change unpredictably
変装	ヘンソウ	disguise —*vi.* be disguised
変造	ヘンゾウ	alteration; defacement; forgery
変速	ヘンソク	changing speed/gears
変則	ヘンソク	irregular; abnormal
変態	ヘンタイ	metamorphosis; abnormal; perverted
変調	ヘンチョウ	change of tone/key; irregular; abnormal
変哲もない	ヘンテツもない	commonplace; ordinary
変転	ヘンテン	great changes; vicissitudes —*vi.* change unpredictably
変動	ヘンドウ	change; fluctuation —*vi.* change; fluctuate
変貌	ヘンボウ	transfiguration; transformation —*vi.* be transformed; change one's appearance
変名	ヘンメイ（ヘンミョウ）	assumed name; name change —*vi.* change one's name; assume an alias
変容	ヘンヨウ	changed appearance —*v.* change appearance
変乱	ヘンラン	upheaval; disturbance

訓
変える	かえる	*vt.* change; alter; move
変わる	かわる	*vi.* change; be different/strange
変わり種	かわりだね	exceptional case; different from the rest
変わり果てる	かわりはてる	*vi.* change completely
変わり目	かわりめ	change; turning point; transition
変わり者	かわりもの	odd person; eccentric

¥
変動所得	ヘンドウショトク	transitory income
変動相場	ヘンドウソウバ	floating exchange rate
変動費	ヘンドウヒ	variable costs

402

夏 ⑩ 一 ア 丆 丙 页 百 頁 頁 夏 夏

音
| 夏 | カ | summer |
| | （ゲ） | summer |

熟
夏季	カキ	summer season
夏期	カキ	summer period
夏至	ゲシ	summer solstice

訓
夏	なつ	summer
夏場	なつば	summertime; summer resort
夏休み	なつやすみ	summer holiday/vacation

3　夕　た／ゆうべ　*ta* (katakana); evening

403

夕 ③ 　ノ ク 夕

音	夕	セキ	evening
訓	夕	ゆう	evening
	夕方	ゆうがた	evening
	夕刊	ゆうカン	evening paper/edition
	夕暮れ	ゆうぐれ	evening
	夕食	ゆうショク	dinner; evening meal
	夕立	ゆうだち	sudden shower in the evening or late afternoon
	夕飯	ゆうハン	dinner; evening meal
	夕日	ゆうひ	setting sun
	夕焼け	ゆうやけ	sunset

404

外 ⑤ 　ノ ク 夕 夘 外

音	外	ガイ	appearance; outside; unfasten
		ゲ	outside
熟	外圧	ガイアツ	external/foreign pressure
	外苑	ガイエン	outer garden (of a palace, etc.)
	外界	ガイカイ	external world; outside; physical world
	外海	ガイカイ (そとうみ)	open sea
	外角	ガイカク	*bas*. outcorner; external angle
	外患	ガイカン	external/foreign troubles
	外観	ガイカン	external appearance
	外気	ガイキ	open air
	外勤	ガイキン	outside duty; canvassing
	外見	ガイケン	outward appearance; faces
	外交	ガイコウ	diplomacy
	外交官	ガイコウカン	diplomat
	外耳	ガイジ	*med*. external ear; concha
	外出	ガイシュツ	going out; outing; airing —*vi*. go out
	外傷	ガイショウ	external wound
	外食	ガイショク	eating/dining out —*vi*. dine/eat out

口
口
土
士
夂
● 夕
大
女
子
宀
寸
小
⺌
⺍
尤
尸
山
川
工
己
巾
干
幺
广
廴
廾
弋
弓
ヨ
彡
彳
艹
⻌
阝
阝
丷
忄
扌
氵
犭

外人	ガイジン	foreigner
外地	ガイチ	foreign area; overseas land
外電	ガイデン	foreign telegram; dispatch from overseas
外泊	ガイハク	sleeping/stopping/staying out (overnight) —*vi.* sleep over; stop out overnight
外部	ガイブ	outside; outer; external
外米	ガイマイ	imported/foreign rice
外面	ガイメン	outward appearance; the outside; exterior
外遊	ガイユウ	foreign travel —*vi.* take a trip abroad
外洋	ガイヨウ	ocean
外用薬	ガイヨウヤク	external remedy; medicine for external use
外来	ガイライ	from abroad; outpatients
外来語	ガイライゴ	*gram.* adopted word; loanword
外科	ゲカ	surgery; department of surgery in a hospital
外道	ゲドウ	non-Buddhist beliefs; demon(-mask)

訓 外	そと	outside
外す	はずす	*vt.* remove; miss; avoid
外れる	はずれる	*vi.* be off; be contrary to; miss
外	ほか	other; another
※外様	とざま	*hist. Tozama* -daimyo (non-Tokugawa daimyo, Edo period)

¥ 外貨	ガイカ	foreign currency/goods
外貨準備	ガイカジュンビ	foreign exchange reserves
外国為替 (外為)	ガイコクかわせ (ガイタメ)	foreign exchange
外国銀行 (外銀)	ガイコクギンコウ (ガイギン)	foreign bank
外国債権 (外債)	ガイコクサイケン (ガイサイ)	foreign bond/loan
外国資本 (外資)	ガイコクシホン (ガイシ)	foreign capital
外国需要 (外需)	ガイコクジュヨウ (ガイジュ)	foreign demand; demand from abroad
外国通貨 (外貨)	ガイコクツウカ (ガイカ)	foreign currency
外債	ガイサイ	foreign bond; foreign debt; foreign loan
外資	ガイシ	foreign capital; foreign investiment
外資系企業	ガイシケイキギョウ	foreign-affiliate; enterprise with foreign capital
外資導入	ガイシドウニュウ	introduction of foreign capital
外部資本	ガイブシホン	outside capital; borrowed capital
外務省	ガイムショウ	Ministry of Foreign Affairs
外務大臣 (外相)	ガイムダイジン (ガイショウ)	minister of foreign affairs

多 ⑥ 　ノ　ク　夕　夕　多　多

音	多	タ	many; much; multiple
熟	多寡	タカ	quantity; number
	多額	タガク	large sum/amount
	多角的	タカクテキ	many sided; versatile; diversified; multilateral
	多角形	タカッケイ	polygon
	多感	タカン	sensibility; susceptibility; sentimentality
	多義	タギ	polysemy; diverse meanings
	多芸	タゲイ	versatility; well versed in the arts
	多元	タゲン	pluralism
	多恨	タコン	numerous regrets; great saddness
	多才	タサイ	versatility; versatile talents
	多彩	タサイ	colorful
	多事	タジ	eventfulness; pressure of business
	多種	タシュ	various kinds
	多種多様	タシュタヨウ	variety; diversity
	多少	タショウ	more or less; approximately; some; a few
	多情	タジョウ	wanton; fickle; inconstant; licentious
	多数	タスウ	large number; multitude; majority; predominance
	多数決	タスウケツ	majority rule
	多勢	タゼイ	great numbers; numerical superiority
	多大	タダイ	great quantity; large amount
	多読	タドク	wide/extensive reading —v. be widely read; read extensively
	多難	タナン	full of difficulties
	多人数	タニンズウ	great number of people
	多年	タネン	many years; number of years
	多分	タブン	plenty; much; many; a great deal; probably; perhaps; maybe
	多忙	タボウ	pressure of work; busy
	多方面	タホウメン	many quarters/directions
	多面	タメン	many faces/sides
	多量	タリョウ	large quantities; abundance; a great deal
訓	多い	おおい	many; much; a lot of
¥	多角化	タカクカ	diversification —v. diversify
	多角経営	タカクケイエイ	diversified/multilateral management
	多国籍企業	タコクセキキギョウ	multinational enterprise

口口土士夂夂 夕 • 大女子宀寸小⺌⻌尢尸山川工己巾干幺广廴廾弋弓彐彡彳艹辶阝阝⺍忄扌犭氵

3

406

夜 ⑧   ' 亠 广 产 产 疒 夼 夜

音	夜	ヤ	night
熟	夜陰	ヤイン	darkness of night
	夜会	ヤカイ	evening party; ball
	夜学	ヤガク	night school; evening classes
	夜間	ヤカン	night; night time
	夜気	ヤキ	night air; stillness of the night
	夜曲	ヤキョク	nocturne
	夜勤	ヤキン	night duty/shift —*vi.* do night duty; work at night
	夜具	ヤグ	bedding
	夜景	ヤケイ	night view
	夜警	ヤケイ	night watch
	夜行	ヤコウ	night train/travel
	夜光虫	ヤコウチュウ	night-glowing insect
	夜叉	ヤシャ	Yasha (female demon in Buddhist mythology)
	夜襲	ヤシュウ	night attack —*v.* make a night attack; attack in darkness
	夜半	ヤハン	midnight; dead of night
	夜分	ヤブン	night; evening
	夜盲症	ヤモウショウ	*med.* night blindness
	夜来	ヤライ	since last night; overnight
訓	夜	よ	night
	夜明かし	よあかし	staying up all night —*vi.* stay up overnight
	夜明け	よあけ	dawn; daybreak
	夜霧	よぎり	night fog
	夜通し	よどおし	overnight
	夜中	よなか	midnight; dead of night
	夜這	よばい	creep in to see a woman at night
	夜目	よめ	watching in the dark
	夜	よる	night

407

夢 ⑬   一 艹 艹 芒 莒 莒 苗 莆 莆 夢 夢 夢

音	夢	ム	dream
熟	夢幻	ムゲン	dreams and fantasies

204

	夢想	ムソウ	dream; vision; fantasy —*v*. dream; fantasize; have a vision
	夢中	ムチュウ	rapture; absorption; intentness; frantic
	夢遊病	ムユウビョウ	sleepwalking
訓	夢	ゆめ	dream
	夢心地	ゆめごこち	trance; ecstasy
	夢路	ゆめじ	dream; dreaming

3 大 だい big

408

大 ③ 一 ナ 大

音	大	タイ	large; many; importance; whole
		ダイ	big; excellent; dimension; prosperity
熟	大安	タイアン （ダイアン）	luck/auspicious day (on the Japanese calendar)
	大意	タイイ	gist; purport; substance; ration; holocaust
	大英帝国	ダイエイテイコク	British Empire
	大家	タイカ	mansion; illustrious family; master; authority
	大火	タイカ	great fire; conflagration
	大会	タイカイ	mass meeting; tournament; convention
	大学	ダイガク	university; college
	大学院	ダイガクイン	graduate school
	大学生	ダイガクセイ	university/college student
	大観	タイカン	general/philosophical/comprehensive view —*v*. take a general view; make a general survey; have a broad outlook
	大寒	ダイカン	the coldest season (the latter part of January); very cold weather
	大気	タイキ	atmosphere; air
	大気圏	タイキケン	atmosphere
	大器	タイキ	great talent; large vessel
	大儀	タイギ	irksome; laborious; tedious
	大規模	ダイキボ	large-scale; mass
	大挙	タイキョ	in great force —*vi*. come in great force
	大局	タイキョク	the whole situation; main issue
	大工	ダイク	carpenter
	大軍	タイグン	large army
	大群	タイグン	large crowd

口 口 土 士 夂 夕 • 大 女 子 宀 寸 小 ⺌ ⺌ 尢 尸 山 川 工 己 巾 干 幺 广 廴 廾 弋 弓 ⺕ 彡 彳 ⺾ ⻌ ⻏ ⻖ ⺍ ⺅ ⺘ ⺩ ⺡

大言壮語	タイゲンソウゴ	big talk; boasting; bragging —*vi.* talk big; boast; brag
大綱	タイコウ	general rules; fundamental principles; outline
大国	タイコク	large/great country
大差	タイサ	great difference; striking contrast
大罪	ダイザイ	great crime; felony; mortal sin
大作	タイサク	major work; masterpiece
大志	タイシ	ambition; aspiration
大使	タイシ	ambassador
大使館	タイシカン	embassy
大師	ダイシ	great teacher of Buddhism; Kobo Daishi
大事	ダイジ	important; grave; serious; valuable
大衆	タイシュウ	masses; crowd of people
大将	タイショウ	general; admiral
大勝	タイショウ	great/landslide victory —*vi.* win by a landslide
大小	ダイショウ	large and small size
大乗	ダイジョウ	Great Vehicle; Mahayana Buddhism
大丈夫	ダイジョウブ	safe; certain; sure; OK
大静脈	ダイジョウミャク	*med.* main vein
大食	タイショク	gluttony; heavy eating —*vi.* eat heavily; eat like a horse
大臣	ダイジン	minister of state
大成	タイセイ	completion; accomplishment —*v.* complete; accomplish; attain; mature
大勢	タイセイ	general trend/tendency/situation
大政奉還	タイセイホウカン	*hist.* restoration of imperial rule (14 October 1867)
大切	タイセツ	important; valuable
大体	ダイタイ	outline; summary; generally; essentially
大々的	ダイダイテキ	on a large scale; great; grand; gigantic; immense
大多数	ダイタスウ	majority
大胆	ダイタン	boldness; daring
大地	ダイチ	earth; ground
大抵	タイテイ	usually; mostly; generally; almost
大敵	タイテキ	powerful enemy
大同小異	ダイドウショウイ	general similarity
大動脈	ダイドウミャク	*med.* main artery
大統領	ダイトウリョウ	president (of a republic)
大任	タイニン	important charge/position
大破	タイハ	ruin; dilapidation; havoc —*v.* be crippled/wrecked/in ruins
大敗	タイハイ	terrible defeat —*vi.* sustain a terrible defeat
大半	タイハン	greater part; majority; bulk

大病	タイビョウ	serious/major illness
大分	ダイブ	very; much
大仏	ダイブツ	great Buddha (statue)
大部分	ダイブブン	the majority (of); mostly; for the most part
大別	タイベツ	broad classification —v. make a general classification; divide into main classes
大変	タイヘン	very; greatly; awfully
大便	ダイベン	feces; stool
大枚	タイマイ	large sum of money
大名	ダイミョウ	*daimyo* (feudal lords of the Edo period)
大役	タイヤク	important task; heavy duty
大洋	タイヨウ	ocean
大陸	タイリク	continent
大量	タイリョウ	large quantity; magnanimity; generosity; liberality
大量生産	タイリョウセイサン	mass production —v. mass produce
大漁	タイリョウ	large catch of fish
大輪	タイリン	large flower/wheel
大老	タイロウ	*hist.* Shogun's chief minister (Edo period)

訓

大	おお	big; large; great
大きい	おおきい	big; large; great; grand
大きさ	おおきさ	size; dimensions; magnitude
大型	おおがた	large size
大柄	おおがら	large pattern/build/frame
大筋	おおすじ	outline
大詰め	おおづめ	final; end; conclusion
大手	おおて	front gate of a castle; major company
大道具	おおドウグ	stage setting
大判	おおバン	large sheet of paper; *ōban* (coinage used during the Edo period)
大水	おおみず	flood; overflow
大物	おおもの	big figure; important person
大家	おおや	landlord; landlady
大いに	おおいに	very; much; far; greatly
※大晦日	おおみそか	New Year's Eve

¥

大口	おおぐち	large lot (amount, size)
大蔵省	おおくらショウ	Ministry of Finance
大蔵大臣	おおくらダイジン	minister of finance
大底	おおそこ	major bottom (stock price trend, etc.)
大台乗せ	おおだいのせ	reaching/hitting a mark
大台割れ	おおだいわれ	dropping below a mark
大手(企業)	おおて(キギョウ)	leading enterprise (company)

口
口
土
士
夂
夕
• 大
女
子
宀
寸
小
⺌
⺍
尢
尸
山
川
工
己
巾
干
幺
广
廴
廾
弋
弓
⺕
彡
彳
艹
辶
阝
阝
亠
忄
扌
氵

大幅	おおはば	full width
大引け	おおびけ	close; closing
大衆相場	タイシュウソウバ	public market
大納会	ダイノウカイ	final session of the year (stock market, etc.)
大発会	ダイハッカイ	first session of the year (stock market, etc.)

409

太 ④ 一 ナ 大 太

音	太	タ	big; fat; thick
		タイ	big; fat; thick; deep; beginning
熟	太古	タイコ	remote ages; ancient times; prehistoric days
	太鼓	タイコ	drum
	太子	タイシ	crown prince; prince
	太平洋	タイヘイヨウ	Pacific Ocean
	太陽	タイヨウ	sun
	太陽熱	タイヨウネツ	solar heat; heat of the sun's rays
	太刀	タチ	long sword
訓	太い	ふとい	big; large; fat; thick
	太さ	ふとさ	thickness
	太る	ふとる	*vi*. grow fat; put on weight

410

天 ④ 一 二 チ 天

音	天	テン	sky; air; the heavens; heaven; nature; fate; destiny
熟	天王星	テンオウセイ	the planet Jupiter
	天下	テンカ	whole country; land; realm
	天下一品	テンカイッピン	beyond comparison; unrivalled
	天涯	テンガイ	horizon; skyline; far-off country
	天蓋	テンガイ	canopy/sunshade (for Buddhist statues or priests)
	天気	テンキ	the weather/elements; atmospheric conditions
	天気予報	テンキヨホウ	weather forecast
	天球	テンキュウ	celestial sphere
	天狗	テング	*tengu* (long-nosed goblin)
	天空	テンクウ	the sky/air/firmament
	天恵	テンケイ	heaven's blessing; gift of nature
	天候	テンコウ	weather; elements

天国	テンゴク	heaven
天才	テンサイ	genius
天災	テンサイ	natural disaster/calamity; act of God
天子	テンシ	son of heaven; emperor
天使	テンシ	angel
天竺	テンジク	*clas.* India
天寿	テンジュ	natural span of life
天守閣	テンシュカク	castle tower; donjon; keep
天上	テンジョウ	the heavens
天井	テンジョウ	ceiling; roof; top
天井桟敷	テンジョウさじき	upper gallery of a theater
天職	テンショク	mission; vocation
天神	テンジン	heavenly gods
天真爛漫	テンシンランマン	innocence; naivety
天性	テンセイ	nature; by nature; naturally
天体	テンタイ	heavenly body
天地	テンチ	heaven and earth; top and bottom
天頂	テンチョウ	zenith
天童	テンドウ	Buddhist angel
天女	テンニョ	celestial nymph
天人	テンニン	angel; heavenly being
天然	テンネン	nature; spontaneity
天然記念物	テンネンキネンブツ	natural monument
天然資源	テンネンシゲン	natural resources
天然色	テンネンショク	natural color
天然痘	テンネントウ	*med.* smallpox
天皇	テンノウ	emperor (Japanese only)
天罰	テンバツ	divine wrath
天火	テンび	oven
天引き	テンびき	deduction; deduction in advance —*v.* deduct; knock off
天秤	テンビン	balance; scales
天秤座	テンビンザ	Libra, seventh sign of the zodiac
天賦	テンプ	nature; given by nature
天分	テンブン	one's nature; natural gifts
天変地異	テンペンチイ	natural disasters
天幕	テンマク	tent; pavilion; marquee; awning
天窓	テンまど	skylight
天命	テンメイ	will of the gods; fate; destiny; life
天文	テンモン	astromony; astrology
天文学	テンモンガク	astronomy

口 口 土 士 夕 夕 大 女 子 宀 寸 小 ⺌ ⺌ 尢 尸 山 川 工 己 巾 干 幺 广 廴 廾 弋 弓 彐 彡 彳 艹 辶 阝 丷 忄 扌 氵

209

口口土士夕夕
●大女子宀寸小ⁿˡ⋯
尤尸山川工己巾
干幺广廴廾弋弓ㅋ彡彳艹辶阝丬忄扌犭氵

天文台	テンモンダイ	astronomical observatory
天与	テンヨ	gift of heaven; godsend
天理教	テンリキョウ	Tenriism (new religion)

訓
天	あま	the heavens; heaven
天下り	あまくだり	descent from heaven *fig.* appointment of a former official to an important post in a private company (through influence from above)
天照大神	あまてらすおおみかみ	Sun Goddess (in Japanese mythology)
天の河	あまのがわ	Milky Way
天	あめ	heaven; the sky; the heavens

411

 ④ 一 二 チ 夫

音
| 夫 | フ（フウ） | husband |

熟
夫婦	フウフ	man and wife; husband and wife; married couple
夫妻	フサイ	husband and wife
夫唱婦随	フショウフズイ	"The husband speaks and the wife obeys"
夫人	フジン	woman; lady; female

訓
| 夫 | おっと | husband; man |
| ※夫婦 | めおと | man and wife; husband and wife; married couple |

412

 ⑤ 丿 冂 口 中 央

音
| 央 | オウ | center; middle |

413

失 ⑤ 丿 � ㇏ 二 牛 失

音
| 失 | シツ | lose; error; failure |

熟
失する	シッする	*vt.* miss; forget
失意	シツイ	disappointment
失火	シッカ	accidental fire —*vi.* catch on fire accidentally
失格	シッカク	disqualification; elimination —*vi.* disqualify;

eliminate

失脚	シッキャク	fall; downfall —*vi.* lose; bring about one's downfall
失禁	シッキン	incontinence —*vi.* be incontinent
失敬	シッケイ	rudeness; theft —*vi.* steal; take; help oneself to
失言	シツゲン	slip of the tongue —*vi.* make a slip of the tongue
失効	シッコウ	invalidation —*vi.* lapse; lose validity; expire; run out
失策	シッサク	error; mistake —*vi.* err; blunder
失笑	シッショウ	spontaneous laughter —*vi.* burst out laughing
失職	シッショク	unemployment —*vi.* lose one's job; become unemployed
失神	シッシン	faint —*vi.* faint; lose consciousness
失政	シッセイ	misgovernment; misrule
失踪	シッソウ	disappearance —*vi.* disappear; vanish; go missing
失速	シッソク	stall —*vi.* stall
失態	シッタイ	blunder
失墜	シッツイ	loss; fall —*v.* lose; fall
失敗	シッパイ	failure; mistake; blunder —*vi.* fail; blunder be unsuccessful
失望	シツボウ	disappointment; despair —*vi.* be disappointed
失明	シツメイ	loss of sight; blindness —*vi.* lose one's eyesight; become blind
失礼	シツレイ	impoliteness; rudeness; bad manners —*vi.* be impolite/rude; have bad manners
失恋	シツレン	unrequited love —*vi.* be unlucky in love; have a broken heart
訓 失う	うしなう	*vt.* lose; miss
¥ 失業	シツギョウ	unemployment —*vi.* lose one's job; be out of work
失業者	シツギョウシャ	the unemployed; unemployed person
失業率	シツギョウリツ	unemployment rate

414

奇 ⑧

音 奇	キ	strange; novel
熟 奇異	キイ	strange; queer; singular; odd
奇禍	キカ	accident; disaster; mishap
奇怪	キカイ	mysterious; weird; strange; outrageous; uncanny
奇遇	キグウ	chance meeting
奇形	キケイ	deformation; malformation
奇習	キシュウ	strange custom

口 口 土 士 夕 夕 ● 大 女 子 宀 寸 小 ⺌ ⺌ 尢 尸 山 川 工 己 巾 干 幺 广 廴 廾 弋 弓 ⺕ 彡 彳 艹 辶 阝 阝 ⺮ 忄 扌 犭 氵

	奇襲	キシュウ	surprise attack —*v*. make a surprise attack
	奇術	キジュツ	jugglery; conjuring tricks; sleight of hand; magic
	奇人	キジン	eccentric person; crank
	奇数	キスウ	*math*. odd number
	奇跡	キセキ	miracle
	奇想天外	キソウテンガイ	original idea; unexpected
	奇抜	キバツ	novel; original; uncoventional
	奇妙	キミョウ	strange; curious; weird; queer
	奇麗	キレイ	beautiful; pretty

415

 ⑧　一　二　三　丰　夫　表　表　奉

音	奉	ホウ	offer
		（ブ）	offer
熟	奉じる	ほうじる	*vt*. present; dedicate; obey; follow; believe in; serve
	奉迎	ホウゲイ	welcoming/meeting (a person of high social standing) —*v*. welcome/meet (a person of high social standing)
	奉献	ホウケン	dedication; offering; consecration —*v*. dedicate; offer; consecrate
	奉公	ホウコウ	public duty; service —*vi*. be of service; carry out one's duties; serve one's master
	奉仕	ホウシ	service (to country, society, elders, etc.) —*vi*. serve (one's country, society, elders, etc.)
	奉書	ホウショ	thick, high-quality paper *hist*. edict from daimyo to lower classes (Edo period)
	奉職	ホウショク	public service —*vi*. be in the service of; hold a post
	奉納	ホウノウ	dedication/offering (to Buddhas, gods) —*v*. dedicate/offer (to Buddhas, gods)
訓	奉る	たてまつる	offer; present; revere

416

 ⑧　一　ナ　大　太　本　本　奔　奔

音	奔	ホン	run
熟	奔走	ホンソウ	running about to achieve a purpose; busily making arrangements —*vi*. run about for a purpose; be busy arranging something
	奔放	ホンポウ	wild; extravagant; uninhibited

奔流　ホンリュウ　rapids; torrent; rushing current

417

契 ⑨ 一 十 キ 主 刧丅 刧刀 刧刀 契刀 契

音	契	ケイ	promise; pledge; oath
熟	契機	ケイキ	opportunity; chance
訓	契り	ちぎり	pledge; vow; plight
	契る	ちぎる	*vt.* pledge; vow; promise; plight one's troth; promise to marry
¥	契約	ケイヤク	contract; agreement —*v.* enter into/sign a contract
	契約書	ケイヤクショ	written contract

418

奏 ⑨ 一 二 三 声 夫 表 表 奉 奏 奏

音	奏	ソウ	play; present; report; take effect
熟	奏する	ソウする	*vt.* play a musical instrument; report to the emperor
	奏楽	ソウガク	instrumental music
	奏功	ソウコウ	achieving one's aim —*vi.* succeed in achieving the aim
	奏効	ソウコウ	effectiveness —*vi.* be effective
	奏上	ソウジョウ	reporting to the emperor —*v.* report to the emperor
訓	奏でる	かなでる	*vt.* play (a musical instrument)

419

奥 ⑫ 丶 丿 冂 冂 冋 向 南 南 南 南 奥 奥 奥

音	奥	オウ	deep; profound; recesses; interior
熟	奥義	オウギ（おくぎ）	secret principles; esoteric mysteries
訓	奥	おく	inner part; innermost part; interior
	奥まる	おくまる	*vi.* extend far back; lie deep within
	奥書	おくがき	postscript; endorsement
	奥様	おくさま	*hon.* (your) wife; married woman
	奥さん	おくさん	*hon.* (your) wife; married woman
	奥底	おくそこ	the depth; the bottom

口口土士夂夕大女子宀寸小⺌⺍尢尸山川工己巾干幺广廴廾弋弓ヨ彡彳艹辶阝⺍忄扌犭氵

奥地	おくチ	the interior; hinterland
奥手	おくて	slow to mature; late to develop
奥の手	おくのて	the last resort; one's best card
奥の間	おくのま	the inner room
奥歯	おくば	*med*. molar
奥床しい	おくゆかしい	graceful; elegant; refined
奥行き	おくゆき	depth; length

420

⑬　｜　｀　丬　ヰ　ヺ　ヺ　ヺ　ヺ　将　将　将　奨

音	奨	ショウ	recommend
熟	奨学金	ショウガクキン	scholarship; fellowship
	奨励	ショウレイ	encouragement; incentive —*v*. encourage

421

奪 ⑭　六　六　木　夲　夲　夲　夲　奞　奞　奪　奪　奪

音	奪	ダツ	plunder; take; seize; wrest; snatch
熟	奪回	ダッカイ	recapture; recovery; retaking —*v*. recapture; recover; retake
	奪還	ダッカン	recapture; recovery; retaking —*v*. recapture; recover; retake
	奪取	ダッシュ	capture; seizure; wrestling —*v*. capture; carry; wrest; seize; snatch
訓	奪う	うばう	*vt*. take by force; seize; wrest; plunder; usurp

422

⑯　六　六　木　夲　夲　夲　奞　奞　奞　奞　奮　奮

音	奮	フン	be enlivened/invigorated
熟	奮起	フンキ	inspiration —*vi*. rouse oneself; be inspired
	奮戦	フンセン	hard fighting —*vi*. fight hard/furiously
	奮然	フンゼン	vigorously; courageously; resolutely
	奮闘	フントウ	struggle; striving —*vi*. struggle/strive for
	奮発	フンパツ	exertion; strenuous efforts; extravagance with money —*vi*. exert oneself; splurge
訓	奮う	ふるう	screw up courage; be inspired; wield; flourish
	奮って	ふるって	voluntarily; willingly; heartily

3 女　おんな／おんなへん　woman

423

女 ③　く　女　女

音	女	ジョ	woman; girl; female
		ニョ	woman; girl
		（ニョウ）	

熟	女医	ジョイ	woman doctor
	女王	ジョオウ	queen
	女系	ジョケイ	female line; maternal relatives
	女子	ジョシ	girl; woman
	女子学生	ジョシガクセイ	female student
	女史	ジョシ	Mrs.; Ms.; Miss
	女児	ジョジ	girl
	女色	ジョショク	amorous involvement with women
	女性	ジョセイ	woman; female
	女性的	ジョセイテキ	feminine; womanish; effeminate
	女装	ジョソウ	women's clothing —*vi.* dress up like a woman; put on women's clothing
	女中	ジョチュウ	maid
	女難	ジョナン	woman trouble
	女優	ジョユウ	actress
	女流	ジョリュウ	women; female
	女流作家	ジョリュウサッカ	woman writer
	女房	ニョウボウ	court lady; one's wife
	女人	ニョニン	woman
訓	女	おんな	woman; female
	女盛り	おんなざかり	peak of womanhood
	女手	おんなで	woman's handwriting
	女	め	woman
	女神	めがみ	goddess

424

妄 ⑥　`　亠　亡　亡　妄　妄

| 音 | 妄 | ボウ | |
| | | モウ | incoherent; reckless; false |

口口土士夂夕大女子宀寸小⺌⺍尢尸山川工己巾干幺广廴廾弋弓⺕彡彳⺾辶阝阝⺌⺖扌犭氵

口口土士夂夕大女子宀寸小ツ冫尢尸山川工己巾干幺广廴廾弋弓ヨ彡彳艹辶阝阝灬忄扌犭氵

熟	妄執	モウシュウ	*Bud.* blind attachment; obsession
	妄信	モウシン	blind acceptance —*v.* accept blindly
	妄想	モウソウ	wild fantasy; delusion —*v.* be deluded
	妄念	モウネン	irrelevant/incoherent thoughts

425

妥 ⑦ 　一 　く 　く 　ワ 　叉 　妥 　妥

音	妥	ダ	moderate; stable; calm
熟	妥協	ダキョウ	compromise; agreement; understanding —*vi.* compromise; make a compromise; reach an agreement
	妥結	ダケツ	compromise settlement; agreement —*vi.* compromise; reach an agreement
	妥当	ダトウ	proper; appropriate; valid —*vi.* apply; hold good
	妥当性	ダトウセイ	propriety; appropriateness; adequacy; pertinence

426

委 ⑧ 　一 　二 　千 　禾 　禾 　禾 　委 　委

音	委	イ	leave to; entrust; minute; detailed
熟	委棄	イキ	relinquishing; abandonment
	委細	イサイ	details; particulars; circumstances
	委縮	イシュク	shrivelling; atrophy —*vi.* shrivel up; waste away
	委譲	イジョウ	transfer —*vt.* transfer to; delegate
	委嘱	イショク	committing with trust and confidence; commission; entrusting; nomination; appointment —*v.* entrust; commission; request; nominate; appoint
	委託	イタク	consignment; trust; charge; commission —*v.* consign; entrust; charge; deposit; put a matter to a person
	委任	イニン	proxy; trust; charge; commission; delegation —*v.* entrust; commission; charge; delegate
訓	委せる	まかせる	*vt.* entrust; leave to; delegate
	委ねる	ゆだねる	*vt.* commit; entrust; delegate
	※委しい	くわしい	details; particulars; circumstances
¥	委員	イイン	member of the committee; commissioner
	委員会	イインカイ	committee; commission
	委託売買	イタクバイバイ	brokerage; agency; transaction

---

427 妻 (8) 一 ㄱ ㅋ ㅌ 争 妻 妻 妻

音	妻	サイ	wife
熟	妻子	サイシ	one's wife and children
	妻女	サイジョ	one's wife and daughter(s); women
	妻帯	サイタイ	married; connubial; matrimonial —*vi.* get married; marry
	妻帯者	サイタイシャ	married man
訓	妻	つま	wife

428 威 (9) ノ 厂 厂 厍 反 反 威 威 威

音	威	イ	power; authority; threat
熟	威圧	イアツ	coercion; overpowering; high-handedness —*v.* restrain or dominate by force; coerce; overpower; overawe
	威圧的	イアツテキ	coercive; overbearing; domineering
	威嚇	イカク	menace; intimidation; threat —*v.* menace; intimidate; threaten
	威厳	イゲン	dignity; majesty; stateliness
	威光	イコウ	influence; authority; power
	威勢	イセイ	vigor; influence; high spirits
	威張る	イばる	*vi.* be proud/haughty; put on airs
	威力	イリョク	power; might; authority; influence
訓	威かす	おどかす	*vt.* threaten; menace; intimidate
	威す	おどす	*vt.* threaten; menace; intimidate

429 姿 (9) 丶 冫 ﾝ 广 ﾅ 次 姿 姿 姿

音	姿	シ	figure
熟	姿勢	シセイ	posture; attitude; profile
	姿態	シタイ	figure; pose
訓	姿	すがた	figure; image; appearance; looks
	姿見	すがたみ	full-length mirror

217

3

口口土士夂夕大 ●女子宀寸小 ⺌尢尸山川工己巾干幺广廴廾弋弓彐彡彳艹辶阝阝䒑忄扌犭氵

430

婆 ⑪ 丶 丷 氵 氵 氵 沪 泸 波 波 波 婆

音	婆	バ	old woman
訓	※婆	ばば	old woman
	※お婆さん	おばあさん	one's grandmother; old woman

431

奴 ⑤ く 夂 女 奴 奴

音	奴	ド	servant
		ヌ	
熟	奴隷	ドレイ	slave
	奴婢	ヌヒ	servant; slave
訓	※奴	やつ	*col.* fellow; chap; guy; he; she
	※奴	やっこ	servant; valet; footman; clown

432

好 ⑥ く 夂 女 女 好 好

音	好	コウ	good; favorable; prefer; like; love
熟	好意	コウイ	goodwill; good wishes; regard; kindness; favor; friendliness
	好感	コウカン	favorable/good impression; good feeling/will
	好機	コウキ	good opportunity/time
	好奇心	コウキシン	curiosity; inquisitiveness
	好色	コウショク	sensuality; amorousness; lust; eroticism
	好人物	コウジンブツ	good-natured person; good fellow; nice chap
	好調	コウチョウ	good condition; favorable; satisfactory; promising
	好都合	コウツゴウ	favorable; convenient; fortunate; prosperous
	好適	コウテキ	suitable; ideal; good best
	好敵手	コウテキシュ	good match; worthy opponent
	好転	コウテン	favorable turn; change for the better; improvement —*vi.* take a favorable turn; change for the better; improve
	好評	コウヒョウ	favorable criticism/comment; public favor
	好物	コウブツ	favorite; delight; favorite food

218

訓	好む	このむ	*vt*. like; fancy; be fond of; love; care for; prefer
	好ましい	このましい	desirable; welcome; nice; good
	好み	このみ	taste; liking; choice; preference
	好き	すき	like; favorite; preference
	好く	すく	*vt*. like; love; be fond of; care for
	※好い	いい（よい）	good; favorable; desirable
¥	好況	コウキョウ	good business conditions; prosperity; boom; brisk market
	好景気	コウケイキ	prosperity; good times; boom
	好材料	コウザイリョウ	good news; favorable factor

433

如 ⑥ く タ 女 如 如 如

音	如	ジョ	the same
		ニョ	like
熟	如才無い	ジョサイない	cautious; clever; adroit; considerate
	如実	ニョジツ	realistically; vividly; graphic
	如来	ニョライ	Buddha
訓	※如何	いかが	how; what

434

妃 ⑥ く タ 女 妃 妃 妃

| 音 | 妃 | ヒ | queen; (married) princess |
| 熟 | 妃殿下 | ヒデンカ | Her Highness |

435

妊 ⑦ く タ 女 妊 妊 妊 妊

音	妊	ニン	conceive
熟	妊産婦	ニンサンプ	pregnant and nursing mothers
	妊娠	ニンシン	conception; pregnancy; gestation — *vi*. conceive; become pregnant
	妊娠中絶	ニンシンチュウゼツ	*med*. abortion; termination of pregnancy
	妊婦	ニンプ	pregnant woman; woman with child
訓	妊む	はらむ	*v*. conceive; become pregnant

口 口 土 士 夂 夕 大 女 子 宀 寸 小 ⺌ ⺌ 尤 尸 山 川 工 己 巾 干 幺 广 廴 廾 弋 弓 ヨ 彡 彳 艹 辶 阝 阝 ⺗ 忄 扌 氵 氵

3

口口土士夂夕大女子宀寸小尢尸山川工己巾干幺广廴廾弋弓彐彡彳艹辶阝阝⺩忄扌犭氵

436

妨 ⑦ 〡 刀 女 女` 妒 妨 妨

音	妨	ボウ	prevent; obstruct; hinder
熟	妨害	ボウガイ	obstruction; disturbance; interference —*v.* obstruct; disturb; interfer
	妨害物	ボウガイブツ	obstacle
訓	妨げる	さまたげる	*vt.* hinder; prevent; obstruct

437

妙 ⑦ 〡 刀 女 妁 奻 妙 妙

音	妙	ミョウ	strange; odd; mystery
熟	妙案	ミョウアン	good idea; ingenious plan
	妙技	ミョウギ	extraordinary skill
	妙手	ミョウシュ	master; expert; virtuoso
	妙味	ミョウミ	delicious taste; charm; exquisite beauty
	妙薬	ミョウヤク	wonder drug
訓	※妙なる	たえなる	exquisite; superb; delicate; charming

438

姉 ⑧ 〡 刀 女 女` 妡 妡 姉 姉

音	姉	シ	elder sister; lady
熟	姉妹	シマイ	sisters
	姉妹都市	シマイトシ	sister city; twin town
訓	姉	あね	one's elder sister
	姉御	あねゴ	one's elder sister; the boss's wife; proprietress; woman boss
	姉さん女房	あねさん ニョウボウ	wife who is older than her husband
	※お姉さん	おねえさん	elder sister; (term of address for a girl older than oneself)

439

始 ⑧ 〡 刀 女 妙 奻 始 始 始

音	始	シ	beginning; start; origin

220

熟	始球式	シキュウシキ	**bas.** opening ceremony of a baseball game in which an honorary guest throws the first ball
	始業	シギョウ	beginning of work or class —**vi.** start work or class
	始業式	シギョウシキ	opening ceremony for school or work
	始終	シジュウ	whole story; from beginning to end; always; constantly; frequently; the beginning and the end
	始祖	シソ	founder; ancestor
	始動	シドウ	starting an engine —**v.** start up an engine
	始発	シハツ	station of origin; first train of the day
	始発駅	シハツエキ	station of origin; first station on a line
	始末	シマツ	ordering; taking care of —**v.** put in order; take care of; come to pass
	始末書	シマツショ	written explanation/apology (for an accident, etc.)
訓	始まり	はじまり	opening; beginning; start
	始まる	はじまる	**vi.** begin; start; date from
	始める	はじめる	**vt.** begin; start; commence
	始め	はじめ	beginning; founding; origin

440

姓 ⑧ 　く　々　女　女　女一　姓　姓　姓

音	姓	ショウ	birth
		セイ	surname
熟	姓名	セイメイ	full name

441

妹 ⑧ 　く　々　女　女　女二　妹　妹　妹

| 音 | 妹 | マイ | younger sister |
| 訓 | 妹 | いもうと | younger sister |

442

姻 ⑨ 　く　々　女　女　妁　妑　妽　姻　姻

| 音 | 姻 | イン | marriage; relative |
| 熟 | 姻戚 | インセキ | relative by marriage |

221

口 口 土 士 夂 夕 大 女 子 宀 寸 小 ⺌ 尢 尸 山 川 工 己 巾 干 幺 广 廴 廾 弋 弓 彐 彡 彳 艹 辶 阝 阝 亠 忄 扌 氵 氵

口口土士夂夕大女子宀寸小业灬尤尸山川工己巾干幺广廴廾弋弓ヨ彡彳艹辶阝丷忄扌氵犭

443

娯 ⑩ く 夕 女 女゛女 娛 娛 娛 娛 娯

| 音 | 娯 | ゴ | amuse oneself |
| 熟 | 娯楽 | ゴラク | amusement; recreation |

444

娠 ⑩ く 夕 女 女゛妒 妒 妮 娠 娠

| 音 | 娠 | シン | pregnant |

445

姫 ⑩ く 夕 女 如 妒 妒 妒 妒 姫 姫

音	姫	キ	princess
訓	姫	ひめ	princess
	姫君	ひめぎみ	princess

446

娘 ⑩ く 夕 女 女゛妒 妒 妒 娘 娘 娘

音	娘	ジョウ	daughter; girl; young woman
訓	娘	むすめ	daughter; girl; young woman
	娘心	むすめごころ	girlish innocence
	娘盛り	むすめざかり	the prime of young womanhood
	娘婿	むすめむこ	son-in-law

447

婚 ⑪ く 夕 女 女゛妒 妒 婚 婚 婚 婚 婚

音	婚	コン	marriage; matrimony; wedlock
熟	婚姻	コンイン	marriage; matrimony; wedlock —*vi.* marry; be married
	婚期	コンキ	marriageable age
	婚約	コンヤク	engagement —*vi.* get engaged
	婚礼	コンレイ	wedding ceremony

448 婦 ⑪

く　乄　女　女ヿ　女ヲ　女ヺ　女ヺ　妒　娟　娟　婦

音	婦	フ	woman; wife
熟	婦警	フケイ	policewoman
	婦女	フジョ	woman
	婦人	フジン	woman; lady
	婦人用	フジンヨウ	for ladies; women's
	婦長	フチョウ	head nurse

449 婿 ⑫

く　乄　女　女゛　女゛　妒　妒　妬　婿　婿　婿　婿

音	婿	セイ	son-in-law
訓	婿	むこ	son-in-law; bridegroom
	婿養子	むこヨウシ	son-in-law taken into the family; adopted son-in-law

450 媒 ⑫

く　乄　女　女゛　妒　妣　妣　妣　媒　媒　媒　媒

音	媒	バイ	intermediation
熟	媒介	バイカイ	agency; intervention; intermediation; matchmaking —*v*. mediate; intervene; act as an agent; matchmake
	媒酌	バイシャク	matchmaking —*v*. arrange a marriage; act as a go-between
	媒酌人	バイシャクニン	matchmaker; go-between
	媒体	バイタイ	medium

451 嫁 ⑬

く　乄　女　女゛　妒　妒　妒　妵　嫁　嫁　嫁　嫁

音	嫁	カ	marry
訓	嫁ぐ	とつぐ	*vi*. marry; be married
	嫁	よめ	bride; daughter-in-law
	嫁入り	よめいり	wedding; matrimony —*vi*. get married; marry into (women only)

口口土士夂夕大女子宀寸小⺍⺌尤尸山川工己巾干幺广廴廾弋弓彐彡彳艹辶阝阝䒑忄扌犭氵

452

嫌 ⑬ く ㄆ 女 女⁻ 女⁼ 妒 妒 婶 婶 嫌 嫌

音	嫌	ケン	hate; dislike; detest
		ゲン	temper; disposition
熟	嫌悪	ケンオ	hated —v. hate; loathe; detest
	嫌疑	ケンギ	suspicion of a crime
訓	嫌	いや	disagreeable; unpleasant; distasteful
	嫌がる	いやがる	*vt.* dislike; be unwilling to do
	嫌気	いやケ	disgust; bearish sentiment
	嫌味	いやミ	sarcasm; catty remarks
	嫌い	きらい	hateful; unpleasant; disagreeable
	嫌う	きらう	*vt.* dislike; hate; detest; loathe

453

嫡 ⑭ く ㄆ 女 女⁻ 女⁼ 妒 妟 妟 嫡 嫡 嫡 嫡

音	嫡	チャク	legitimate child; descendant
熟	嫡子	チャクシ	heir; legitimate son
	嫡出	チャクシュツ	legitimacy
	嫡男	チャクナン	eldest son; heir

454

嬢 ⑯ く ㄆ 女 女⁻ 女⁼ 妒 姉 媷 嫭 嬢 嬢 嬢 嬢

| 音 | 嬢 | ジョウ | girl |
| 訓 | ※嬢 | むすめ | girl; one's daughter |

---

3 子 こ／こへん child

455

子 ③ ㇐ 了 子

| 音 | 子 | シ | child; son; man; Confucius |
| 熟 | 子宮 | シキュウ | *med.* womb; uterus |

	子細	シサイ	details; particulars; reasons; circumstances; meaning
	子爵	シシャク	viscount
	子息	シソク	son
	子孫	シソン	posterity; descendant
	子弟	シテイ	boys; children; younger people
	子葉	ショウ	*bio.* cotyledon
訓	子	こ	child
	子供	こども	child; children
	子分	こブン	follower; henchman
	子煩悩	こボンノウ	fond; doting
	子持ち	こもち	parent
	子守	こもり	baby-sitting
	子役	こヤク	child actor
	※子	ね	the rat (first sign of the Chinese zodiac)
¥	子会社	こガイシャ	subsidiary; affiliated company

456

孔 ④ 　 了 子 孔

音	孔	コウ	hole; Confucius
熟	孔子	コウシ	Confucius
	※孔雀	クジャク	peacock; peahen
訓	※孔	あな	hole

457

字 ⑥ 　ハ 宀 宀 宁 字

音	字	ジ	letter; character
熟	字音	ジオン	the Japanized pronunciation of a Chinese character
	字義	ジギ	meaning of a Chinese character
	字句	ジク	words; phrases; wording; expression; letters and phrases
	字書	ジショ	dictionary
	字体	ジタイ	form of a character; typeface
	字典	ジテン	dictionary
	字引	じびき	dictionary
	字幕	ジマク	movie subtitle
訓	字	あざ	section of a village

3

口口土士夂夕大女子宀寸小⺌

尤尸山川工己巾干幺广廴廾弋弓彐彡彳⻌

阝阝艹宀忄扌氵

458

存 ⑥ 一 ナ ナ 在 存 存

音	存	ソン	be; exist
		ゾン	be; exist
熟	存外	ゾンガイ	unexpectedly; beyond expectations; contrary to expectations
	存在	ソンザイ	existence —v. exist
	存続	ソンゾク	continued existence; duration —v. continue (to exist); endure; last
	存念	ゾンネン	idea; thought; concept
	存分	ゾンブン	to one's heart's content; as much as one wants; without reserve
	存命	ゾンメイ	living —v. be alive
	存立	ソンリツ	existence; substistence —v. exist; subsist

459

孝 ⑦ 一 十 土 耂 耂 考 孝

| 音 | 孝 | コウ | filial piety; obedience to one's parents |
| 熟 | 孝行 | コウコウ | filial piety; obedience to one's parents —vi. be dutiful to one's parents; be a good son/daughter |

460

学 ⑧ 丶 丷 ⺍ ⺍ 兴 学 学 学

音	学	ガク	study; science
熟	学位	ガクイ	academic degree
	学園	ガクエン	school; educational institution
	学業	ガクギョウ	studies; schoolwork
	学芸	ガクゲイ	art and science
	学士	ガクシ	bachelor's degree
	学資	ガクシ	educational fund
	学識	ガクシキ	scholarship; learning
	学者	ガクシャ	scholar; learned person
	学習	ガクシュウ	study; learning —v. study; learn
	学術	ガクジュツ	science; learning
	学生	ガクセイ	student
	学制	ガクセイ	educational system

学説	ガクセツ	theory; doctrine
学長	ガクチョウ	chancellor/president of a university
学徒	ガクト	students and pupils
学童	ガクドウ	schoolchild; pupil
学年	ガクネン	school year; grade
学閥	ガクバツ	clique of alumni
学費	ガクヒ	school expenses; tuition fees
学名	ガクメイ	scientific name
学問	ガクモン	learning and research —*vi.* pursue learning
学友	ガクユウ	schoolmate
学用品	ガクヨウヒン	school supplies
学力	ガクリョク	academic ability
学歴	ガクレキ	school career; educational background
学割	ガクわり	student discounts
学科	ガッカ	school subject; branch of learning
学会	ガッカイ	learned society; academia; meeting of scholars
学界	ガッカイ	academic world; academia
学期	ガッキ	school term
学区	ガック	school precincts
訓 学ぶ	まなぶ	*vt.* learn; study

461

季 ⑧ 　一　二　千　禾　禾　秂　季　季

音 季	キ	season
熟 季刊	キカン	quarterly publication
季節	キセツ	season
季節風	キセツフウ	monsoon

462

孤 ⑨ 　了　了　子　孑　孔　孤　孤　孤

音 孤	コ	orphan; alone; isolated
熟 孤軍奮闘	コグンフントウ	single-handed struggle —*v.* fight alone against all odds; struggle single-handedly
孤児	コジ	orphan
孤児院	コジイン	orphanage
孤島	コトウ	solitary island
孤独	コドク	solitude; loneliness; isolation
孤立	コリツ	isolation —*v.* stand alone; be in isolation

孫 ⑩　 ⁷ ⁷ ⁷ ⁷ ⁷ 孫 孫 孫 孫 孫

音	孫	ソン	descendants
訓	孫	まご	grandchild
	孫子	まごこ	children and grandchildren; descendants

---

3 宀　うかんむり　*u* (katakana)

安 ⑥　 ' ' 宀 安 安 安

音	安	アン	safe; stable; easy; peaceful; inexpensive
熟	安易	アンイ	easy; simple; straightforward; easygoing; carefree
	安価	アンカ	cheapness; low price
	安閑	アンカン	leisure; idleness
	安産	アンザン	easy birth/delivery —*v.* have an easy birth; give birth easily
	安住	アンジュウ	peaceful living —*vi.* live in peace
	安心	アンシン	peace of mind; relief; safety —*vi.* feel at rest/relieved/assured
	安静	アンセイ	free from activity or labor; rest; quiet; repose
	安全	アンゼン	free from harm or risk; safety; security
	安全第一	アンゼンダイイチ	safety first
	安全地帯	アンゼンチタイ	safety zone
	安息	アンソク	repose; rest —*vi.* rest; take a break
	安泰	アンタイ	peace; tranquillty; safety; security
	安置	アンチ	installation —*v.* install; enshrine
	安着	アンチャク	comfort; safe arrival —*vi.* arrive safely
	安直	アンチョク	inexpensive
	安定	アンテイ	stability; stabilization; steadiness —*vi.* be stable/steady/balanced/settled
	安定性	アンテイセイ	stability
	安否	アンピ	safety; welfare
	安眠	アンミン	quiet/restful sleep —*vi.* sleep well; have a good sleep
	安楽死	アンラクシ	painless death; mercy killing; euthanasia
訓	安い	やすい	cheap; easy; calm

安上がり	やすあがり	doing something cheaply
安らか	やすらか	peaceful; tranquil; calm
安らぎ	やすらぎ	peace of mind; serenity; calmness
安んじる	やすんじる	*v.* be reassured; have peace of mind; be contented

¥ 安全保障 アンゼンホショウ security
（安保）（アンポ）

安定市況	アンテイシキョウ	stable market
安値	やすね	low price/rate; low level

465

宇 ⑥ 　 ′ ′′ 宀 宀 宇 宇

音	宇	ウ	expanse; universe; cosmos; space; eaves; roof
熟	宇宙	ウチュウ	the universe; outer space
	宇宙船	ウチュウセン	spaceship; spacecraft
	宇宙飛行士	ウチュウヒコウシ	astronaut; spaceman

466

守 ⑥ 　 ′ ′′ 宀 宀 守 守

音	守	シュ	defend
		（ス）	protect
熟	守衛	シュエイ	guard; doorman; doorkeeper
	守護	シュゴ	protection —*v.* protect; guard
	守護神	シュゴシン	guardian diety
	守勢	シュセイ	defensive
	守銭奴	シュセンド	miser
	守備	シュビ	defense —*v.* defend; guard
訓	守る	まもる	*vt.* defend; protect; keep one's word; abide by
	守り	まもり	defense; protection; safeguard
	守	もり	nursemaid

467

宅 ⑥ 　 ′ ′′ 宀 宀 宀 宅

音	宅	タク	home; house; residence; our home; my husband
熟	宅地	タクチ	building lot; land for housing; residential land

229

3

口
口
土
士
夂
夕
大
女
子
宀 ●
寸
小
⺌
⺌
尢
尸
山
川
工
己
巾
干
幺
广
廴
廾
弋
弓
ヨ
彡
彳
⺾
⻌
阝
阝
⺍
忄
扌
犭
氵

口口土士夕夕大女子宀寸小⺌⺍尢尸山川工己巾干幺广廴廾弋弓ヨ彑彡彳⺾辶阝⻏⺕忄扌氵

完 ⑦

`丶 冖 宀 宀 宇 宇 完`

音	完	カン	complete; perfect
熟	完結	カンケツ	completion; conclusion; termination —*v*. complete; conclude; finish; end
	完済	カンサイ	full payment of debts —*vt*. pay off one's all debts
	完勝	カンショウ	complete victory —*vi*. defeat decisively; win a landslide victory
	完遂	カンスイ	successful execution; accomplishment —*v*. complete; carry through
	完成	カンセイ	completion; accomplishment; perfection —*v*. complete; conclude; finish; accomplish
	完全	カンゼン	perfection; completeness
	完投	カントウ	*bas*. pitching a whole game —*vi*. pitch a whole game
	完納	カンノウ	full payment —*v*. pay in full
	完敗	カンパイ	complete defeat —*vi*. suffer a complete defeat
	完備	カンビ	perfection; completion —*v*. be perfect/complete
	完封	カンプウ	complete blockade —*v*. blockade
	完璧	カンペキ	perfection
	完了	カンリョウ	completion; conclusion —*v*. complete; conclude
訓	※完うする	まっとうする	*vt*. accomplish; fulfill; complete

官 ⑧

`丶 冖 宀 宀 宁 官 官 官`

音	官	カン	official; government; senses
熟	官軍	カングン	government forces; Imperial Army
	官公庁	カンコウチョウ	government and municipal offices
	官舎	カンシャ	official residence
	官職	カンショク	government/official post
	官製	カンセイ	government manufacture
	官庁	カンチョウ	government office
	官邸	カンテイ	residence of a high official or Cabinet minister
	官能	カンノウ	senses; sensual
	官能的	カンノウテキ	sensual
	官報	カンポウ	official gazette
	官吏	カンリ	government official; civil servant
	官僚	カンリョウ	bureaucracy

実 ⑧

`ヽ ハ 宀 宀 宀 宣 実 実`

音	実	ジツ	substance; sincerity; truth; reality; actual
熟	実印	ジツイン	registered seal
	実益	ジツエキ	practical use; usefulness; actual profit
	実演	ジツエン	stage show; demonstration
	実家	ジッカ	one's parents' home
	実害	ジツガイ	actual harm
	実学	ジツガク	practical science; studies of use in everyday life
	実感	ジッカン	actual feeling; atmosphere —v. realize
	実技	ジツギ	actual technique; practical skills; technical skill
	実況	ジッキョウ	real/actual condition
	実況放送	ジッキョウ ホウソウ	live broadcasting
	実兄	ジッケイ	one's real brother
	実刑	ジッケイ	prison sentence
	実権	ジッケン	real power; actual control
	実験	ジッケン	experimentation; experiment; test —v. experiment
	実験室	ジッケンシツ	laboratory
	実験的	ジッケンテキ	experimental
	実現	ジツゲン	realization; materialization —v. be realized; materialize
	実行	ジッコウ	practice; action; execution —v. carry out; put into practice; execute
	実行可能	ジッコウカノウ	practical; feasible
	実際	ジッサイ	in practice; fact; truth; reality; actuality; really; indeed
	実在	ジツザイ	real/actual existence —vi. exist
	実在論	ジツザイロン	realism
	実子	ジッシ	one's real/own child
	実施	ジッシ	execution; enforcement —v. put into effect/operation/force
	実質	ジッシツ	substance; essence
	実写	ジッシャ	photograph or movie of actual scenery or people —v. photograph or film actual scenery or people
	実社会	ジッシャカイ	the real world
	実習	ジッシュウ	practical training —v. practice; have training
	実証	ジッショウ	proof —v. prove; demonstrate
	実情	ジツジョウ	actual conditions
	実数	ジッスウ	*math*. real/actual number

口 口 土 士 夕 大 女 子 宀 寸 小 ⺌ ⺌ 尢 尸 山 川 工 己 巾 干 幺 广 廴 廾 弋 弓 ∃ 彡 彳 艹 辶 阝 阝 ⺍ 忄 扌 氵 冫

口口土士夂夕大女子宀寸小⺌⺍尢尸山川工己巾干幺广廴廾弋弓彐彡彳⺾辶阝⺹忄扌犭氵

実績	ジッセキ	actual results; achievements
実践	ジッセン	practice —v. practice
実戦	ジッセン	actual fighting/service; combat
実測	ジッソク	actual survey/measurement —v. measure; survey
実存	ジツゾン	existence —vi. exist
実存主義	ジツゾンシュギ	existentialism
実体	ジッタイ	substance; solid
実態	ジッタイ	actual condition
実弾	ジツダン	live cartridge/ammunition
実地	ジッチ	in actual practice; the scene (of a crime)
実直	ジッチョク	honest; steady; conscientious
実費	ジッピ	actual expenses
実否	ジッピ	true or not
実父	ジップ	one's real/own father
実物	ジツブツ	the real thing; the genuine article; real life
実物大	ジツブツダイ	actual/life/full size
実母	ジツボ	one's real/own mother
実名	ジツメイ	one's real name
実用	ジツヨウ	practical use
実用化	ジツヨウカ	practicality —v. put a thing to practical use
実用主義	ジツヨウシュギ	pragmatism
実用的	ジツヨウテキ	practical
実用品	ジツヨウヒン	daily necessities; domestic articles
実利	ジツリ	utility; actual benefit
実利的	ジツリテキ	utilitarian
実力	ジツリョク	real ability; force; arms
実力行使	ジツリョクコウシ	use of force
実力者	ジツリョクシャ	influential person; powerful figure
実例	ジツレイ	instance; example
実録	ジツロク	true record
実話	ジツワ	true story; story taken from real life
訓 実	み	seed; berry; fruit; nut; ingredients; content; substance
実る	みのる	vi. bear fruit; bear fruitful results
実り	みのり	ripening; fruitful; productive
¥ 実株	ジツかぶ	spot stocks/shares; real stock
実業家	ジツギョウカ	business man
実業界	ジツギョウカイ	business world/circles/community
実行委員	ジッコウイイン	executive committee
実行予算	ジッコウヨサン	working budget
実質所得	ジッシツショトク	real income
実質賃金	ジッシツチンギン	real wages

実収	ジッシュウ	net income/profit
実地訓練	ジッチクンレン	on-the-job training
実働時間	ジツドウジカン	actual working hours
実物取引	ジツブツとりひき	spot/cash transaction
実務	ジツム	practical business affairs
実力主義	ジツリョクシュギ	merit system

471 宗 ⑧ ` 丷 宀 宀 宀 宇 宗 宗

音	宗	シュウ	sect; religion; denomination
		ソウ	founder; head; leader
熟	宗教	シュウキョウ	religion
	宗教家	シュウキョウカ	man of religion
	宗旨	シュウシ	tenets; doctrine; sect; religion
	宗祖	シュウソ	founder of a sect
	宗徒	シュウト	believer; adherent
	宗派	シュウハ	sect; denomination
	宗家	ソウケ	head family; originator
	宗匠	ソウショウ	master; teacher

472 宙 ⑧ ` 丷 宀 宀 宀 宙 宙 宙

音	宙	チュウ	sky; air; space
熟	宙返り	チュウがえり	somersault; looping the loop —*vi.* turn a somersault; turn loops

473 定 ⑧ ` 丷 宀 宀 宁 宇 定 定

音	定	テイ	fixed; constant; regular
		ジョウ	
熟	定規	ジョウギ	ruler; scale
	定圧	テイアツ	constant pressure
	定員	テイイン	capacity; seating/passenger capacity; regular staff
	定期	テイキ	fixed period
	定期券	テイキケン	pass; season ticket

233

口
口
土
士
夂
夕
大
女
子
宀
寸
小
⺌
⺍
尢
尸
山
川
工
己
巾
干
幺
广
廴
廾
弋
弓
彐
彡
彳
⺘
⻌
阝
阝
⺮
忄
扌
氵
犭

	定期船	テイキセン	liner
	定義	テイギ	definition —*v.* define
	定休日	テイキュウび	regular holiday
	定形	テイケイ	fixed form; regular shape
	定型	テイケイ	type; definate form
	定型的	テイケイテキ	typical; stereotyped
	定見	テイケン	definite view; firm conviction
	定限	テイゲン	fixed limit; limits; limitation; restriction —*v.* limit; restrict; confine
	定刻	テイコク	appointed hour; scheduled time
	定時	テイジ	regular/fixed time
	定住	テイジュウ	settlement; domicile —*v.* settle down; reside
	定住者	テイジュウシャ	permanent resident; settler
	定食	テイショク	set meal
	定数	テイスウ	fixed number; constant; invariable; fate
	定説	テイセツ	established theory
	定足数	テイソクスウ	quorum
	定置	テイチ	fixing in a set position —*vt.* fix; set; station
	定着	テイチャク	fixing; fastening; fixation; anchoring —*v.* fix; fasten; anchor; take root
	定点	テイテン	fixed point
	定年	テイネン	age limit; retirement age
	定評	テイヒョウ	established reputation; fixed opinion
	定本	テイホン	standard/authentic text
	定理	テイリ	theorem
	定率	テイリツ	fixed rate
	定量	テイリョウ	fixed quantity; measurement; dose —*v.* measure
	定例	テイレイ	established usage; precedent
訓	定まる	さだまる	*vi.* be decided/determined/fixed/settled
	定める	さだめる	*vt.* decide; determine; appoint; set; lay down; prescribe
	定か	さだか	certain; fixed
¥	定価	テイカ	fixed/marked/labled/list price
	定額	テイガク	fixed/required amount; flat sum
	定額貯金	テイガクチョキン	fixed amount; savings; fixed deposit
	定款	テイカン	articles of association
	定期預金	テイキヨキン	fixed term deposit; time deposit
	定収	テイシュウ	fixed income
	定職	テイショク	regular occupation; fixed employment
	定率法	テイリツホウ	fixed rate method

474

宝 ⑧ 　ヽ ′ 宀 宀 宀 宇 宝 宝

音	宝	ホウ	treasure
熟	宝玉	ホウギョク	jewel; gem; precious stone
	宝庫	ホウコ	treasure house
	宝石	ホウセキ	jewel; gem; precious stone
	宝典	ホウテン	valued/useful book; book of Buddhist sutras
	宝刀	ホウトウ	treasured sword
	宝物	ホウモツ	treasure
訓	宝	たから	treasure
	宝籤	たからくじ	lottery; raffle
	宝島	たからじま	treasure island
	宝物	たからもの	treasure

475

宣 ⑨ 　ヽ ′ 宀 宀 宀 宁 官 宣 宣

音	宣	セン	declare; edict; announce
熟	宣教師	センキョウシ	missionary
	宣言	センゲン	declaration; statement —v. declare; state
	宣告	センコク	pronouncement; sentence; verdict —v. pronounce; sentence; give a verdict
	宣誓	センセイ	oath; vow; pledge —v. make an oath; vow; pledge
	宣戦	センセン	declaration of war —vi. declare war
	宣伝	センデン	propaganda; advertising; publicity —v. propagate; advertise; publicize
訓	※宣べる	のべる	vt. state; declare

476

客 ⑨ 　ヽ ′ 宀 宀 宀 タ 突 客 客

音	客	キャク (カク)	guest; visitor; visiting; traveler; customer; client; the past
熟	客死	カクシ (キャクシ)	dying away from home; dying in a foreign country —vi. die away from home; die overseas
	客員教授	キャクイン キョウジュ	visiting/guest professor
	客受け	キャクうけ	customer appeal

口 口 土 士 夂 夕 大 女 子 宀 • 寸 小 ⺌ ⼮ 尢 尸 山 川 工 己 巾 干 幺 广 廴 廾 弋 弓 彐 彡 彳 艹 辶 阝 阝 ⺍ 忄 扌 氵 犭

3

口 口 土 士 夂 夕 大 女 子 宀 寸 小 ⺌ ⺌ 尢 尸 山 川 工 己 巾 干 幺 广 廴 廾 弋 弓 ⺕ 彡 彳 艹 辶 阝 阝 亠 忄 扌 氵

	客室	キャクシツ	guest room
	客車	キャクシャ	passenger vehicle; coach; carriage
	客商売	キャクショウバイ	service industry
	客筋	キャクすじ	quality of clientele
	客席	キャクセキ	audience seat
	客船	キャクセン	passenger vessel/liner
	客引き	キャクひき	barker —*vi.* pull in/attract customers
	客間	キャクま	drawing room; parlor; guest room
	客観	キャッカン	object (in philosophy)
	客観的	キャッカンテキ	objective
¥	客注	キャクチュウ	customer order

477 室 ⑨

' 宀 宀 宀 宔 宔 室 室 室

音	室	シツ	room; wife; concubine
熟	室温	シツオン	room temperature
	室外	シツガイ	outside the room
	室内	シツナイ	inside the room
	室内楽	シツナイガク	chamber music
訓	室	むろ	cellar; hot house; drying room
	室町	むろまち	*hist.* Muromachi period/culture (1338-1573)

478 宜 ⑧

' 宀 宀 宁 宜 宜 宜 宜

音	宜	ギ	right; good; suitable
訓	*宜しい	よろしい	good; suitable; right
	*宜しく	よろしく	well; suitably; properly; send one's best regards

479 宴 ⑩

' 宀 宀 宀 宊 宴 宴 宴 宴

音	宴	エン	banquet
熟	宴会	エンカイ	feast; banquet; social party
	宴席	エンセキ	dinner party; banquet
訓	*宴	うたげ	party; banquet; feast

家 ⑩　` ` ⼧ ⼧ ⼧ ⼧ 宇 宇 家 家 家

音	家	カ	house; family
		ケ	house; family
熟	家屋	カオク	house
	家業	カギョウ	one's trade or business
	家具	カグ	furniture
	家系	カケイ	family line; lineage
	家計	カケイ	household economy; housekeeping expenses
	家財	カザイ	household goods
	家事	カジ	housework
	家臣	カシン	*hist*. retainer/vassal (Edo period)
	家政	カセイ	housekeeping
	家政婦	カセイフ	housekeeper
	家族	カゾク	family
	家畜	カチク	domestic animals
	家庭	カテイ	home; household; family
	家伝	カデン	handed down from father to son; hereditary
	家内	カナイ	family; one's wife
	家風	カフウ	family custom
	家宝	カホウ	heirloom
	家名	カメイ	family name
	家老	カロウ	*hist*. chief/principal retainer (Edo period)
	家来	ケライ	subordinates loyal to a lord; vassal; retinue
訓	家	いえ	house; home; ancestry
	家柄	いえがら	birth; status
	家主	いえぬし (やぬし)	landlady; landlord; houseowner
	家元	いえもと	*hist*. the head of a school (of a traditional art)
	家屋敷	いえやしき	*hist*. estate; mansion
	家	や	house
	家賃	やチン	rent for a house, apartment, etc.

害 ⑩　` ` ⼧ ⼧ 宀 宀 宇 宇 害 害

音	害	ガイ	harm; damage
熟	害する	ガイする	*vt*. injure; harm; hurt; impair

口口土士夂夕大女子宀寸小⺌⺍尢尸山川工己巾干幺广廴廾弋弓彐彡彳艹辶阝阝兰忄扌犭氵

害悪	ガイアク	evil; vice
害虫	ガイチュウ	harmful/noxious insect
害毒	ガイドク	evil influence; evil; harm

482

宮 ⑩   ヽ ⸌ 宀 宀 宀 宀 宀 宮 宮 宮

音	宮	キュウ	palace; imperial dwelling; shrine
		グウ	
		（ク）	
熟	宮城	キュウジョウ	imperial palace
	宮廷	キュウテイ	court; palace
	宮殿	キュウデン	palace
	宮内庁	クナイチョウ	Imperial Household Agency
訓	宮	みや	(Shinto) shrine; imperial prince

483

宰 ⑩   ヽ ⸌ 宀 宀 宀 宀 宰 宰 宰 宰

音	宰	サイ	govern; minister; control; supervise
熟	宰相	サイショウ	prime minister
	宰領	サイリョウ	supervision; superintendence; supervisor; superintendent —*v.* supervise; oversee; organize

484

宵 ⑩   ヽ ⸌ 宀 宀 宀 宀 宵 宵 宵

音	宵	ショウ	evening
訓	宵	よい	early evening
	宵の口	よいのくち	early evening
	宵闇	よいやみ	dusk; twilight

485

容 ⑩   ヽ ⸌ 宀 宀 宀 容 容 容 容 容

音	容	ヨウ	form; appearance; content
熟	容易	ヨウイ	easy; simple
	容器	ヨウキ	vessel; container

容疑	ヨウギ	suspicion (of a crime)
容疑者	ヨウギシャ	suspect
容姿	ヨウシ	face and figure; looks; appearances
容赦	ヨウシャ	pardon; mercy; forgiveness —*v.* pardon; forgive
容色	ヨウショク	features; looks; personal appearance
容積	ヨウセキ	capacity; volume
容体	ヨウダイ	condition (of an illness)
容認	ヨウニン	admission; approval; acceptance —*v.* admit; approve; accept
容貌	ヨウボウ	looks; personal appearance
容量	ヨウリョウ	capacity; volume
訓 ＊容れる	いれる	*vt.* put/let in; admit; accept

486

寄 ⑪ 　 ' 宀 宀 宀 宀 宀 宇 宇 宇 宇 寄

音	寄	キ	call at; depend on; approach; contribute; donation
熟	寄港	キコウ	port call —*vi.* call at port
	寄稿	キコウ	newspaper/magazine contributor —*vi.* contribute to a newspaper; write for a magazine
	寄宿舎	キシュクシャ	dormitory
	寄食	キショク	dependence —*vi.* sponge off one friends or relatives
	寄進	キシン	donation; contribution —*vt.* make a donation
	寄生	キセイ	parasitism —*vi.* be parasitic; be a parasite
	寄贈	キゾウ	presentation; donation; gift —*v.* present; donate; make a gift
	寄付	キフ	contribution; donation —*v.* contribute; donate
	寄与	キヨ	contribution; services —*v.* contribute; render services
	寄留	キリュウ	sojourn; temporary residence —*vi.* sojourn; reside temporarily
訓	寄る	よる	*vi.* draw near; drop in; come together; stop at a place
	寄せる	よせる	*v.* allow (a person); put (a thing) aside; send (a letter); be dependent on (a person); contribute an article (to a magazine)
	寄り合い	よりあい	meeting; assembly; gathering
	寄り道	よりみち	dropping in on the way —*vi.* drop in on the way
	＊寄席	よせ	variety entertainment/show
¥	寄りつき	よりつき	open; opening price; opening of the session/market

口口土士夂夕大女子宀寸小⺌⺍尤尸山川工己巾干幺广廴廾弋弓彐彡彳�…辶阝阝⺹⺾忄扌犭氵

寂 ⑪ 　 丶 丷 宀 宀 宀 宀 宀 宇 宋 宋 宋 宋 寂

音	寂	ジャク（セキ）	lonely
熟	寂然	セキゼン（ジャクネン）	loneliness; desolation; seclusion
	寂寞	セキバク	solitude; loneliness; desolation
	寂寥	セキリョウ	loneliness; desolation
訓	寂しい	さびしい	lonely; sad; deserted; empty
	寂れる	さびれる	*vi.* decline; be deserted; become desolate
	寂	さび	mellow; seasoned; grace; aged beauty

宿 ⑪ 　 丶 丷 宀 宀 宀 宀 宀 宿 宿 宿 宿

音	宿	シュク	inn; stay
熟	宿縁	シュクエン	destiny; fate
	宿願	シュクガン	long-cherished desire; dream
	宿舎	シュクシャ	dormitory; housing; lodgings; accomodations
	宿題	シュクダイ	homework; assignment
	宿直	シュクチョク	night duty
	宿敵	シュクテキ	old foe; archenemy
	宿泊	シュクハク	lodging —*vi.* lodge
	宿命	シュクメイ	fate; destiny
	宿命論	シュクメイロン	fatalism
訓	宿	やど	inn; hotel; lodgings; shelter
	宿る	やどる	*vi.* dwell; live; stay; lodge; harbor
	宿す	やどす	*vt.* be pregnant; harbor; give lodgings to
	宿帳	やどチョウ	hotel register
	宿賃	やどチン	hotel bill
	宿無し	やどなし	homeless person; vagabond; tramp
	宿屋	やどや	inn; hotel

密 ⑪ 　 丶 丷 宀 宀 宀 宓 宓 宓 宓 密 密

音	密	ミツ	close; dense; crowded; minute; fine; secret

熟	密画	ミツガ	detailed drawing
	密会	ミッカイ	clandestine meeting —*vi.* meet secretly; have a secret rendezvous
	密議	ミツギ	secret conference/consultation
	密航	ミッコウ	stow away; secret passage on a ship —*vi.* stowaway
	密行	ミッコウ	prowling —*v.* prowl about; go secretly
	密告	ミッコク	secret information —*v.* provide secret information
	密告者	ミッコクシャ	informer; betrayer
	密旨	ミッシ	secret orders
	密事	ミツジ	secret
	密室	ミッシツ	secret/locked room
	密集	ミッシュウ	crowd —*vi.* mass together
	密書	ミッショ	secret written message
	密生	ミッセイ	thick/luxurious growth —*vi.* grow thick/luxuriantly
	密接	ミッセツ	close; intimate —*vi.* be close/intimate
	密造	ミツゾウ	illegal manufacture —*v.* manufacture illegally
	密談	ミツダン	secret talk —*vi.* take part in secret conversations
	密着	ミッチャク	sticking; adherence —*vi.* stick/adhere to
	密通	ミッツウ	adultery; secret relationship —*vi.* commit adultery; have an affair
	密偵	ミッテイ	spy; undercover agent
	密度	ミツド	density
	密入国	ミツニュウコク	illegal immigration —*vi.* enter a country illegally
	密売	ミツバイ	illicit sale; smuggling; bootlegging —*v.* smuggle; bootleg
	密封	ミップウ	sealed up/tight —*v.* seal up/tight
	密閉	ミッペイ	shut tight —*v.* seal airtight
	密約	ミツヤク	secret agreement —*vi.* make a secret agreement
	密輸	ミツユ	smuggling; contraband —*v.* smuggle
	密猟	ミツリョウ	poaching —*v.* poach
	密漁	ミツリョウ	fish poaching —*v.* poach fish
	密林	ミツリン	jungle; dense forest

490

寒 ⑫　　、 䒑 宀 宀 宀 宀 审 宲 実 実 寒 寒

音	寒	カン	cold; poor
熟	寒気	カンキ	cold weather

241

3

口
口
土
士
夂
夕
大
女
子
宀
寸
小
⺌
⺍
尢
尸
山
川
工
己
巾
干
幺
广
廴
廾
弋
弓
彐
彡
彳
艹
辶
阝
亠
忄
扌
氵

寒暑	カンショ	heat and cold; temperature
寒村	カンソン	remote/lonely village
寒帯	カンタイ	frigid zone; arctic regions
寒暖	カンダン	hot and cold; temperature
寒暖計	カンダンケイ	thermometer
寒中	カンチュウ	midwinter; depth of winter
寒波	カンパ	cold wave
寒流	カンリュウ	cold current
寒冷	カンレイ	coldness; chill
訓 寒い	さむい	cold; chilly
寒気	さむケ	chill; cold fit; rigor
寒さ	さむさ	coldness; the cold

491

 富 ⑫　　、　丶　宀　宀　宀　宀　宁　宫　宫　富　富　富

音 富	フ	wealth; rich; affluent; ample
	（フウ）	
熟 富貴	フウキ	wealth and rank
富強	フキョウ	rich and powerful (country)
富鉱	フコウ	rich ore/deposit
富豪	フゴウ	rich man; millionaire
富国	フコク	rich country
富農	フノウ	wealthy farmer
富裕	フユウ	rich; wealthy; affluent
富有	フユウ	wealthy; affluent; rich
富力	フリョク	wealth; resources
訓 富	とみ	wealth; resources; assets
富む	とむ	*vi*. be rich; abound in

492

 寛 ⑬　　、　丶　宀　宀　宀　宀　宵　宵　宵　窨　寛　寛

音 寛	カン	tolerant; broad-minded; lenient
熟 寛大	カンダイ	generosity; broad-mindedness; liberality; leniency
寛容	カンヨウ	magnanimity; tolerance; forbearance
訓 ※寛ぐ	くつろぐ	*vi*. be at ease; relax
※寛い	ひろい	generous; broad-minded; magnanimous

242

493 寝 ⑬ 　 丶 丶 宀 宀 宀 宀 宀 宀 宀 宀 寢 寝

音	寝	シン	sleep
熟	寝具	シング	bedclothes; bedding
	寝室	シンシツ	bedroom
	寝食	シンショク	eating and sleeping
	寝台	シンダイ	bed; sleeping berth
	寝台車	シンダイシャ	sleeping car; sleeper
訓	寝る	ねる	*vi.* lie down; sleep
	寝返り	ねがえり	tossing and turning (in one's sleep); betrayal
	寝顔	ねがお	face of a sleeping person
	寝かす	ねかす	*vt.* put to bed; lay down
	寝言	ねごと	talking in one's sleep
	寝床	ねどこ	bed
	寝冷え	ねびえ	catching cold (in one's sleep) —*vi.* catch cold (in one's sleep)
	寝坊	ねボウ	oversleeping; late riser —*vi.* oversleep; get up late
	寝間着	ねまき	nightclothes; nightgown; nightdress; pajamas

494 寡 ⑭ 　 宀 宀 宀 宀 帘 宕 宜 宣 寊 寊 寡 寡

音	寡	カ	few; widow
熟	寡少	カショウ	little; few
	寡婦	カフ	widow
	寡聞	カブン	ill-informed; little knowledge
	寡黙	カモク	speaking few words; taciturn
訓	寡	やもめ	widow
	＊寡ない	すくない	not many; a few

495 察 ⑭ 　 宀 宀 宀 宀 宀 宀 宊 宨 宨 寠 寠 察

音	察	サツ	investigate; guess
熟	察する	サッする	*vt.* investigate; guess
	察知	サッチ	perception; sense —*v.* perceive; sense; gather; infer

243

口口土士夂夕大女子宀寸小⺌尤尸山川工己巾干幺广廴廾弋弓彐彡彳艸辶阝⺍忄扌犭氵

496

寧 ⑭

宀 宀 宧 宧 宧 宁 寍 寍 寍 寍 寧 寧

| 音 | 寧 | ネイ | peaceful; calm |

497

審 ⑮

宀 宀 宧 宧 宋 宋 宋 宋 寀 審 審 審

音	審	シン	judge
熟	審議	シンギ	deliberation; discussion —v. deliberate; discuss
	審査	シンサ	judgment; examination; inspection —v. examine; inspect; screen; judge
	審判	シンパン	referee; judgment —v. referee; umpire; judge

498

寮 ⑮

宀 宀 宀 宎 宎 宎 宷 宷 寮 寮 寮 寮

音	寮	リョウ	dormitory; hotel
熟	寮生	リョウセイ	dormitory student; boarder
	寮長	リョウチョウ	dormitory director

3 寸 すん inch

499

寸 ③

一 寸 寸

音	寸	スン	*sun* (unit of length, approx. 3.03 cm); small; tiny
熟	寸暇	スンカ	moment's leisure; spare moment
	寸劇	スンゲキ	short play; sketch; skit
	寸志	スンシ	small present (small amount of money)
	寸前	スンゼン	just/right/immediately before
	寸断	スンダン	*vt.* tear/cut to pieces
	寸評	スンピョウ	short review; brief comment
	寸分	スンブン	bit; little
	寸法	スンポウ	measure; measurements; dimensions; plan

3

口口土士夂夕大女子宀寸小⺌⺍尢尸山川工己巾干幺广廴廾弋弓ヨ彡彳艹辶阝⺍忄扌氵氵

500

寺 ⑥ 一 十 土 土 寺 寺

音	寺	ジ	temple
熟	寺院	ジイン	temple
	寺社	ジシャ	shrines and temples
訓	寺	てら	Buddhist temple

501

寿 ⑦ 一 二 三 丰 丰 寿 寿

音	寿	ジュ	age; congratulations
熟	寿命	ジュミョウ	life; life-span; life expectancy
	※寿司	スシ	*sushi* (vinegared rice and raw fish)
訓	寿	ことぶき	congratulations; happiness; long life

502

対 ⑦ 丶 亠 ナ 文 文 対 対

音	対	タイ ツイ	set; couple; response; oppose; face
熟	対する	タイする	*vi.* be against; oppose; face
	対応	タイオウ	correspondence; equivalence; counterpart —*vi.* correspond to; be equivalent to; tackle; deal with; cope
	対角線	タイカクセン	diagonal (line)
	対決	タイケツ	confrontation; face-to-face meeting —*vi.* confront; have a showdown; stand face-to-face
	対向	タイコウ	opposite
	対抗	タイコウ	opposition; confrontation; antagonism —*vi.* oppose; confront; antagonize
	対策	タイサク	countermeasure; counterplan; countermove
	対処	タイショ	coping; dealing; tackling —*vi.* cope/deal with; tackle
	対称	タイショウ	symmetry *gram.* the second person
	対象	タイショウ	object; subject; target
	対照	タイショウ	contrast; comparison —*v.* contrast; compare
	対戦	タイセン	competition —*vi.* compete; oppose

245

3

口口土士夂夕大女子宀寸小ﾘｲ・尢尸山川工己巾干幺广廴廾弋弓ヨ彡彳艹辶阝丷忄扌犭彡

対談	タイダン	talk; conversation; dialog; interview —*vi*. talk/converse with; have an interview with
対等	タイトウ	equality; equal footing; equal terms; parity
対比	タイヒ	contrast; comparison; opposition; analogy —*v*. contrast; compare; oppose; analogize
対面	タイメン	interview; meeting —*vi*. interview; meet; see; have an interview
対立	タイリツ	opposition; confrontation; contrast —*vi*. be opposed/confronted with
対話	タイワ	dialog; conversation —*vi*. have a dialog/conversation with
対句	ツイク	antithesis; parallelism
対語	ツイゴ	*gram*. antonym

503

一 厂 厂 币 甫 吏 車 専 専
⑨

音	専	セン	solely; exclusive
熟	専横	センオウ	despotism; tyranny
	専科	センカ	special course (of study)
	専業	センギョウ	profession; main occupation
	専攻	センコウ	one's major (at university, etc.) —*v*. major in (biochemistry, etc.)
	専従	センジュウ	exclusive obedience; full-time employment
	専心	センシン	devotion; concentration; undivided attention —*vi*. be devoted; concentrate; give one's undivided attention
	専制	センセイ	absolutism; autocracy
	専制政治	センセイセイジ	absolute/despotic government
	専任	センニン	full-time
	専念	センネン	close/undivided attention —*vi*. give one's close/undivided attention
	専売	センバイ	monopoly —*v*. monopolize
	専務	センム	managing director
	専門	センモン	specialty
	専門家	センモンカ	person specialized in certain fields
	専門店	センモンテン	specialty store
	専有	センユウ	exclusive possession; monopoly —*v*. possess exclusively; monopolize
	専用	センヨウ	exclusive use; private/personal use —*v*. have exclusive use of
訓	専ら	もっぱら	exclusively
¥	専売特許	センバイトッキョ	patent

封 ⑨

一 十 土 𡈼 丰 圭 圭 封 封

音	封	フウ	seal
		ホウ	fief
熟	封じる	フウじる	*vt.* seal; blockade; silence
	封印	フウイン	seal —*v.* seal (a letter)
	封緘	フウカン	seal an envelope
	封切り	フウきり	(film/movie) release; opening a letter
	封鎖	フウサ	blockade; freezing —*v.* blockade; block; freeze
	封殺	フウサツ	*bas.* force out —*vt.* force out
	封書	フウショ	sealed letter
	封筒	フウトウ	envelope
	封入	フウニュウ	enclosure (in a letter) —*v.* enclose (in a letter)
	封建	ホウケン	feudalism
	封建時代	ホウケンジダイ	feudal age
	封建社会	ホウケンシャカイ	feudal society
	封建制度	ホウケンセイド	feudalism
	封建的	ホウケンテキ	feudal

射 ⑩

' イ 勹 甸 甸 身 身 身 射 射

音	射	シャ	archery; fire
熟	射角	シャカク	angle of fire
	射撃	シャゲキ	shooting —*v.* shoot; fire
	射幸	シャコウ	speculation
	射幸心	シャコウシン	speculative spirit
	射幸的	シャコウテキ	speculative
	射殺	シャサツ	death by shooting —*v.* shoot to death
	射手	シャシュ	marksman; archer
	射出	シャシュツ	ejection; radiation; discharge —*v.* fire; eject; spout; radiate
	射精	シャセイ	ejaculation; seminal emission —*vi.* ejaculate
	射程	シャテイ	shooting/firing range
	射的	シャテキ	target practice
	射利心	シャリシン	mercenary spirit
訓	射る	いる	*vt.* shoot; fire

口口土士夂夕大女子宀寸小 ・ 小 ⺍ 尢尸山川工己巾干幺广廴廾弋弓ヨ彡彳彑阝阝亠忄扌犭氵

506

将 ⑩

丿 丬 丬 丬 丬 丬 丬 丬 丬 将 将

音	将	ショウ	commander; general
熟	将棋	ショウギ	*shōgi* (Japanese chess)
	将軍	ショウグン	shogun; military dictator; general
	将来	ショウライ	the future

507

尉 ⑪

⼀ ⼀ ⼾ ⼾ ⼾ ⼾ ⼾ ⼾ ⼾ 尉 尉

音	尉	イ	military company officer
熟	尉官	イカン	military company officer

508

尋 ⑫

⼀ ⼀ ⼀ ⼀ ⼀ ⼀ ⼀ ⼀ ⼀ ⼀ 尋 尋

音	尋	ジン	ask
熟	尋常	ジンジョウ	ordinary; mediocre
	尋問	ジンモン	questioning —*v*. question; examine
訓	尋ねる	たずねる	*vt*. search for; ask; inquire

509

尊 ⑫

丶 ⼀ ⼀ ⼀ ⼀ ⼀ ⼀ 酋 酋 酋 尊 尊

音	尊	ソン	esteem; value; respect
熟	尊敬	ソンケイ	respect; esteem; honor —*v*. respect; hold in esteem; honor
	尊厳	ソンゲン	dignity
	尊大	ソンダイ	haughty; arrogant; self-important
	尊重	ソンチョウ	respect; esteem —*v*. respect; hold in esteem
	尊王	ソンノウ	reverence for the emperor; advocacy of imperial rule
	尊父	ソンプ	**hon**. your father
訓	尊い	たっとい	exalted; valuable; precious; noble
	尊ぶ	たっとぶ	*vt*. respect; esteem; value
	尊い	とうとい	noble; precious; exalted valulable

尊ぶ　とうとぶ　*vt*. respect; value; esteem

510

导⑮　　⺉　⺍　⼴　芐　芐　首　首　`首　渞　道　道　導

音	導	ドウ	guide; transmit; conduct
熟	導火線	ドウカセン	fuse; cause; agency; impetus; incentive
	導線	ドウセン	leading wire
	導体	ドウタイ	conductor (of electricity, heat, etc.)
	導入	ドウニュウ	introduction; induction; invitation —*v*. introduce; induce; invite
訓	導き	みちびき	guidance; showing the way; instruction
	導く	みちびく	*vt*. guide; lead; conduct; show; introduce; instruct

3　小　しょう　small

511

小③　　亅　小　小

音	小	ショウ	small; little; younger; (prefix) sub-
熟	小異	ショウイ	minor differences
	小学生	ショウガクセイ	elementary school pupil
	小学校	ショウガッコウ	elementary/primary school
	小休止	ショウキュウシ	break; breather —*v*. take a break/breather
	小計	ショウケイ	subtotal
	小康	ショウコウ	lull; letup; remission
	小国	ショウコク	little country; minor power
	小差	ショウサ	narrow margin
	小冊子	ショウサッシ	pamphlet; booklet
	小市民	ショウシミン	petty bourgeois
	小食	ショウショク	light eating
	小心	ショウシン	timidity; cowardice
	小心者	ショウシンもの	coward; timid person
	小数	ショウスウ	*math*. decimal
	小数点	ショウスウテン	*math*. decimal point
	小生	ショウセイ	*hum*. I; me
	小節	ショウセツ	bar of music; measure

249

口
口
土
士
夕
大
女
子
宀
寸　●
小　●
⺌
⺍
尢
尸
山
川
工
己
巾
干
幺
广
廴
廾
弋
弓
彐
彡
彳
艹
辶
阝
阝
⺍
忄
扌
氵
犭

口
口
土
士
夂
夕
大
女
子
宀
寸
●小
⺌
⺍
尤
尸
山
川
工
己
巾
干
幺
广
廴
廾
弋
弓
ヨ
彡
彳
艹
辶
阝
丷
忄
扌
犭
氵

小説	ショウセツ	novel; fiction
小説家	ショウセツカ	novelist
小児	ショウニ	small child; infant
小児科	ショウニカ	*med*. pediatrics
小便	ショウベン	urine; piss; pee —*vi*. pass urine; piss; pee

訓

小さい	ちいさい	small; little; tiny; young
小	お	(prefix) small; little; sub-
小	こ	(prefix) small; little; sub-
小型	こがた	small size; small; compact
小型化	こがたカ	miniature; small; compact —*v*. miniaturize; compact
小柄	こがら	small build/size/stature
小言	こごと	scolding; rebuke; preaching; lecture; grumbling
小細工	こザイク	cheap/petty tricks
小雨	こさめ	light/fine rain; drizzle
小銭	こぜに	small change
小僧	こゾウ	priestling; novice; shop boy; errand boy; urchin; brat
小遣い	こづかい	spending/pocket money
小包	こづつみ	parcel; package
小手先	こてさき	cheap/petty tricks
小話	こばなし	short tale; anecdote
小人	こびと	dwarf; pygmy
小間使い	こまづかい	maid
小間物屋	こまものや	notions dealer; haberdasher
小麦	こむぎ	wheat
小麦粉	こむぎこ	flour
小屋	こや	hut; shed; shack; cabin

¥

小売店	こうりテン	kiosk (selling magazines, newspapers, sweets, etc.)
小売り	こうり	retail
小切手	こぎって	check
小切手帳	こぎってチョウ	checkbook
小口	こぐち	small lots

512

少 ④ 丿 丄 小 少

音

| 少 | ショウ | few; young |

熟

| 少額 | ショウガク | small sum/amount of money |
| 少女 | ショウジョ | girl |

少々	ショウショウ	just a little; few
少食	ショウショク	light eating; small appetite
少数	ショウスウ	small number
少年	ショウネン	boy; juvenile
少量	ショウリョウ	small quantity; morsel
訓 少ない	すくない	few; not many; little
少し	すこし	little; not much

---

3 ソパソ さかさしょう small on top

513

当 ⑥ 　 丶 ゛ ゛ 当 当 当

音 当	トウ	right; justice; fairness; this; the present; the current; right now
熟 当局	トウキョク	authorities; the powers that be
当座	トウザ	the time being; the present
当時	トウジ	at the present time; then; in those days
当事者	トウジシャ	party concerned; interested party
当日	トウジツ	that/the day; the appointed day
当初	トウショ	at first; at the beginning
当世	トウセイ	present day; the day/age/era
当選	トウセン	winning; return to office; election —*vi.* be elected/returned to office; win an election
当然	トウゼン	naturally; justly; properly; as a matter of course
当地	トウチ	this place/area here
当直	トウチョク	being on duty/watch —*vi.* be on duty; keep watch
当人	トウニン	the said person; the person in question; the man himself
当年	トウネン	this year; that year; those days
当番	トウバン	being on duty/watch/guard
当否	トウヒ	right or wrong; justice; propriety; fitness; suitability
当分	トウブン	for the time being
当方	トウホウ	our part; I; we
当面	トウメン	present; urgent; pressing; immediate —*vi.* face; confront
当落	トウラク	result of an election

口口土士攵夕大女子宀寸小⺌⺌尢尸山川工己巾干幺广廴廾弋弓彐彡彳⺾阝阝⺌忄扌犭氵

	当惑	トウワク	perplexity; embarrassment; discomfiture; dilemma; confusion —*vi.* be perplexed/bewildered
訓	当たる	あたる	hit; strike; touch; be touched; be equal; match; *col.* have food poisoning
	当たり	あたり	hit; success; strike
	当たり前	あたりまえ	proper; right; just; fair; common; normal; usual
	当てる	あてる	apply; lay; hold; hit; strike; guess; succeed; expose
¥	～当たり	～あたり	(suffix) per-
	当期未処分 利益	トウキミショブン リエキ	unappropriated retained earnings
	当期利益	トウキリエキ	net income
	当局	トウキョク	the authorities concerned
	当座貸越	トウザかしこし	overdraft; overdrawn
	当座資産	トウザシサン	liquid assets
	当座預金	トウザヨキン	current account; deposit
	当日取引	トウニチとりひき	cash delivery

514
尚 ⑧ 丿 丨 ⺌ � 尚 尚 尚 尚

音	尚	ショウ	respect
熟	尚早	ショウソウ	too early/soon
訓	※尚	なお	moreover; furthermore

515
党 ⑩ 丿 丨 ⺌ ⺌ 党 党 党 党 党 党

音	党	トウ	company; (political) party
熟	党員	トウイン	party member
	党規	トウキ	(political) party regulations
	党紀	トウキ	(political) party discipline
	党議	トウギ	party policy; platform; party decision
	党首	トウシュ	party leader
	党籍	トウセキ	party register
	党派	トウハ	party/action/school of thought
	党風	トウフウ	(political) party character
	党利	トウリ	party interests
	党略	トウリャク	party platform/policy

516

単 ⑨ ＼ ＼＼ ＼＼ノ ｜＼ノ ＼ノ ＼ノ ＼ノ ＼ノ ＼ノ

音	単	タン	single; simple
熟	単位	タンイ	unit
	単元	タンゲン	unit
	単語	タンゴ	word
	単行本	タンコウボン	separate volume; one volume (not a series, etc.); hardcover book
	単純	タンジュン	simplicity
	単身	タンシン	alone; by oneself; unaccompanied
	単数	タンスウ	singular number
	単線	タンセン	single track
	単調	タンチョウ	monotony; dullness; humdrum
	単刀直入	タントウ チョクニュウ	straightforward; direct; frank; to the point
	単独	タンドク	singleness; independence; separateness
	単文	タンブン	simple sentence
¥	単価	タンカ	unit cost/price
	単式	タンシキ	single entry bookkeeping; simple system
	単利	タンリ	simple interest

517

巣 ⑪ ＼ ＼＼ ＼＼ノ ｜＼ノ ＼ノ ＼ノ ＼ノ ＼ノ ＼ノ 単 単 巣

音	巣	ソウ	nest; web; hive
熟	巣窟	ソウクツ	den; hangout
訓	巣	す	nest; shelter; web; hive
	巣くう	すくう	*vi*. build a nest
	巣立つ	すだつ	*vi*. leave the nest; graduate; start out in life

518

営 ⑫ ＼ ＼＼ ＼＼ノ ｜＼ノ 学 学 学 営 営 営 営 営

音	営	エイ	run; manage; administer

3

口
口
土
士
夂
夕
大
女
子
宀
寸
小
ツ

• 尢
戸
山
川
工
己
巾
干
幺
广
廴
廾
弋
弓
ヨ
彡
彳
⺾
辶
阝
⺶
忄
扌
氵

訓	営み	いとなみ	business; trade
	営む	いとなむ	*vt*. run a business; engage in commercial activities
¥	営業	エイギョウ	business; trade; commerce —*v*. conduct business; trade
	営業外収益	エイギョウガイシュウエキ	non-operating income or revenue; other income
	営業外費用	エイギョウガイヒヨウ	non-operating expenses
	営業外利益	エイギョウガイリエキ	non-operating profit
	営業収益	エイギョウシュウエキ	operating profit
	営業実績	エイギョウジッセキ	business result
	営業費用	エイギョウヒヨウ	operating expenses
	営業不振	エイギョウフシン	slump in business
	営業妨害	エイギョウボウガイ	obstruction of business
	営業報告書	エイギョウホウコクショ	business report
	営業利益	エイギョウリエキ	operating profit
	営団	エイダン	management corporation
	営利	エイリ	gain; profit-making
	営林	エイリン	forest management; forestry

519

厳 ⑰ 　 ヽ　丷　广　严　严　严　严　屵　屵　屵　厳　厳

音	厳	ゲン（ゴン）	strict; severe; stern; solemn
熟	厳戒	ゲンカイ	strict guard/alert —*v*. keep strict guard; be on strict alert
	厳格	ゲンカク	strict; severe; stern; rigid
	厳禁	ゲンキン	strict prohibition —*v*. be strictly prohibited
	厳守	ゲンシュ	strict observance —*v*. keep strictly to; adhere rigidly; obey
	厳重	ゲンジュウ	stern; severe; strict; tight; close
	厳粛	ゲンシュク	solemn; grave; awesome
	厳正	ゲンセイ	strict; rigid; fair; impartial
	厳選	ゲンセン	careful selection —*v*. select carefully; hand pick
	厳然	ゲンゼン	grim; grave; solemn
	厳冬	ゲントウ	severe/hard winter
	厳罰	ゲンバツ	severe/heavy punishment
	厳父	ゲンプ	strict father; (another person's) father
	厳密	ゲンミツ	strict; close; clear cut;

254

厳命	ゲンメイ	strict command —*v*. give a strict command
訓 厳か	おごそか	solemn; stately
厳しい	きびしい	severe; strict; stern

---

3 尢 だいのまげあし crooked leg

520

就⑫ ' ㇒ ㇖ ㇇ 古 古 亨 亨 京 京 京 尌 就 就

音 就	シュウ （ジュ）	get a job; install; study with; set out
熟 就役	シュウエキ	going into commission —*vi*. go into commission; undergo punishment
就学	シュウガク	entering/starting school —*vi*. enter/start school
就学率	シュウガクリツ	percentage of pupils attending school
就航	シュウコウ	commission/service (of ships/aircraft)
就寝	シュウシン	going to bed —*vi*. go to bed
就任	シュウニン	inauguration/installation in a new position —*vi*. take up a position
就任式	シュウニンシキ	inauguration; inaugural ceremony
訓 就く	つく	*vi*. get a job; become; study under
就ける	つける	*vt*. seat; appoint a person; install
¥ 就業	シュウギョウ	arriving at work; starting work —*vi*. start/begin work
就業時間	シュウギョウ ジカン	working hours
就業人口	シュウギョウ ジンコウ	work force
就職	シュウショク	finding employment; job hunting —*vi*. find work; get a job
就職活動	シュウショク カツドウ	job hunting
就職口	シュウショクグチ	position; situation; opening
就職先	シュウショクサキ	place of employment
就職試験	シュウショクシケン	examination for employment
就職難	シュウショクナン	job shortage
就職率	シュウショクリツ	rate of employment
就労	シュウロウ	starting work; being employed —*vi*. get to work; start working; be employed

ロ口土士夕大女子宀寸小⺌⺍尢尸山川工己巾干幺广廴廾弋弓彐彡彳艹辶阝阝亠忄扌犭氵

3 尸　しかばね　corpse; flag

521

尺 ④　　 一 コ 尸 尺

音	尺	シャク	*shaku* (unit of measurement, approx. 30.3 cm)
熟	尺度	シャクド	measure; standard; criterion
	尺八	シャクハチ	*shakuhachi* (bamboo flute)
	尺貫法	シャッカンホウ	the *shaku-kan* system of weights and measures

522

尼 ⑤　　 一 コ 尸 尸 尼

音	尼	ニ	nun
熟	尼僧	ニソウ	nun; sister; priestess
訓	尼	あま	nun; sister
	尼寺	あまでら	nunnery; convent

523

尽 ⑥　　 一 コ 尸 尺 尺 尽

音	尽	ジン	serve; run out
熟	尽力	ジンリョク	exertion; effort; endeavor —*vi*. exert; make an effort/endeavor
訓	尽かす	つかす	*vt*. run out of; use up
	尽きる	つきる	*vi*. run out; be spent/exhausted
	尽くす	つくす	*vt*. make an effort; exhaust; try hard

524

局 ⑦　　 一 コ 尸 尸 局 局 局

音	局	キョク	part; bureau; chamber
熟	局所	キョクショ	local; part of the body (normally sexual organs)
	局地	キョクチ	locality
	局部	キョクブ	limited part; section
	局面	キョクメン	position; situation; phase

525

尿 ⑦ ⁻ ⁼ ⼾ ⼰ ⼰ ⼰ 尿

音	尿	ニョウ	urine
熟	尿意	ニョウイ	desire to pass water
	尿道	ニョウドウ	*med.* urethra

526

尾 ⑦ ⁻ ⁼ ⼾ ⼰ ⼰ ⼰ 尾

音	尾	ビ	tail
熟	尾行	ビコウ	follow —*vi.* follow; shadow; tail
	尾骨	ビコツ	*med.* coccyx
	尾灯	ビトウ	taillight
	尾翼	ビヨク	tail (of a plane)
	尾篭	ビロウ	indecent; indelicate
訓	尾	お	tail
	尾根	おね	mountain ridge

527

居 ⑧ ⁻ ⁼ ⼾ ⼰ ⼰ ⼰ 居 居

音	居	キョ	be; live; sit
熟	居住	キョジュウ	residence; abode; dwelling —*vi.* reside; dwell
	居所	キョショ	one's abode; one's place of residence
	居留地	キョリュウチ	settlement; concession
訓	居心地	いごこチ	comfortable; at ease; cosy; smug
	居酒屋	いざかや	tavern; bar
	居間	いま	living room
	居る	いる	*vi.* be; exist; live; sit
	居留守	いルス	pretend to be out

528

屈 ⑧ ⁻ ⁼ ⼾ ⼰ ⼰ ⼰ 屈 屈

音	屈	クツ	stoop; bow; lean over; be broken/crushed/sprained

257

3

熟	屈する	クッする	*v.* bend; yield; submit; give in
	屈強	クッキョウ	strong; sturdy; stalwart
	屈曲	クッキョク	bend; flex —*vi.* bend; curve; turn
	屈指	クッシ	leading; foremost; prominent
	屈辱	クツジョク	humiliation; indignity
	屈伸	クッシン	expansion and contraction; bending and stretching —*vi.* expand and contract; bend and stretch
	屈折	クッセツ	bend; turn —*vi.* bend; curve; turn
	屈服	クップク	submission; surrender —*vi.* submit; surrender

529

届 ⑧　　　一 コ ヨ 尸 尺 戸 屇 届 届

音	届	（カイ）	send; report
訓	届く	とどく	*vi.* reach; attain
	届ける	とどける	*vt.* report; notify; send; forward
	届け	とどけ	report; notice; forwarding; delivery
	届け出で	とどけいで	notification; entry
	届け先	とどけさき	destination; receiver's address; consignee
	届け出る	とどけでる	*vt.* submit/give notice

530

屋 ⑨　　　一 コ 尸 尸 尸 层 屋 屋 屋

音	屋	オク	house; roof
熟	屋外	オクガイ	the outdoors/open air
	屋上	オクジョウ	rooftop; roof
	屋内	オクナイ	indoors
訓	屋	や	house; roof; store name; seller
	屋号	やゴウ	store name
	屋敷	やしき	mansion; residence
	屋台	やタイ	pushcart/mobile stall
	屋根	やね	roof

531

展 ⑩　　　一 コ 尸 尸 尸 屛 屛 屛 屛 展

音	展	テン	display; spread

熟	展開	テンカイ	unfolding; development; evolution; discovery; deployment —*v.* unfold; develop; evolve; deploy
	展示	テンジ	display; exhibition —*v.* exhibit; display; have on view
	展望	テンボウ	view; prospect; outlook; review —*v.* have a view of; look over; survey; review; pass
	展望鏡	テンボウキョウ	telescope
	展望台	テンボウダイ	observatory; observation post
	展覧	テンラン	exhibition; show —*v.* exhibit; display; show
	展覧会	テンランカイ	exhibition; exhibit; show

532 ⑫ 　 ¬ ¬ ⼫ ⼫ ⼫ ⼫ ⼫ ⼫ 属 属 属 属

音	属	ショク	
		ゾク	belong to; be attached to; genus
熟	属目	ショクモク	attention; observation
	属性	ゾクセイ	attribute
	属地	ゾクチ	territory; possession
	属領	ゾクリョウ	territory; possession; dependency
	属国	ゾッコク	dependency; vassal state

533 層 ⑭ 　 ⼫ ⼫ ⼫ ⼫ 屈 屈 屈 届 届 層 層 層

| 音 | 層 | ソウ | layer; class; stratum |
| 熟 | 層雲 | ソウウン | stratus |

534 履 ⑮ 　 ⼫ ⼫ ⼫ ⼫ ⼫ ⼫ 屈 屈 屈 屈 履 履

音	履	リ	footwear; do
熟	履行	リコウ	implementation; execution —*v.* perform; fulfill; implement; carry out
	履歴	リレキ	personal history; background; career
	履歴書	リレキショ	one's personal/life history; résumé
訓	履く	はく	put on (footwear, socks, trousers, a skirt)
	履物	はきもの	footwear

3 山　やま　mountain

535

山　｜ 山 山 ③

音	山	サン	mountain
熟	山河	サンガ	mountains and rivers
	山岳	サンガク	mountains
	山間	サンカン	in the mountains
	山菜	サンサイ	edible wild plants
	山水画	サンスイガ	landscape (painting)
	山積	サンセキ	pile; accumulation —*vi*. pile up; accumulate
	山荘	サンソウ	mountain cottage/villa
	山村	サンソン	mountain village
	山頂	サンチョウ	mountaintop; summit; peak
	山腹	サンプク	hillside; mountainside
	山脈	サンミャク	mountain range
	山門	サンモン	temple gate; main gate of a Buddhist temple
	山野	サンヤ	hills and fields; countryside
	山林	サンリン	forest in the mountains; mountains and forest
	山麓	サンロク	foot of a mountain
訓	山	やま	mountain; hill; mine; heap; pile; climax; peak; crisis (of an illness)
	山男	やまおとこ	woodsman; mountain laborer
	山崩れ	やまくずれ	landslide
	山小屋	やまごや	mountain hut/lodge
	山里	やまざと	mountain hamlet/village
	山師	やまシ	prospecter; miner; speculator; imposter; swindler
	山津波	やまつなみ	landslide
	山積み	やまづみ	heap; huge amount
	山の手	やまのて	uptown; residential
	山登り	やまのぼり	mountain-climbing —*vi*. climb mountains

536

岐　｜ 丨 屮 屮 屵 屵 屵 岐 ⑦

音	岐	キ	branch; fork
熟	岐路	キロ	forked road

537

岳 ⑧ ノ ノ ケ ゲ 丘 丘 岳 岳

音	岳	ガク	high mountain
熟	岳父	ガクフ	one's wife's father/father-in-law
訓	岳	たけ	mountain peak

538

岩 ⑧ 丨 山 山 屵 岩 岩 岩

音	岩	ガン	rock
熟	岩塩	ガンエン	rock salt
	岩窟	ガンクツ	cavern; cave; grotto
	岩礁	ガンショウ	reef; rocks covered by the water
	岩石	ガンセキ	rock; crag; stones and rocks
	岩頭	ガントウ	top of a rock; rock head
	岩盤	ガンバン	bedrock
	岩壁	ガンペキ	rock wall/face
訓	岩	いわ	rock; crag; reef
	岩陰	いわかげ	shade of a rock
	岩清水	いわしみず	spring water
	岩場	いわば	rock face; cliff
	岩屋	いわや	cave; cavedwelling

539

岸 ⑧ 丨 山 山 屵 岸 岸 岸 岸

音	岸	ガン	shore
熟	岸壁	ガンペキ	quay; rock; sea wall
訓	岸	きし	seashore; cliff

540

岬 ⑧ 丨 屮 山 山 屾 岘 岬 岬

| 音 | 岬 | （コウ） | cape |
| 訓 | 岬 | みさき | cape; point; headland; promontory |

口口土士夂夕大女子宀寸小⺌⺍尢尸山川工己巾干幺广廴廾弋弓彐彡彳艹辶阝阝宀忄扌氵

3

口口土士夂夕大女子宀寸小⺌⺍尤尸山川工己巾干幺广廴廾弋弓彐彡彳艹辶阝⺌忄扌氵

541

峡 ⑨　丨　丨　山　山⁻　山′　山⁻　山⁻　峡　峡

音	峡	キョウ	ravine; gorge; narrow valley
熟	峡谷	キョウコク	gorge; ravine; glen
	峡路	キョウロ	defile; narrow (pass)

542

峠 ⑨　丨　丨　山　山′　山′　山ᵗ　峠　峠　峠

| 訓 | 峠 | とうげ | ridge; pass; crisis |

543

島 ⑩　ᐟ　ᐟ′　ᐟ冖　戸　戸　皀　鳥　鳥　島　島

音	島	トウ	island
熟	島民	トウミン	islanders; natives of an island
訓	島	しま	island
	島影	しまかげ	sight of an island
	島国	しまぐに	island nation
	島国根性	しまぐにコンジョウ	insular spirit; insularism
	島田	しまだ	(traditional Japanese coiffure for unmarried women)
	島流し	しまながし	exile; banishment

544

峰 ⑩　丨　山　山　山′　山⁾　屮　岮　峯　峰

音	峰	ホウ	peak; summit; back (of a sword)
訓	峰	みね	peak; summit; back (of a sword)
	峰打ち	みねうち	*vt.* strike (a person) with the back of one's sword

545

崎 ⑪　丨　山　山　山⁻　山ᵗ　山ᵗ　崎　崎　崎　崎

| 訓 | 崎 | さき | cape; headland |

262

546

崇 ⑪　　` ⊥ 屮 中 屵 峃 峃 峃 峃 崇 崇

音	崇	スウ	noble; worship
熟	崇敬	スウケイ	reverence; veneration —v. venerate; revere; pay respect; hold in esteem
	崇高	スウコウ	sublime; lofty; grand; noble
	崇拝	スウハイ	worship; adoration; admiration; cult —v. worship; venerate; adore; admire; idolize
	崇拝者	スウハイシャ	worshipper; admirer
訓	※崇める	あがめる	vt. worship; revere; venerate

547

崩 ⑪　　` ⊥ 屮 广 屵 屵 屵 峅 崩 崩 崩

音	崩	ホウ	crumble; fall to pieces; collapse
熟	崩じる	ホウじる	vi. die; pass away (use of the emperor)
	崩壊	ホウカイ	collapse; disintegration —vi. collapse; disintegrate
	崩御	ホウギョ	demise/death of the emperor —vi. (the emperor) passes away
訓	崩す	くずす	vt. demolish; change/break (a large bill); simplify (the way of writing a *kanji*)
	崩れる	くずれる	vi. crumble; fall to pieces; collapse; break

3　川　かわ river

548

川 ③　　ノ 丿 川

音	川	セン	river
熟	川柳	センリュウ	*senryū* (satirical haiku)
訓	川	かわ	river
	川上	かわかみ	upper stream
	川下	かわしも	lower stream
	川瀬	かわせ	shallows; rapids
	川床	かわどこ	riverbed

川面　　かわも　　surface of a river
※川原　　かわら　　dry riverbed

549

州 ⑥　　' 丿 丿 州 州 州

| 音 | 州 | シュウ | province; state; continent |
| 訓 | 州 | す | sand bank |

3 エ　え　*e* (katakana)

550

工 ③　　一 丁 工

音	工	コウ (ク)	artisan; work; craft; construction
熟	工夫	クフウ	device; idea
	工面	クメン	contrivance; management —*v.* contrive; manage
	工員	コウイン	factory worker
	工学	コウガク	engineering
	工業	コウギョウ	industry; manufacturing
	工具	コウグ	tool; implement
	工芸	コウゲイ	industrial arts
	工作	コウサク	handicraft; handiwork; construction —*v.* make; construct
	工事	コウジ	construction work
	工場	コウジョウ (コウば)	factory
	工賃	コウチン	pay; wages
	工程	コウテイ	process
¥	工業化	コウギョウカ	industrialization —*v.* industrialize
	工費	コウヒ	construction costs

551

巧 ⑤　　一 丁 工 工 巧

| 音 | 巧 | コウ | skill |

口口土士夂夕大女子宀寸小⺌⺍尤尸山川工己巾干幺广廴廾弋弓ヨ彡彳艹⻌阝⻏亠忄扌犭氵

熟	巧者	コウシャ	clever; skillful; dexterous
	巧妙	コウミョウ	skill; dexterity; ingenuity
訓	巧み	たくみ	skill; dexterity; cunning

552

左 ⑤　一 ナ ナ ナ 左

音	左	サ	left
熟	左官	サカン	plasterer
	左記	サキ	the following; the above
	左折	サセツ	left turn —*vi.* make a left turn; turn to the left
	左折禁止	サセツキンシ	No Left Turn (road marking)
	左遷	サセン	relegation; demotion —*v.* relegate; demote
	左派	サハ	left-wing party; the left
	左右	サユウ	right and left; both ways; opposite directions —*v.* control; influence
	左翼	サヨク	the left wing; leftist
訓	左	ひだり	left
	左手	ひだりて	left hand
	左前	ひだりまえ	wrong way; adversity; downward course

553

差 ⑩　ヽ ヽ ン ソ 芏 羊 差 差 差 差

音	差	サ	point; indicate; difference; distinguish
熟	差異(差違)	サイ	difference
	差額	サガク	balance; margin; difference
	差別	サベツ	discrimination; prejudice —*v.* discriminate (against)
	差別待遇	サベツタイグウ	discrimination among people; treating people differently
	差別用語	サベツヨウゴ	discriminatory language; derogatory term
訓	差す	さす	*v.* pour; fill; add; apply; offer; point at -*vi.* shine
	差し上げる	さしあげる	*vi.* give; present; offer
	差し入れる	さしいれる	*vt.* insert; put into
	差し押さえる	さしおさえる	*vt.* seize; attach; distrain
	差し金	さしがね	instigation; suggestion
	差し込む	さしこむ	insert; plug in

口 口 土 士 夂 夕 大 女 子 宀 寸 小 ⺌ ⺍ 尢 尸 山 川 工 己 巾 干 幺 广 廴 廾 弋 弓 彐 彡 彳 艹 辶 阝 阝 ⺾ 扌 ⺘ 氵

口口土士夂夕大女子宀寸小⺌⺍尢尸山川・己⺟巾干幺广廴廾弋弓彐彡彳⺾辶阝亠忄扌犭氵

差出人	さしだしニン	sender	
差し支える	さしつかえる	*vi*. interfere	
差止め	さしどめ	prohibition; ban; suspension	
差し引く	さしひく	*vt*. deduct	
差向い	さしむかい	face to face	
差し戻し	さしもどし	returning; sending back; referring (a case) back (to the original court)	

¥
差益	サエキ	profit margin
差額税	サガクゼイ	differential tarriff
差金	サキン	balance; difference; margin
差金決済	サキンケッサイ	making up differences
差損	サソン	loss from the difference of quotations
差別関税	サベツカンゼイ	selective taxes

3 　己　おのれ　self; snake

554 己 ③ 　フ コ 己

音	己	キ	myself
		コ	self
訓	己	おのれ	oneself *col*. you bastard (term of abuse)

555 巻 ⑨ 　丶 ⺌ ⺍ 半 半 关 关 巻 巻

音	巻	カン	volume; scroll
熟	巻頭	カントウ	beginning of a book
	巻末	カンマツ	end of a book
訓	巻き	まき	roll; volume; tome; book
	巻網	まきあみ	round haul net
	巻き貝	まきがい	snail; conch
	巻紙	まきがみ	wrapping paper
	巻き舌	まきじた	trilling (one's r's)
	巻き尺	まきジャク	tape measure
	巻き添え	まきぞえ	involvement; entanglement; embroilment
	巻物	まきもの	scroll
	巻く	まく	*v*. roll; coil

3 巾　はば／はばへん　width; cloth

556

市 ⑤　丶　一　广　亣　市

音	市	シ	market; city; municipality; urban; municipal
熟	市営	シエイ	municipal management
	市街	シガイ	the streets; the city
	市外	シガイ	outskirts of a town; out of town
	市議会	シギカイ	city assembly/council
	市制	シセイ	municipal organization
	市政	シセイ	municipal government/administration
	市長	シチョウ	mayor
	市民	シミン	citizen
	市民権	シミンケン	citizenship
	市役所	シヤクショ	city hall; municipal office
	市立	シリツ (いちリツ)	municipal
訓	市	いち	market; fair
	市場	いちば	market
	市松模様	いちまつモヨウ	checked pattern
¥	市価	シカ	market price
	市況	シキョウ	market condition
	市場	シジョウ	market; exchange; marketplace
	市場価格	シジョウカカク	market price/value
	市場性	シジョウセイ	marketability
	市場占有率	シジョウセンユウリツ	market share
	市場相場	シジョウソウば	market prices
	市場調査	シジョウチョウサ	market survey/research —v. carry out market research
	市販	シハン	marketing; offering for sale —v. market; put on the market

557

布 ⑤　ノ　ナ　ナ　右　布

音	布	フ	cloth; spread
熟	布教	フキョウ	propagation of religion; missionary work —v. propagate religion

3

	布巾	フキン	dishcloth
	布告	フコク	declaration; proclamation; notification —*v.* declare; proclaim; announce; decree
	布陣	フジン	the line-up/lines —*vi.* take up one's position (for a battle, contest, etc.)
	布施	フセ	offering; alms; charity
	布石	フセキ	initial stage in a go match; arrangements; preparations
	布団	フトン	futon; quilt; mattress
訓	布	ぬの	cloth; material
	布地	ぬのジ	cloth; material

558

帆 ⑥ 丿 冂 巾 帄 帆 帆

音	帆	ハン	sail
熟	帆船	ハンセン	sailing ship
	帆走	ハンソウ	sailing —*vi.* sail; go by ship
訓	帆	ほ	sail
	帆柱	ほばしら	mast

559

希 ⑦ 丿 乂 メ 产 予 希 希

音	希	キ	rare; wish
熟	希少	キショウ	scarce; rare
	希少価値	キショウカチ	scarcity value
	希代	キダイ	rarity; uniqueness
	希薄	キハク	thinness; rarefaction
	希望	キボウ	hope; wish; desire; ambition —*v.* hope; wish; desire; aspire to
	希硫酸	キリュウサン	dilute sulfuric acid
※	希有	ケウ	rarity; unusual; uncommon
訓 ※	希	まれ	rare; uncommon; unusual

560

帥 ⑨ 丿 丆 厃 厃 肖 自 自 帥 帥

音	帥	スイ	command; leader

口 口 土 士 夂 夕 大 女 子 宀 寸 小 ⺌ ⺍ 尤 尸 山 川 工 己 巾 干 幺 广 廴 廾 弋 弓 彐 彡 彳 艹 辶 阝 阝 丷 忄 扌 犭 氵

561

帝 ⑨ `' 亠 亠 亠 产 产 产 产 帝`

音	帝	テイ	emperor
熟	帝王	テイオウ	sovereign; monarch; emperor
	帝国	テイコク	empire
	帝政	テイセイ	imperial government/rule; imperialism
	帝都	テイト	imperial capital/metropolis
訓	※帝	みかど	emperor

562

帰 ⑩ `' 丿 丿┐ 丿┒ 丿╕ 尸 归 归 帰 帰`

音	帰	キ	return
熟	帰依	キエ	*Bud*. becoming a believer —*vi*. become a believer
	帰化	キカ	naturalization —*vi*. become naturalized
	帰還	キカン	return; repatriation —*vi*. return; be repatriated
	帰京	キキョウ	returning to Tokyo —*vi*. return to Tokyo
	帰郷	キキョウ	going home; returning to one's home town —*vi*. return to one's home town
	帰結	キケツ	conclusion; end; result; consequence —*vi*. be concluded; end
	帰国	キコク	return to one's country —*vi*. return/come back to one's country; go/come home
	帰省	キセイ	coming home; homecoming —*vi*. go/come/return home; visit one's native place
	帰着	キチャク	return; coming back; conclusion —*vi*. return; come back; conclude; bring to a conclusion
	帰途	キト	on one's way back
	帰路	キロ	homeward journey
訓	帰す	かえす	*vt*. dismiss; release
	帰る	かえる	*vi*. return; go home; leave

563

師 ⑩ `' 亻 ⼓ ⼓ 自 自 ⼓ 師 師 師`

音	師	シ	army; teacher; missionary
熟	師事	シジ	studying under a person —*vi*. study under a person; become a person's student

口口土士夂夕大女子宀寸小⺌⺍尢尸山川工己巾干幺广廴廾弋弓彐彡彳艹⻌阝阝⺍扌犭氵

3

口 口 土 士 夂 夕 大 女 子 宀 寸 小 ⺌ ⺍ 尢 尸 山 川 工 己 巾 干 幺 广 廴 廾 弋 弓 彐 彡 彳 艹 辶 阝 阝 艹 忄 扌 氵

	師匠	シショウ	teacher; master
	師団	シダン	division of soldiers
	師弟	シテイ	master and pupil; teacher and student
	師範	シハン	instructor
訓	※師走	しわす （しはす）	the twelfth month of the lunar calendar; December

---

564

席 ⑩　' 一 广 广 广 产 产 产 庐 庐 席

音	席	セキ	seat; place
熟	席次	セキジ	ranking; precedance; seating order
	席上	セキジョウ	at the meeting; on the occasion
	席巻	セッケン	sweeping; conquest

565

帯 ⑩　一 十 卅 卅 冊 冊 卅 带 带 带

音	帯	タイ	belt; band; wear; zone
熟	帯出	タイシュツ	borrowing —*v.* carry out; take out; borrow
訓	帯	おび	*obi* (sash used to tie around a kimono); belt; sash; girdle
	帯状	おびジョウ	long, narrow strip
	帯封	おびフウ	wrapper around a posted newspaper, magazine, etc.
	帯びる	おびる	*vt.* wear; put on; bear; carry; be entrusted/vested with

---

566

常 ⑪　' ⺌ ⺌ ⺌ 心 心 学 学 常 常 常

音	常	ジョウ	ordinary; common; normal
熟	常温	ジョウオン	normal/room/average/uniform temperature
	常軌	ジョウキ	normal/proper/common course
	常客	ジョウキャク	regular customers; a regular
	常勤	ジョウキン	full-time/regular employment —*vi.* be in full-time/regular employment
	常時	ジョウジ	always; habitually
	常識	ジョウシキ	common sense/decency/practice; reasonable; sensible

常習	ジョウシュウ	bad habit —*v*. be in the habit of
常習者	ジョウシュウシャ	addict
常習犯	ジョウシュウハン	habitual offender; confirmed criminal
常食	ジョウショク	diet; staple food —*v*. eat everyday; live on a diet of
常人	ジョウジン	ordinary man
常数	ジョウスウ	***math.*** constant
常設	ジョウセツ	permanent; standing —*v*. establish permanently
常態	ジョウタイ	normal condition
常道	ジョウドウ	regular/usual way; proper behavior/conduct
常任	ジョウニン	permanent; regular; standing
常備	ジョウビ	standing; reserve —*v*. have always ready; be provided with
常用	ジョウヨウ	common/everyday use —*v*. use commonly/regularly; have everyday use of
常用漢字	ジョウヨウカンジ	*jōyō kanji* (the 1,945 Chinese characters in common use)
常緑樹	ジョウリョクジュ	evergreen tree
常連	ジョウレン	regular customer; frequenters

訓 常 — つね — common; everyday; ordinary; normal; always; constantly

常々	つねづね	always; at all times
常	とこ	(prefix) everlasting; permanent
常夏	とこなつ	everlasting/permanent summer

¥ 常任理事国 — ジョウニンリジコク — permanent member (of the U.N. Security Council)

567

帳 ⑪ ⺀ 冂 巾 忄 忦 忯 忰 帳 帳 帳 帳

音 帳 — チョウ — curtain; book; register; album

熟
帳尻	チョウジリ	balance of accounts
帳場	チョウば	counter; counting house; office; front desk
帳簿	チョウボ	account book; ledger; register
帳面	チョウメン	notebook; register; account book

訓 ※帳 — とばり — curtain; hangings

568

幅 ⑫ ⺀ 冂 巾 忄 忦 忯 忰 忱 幅 幅 幅 幅

音 幅 — フク — width; (counter for hanging scrolls)

3

口口土士夂夕大女子宀寸小⺌⺍尢戸山川工己巾干幺广廴廾弋弓ヨ彑彡彳辶阝⻏亠忄扌犭氵

熟	幅員	フクイン	width; breadth; extent
訓	幅	はば	width; breadth; range; influence
	幅跳び	はばとび	long jump
	幅広い	はばひろい	broad; extensive

569

帽 ⑫ ⺈ 冂 巾 巾 帄 帄 帍 帆 帽 帽 帽 帽

音	帽	ボウ	hat; cap
熟	帽子	ボウシ	hat
	帽章	ボウショウ	badge on a cap

570

 幕 ⑬ 一 艹 艹 芇 苎 昔 莒 莫 莫 莫 幕 幕

音	幕	バク	Japanese feudal government
		マク	curtain; act
熟	幕府	バクフ	shogunate; military government
	幕末	バクマツ	*hist*. last years of the Tokugawa shogunate
	幕僚	バクリョウ	staff of an important project; staff officers
	幕間	マクあい	intermission
	幕開き	マクあき	start of a play
	幕内	マクうち	senior-grade sumo wrestler
	幕切れ	マクぎれ	end
	幕下	マクした	junior-grade sumo wrestler
	幕の内	マクのうち	behind the curtain

571

幣 ⑮ ⺊ ⺌ ⺌ 广 屵 芇 芇 芇 敝 敝 敝 敝 幣

音	幣	ヘイ	offering to the gods/emperor/guest; money; currency
熟	幣制	ヘイセイ	monetary system
	幣束	ヘイソク	Shinto offerings of cloth, rope, or cut paper
	幣帛	ヘイハク	Shinto offerings of cloth, rope, or cut paper
	幣物	ヘイモツ（ヘイブツ）	Shinto offerings of cloth, rope, or cut paper; offering; gift
訓	※幣	ぬさ	Shinto offerings of cloth, rope, or cut paper

272

3 干　かん　dry; one ten

572

干 ③　一 二 干

音	干	カン	dry; concern; perpetrate; ebb
熟	干害	カンガイ	drought disaster/damage
	干渉	カンショウ	interference; meddling; intervention —*v.* interfere; meddle; intervene
	干拓	カンタク	land reclamation by drainage —*v.* reclaim land by drainage; drain off
	干潮	カンチョウ	ebb/low tide
	干満	カンマン	ebb and flow; tide
訓	干潟	ひがた	dry beach
	干物	ひもの	dried fish
	干る	ひる	*vi.* dry; parch; recede; fall; ebb
	干す	ほす	*vt.* dry; drain; drink up

573

平 ⑤　一 ⺀ 公 平 平

音	平	ヘイ	flat; level; even; calm; ordinary; common; peaceful
		ビョウ	
熟	平等	ビョウドウ	equality; impartiality
	平安	ヘイアン	peace; safety and security *hist.* Heian period/court (794-1185)
	平易	ヘイイ	easy; simple; straightforward
	平温	ヘイオン	usual temperature
	平穏	ヘイオン	calm; peaceful
	平気	ヘイキ	calm; unconcerned; nonchalant
	平均	ヘイキン	average; mean
	平原	ヘイゲン	plain; prairie
	平行	ヘイコウ	parallel —*vi.* be parallel
	平行線	ヘイコウセン	parallel line
	平日	ヘイジツ	weekdays; every day apart from Sundays and National Holidays
	平常	ヘイジョウ	usual; common; everyday
	平身低頭	ヘイシンテイトウ	bowing; prostration —*vi.* bow to the ground; prostrate oneself

平静	ヘイセイ	tranquillity; calmness; peacefulness
平生	ヘイゼイ	usual; everyday; ordinary
平然	ヘイゼン	calmness; nonchalance
平素	ヘイソ	usual; commonplace; ordinary
平坦	ヘイタン	even surface; flat; regular
平地	ヘイチ	level/flat land; even surface
平熱	ヘイねつ	normal body temperature
平年	ヘイネン	normal year; not a leap year
平服	ヘイフク	plain/everyday clothes
平方	ヘイホウ	*math.* square of a number; square (meter, etc.) —*v.* square a number
平方根	ヘイホウコン	*math.* square root
平凡	ヘイボン	common; ordinary; mediocre
平民	ヘイミン	common people
平野	ヘイヤ	plain; open field
平和	ヘイワ	peace

訓

平ら	たいら	flat; level
平	ひら	common; ordinary; average
平謝り	ひらあやまり	humble apology
平泳ぎ	ひらおよぎ	breast stroke
平仮名	ひらがな	*hiragana* (the cursive syllabary)
平たい	ひらたい	flat; level
平屋	ひらや	one-story house

574

年 ⑥ 　　ノ　ー　ヒ　丘　生　年

音 年	ネン	year; age
熟 年賀	ネンガ	New Year's greetings
年賀状	ネンガジョウ	New Year's greeting card
年月日	ネンガッぴ	date; year, month, and date
年刊	ネンカン	yearly publication; annual
年間	ネンカン	period of a year
年鑑	ネンカン	yearbook
年忌	ネンキ	anniversary service for a dead person
年季	ネンキ	apprenticeship; experience; training
年期	ネンキ	period of years; length of time (in years)
年貢	ネング	land tax; ground rent
年月	ネンゲツ	a long period of time
年限	ネンゲン	period of years; length of time (in years)
年功	ネンコウ	long experience/service

	年号	ネンゴウ	name of an era
	年始	ネンシ	beginning of the year
	年次	ネンジ	annual; yearly
	年収	ネンシュウ	yearly income; annual salary
	年中	ネンジュウ	whole year; always; perpetually
	年中行事	ネンチュウギョウジ	annual functions; regular events
	年少	ネンショウ	youth
	年代	ネンダイ	era; age; epoch; period
	年長	ネンチョウ	seniority
	年度	ネンド	year; term; fiscal/financial year
	年頭	ネントウ	beginning of the year
	年内	ネンナイ	within the year; before the year is out
	年輩	ネンパイ	elderly age; age; years
	年表	ネンピョウ	chronological table
	年譜	ネンプ	chronological record; chronology
	年別	ネンベツ	annual variation; classification by year
	年俸	ネンポウ	annual salary; yearly stipend
	年報	ネンポウ	annual report
	年末	ネンマツ	year-end; end of the year
	年齢	ネンレイ	age; years
訓	年	とし	year; age; years
	年上	としうえ	older
	年子	としご	children born in consecutive years
	年下	としした	younger
¥	年額	ネンガク	annual sum; yearly amount
	年給	ネンキュウ	annual salary
	年金	ネンキン	pension; annuity
	年産	ネンサン	yearly output; annual production
	年度	ネンド	fiscal year
	年利	ネンリ	annual interest

575

幸 ⑧   一 十 土 士 击 圭 㚏 幸

音	幸	コウ	happiness; good luck; felicity
熟	幸運	コウウン	good fortune/luck; happiness
	幸福	コウフク	happiness; felicity; well-being; bliss
訓	幸い	さいわい	happiness; felicity; bliss; good luck/fortune
	幸	さち	happiness; fortune; luck

口口土士夂夕大女子宀寸小丷ⅶ尢尸山川工己巾干幺广廴廾弋弓彐彡彳艹辶阝阝卄忄扌氵犭

幸せ　　しあわせ　　happiness; felicity; bliss

幸せ　　しあわせ　　happiness; felicity; bliss

左側縦書き部首：
口 口 土 士 夂 夕 大 女 子 宀 寸 小 ⺌ ⅋ 尢 尸 山 川 工 己 巾 干 幺 广 廴 廾 弋 弓 彐 彡 彳 艹 辶 阝 阝 丷 忄 扌 犭 氵

576

幹 ⑬　一 十 ⺌ 古 吉 吉 直 卓 斡 幹 幹 幹

音	幹	カン	tree trunk; body; ability
熟	幹事	カンジ	manager; secretary; person in charge of a party
	幹線	カンセン	trunk/main line
訓	幹	みき	tree trunk; important part
¥	幹事長	カンジチョウ	chief secretary; secretary-general
	幹部	カンブ	leading members; managing staff; executives; party organizers

---

3　幺　いとがしら　short thread

577

幻 ⑤　く 幺 幺 幻

音	幻	ゲン	phantom; illusion; fantasy
熟	幻影	ゲンエイ	illusion; vision; dream
	幻覚	ゲンカク	hallucination
	幻想	ゲンソウ	fantasy; illusion; dream —v. fantasize; hallucinate; dream
	幻想的	ゲンソウテキ	fantastic; illusory; dreamy
	幻灯	ゲントウ	slide
	幻滅	ゲンメツ	disillusionment —vi. be disillusioned
	幻惑	ゲンワク	dazzling; bewitching —v. dazzle; bewitch
訓	幻	まぼろし	phantom; illusion; hallucination

578

幼 ⑤　く 幺 幺 幻 幼

音	幼	ヨウ	infant; small child
熟	幼魚	ヨウギョ	young fish
	幼児	ヨウジ	infant; toddler; baby
	幼時	ヨウジ	childhood; infancy
	幼少	ヨウショウ	childhood; infancy

幼稚	ヨウチ	childish; infantile; puerile
幼稚園	ヨウチエン	kindergarten
幼虫	ヨウチュウ	larva
幼年	ヨウネン	childhood; infancy; child
幼名	ヨウメイ	one's infant name

訓
幼い	おさない	young; infantile; childish
幼な顔	おさながお	how one looked as a baby
幼子	おさなご	little child; baby
幼心	おさなごころ	child's mind/heart
※幼ない	いとけない	young; infant

579

 ⑨ 　丨　彳　彳　幺　纟　纟　纟　幽　幽

音
| 幽 | ユウ | confine to a room; faint; dim; weak; indistinct |

熟
幽界	ユウカイ	Hades; realm of the dead
幽鬼	ユウキ	ghost; devil; fairy
幽居	ユウキョ	isolated retreat
幽玄	ユウゲン	mystery; the occult
幽谷	ユウコク	deep valley; ravine; glen
幽囚	ユウシュウ	confinement; captivity
幽閉	ユウヘイ	confinement; house arrest; imprisonment —*v.* confine; shut up
幽明	ユウメイ	darkness and light
幽門	ユウモン	*med*. pylorus
幽霊	ユウレイ	ghost; apparition; spirit

訓
| ※幽かな | かすかな | faint; dim; weak; indistinct; hazy; poor; wretched |

580

 ⑫ 　⼂　幺　幺　幺′　幺′　幺幺　幺幺　幺′′　㦮　幾　幾

音
| 幾 | キ | nearly; almost |

熟
| 幾何学 | キカガク | geometry |

訓
幾	いく	how much/many
幾重	いくえ	how many folds/ply; repeatedly; earnestly
幾星霜	いくセイソウ	time
幾多	いくタ	many
幾つ	いくつ	how much/many
幾日	いくニチ	how many days

口口土士夕大女子宀寸小⺌⻭尢尸山川工己巾干幺广廴廾弋弓ヨ彡彳艹辶阝⺍忄扌氵犭

3 广　まだれ　dotted cliff

581

広 ⑤　` 一 广 広 広

音	広	コウ	wide; broad; spacious; spread
熟	広義	コウギ	broad sense
	広言	コウゲン	big talk; brag; boast; boasting —*vi.* talk big; brag; boast
	広原	コウゲン	vast plain; open country
	広告	コウコク	advertisement; notice; announcement —*v.* advertise; announce; give publicity to
	広大	コウダイ	vast; extensive; immense; huge
	広報	コウホウ	public information; publicity; public relations
訓	広い	ひろい	wide; broad; spacious; large
	広場	ひろば	open space; square; plaza
	広々	ひろびろ	wide; open; vast
	広間	ひろま	hall; saloon
	広がる	ひろがる	*vi.* spread out; expand; extend; stretch
	広げる	ひろげる	*vt.* extend; expand; enlarge; widen; unfold; open; lay out
	広さ	ひろさ	area; extent; dimensions
	広まる	ひろまる	*vi.* spread; be diffused/propagated
	広める	ひろめる	*vt.* extend; widen; broaden; spread; diffuse; propagate

582

庁 ⑤　` 一 广 庁 庁

音	庁	チョウ	agency; office; board
熟	庁舎	チョウシャ	government building

583

序 ⑦　` 一 广 庐 庐 序 序

音	序	ジョ	introduction
熟	序曲	ジョキョク	overture
	序文	ジョブン	preface; foreword; introduction

序幕	ジョマク	opening/first act
序列	ジョレツ	order; rank; ranking
序論	ジョロン	introduction

584

床 ⑦ ' 一 广 广 庁 庄 床

音	床	ショウ	bed; seat; the ground
訓	床	とこ	bed
	床の間	とこのま	*tokonoma* (alcove in a traditional Japanese home)
	床屋	とこや	barbershop; barber
	床	ゆか	floor
	床板	ゆかいた	floorboard
	床上	ゆかうえ	above the floor
	床下	ゆかした	under the floor

585

底 ⑧ ' 一 广 广 庐 庐 底 底

音	底	テイ	bottom; base; kind; sort
熟	底止	テイシ	cessation —*v.* cease; stop; end
	底辺	テイヘン	*math.* base (of a triangle) *fig.* bottom/lower levels (of society)
	底本	テイホン	original text; source book
	底流	テイリュウ	undercurrent; underflow
訓	底	そこ	base; bottom; lower part
	底力	そこぢから	latent energy; hidden power
¥	底値	そこね	rock-bottom/bedrock price

586

店 ⑧ ' 一 广 广 庐 庐 店 店

音	店	テン	shop
熟	店員	テンイン	clerk; shop assistant; salesman; saleswoman
	店主	テンシュ	shopkeeper; storekeeper; store owner
	店頭	テントウ	shop front; counter; shop; store
	店屋物	テンやもの	dishes from a caterer; dishes prepared at a store

口 口 土 士 夕 夕 大 女 子 宀 寸 小 ⺌ ⺍ 尢 尸 山 川 工 己 巾 干 幺 广 廴 廾 弋 弓 彐 彡 彳 艹 辶 阝 阝 ⺍ 忄 扌 氵 氵

3

口口土士夕夕大女子宀寸小⺌⺍尤尸山川工己巾干幺广廴廾弋弓彑彡彳⺾辶阝⻌忄扌犭氵

訓	店	みせ	stall; shop; office; place of business
	店先	みせさき	storefront
	店仕舞い	みせじまい	closing down of a business —*v.* close down a business
	店番	みせバン	tending a store; store tender; salesman
	店開き	みせびらき	opening of business —*v.* open business
	※店	たな	shop; store; house to let
¥	店頭株	テントウかぶ	over-the-counter stock; counter share
	店頭販売	テントウハンバイ	over-the-counter transaction
	店舗	テンポ	store; shop; outlet
	※店卸し	たなおろし	stocktaking; inventory; faultfinding; disparagement —*v.* take stock; take an inventory
	※店晒し	たなざらし	shop-soiled goods

587

府 ⑧ 　 ` 一 广 广 广 庁 府 府

音	府	フ	capital; prefecture (used only for Osaka and Kyoto)
熟	府議会	フギカイ	prefectural assembly
	府庁	フチョウ	prefectural office
	府立	フリツ	prefectural

588

度 ⑨ 　 ` 一 广 广 庐 庐 庐 度 度

音	度	ド	degree; frequency; extent; measure; time
		(タク)	
		(ト)	
熟	度合い	ドあい	degree; extent; rate
	度外視	ドガイシ	neglect; disregard —*v.* neglect; disregard; overlook; ignore
	度胸	ドキョウ	courage; pluck; mettle; guts; nerve
	度数	ドスウ	number of times; frequency; incidence; degree
	度量	ドリョウ	generosity; liberality; magnanimity; length and volume
	度量衡	ドリョウコウ	weights and measures
訓	度	たび	time; occasion; every time
	度重なる	たびかさなる	*vi.* be repeated/repetitive
	度々	たびたび	often; repeatedly; over and over

280

589

庫 ⑩   ` 一 广 广 广 广 庐 庐 庫 庫

| 音 | 庫 | コ (ク) | warehouse; store |
| 訓 | ※庫 | くら | warehouse; store; emporium |

590

座 ⑩   ` 一 广 广 广 广 庐 庐 座 座

音	座	ザ	sitting; gathering; theater
熟	座金	ザがね	metal washer
	座興	ザキョウ	joke; entertainment; fun
	座高	ザコウ	one's height when sitting
	座敷	ザシキ	Japanese-style room; guest room
	座礁	ザショウ	running aground; stranding —*vi.* run aground; be stranded
	座席	ザセキ	seat
	座禅	ザゼン	*zazen* (Zen meditation)
	座像	ザゾウ	seated statue; seated figure
	座談	ザダン	conversation; discussion —*vi.* converse; discuss
	座長	ザチョウ	chairman; chairperson
	座標	ザヒョウ	coordinates
	座布団	ザブトン	cushion
	座右	ザユウ	at one's side; within arm's reach
訓	座る	すわる	*vi.* sit down; be seated

591

庭 ⑩   ` 一 广 广 广 庄 庄 庭 庭 庭

音	庭	テイ	garden
熟	庭園	テイエン	garden; park
	庭球	テイキュウ	tennis
	庭前	テイゼン	garden
訓	庭	にわ	garden
	庭石	にわいし	garden stone
	庭先	にわさき	in the garden
	庭師	にわシ	landscape gardener; garden designer

口 口 土 士 夂 夕 大 女 宀 寸 小 ⺌ ⺌ 尢 尸 山 川 工 己 巾 干 幺 广 廴 廾 弋 弓 彐 彡 彳 艹 辶 阝 阝 ⺍ 忄 扌 氵 氵

ロロ土士夂夕大女子宀寸小⺌⻌尤尸山川工己巾干幺广廴廾弋弓彐彡彳艹辶阝阝⺍忄扌氵

592

康 ⑪

` 一 广 广 广 广 庐 庐 庚 康

音	康	コウ	peaceful; healthy

593

庶 ⑪

` 一 广 广 广 庐 庐 庐 庶 庶 庶

音	庶	ショ	people; many
熟	庶子	ショシ	illegitimate child
	庶民	ショミン	the common people
	庶務	ショム	general affairs

594

庸 ⑪

` 一 广 广 广 広 庐 庐 肩 肩 庸

音	庸	ヨウ	employ; ordinary

595

廃 ⑫

` 一 广 庐 庐 庐 庆 庆 庆 庨 摩 廃

音	廃	ハイ	become obsolete
熟	廃する	ハイする	*vt.* abolish; abandon; repeal; dethrone; discontinue
	廃刊	ハイカン	discontinued publication; out-of-print —*v.* discontinue publication
	廃棄	ハイキ	abandonment; disuse; abolition —*v.* do away with; annul; abolish; abandon
	廃虚	ハイキョ	ruins; remains
	廃業	ハイギョウ	discontinuance of business —*v.* give up one's business; shut up shop
	廃坑	ハイコウ	abandoned/disused mine
	廃校	ハイコウ	closing down of a school
	廃止	ハイシ	abolition; disuse; discontinuance; annulment —*v.* abolish; disuse; discontinue; annul; nullify
	廃人	ハイジン	person maimed for life; confirmed invalid
	廃絶	ハイゼツ	extinction —*v.* become extinct; be discontinued
	廃藩置県	ハイハンチケン	*hist.* abolition of clans and establishment of prefectures (Meiji period)

廃品	ハイヒン	scrap; junk; waste
廃品回収	ハイヒンカイシュウ	scrap collection
廃物	ハイブツ	scrap; useless thing; waste; trash

訓 廃る　すたる　*vi.* go out of use; fall into disuse; become obsolete; die out

廃れる　すたれる　*vi.* go out of use; fall into disuse; become obsolete; die out

---

596

廊 ⑫ 　` 一 广 广 庐 庐 庐 启 郎 庐 庐 廊 廊

| 音 廊 | ロウ | corridor; hall |
| 熟 廊下 | ロウカ | corridor; hall |

597

廉 ⑬ 　` 广 广 广 产 庐 庐 庐 庐 庐 庶 廉 廉

音 廉	レン	purity; honest; low price
熟 廉価	レンカ	low price
廉潔	レンケツ	honest; upright
廉直	レンチョク	honesty; integrity
廉売	レンバイ	bargain sale —*v.* sell cheaply

---

3 廴　えんにょう　stretching

598

廷 ⑦ 　一 二 千 壬 任 廷 廷

音 廷	テイ	court
熟 廷臣	テイシン	court official; courtier
廷吏	テイリ	sergeant

599

延 ⑧ 　一 千 千 正 正 延 延 延

| 音 延 | エン | extend; lengthen; postpone |

283

口口土士夂夕大女子宀寸小ザ巛尤尸山川工己巾干幺广廴廾弋弓ヨ彡彳忄扌氵

熟	延引	エンイン	delay; postponement; procrastination —*vi.* be delayed/postponed/put off
	延期	エンキ	delay; postponement; procrastination —*v.* delay; postpone; procrastinate; put off
	延焼	エンショウ	spread of a fire —*vi.* spread; catch fire
	延着	エンチャク	delayed/late arrival —*vi.* arrive late; be delayed
	延長	エンチョウ	extension; continuation —*v.* lengthen in time, scope, or range; extend; continue; prolong
訓	延ばす	のばす	*vt.* lengthen; stretch; extend; postpone; put off
	延びる	のびる	*vi.* lengthen; stretch; extend; be put off; be delayed
	延び	のび	postponement; putting off; stretching; growth; extension
	延び延び	のびのび	long delay
	延べる	のべる	*vt.* spread; extend; postpone; put off
	延べ	のべ	total; aggregate
¥	延滞	エンタイ	delay (in payment) —*vi.* be behind (with payments); be in arrears
	延べ払い	のべばらい	deferred payment

600

 ⑨　フ　ユ　ヨ　ヨ　ヨ　聿　肀　建　建

音	建	ケン (コン)	build
熟	建国	ケンコク	foundation of a state
	建設	ケンセツ	construction; building; establishment —*v.* construct; build; establish
	建造	ケンゾウ	building; construction —*v.* build; construct
	建造物	ケンゾウブツ	structure
	建築	ケンチク	building; construction; architecture —*v.* build; construct
	建築家	ケンチクカ	architecture
	建立	コンリュウ	erection/construction (of a shrine or a temple) —*v.* erect/construct (a shrine or temple)
訓	建つ	たつ	*vi.* be built/set up/erected
	建てる	たてる	*vt.* build; construct; erect
	建具	たてグ	door; sliding door; window frames; fittings; fixtures
	建具屋	たてグや	joiner
	建坪	たてつぼ	floor space
	建て前	たてまえ	*tatemae* (principle); roof-raising ceremony
	建物	たてもの	building

284

¥	建設省	ケンセツショウ	Ministry of Construction
	建て玉	たてだま	commitment; outstanding loan
	建て値	たてね	market price

---

3 廾 こまぬき twenty legs

601

弊 ⑮ 丶 丷 丷 丷 尚 尚 尚 尚 尚 敝 敝 弊

音	弊	ヘイ	abuse; evil; get old/shabby/tired (humble)
熟	弊害	ヘイガイ	evil; ill effects
	弊社	ヘイシャ	*hum*. our company; we
	弊習	ヘイシュウ	bad habit/manners
	弊村	ヘイソン	impoverished village; *hum*. our village
	弊風	ヘイフウ	bad habit/manners

---

3 弋 しきたすき／しきがまえ ceremony

602

式 ⑥ 一 二 テ 王 式 式

音	式	シキ	ceremony; formula; system; equation; expression
熟	式辞	シキジ	address (at a ceremony)
	式次	シキジ	order of ceremonies
	式日	シキジツ	day of a ceremony
	式場	シキジョウ	ceremonial hall
	式台	シキダイ	step in a Japanese entryway
	式典	シキテン	ceremony
	式服	シキフク	formal/ceremonial dress

603

弐 ⑥ 一 二 二 弍 弍 弐

音	弐	ニ	two (used on official documents)
熟	弐万円	ニマンエン	twenty thousand yen

弓 ゆみ／ゆみへん bow

3

604

弓 ③ ⁊ ⁊ 弓

音	弓	キュウ	bow; bow-shaped
熟	弓術	キュウジュツ	archery; bowmanship
	弓状	キュウジョウ	bow-shaped; arched
	弓道	キュウドウ	*kyūdō* (Japanese archery)
訓	弓	ゆみ	bow
	弓矢	ゆみや	bow and arrow

605

引 ④ ⁊ ⁊ 弓 引

音	引	イン	pull; attract; guide; lead
熟	引火	インカ	ignition; combustion —*vi.* ignite; set fire to; combust
	引責	インセキ	assumption of responsibility —*vi.* assume responsibility
	引率	インソツ	leadership; command —*v.* lead; head; command
	引退	インタイ	retirement —*vi.* retire; withdraw from public life
	引用	インヨウ	quotation; citation —*v.* quote; cite
	引力	インリョク	gravitation
	引例	インレイ	quotation; citation
訓	引く	ひく	*vt.* pull; draw; reduce; retire; drag; lay on; refer to
	引き受ける	ひきうける	*vt.* accept an offer; assume; take over; guarantee
	引き換える	ひきかえる	*vt.* change; exchange; convert
	引き算	ひきザン	*math.* subtraction
	引き出し	ひきだし	drawer
	引き立てる	ひきたてる	*vt.* make (someone/something) stand out
	引き取る	ひきとる	*vt.* take over
	引き抜く	ひきぬく	*vt.* pull out
	引き分ける	ひきわける	*v.* draw; tie
	引け目	ひけめ	inferiority complex
	引っ越す	ひっこす	*vi.* move house

口口土士夂夕大女子宀寸小⺌⺍尤尸山川工己巾干幺广廴廾弋弓彐彡彳艹辶阝阝宀忄扌犭氵

引っ張る	ひっぱる	**vt**. pull
¥ 引き合い	ひきあい	inquiry; deal
引き上げ	ひきあげ	pulling up; raise; increase
引当金	ひきあてキン	allowance; revenues
引き受け	ひきうけ	underwriting
引受会社	ひきうけガイシャ	accepting corporation; underwriter
引け	ひけ	closing; close

606

弔 ④   ⌐ ⊐ 弓 弔

音	弔	チョウ	mourn
熟	弔意	チョウイ	condolence; mourning; sympathy
	弔辞	チョウジ	memorial address
	弔電	チョウデン	condolatory telegram
	弔文	チョウブン	funeral address
	弔問	チョウモン	sympathy call —**v.** make a sympathy call
訓	弔い	とむらい	funeral; burial; mass for the dead; condolence
	弔う	とむらう	**vt**. mourn; condole; perform a Buddhist memorial service

---

607

弟 ⑦   丶 丷 䒑 䒑 弟 弟 弟

音	弟	テイ	younger brother
		（ダイ）	
		（デ）	
熟	弟妹	テイマイ	younger brothers and sisters
	弟子	デシ	disciple
訓	弟	おとうと	younger brother

608

弦 ⑧   ⌐ ⊐ 弓 弓' 弙 弙 弦 弦

音	弦	ゲン	bowstring; string
熟	弦楽	ゲンガク	music of stringed instruments
	弦楽器	ゲンガッキ	stringed instrument
訓	弦	つる	string (on an instrument)

口口土士夕大女子宀寸小⺌⺍尢尸山川工己巾干幺广廴廾弋弓彐彡彳⺅⺾辶阝阝亠忄扌氵

609

弧 ⑨
丶 丶 弓 弖 弧 弧 弧 弧 弧

音	弧	コ	arc
熟	弧状	コジョウ	arch

610

弱 ⑩
丶 コ 弓 弓 弓 弓 弱 弱 弱 弱

音	弱	ジャク	weak
熟	弱酸	ジャクサン	weak acid
	弱視	ジャクシ	weak sight; amblyopia
	弱小	ジャクショウ	small and weak; young
	弱震	ジャクシン	minor earthquake; tremor
	弱卒	ジャクソツ	weak soldier/subordinate
	弱体	ジャクタイ	weak body/system
	弱敵	ジャクテキ	unworthy enemy
	弱点	ジャクテン	weakness; weak point; shortcoming; defect
	弱電機	ジャクデンキ	light electric appliance
	弱肉強食	ジャクニクキョウショク	survival of the fittest; law of the jungle
	弱年	ジャクネン	youth
	弱輩	ジャクハイ	young fellow; kid
	弱化	ジャッカ	weakening —v. weaken
	弱冠	ジャッカン	youth
訓	弱い	よわい	weak; frail; feeble; poor; bad
	弱気	よわキ	timid; fainthearted
	弱腰	よわごし	weak attitude
	弱音	よわね	complaint
	弱火	よわび	slow flame; low heat
	弱虫	よわむし	coward; weakling
	弱々しい	よわよわしい	feeble; faint; frail; delicate; fragile
	弱さ	よわさ	weakness; feebleness; frailty
	弱まる	よわまる	vi. get weak; abate; drop; calm down
	弱み	よわみ	weak position; vulnerability; weak point
	弱める	よわめる	vt. weaken; impair; decrease; turn down; lower; dilute
	弱る	よわる	vi. grow weak; weaken; be at a loss what to do; be in a fix
	弱り果てる	よわりはてる	vi. be weak with exhaustion; be annoyed; be fed up

288

強 ⑪

ㄱ ㄱ 弓 弘 弘 弘 弘 弘 強 強 強

音	強	キョウ	strong; strengthen; force
		ゴウ	strong
熟	強化	キョウカ	strengthening; intensification; reinforcement —v. strengthen; solidify; build up; intensify
	強健	キョウケン	robust health; strong constitution
	強権	キョウケン	authority; state power
	強固	キョウコ	firmness; stability; solidity; security; strength
	強行	キョウコウ	enforcement; force —v. enforce; force
	強硬	キョウコウ	tough elements; hard-liners
	強豪	キョウゴウ	veteran; strong player
	強震	キョウシン	strong earthquake
	強勢	キョウセイ	emphasis; stress
	強制	キョウセイ	compulsion; coercion; duress —v. compel; force; coerce
	強壮	キョウソウ	robustness
	強大	キョウダイ	mighty; powerful; strong
	強調	キョウチョウ	emphasis —v. emphasize
	強度	キョウド	intensity; strength
	強要	キョウヨウ	persistent demand; extortion —v. exact; compel; force; coerce
	強力	キョウリョク	power; might
	強烈	キョウレツ	intense; strong; severe
	強引	ゴウイン	force
	強情	ゴウジョウ	obstinacy; stubbornness
	強奪	ゴウダツ	seizure; extortion; robbery —v. seize; rob with violence
	強盗	ゴウトウ	burglar; robber; housebreaker
	強欲	ゴウヨク	avarice; greed; greediness
訓	強い	つよい	strong
	強まる	つよまる	vi. become strong; be intensified; increase; be emphasized
	強める	つよめる	vt. strengthen; intensify; increase; emphasize
	強いる	しいる	vt. force; compel; press
¥	強行採決	キョウコウサイケツ	forcing a vote —v. force a vote (in the House of Representatives)
	強制的	キョウセイテキ	mandatory; compulsory
	強制破産	キョウセイハサン	forced liquidation
	強気筋	つよキすじ	bull (long) account (interest)
	強含み	つよふくみ	strengthening; strong feeling (market)

口 口 土 士 夂 夕 大 女 子 宀 寸 小 ⺌ ⺍ 尢 尸 山 川 工 己 巾 干 幺 广 廴 廾 弋 弓 ⺕ 彡 彳 ⺾ 辶 阝 阝 ⺶ 扌 氵 犭

3

口 口 土 士 夕 大 女 子 宀 寸 小 ⺌ ⺌ 尢 尸 山 川 工 己 巾 干 幺 广 廴 廾 弋 弓 ⼹ ⼹ ⺕ ⼺ 彳 ⾋ 辶 ⻏ ⻏ ⺍ 忄 扌 犭 氵

612

張 ⑪　　ᐟ ᑕ 引 引 引 引 引 張 張 張 張

音	張	チョウ	stretch
熟	張本人	チョウホンニン	ringleader
	張力	チョウリョク	tension; tensile force
訓	張る	はる	*v.* stretch; spread; extend; strain; tighten
	張り合う	はりあう	*vi.* rival; emulate; compete
	張り切る	はりきる	*vi.* be in high spirits
	張り子	はりこ	papier-mâché
	張り込む	はりこむ	*vi.* keep watch/lookout; be eager; invest

613

弾 ⑫　　ᐟ ᑕ 弓 弓 弓 弓 弓 弾 弾 弾 弾 弾

音	弾	ダン	bullet; projectile; missile; bounce; spring; rebound
熟	弾圧	ダンアツ	oppression; suppression; pressure; coercion —*v.* oppress; surpress; repress; crush
	弾劾	ダンガイ	impeachment; denunciation; accusation; censure —*v.* impeach; denounce; accuse
	弾丸	ダンガン	bullet; projectile; cannonball
	弾性	ダンセイ	elasticity
	弾道	ダンドウ	trajectory; line of fire
	弾薬	ダンヤク	ammunition; munitions
	弾力	ダンリョク	elasticity; elastic force; resilience; spring
訓	弾む	はずむ	*v.* spring; bound; rebound; be stimulated/encouraged
	弾く	ひく	*vt.* play (a musical instrument)
	弾	たま	bullet

---

3 彐 けいがしら pig's head

614

粛 ⑪　　ᐟ ⼺ ⼺ 聿 聿 聿 聿 肅 肅 肅 肅

音	粛	シュク	be discreet

290

熟	粛正	シュクセイ	enforcement; cleanup —*v.* enforce; clean up
	粛清	シュクセイ	political purge —*v.* purge
	粛然	シュクゼン	silently; quietly; solemnly

---

3 彡 さんづくり short hair

615

形⑦ 一 ニ テ 开 开 形 形

音	形	ケイ	shape; form; appearance
		ギョウ	form; figure; model
熟	形相	ギョウソウ	looks; figure; face
	形骸化	ケイガイカ	becoming a mere name; taking the teeth out —*vi.* become a mere name; take the teeth out
	形式	ケイシキ	formation
	形式的	ケイシキテキ	formally; perfunctory
	形而上	ケイジジョウ	metaphysical
	形状	ケイジョウ	shape; state
	形勢	ケイセイ	situation; state of affairs
	形成	ケイセイ	formation —*v.* form; build/make up
	形成外科	ケイセイゲカ	plastic/cosmetic surgery
	形跡	ケイセキ	traces; evidence
	形態	ケイタイ	form; shape
	形容	ケイヨウ	description; qualification; modification —*v.* describe; modify; qualify
	形容詞	ケイヨウシ	*gram.* adjective
	形容動詞	ケイヨウドウシ	*gram.* adjectival verb (verb used to qualify/modify a noun)
訓	形	かた	shape; form; model; pattern
	形	かたち	shape; form
	形見	かたみ	keepsake; memento

616

彩⑪ 一 ⺈ ⺈ ⺈ ⺈ 平 平 采 采 彩 彩

| 音 | 彩 | サイ | color |
| 熟 | 彩色 | サイショク (サイシキ) | coloring —*v.* color |

訓	彩る	いろどる	*vt*. color; be bright
	彩り	いろどり	coloring; color scheme

617 彫 ⑪
） 刀 刀 門 用 用 周 周 周ʼ 彫 彫

音	彫	チョウ	engrave
熟	彫金	チョウキン	metal carving; chasing
	彫刻	チョウコク	sculpture; carving; engraving —*v.* sculpture; carve; engrave
	彫刻家	チョウコクカ	sculptor; engraver; carver
	彫塑	チョウソ	carving and modeling; clay model
	彫像	チョウゾウ	statue
訓	彫る	ほる	*vt*. carve; engrave; sculpture; tattoo

618 彰 ⑭
、 亠 立 产 音 音 音 童 章 彰

音	彰	ショウ	manifest

619 影 ⑮
ノ 口 日 旦 早 昗 昗 景 景 影

音	影	エイ	shadow; shape
熟	影響	エイキョウ	influence; effect —*vi.* influence; affect
訓	影	かげ	shadow; image; ghost
	影絵	かげえ	shadow picture
	影法師	かげボウシ	shadow; silhouette
	影武者	かげムシャ	dummy general

3	彳	ぎょうにんべん	going man

620 役 ⑦
ノ ク 彳 彳 彳 役 役

音	役	エキ	war; battle; service

	役	ヤク	post; role; duty; charge
熟	役者	ヤクシャ	actor
	役所	ヤクショ	government office
	役立つ	ヤクだつ	*vi*. be useful; serve a purpose
	役立てる	ヤクだてる	*vt*. put to use; make use of
	役人	ヤクニン	officer
	役場	ヤクば	town office
	役割	ヤクわり	part; role
¥	役員	ヤクイン	director on the board; corporate executive
	役員賞与	ヤクインショウヨ	bonus for directors and auditors

621

往 ⑧   ノ ク イ 彳 彳 行 行 往

音	往	オウ	go; former; past
熟	往々	オウオウ	sometimes; occasionally; now and then
	往時	オウジ	the past; things past
	往生	オウジョウ	death; submission —*vi*. die; pass away; submit
	往信	オウシン	outgoing letter; letter sent
	往診	オウシン	physician's house call —*vi*. make a house call
	往年	オウネン	former years; formerly; the past
	往復	オウフク	round/return trip —*v*. go and come back; make a round trip
	往来	オウライ	coming and going; street traffic —*vi*. come and go
	往路	オウロ	outward trip/journey
訓	往く	ゆく	*vi*. go

622

径 ⑧   ノ ク イ 彳 彳 径 径 径

音	径	ケイ	lane; small road; path; diameter
熟	径路	ケイロ	course; route; process

623

征 ⑧   ノ ク イ 彳 彳 征 征 征

音	征	セイ	attack

3

口 口 土 士 夂 夕 大 女 子 宀 寸 小 ⺌ ⺍ 尤 尸 山 川 工 己 巾 干 幺 广 廴 廾 弋 弓 彐 彡 彳 • 艹 辶 阝 阝 亠 忄 扌 氵 犭

熟	征伐	セイバツ	subjugation; conquest —*v.* conquer; subjugate
	征服	セイフク	conquest —*v.* conquer; overcome; subdue
	征服者	セイフクシャ	conqueror

624

彼 ⑧ ′ �ノ イ ⼻ 行 扩 护 彼 彼

音	彼	ヒ	he; that
熟	彼我	ヒガ	oneself and others; each other
	彼岸	ヒガン	equinoctial week; the other shore; that
訓	彼	かれ	he; boyfriend; lover
	彼氏	かれシ	he; boyfriend; lover
	彼等	かれら	they
	彼	かの	that
	彼女	かのジョ	she; girlfriend; lover
	※彼方	かなた	there; yonder; the other side

625

後 ⑨ ′ ⼻ イ ⼿ 彳 祥 徉 移 移 後

音	後	ゴ	after; post; later
		（コウ）	
熟	後遺症	コウイショウ	*med.* prognostic symptoms; aftereffect
	後援	コウエン	support; backing —*v.* support; give support to; back up
	後悔	コウカイ	repentance; regret; remorse —*v.* repent; regret; show remorse
	後学	コウガク	future scholars; future reference
	後記	コウキ	postscript
	後期	コウキ	latter period
	後継者	コウケイシャ	successor; heir; heiress
	後見人	コウケンニン	guardian
	後者	コウシャ	latter
	後進	コウシン	reversing —*v.* reverse; back up; go backwards
	後進国	コウシンコク	developing country
	後世	コウセイ	future generations; ages to come
	後続	コウゾク	following; succeeding; next
	後退	コウタイ	retreat; recession; retrogression; step back —*vi.* retreat; retrogress; go backwards; step back
	後天的	コウテンテキ	acquired; postnatal

294

後任	コウニン	successor	
後年	コウネン	future years; in years to come; later; afterwards	
後輩	コウハイ	one's junior; underclassmen	
後半	コウハン	latter/second half	
後半生	コウハンセイ	the latter half of life	
後尾	コウビ	end of the line; tail end	
後部	コウブ	back end; rear	
後家	ゴケ	widow	
後光	ゴコウ	halo	
後妻	ゴサイ	second wife	
後日	ゴジツ	later date; later on; in the future	
後手	ゴテ	one step behind; too late; second player (in go or shōgi)	

訓 後 あと — later; after; next; the rest

後押し	あとおし	push; support; backup —v. push; support; back up
後始末	あとシマツ	settlement
後ずさり	あとずさり	stepping back —vi. step back
後回し	あとまわし	postponement; putting off
後ろ	うしろ	back; behind
後ろめたい	うしろめたい	feel uneasy/guilty; have a bad conscience
後ろ指	うしろゆび	suspicion
後れる	おくれる	vi. be late; be backward
後	のち	later; afterwards; in the future

¥
後入れ先出し法	あといれさきだしホウ	last-in first-out method
後配株	コウハイかぶ	deferred stock
後場	ゴば	afternoon session

626

待 ⑨　ノ ラ イ 彳 彳 社 往 待 待

音 待	タイ	wait; treat	
熟 待機	タイキ	waiting for a chance —vi. watch and wait; wait and see	
待遇	タイグウ	treatment; reception; service; pay; salary —v. treat; receive; entertain	
待避	タイヒ	sheltering —v. take shelter	
待望	タイボウ	eager waiting —v. wait eagerly	
訓 待つ	まつ	vt. wait	
待合室	まちあいシツ	waiting room	

口 口 土 士 夂 夕 大 女 子 宀 寸 小 ⺌ ⺍ 尢 尸 山 川 工 己 巾 干 幺 广 廴 廾 弋 弓 彐 彡 彳 艹 辶 阝 阝 丷 忄 扌 氵 犭

3

口口土士夂夕大女子宀寸小⺌⺍尢尸山川工已巾干幺广廴廾弋弓彐彡彳⺾⻌阝⺍忄扌犭氵

627

律 ⑨

丶 �ノ ⼻ イ 彳 彳 律 律 律 律

音	律	リツ （リチ）	law; regulation; rhythm
熟	律する	リッする	*vt*. judge; measure
	律儀	リチギ	honesty; integrity; loyalty
	律動	リツドウ	rhythm —*vi*. have rhythm; be rhythmic
	律法	リッポウ	law; rule
	律令	リツリョウ	code of laws; laws and orders

628

従 ⑩

丶 ノ イ 彳 彳 彳 彳 彷 従 従

音	従	ジュウ （ジュ） （ショウ）	obey; follow; engage in junior grade
熟	従業員	ジュウギョウイン	employee
	従軍	ジュウグン	going to the front with the army —*vi*. go to the front with the army
	従事	ジュウジ	engagement; involvement —*vi*. engage in; be involved in
	従順	ジュウジュン	obedience; submission
	従属	ジュウゾク	subordination —*vi*. be subordinate to
	従来	ジュウライ	hitherto; as in the past; as usual
訓	従う	したがう	*vi*. follow; accompany; obey; conform; comply
	従える	したがえる	*vt*. be attended/followed by
	従って	したがって	accordingly; consequently; therefore; in obedience to; as; in proportion to

---

629

徐 ⑩

丶 ノ イ 彳 彳 彳 彴 徐 徐 徐

音	徐	ジョ	slow
熟	徐行	ジョコウ	slow speed; slowly —*vi*. go slowly; go at slow speed
	徐々に	ジョジョに	gradually; little by little; slowly

630

徒 ⑩ ノ ク イ 犭 犳 彴 彴 祏 徙 徒

音	徒	ト	on foot; empty; vain; companions; disciple; punishment
熟	徒競争	トキョウソウ	footrace; race on foot
	徒弟	トテイ	apprentice; disciple
	徒党	トトウ	faction; conspirators; league
	徒歩	トホ	walking; going on foot
	徒労	トロウ	futile effort; vain attempt; fruitless labor
訓	※徒	あだ	empty; vain

631

得 ⑪ ノ ク イ 彴 狗 袒 袒 得 得 得

音	得	トク	obtain; acquire; ability
熟	得する	トクする	*vi.* obtain; acquire; get
	得意	トクイ	pride; triumph; forte; strong point; customer; patron
	得策	トクサク	good policy; best plan
	得失	トクシツ	relative merits; advantages and disadvantages; profit and loss
	得心	トクシン	conviction; consent; compliance —*vi.* consent to; comply with; be convinced of
	得点	トクテン	score; marks obtained —*vi.* score; gain marks
	得票	トクヒョウ	polling score —*vi.* poll; gain/win votes
	得票数	トクヒョウスウ	number of votes polled
訓	得る	うる	*vt.* obtain; acquire; get; can; be able to
	得る	える	*vt.* get; have; obtain; acquire; can; be able to
	得手	えて	strong point; forte

632

御 ⑫ ノ ク イ 彳 彳 彴 彴 得 得 御 御

音	御	ギョ	skilled driving; control; manage
		ゴ	(honorific prefix)
熟	御する	ギョする	*vt.* control; manage
	御者	ギョシャ	coach driver; carriage handler
	御所	ゴショ	imperial palace

297

3

口口土士夊夕大女子宀寸小⺌⺍尢尸山川工己巾干幺广廴廾弋弓彐彡彳⺾辶⻏⻏亠忄扌犭氵

	御破算	ゴハサン	calculating anew; calling the whole thing off; making a fresh start
	御用	ゴヨウ	business; order; government service
	御来光	ゴライコウ	view of the rising sun from a mountain top
	御陵	ゴリョウ	imperial tomb
訓	御	おん	(honorific prefix)
	御中	おんチュウ	Messrs

633

循 ⑫ 　ヽ ノ 彳 彳 彳 彳 彳 彳 循 循 循 循

音	循	ジュン	follow; circulate
熟	循環	ジュンカン	circulation; cycle —*vi.* circulate; go in circles
	循環器	ジュンカンキ	*med.*/circulatory organ

634

復 ⑫ 　ヽ ノ 彳 彳 彳 彳 彳 彳 彳 復 復 復

音	復	フク	return; repeat; be restored
熟	復する	フクする	*v.* return; be restored; reply; take revenge
	復位	フクイ	restoration; reinstatement —*vi.* be restored/reinstated
	復員	フクイン	demobilization —*v.* be demobilized and sent home
	復縁	フクエン	reconciliation (with one's husband/wife) —*vi.* be reconciled (with one's husband/wife)
	復元	フクゲン	restoration (to the original state) —*v.* restore; reconstruct
	復習	フクシュウ	review; revision —*v.* review; revise
	復讐	フクシュウ	revenge —*vi.* revenge oneself; avenge
	復唱	フクショウ	repeat —*v.* repeat an order aloud
	復職	フクショク	reinstatement; reappointment —*vi.* be reinstated/reappointed in one's job
	復命	フクメイ	report —*v.* report (to one's superior)
	復路	フクロ	return trip
	復活	フッカツ	rebirth; revival —*v.* be reborn/brought back to life
	復活祭	フッカツサイ	Easter
	復刊	フッカン	republication; reissue —*v.* republish; reissue
	復帰	フッキ	return; reinstatement —*vi.* return; reinstate; come back
	復旧	フッキュウ	restoration; recovery —*v.* restore; be restored

298

復古	フッコ	restoration (of the old régime/situation) —v. restore; be restored
復古調	フッコチョウ	reactionary mood
復興	フッコウ	reconstruction; revival —v. reconstruct; revive
復刻	フッコク	republication; reissue —v. republish; reissue

訓 ※復 | また | again

635

微 ⑬ 　ｿ 亻 犭 彴 犲 犲 犲 徉 徿 微 微

音 微	ビ (ミ)	minute; slight

熟 微温	ビオン	lukewarm; tepid
微行	ビコウ	traveling incognito —vi. travel incognito
微光	ビコウ	faint light; glimmering
微細	ビサイ	minute; tiny
微視的	ビシテキ	microscopic
微弱	ビジャク	faint; feeble
微小	ビショウ	microscopic; minute; tiny
微少	ビショウ	minute quantity
微笑	ビショウ	smile
微震	ビシン	slight earthquake/tremor
微生物	ビセイブツ	*bio.* microorganism; microbe
微動	ビドウ	tremor; quiver; slight shock
微熱	ビネツ	*med.* slight fever
微風	ビフウ	gentle breeze
微分	ビブン	*math.* differential calculus
微妙	ビミョウ	delicate; subtle
微粒子	ビリュウシ	tiny particle; fine-grained
微量	ビリョウ	minute amount
微力	ビリョク	*hum.* my (poor) ability
微々たる	ビビたる	slight; meager; trifling
微塵	ミジン	particle; bit; iota

訓 ※微か | かすか | faint; dim

636

徴 ⑭ 　彳 彳 彳 彷 彷 徍 徉 徏 徎 徴 徴

音 徴	チョウ	sign; symbol; indication; omen; demand; call

3

口口土士夂夕大女子宀寸小⺌⺍尢尸山川工己巾干幺广廴廾弋弓彐彡彳

•⺿⻌阝丷忄扌犭氵

熟	徴候	チョウコウ	sign; indication; omen
	徴収	チョウシュウ	collection; levy; imposition —*v.* collect; levy; impose
	徴集	チョウシュウ	levy; enlistment; enrollment; recruitment —*v.* levy; enlist; conscript; recruit; call up
	徴税	チョウゼイ	tax collection —*v.* collect/raise/levy taxes
	徴発	チョウハツ	requisition; commandeering —*v.* requisition; commandeer
	徴兵	チョウヘイ	conscription; enlistment; the draft —*vi.* conscript; enlist; draft
	徴兵制度	チョウヘイセイド	conscription system
	徴募	チョウボ	recruitment —*vt.* recruit
	徴用	チョウヨウ	commandeering; drafting; requisition —*v.* commandeer; draft; requisition; levy

637

徳⑭ 彳 彳 彳 彳 徏 徏 徏 徳 徳 徳 徳 徳

音	徳	トク	virtue; goodness; grace; character
熟	徳育	トクイク	moral education/training
	徳政	トクセイ	benevolent administration
	徳性	トクセイ	morality
	徳操	トクソウ	strong moral sense/character
	徳望	トクボウ	moral influence
	徳目	トクモク	individual article of ethics
	徳用	トクヨウ	economical
	徳利	トクリ	flask; liquor bottle; turtleneck
	徳化	トッカ	*v.* influence by good moral example
	徳行	トッコウ	virtuous conduct; virtue; goodness

638

徹⑮ 彳 彳 彳 彳 徍 徎 徎 徎 徹 徹 徹 徹

音	徹	テツ	penetrate
熟	徹する	テッする	*vi.* penetrate; go right through; be thorough/complete
	徹底	テッテイ	thoroughness; completeness —*vi.* be thorough/complete/exhaustive
	徹底的	テッテイテキ	thorough; complete; perfect
	徹頭徹尾	テットウテツビ	throughout; thoroughly; from beginning to end
	徹夜	テツヤ	all-night vigil/sitting —*vi.* sit/stay up all night; keep vigil

300

3　艹　くさかんむり　grass crown

639

芋 ⑥　一 十 ヤ サ 芏 芋

訓	芋	いも	potato

640

芝 ⑥　一 十 ヤ サ 芝 芝

訓	芝	しば	lawn; turf
	芝居	しばい	play; drama; theater
	※芝生	しばふ	lawn; turf

641

花 ⑦　一 十 ヤ サ 艾 花 花

音	花	カ	flower; gaudy
熟	花壇	カダン	flower bed
	花鳥風月	カチョウフウゲツ	beauties of nature; elegant pursuits
	花瓶	カビン	vase
	花粉	カフン	pollen
	花弁	カベン	petal
訓	花	はな	flower; cherry blossoms; gratuity; flower arrangement
	花形	はながた	floral pattern; celebrity; popular star
	花束	はなたば	bouquet; bunch of flowers
	花火	はなび	fireworks
	花見	はなみ	cherry-blossom viewing
	花婿	はなむこ	bridegroom
	花嫁	はなよめ	bride

642

芸 ⑦　一 十 ヤ サ 兰 芸 芸

音	芸	ゲイ	learning; art; entertainment

301

3

口 口 土 士 夂 夕 大 女 子 宀 寸 小 ⺌ 尢 尸 山 川 工 己 巾 干 幺 广 廴 廾 弋 弓 彐 彡 彳 艹 辶 阝 阝 丷 忄 扌 氵 犭

口
口
土
士
夂
夕
大
女
子
宀
寸
小
⺌
⺍
尢
尸
山
川
工
己
巾
干
幺
广
廴
廾
弋
弓
ヨ
彡
彳
⺾
⻌
⻏
⻖
⺗
⺘
⺡

熟	芸者	ゲイシャ	geisha
	芸術	ゲイジュツ	art; the arts
	芸当	ゲイトウ	feat; trick; stunt; performance
	芸道	ゲイドウ	art; accomplishments
	芸人	ゲイニン	artist; entertainer; public performer
	芸能	ゲイノウ	public entertainment; performing arts
	芸名	ゲイメイ	stage name

643

芳 ⑦ 一 十 艹 芒 芋 芳 芳

音	芳	ホウ	fragrance; (honorific prefix)
熟	芳香	ホウコウ	fragrance; perfume; aroma
	芳志	ホウシ	*hon*. your good wishes/kindness
	芳醇	ホウジュン	mellow/rich (saké)
	芳書	ホウショ	*hon*. your kind letter
	芳情	ホウジョウ	*hon*. your kindness
	芳心	ホウシン	*hon*. your good wishes/kindness
	芳墨	ホウボク	scented ink *hon*. your kind letter
	芳名	ホウメイ	*hon*. your name; good name/reputation
	芳名録	ホウメイロク	visitor's book; name list
	芳烈	ホウレツ	perfume; fragrance; aroma
訓	芳しい	かんばしい	fragrant; aromatic; excellent; superior
	※芳ばしい	こうばしい	fragrant; aromatic

644

英 ⑧ 一 十 艹 苎 苎 苙 革 英

音	英	エイ	brilliant; eminent; England; English
熟	英気	エイキ	virility; energy; vigor
	英語	エイゴ	the English language
	英国	エイコク	England; Britain
	英才	エイサイ	genius; talent
	英断	エイダン	decisive judgment
	英知	エイチ	wisdom; intelligence
	英文	エイブン	English writing
	英文学	エイブンガク	English literature
	英文法	エイブンポウ	English grammar
	英米	エイベイ	England and America; English and American

英訳	エイヤク	English translation —*v*. translate into English
英雄	エイユウ	hero
英霊	エイレイ	the spirits of the war dead; the souls of those killed in battle

---

645

芽 ⑧ 一 ＋ ＋ 丗 丗 芒 芽 芽

音	芽	ガ	bud
訓	芽	め	bud; good luck
	芽生え	めばえ	sprout; bud
	芽生える	めばえる	*vi*. spring up; sprout

646

苦 ⑧ 一 ＋ ＋ 丗 芒 芢 苦 苦

音	苦	ク	bitter; pain; hard work
熟	苦学	クガク	self-support through university —*vi*. pay one's way/work through university
	苦境	クキョウ	distressed circumstances; dire straits
	苦行	クギョウ	penance; aseticism —*vi*. do penance; practice aseticism
	苦言	クゲン	outspoken advice; bitter counsel
	苦汁 (をなめる)	クジュウ (をなめる)	experience the bitterness of life
	苦笑	クショウ	wry smile; strained laugh —*vi*. smile wryly
	苦情	クジョウ	complaint; grievance; objection
	苦心	クシン	pains; effort; labor; trouble; hard work —*vi*. make painstaking efforts
	苦戦	クセン	hard fight; desperate battle —*vi*. fight hard; battle desperately
	苦痛	クツウ	pain; anguish
	苦闘	クトウ	bitter struggle; hard fight —*vi*. put up a bitter struggle/hard fight
	苦難	クナン	distress; suffering; affliction
	苦肉の策	クニクのサク	last resort; desperate/clumsy measure taken under the pressure of necessity
	苦悩	クノウ	suffering; distress; affliction —*vi*. suffer; be distressed/afflicted
	苦杯	クハイ	bitter cup/experience
	苦楽	クラク	joys and sorrows
	苦慮	クリョ	anxiety; worry; concern —*vi*. be anxious; worry; feel concern

3

苦労　　　クロウ　　　trouble; hardship; suffering —*vi.* be troubled; suffer hardship

訓　苦しい　　くるしい　　painful; hard; difficult; embarrassing
　　苦しむ　　くるしむ　　*vi.* suffer from; groan; agonize; be troubled with; worry oneself; be at a loss
　　苦しめる　くるしめる　*vt.* torment; torture; distress; trouble; inflict pain
　　苦い　　　にがい　　　bitter; hard; trying
　　苦手　　　にがて　　　weak point; be bad (at)
　　苦り切る　にがりきる　*vi.* pull a sour face

647

茎⑧　　一　十　艹　芏　艼　苙　茎　茎

音　茎　　　ケイ　　　stalk; stem; stalk shaped
訓　茎　　　くき　　　stalk; stem

648

若⑧　　一　十　艹　艹　芍　芒　若　若

音　若　　　ジャク　　　young
　　　　　　（ニャク）

熟　若年　　ジャクネン　　youth
　　若輩　　ジャクハイ　　young fellow
　　若干　　ジャッカン　　some; a few
訓　若い　　わかい　　　young; immature; green
　　若草　　わかくさ　　green/young grass
　　若気　　わかゲ　　　youthful impatience
　　若様　　わかさま　　prince
　　若衆　　わかシュウ　　young person
　　若造　　わかゾウ　　stripling
　　若旦那　わかダンナ　　young master
　　若作り　わかづくり　　making oneself up to look young; mutton dressed up as lamb
　　若手　　わかて　　　young person
　　若向き　わかむき　　suitable for younger people
　　若者　　わかもの　　young man/people; youth
　　若し　　もし　　　if; in case of; suppose
　　若しくは　もしくは　　or; either
※　若人　　わこうど　　young person/people

口
口
土
士
夂
夕
大
女
子
宀
寸
小
⺌
⺍
尢
尸
山
川
工
己
巾
干
幺
广
廴
廾
弋
弓
ヨ
彡
彳
⺾
⻌
⻏
⻏
亠
忄
扌
氵

304

649 苗 ⑧

一 艹 艹 艹 芇 芇 苗 苗

音	苗	ビョウ	seedling; sapling; shoot
熟	※苗字	ミョウジ	surname; family name
訓	苗	なえ	young plant; (rice) seedling
	苗木	なえぎ	sapling; young tree
	苗床	なえどこ	seedbed

650 茂 ⑧

一 艹 艹 艹 产 芦 芪 茂 茂

| 音 | 茂 | モ | grow thickly/luxuriantly |
| 訓 | 茂る | しげる | *vi.* grow thickly/luxuriantly |

651 荒 ⑨

一 艹 艹 艹 艹 芒 芒 芦 芹 荒

音	荒	コウ	barren; wild; rough; savage
熟	荒天	コウテン	stormy weather
	荒土	コウド	barren land; wasteland; waste
	荒廃	コウハイ	devastation; desolation; waste; ruin —*vi.* be devastated; go to ruin
	荒涼	コウリョウ	desolate; dreary; bleak; deserted; inhospitable
訓	荒い	あらい	rude; wild; rough; savage; violent
	荒らす	あらす	*vt.* devastate; lay waste; damage; harm
	荒物	あらもの	kitchenware; kitchen utensils; sundry goods used for daily life
	荒れる	あれる	*vi.* become rough; rage; be wild; ran waste; be devasted

652 草 ⑨

一 艹 艹 艹 芇 芇 苩 苩 草 草

音	草	ソウ	grass; small plants; original; draft; cursive handwriting
熟	草案	ソウアン	(rough) draft; rough copy
	草原	ソウゲン	grassy plain; grass land
	草稿	ソウコウ	draft; notes; manuscript

口口土士夕夕大女子宀寸小小ツ尢尸山川工己巾干幺广廴廾弋弓ヨ彡彳艹辶阝阝艹忄扌氵犭

口口土士夂夕大女子宀寸小⺌尢戸山川工己巾干幺广廴廾弋弓彐彡彳艹辶阝⺧⺮扌氵

	草書	ソウショ	cursive form of a Chinese character
	草食	ソウショク	herbivorous
	草々	ソウソウ	In haste (closing words of a letter)
	草創	ソウソウ	inauguration; inception; beginning of construction of a temple or shrine
	草木	ソウモク	plants and trees; vegetation
※	草履	ゾウリ	*zōri* (sandals)
訓	草	くさ	grass; small plants
	草分け	くさわけ	early settler; pioneer

653

荘 ⑨　一 ⼗ 艹 ヤ 芢 荘 荘 荘 荘 荘

	荘	ショウ	manor
音		ソウ	solemn; villa; inn; village
熟	荘園	ショウエン	*hist*. manor (of Heian period nobles)
	荘厳	ソウゴン	sublime; grand; majestic
	荘重	ソウチョウ	solemn; sublime; impressive

654

茶 ⑨　一 ⼗ 艹 ⺾ 艾 芣 苂 茶 茶

	茶	チャ	tea plant; tea; light brown
音		サ	tea
熟	茶菓	サカ / チャカ	tea and candy
	茶会	サカイ / チャカイ	gathering for tea ceremony
	茶道	サドウ	tea ceremony
	茶飯事	サハンジ	everyday affair
	茶話会	サワカイ	tea party
	茶色	チャいろ	brown
	茶菓子	チャガシ	tea cake
	茶釜	チャがま	tea kettle
	茶器	チャキ	tea ceremony paraphernalia
	茶室	チャシツ	tea arbor; tea ceremony room
	茶所	チャどころ	tea-growing district; tea-producing center
	茶の間	チャのま	living/sitting room
	茶番	チャバン	tea maker; farce
	茶目	チャめ	playful
	茶碗	チャワン	(rice) bowl; teacup

655 荷 ⑩ 一 十 十 井 芒 芢 芢 荷 荷 荷

音	荷	カ	load; burden; cargo
熟	荷担	カタン	help; assistance; support; aid —*vi.* help; assist; support; aid
訓	荷	に	load; burden
	荷札	にふだ	luggage tag
	荷物	にモツ	load; burden; luggage; baggage
¥	荷受人	にうけニン	consignee
	荷送人	におくりニン	shipper
	荷為替手形	にがわせてがた	(documentary) bill of exchange

656 華 ⑩ 一 十 十 艹 艹 苎 苹 荳 莖 華

音	華	カ	floweriness; flower; gaudy
		（ケ）	flower
熟	華道	カドウ	art of flower arrangement
	華美	カビ	gaudiness; splendor
	華麗	カレイ	gorgeousness; magnificence
訓	華	はな	flower; cherry blossoms
	華々しい	はなばなしい	splendid; brilliant; glorious
	華やか	はなやか	showy; gaudy; colorful

657 菓 ⑪ 一 十 十 艹 艹 芢 苩 苩 苩 華 菓 菓

音	菓	カ	cake; candy; fruit
熟	菓子	カシ	cake; candy

658 菊 ⑪ 一 十 十 艹 艹 芍 芍 芍 菊 菊 菊

音	菊	キク	chrysanthemum
熟	菊花	キクカ	chrysanthemum
		（キッカ）	

3

口 口 土 士 夂 夕 大 女 子 宀 寸 小 ⺌ ⺌ 尢 尸 山 川 工 己 巾 干 幺 广 廴 廾 弋 弓 ⺕ 彡 彳 艹 辶 阝 阝 丬 忄 扌 犭 氵

口口土士夕夕大女子宀寸小䒑ソ尢尸山川工己巾干幺广廴廾弋弓ヨ彐彡彳艹⻌阝⻏丬忄扌氵犭

659

菌 ⑪ 一 十 丷 艹 广 芦 芦 芦 菌 菌 菌 菌

音	菌	キン	mushroom; toadstool; bacteria
熟	菌糸	キンシ	spawn; hypha
	菌類	キンルイ	fungi

660

菜 ⑪ 一 十 丷 艹 艹 芍 芍 莖 莖 莖 菜

音	菜	サイ	vegetables; greens
熟	菜園	サイエン	vegetable/kitchen garden
	菜根	サイコン	vegetable roots; simple meal
	菜食	サイショク	vegetable diet; vegetarian meal —vi. live on vegetables; follow a vegetarian diet
	菜食主義者	サイショクシュギシャ	vegetarian
訓	菜	な	vegetables; greens
	菜種	なたね	rapeseed
	菜の花	なのはな	rape blossoms

661

著 ⑪ 一 十 丷 艹 艹 艼 芏 芌 芋 著 著 著

音	著	チョ	work; written by; author; remarkable
熟	著作	チョサク	literary work; writing; authorship —v. write (a novel, etc.)
	著作権	チョサクケン	copyright; literary property
	著作者	チョサクシャ	author; writer
	著者	チョシャ	author; writer
	著述	チョジュツ	writing books; book; literary work —v. write a book
	著書	チョショ	literary work; book
	著名	チョメイ	prominence; eminence; distinction; celebrity
	著明	チョメイ	renowned; famous
訓	著す	あらわす	vt. write; publish
	著しい	いちじるしい	remarkable; distinguished; striking

308

662 葬 ⑫

一 ⼀ ⼂ ⼃ ⼚ ⼛ 芀 芀 芀 苑 荶 葬 葬

音	葬	ソウ	bury; inter
熟	葬儀	ソウギ	funeral
	葬儀屋	ソウギや	undertaker
	葬式	ソウシキ	funeral
	葬礼	ソウレイ	funeral
訓	葬る	ほうむる	*vt*. bury; inter

663 葉 ⑫

一 ⼀ ⼂ ⼃ ⼚ ⼛ ⼜ ⼝ 苩 䒷 莱 葉 葉

音	葉	ヨウ	leaf; (counter for flat, thin objects)
熟	葉柄	ヨウヘイ	leaf stem
	葉脈	ヨウミャク	vein (of a leaf)
	葉緑素	ヨウリョクソ	chlorophyl
訓	葉	は	leaf
	葉書	はがき	postcard
	葉末	はずえ	leaf tip
	葉月	はづき	eighth lunar month
	葉巻	はまき	cigar

664 落 ⑫

一 ⼀ ⼂ ⼃ ⼚ 汁 茫 莎 茨 茨 落 落

音	落	ラク	fall; fail; be defeated
熟	落書き	ラクがき	graffiti —*v*. scribble; scrawl; doodle
	落伍	ラクゴ	falling/dropping behind; falling out of —*vi*. fall behind; drop/fall out of line; drop to the rear
	落語	ラクゴ	*rakugo* (comic story telling)
	落差	ラクサ	water head/level; difference in height
	落日	ラクジツ	setting sun
	落城	ラクジョウ	fall of a castle —*vi*. fall; surrender
	落成	ラクセイ	completion of construction —*vi*. be completed/finished/ready for occupancy
	落成式	ラクセイシキ	building-completion ceremony

口口土士夂夕大女子宀寸小⺌⺍尢尸山川工己巾干幺广廴廾弋弓彐彡彳⺊阝⻏亠忄扌氵

落選	ラクセン	defeat in an election; failure to get elected —*vi.* be defeated/unsuccessful in an election
落第	ラクダイ	failure in an examination —*vi.* fail to pass an examination
落胆	ラクタン	discouragement; disheartenment —*v.* be discouraged/disheartened
落着	ラクチャク	settlement —*vi.* come to a settlement; be settled
落丁	ラクチョウ	missing pages (in a book)
落馬	ラクバ	fall from one's horse —*vi.* fall/be thrown off one's horse
落盤	ラクバン	cave-in —*vi.* cave in
落命	ラクメイ	death —*vi.* die; pass away; be killed
落葉	ラクヨウ	fallen leaves —*vi.* shed/cast leaves
落葉樹	ラクヨウジュ	deciduous tree
落陽	ラクヨウ	setting sun
落雷	ラクライ	falling of a thunderbolt —*vi.* be struck by lightning
落下	ラッカ	fall; descend; drop —*vi.* fall; descend; drop
落下傘	ラッカサン	parachute
落花生	ラッカセイ	peanuts
訓 落ちる	おちる	*vi.* fall; fail
落ち着く	おちつく	calm/settle down
落ち目	おちめ	decline of fortune; adversity
落とす	おとす	*vt.* drop; let fall; lose
落とし穴	おとしあな	pitfall; pit; trap; tricky
落とし子	おとしご	illegitimate child
落とし物	おとしもの	lost article; article accidentally dropped
¥ 落札	ラクサツ	successful bid

665

 蒸 ⑬　一 艹 艹 艻 芽 茅 苤 莁 蒥 蒸 蒸 蒸

音 蒸	ジョウ	vapor
熟 蒸気	ジョウキ	steam; vapor
蒸気機関	ジョウキキカン	steam engine
蒸発	ジョウハツ	evaporation; vaporization —*vi.* evaporate; vaporize
蒸留	ジョウリュウ	distillation —*v.* distill
蒸留酒	ジョウリュウシュ	distilled/hard liquor
訓 蒸す	むす	*v.* steam; be sultry; be hot and humid
蒸し暑い	むしあつい	muggy; sultry; hot and humid
蒸し焼き	むしやき	baking; roasting

| 蒸らす | むらす | *vt*. steam |
| 蒸れる | むれる | *vi*. be steamed/stuffy; get sticky |

666

蓄 ⑬　一 艹 芒 苎 苎 苔 萎 萎 菩 蔷 蓄 蓄 蓄

音	蓄	チク	store; stock; accumulate
熟	蓄音機	チクオンキ	phonograph; record player
	蓄財	チクザイ	accumulation of wealth —*vi*. accumulate wealth; make/amass money
	蓄積	チクセキ	accumulation; stockpiling —*v*. accumulate; amass; hoard
訓	蓄える	たくわえる	*vt*. store; stock; stay up; lay up

667

蔵 ⑮　艹 疒 芦 芹 莎 茊 莀 莀 莀 蔵 蔵 蔵

音	蔵	ゾウ	warehouse; storehouse; repository
熟	蔵書	ゾウショ	private library; book collection
訓	蔵	くら	warehouse
¥	蔵相 (大蔵大臣)	ゾウショウ (おおくら ダイジン)	Finance Minister

668

薫 ⑯　艹 苹 苹 苹 苧 营 董 菫 菫 董 董 薫

音	薫	クン	fragrance
熟	薫陶	クントウ	discipline; training; education —*v*. discipline; train; educate
	薫風	クンプウ	light balmy/summer breeze
訓	薫る	かおる	*vi*. smell sweet; be fragrant

669

薪 ⑯　艹 艹 茸 苙 荳 莘 莘 莘 莘 薪 薪 薪

| 音 | 薪 | シン | firewood |
| 熟 | 薪炭 | シンタン | firewood and charcoal; winter fuel |

311

口口土士夂夕大女子宀寸小⺌⺍尢尸山川工己巾干幺广廴廾弋弓ヨ彡彳⺾⻌⻏⺍忄扌氵

訓 薪　　たきぎ　　firewood

670
薦 ⑯　　艹 艹 芦 芦 芦 芦 芦 芦 芦 薦 薦 薦

音 薦　　セン　　recommend
訓 薦める　すすめる　*vt.* recommend

671
薄 ⑯　　艹 艻 芦 芦 芦 芦 蓮 蒲 蒲 蓮 薄 薄

音 薄　　ハク　　thin

熟 薄謝　ハクシャ　***hum.*** token of gratitude
　薄弱　ハクジャク　weakness; feebleness; flimsiness; infirmity
　薄情　ハクジョウ　heartless; unfeeling; coldhearted
　薄氷　ハクヒョウ　thin ice; thin coat of ice
　薄命　ハクメイ　unhappiness; misfortune; short life
　薄利　ハクリ　small profits; narrow profit margin
　薄給　ハッキュウ　small salary; low wages; pittance
　薄幸　ハッコウ　ill fated; unfortunate; unlucky; hapless

訓 薄い　うすい　thin; weak; scanty; sparse
　薄明かり　うすあかり　twilight; dim light; glimmer
　薄まる　うすまる　*v.* become thin/weak
　薄める　うすめる　*vt.* make thin; weaken; dilute
　薄らぐ　うすらぐ　*vi.* thin; wear thin; fade; grow pale
　薄れる　うすれる　*vi.* thin; wear thin; fade; grow pale
　薄着　うすぎ　light dress; scanty clothing —*vi.* be lightly dressed
　薄暗い　うすぐらい　gloomy; somber; dusky
　薄化粧　うすゲショウ　light make-up
　薄手　うすで　slight cut; minor injury; thin article (material, china, etc.)
　薄目　うすめ　comparative lightness; half-closed eyes
　薄笑い　うすわらい　half-smile

672
薬 ⑯　　艹 艹 艹 艹 甘 甘 甘 苩 薬 蕐 薬 薬 薬

音 薬　　ヤク　　medicine; chemical

熟	薬学	ヤクガク	pharmacology
	薬剤	ヤクザイ	medicine; drugs
	薬剤師	ヤクザイシ	pharmacist
	薬師如来	ヤクシニョライ	Buddha who can cure any ailment
	薬草	ヤクソウ	medicinal herbs
	薬品	ヤクヒン	drugs; chemicals
	薬方	ヤクホウ	prescription
	薬味	ヤクミ	spices; seasoning
	薬用	ヤクヨウ	medicinal
	薬局	ヤッキョク	pharmacy; chemist's shop
	薬効	ヤッコウ	effect of medicine
訓	薬	くすり	medicine; drugs; chemicals
	薬屋	くすりや	drugstore; chemist's shop
	薬指	くすりゆび	ring/fourth finger

673

艹 艹 艹 苎 芳 芦 茮 萍 萍 薄 藩 藩 藩 ⑱

音	藩	ハン	feudal clan; fief; feudal domain
熟	藩士	ハンシ	clansman; retainer of a daimyo
	藩主	ハンシュ	feudal lord

674

藻 艹 艹 艹 莎 莎 莎 莎 藻 藻 藻 藻 藻 ⑲

| 音 | 藻 | ソウ | duckweed |
| 訓 | 藻 | も | waterweed |

---

3 辶 しんにょう road

675

丶 入 丶入 込 込 ⑤

訓	込む	こむ	*vi.* be crowded; be congested; be packed
	込み合う	こみあう	*vi.* crowded
	込み入る	こみいる	*vi.* complicated
	込める	こめる	*vt.* load; include; put into; concentrate

313

3

口 口 土 士 夂 夕 大 女 子 宀 寸 小 ⺌ � 尢 尸 山 川 工 已 巾 干 幺 广 廴 廾 弋 弓 ヨ 彡 彳 艹 辶 阝 阝 ⺌ 忄 扌 犭 氵

口口土士夕大女子宀寸小ㇳㇳ尤尸山川工己巾干幺广ㄡ廾弋弓ㅌ彡彳艹辶阝阝⺍忄扌犭氵

676

辺 ⑤   フ カ ゙カ 辺 辺

音	辺	ヘン	edge; boundary; border; vicinity; neighborhood; surrounding area
熟	辺境	ヘンキョウ	remote frontier; border country
	辺地	ヘンチ	remote place; out-of-the-way location
	辺土	ヘンド	place long way away from the city; remote region
	辺鄙	ヘンピ	remote; out-of-the-way; rural
	辺幅	ヘンプク	outward appearance
訓	辺り	あたり	neighborhood; surrounding area; vicinity
	辺	べ	neighborhood; surrounding area; vicinity
	※辺	ほとり	neighborhood; surrounding area; vicinity

677

巡 ⑥   く 《 巛 ゙巛 巡 巡

音	巡	ジュン	make a round; tour
熟	巡回	ジュンカイ	patrol; round —*vi*. go around; make one's round; patrol
	巡業	ジュンギョウ	tour; touring —*vi*. make a provincial tour
	巡検	ジュンケン	inspection —*vt*. inspect; patrol
	巡航	ジュンコウ	cruise; cruising —*vi*. cruise
	巡査	ジュンサ	policeman
	巡察	ジュンサツ	patrol; inspection
	巡視	ジュンシ	patrol; round of inspection —*v*. patrol; make an inspection
	巡洋艦	ジュンヨウカン	cruiser
	巡礼	ジュンレイ	*Bud*. pilgrimage; pilgrim —*vi*. make a pilgrimage
訓	巡る	めぐる	*vi*. travel around; circle; circulate
	巡り合わせ	めぐりあわせ	fortune; good/bad luck
	※お巡りさん	おまわりさん	policeman

678

迅 ⑥   て ㇆ 凡 ゙凡 迅 迅

音	迅	ジン	swift
熟	迅速	ジンソク	prompt; quick; swift; rapid

近 ⑦ ノ ∫ ୮ ୮ ゲ 斤 斤 沂 近 近

音	近	キン	near; approach; recent; close
熟	近影	キンエイ	recent photograph; new portrait
	近刊	キンカン	recent publication/issue
	近眼	キンガン	nearsightedness; myopia
	近況	キンキョウ	recent condition; present situation
	近々	キンキン	shortly; before long
	近郊	キンコウ	suburbs; outskirts
	近視	キンシ	nearsightedness; myopia
	近日	キンジツ	soon; shortly; in a few days
	近所	キンジョ	neighborhood; vicinity
	近親	キンシン	close relation
	近世	キンセイ	modern/recent times
	近接	キンセツ	approach; contiguity —*vi*. approach; be contiguous
	近代	キンダイ	the modern age
	近代化	キンダイカ	modernization
	近代的	キンダイテキ	modern
	近年	キンネン	recent years
	近辺	キンペン	neighborhood; vicinity
	近隣	キンリン	neighborhood; vicinity
訓	近い	ちかい	close; nearby
	近頃	ちかごろ	recently; nowadays
	近々	ちかぢか	before long
	近づく	ちかづく	*vi*. come/go near; approach
	近道	ちかみち	short cut

迎 ⑦ ′ ୮ 匚 ഥ ഥ 迎 迎

音	迎	ゲイ	welcome
熟	迎合	ゲイゴウ	getting along easily with other —*vi*. accommodate oneself; cater; get along easily with others
	迎春	ゲイシュン	New Year greetings
	迎賓館	ゲイヒンカン	reception hall; guest house
訓	迎える	むかえる	*vt*. meet; greet; receive; welcome
	迎え	むかえ	meeting

口口土士夂夕大女子宀寸小⺌⺍尢尸山川工已巾干幺广廴廾弋弓彐彡彳艹辶阝⺍忄扌氵犭

口口土士夂夕大女子宀寸小�宀尢尸山川工己巾干幺广廴廾弋弓彐彡彳艹辶阝阝丷忄扌犭氵

681

返 ⑦

一 厂 厂 反 反 返 返

音	返	ヘン	return
熟	返還	ヘンカン	returning (to original owner/place) —v. return; give back
	返却	ヘンキャク	returning; repaying; refunding —v. return; repay; refund
	返事	ヘンジ	answer; reply; response —vi. answer; reply; respond
	返書	ヘンショ	letter of reply
	返上	ヘンジョウ	returning; sending back —v. return; send back; give back
	返信	ヘンシン	letter of reply
	返送	ヘンソウ	sending back; returning —v. send back; return
	返電	ヘンデン	telegram in reply
	返答	ヘントウ	answer; reply; response —vi. answer; reply; respond
	返杯	ヘンパイ	offering back a cup of saké (in return for a previously accepted cup) —vi. offer a return cup of saké
	返本	ヘンポン	returning unsold books to the publisher; returns —v. return unsold books to the publisher
	返礼	ヘンレイ	return present; giving a present in return for a previously received gift —vi. make a gift in return for a previous gift/favor
訓	返す	かえす	vt. return; give/send/bring back
	返す返す	かえすがえす	repeat; do over and over again
	返り討ち	かえりうち	die while trying to kill an enemy
	返る	かえる	vi. return; be given/sent back; come back
¥	返金	ヘンキン	repayment (of money); refundment —vi. pay back; refund
	返済	ヘンサイ	repayment (of a loan); returning (borrowed goods) —v. repay; return
	返納	ヘンノウ	returning (to original owner/place)
	返品	ヘンピン	return of unsold goods; returns —v. return (unsold goods)

682

述 ⑧

一 十 才 木 术 术 沭 述

音	述	ジュツ	state; mention; say

熟	述懐	ジュッカイ	recollection; expression (of one's thoughts); relation —*v*. express one's thoughts; relate; reminisce
	述語	ジュツゴ	*gram*. predicate
訓	述べる	のべる	*vt*. state; describe; mention

683 迭 ⑧
`丿 ﾉ ﾆ 𠂉 失 ﹁失 迭 迭`

| 音 | 迭 | テツ | change |

684 迫 ⑧
`丿 ﹅ 冂 白 白 ﹁白 泊 迫`

音	迫	ハク	gain upon
熟	迫害	ハクガイ	persecution; oppression; torment —*v*. persecute; oppress; torment
	迫力	ハクリョク	force; power; drive
訓	迫る	せまる	*v*. press; urge; draw near; gain upon

685 逆 ⑨
`丶 丷 丷 ﾊ 屰 屰 ﹁逆 逆 逆`

音	逆	ギャク	opposite; reverse
熟	逆効果	ギャクコウカ (ギャッコウカ)	adverse reaction; boomerang effect
	逆光	ギャクコウ	against the light
	逆算	ギャクサン	inverse operation —*v*. operate inversely
	逆襲	ギャクシュウ	counterattack; retort —*v*. counterattack; retort
	逆上	ギャクジョウ	dizziness; vertigo; frenzy; madness —*vi*. be dizzy; suffer from vertigo; go mad
	逆説	ギャクセツ	paradox
	逆手	ギャクて	dirty trick; backhander; using an opponent's strength against him
	逆転	ギャクテン	reversal; turnabout —*v*. reverse positions; turn about
	逆風	ギャクフウ	headwind; adverse wind
	逆用	ギャクヨウ	reverse use —*v*. use in an opposite way
	逆流	ギャクリュウ	countercurrent; counterflow —*vi*. flow against the current
	逆境	ギャッキョウ	adversity; adverse circumstances

口口土士夂夕大女子宀寸小⺌⺍尢尸山川工己巾干幺广廴廾弋弓彐彡彳⺾辶阝⺌⺾扌犭氵

	逆行	ギャッコウ	retrogression; retrogradation —*vi.* retrogress
訓	逆	さか	inverse; upside down
	逆さま	さかさま	inverse; inverted; upside down; topsy-turvy
	逆夢	さかゆめ	dreaming the opposite of reality
	逆らう	さからう	*vi.* oppose; go against; act contrary to
¥	逆指値	ギャクさしね	counterbid
	逆ざや	ギャクざや	negative spread
	逆調	ギャクチョウ	adverse balance of trade; unfavorable trade balance
	逆日歩	ギャクひぶ	negative interest per diem
	逆輸入	ギャクユニュウ	reimporting

686

送 ⑨　 丶 丷 ḧ ᝍ 关 关 送 送

音	送	ソウ	send
熟	送還	ソウカン	sending back; repatriation —*v.* send back; repatriate
	送球	ソウキュウ	passing/throwing a ball —*vi.* pass/throw a ball
	送金	ソウキン	remittance —*vi.* send a remittance/money
	送迎	ソウゲイ	greeting and farewell —*v.* see someone off and meet them upon return; drop off and pick up
	送検	ソウケン	being sent to the procurator's office —*v.* send to the procurator's office
	送信	ソウシン	(radio/wireless) transmission —*v.* transmit
	送電	ソウデン	power transmission —*v.* transmit power
	送付	ソウフ	sending; forwarding —*v.* send; forward; remit
	送別	ソウベツ	farewell; send off —*v.* see someone off; say farewell
	送料	ソウリョウ	postage; shipping charges
	送話器	ソウワキ	transmitter (of sound)
訓	送る	おくる	*vt.* send
	送り仮名	おくりがな	inflectional *kana* ending

687

退 ⑨　 ᒤ ᒣ ᒧ 艮 艮 艮 艮 退 退

音	退	タイ	retreat; recede; withdraw; expel; drive away; refuse
熟	退位	タイイ	abdication —*vi.* abdicate

退院	タイイン	leaving hospital; discharge from hospital —*vi*. be discharged from hospital
退化	タイカ	degeneration; degradation; regression —*vi*. degenerate; degrade; retrograde
退学	タイガク	leaving school/college; expulsion —*vi*. leave school; withdraw from college; be expelled
退却	タイキャク	retreat; withdrawal; retirement —*vi*. retreat; withdraw; retire
退去	タイキョ	leaving; quitting; withdrawl; evacuation —*v*. leave; quit; withdraw; evacuate
退屈	タイクツ	tedium; boredom —*vi*. be bored
退校	タイコウ	dismissal/expulsion from school —*vi*. give up school; be expelled
退散	タイサン	dispersion; melting —*vi*. disperse; break up; melt
退治	タイジ	subdual; subjugation; elimination; crusade —*v*. subdue; subjugate; suppress; eliminate; crusade
退社	タイシャ	retirement from a company; leaving the office —*vi*. retire; leave the office
退出	タイシュツ	leaving; withdrawal —*vi*. leave; withdraw
退場	タイジョウ	exit; leaving; walk out —*vi*. leave; go away; make one's exit; walk out
退陣	タイジン	decampment; retirement —*vi*. decamp; withdraw; retire; step down
退席	タイセキ	leaving one's seat; retirement; withdrawal —*vi*. leave one's seat; retire; withdraw
退任	タイニン	retirement —*v*. retire
退避	タイヒ	evacuation —*vi*. evacuate; escape; flee
訓 退く	しりぞく	*vi*. retreat; recede; withdraw; retire
退ける	しりぞける	*vt*. drive; send away; repel; expel; retire; refuse
¥ 退職	タイショク	retirement —*v*. retire from work
退職金	タイショクキン	retirement allowance

688

追 ⑨ 　 ′ ｀ ｒ ｒ ｒ 自 自 ﾞ自 追 追

音 追	ツイ	run/hunt after
熟 追憶	ツイオク	remembrance; recollection; retrospection; review —*v*. remember; recollect; retrospect; review
追加	ツイカ	addition; addendum; appendix; supplement —*v*. add; append; supplement
追及	ツイキュウ	overtaking; catching up —*v*. overtake; catch up with; gain on

3

口口土士夂夕大女子宀寸小⺌⺌尢尸山川工己巾干幺广廴廾弋弓彐彡彳艹⻌⻏阝爿忄扌犭氵

	追求	ツイキュウ	pursuit; chase; search —*v.* pursue; chase; follow
	追究	ツイキュウ	close inquiry; thorough investigation —*v.* inquire into; investigate closely; cross-examine
	追撃	ツイゲキ	chase; pursuit; follow up attack —*v.* chase; pursue
	追従	ツイジュウ	following; servility —*vi.* follow; be servile; kowtow
	追従	ツイショウ	flattery; adulation; sycophancy —*vi.* flatter; adulate
	追随	ツイズイ	following —*vi.* follow
	追跡	ツイセキ	pursuit; chase; tracking; stalking —*v.* pursue; chase; track; stalk
	追想	ツイソウ	remembrance; recollection; retrospection; reminiscence —*v.* remember; recollect; retrospect; reminisce
	追徴	ツイチョウ	additional collection; supplementary charge —*v.* make an additional charge of; impose a penalty of
	追徴金	ツイチョウキン	additional charge; imposition; forfeit
	追悼	ツイトウ	mourning —*v.* mourn for
	追突	ツイトツ	rear-end collision —*vi.* collide from behind
	追認	ツイニン	ratification; confirmation —*v.* ratify; confirm
	追放	ツイホウ	banishment; eviction; exile; deportation; purge —*v.* banish; exile; evict; deport; purge
訓	追う	おう	*vt.* drive away; pursue; chase; follow
	追い返す	おいかえす	*vt.* repel; repulse; beat off; drive back
	追い出す	おいだす	*vt.* expel; turn out; throw out; discharge; dismiss
	追い払う	おいはらう	*vt.* drive/turn/send away; repel
¥	追い証	おいショウ	re-margin; additional cover (margin)
	追加予算	ツイカヨサン	supplementary budget

689

ノ ｊ ｊ 丬 北 兆 ｀兆 逃 逃

⑨

音	逃	トウ	run away; escape; flee
熟	逃走	トウソウ	flight; desertion; escape; getaway —*vi.* fly; flee; desert; escape; run away
	逃避	トウヒ	escape; evasion; flight —*vi.* escape; evade; fly; take flight
	逃亡	トウボウ	flight; escape; desertion —*vi.* flee; fly; take flight; escape
訓	逃がす	にがす	*vt.* let go; set free; liberate; let loose

320

逃げ	にげ	escape; getaway; evasion
逃げ道	にげみち	way of escape; way out
逃げる	にげる	*vi*. fly; flee; run away; escape
逃す	のがす	*vt*. let go; set free; liberate; let loose
逃れる	のがれる	*vi*. escape; flee; get away; take flight; evade

690

迷 ⑨ 、 丷 丷 半 米 米 ˋ米 迷 迷

音	迷	メイ	get lost; go astray; be perplexed
熟	迷宮	メイキュウ	labyrinth; maze
	迷彩	メイサイ	camouflage
	迷信	メイシン	superstition
	迷想	メイソウ	illusion; fallacy
	迷妄	メイモウ	illusion; delusion
	迷路	メイロ	labyrinth; maze
	迷惑	メイワク	trouble; annoyance; inconvenience —*vi*. trouble; annoy; be inconvenient
訓	迷う	まよう	*vi*. hesitate; lose one's way
	迷い	まよい	perplexity; doubt; delusion
	迷わせる	まよわせる	*vt*. perplex; lead astray; charm; seduce
	※迷子	まいご	lost child

691

逝 ⑩ 一 亅 扌 扩 护 折 折 ˋ折 浙 逝

音	逝	セイ	die
熟	逝去	セイキョ	death —*vi*. die; pass away
訓	逝く	ゆく	*vi*. die; pass away

692

造 ⑩ ′ ⺧ ⺧ 生 牛 告 告 ˋ告 浩 造

音	造	ゾウ	build; make; produce
熟	造営	ゾウエイ	erection; building; construction —*v*. erect; build; construct
	造花	ゾウカ	artificial flowers
	造形	ゾウケイ	molding; modeling —*v*. mold; model
	造詣	ゾウケイ	attainments; scholarship

口
口
土
士
夂
夕
大
女
子
宀
寸
小
⺌
⺍
尢
尸
山
川
工
己
巾
干
幺
广
廴
廾
弋
弓
ヨ
彡
彳
艹
辶
阝
阝
⺍
忄
扌
氵
犭

口口土士夂夕大女子宀寸小⺌⺍尢尸山川工己巾干幺广廴廾弋弓彐彡彳⺾⻌阝⺋⺍忄扌犭氵

造作	ゾウサ	trouble; difficulty
造作	ゾウサク	fixtures; facial features
造成	ゾウセイ	construction —*v.* construct; build
造船	ゾウセン	shipbuilding —*v.* build/construct a ship
造幣局	ゾウヘイキョク	the Mint
造林	ゾウリン	forestation
訓 造る	つくる	*vt.* make; build; produce

693 速 ⑩ 一 ｆ 戸 戸 申 東 束 ᐟ凍 涑 速

音 速	ソク	fast
熟 速成	ソクセイ	intensive training; short course —*v.* train quickly; give intense training
速達	ソクタツ	express/special delivery
速度	ソクド	speed; velocity
速報	ソクホウ	bulletin; news flash —*v.* report promptly; announce quickly
速力	ソクリョク	speed; velocity
速記	ソッキ	shorthand —*v.* write/take down in shorthand
速攻	ソッコウ	swift attack —*v.* launch a swift attack
速効	ソッコウ	quick effect
訓 速い	はやい	fast
速める	はやめる	*vt.* quicken; accelerate
速やか	すみやか	prompt; speedy

694 逐 ⑩ 一 ｆ 丆 牙 豸 豸 豕 ᐟ豕 逐 逐

音 逐	チク	dispel; pursue; drive away
熟 逐一	チクイチ	one by one; minutely; in detail
逐次	チクジ	successively; one after another
訓 逐う	おう	*vt.* drive away; pursue; chase

695 通 ⑩ 一 マ マ 亓 丏 甬 甬 ᐟ甬 涌 通

音 通	ツウ (ツ)	pass; go to and from; inform; know thoroughly

熟	通じる	ツウじる	*vi*. pass; run; be open to traffic; transmit; be understood
	通じて	ツウじて	through; throughout; all over; in total; together with
	通院	ツウイン	regular hospital visits —*vi*. go to hospital regulary
	通運	ツウウン	transportation; forwarding; express
	通過	ツウカ	passage; passing; pass; transit; carriage —*vi*. pass; pass/go through
	通学	ツウガク	attending school —*vi*. attend school
	通気	ツウキ	ventillation; draft; airing; aeration
	通勤	ツウキン	commuting; going to work —*vi*. commute; go to work
	通行	ツウコウ	traffic; passing; passage; transit —*vi*. pass; go past/through
	通告	ツウコク	notification; notice; announcement; warning —*v*. notify; give notice; announce; warn
	通算	ツウサン	sum total; aggregate; summing-up —*v*. total; include; aggregate; sum up
	通称	ツウショウ	common name; alias
	通常	ツウジョウ	usually; normally; generally
	通信	ツウシン	correspondence; communication; intelligence; dispatch; news —*vi*. correspond; communicate
	通信販売	ツウシンハンバイ	mail order
	通説	ツウセツ	common opinion; popular view
	通俗	ツウゾク	popularity; conventionality
	通達	ツウタツ	notification; communication; circular notice —*v*. notify; communicate
	通知	ツウチ	notice; notification; communication; information; advice —*v*. notify; communicate; inform; advise
	通帳	ツウチョウ	bankbook; passbook
	通読	ツウドク	reading (a book) from cover to cover —*v*. read from cover to cover
	通報	ツウホウ	report; dispatch; advice; bulletin; information —*vi*. report; notify; advise
	通訳	ツウヤク	interpretation; interpreter —*v*. interpret; act as an interpreter
	通用	ツウヨウ	common/popular use; circulation; currency —*vi*. be in common use; circulate; run current
	通例	ツウレイ	usually; commonly; generally; as a rule
	通路	ツウロ	path; passageway
	通話	ツウワ	telephone call/conversation
	通夜	ツヤ	wake; vigil
訓	通う	かよう	*vi*. go to and from; frequent; attend (school, lessons, etc.)
	通る	とおる	*vi*. go along; pass by

口 口 土 士 夂 夕 大 女 子 宀 寸 小 屮 ⺍ 尤 尸 山 川 工 己 巾 干 幺 广 廴 廾 弋 弓 ⺕ 彡 彳 艹 辶 阝 ⺍ ⺶ 扌 氵

通す	とおす	*vt*. pass through; pierce; admit; let a person pass
通り	とおり	road; street; passage; understanding; way; manner
通り掛かる	とおりかかる	*vi*. happen/chance to pass
通り越す	とおりこす	*vt*. walk/pass by; be more than; exceed
通り過ぎる	とおりすぎる	*vi*. go past/by
通り抜ける	とおりぬける	*vi*. pass/walk through; cut across/through
¥ 通貨	ツウカ	currency
通貨供給量	ツウカ キョウキュウ リョウ	money supply
通貨単位	ツウカタンイ	currency/monetary unit
通産省 （通商産 業省）	ツウサンショウ （ツウショウサン ギョウショウ）	Ministry of International Trade and Industry (MITI)
通産大臣	ツウサンダイジン	Minister of International Trade and Industry
通常国会	ツウジョウ コッカイ	ordinary session of the Diet
通知預金	ツウチヨキン	deposit at call

696

⑩ 一 厂 厂 戶 戶 后 禹 ʼ禹 漏 逓

音 逓	テイ	send from stage to stage
熟 逓減	テイゲン	gradual diminution/decrease —*v*. decrease gradually; diminish successively
逓信	テイシン	communications; transmission
逓増	テイゾウ	gradual increase —*v*. increase gradually

697
途 ⑩ ノ 八 今 今 余 余 ʼ余 涂 途

音 途	ト	way; road
熟 途上	トジョウ	on the way/road; en route
途絶	トゼツ	interruption; stoppage; cessation; suspension —*vi*. be stopped/cut off/obstructed/interrupted
途端	トタン	just as; in the act of; the very moment/minute
途中	トチュウ	on the way; en route; halfway; midway; unfinished; incomplete
途轍もない	トテツもない	wild; absurd; preposterous
途方	トホウ	way; means; reason; logic

698

透 ⑩　一　二　千　禾　禾　禾　秀　秀　透　透

音	透	トウ	be transparent
熟	透視	トウシ	seeing through; fluoroscopy; radiology —*v.* see through; examine by fluoroscopy
	透写	トウシャ	tracing —*v.* trace out
	透明	トウメイ	transparency; clearness; clarity
	透明人間	トウメイニンゲン	invisible man
訓	透く	すく	*vi.* be transparent; become sparse
	透ける	すける	*vi.* be transparent
	透かす	すかす	*vt.* make transparent; look through; peer into; hold up to the light
	透き通る	すきとおる	*vi.* be transparent; be seen through
	透き間	すきま	small gap/opening
	透き間風	すきまかぜ	draft

699

連 ⑩　一　厂　厂　戸　百　盲　車　車　連　連

音	連	レン	company; relation
熟	連記	レンキ	list —*v.* list up; make a list
	連休	レンキュウ	consecutive holidays
	連係	レンケイ	connection; liaison; contact
	連携	レンケイ	in cooperation/concert with —*vi.* cooperate with; be in concert
	連結	レンケツ	connection; coupling; consolidated —*v.* connect; couple; consolidate
	連呼	レンコ	repeated calls/shouts —*v.* call/shout repeatedly
	連行	レンコウ	escorting/accompanying (a criminal, etc.) —*v.* escort/accompany (a criminal etc.)
	連合	レンゴウ	union; league; federation —*v.* be in alliance/league with
	連座	レンザ	involvement; accompanying —*vi.* be involved in; accompany
	連載	レンサイ	(magazine/newspaper) serialization —*v.* serialize (in a magazine/newspaper); run a serial
	連作	レンサク	repeated cultivation of the same crop; linked short stories/*tanka* —*v.* plant (a field) with same crop every year
	連鎖反応	レンサハンノウ	chain reaction

口
口
土
士
夂
夕
大
女
子
宀
寸
小
⺌
尢
尸
山
川
工
己
巾
干
幺
广
廴
廾
弋
弓
彐
彡
彳
⺾
辶
阝
阝
亠
忄
扌
氵
⺡

連山	レンザン	mountain range
連日	レンジツ	day after day; every day
連勝	レンショウ	consecutive victories; winning streak —*vi.* keep on winning; be on a winning streak
連戦	レンセン	series of battles; battle after battle
連想	レンソウ	association of ideas —*v.* associate (A with B); be reminded of
連続	レンゾク	continuation; consecutive; in a row —*v.* continue; be consecutive
連打	レンダ	repeated blows —*v.* hit back; offer repeated blows/strikes
連帯	レンタイ	solidarity
連中	レンチュウ	particular group of people; they; crowd
連動	レンドウ	gears; linkage; drive —*vi.* link; drive
連破	レンパ	successive wins; winning streak —*v.* win successively; keep on winning; have a winning streak
連敗	レンパイ	successive defeats; losing streak —*vi.* keep on losing; suffer a losing streak
連発	レンパツ	rapid machine-gun fire —*v.* fire shots rapidly one after another
連邦	レンポウ	federation
連峰	レンポウ	mountain range
連名	レンメイ	joint signature
連盟	レンメイ	league; federation; union
連綿	レンメン	unbroken; consecutive
連夜	レンヤ	night after night; nightly
連絡	レンラク	connection; contact; liaison; communicate —*v.* connect; make contact; liaise; communicate
連絡船	レンラクセン	ferryboat
連立	レンリツ	alliance; coalition —*v.* make an alliance/coalition
訓 連なる	つらなる	*vi.* stand in a row
連ねる	つらねる	*vt.* put in a row
連れる	つれる	*v.* take along; accompany
連れ	つれ	companion
連れ子	つれこ	child by a previous marriage
¥ 連銀 (連邦銀行)	レンギン (レンポウギンコウ)	Federal/Central Bank (U.S.)
連結決済	レンケツケッサイ	consolidated statement of accounts
連結財務諸表	レンケツザイムショヒョウ	consolidated financial statements
連結指数	レンケツシスウ	chain-index

連帯責任　レンタイセキニン　solidarity
連邦準備　レンボウジュンビ　Federal Reserve Bank (U.S.)
　　銀行　ギンコウ

口口土士夕大女子宀寸小⺌⺍尢尸山川工己巾干幺广廴廾弋弓ヨ彡彳⺌辶阝爿忄扌犭氵

700

逸 ⑪　　ノ　ク　⺅　⺈　⺤　岙　夕　免　⺈免　逸免　逸

音	逸	イツ	deviate; flee; miss; lose; leisure; excellent
熟	逸する	イッする	*v.* fail to catch; let go; lose
	逸材	イツザイ	person of talent; able person
	逸脱	イツダツ	departure; deviation; breakaway —*v.* deviate; depart; breakaway
	逸話	イツワ	anecdote
訓	逸らす	そらす	*vt.* let slip; miss; lose; let go
	逸れる	それる	*vi.* deviate from; swerve

701

週 ⑪　　丿　冂　月　円　円　用　周　周　⺈周　週　週

音	週	シュウ	week
熟	週間	シュウカン	week
	週刊	シュウカン	weekly publication
	週刊誌	シュウカンシ	weekly magazine
	週休	シュウキュウ	weekly holiday
	週給	シュウキュウ	weekly pay/salary
	週日	シュウジツ	weekdays (mon-sat)
	週番	シュウバン	week-long duty
	週末	シュウマツ	weekend
¥	週休二日制	シュウキュウ ふつかセイ	five-day work week

702

進 ⑪　　ノ　亻　亻　⺊　什　件　隹　⺈隹　進　進

音	進	シン	advance
熟	進化	シンカ	evolution —*vi.* evolve; develop
	進学	シンガク	educational progress; development —*vi.* go on to the next stage of one's education

3

口 口 土 士 夂 夕 大 女 子 宀 寸 小 ⺌ ⺍ 尢 尸 山 川 工 己 巾 干 幺 广 廴 廾 弋 弓 ヨ 彡 彳 艹 辶 阝 丷 忄 扌 犭 氵

進学志望者	シンガク シボウシャ	applicants to high school or college
進学塾	シンガクジュク	cram school
進学率	シンガクリツ	ratio of students who go on to higher education
進級	シンキュウ	promotion —*vi.* be promoted
進軍	シングン	advance; march; marching —*vi.* advance; march on
進撃	シンゲキ	attack; advance; charge —*vi.* advance; attack; make an attack
進言	シンゲン	advice; counsel; proposal —*v.* advise; counsel; make a proposal
進行	シンコウ	advance; progress —*vi.* move forward; advance; make progress
進攻	シンコウ	attack —*v.* attack; advance
進航	シンコウ	progress of a boat or ship
進取	シンシュ	enterprising; enterprise
進出	シンシュツ	advance —*vi.* advance; make inroads into; go into
進退	シンタイ	advance or retreat; movement; behavior
進駐軍	シンチュウグン	Occupation Forces
進捗状況	シンチョク ジョウキョウ	progress
進呈	シンテイ	presentation —*v.* present
進展	シンテン	development; progress —*vi.* develop; progress
進度	シンド	progress; degree of progress
進入	シンニュウ	entry; approach —*vi.* march; make their way; enter; approach
進歩	シンポ	progress; advance; improvement —*vi.* make progress; advance; improve
進歩的	シンポテキ	progressive; advanced
進物	シンモツ	gift
進路	シンロ	course; route; way
訓 進む	すすむ	*vi.* advance; progress; travel; go forward *vt.* lead; move; go ahead
進める	すすめる	*vt.* lead; move; advance; proceed; go ahead; be promoted

703

 ⑪ 　 コ ⁁ ⺕ 肀 聿 肀 肀 隶 ⁁隶 隶 逮

音	逮	タイ	arrest; capture; chase; reach
熟	逮捕	タイホ	arrest; apprehension; capture —*v.* arrest; apprehend; capture; put into custody

704

運 ⑫　　` ＾ ＾ ＾ ＾ ＾ ＾ ＾ ＾ 軍 軍 運 運

音	運	ウン	carry; ship; transport; fate; luck; destiny
熟	運営	ウンエイ	management; operation; administration —*v.* manage; operate; administer
	運河	ウンガ	canal
	運休	ウンキュウ	suspension (of a scheduled train, flight, etc.) —*v.* suspend (a train, flight) etc.
	運行	ウンコウ	revolution; movement; motion —*vi.* revolve; orbit; move around
	運航	ウンコウ	shipping; airline service —*vi.* operate; run; ply
	運勢	ウンセイ	one's stars; fortune; luck
	運送	ウンソウ	transportation; conveyance; shipping; transporting; traffic —*v.* transport; convey; carry; forward; ship
	運賃	ウンチン	freight; shipping charge; tarrif; passenger fare; (goods) rate
	運転	ウンテン	driving; operation —*v.* drive; operate
	運転手	ウンテンシュ	driver
	運転免許	ウンテンメンキョ	driver's license
	運動	ウンドウ	motion; exercise; canvassing; campaign —*vi.* move; exercise; canvass; campaign
	運搬	ウンパン	forwarding; shipping; transporting; carriage —*v.* carry; transport; convey; deliver
	運命	ウンメイ	destiny; fate; luck; fortune; the inevitable
	運輸	ウンユ	transport; traffic
訓	運ぶ	はこぶ	*vt.* carry; ship; progress
Y	運行	ウンコウ	movement; operation; service
	運転資金	ウンテンシキン	operational funds; working capital
	運輸省	ウンユショウ	Ministry of Transport
	運輸大臣	ウンユダイジン	minister of transport

705

過 ⑫　　` ＾ ロ ロ ロ ロ 丹 咼 咼 咼 渦 渦 過

音	過	カ	pass; spend; error; excessive
熟	過激	カゲキ	extreme/radical (thought or action)
	過去	カコ	the past; one's past life —*gram.* past tense
	過酷	カコク	severe; harsh; cruel; hard; merciless
	過言	カゴン	saying too much; exaggeration

口口土士夂夕大女子宀寸小⺌⺍尢尸山川工己巾干幺广廴廾弋弓彐彡彳艹辶⻏⺍忄扌氵

過失	カシツ	unintentional mistake; error; negligence
過日	カジツ	the other day; some days ago
過重	カジュウ	too great a load; overload
過小	カショウ	too small
過少	カショウ	too few/little
過剰	カジョウ	surplus; excess
過信	カシン	overconfidence —*v.* have too much confidence
過疎	カソ	sparseness; depopulation
過多	カタ	excess; surplus; too much/many
過大	カダイ	too big; excessive
過程	カテイ	process; course
過度	カド	beyond a reasonable limit; excess
過渡期	カトキ	transition; transitional period
過熱	カネツ	overheating —*v.* overheat
過半数	カハンスウ	majority
過敏	カビン	oversensitive
過不足	カフソク	excess or deficiency
過分	カブン	generous; excessive; unworthy
過密	カミツ	overcrowded; overpopulated
過労	カロウ	overwork; overexertion

訓
過ぎる	すぎる	*vi.* pass; exceed
過ごす	すごす	*vt.* pass/spend (time); live; stay
過ち	あやまち	mistake; fault; error
過つ	あやまつ	*vt.* err; make a mistake

¥ 過労死　カロウシ　death from overwork —*vi.* die from working too hard

---

706

遇 ⑫　丶 冂 冂 曰 罒 禺 禺 禺 禺 丶遇 遇

音 遇　グウ　unexpected; treatment
熟 遇する　グウする　*vt.* treat; use; deal with; entertain; receive

707

遂 ⑫　丶 ⺍ ⺌ 芢 芳 芳 芽 㒸 ⺍㒸 遂 遂

音 遂　スイ　carry out
熟 遂行　スイコウ　execution; accomplishment; performance —*v.* execute; accomplish; perform; carry out
訓 遂げる　とげる　*vt.* accomplish; achieve; attain; realize; effect

※遂に　　　　ついに　　　　　at last; finally

708
達 ⑫　　一　十　土　丯　圥　坴　幸　查　查　幸　達　達

音	達	タツ	lead; deliver; announcement
熟	達する	タッする	*v.* reach; attain; achieve
	達観	タッカン	farsighted-view; philosophic view —*v.* take a farsighted view
	達者	タッシャ	healthy; well; strong; expert; proficient; clever
	達人	タツジン	expert; master
	達成	タッセイ	attainment; achievement; accomplishment —*v.* achieve; attain; accomplish
	達筆	タッピツ	good handwriting/writing style

709
遅 ⑫　　フ　ヲ　尸　尸　尺　戽　屋　屋　犀　犀　遅　遅

音	遅	チ	be late/delayed/slow
熟	遅延	チエン	delay; postponement —*v.* delay; postpone
	遅刻	チコク	lateness; being late —*v.* be/come late
	遅々	チチ	slowly; lagging; tardy
	遅配	チハイ	delay (in delivery, pay, etc.) —*v.* delay (delivery, payment, etc.)
訓	遅らす	おくらす	*vt.* delay; defer; put off
	遅れる	おくれる	*vi.* be late/behind schedule/delayed; fall behind
	遅い	おそい	late; slow

710
道 ⑫　　丶　ソ　ソ　ゾ　ゲ　首　首　首　首　首　道　道

音	道	ドウ (トウ)	road; reason; method; district; way
熟	道義	ドウギ	morality; morals; moral principles
	道具	ドウグ	instrument; appliance; tool; furniture
	道具箱	ドウグばこ	tool box
	道化	ドウケ	buffoonery; tomfoolery
	道化師	ドウケシ	clown
	道場	ドウジョウ	drill hall for martial arts

口口土士攵夕大女子宀寸小ル丷尢尸山川工已巾干幺广廴廾弋弓彐彡彳艹辶阝艹扌犭氵

口 口 土 士 夂 夕 大 女 子 宀 寸 小 ⺌ ⺍ 尢 尸 山 川 工 己 巾 干 幺 广 廴 廾 弋 弓 彐 彡 彳 ⺾ ⻌ 阝 ⺀ 忄 扌 氵 犭

道中	ドウチュウ	on a journey; travel on a tour
道程	ドウテイ	distance; journey
道徳	ドウトク	morality
道破	ドウハ	declaration; strong statement —*v*. declare; state strongly
道標	ドウヒョウ（みちしるべ）	guidepost; signpost
道楽	ドウラク	hobby; pastime; dissipation; debauchery
道楽者	ドウラクもの	playboy
道理	ドウリ	reason; right; justice; truth
道路	ドウロ	road; way; street
道路標識	ドウロヒョウシキ	road sign

訓

道	みち	road; way; street; journey; distance; duty; morality
道案内	みちアンナイ	guidance; guide
道草を食う	みちくさをくう	*vi*. loiter/tarry on the way —*fig*. lose/waste time
道順	みちじゅん	route; itinerary

711

 ⑫ 　 一 ㇕ ㇌ 戸 戸 戸 肩 肩 扁 扁 漏 遍 遍

音

遍	ヘン	widely; generally; everywhere; (number) of times

熟

遍在	ヘンザイ	ubiquitous; omnipresent —*vi*. be ubiquitous/omnipresent
遍歴	ヘンレキ	traveling to various countries; experiencing many things —*vi*. travel abroad; experience
遍路	ヘンロ	pilgrim; pilgrimage

712

遊 ⑫ 　 ` ㇒ ㇌ 方 方 ガ 疒 斿 斿 斿 游 遊

音

遊	ユウ（ユ）	play; tour; enjoy; oneself; be idle

熟

遊泳	ユウエイ	swimming
遊園地	ユウエンチ	amusement park; recreation area; playground
遊学	ユウガク	studying away from home —*v*. study away from home
遊戯	ユウギ	play; games; sport; entertainment; amusement; pastime
遊休	ユウキュウ	idle; unused

遊撃	ユウゲキ	commando attack; shortstop -*bas*. hit and run attack	
遊星	ユウセイ	planet	
遊説	ユウゼイ	canvassing; campaign —*vi*. canvass; campaign	
遊牧民	ユウボクミン	nomads	
遊覧	ユウラン	sightseeing; excursion —*vi*. go sightseeing; go on an excursion	
遊離	ユウリ	isolation; separation —*v*. be isolated/separated	
遊山	ユサン	picnic/outing/excursion to the mountains	
訓 遊ぶ	あそぶ	*vi*. play; enjoy oneself; be idle	
遊び	あそび	play; game; sport; amusement; recreation	
遊ばせる	あそばせる	amuse; let play; leave something as it is	

713

 ⑬ ノ ナ 五 キ キ 吾 音 音 音 韋 違 違

音 違	イ	differ from; unlike; mistake	
熟 違憲	イケン	violation of the constitution	
違反	イハン	violation; offense; infringement; breach —*vi*. violate; infringe; disobey; break the law	
違犯	イハン	violation; offense; infringement; breach —*vi*. violate; infringe; disobey; break the law	
違法	イホウ	illegality; lawbreaking; unlawfulness	
違約	イヤク	breach of contract; break a promise; default —*vi*. infringe a contract; break a promise; default	
違和感	イワカン	feeling of being out of place; incongruity	
訓 違い	ちがい	difference; mistake	
違う	ちがう	*vi*. differ; be wrong; disagree; oppose	
違える	ちがえる	*vt*. change; alter; vary	
※違う	たがう	*vi*. differ; be different in opinion	
※違える	たがえる	*vt*. change; alter; mistake; confuse	
¥ 違約金	イヤクキン	penalty; forfeit	

714

 ⑬ 一 十 土 キ 吉 吉 声 声 亨 袁 遠 遠

音 遠	エン	distant; far; profound; perspective	
	（オン）	far; eternity	
熟 遠因	エンイン	remote cause; underlying factor; indirect cause	
遠泳	エンエイ	long-distance swim	

口口土士夂夕大女子宀寸小⺌⺍尢尸山川工己巾干幺广廴廾弋弓彐彡彳艹辶阝阝丷⺌扌犭氵

遠海	エンカイ	the open sea; the deep
遠隔	エンカク	remote; faraway; distant
遠距離	エンキョリ	long distance
遠近	エンキン	far and near; distance
遠景	エンケイ	distant view
遠視	エンシ	farsightedness; hyperopia
遠日点	エンジツテン	aphelion
遠心力	エンシンリョク	centrifugal force
遠征	エンセイ	military expedition; expedition —*vi*. invade; go on an expedition
遠足	エンソク	excursion; day-trip; school trip
遠大	エンダイ	having wide range or effect; far-reaching
遠望	エンボウ	distant view; perspective —*v*. view from a distance
遠方	エンポウ	faraway
遠洋	エンヨウ	the open sea; the deep
遠来	エンライ	coming from afar
遠慮	エンリョ	reserve; modesty; forethought; foresight —*v*. be modest; keep a distance; refrain
遠路	エンロ	long way; roundabout way

訓

遠浅	とおあさ	shallow for a considerable distance; shoal
遠い	とおい	far; remote; distant
遠縁	とおエン	distant relative
遠回し	とおまわし	indirect; roundabout; vague
遠回り	とおまわり	detour

715

 ⑬

、　丶　口　口　中　虫　串　串　串　貴　書　遣　遣

音	遣	ケン	dispatch; send
熟	遣唐使	ケントウシ	*hist*. Japanese envoys sent to Tang Dynasty China
訓	遣う	つかう	*vt*. spend; consume; waste; worry
	遣わす	つかわす	*vt*. dispatch; send

716

 ⑭

一　广　广　庐　府　府　府　庶　庶　庶　遮　遮

| **音** | 遮 | シャ | interrupt |
| **熟** | 遮光 | シャコウ | preventing light from leaking outside —*v*. shade; shield |

遮断	シャダン	interruption; isolation —v. cut off; stop; interrupt traffic
遮断器	シャダンキ	railroad crossing gate
遮二無二	シャニムニ	furious; all one's might; like crazy
遮蔽	シャヘイ	shelter; cover —v. shelter; shade; cover
訓 遮る	さえぎる	*vt.* interrupt; obstruct; block; intercept
遮り	さえぎり	obstruct; cut off; block; interrupt

717

遭 ⑭   一 戸 市 市 曲 曲 曹 曹 曹 曹 遭 遭

音 遭	ソウ	encounter; meet
熟 遭遇	ソウグウ	encounter; meeting —v. encounter; meet
遭難	ソウナン	accident; disaster; mishap —v. meet with accident/disaster
訓 遭う	あう	*vi.* meet

718

適 ⑭   ` 亠 ナ 广 产 产 产 商 商 商 滴 適

音 適	テキ	suit
熟 適する	テキする	*vi.* fit; suit; agree; be adapted/qualified
適応	テキオウ	adaptation; accommodation; conformity —v. be adaptable; be suitable/fitted to
適応性	テキオウセイ	adaptability; flexibility
適格	テキカク	competency
適宜	テキギ	suitable; appropriate; fitting; proper
適合	テキゴウ	conformity; agreement; compatibility —v. conform; suit; fit; be compatible
適材適所	テキザイテキショ	right man in the right place
適時	テキジ	timely; opportune
適正	テキセイ	proper; appropriate; right; just
適正化	テキセイカ	rationalization
適性	テキセイ	aptitude
適性検査	テキセイケンサ	aptitude test —v. give an aptitude test
適切	テキセツ	pertinent; fit; suitable; adequate; proper; relevent
適中	テキチュウ	hit
適度	テキド	moderation; proper degree; temperance; measure
適当	テキトウ	suitable; fit; proper; adequate

335

口口土士夂夕大女子宀寸小⺌尢尸山川工己巾干幺广廴廾弋弓彐彡彳⺾辶⻏⻏⺪忄扌犭氵

適任	テキニン	fitness; suitability; competence
適否	テキヒ	propriety; suitability; fitness; aptitude
適法	テキホウ	legality; lawfulness
適役	テキヤク	fit post/role
適用	テキヨウ	application —*v.* apply
適量	テキリョウ	proper quantity/dose; dosage
適例	テキレイ	good example
適齢	テキレイ	marriageable age
訓※適う	かなう	*vi.* suit; fit; be consistent/agreeable

719

遺 ⑮　丶 冖 口 虫 虫 串 虫 贵 贵 贵 贵 贵 遗 遺

音	遺	イ	leave; abandon
		（ユイ）	

熟	遺影	イエイ	portrait of the deceased
	遺憾	イカン	regrettable; lamentable; deplorable
	遺棄	イキ	abandonment; desertion —*v.* abandon; desert; leave unattended
	遺業	イギョウ	work left unfinished by the deceased; unfinished work
	遺訓	イクン	maxims left by the dead
	遺骨	イコツ	(one's) ashes; skeletal remains
	遺作	イサク	posthumous work
	遺産	イサン	inheritance; legacy; estate; bequest
	遺志	イシ	one's dying wish; unfulfilled wish of a dying person
	遺児	イジ	child of the deceased; orphaned child
	遺失	イシツ	loss —*v.* lose; leave behind
	遺失物	イシツブツ	lost article/property
	遺書	イショ	note left behind by a dead person; suicide note
	遺跡	イセキ	ruins; relics; remains
	遺族	イゾク	bereaved family; family of the deceased; survivors
	遺体	イタイ	dead body; corpse; remains
	遺伝	イデン	heredity; hereditary transmission; genetic inheritance —*vi.* be inherited; be transmitted; be handed down
	遺伝子	イデンシ	gene
	遺品	イヒン	article left by the departed
	遺物	イブツ	relic; remains; antiquity; memento
	遺言	ユイゴン	(one's) will; will and testament; one's spoken will and testament —*v.* leave/make a will

720

遵 ⑮ 　亠 广 芦 芦 芮 首 首 酋 尊 尊 導 遵

音	遵	ジュン	observe
熟	遵守	ジュンシュ	observance (of the law) —*v.* obey (the law)
	遵法	ジュンポウ	law-abiding

721

選 ⑮ 　丷 丷 ユ 巳 吕 吕 严 珝 巽 巽 巽 選 選

音	選	セン	choose; select
熟	選外	センガイ	left out; not chosen
	選挙	センキョ	election —*v.* elect
	選挙権	センキョケン	right to vote; suffrage
	選考	センコウ	selection; screening —*v.* select; screen
	選者	センジャ	selector; judge
	選手	センシュ	sports player; athlete
	選手権	センシュケン	championship title
	選集	センシュウ	selection; anthology
	選出	センシュツ	election; select —*v.* elect; select; pick out
	選択	センタク	selection; choice —*v.* choose; select
	選定	センテイ	selection; choice —*v.* select; choose
	選抜	センバツ	selection; choice —*v.* select; choose; single out
	選別	センベツ	selection; grading; sorting —*v.* select; grade; sort
	選良	センリョウ	the elite; member of a parliament
訓	選ぶ	えらぶ	*vt.* choose; select
	※選る	える	*vt.* choose; select
	※選る	すぐる	*v.* choose; select
	※選る	よる	*vt.* choose; select
¥	選別買い	センベツがい	selective buying

722

遷 ⑮ 　一 币 币 西 要 覀 覀 悪 悪 遷 遷

音	遷	セン	remove; change
熟	遷都	セント	transfer of the capital city —*vi.* transfer the capital city

337

口 口 土 士 夂 夕 大 女 子 宀 寸 小 ⺌ 尢 尸 山 川 工 己 巾 干 幺 广 廴 廾 弋 弓 ヨ 彡 彳 艹 辶 阝 阝 ⺍ 扌 氵 氵

口口土士夂夕大女子宀寸小⺌⺍尤尸山川工己巾干幺广廴廾弋弓彐彡彳艹⻌阝⺬忄扌犭氵

723 還 ⑯

口　罒　罒　罒　睘　睘　睘　睘　睘　景　還　還

音 還	カン	return
	（ゲン）	
熟 還元	カンゲン	restoration; chemical reduction —v. restore; reduce; resolve
還付	カンプ	return; restoration; restitution —v. return; restore; retrocede
還暦	カンレキ	one's sixty-first birthday
還俗	ゲンゾク	secularization —vi. return to secular life; renounce the cloth
訓 ※還る	かえる	vi. return; come back
※還る	めぐる	vi. circulate; come around; return

724 避 ⑯

丶　コ　尸　居　居　居　居　辟　辟　辟　避　避

音 避	ヒ	avoid
熟 避暑	ヒショ	summering (in a cool place) —vi. spend/pass the summer (in a cool place)
避暑地	ヒショチ	summer resort
避難	ヒナン	refuge; shelter; evacuation —vi. take/seek refuge/shelter; evacuate
避難民	ヒナンミン	refugees; evacuees
避妊	ヒニン	contraception; birth control —vi. prevent conception; practice birth control
避雷針	ヒライシン	lightning rod
訓 避ける	さける	vt. avoid; escape
※避ける	よける	vt. avoid; escape

3 阝　こざとへん　left village

725 防 ⑦

丶　ろ　阝　阝'　阝宀　防　防

| 音 防 | ボウ | defend; protect; prevent; (prefix) anti-; -proof; -resistant |

338

熟	防衛	ボウエイ	defense —v. defend
	防疫	ボウエキ	prevention against epidemics —v. prevent epidemics
	防音	ボウオン	soundproof —vi. be soundproof
	防火	ボウカ	fire prevention; fire fighting; fireproof
	防火栓	ボウカセン	fire hydrant
	防火壁	ボウカヘキ	fire wall
	防寒	ボウカン	protection against the cold
	防寒服	ボウカンフク	winter/arctic clothing
	防御	ボウギョ	defense —v. defend (against an enemy attack)
	防具	ボウグ	armor; protective gear
	防空	ボウクウ	air defense
	防空壕	ボウクウゴウ	air-raid/bomb shelter
	防護	ボウゴ	protection; custody —v. protect (against injury)
	防塞	ボウサイ	roadblock; barricade; fort
	防災	ボウサイ	prevention of disaster
	防止	ボウシ	prevention —v. prevent
	防湿	ボウシツ	dampproof
	防臭剤	ボウシュウザイ	deodorant
	防縮	ボウシュク	shrinkage prevention —vi. prevent shrinkage
	防食剤	ボウショクザイ	anti-corrosive
	防塵	ボウジン	dustproof
	防水	ボウスイ	waterproof; watertight —v. make waterproof/watertight
	防雪	ボウセツ	snow protection
	防雪林	ボウセツリン	snowbreak (forest)
	防戦	ボウセン	defensive battle/fight —vi. fight a defensive battle
	防弾	ボウダン	bulletproof; bombproof
	防虫	ボウチュウ	insect repellent
	防虫剤	ボウチュウザイ	insecticide
	防毒	ボウドク	gasproof
	防波堤	ボウハテイ	breakwater
	防犯	ボウハン	crime prevention
	防備	ボウビ	defensive preparations —v. make preparations to defend/protect (against an enemy attack)
	防風	ボウフウ	wind protection/shelter
	防風林	ボウフウリン	windbreak (forest)
	防腐剤	ボウフザイ	preservative
	防壁	ボウヘキ	barrier; bulwark
訓	防ぐ	ふせぐ	vt. defend; prevent; protect (from)
¥	防衛庁	ボウエイチョウ	Defense Agency

口口土士夕大女子宀寸小⺌⺍尤尸山川工己巾干幺广廴廾弋弓彐彡彳艹辶阝阝丷忄扌氵

339

ロ口土士夂夕大女子宀寸小⺌⺍尤尸山川工己巾干幺广廴廾弋弓彐彡彳艹⻌阝阝⺊忄扌氵

726 阻 ⑧
` ` ⻖ ⻖ ⻖| ⻖⊓ ⻖⊓ ⻖目 阻

音	阻	ソ	obstruct; prevent; impede; block; hamper
熟	阻害	ソガイ	obstruction; hindrance —*v.* obstruct; hinder; impede; check; retard
	阻止	ソシ	deterrence; hinderance; obstruction —*vt.* check; deter; hinder; obstruct
	阻喪	ソソウ	discouraged; disheartened; depressed —*vi.* be discouraged/disheartened/depressed
訓	阻む	はばむ	*vt.* impede; obstruct; prevent; block; hamper

727 附 ⑧
` ` ⻖ ⻖ ⻖ ⻖⊣ 附 附

| 音 | 附 | フ | attach |
| 訓 | ※附く | つく | *vi.* be attached/affixed/added |

728 限 ⑨
` ` ⻖ ⻖⊓ ⻖⊒ ⻖∃ 阻 阻 限

音	限	ゲン	limit; boundary; restriction
熟	限界	ゲンカイ	limit; boundary; margin
	限外	ゲンガイ	beyond the limit; excessive
	限局	ゲンキョク	strict limitation; limit strictly
	限定	ゲンテイ	limitation; restriction —*v.* limit; restrict
	限度	ゲンド	limit
訓	限る	かぎる	*vt.* restrict; limit
	限り	かぎり	limits; restriction
¥	限月	ゲンゲツ	delivery month

729 院 ⑩
` ` ⻖ ⻖' ⻖' ⻖⊓ 陀 陀 陀 院

音	院	イン	public place or building (such as hospital or Diet)
熟	院議	インギ	parliamentary/Diet decision
	院長	インチョウ	the director (of a hospital)

730

陥 ノ 了 3 阝 阝′ 阝″ 阝″ 阽 陥 陥

音	陥	カン	fall; fall into
熟	陥没	カンボツ	depression; subsidence; cave-in —*vi.* subside; sink; cave in
	陥落	カンラク	fall; surrender —*vi.* fall; surrender
訓	陥る	おちいる	*vi.* fall into; sink; cave in; subside
	陥れる	おとしいれる	*vt.* entrap; ensnare; capture

731

降 ノ 了 3 阝 阝′ 阝″ 降 降 降 降

音	降	コウ	fall; descend; alight; drop; surrender
熟	降雨	コウウ	rainfall; precipitation
	降下	コウカ	descent; falling; dropping; fall; landing —*vi.* descend; fall; drop; land
	降参	コウサン	surrender; submission; capitulation —*vi.* surrender; submit; capitulate
	降車	コウシャ	alighting; getting off —*vi.* alight; get off/down
	降水量	コウスイリョウ	amount of precipitation/rainfall
	降雪	コウセツ	snowfall; snow
	降誕	コウタン	nativity; birth; advent; incarnation —*vi.* be born; be incarnated; see the light
	降伏	コウフク	surrender; submission; capitulation —*vi.* surrender; submit; capitulate
訓	降りる	おりる	*vi.* come/get down; descend; alight; leave; quit
	降ろす	おろす	*vt.* take down; lower; bring down; drop; have an abortion; grate
	降る	ふる	*vi.* fall; come down; descend; rain; snow

732

除 ノ 了 3 阝 阝′ 阝ヽ 阸 阾 除 除 除

音	除	ジョ (ジ)	remove; divide
熟	除外	ジョガイ	exception; exclusion —*v.* exclude; leave out
	除去	ジョキョ	removal; riddance —*v.* remove; get rid of
	除籍	ジョセキ	removal from a (family) register —*v.* remove a person's name from a (family) register

口口土士夕夕大女子宀寸小⺌⺍尢尸山川工己巾干幺广廴廾弋弓彐彡彳艹辶阝⺍忄扌氵犭

口口土士夂夕大女子宀寸小灬 "尢尸山川工己巾干幺广廴廾弋弓彐彡彳艹辶阝阝并忄扌犭氵

	除雪	ジョセツ	snow removal —*vi.* clear away the snow
	除草	ジョソウ	weeding —*vi.* weed
	除幕式	ジョマクシキ	unveiling ceremony
	除名	ジョメイ	expulsion —*v.* expel from (association, political party, etc.)
	除夜	ジョヤ	New Year's Eve
訓	除く	のぞく	*vt.* remove; exclude; expel; leave/take out

733

陣 ⑩　　 ⁊ 　ㇵ 　阝 　阝¯ 　阝一 　阿 　阿 　陌 　陏 　陣

音	陣	ジン	disposition of an army
熟	陣営	ジンエイ	camp
	陣痛	ジンツウ	*med.* labor pains
	陣頭	ジントウ	the front/head
	陣容	ジンヨウ	battle formation

734

陛 ⑩　　 ⁊ 　ㇵ 　阝 　阝¯ 　阰 　阰¯ 　阰 　陛 　陛 　陛

音	陛	ヘイ	stairway in the imperial palace; (honorific word used to describe a monarch)
熟	陛下	ヘイカ	His/Her/Your Majesty

735

陰 ⑪　　 ⁊ 　ㇵ 　阝 　阝¯ 　阝⌃ 　阽 　阽 　陰 　陰 　陰 　陰

音	陰	イン	shade; secret; shadow; negative
熟	陰影	インエイ	shadow; shading; gloom
	陰気	インキ	gloominess; gloom; dismalness; melancholy
	陰険	インケン	crafty; treacherous
	陰惨	インサン	disastrous; dismal; weird; gloomy
	陰性	インセイ	negative (of a medical test); dormant
	陰謀	インボウ	plot; intrigue; conspiracy
	陰暦	インレキ	lunar calendar
訓	陰	かげ	shade; behind the scenes
	陰口	かげぐち	backbiting
	陰る	かげる	*vi.* darken; get dark; become cloudy; be obscured

736

険 ⑪ ⟨ ⟩ ⟨ ⟩ ⟨ ⟩ ⟨ ⟩ ⟨ ⟩ ⟨ ⟩ ⟨ ⟩ ⟨ ⟩ ⟨ ⟩ ⟨ ⟩ 険

音	険	ケン	steep
熟	険悪	ケンアク	threatening; hostile; cross
訓	険しい	けわしい	steep; stern; sharp

737

陳 ⑪ ⟨ ⟩ ⟨ ⟩ ⟨ ⟩ ⟨ ⟩ ⟨ ⟩ ⟨ ⟩ ⟨ ⟩ ⟨ ⟩ 陣 陳 陳

音	陳	チン	display; state; declare
熟	陳謝	チンシャ	apology; regret —*v.* apologize; express one's regret
	陳述	チンジュツ	statement; declaration; desposition —*v.* state; declare; set forth
	陳情	チンジョウ	appeal; representation; petition —*v.* make an appeal/representation; petition
	陳情書	チンジョウショ	representation; petition
	陳腐	チンプ	commonplace; old-fashioned; antiquated
	陳弁	チンベン	justification —*vt.* justify; explain
	陳列	チンレツ	exhibition; show; display —*v.* exhibit; show; display

738

陶 ⑪ ⟨ ⟩ ⟨ ⟩ ⟨ ⟩ ⟨ ⟩ ⟨ ⟩ ⟨ ⟩ ⟨ ⟩ 陶 陶 陶 陶

音	陶	トウ	earthenware
熟	陶器	トウキ	earthenware; ceramics; pottery
	陶芸	トウゲイ	ceramic art
	陶工	トウコウ	potter; porcelain maker
	陶工術	トウコウジュツ	ceramics; pottery
	陶磁器	トウジキ	china and porcelain; ceramics; pottery
	陶酔	トウスイ	intoxication; fascination; rapture —*vi.* be intoxiated/fascinated/charmed
	陶製	トウセイ	made of ceramics
	陶然	トウゼン	mellow with drink; tipsy
	陶土	トウド	potter's clay; kaolin; china clay
	陶冶	トウヤ	cultivation; training; education —*v.* cultivate; train; educate
訓	※陶	すえ	china; earthenware; ceramics

口 口 土 士 夂 夕 大 女 子 宀 寸 小 ⺌ ⺍ 尢 尸 山 川 工 己 巾 干 幺 广 廴 廾 弋 弓 ヨ 彡 彳 艹 辶 ⻏ ⻖ 丷 忄 扌 犭 氵

739 陪 ⑪

丿 ⼻ ⻖ ⻖' ⻖⁻ ⻖⁺ ⻖⼂ 陉 陪 陪 陪

音	陪	バイ	accompany a superior
熟	陪審	バイシン	jury
	陪審員	バイシンイン	juror; member of the jury
	陪席	バイセキ	sitting with one's superior —*vi.* sit with one's superior

740 陸 ⑪

丿 ⼻ ⻖ ⻖⁻ ⻖⁺ 陆 陆 陆 陸 陸

音	陸	リク	land
熟	陸運	リクウン	land transport
	陸軍	リクグン	army
	陸上競技	リクジョウキョウギ	field and track events
	陸続	リクゾク	in succession; continuously
	陸地	リクチ	land
	陸路	リクロ	overland route
	陸橋	リッキョウ	overpass; viaduct
訓	※陸	おか	land

741 隆 ⑪

丿 ⼻ ⻖ ⻖' ⻖� ⻖⼂ ⻖⼃ 降 降 降 隆

音	隆	リュウ	high; noble; flourishing
熟	隆起	リュウキ	rise; bulge; elevation; protruberance —*vi.* rise; bulge; elevate; protrude
	隆盛	リュウセイ	prosperous; flourishing; thriving
	隆々	リュウリュウ	prosperous; thriving; muscular

742 陵 ⑪

丿 ⼻ ⻖ ⻖⁻ ⻖⁺ 陆 陆 陆 陵 陵 陵

音	陵	リョウ	imperial tomb; insult; outrage; rape; violation
熟	陵辱	リョウジョク	indignity; insult; outrage; rape —*v.* insult; rape; violate; make fun of; embarrass

344

	陵墓	リョウボ	imperial tomb
訓	陵	みささぎ	imperial tomb

階 ⑫　　， ３ 阝 阝- 阝⺊ 阝⺊' 阝比 阝比 阝阹 階 階 階

音	階	カイ	stairs; floor; staircase; rank
熟	階下	カイカ	downstairs
	階級	カイキュウ	class
	階上	カイジョウ	upstairs
	階層	カイソウ	class; layer; stratum
	階段	カイダン	stairs

隅 ⑫　　， ３ 阝 阝ⁱ 阝尸 阝尸 阝甲 阝甲 阴 隅 隅 隅

音	隅	グウ	corner
訓	隅	すみ	corner
	隅田川	すみだがわ	Sumida River (Tokyo)

随 ⑫　　， ３ 阝 阝ノ 阝⺮ 阝㐄 阼 陏 陏 隋 随 随

音	随	ズイ	follow
熟	随意	ズイイ	voluntary; optional
	随一	ズイイチ	foremost; most
	随員	ズイイン	suite; attendant
	随行	ズイコウ	attendance —*vi.* attend; accompany; follow
	随行者	ズイコウシャ	attendant
	随時	ズイジ	any time; all times
	随従	ズイジュウ	following (a lead) —*vi.* follow; play second fiddle
	随従者	ズイジュウシャ	henchman; follower
	随所	ズイショ	everywhere; anywhere
	随想	ズイソウ	occasional/random thoughts
	随伴	ズイハン	accompanying —*vi.* escort; follow
	随筆	ズイヒツ	essay
	随分	ズイブン	fairly; pretty; tolerably

口口土士夕大女子宀寸小⺌⺍尤尸山川工己巾干幺广廴廾弋弓彐彡彳艹辶阝阝立⺾忄扌犭氵

左 margin vertical characters:
口 口 土 士 夂 夕 大 女 子 宀 寸 小 ⺌ ⺌ 尢 尸 山 川 工 己 巾 干 幺 广 廴 廾 弋 弓 彐 彡 彳 艹 辶 阝 阝 ⺍ 忄 扌 犭 氵

746

隊 ⑫ ⺂ ⻖ ⻖ ⻖ ⻖ ⻖ ⻖ 阝 阝 陟 陟 隊

音	隊	タイ	crew; party
熟	隊員	タイイン	crew member
	隊商	タイショウ	caravan
	隊長	タイチョウ	captain; leader; commanding officer
	隊列	タイレツ	file; rank

747

陽 ⑫ ⺂ ⻖ 阝 阝 阝 阝 阝 阝 阝 陽 陽 陽

音	陽	ヨウ	the sun; positive; yang
熟	陽気	ヨウキ	weather; cheerful; gay; happy
	陽極	ヨウキョク	positive pole; anode
	陽光	ヨウコウ	sunlight; sunshine
	陽子	ヨウシ	proton
	陽春	ヨウシュン	warm spring; New Year (of the lunar calendar)
	陽性	ヨウセイ	cheerful; positive
	陽転	ヨウテン	positive reaction (to a medical test) —*vi*. react positively (to a medical test)
	陽暦	ヨウレキ	solar calendar
訓	※陽	ひ	sun
	※陽当たり	ひあたり	exposure to the sun

748

隔 ⑬ ⺂ 阝 阝 阝 阝 阝 阝 隔 隔 隔 隔 隔

音	隔	カク	separate
熟	隔月	カクゲツ	every other month
	隔日	カクジツ	every other day
	隔週	カクシュウ	every other week
	隔世	カクセイ	distant age
	隔絶	カクゼツ	separation; isolation; segregation —*vi*. be separated/isolated/segregated from
	隔年	カクネン	every other year
	隔離	カクリ	isolation; quarantine; segregation —*v*. isolate; quarantine; segregate

訓	隔たる	へだたる	*vi.* be distant from; be isolated/estranged
	隔てる	へだてる	*vt.* part; separate; segregate; isolate; alienate; estrange
	隔たり	へだたり	distance; interval; difference; estrangement

749

隠 ⑭   阝 阝′ 阝″ 阝‴ 阝‴ 阿 阿 隠 隠 隠 隠 隠

音	隠	イン	conceal; retire; retirement
		(オン)	
熟	隠居	インキョ	retirement; retired person; old gentleman or lady (retire from active life) —*vi.* retire from active life; go into retirement
	隠語	インゴ	secret language; jargon
	隠匿	イントク	concealment; secretion —*v.* hide; conceal; secrete
	隠密	オンミツ	privacy; secrecy; spy
訓	隠れる	かくれる	*vi.* disappear; hide; retire
	隠す	かくす	*vt.* hide

750

際 ⑭   阝 阝′ 阝″ 阝″ 阝″ 阝″ 際 際 際 際 際 際

音	際	サイ	case; associate; mix; limit; occasion
熟	際限	サイゲン	limits; bounds
訓	際	きわ	brink; verge
	際立つ	きわだつ	*vi.* stand out; be conspicuous
	際どい	きわどい	risky; close; narrow; indecent
	際物	きわもの	seasonal goods

751

障 ⑭   阝 阝′ 阝″ 阝″ 阝″ 阵 阵 陪 陪 障 障 障

音	障	ショウ	obstacle; hurdle
熟	障害	ショウガイ	obstacle; hindrance; difficulty; handicap; disorder; impediment
	障害者	ショウガイシャ	handicapped person
	障害物	ショウガイブツ	obstacle; hurdle
	障子	ショウジ	*shōji* (paper sliding door)
	障壁	ショウヘキ	barrier; wall

口口土士夂夕大女子宀寸小㐅尢尸山川工己巾干幺广廴廾弋弓彐彡彳艹辶阝⻖忄扌氵犭

訓 障る　　さわる　　*vi*. interfere; obstruct; be bad for
　　障り　　さわり　　obstacle; obstruction

752 隣 ⑯　阝 阝 阝 阝 阼 阼 阼 阼 阼 阼 隣 隣

音 隣　　リン　　neighboring; adjacent; adjoin
熟 隣人　　リンジン　　neighbor
　　隣接　　リンセツ　　adjacent; contiguous; bordering —*vi*. adjoin; be contiguous; border on
訓 隣　　となり　　next-door; adjoining

3　阝　おおざと　right village

753 邦 ⑦　一 二 三 丰 丰 邦 邦

音 邦　　ホウ　　country; our country (Japan)
熟 邦画　　ホウガ　　Japanese film/picture
　　邦楽　　ホウガク　　Japanese music
　　邦人　　ホウジン　　Japanese person
　　邦文　　ホウブン　　Japanese language
訓 邦　　くに　　country (Japan)
¥ 邦銀　　ホウギン　　Japanese commercial banks

754 邪 ⑧　一 一 工 牙 牙 牙 邪 邪

音 邪　　ジャ　　wicked
熟 邪悪　　ジャアク　　wicked; malicious; viscious
　　邪気　　ジャキ　　malicious; wicked
　　邪教　　ジャキョウ　　heretical religion
　　邪険　　ジャケン　　cruel; harsh; unkind
　　邪心　　ジャシン　　wicked heart
　　邪推　　ジャスイ　　groundless suspicion —*v*. suspect without reason
　　邪説　　ジャセツ　　heresy

邪道	ジャドウ	evil way; misleading
邪念	ジャネン	wicked thought; evil desire
邪魔	ジャマ	obstacle; hindrance; interference; nuisance; bother —*v.* interrupt; disturb; trouble

---

755

邸 ⑧

`, ㄈ ㄥ 氏 氏 氐 氐 氐 邸`

音	邸	テイ	mansion
熟	邸宅	テイタク	mansion; residence
訓	※邸	やしき	mansion; residence

756

郊 ⑨

`, 亠 宀 六 交 交 交 郊`

| 音 | 郊 | コウ | suburbs; the country |
| 熟 | 郊外 | コウガイ | suburbs; outskirts |

757

郎 ⑨

`, ㄋ ㄋ ㅌ 自 自 自 郎 郎`

| 音 | 郎 | ロウ | man; husband |
| 熟 | 郎党 | ロウトウ | vassals; retainers |

758

郡 ⑩

`ㄱ ㄋ ㅌ 尹 尹 君 君 君 郡 郡`

| 音 | 郡 | グン | territorial division; (suffix) *-gun* (county; district) |
| 熟 | 郡部 | グンブ | rural section; suburban districts; districts classified as *gun* |

759

郭 ⑪

`, 亠 宀 古 古 亯 亨 享 享 郭 郭`

| 音 | 郭 | カク | land enclosure; outline |
| 訓 | ※郭 | くるわ | quarter; district |

口口土士夕夕大女子宀寸小ㅗㅛ尢尸山川工己巾干幺广廴廾弋弓ヨ彡彳艹廴阝普忄扌犭氵

760

郷 ⑪

′ ⺃ ⺁ ⺈ ⺈ ⺈ ⺈ ⺈ ⺈ ⺈ 郷

音	郷	キョウ	town; hometown; country; province
		ゴウ	
熟	郷愁	キョウシュウ	homesickness
	郷土	キョウド	one's hometown/town of birth
	郷土色	キョウドショク	local color
	郷里	キョウリ	one's hometown

761

都 ⑪

一 十 土 耂 耂 者 者 者 者 者 都

音	都	ト	city; Tokyo
		ツ	all
熟	都合	ツゴウ	arrangements; circumstances
	都度	ツド	every time; each occasion; whenever
	都営	トエイ	metropolitan Tokyo-run (subway)
	都下	トカ	metropolis; capital; Tokyo
	都会	トカイ	city; town
	都市	トシ	city; town; urban area
	都心	トシン	city center
	都内	トナイ	within Tokyo
	都立	トリツ	metropolitan; municipal
訓	都	みやこ	capital; metropolis; seat of government
	都落ち	みやこおち	rustification —*vi.* flee the capital city
¥	都市銀行	トシギンコウ	city bank

762

部 ⑪

′ ㇒ ㇒ ㇏ 立 产 音 音 音 部 部

音	部	ブ	section; department; club; category; (counter for copies of books, etc.)
熟	部員	ブイン	staff; member of a club
	部下	ブカ	subordinate (worker)
	部首	ブシュ	radicals of Chinese characters
	部署	ブショ	one's post/duty/station
	部数	ブスウ	number of copies; circulation

350

部族	ブゾク	tribe
部隊	ブタイ	(military) unit; corps; detachment
部長	ブチョウ	department head; head of a club
部分	ブブン	part
部落	ブラク	village; community
部類	ブルイ	classification; category
※部屋	へや	room
¥ 部品	ブヒン	machine/spare parts
部門	ブモン	department; field; branch; section; class; division

763
郵 ⑪ 　一　二　三　手　丐　香　垂　垂　垂　郵゛郵

音	郵	ユウ	mail; post
熟	郵政	ユウセイ	postal system
	郵税	ユウゼイ	postage; rate of postage
	郵送	ユウソウ	mailing —v. mail; post
	郵便	ユウビン	mail; post
	郵便局	ユウビンキョク	post office
	郵便箱	ユウビンばこ	mailbox
¥	郵政省	ユウセイショウ	Ministry of Posts and Telecommunications

3　立　そいち　lining up (artificial radical)

764
並 ⑧ 　丶　丷　丷　丷　丷　並　並　並

音	並	ヘイ	side-by-side; together; ordinary
熟	並行	ヘイコウ	parallel; side-by-side; together —vi. line up in a row; occur simultaneously
	並存 （ヘイソン）	ヘイゾン	coexistence —vi. coexist
	並立	ヘイリツ	standing side-by-side —vi. stand side-by-side
	並列	ヘイレツ	parallel (circuit); arranged in a row —v. arrange in a row
訓	並	なみ	ordinary; average; regular
	並木	なみき	row of trees on either side of a street
	並外れる	なみはずれる	vi. be out of the ordinary

口口土士夂夕大女子宀寸小⺌⺍尤尸山川工己巾干幺广廴廾弋弓彐彡彳⺾辶⻏⻖⺾⺄忄扌犭氵

並幅	なみはば	standard width (about 36 cm)
並ぶ	ならぶ	*vi*. be in a row; rank with; queue up
並べる	ならべる	*vt*. arrange/place in a row; display; lay out; compare
並びに	ならびに	both; and; as well as

765

兼 ⑩ 　 ` ⸜ ⸝ ⸜ ⸝ ⸝ ⸝ ⸝ 兼

音	兼	ケン	concurrent
熟	兼営	ケンエイ	running two or more businesses at once —*vt*. run two or more businesses at once
	兼業	ケンギョウ	side job
	兼行	ケンコウ	round the clock; twenty-four hours a day —*v*. work around the clock
	兼帯	ケンタイ	combined use —*vi*. can be used both as
	兼任	ケンニン	additional post; side job —*v*. hold an additional post
	兼務	ケンム	additional post; side job —*v*. hold an additional post
	兼用	ケンヨウ	double-use; double purpose —*v*. also serves; can be used both as
訓	兼ねる	かねる	*vt*. be concurrent; combine; serve both as; be both; (suffix) cannot; be hard to; be not in a position to
¥	兼営業務	ケンエイギョウム	multiple businesses —*v*. operate in addition to some other business

3	忄	see ⇨p.370
3	扌	see ⇨p.389
3	犭	see ⇨p.572
3	氵	see ⇨p.516

766

心 ⌂   ⌂ 心 心 心
④

音	心	シン	mind; core; heart; soul
熟	心音	シンオン	*med.* heart beat
	心外	シンガイ	regrettable; unexpected; unthinkable
	心眼	シンガン	mind's eye; insight
	心機一転	シンキイッテン	changing one's mind; turning over a new leaf —*v.* change one's mind; turn over a new leaf
	心境	シンキョウ	state of mind; feelings
	心中	シンジュウ	double/lovers' suicide —*vi.* commit suicide together
	心証	シンショウ	firm belief; conviction; impression
	心象	シンショウ	image; mental picture
	心情	シンジョウ	feelings; emotions
	心身	シンシン	body and mind; mentally and physically
	心身症	シンシンショウ	*med.* psychosomatic disorders
	心酔	シンスイ	ardent admiration —*v.* adore; be an ardent admirer of
	心臓	シンゾウ	*med.* heart
	心臓外科	シンゾウゲカ	open heart surgery
	心中	シンチュウ	at heart; inwardly; feelings
	心痛	シンツウ	worry; concern —*v.* be worried/concerned
	心的	シンテキ	mental; psychological
	心電図	シンデンズ	*med.* electrocardiogram (ECG)
	心配	シンパイ	anxiety; worry; care —*v.* be worried/troubled; worry; care
	心拍	シンパク	heartbeat
	心拍数	シンパクスウ	*med.* pulse rate
	心理	シンリ	mentally; mental state; psychology
	心理学	シンリガク	psychology
	心理的	シンリテキ	psychological; mental
	心霊	シンレイ	spirit; psychic; spiritual
	心霊術	シンレイジュツ	spiritualism
	心労	シンロウ	cares; anxieties; worries
訓	心	こころ	mind; heart; feeling; consideration; attention
	心当たり	こころあたり	in mind; could think of
	心有る	こころある	thoughtful; considerate; sensible; sensitive

4

心意気	こころイキ	spirit; determination
心得	こころえ	knowledge; understanding; rules; regulations; directions; instructions
心得る	こころえる	*vt.* know; understand; regard; think; be aware of
心掛け	こころがけ	intention; care; prudence
心配り	こころくばり	consideration; thoughtfulness
心苦しい	こころぐるしい	feeling sorry/bad about
心して	こころして	determinedly; carefully
心強い	こころづよい	reassuring; encouraging
心残り	こころのこり	regret
心細い	こころぼそい	lonely; helpless; hopeless; discouraging
※心地	ここち	feeling; sensation

767

必 ⑤　｀ ｿ 必 必 必

音	必	ヒツ	certain; sure; necessary
熟	必携	ヒッケイ	indispensable; handbook; manual
	必見	ヒッケン	required reading/viewing
	必殺	ヒッサツ	inevitable killing; deadly
	必死	ヒッシ	certain death; desperate; frantic; with all one's might
	必至	ヒッシ	inevitable; desperate; frantic
	必修科目	ヒッシュウカモク	required/obligatory/compulsory subject
	必需品	ヒツジュヒン	necessities; essentials
	必勝	ヒッショウ	sure victory; desperate to win
	必定	ヒツジョウ	inevitable; unavoidable
	必須	ヒッス	indispensable; essential; requisite; compulsory
	必然	ヒツゼン	inevitability; necessity; certainty
	必然性	ヒツゼンセイ	necessity; inevitability
	必然的	ヒツゼンテキ	inevitable; of necessity; as a matter of course
	必着	ヒッチャク	required arrival time
	必中	ヒッチュウ	always hits the target —*vi.* never fails to hit the target
	必読	ヒツドク	required reading
	必要	ヒツヨウ	necessary; essential
	必要悪	ヒツヨウアク	necessary evil
	必要条件	ヒツヨウジョウケン	necessary condition
訓	必ず	かならず	surely; certainly; without fail; certainly

心 忄 小 戈 戸 手 扌 支 攵 文 斗 斤 方 日 曰 月 肉 月 木 欠 止 歹 殳 母 毋 比 毛 氏 气 水 氷 氵 火 灬 爫 父 片 牛 犬 犭 王 礻 耂

応 ⑦ 　　 ' 一 广 广 応 応 応

音	応	オウ	respond; meet; consent
熟	応じる	オウじる	*vi.* respond to; act in accordance with; consent; be suitable
	応援	オウエン	aid; assistance; support; moral support; cheering —*v.* help; assist; support; give moral support; cheer
	応急	オウキュウ	emergency
	応接	オウセツ	reception —*vi.* receive/see a guest
	応接間	オウセツま	waiting room; reception
	応戦	オウセン	returning fire; fight back —*vi.* return fire; fight back
	応対	オウタイ	reception —*vi.* see one's guests; grant an interview
	応諾	オウダク	consent; assent —*v.* consent/assent to
	応答	オウトウ	reply; response; answer —*vi.* reply; respond; answer
	応分	オウブン	fitting; suitable; appropriate; reasonable
	応募	オウボ	application; enlistment; subscription; enrollment —*vi.* apply for; enlist; subscribe for (to); enroll
	応用	オウヨウ	application; adaptation; improvement —*v.* apply; adapt; put into practice
訓	応える	こたえる	*vi.* respond to; have effect on
¥	応札	オウサツ	tender for
	応募者 利回り	オウボシャ りまわり	yield/return to subscriber
	応募資金	オウボシキン	subscribed capital (fund)

忌 ⑦ 　　 ㇕ コ 己 忌 忌 忌 忌

音	忌	キ	abominate; mourning
熟	忌中	キチュウ	in mourning
	忌日	キニチ (キジツ)	anniversary of the day someone died
	忌避	キヒ	evasion —*v.* evade; shirk
訓	忌まわしい	いまわしい	abominable; disgusting; offensive
	忌み	いみ	abstinence; taboo
	忌む	いむ	*vt.* hate; loathe; abhor; detest; abstain

4

心 忄 小 戈 戸 手 扌 支 攵 文 斗 斤 方 日 曰 月 肉 月 木 欠 止 歹 殳 母 毌 比 毛 氏 气 水 氺 氵 火 灬 ⺤ 父 片 牛 犬 犭 王 ⺩ 耂

4

志 ⑦ 一 十 士 志 志 志

音	志	シ	will; intention; desire; wish
熟	志願	シガン	wish; desire; ambition —*v*. apply; volunteer; wish; want
	志願者	シガンシャ	applicant; candidate
	志願兵	シガンヘイ	volunteer soldier
	志向	シコウ	intention —*v*. intend
	志望	シボウ	wish; desire; ambition —*v*. wish for; desire; aspire
	志望者	シボウシャ	applicant; candidate
訓	志	こころざし	will; resolution; aim; purpose; intention; wish; gift; kindness; consideration
	志す	こころざす	*vi*. intend; aim; aspire; make up one's mind

771

忍 ⑦ フ カ 刃 刃 忍 忍 忍

音	忍	ニン	bear; endure; conceal; hide; spy
熟	忍苦	ニンク	endurance; stoicism —*vi*. be patient; endure
	忍者	ニンジャ	spy; ninja
	忍従	ニンジュウ	submission; subservience; resignation; passiveness —*vi*. submit; suffer; lie down
	忍術	ニンジュツ	art of invisibility; ninja arts
	忍耐	ニンタイ	perseverance; patience; endurance; fortitude; stoicism —*v*. persevere; be patient; endure
訓	忍ぶ	しのぶ	*vt*. bear; stand; endure; hide oneself; conceal
	忍ばせる	しのばせる	*vt*. conceal; hide; secrete
	忍び	しのび	mystification; spy
	忍び足	しのびあし	stealthy steps
	忍び込む	しのびこむ	*vi*. steal/creep into

772

忘 ⑦ 、 亠 亡 亡 忘 忘 忘

音	忘	ボウ	forget
熟	忘恩	ボウオン	ingratitude
	忘我	ボウガ	self-oblivion; trance; ecstasy

| 忘却 | ボウキャク | oblivion; forgetting —v. be oblivious to; forget |
| 忘年会 | ボウネンカイ | year-end party |

訓 忘れる　わすれる　v. forget
忘れ形見　わすれがたみ　memento; keepsake; posthumous child
忘れ物　わすれもの　lost property; item left behind accidentally

773

忠 ⑧ 丶 ロ ロ 中 中 忠 忠 忠

音 忠 チュウ loyalty; devotion; fidelity; faithfulness

熟 忠義 チュウギ loyalty; fidelity; devotion
忠孝 チュウコウ loyalty and filial piety
忠告 チュウコク advice; warning; caution; admoniton
　　　　　　　　　　—v. advise; warn; caution; admonish
忠実 チュウジツ honesty; faithfulness; devotion; fidelity; faith
忠臣 チュウシン loyal retainer
忠誠 チュウセイ allegiance; loyalty; fidelity; devotion; integrity
忠節 チュウセツ loyalty; allegiance; fidelity; devotion

774

念 ⑧ ノ 人 人 今 今 念 念 念

音 念 ネン think

熟 念じる ネンじる vt. wish; pray
念願 ネンガン wish; desire; prayer —v. wish; desire; pray
念頭 ネントウ mind
念仏 ネンブツ Buddhist prayer
念力 ネンリキ willpower; will; faith

775

急 ⑨ ノ ク ク ヲ 刍 刍 急 急 急

音 急 キュウ make haste; hasten; acute

熟 急患 キュウカン emergency case/patient
急激 キュウゲキ sudden; abrupt; precipitous
急行 キュウコウ express (train/bus) —vi. hasten; go posthaste
急降下 キュウコウカ nose dive —vi. nose-dive
急告 キュウコク urgent notice

心 忄 小 戈 戸 手 扌 支 攵 文 斗 斤 方 日 曰 月 肉 月 木 欠 止 歹 殳 母 毋 比 毛 氏 气 水 氷 氵 火 灬 灬 父 片 牛 犬 犭 王 衤 耂

357

心忄小戈戸手扌支攵文斗斤方日曰月肉月木欠止歹殳母毋比毛氏气水氺氵火灬爪父片牛犬犭王礻耂

急死	キュウシ	sudden death —*vi*. die suddenly
急襲	キュウシュウ	surprise attack/raid —*v*. attack suddenly
急所	キュウショ	vital part of the body
急進	キュウシン	rapid progress —*vi*. make rapid progress
急性	キュウセイ	acute (sickness)
急逝	キュウセイ	sudden death —*vi*. die suddenly
急送	キュウソウ	dispatching hurriedly —*v*. send a thing in haste
急増	キュウゾウ	sudden increase; jump —*vi*. increase rapidly/suddenly
急速	キュウソク	rapid; swift; prompt
急停止	キュウテイシ	sudden stop —*vi*. stop suddenly
急転	キュウテン	sudden change —*vi*. change suddenly; take a sudden turn
急場	キュウば	emergency; crisis
急迫	キュウハク	urgency; imminence —*vi*. be imminent/pressing
急病	キュウビョウ	sudden attack of illness
急変	キュウヘン	sudden change/transition —*vi*. change suddenly
急募	キュウボ	urgent recruitment —*v*. recruit in haste
急報	キュウホウ	urgent message/report —*v*. send an urgent message; report promptly
急務	キュウム	urgent business; pressing need
急用	キュウヨウ	urgent business; business demanding immediate attention
急流	キュウリュウ	rapidly flowing stream
訓 急ぐ	いそぐ	*vi*. hasten; hurry up; go quickly
¥ 急騰	キュウトウ	sudden rise; jump
急落	キュウラク	sudden/sharp drop; fall

776

思 ⑨ 丶 冂 冂 田 用 田 甲 思 思 思

音 思	シ	think; thought; idea
熟 思案	シアン	thought; consideration; reflection; worry —*v*. think; consider; reflect; worry
思考	シコウ	thought; thinking —*v*. think
思索	シサク	meditation; contemplation —*v*. think; meditate; comtemplate; ponder
思春期	シシュンキ	puberty; adolescence
思想	シソウ	thought; idea; thoughts
思想家	シソウカ	thinker
思慕	シボ	yearning —*v*. yearn/long for; love
思慮	シリョ	prudence; consideration; careful thought

訓	思う	おもう	***vt.*** think; consider; suspect; wonder; guess; suppose; imagine; fancy; be in love; wish; desire; recall; remember
	思う存分	おもうゾンブン	as much as one likes
	思い	おもい	thought; feeling; wish; desire; love
	思い浮かべる	おもいうかべる	***vt.*** recall; remember
	思い切って	おもいきって	bravely
	思い出す	おもいだす	***vt.*** recall; remember
	思い出	おもいで	memory; recollections
¥	思惑買い	おもワクがい	speculative buying

777

 ⑨ ㇐ ㇛ ㇜ 台 台 台 怠 怠 怠

音	怠	タイ	idle; neglect; negligence
熟	怠惰	タイダ	idleness; laziness; indolence; sloth
	怠慢	タイマン	negligence; neglect; procrastination
訓	怠る	おこたる	***vi.*** neglect; be negligent/idle
	怠け者	なまけもの	idler; lazybones
	怠ける	なまける	***v.*** be idle/lazy

778

怒 ⑨ ㇛ ㇜ 女 奵 奴 奴 怒 怒 怒

音	怒	ド	anger; indignation; rage; fury
熟	怒気	ドキ	anger; angry mood; fume; indignation; wrath; resentment
	怒号	ドゴウ	roar; outcry; bellow —***vi.*** roar; bellow; howl
	怒声	ドセイ	angry voice
	怒涛	ドトウ	angry waves; high seas; rough waters
訓	怒る	いかる	***vi.*** become angry; get upset
	怒り	いかり	anger; rage; passion; wrath; indignation
	怒る	おこる	***vi.*** become/get angry; lose one's temper

779

恩 ⑩ ㇐ 冂 冃 冄 冈 因 因 恩 恩 恩

| 音 | 恩 | オン | kindness; favor; grace |

359

4

心 ㇜ 小 戈 戸 手 扌 支 攵 文 斗 斤 方 日 曰 月 肉 月 木 欠 止 歹 殳 母 毋 比 毛 氏 气 水 氺 氵 火 灬 ㄊ 父 片 牛 犬 犭 王 礻 耂

心 忄 小 戈 戸 手 扌 支 攵 文 斗 斤 方 日 曰 月 肉 月 木 欠 止 歹 殳 母 毋 比 毛 氏 气 水 氷 氵 火 灬 爫 父 片 牛 犬 犭 王 礻 耂

熟	恩返し	オンがえし	repayment of a favor
	恩義	オンギ	favor; obligation; moral obligation
	恩給	オンキュウ	pension
	恩恵	オンケイ	favor; benefit
	恩師	オンシ	one's former teacher
	恩賜	オンシ	imperial gift
	恩赦	オンシャ	amnesty; general pardon
	恩情	オンジョウ	compassion
	恩知らず	オンしらず	ingratitude; ingrate
	恩人	オンジン	benefactor; patron
	恩寵	オンチョウ	grace; favor
	恩典	オンテン	grace; act of grace

780

恐 ⑩

一 丁 工 卫 巩 巩 巩 恐 恐 恐

音	恐	キョウ	fear; fright
熟	恐喝	キョウカツ	threat; menace; blackmail —v. threaten; menace; blackmail
	恐慌	キョウコウ	panic; scare; alarm
	恐縮	キョウシュク	gratitude; appreciation; fear —vi. be grateful; appreciate; be frightened
	恐怖	キョウフ	fear; terror; fright
	恐怖症	キョウフショウ	phobia; morbid fear
	恐竜	キョウリュウ	dinosaur
訓	恐れる	おそれる	vi. fear; be afraid of; dread
	恐ろしい	おそろしい	terrible; frightening; dreadful
	恐らく	おそらく	perhaps; probably; maybe
	恐れ入る	おそれいる	vi. be overwhelmed (with gratitude/shame); be astonished; be sorry to trouble; beg pardon; be defeated; yield; plead quilty
¥	恐慌	キョウコウ	financial panic/crisis

781

恵 ⑩

一 厂 戸 戸 百 申 声 恵 恵 恵

音	恵	エ	happiness
		ケイ	mercy
熟	恵比寿	エビス	Ebisu (god of wealth)
	恵贈	ケイゾウ	(phrase used to express gratitude after receiving a gift)

| 訓 | 恵む | めぐむ | *vt.* bless; favor |
| | 恵み | めぐみ | blessings; favors |

782

息 ⑩ ＇ ＜ ㇒ 白 自 自 自 息 息 息

音	息	ソク	breath; son
熟	息災	ソクサイ	healthy; safety; safe and sound
	息女	ソクジョ	daughter
訓	息	いき	breath
	※息子	むすこ	son

783

恥 ⑩ 一 ＜ Ｆ Ｆ 耳 耳 耳 耳 恥 恥

音	恥	チ	shyness; bashfulness; shame; disgrace
熟	恥辱	チジョク	disgrace; dishonor; shame; indignity; stigma
訓	恥	はじ	shame; disgrace; dishonor; embarrassment
	恥知らず	はじしらず	shameless; thick-skinned
	恥じらう	はじらう	*vi.* be shy/coy/bashful
	恥じる	はじる	*vi.* feel shame; be ashamed of
	恥ずかしい	はずかしい	shy; shameful; disgraceful; embarrassing
	恥ずかしがり屋	はずかしがりや	shy person

784

恋 ⑩ ＇ 亠 ナ 亢 亣 亦 亦 恋 恋 恋

音	恋	レン	love
熟	恋愛	レンアイ	love —*v.* love
	恋歌	レンカ	love song/poem
	恋情	レンジョウ	love; affection
	恋慕	レンボ	falling in love —*vi.* fall in love with
訓	恋	こい	love
	恋しい	こいしい	dear; beloved
	恋人	こいびと	sweetheart; boyfriend; girlfriend
	恋文	こいぶみ	love letter
	恋う	こう	*vt.* yearn for

361

4

悪 ⑪ 　一 ⼁ 亠 亍 亜 亜 亜 亜 悪 悪 悪

心忄小戈戸手扌支攵文斗斤方日曰月肉月木欠止歹殳母毋比毛氏气水氺氵火灬一父片牛犬犭王礻老

音	悪	アク	wrong; incorrect; bad; evil; immoral; ugly; poor quality; inferior; hate
		オ	hate
熟	悪意	アクイ	evil intention; wrongful intent
	悪運	アクウン	the devil's luck
	悪行	アクギョウ	evildoing; wicked act
	悪事	アクジ	evil deed; wrongdoing; wrong; crime
	悪質	アクシツ	full of faults; vicious; corrupt; of poor quality; faulty; defective
	悪臭	アクシュウ	bad smell; stink; stench
	悪習	アクシュウ	bad habit; abuse; vice
	悪循環	アクジュンカン	vicious circle
	悪性	アクセイ	evil nature; malignancy; malevolence
	悪戦苦闘	アクセントウ	struggle; desperate fight —vi. struggle; fight desperately
	悪態	アクタイ	foul language; curse; slander; abuse
	悪党	アクトウ	bad person; villain; scoundrel; rogue
	悪徳	アクトク	vice; corruption; immorality
	悪人	アクニン	wicked person; wrongdoer
	悪筆	アクヒツ	poor handwriting
	悪評	アクヒョウ	ill repute; bad reputation; notoriety
	悪風	アクフウ	bad custom; vice
	悪文	アクブン	poor writing; writing that is difficult to understand
	悪魔	アクマ	devil; demon; fiend; Satan
	悪夢	アクム	nightmare; bad dream
	悪名	アクメイ	bad reputation; infamy; notoriety
	悪用	アクヨウ	abuse; misuse —v. abuse; misuse; put to a bad use
	悪化	アッカ	worsening; deterioration —vi. get worse; become impaired; deteriorate
	悪寒	オカン	chill; cold
訓	悪い	わるい	wrong; bad; inferior; ugly
	悪賢い	わるがしこい	cunning; sly; crafty
	悪気	わるギ	malice; spite; ill will; harm
	悪口	わるくち	abuse; slander; foul language
	悪者	わるもの	bad person; rogue; villain
	※悪戯	いたずら	mischief; prank; practical joke
	※悪阻	つわり	morning sickness

362

786

患 ⑪ 丶 口 口 口 尸 吊 吕 串 串 患 患 患

音	患	カン	trouble; anxiety
熟	患者	カンジャ	patient
	患部	カンブ	part of the body affected by illness or injury
訓	患う	わずらう	*v.* be ill; feel sick; be worried/tormented
	患い	わずらい	illness; sickness; worry; torment

787

悠 ⑪ ノ イ 仆 竹 伫 攸 攸 攸 悠 悠 悠

音	悠	ユウ	leisure; longtime; distant
熟	悠久	ユウキュウ	eternity; permanence
	悠然	ユウゼン	calm; with perfect composure
	悠長	ユウチョウ	leisurely; slow; easy going
	悠々たる	ユウユウたる	quiet; calm; composed; leisurely

788

悲 78 8) ナ ヲ ヲ 刣 非 非 非 非 悲 悲 悲

音	悲	ヒ	sad
熟	悲哀	ヒアイ	sorrow; grief; sadness
	悲運	ヒウン	misfortune; bad/ill luck
	悲歌	ヒカ	elegy; sad tune; plaintive melody
	悲観	ヒカン	pessimism; disappointment —*v.* be pessimistic/disappointed
	悲願	ヒガン	Buddhist prayer for mankind; earnest wish
	悲喜	ヒキ	joy and sorrow
	悲境	ヒキョウ	adversities; unhappy situation; plight
	悲劇	ヒゲキ	tragedy; tragic play
	悲惨	ヒサン	miserable; pathetic; tragic
	悲壮	ヒソウ	tragic but brave; heroic (death)
	悲愴	ヒソウ	pathetic; grievous; mournful
	悲嘆	ヒタン	grief; sorrow; anguish; lamentation —*vi.* grieve; sorrow; mourn; lament
	悲痛	ヒツウ	bitter; grief; sorrow
	悲報	ヒホウ	sad news

心 忄 小 戈 戸 手 扌 支 攵 文 斗 斤 方 日 曰 月 肉 月 木 欠 止 歹 殳 母 毋 比 毛 氏 气 水 氺 氵 火 灬 爫 父 片 牛 犬 犭 王 礻 耂

心忄小戈戸手扌支攵文斗斤方日曰月肉月木欠止歹殳母毋比毛氏气水氷氵火灬爫父片牛犬犭王礻耂

悲鳴	ヒメイ	scream; shrier
悲恋	ヒレン	tragic love
悲話	ヒワ	sad story
訓 悲しい	かなしい	sorrowful; sad
悲しむ	かなしむ	*vt*. grieve; mourn; sorrow

789

惑 ⑫ 一 厂 厂 戸 戸 弌 或 或 或 或 惑 惑

音 惑	ワク	go astray; be misguided/tempted
熟 惑星	ワクセイ	planet
訓 惑う	まどう	*vi*. go astray; be misguided/tempted

790

愛 ⑬ ノ ハ ャ ぁ 爫 ぜ 严 严 忌 恶 愛 夢 愛

音 愛	アイ	love; affection; attraction; attachment
熟 愛する	アイする	*vt*. love; be attracted to; cherish; hold dear
愛煙家	アイエンカ	habitual smoker
愛嬌	アイキョウ	charms; physical grace or attraction
愛顧	アイコ	favor; patronage —*vt*. favor; patronize
愛護	アイゴ	protection; preservation; conservation —*v*. protect; preserve; conserve
愛好	アイコウ	love; liking —*v*. love; like; be a lover of; be fond of
愛国心	アイコクシン	patriotism; nationalism
愛妻	アイサイ	one's beloved/darling wife
愛妻家	アイサイカ	devoted husband; husband who loves and cares for his wife
愛児	アイジ	beloved/favorite child
愛称	アイショウ	pet name; nickname
愛情	アイジョウ	feeling of love; affection; attachment; devotion
愛人	アイジン	lover; sexual partner
愛惜	アイセキ	attachment —*vt*. long for
愛想	アイソ（ウ）	amiablity; sociability; friendliness; congeniality
愛憎	アイゾウ	love and hatred
愛着	アイチャク	attachment; affection; love —*v*. become attached to; hold dear
愛読	アイドク	enjoyable/regular reading —*v*. enjoy reading; read regularly
愛用	アイヨウ	habitual/regular use —*v*. use habitually; patronize

意 ⑬ 　 ﾉ 　亠 亠 亠 立 产 产 咅 咅 音 音 意 意

音	意	イ	mind; feeling; thought; idea; intention; opinion; reason; meaning
熟	意外	イガイ	unexpected; unforeseen; surprising
	意気	イキ	spirits; disposition; temperament; humor
	意気消沈	イキショウチン	depression; dejection —*vi.* be depressed; feel dejected; be dispirited
	意気投合	イキトウゴウ	mutual understanding; sympathy; affinity —*vi.* get on well with; have an affinity for; be like minded
	意気揚々	イキヨウヨウ	triumphant; exultant
	意気地なし	イクジなし	coward; lack of courage or resolution
	意義	イギ	meaning; sense; significance
	意見	イケン	opinion; view; idea; suggestion —*v.* give advice; admonish; reprove
	意向	イコウ	intention; inclination; disposition
	意志	イシ	will; volition
	意思	イシ	intention; intent; purpose
	意地	イジ	temper; obstinacy; pride; nature; dispositon
	意地悪	イジわる	ill-natured; malevolent; spiteful
	意識	イシキ	consciousness; awareness; senses —*v.* be conscious; feel; be aware
	意匠	イショウ	idea; device; design
	意中	イチュウ	one's mind/thoughts/feelings
	意図	イト	intent; intention; aim; idea —*v.* intend; design; aim
	意表	イヒョウ	unexpectedness; surprise
	意味	イミ	meaning; sense; significance; implication —*v.* mean; signify; imply
	意訳	イヤク	free translation —*v.* translate freely
	意欲	イヨク	will; desire; volition

感 ⑬ 　 ﾉ 厂 厂 厂 斤 后 咸 咸 咸 感 感

音	感	カン	feel; feeling; inspiration; sensation; sentiment; emotion
熟	感じる	カンじる	*v.* be conscious of; suffer; be impressed; feel
	感化	カンカ	inspiration; influence —*v.* inspire; influence
	感慨	カンガイ	deep emotion

心 忄 小 戈 戸 手 扌 支 攵 文 斗 斤 方 日 曰 月 肉 月 木 欠 止 歹 殳 母 毋 比 毛 氏 气 水 氺 氵 火 灬 灬 父 片 牛 犬 犭 王 礻 耂

感慨無量	カンガイムリョウ	filled with deep emotion
感覚	カンカク	sense; sensibility; feeling
感激	カンゲキ	deep emotion; impression; enthusiasm —*vi.* be deeply moved/impressed
感光	カンコウ	exposure to light
感謝	カンシャ	thanks; appreciation; gratitude —*v.* thank; be thankful/grateful for
感受性	カンジュセイ	sensibility; receptivity
感傷	カンショウ	sentimentality
感情	カンジョウ	feeling; sentiment; emotion
感触	カンショク	sense of touch
感染	カンセン	infection —*v.* be infected
感想	カンソウ	impressions; thoughts
感嘆	カンタン	great admiration; wonder; amazement —*vi.* admire; marvel; wonder; be amazed
感知	カンチ	perception; awareness —*v.* perceive; become aware of
感づく	カンづく	*vi.* suspect; sense; get wind of
感電	カンデン	electric shock —*vi.* receive an electric shock
感度	カンド	sensitivity; sensibility
感動	カンドウ	impression; emotion; inspiration —*vi.* be impressed/moved/inspired
感服	カンプク	admiration —*vi.* be impressed by
感冒	カンボウ	*med.* cold; catarrh
感銘	カンメイ	deep impression —*vi.* be deeply impressed; make an impression
感涙	カンルイ	tears of gratitude

793

愚 ⑬ 　 ′ 口 曰 曰 戸 昌 禺 禺 禺 禺 愚 愚

音	愚	グ	stupid; foolish
熟	愚計	グケイ	foolish intention *hum.* (my) plans
	愚行	グコウ	foolish act
	愚作	グサク	poor work; trash; rubbish *hum.* one's own work
	愚痴	グチ	idle complaint; grumble
	愚問	グモン	stupid question *hum.* one's own question
	愚劣	グレツ	stupidity; foolishness; absurdity
	愚弄	グロウ	mockery; derision; ridicule —*v.* fool; befool; make a fool of; jibe
訓	愚か	おろか	foolish; stupid; witless

794

慈 ⑬ 　丶　丶　⺌　⺍　亡　玄　玆　玆　兹　茲　慈　慈

音	慈	ジ	mercy; affection
熟	慈愛	ジアイ	affection; love
	慈雨	ジウ	welcome rain
	慈善	ジゼン	almsgiving; charity
	慈悲	ジヒ	mercy; charity
	慈父	ジフ	affectionate father
	慈母	ジボ	affectionate mother
訓	慈しみ	いつくしみ	love; affection
	慈しむ	いつくしむ	*vt*. love; be tender

795

愁 ⑬ 　一　二　千　禾　禾　禾　秒　秒　秋　秋　愁

音	愁	シュウ	lament; grief; sorrow
熟	愁傷	シュウショウ	grief; deep sorrow
訓	愁い	うれい	grief; sorrow; distress; trouble
	愁える	うれえる	*vt*. lament; worry; be troubled

796

想 ⑬ 　一　十　才　木　机　机　相　相　相　相　想　想

音	想	ソウ	idea; thought
		（ソ）	
熟	想起	ソウキ	recollection; remembrance
	想像	ソウゾウ	imagination —*v*. imagine
	想定	ソウテイ	supposition; hypothesis —*v*. suppose; make a hypothesis
	想念	ソウネン	idea; conception
訓	※想う	おもう	*vt*. think of; call to mind

797

態 ⑭ 　㇐　㇒　㇒　台　育　育　能　能　能　態　態

| 音 | 態 | タイ | figure; posture; attitude |

367

心忄小戈戸手扌支攵文斗斤方日曰月肉月木欠止歹殳母毋比毛氏气水氺氵火灬爫父片牛犬犭王礻衤耂

| 熟 | 態勢 | タイセイ | attitude; condition |
| | 態度 | タイド | attitude; behavior |

798

慰 ⑮ 　 ㇀ ㇖ ㇕ 尸 尼 尽 尉 尉 尉 尉 慰

音	慰	イ	comfort; console
熟	慰安	イアン	comfort; consolation; solace —*v.* comfort; console; solace
	慰謝料	イシャリョウ	consolation money; compensation; damages
	慰問	イモン	consolation; sympathy —*v.* go to console; show sympathy; inquire after
	慰労	イロウ	recognition of services —*v.* acknowledge a person's services
訓	慰む	なぐさむ	*vt.* be diverted; make fun of; make a plaything of
	慰める	なぐさめる	*vi.* comfort; console; amuse

799

慶 ⑮ 　 ㇐ 广 庐 庐 庐 庐 庐 廐 廐 慶 慶 慶

音	慶	ケイ	congratulate; celebrate; auspicious
熟	慶賀	ケイガ	congratulations —*v.* congratulate; celebrate
	慶事	ケイジ	happy event
	慶祝	ケイシュク	celebration —*v.* celebrate
	慶弔	ケイチョウ	congratulations and condolences

800

憂 ⑮ 　 ㇐ ㇐ ㇑ 页 页 百 直 盲 惪 惪 惪 夒 憂

音	憂	ユウ	grieve; be distressed/anxious
熟	憂鬱	ユウウツ	melancholy; dejection; gloom
	憂国	ユウコク	concern about the future of one's country
	憂愁	ユウシュウ	melancholy; grief; gloom
	憂慮	ユウリョ	anxiety; apprehension —*v.* be anxious/apprehensive/concerned; worry
訓	憂い	うい	gloomy; unhappy; sad
	憂い	うれい	grief; anxiety; distress
	憂える	うれえる	*vt.* be distressed/anxious; grieve

801

慮 ⑮ 　 ゝ 　ト 　 ⼾ 　 广 　 ⼾ 　 ⼾ 　 虍 　 虍 　 虐 　 虐 　 虗 　 慮 　 慮

音	慮	リョ	consideration; thought
熟	慮外	リョガイ	unexpected; rude; inconsiderate; thoughtless
訓	※慮る	おもんばかる	*vt*. think; consider; be prudent; fear; be apprehensive

802

憩 ⑯ 　 ー 　 ⼆ 　 千 　 舌 　 舌 　 舌 　 舌 　 刮 　 刮 　 刮 　 憩 　 憩

音	憩	ケイ	rest; relaxation
訓	憩い	いこい	rest; relaxation; respite
	憩う	いこう	*vi*. rest; take a rest; relax

803

憲 ⑯ 　 ゝ 　 宀 　 宀 　 宀 　 宝 　 宝 　 害 　 害 　 害 　 憲 　 憲 　 憲

音	憲	ケン	constitution
熟	憲章	ケンショウ	charter
	憲法	ケンポウ	constitution
訓	憲	のり	law; rule; regulation

804

懇 ⑰ 　 ー 　 ⼎ 　 ⼢ 　 ⼵ 　 豸 　 豸 　 豸 　 貇 　 貇 　 貇 　 懇 　 懇

音	懇	コン	kind; polite; courteous; sincere
熟	懇意	コンイ	intimacy; friendship; kindness
	懇願	コンガン	entreaty; solicitation; petition —*v*. entreat; implore; beseech; appeal; petition
	懇情	コンジョウ	kindness; consideration
	懇親	コンシン	good fellowship; friendship; intimacy
	懇切	コンセツ	kindness; cordiality
	懇談	コンダン	familiar talk; chat —*vi*. have a chat; confabulate
	懇篤	コントク	kindness; cordiality
訓	懇ろ	ねんごろ	politeness; courtesy; kindness

心 忄 小 戈 戸 手 扌 支 攵 文 斗 斤 方 日 曰 月 肉 月 木 欠 止 歹 殳 母 毋 比 毛 氏 气 水 氺 氵 火 灬 ⺍ 父 片 牛 犬 犭 王 衤 耂

4

心
忄
小
戈
戸
手
扌
支
攵
文
斗
斤
方
日
曰
月
肉
月
木
欠
止
歹
殳
母
毋
比
毛
氏
气
水
氺
氵
火
灬
爫
父
片
牛
犬
犭
王
礻
老

805

懲 ⑱　彳　彳　彳　彳　彳　彳　徍　徵　徵　徵　徵　懲

音	懲	チョウ	punish
熟	懲役	チョウエキ	penal servitude
	懲戒	チョウカイ	discipline; official reprimand —*v.* reprimand; discipline; reprove
	懲罰	チョウバツ	chastisement; discipline; punishment —*v.* chastise; discipline; punish
訓	懲らしめる	こらしめる	*vt.* chastise; chasten; punish; correct; discipline
	懲らす	こらす	*vt.* chastise; chasten; punish; correct; discipline
	懲りる	こりる	*vi.* learn by experience; learn from one's mistakes

---

806

懸 ⑳　冂　目　但　県　県　県　県　県　県　県　縣　懸

音	懸	ケン	suspend; hang
		ケ	
熟	懸念	ケネン	anxiety; fear; apprehension —*v.* fear; apprehend
	懸案	ケンアン	pending problem; undecided matter
	懸賞	ケンショウ	prize; reward
	懸垂	ケンスイ	hanging; suspending —*vi.* hang; suspend
	懸命	ケンメイ	eagerly
訓	懸かる	かかる	*vi.* hang; set about; decide; fall into a trap; rest; be supported
	懸ける	かける	*vt.* hang; suspend; offer; risk

---

3 忄　りっしんべん　heart to the left

807

忙 ⑥　丶　丶　忄　忄　忙　忙

音	忙	ボウ	busy
熟	忙殺	ボウサツ	keeping (someone) very busy; being very busy —*v.* keep (someone) very busy
訓	忙しい	いそがしい	busy

| ※忙しい | せわしい | busy; restless |
| ※忙しない | せわしない | restless; in a hurry |

808

快 ⑦　　丶丶忄忄忄快快

音	快	カイ	comfort; pleasure
熟	快活	カイカツ	cheerfulness; liveliness
	快感	カイカン	pleasant sensation; pleasure
	快挙	カイキョ	brilliant achievement; heroic deed
	快勝	カイショウ	easy victory —*vi.* win an easy victory
	快晴	カイセイ	fine weather
	快走	カイソウ	fast running —*vi.* run fast
	快速	カイソク	high/great speed
	快調	カイチョウ	excellent condition; harmony
	快適	カイテキ	comfortable; delightful; agreeable
	快方	カイホウ	convalescence; recovery from illness
	快報	カイホウ	good/welcome news
	快楽	カイラク	pleasure; enjoyment
訓	快い	こころよい	pleasant; comfortable

809

怪 ⑧　　丶丶忄忄怪怪怪怪

音	怪	カイ	strange; suspect; doubtful
		(ケ)	
熟	怪獣	カイジュウ	monstrous beast; monster
	怪談	カイダン	ghost story
	怪物	カイブツ	monster
	怪力	カイリキ	Herculean strength
	怪我	ケガ	injury
訓	怪しい	あやしい	doubtful; mysterious; dubious
	怪しむ	あやしむ	*vt.* doubt

810

怖 ⑧　　丶丶忄忄忄忄怖怖

| 音 | 怖 | フ | fear |

371

心 忄 小 戈 戸 手 扌 支 攵 文 斗 斤 方 日 曰 月 肉 月 木 欠 止 歹 殳 母 毋 比 毛 氏 气 水 氺 氵 火 灬 爫 父 片 牛 犬 犭 王 礻 耂

心忄小戈戸手扌支攵文斗斤方日曰月肉月木欠止歹殳母毋比毛氏气水氷氵火灬爫父片牛犬犭王礻耂

訓 怖い　　こわい　　　　fearful; frightful; scary; awful
　　怖がる　　こわがる　　*vi.* fear; be afraid/scared

811

性 ⑧ 　 ′ 　 ′ 　 忄 　 忄 　 忄 　 忄 　 忄 　 性

音	性	セイ	nature; sex; gender
		ショウ	nature
熟	性根	ショウネ	nature; character
	性分	ショウブン	nature; disposition
	性愛	セイアイ	sexual love
	性格	セイカク	character; personality
	性器	セイキ	sexual organs; genitals
	性急	セイキュウ	hasty; impatient
	性教育	セイキョウイク	sex education
	性交	セイコウ	intercourse; sex; coitus —*vi.* have sex; make love
	性向	セイコウ	disposition; nature
	性行	セイコウ	character and conduct
	性行為	セイコウイ	sexual act
	性質	セイシツ	nature; disposition; property
	性的	セイテキ	sexual
	性転換	セイテンカン	sex change —*v.* change one's sex
	性転換者	セイテンカンシャ	transsexual
	性能	セイノウ	performance; efficiency
	性病	セイビョウ	venereal disease
	性病科	セイビョウカ	department for the treatment of venereal diseases
	性癖	セイヘキ	natural tendency; propensity
	性別	セイベツ	distinction of sex; gender
	性本能	セイホンノウ	sex drive/impulse
	性欲	セイヨク	sexual desire; lust

812

悔 ⑨ 　 ′ 　 ′ 　 忄 　 忄 　 忄 　 忄 　 悔 　 悔 　 悔

音	悔	カイ	regret; repent
熟	悔悟	カイゴ	remorse; regret —*vi.* feel remorse/regret
	悔恨	カイコン	remorse; regret —*vi.* feel remorse/regret
訓	悔いる	くいる	*vi.* repent; regret

| 悔しい | くやしい | regretful; feel frustrated |
| 悔やむ | くやむ | *vt.* condole; lament |

813

恒 ⑨
` , ＼ 忄 忄 忄 忄 忆 恒 恒`

音	恒	コウ	constant; fixed; usual
熟	恒久	コウキュウ	eternal; everlasting
	恒久性	コウキュウセイ	permanency
	恒産	コウサン	estate; steady job
	恒常	コウジョウ	stability; constance; standards
	恒星	コウセイ	fixed star
	恒例	コウレイ	usual practice; established custom

814

恨 ⑨
` , ＼ 忄 忄 忄 忆 恨 恨 恨`

音	恨	コン	bear a grudge; regret
訓	恨み	うらみ	grudge; ill feeling; hatred
	恨む	うらむ	*vt.* regret; bear a grudge; show resentment
	恨めしい	うらめしい	reproachful; rueful; spiteful; hateful

815

悦 ⑩
` , ＼ 忄 忄 忄 忄 忄 忱 忱 悦`

音	悦	エツ	rapture; joy
熟	悦楽	エツラク	joy; happiness; delight —*vi.* be full of joy; be happy/delighted
訓	悦ばす	よろこばす	*vt.* please; gladden; make happy
	悦ぶ	よろこぶ	*vi.* be happy/glad/delighted

816

悟 ⑩
` , ＼ 忄 忄 忄 恬 恬 悟 悟`

音	悟	ゴ	realize; perceive
訓	悟る	さとる	*vt.* realize; perceive; be enlightened
	悟り	さとり	enlightenment; perception

心 忄 小 戈 戸 手 扌 支 攵 文 斗 斤 方 日 日 月 肉 月 木 欠 止 歹 殳 母 毋 比 毛 氏 气 水 氺 氵 火 灬 爪 父 片 牛 犬 犭 王 礻 耂

心忄小戈戸手扌支攵文斗斤方日曰月肉月木欠止歹殳母毋比毛氏气水氺氵火灬爫父片牛犬犭王礻歩

817

悩 ⑩ 　 ＇ ＇ ′ ′ ′ ′ ′ 忄 忄 忄 悩 悩

音	悩	ノウ	worry
熟	悩殺	ノウサツ	fascination; enchantment —*v.* fascinate; enchant; bewitch; captivate; charm
訓	悩ます	なやます	*vt.* afflict; torment; harass; torture
	悩み	なやみ	worry; anguish
	悩む	なやむ	*vi.* be troubled/worried/distressed

818

惨 ⑪ 　 ＇ ＇ ′ 忄 忄 忄 忄 忰 快 惨 惨

音	惨	サン	piteous; wretched; miserable
		ザン	
熟	惨劇	サンゲキ	tragedy; disaster
	惨事	サンジ	disaster; tragic incident; terrible accident
	惨状	サンジョウ	terrible sight; horrible spectacle
	惨敗	ザンパイ	crushing/humiliating defeat —*vi.* suffer a crushing/humiliating defeat
訓	惨め	みじめ	miserable; wretched; pitiable; pathetic

819

情 ⑪ 　 ＇ ＇ ′ 忄 忄 忄 忄 忰 情 情 情 情

音	情	ジョウ	feeling; sentiment; emotions; heart; affection; love
		(セイ)	
熟	情愛	ジョウアイ	affection; love; compassion
	情感	ジョウカン	emotion
	情景	ジョウケイ	scene
	情交	ジョウコウ	sexual intercourse
	情死	ジョウシ	lover's suicide —*vi.* carry out a suicide pact
	情事	ジョウジ	love affair
	情実	ジョウジツ	private considerations; favoritism
	情趣	ジョウシュ	artistic; tasteful; elegant; charming
	情状	ジョウジョウ	circumstances; allowances
	情状酌量	ジョウジョウシャクリョウ	consideration of the extenuating circumstances

374

情勢	ジョウセイ	situation; state of affairs; conditions
情操	ジョウソウ	sentiments
情痴	ジョウチ	blind passion; foolish love
情緒	ジョウチョ	emotion; sentiment
情熱	ジョウネツ	passion; ardor; enthusiasm
情熱的	ジョウネツテキ	passionate; ardent; enthusiastic
情念	ジョウネン	sentiments; feelings
情夫	ジョウフ	male lover
情婦	ジョウフ	female lover
情報	ジョウホウ	information; news; data; report
情報機関	ジョウホウキカン	secret service
情報処理	ジョウホウショリ	data processing
情欲	ジョウヨク	sexual desire; lust
情理	ジョウリ	reason and sentiment
訓 情け	なさけ	sympathy; pity; compassion; charity; love
情けない	なさけない	deplorable; shameful; heartless; miserable; disgraceful

820

惜 ⑪ 　 ， 　 ，， 　 忄 　 忄一 　 忄丷 　 忄丗 　 忰 　 悟 　 惜 　 惜 　 惜

音 惜	セキ	regrettable; precious; wasteful
熟 惜敗	セキハイ	narrow defeat —*vi.* be narrowly defeated
惜別	セキベツ	reluctant parting —*v.* part reluctantly
訓 惜しい	おしい	regretful
惜しむ	おしむ	*vt.* regret; value; be reluctant to part with

821

悼 ⑪ 　 ， 　 ，， 　 忄 　 忄ˊ 　 忄宀 　 忄宀 　 忄白 　 悍 　 悼 　 悼 　 悼

| **音** 悼 | トウ | grieve |
| **訓** 悼む | いたむ | *vi.* moan; grieve; lament |

822

慌 ⑫ 　 ， 　 ，， 　 忄 　 忄一 　 忄亡 　 忄亠 　 忄芒 　 忄芒 　 忄芒 　 慌 　 慌 　 慌

音 慌	コウ	busy; hurry; confused
訓 慌ただしい	あわただしい	busy; bustling; hurried; restless
慌てる	あわてる	*vi.* be confused; hurry; be flurried/disconcerted

心 忄 小 戈 戸 手 扌 支 攵 文 斗 斤 方 日 曰 月 肉 月 木 欠 止 歹 殳 母 毋 比 毛 氏 気 水 氷 氵 火 灬 爫 父 片 牛 犬 犭 王 礻 耂

心忄小戈戸手扌支攵文斗斤方日曰月肉月木欠止歹殳母毋比毛氏气水氺氵火灬宀父片牛犬犭王礻爿

823

惰 ⑫
丶 ハ 忄 忄 忄 忄 忄 忰 忰 惰 惰 惰

音	惰	ダ	neglect; laziness
熟	惰性	ダセイ	inertia
	惰力	ダリョク	inertia; momentum

824

愉 ⑫
丶 ハ 忄 忄 忄 忄 忄 怜 怜 愉 愉 愉

音	愉	ユ	joy; pleasure
	愉快	ユカイ	pleasant; merry; cheerful
	愉楽	ユラク	pleasure; joy
訓	※愉しい	たのしい	pleasant; delightful; fun

825

慨 ⑬
丶 忄 忄 忄 忄 忙 惧 惧 惧 慨 慨

音	慨	ガイ	lament; deplore
熟	慨嘆	ガイタン	deploring; lamentation; regret —v. deplore; lament; regret
訓	※慨く	なげく	v. grieve; moan; lament

826

慎 ⑬
丶 忄 忄 忄 忄 忄 愼 愼 愼 愼 慎 慎

音	慎	シン	prudent
熟	慎重	シンチョウ	careful; prudent; cautious; discreet
訓	慎む	つつしむ	vt. be careful/discreet; refrain; abstain
	慎み	つつしみ	prudence; discretion; modesty
	慎ましい	つつましい	prudent; discreet; modest

827

慣 ⑭
忄 忄 忄 忄 忄 慣 慣 慣 慣 慣 慣

音	慣	カン	custom; get used to

熟	慣行	カンコウ	customary practice; traditional way
	慣習	カンシュウ	rules and conventions
	慣性	カンセイ	inertia
	慣用	カンヨウ	usage; common use
	慣例	カンレイ	custom; usage; convention
訓	慣れる	なれる	*vi*. get used to; grow accustomed to
	慣らす	ならす	*vt*. tame; domesticate; accustom; familiarize

828

憎 ⑭ 忄 忄 忄 忄 忙 忄 憎 憎 憎 憎 憎 憎

音	憎	ゾウ	hate
熟	憎悪	ゾウオ	hatred; abhorrence
訓	憎い	にくい	hateful; horrible; repulsive
	憎む	にくむ	*vt*. hate
	憎しみ	にくしみ	hatred; animosity
	憎らしい	にくらしい	hateful; horrible; repulsive

829

慢 ⑭ 忄 忄 忄 忄 忄 忄 悍 悍 慢 慢 慢 慢

音	慢	マン	lazy; scorn; deride; prolonged; chronic; boasting
熟	慢心	マンシン	self-conceit —*v*. be conceited
	慢性	マンセイ	chronic

830

憤 ⑮ 忄 忄 忄 忱 忱 忱 悄 憤 憤 憤 憤 憤

音	憤	フン	resent; be indignant/enraged
熟	憤慨	フンガイ	indignation; resentment —*v*. be indignant; resent
	憤激	フンゲキ	anger; wrath; indignation —*vi*. become enraged/indignant
	憤死	フンシ	dying in a fit of anger —*vi*. die in a fit of anger —*bas*. be put out (with men on base)
	憤然	フンゼン	indignantly
	憤怒	フンヌ (フンド)	anger; wrath; indignation —*vi*. be angry/indignant
訓	憤る	いきどおる	get angry; resent; be indignant/enraged

4

心 忄 小 戈 戸 手 扌 支 攵 文 斗 斤 方 日 曰 月 肉 月 木 欠 止 歹 殳 母 毋 比 毛 氏 气 水 氺 氵 火 灬 爫 父 片 牛 犬 犭 王 尹 耂

心忄小戈戸手扌支攵文斗斤方日曰月肉月木欠止歹殳母毋比毛氏气水氷氵火灬爫父片牛犬犭王礻爿

831 憶 ⑯
忄 忄 忄 忄 忄 忄 忄 忄 忄 憶 憶 憶

音 憶　オク　remember; think; guess
熟 憶説　オクセツ　hypothesis
　　憶測　オクソク　conjecture; surmise; guess —*v.* conjecture; surmise; guess
　　憶病　オクビョウ　timid; cowardly
訓 ※憶える　おぼえる　*vi.* remember; learn; feel
　　※憶う　おもう　*vt.* think; guess; conjecture

832 懐 ⑯
忄 忄 忄 忄 忄 忄 忄 忄 忄 懐 懐 懐

音 懐　カイ　long for; recollect
熟 懐疑　カイギ　doubt; skepticism; disbelief —*v.* doubt; be skeptical; disbelieve
　　懐古　カイコ　nostalgia; yearning for the past —*vi.* remember the past; recollect the old days
　　懐柔　カイジュウ　appeasememt; conciliation; pacification —*v.* appease; conciliate; pacify
　　懐石料理　カイセキリョウリ　light meal served before a tea ceremony; *kaiseki* cuisine
　　懐中　カイチュウ　pocket (watch, flashlight, etc.); wallet
　　懐妊　カイニン　conception; pregnancy —*vi.* conceive; become pregnant
　　懐炉　カイロ　body heater
訓 懐かしい　なつかしい　dear; beloved; longed/yearned for
　　懐かしむ　なつかしむ　*vt.* yearn/long for; miss; think fondly of
　　懐く　なつく　*vi.* become attached to; become familiar with
　　懐ける　なつける　*vt.* win someone's heart; make someone fall in love with you
　　懐　ふところ　bosom; breast; pocket; purse

833 憾 ⑯
忄 忄 忄 忄 忄 忄 憾 憾 憾 憾 憾 憾

音 憾　カン　regret
訓 ※憾み　うらみ　regret
　　※憾む　うらむ　*vt.* be sorry for; regret

4 小 したごころ bottom heart

834

恭 ⑩   一 十 艹 艹 并 芉 共 恭 恭 恭 恭

音	恭	キョウ	respectful; reverent
熟	恭賀	キョウガ	respectful congratulations
	恭賀新年	キョウガシンネン	Happy New Year
	恭順	キョウジュン	submission; obedience
訓	恭しい	うやうやしい	respectful; reverent

835

慕 ⑭   艹 艹 艹 芦 苩 昔 莫 莫 莫 菒 蔂 慕 慕

音	慕	ボ	yearn for; desire; love dearly; idolize
熟	慕情	ボジョウ	affection; love; longing
訓	慕う	したう	*vt*. yearn for; desire; love dearly; idolize; admire
	慕わしい	したわしい	dear; beloved

4 戈 ほこがまえ tasseled spear

836

成 ⑥   ) 厂 厅 成 成 成

音	成	セイ (ジョウ)	be completed; achieve; accomplish
熟	成就	ジョウジュ	accomplishment; attainment —*v*. accomplish; attain
	成仏	ジョウブツ	death; Buddhahood —*vi*. enter Nirvana; die; pass away
	成育	セイイク	growth; development —*v*. grow; develop; raise
	成因	セイイン	origin; cause
	成果	セイカ	result; fruits; achievement
	成句	セイク	set phrase; idiomatic expression; common saying; proverb

379

心 忄 小 戈 戸 手 扌 支 攵 文 斗 斤 方 日 曰 月 肉 月 木 欠 止 歹 殳 母 毋 比 毛 氏 气 水 氺 氵 火 灬 爪 父 片 牛 犬 犭 王 衤 耂

心
忄
小
戈
戸
手
扌
支
攵
文
斗
斤
方
日
曰
月
肉
月
木
欠
止
歹
殳
母
毋
比
毛
氏
气
水
氺
氵
火
灬
爪
父
片
牛
犬
犭
王
礻
耂

成形	セイケイ	molding —*v.* mold	
成型	セイケイ	casting —*v.* cast	
成功	セイコウ	success; achievement —*vi.* succeed; be successful; pass; achieve	
成熟	セイジュク	maturity; ripeness —*vi.* ripen; mature	
成熟期	セイジュクキ	adolescence; puberty; period of maturity	
成人	セイジン	adult; grown-up —*vi.* grow-up; attain adulthood	
成人教育	セイジンキョウイク	adult education	
成人式	セイジンシキ	*seijinshiki* (coming-of-age ceremony)	
成績	セイセキ	result; record; grade; mark; performance; showings	
成層圏	セイソウケン	stratosphere	
成虫	セイチュウ	imago	
成長	セイチョウ	growth; development —*vi.* grow; grow up; develop	
成長率	セイチョウリツ	growth rate	
成年	セイネン	adult age; majority	
成敗	セイハイ	success and failure	
成敗	セイバイ	judgment; punishment —*v.* judge; punish	
成否	セイヒ	success or failure; result	
成分	セイブン	ingredient; component; constituent	
成立	セイリツ	formation —*vi.* come into existence/being; be organized/concluded	

訓

成す	なす	*vt.* accomplish; achieve; take shape; form
成る	なる	*vi.* become; be completed; consist; be made up; be promoted
成り上がり者	なりあがりもの	upstart
成金	なりキン	upstart; newly rich
成り立ち	なりたち	history; the origin; structure; formation
成り行き	なりゆき	course of events; developments

¥

成り行き（注文）	なりゆき（チュウモン）	market order; at the market

837

⑦

丶 ノ 二 千 手 我 我 我

音

我	ガ	self; selfish; ego; obstinacy

熟

我意	ガイ	self-will; obstinacy
我田引水	ガデンインスイ	drawing water for one's own field *fig.* promoting one's own interests

我慢	ガマン	patience; tolerance; perseverance; endurance —v. be patient/tolerant; persevere; endure	
我流	ガリュウ	self-taught method; one's own way (of doing something)	

訓

我	わ	I
我輩	わがハイ	*clas.* I; myself; me
我	われ	I; one's side
我等	われら	we; our; us
我々	われわれ	we; our; us

838

戒 ⑦ 一 二 テ 开 开 戒 戒

音 戒 カイ admonition; remonstrance

熟

戒厳令	カイゲンレイ	martial law
戒告	カイコク	admonition; reprimand; warning —v. admonish; reprimand; warn
戒名	カイミョウ	posthumous Buddhist name
戒律	カイリツ	Buddhist precepts

訓

戒め	いましめ	warning; admonition
戒める	いましめる	*vt.* warn; prohibit

839

戦 ⑬ ゛ ゛ ヽ ゛ ゛ ゛ ヽ ゛ 丷 尚 単 単 戦 戦 戦

音 戦 セン war; battle

熟

戦域	センイキ	war zone; theater of war
戦火	センカ	(the flames of) war
戦艦	センカン	battleship
戦記物	センキもの	account of a war
戦況	センキョウ	war situation
戦局	センキョク	war situation
戦後	センゴ	after the war; post war (in particular, World War Ⅱ)
戦国	センゴク	country torn apart by civil war
戦国時代	センゴクジダイ	*hist.* era of civil wars (1467-1568)
戦災	センサイ	war devastation
戦士	センシ	warrior; soldier
戦死	センシ	death in battle; killed in action —vi. be killed/die in action

4

心 忄 小 戈 戸 手 扌 支 攵 文 斗 斤 方 日 曰 月 肉 月 木 欠 止 歹 殳 母 毋 比 毛 氏 气 水 氺 氵 火 灬 爪 父 片 牛 犬 犭 王 礻 歺

戦時	センジ	wartime; war period
戦車	センシャ	tank
戦術	センジュツ	tactics
戦勝	センショウ	victory —*vi*. be victorious in battle
戦傷	センショウ	war wound —*vi*. be wounded in battle
戦場	センジョウ	battlefield; front
戦績	センセキ	war record
戦線	センセン	battle line; front
戦前	センゼン	before the war; prewar (in particular, World War II)
戦争	センソウ	war —*vi*. fight; go to war
戦隊	センタイ	corps; squadron
戦端	センタン	opening of hostilities
戦地	センチ	battlefield; front
戦中	センチュウ	during the war
戦闘	セントウ	action; combat; battle; fighting —*vi*. go into action/combat; battle; fight
戦犯	センパン	war crime/criminal
戦費	センピ	costs of war
戦没者	センボツシャ	fallen soldier
戦友	センユウ	con/comrade-in-arms rade-in-arms
戦乱	センラン	upheavals of war
戦慄	センリツ	shivering; trembling with fear —*vi*. shiver; tremble with fear
戦利品	センリヒン	war spoils; booty
戦略	センリャク	strategy
戦力	センリョク	war fighting capacity
戦歴	センレキ	war experience; combat record
戦列	センレツ	ranks; battle line
訓 戦う	たたかう	*vt*. fight; wage war
戦	いくさ	war
※戦く	おののく	*vi*. shudder; tremble; shiver
※戦ぐ	そよぐ	*vi*. rustle; stir; sway; tremble; quiver

840

戯 ⑮　丶 卜 卜 广 戸 声 卢 虎 虚 虚 戯 戯 戯

音 戯	ギ	play; joke
熟 戯画	ギガ	caricature; cartoon
戯曲	ギキョク	drama; play
訓 戯れる	たわむれる	*vi*. play; tease; joke; flirt
戯れ	たわむれ	play; joke; fun; flirtation

382

4 戸 と door

841 戸 ④ 一 ヲ 弖 戸

音	戸	コ	door; house; (counter for houses and buildings)
熟	戸外	コガイ	outdoors; out of doors; open air
	戸籍	コセキ	census; registration; person's family register
	戸籍抄本	コセキショウホン	abstract of one's family register
	戸籍謄本	コセキトウホン	copy of one's family register
	戸別	コベツ	from door to door; each house
訓	戸	と	door
	戸締り	とじまり	locking up —*vi.* lock up
	戸棚	とだな	cabinet; cupboard; sideboard; closet
	戸惑う	とまどう	*vi.* be puzzled; be at a loss

842 戻 ⑦ 一 ヲ 弖 戸 戸 戻 戻

音	戻	レイ	go back; come back; return
訓	戻す	もどす	*vt.* return; go back; come back; throw up; vomit
	戻る	もどる	*vi.* return; give back; send back; restore

843 所 ⑧ 一 ヲ 弖 戸 戸 戸 所 所

音	所	ショ	place
熟	所轄	ショカツ	jurisdiction
	所管	ショカン	jurisdiction
	所感	ショカン	impressions; thoughts; feelings
	所見	ショケン	one's view/opinion
	所在	ショザイ	site; one's whereabouts; location
	所産	ショサン	product; fruit of one's efforts
	所持	ショジ	possession —*v.* possess; have; store/put away one's possessions
	所信	ショシン	one's beliefs/opinions/views

心忄小戈戸手扌支攵文斗斤方日曰月肉月木欠止歹殳母毋比毛氏气水氺氵火灬爪父片牛犬犭王礻耂

所詮	ショセン	after all; any way
所蔵	ショゾウ	possession —*v.* possess; own; store/put away one's possessions
所属	ショゾク	one's position —*vi.* belong to; be with; be attached to
所存	ショゾン	thoughts; intentions
所帯	ショタイ	property; household
所長	ショチョウ	the head
所定	ショテイ	fixed; appointed
所望	ショモウ	desire; wish; request —*v.* wish; desire; ask for; request
所有	ショユウ	ownership; possession —*vt.* own; possess
所有権	ショユウケン	ownership; title
所用	ショヨウ	business
訓 所	ところ	place; spot; locality
¥ 所持人	ショジニン	bearer; holder
所得	ショトク	income; earnings
所得税	ショトクゼイ	income tax
所有	ショユウ	possession —*v.* own; possess

---

844 ⑧ 一 � �W 戸 戸 戸 房 房

音 房	ボウ	chamber; room; tassel
熟 房中	ボウチュウ	in the room/bedroom
訓 房	ふさ	tassel; tuft; cluster; bunch (of grapes)
房々	ふさふさ	tufty/bushy/profuse (hair)

---

845 ⑩ 一 � W 戸 戸 戸 肩 扇 扇 扇

音 扇	セン	folding fan
熟 扇形	センケイ	fan shape; sector; segment
扇情	センジョウ	inflammatory; provocative
扇状地	センジョウチ	alluvial fan; delta
扇子	センス	fan
扇動	センドウ	instigation; incitement; agitation —*v.* instigate; incite; agitate
扇風機	センプウキ	electric fan
訓 扇	おうぎ	fan

846

扉 ⑫　一 ＝ ＝ 尸 戸 戶 戶 扉 扉 扉 扉 扉 扉

音	扉	ヒ	door
訓	扉	とびら	door; title page (of a book); frontispiece

4 手 て hand　　扌 (p.389)

847

手 ④　一 ＝ ＝ 手

音	手	シュ	hand
熟	手記	シュキ	note; memorandum; private papers
	手芸	シュゲイ	handicrafts
	手工業	シュコウギョウ	handicraft/manual industry
	手術	シュジュツ	*med.* operation; surgery —*v.* operate; perform an operation
	手段	シュダン	means; step; measure
	手動	シュドウ	manual operation
	手法	シュホウ	technique; technical skill
	手練	シュレン	skill; dexterity
	手腕	シュワン	ability; capability
訓	手	て	hand; handle; trouble; means
	手足	てあし	hands and feet; arms and legs; limbs
	手当たり次第	てあたりシダイ	at random
	手当	てあて	medical treatment/care; salary; allowance; cover; provision —*v.* treat (a burn, etc.)
	手薄	てうす	short of hands
	手書き	てがき	handwriting —*v.* write; draft
	手数	てかず (てスウ)	trouble
	手堅い	てがたい	steady; sound; safe; trustworthy; reliable
	手紙	てがみ	letter; note
	手柄	てがら	exploit; great deed; feat
	手軽	てがる	light; simple
	手際	てぎわ	skill
	手口	てぐち	method; way; trick; *modus operandi*
	手首	てくび	wrist

心
忄
小
戈
戸
● 手
扌
支
攵
文
斗
斤
方
日
曰
月
肉
月
木
欠
止
歹
殳
母
毋
比
毛
氏
气
水
氺
氵
火
灬
爪
父
片
牛
犬
犭
王
礻
耂

手心 (を加える)	てごころ (をくわえる)	consideration; allowance —v. consider; allow for
手応え	てごたえ	effect; resistance; response
手頃	てごろ	proper; handy; suitable; reasonable; moderate
手強い	てごわい	strong; tough; formidable
手細工	てザイク	handiwork; handicraft
手先	てさき	fingertips
手探り	てさぐり	groping
手提げ	てさげ	handbag; bag
手下	てした	underling; henchmen
手品	てじな	magic; conjuring trick; sleight of hand
手品師	てじなシ	magician; conjurer
手順	てジュン	order; plan; arrangements; process; procedure
手錠	てジョウ	handcuffs
手製	てセイ	handmade; homemade
手相	てソウ	palmistry
手出し	てだし	interference —vi. meddle; interfere; make advances; dabble
手立て	てだて	means; process; order
手近	てぢか	close at hand; within reach
手違い	てちがい	mistake; blunder; accident
手帳	てチョウ	notebook; pocket diary
手作り	てづくり	homemade; handmade
手伝う	てつだう	vt. help; assist; aid
手続き	てつづき	procedure; formalities
手並み	てなみ	skill; dexterity
手習い	てならい	practice; learning
手慣れる	てなれる	vi. get used (to); get skillful (in)
手荷物	てにモツ	baggage
手拭い	てぬぐい	towel
手配	てハイ	arrangements; preparations; search —v. arrange; prepare
手放す	てばなす	vt. dispose; do away with; part; sell
手引き	てびき	guidance; guide; introduction; manual
手袋	てぶくろ	gloves; mittens
手解き	てほどき	initiation
手本	てホン	copy; model; copy book
手前	てまえ	before; near; in front
手間取る	てまどる	vi. take time; be delayed; be kept long
手回し	てまわし	preparation; arrangements
手短か	てみじか	brief; short
手持ち	てもち	on a hand; in stock; holdings

手元	てもと	at hand
手料理	てリョウリ	home cooking
¥ 手当	てあて	allowance; cover; procurement; purchase
手形	てがた	handprint; document; bill; draft; note
手形割引	てがたわりびき	discount of bills
手仕舞	てジまい	evening up
手数料	てスウリョウ	fee; change; commission
手付金	てつけキン	earnest; deposit; bargain deposit; bargain-money deposit paid on contracts; security money; hand money
手取り	てどり	net profit/income/receipts; one's salary after tax/deduction; clear gain
手直し	てなおし	later adjustment; readjustment
手控え	てびかえ	holding off
手引書	てびきショ	introduction; manual; handbook

848
⑧

音	承	ショウ	consent; agree; accept
熟	承諾	ショウダク	consent; agreement; acceptance; assent —v. consent; agree; give one's consent
	承知	ショウチ	consent; agreement; assent —v. know; understand; be aware; consent; agree; permit; allow
	承認	ショウニン	approval; consent; assent —v. approve; consent; acknowledge
	承服	ショウフク	submission —v. yield to; accept; consent
訓	承る	うけたまわる	vt. hear; understand; comply; consent

849
⑩

音	挙	キョ	raise; lift; enumerate; list; happen; occur; move; shake
熟	挙行	キョコウ	performance; celebration —v. perform (a ceremony); hold (a reception); celebrate (a marriage)
	挙国一致	キョコクイッチ	the whole country; nationwide
	挙式	キョシキ	(bridal) ceremony; celebration —vi. hold a ceremony; celebrate
	挙手	キョシュ	raising one's hand; show of hands —vi. raise one's hand; give a show of hands

心 忄 小 戈 戸 手 扌 支 攵 文 斗 斤 方 日 曰 月 肉 月 木 欠 止 歹 殳 母 毋 比 毛 氏 气 水 氺 氵 火 灬 爪 父 片 牛 犬 犭 王 礻 耂

挙措	キョソ	deportment; behavior; manner
挙動	キョドウ	behavior; conduct; demeanor
挙兵	キョヘイ	raising an army; taking up arms —*vi*. raise an army; take up arms
訓 挙がる	あがる	*vi*. raise; be lifted/elevated
挙げる	あげる	*vt*. raise; lift; elevate

850

掌 ⑫ ` ` ⺍ ⻗ 尚 尚 尚 尚 営 堂 堂 掌

音 掌	ショウ	palm; administer
熟 掌握	ショウアク	control; command; power —*v*. control; command; come into power
掌中	ショウチュウ	in (his/her) hands

851

撃 ⑮ 一 厂 冖 百 車 車 車 軖 軗 軗 墼 撃

音 撃	ゲキ	strike; attack
熟 撃砕	ゲキサイ	destruction —*vt*. destroy; shatter; defeat
撃退	ゲキタイ	repulsion; rejection; refusal —*v*. drive back; repulse; reject; refuse
撃沈	ゲキチン	sinking a ship —*v*. sink a ship; send a ship to the bottom
撃墜	ゲキツイ	shooting down a plane —*v*. shoot down a plane
撃破	ゲキハ	defeat; destruction —*v*. defeat; beat; destroy
撃滅	ゲキメツ	destruction; extermination —*v*. destruct; exterminate
訓 撃つ	うつ	*vt*. fire; shoot

852

摩 ⑮ ` 一 广 广 庐 庐 庐 庐 麻 麻 麼 摩

音 摩	マ	rub; scrape
熟 摩擦	マサツ	friction —*v*. create/feel/apply friction
摩天楼	マテンロウ	skyscraper
摩滅	マメツ	abrasion; wear —*v*. wear out
訓 ※摩る	さする	*vt*. pat; stroke; rub

3 扌 てへん hand at left

853 才 ③ 一 十 才

音	才	サイ	wit; talent; ability
熟	才覚	サイカク	wit; resources; contrivance; device
	才気	サイキ	quick-witted; gifted; brilliant
	才女	サイジョ	talented woman
	才能	サイノウ	talent; ability; gift

854 打 ⑤ 一 十 扌 扌 打

音	打	ダ	beat; bat; strike; hit; shoot
熟	打開	ダカイ	breakthrough; development; solution —*v.* breakthrough; effect a development
	打楽器	ダガッキ	percussion instrument
	打球	ダキュウ	*bas.* batting
	打撃	ダゲキ	blow; hit; knock; shock
	打算的	ダサンテキ	calculating; selfish; self-centered; mercenary
	打者	ダシャ	*bas.* batter
	打順	ダジュン	*bas.* batting order
	打診	ダシン	inquire; percussion —*med.* tapping —*v.* inquire; sound out —*med.* tap
	打席	ダセキ	*bas.* at bat
	打線	ダセン	*bas.* the batting line-up
	打倒	ダトウ	overthrow —*v.* overthrow; defeat; knock down; topple
	打破	ダハ	breaking; destruction; defeat; conquest; overthrow —*v.* break down; overthrow; conquer; destroy; defeat
	打撲	ダボク	blow; strike; hit —*v.* blow; strike; hit
	打撲傷	ダボクショウ	bruise; contusion
	打率	ダリツ	*bas.* batting average
訓	打つ	うつ	*vt.* hit; strike; shoot; make noodles; send a telegram; gamble
	打ち勝つ	うちかつ	*vi.* overcome; get over; conquer
	打ち切る	うちきる	*vt.* stop doing something; call off
	打ち込む	うちこむ	*vt.* devote oneself (to); drive in; shoot into

心 忄 小 戈 戸 手 扌 支 攵 文 斗 斤 方 日 曰 月 肉 月 木 欠 止 歹 殳 母 毌 比 毛 氏 气 水 氺 氵 火 灬 宀 父 片 牛 犬 犭 王 礻 耂

心忄小戈戸手扌
●扌支攵文斗斤方
日曰月肉月木欠
止歹殳母毋比毛
氏气水氺氵火灬
⺤父片牛犬犭王
礻耂

855

払 ⑤
一 す 扌 払 払

音	払	フツ	pay; sweep/drive away
熟	払拭	フッショク	sweeping away; wiping out —v. sweep away; wipe out
訓	払う	はらう	**vt.** pay; sweep/drive away; sell; dispose; pay; pay (attention)
	払い	はらい	payment; defrayment; discharge; quittance; acquittance; settlement; clearance; liquidation; repayment
¥	払い込み	はらいこみ	payment; installment
	払い下げる	はらいさげる	**vt.** sell; dispose of
	払い済み	はらいずみ	paid up; settled
	払い出し	はらいだし	payment
	払出銀行	はらいだしギンコウ	paying bank
	払い戻し	はらいもどし	refund; repayment

856

扱 ⑥
一 す 扌 扌 扨 扱

音	扱	(ソウ)	manage; handle; deal
訓	扱う	あつかう	**vt.** manage; handle; deal; arbitrate; treat
	※扱く	しごく	**vt.** squeeze through one's hands; draw through one's hands; put a person through hard training

857

技 ⑦
一 十 扌 扩 扌 technique 技

音	技	ギ	skill; art; craft
熟	技巧	ギコウ	craftmanship; workmanship; technical skill
	技師	ギシ	engineer; technician
	技術	ギジュツ	technique; technology; technical skill
	技能	ギノウ	technical skill; ability
	技法	ギホウ	technique
	技量	ギリョウ	skill; ability; talent; capability
訓	技	わざ	art; trick; skill

858

抗 ⑦   一 十 才 扌 扩 扩 抗

音	抗	コウ	resist; protest; oppose
熟	抗議	コウギ	protest; objection; complaint —*vi.* protest; object; complain
	抗生物質	コウセイブッシツ	*med.* antibiotics
	抗争	コウソウ	contention; dispute —*vi.* contend; struggle against; resist
	抗体	コウタイ	*med.* antibody

859

抄 ⑦   一 十 才 扌 扚 抄 抄

音	抄	ショウ	extract
熟	抄本	ショウホン	abridgment; abridged version of one's family register
	抄録	ショウロク	extract; summary —*v.* extract; summarize

860

折 ⑦   一 十 才 扌 扩 扩 折

音	折	セツ	break; divide; be folded
熟	折角	セッカク	kindly; with much effort; go to the trouble of
	折衷	セッチュウ	compromise; cross; blending —*v.* compromise; cross; blend
	折半	セッパン	halving —*v.* halve; divide into two
訓	折る	おる	*v.* fold; break; bend
	折れる	おれる	*vi.* break; be folded; bend; turn; yield
	折	おり	occasion; opportunity
	折り合う	おりあう	*vi.* agree; come to terms
	折り返す	おりかえす	*v.* make a turn; turn back
¥	折衝	セッショウ	negotiation —*vi.* negotiate

861

択 ⑦   一 十 才 扩 扩 护 択

音	択	タク	choose; select

心忄小戈戸手扌支攵文斗斤方日曰月肉月木欠止歹殳母毋比毛氏气水氺氵火灬爪父片牛犬犭王礻牙

862

投 ⑦　一　十　扌　扌　扩　捗　投

音	投	トウ	throw; fling; cast
熟	投影	トウエイ	casting a shadow; projection —v. project; reflect; cast a refection
	投下	トウカ	dropping; throwing down —v. drop; throw down
	投函	トウカン	mailing; posting —v. mail; post
	投球	トウキュウ	**bas**. pitching —v. **bas**. throw; pitch
	投降	トウコウ	surrender —vi. surrender; lay down one's arms
	投稿	トウコウ	magazine/newspaper contribution —vi. contribute/write for (a magazine, newspaper, etc.)
	投合	トウゴウ	agreement; coincidence —vi. agree/coincide with
	投獄	トウゴク	imprisonment; confinement —v. imprison; confine
	投資	トウシ	investment —vi. invest; make investments
	投宿	トウシュク	registering/staying at a hotel —vi. register/stay at a hotel
	投書	トウショ	contribution; reader's letter; letter to the editor —vi. write a letter to the editor; contribute to (a magazine, newspaper, etc.)
	投身	トウシン	suicide by drowning —vi. commit suicide by drowning
	投石	トウセキ	stone throwing —vi. throw stones
	投入	トウニュウ	investment; capital injection; commitment —v. invest in; commit to
	投票	トウヒョウ	vote; suffrage; poll; ballot; voting; election —vi. ballot; cast a vote; elect; vote
	投薬	トウヤク	prescription —v. prescribe medicine; medicate
訓	投げる	なげる	vt. throw; fling; cast; abandon; give up
	※投網	とあみ	cast net
¥	投機	トウキ	speculation; venture
	投資家	トウシカ	investor
	投資顧問業	トウシコモンギョウ	investment advisor
	投資信託（投信）	トウシシンタク（トウシン）	investment trust
	投資有価証券	トウシユウカショウケン	investments in securities
	投げ	なげ	sacrifice; shaking out

把 ⑦

一 十 扌 扌 扩 扣 押 把

音	把	ハ	grasp
熟	把握	ハアク	grasp; hold; grip —*v.* grasp; get hold of; grip; seize

抜 ⑦

一 十 扌 扌 扩 抜 抜

音	抜	バツ	pull out
熟	抜群	バツグン	preeminent; conspicuous; distinguished; outstanding
	抜糸	バッシ	removal of stitches —*vi.* remove stitches
	抜歯	バッシ	tooth extraction —*vi.* extract a tooth
	抜粋	バッスイ	extraction; excerpt; selection —*v.* extract; excerpt; select
	抜擢	バッテキ	choice; selection —*v.* choose; select
	抜刀	バットウ	unsheathed blade —*vi.* draw one's sword
	抜本的	バッポンテキ	radical; drastic; rigorous
訓	抜かす	ぬかす	*vt.* omit; leave out; look over; skip
	抜かる	ぬかる	*vi.* commit a blunder; make a slip
	抜く	ぬく	*v.* draw/pull out; extract; remove; omit
	抜け道	ぬけみち	byway; secret passage; excuse
	抜け目	ぬけめ	something missing/lacking; incomplete
	抜ける	ぬける	*vi.* come/fall out; be left out/omitted

批 ⑦

一 十 扌 扌 扌 批 批 批

音	批	ヒ	criticize
熟	批准	ヒジュン	ratification (of a treaty); sanction —*v.* ratify (a treaty); sanction
	批判	ヒハン	criticism; comment; critique —*v.* criticize; comment
	批評	ヒヒョウ	criticism; critique; critical essay —*v.* criticize; comment
	批評家	ヒヒョウカ	critic; reviewer
	批評眼	ヒヒョウガン	critical eye
	批難	ヒナン	negative criticism; blame —*vt.* denounce; blame

866

扶 ⑦ ー † ‡ ‡ ‡ 扦 扶

音	扶	フ	help
熟	扶助	フジョ	help; aid; assistance —*v.* help; aid; assist
	扶養	フヨウ	support; maintenance —*v.* support; maintain; keep up
訓	※扶ける	たすける	help; assist; aid
¥	扶養控除	フヨウコウジョ	allowance/tax exemption for dependents
	扶養家族	フヨウカゾク	dependent family member; dependent

867

抑 ⑦ ー † ‡ ‡ 扣 抑 抑

音	抑	ヨク	hold; down; control; suppress
熟	抑圧	ヨクアツ	suppression; restraint —*v.* suppress; restrain
	抑制	ヨクセイ	restraint; control; suppression —*v.* restrain; control; suppress
	抑揚	ヨクヨウ	intonation; modulation
	抑留	ヨクリュウ	detention; internment —*v.* detain; intern
訓	抑える	おさえる	*vt.* hold down; control; suppress
	抑え難い	おさえがたい	irrepressible; uncontrollable
	抑え付ける	おさえつける	*vt.* hold down; curb; control

868

押 ⑧ ー † ‡ 扣 扣 押 押 押

音	押	オウ	press; push
熟	押印	オウイン	sealing —*vi.* seal; affix a seal to
	押韻	オウイン	rhyme; rhyming —*v.* rhyme; make a rhyme
	押収	オウシュウ	seizure; confiscation —*v.* seize; impound; confiscate
	押捺	オウナツ	fingerprinting —*v.* fingerprint
訓	押す	おす	*vt.* push; press
	押さえる	おさえる	*vt.* press down; keep down; suppress; restrain; control
	押し	おし	push; pushing
	押入れ	おしいれ	closet; cupboard
	押し花	おしばな	pressed flowers

394

押し問答	おしモンドウ	repeated questioning and answering; argument —*vi*. bandy words with; wrangle with
¥ 押し上げる	おしあげる	*vt*. push up
押し売り	おしうり	high-pressure selling
押し切る	おしきる	*vt*. push through; have one's own way
押目	おしめ	dip; reaction

869

拐 ⑧　一 十 扌 扌 护 护 拐 拐

| 音 拐 | カイ | kidnap |

870

拡 ⑧　一 十 扌 扌゛扩 扩 拡 拡

音 拡	カク	expand; spread
熟 拡散	カクサン	proliferation; diffusion —*v*. spread; proliferate
拡充	カクジュウ	expansion; amplification —*v*. expand; amplify
拡声器	カクセイキ	loudspeaker
拡大	カクダイ	enlargement; magnification —*v*. magnify; expand
拡張	カクチョウ	extension; expansion; enlargement —*v*. extend; expand; enlarge; increase
訓 拡げる	ひろげる	*vt*. spread; widen; expand
¥ 拡散指数	カクサンシスウ	diffusion index
拡大基調	カクダイキチョウ	expansive keynote
拡大再生産	カクダイ サイセイサン	reproduction on an expanded scale; expanded reproduction

---

871

拒 ⑧　一 十 扌 扎 扣 拒 拒 拒

音 拒	キョ	refuse; reject; decline; turn down
熟 拒絶	キョゼツ	refusal; rejection; denial; repudiation —*v*. refuse; reject; deny
拒否	キョヒ	denial; veto; disapproval —*v*. deny; veto; disapprove
訓 拒む	こばむ	*vt*. refuse; reject; decline; turn down
¥ 拒否権	キョヒケン	veto right

心 忄 小 戈 戸 手 扌 • 支 攵 文 斗 斤 方 日 曰 月 肉 月 木 欠 止 歹 殳 母 毋 比 毛 氏 气 水 氺 氵 火 灬 宀 父 片 牛 犬 犭 王 衤 耂

心忄小戈戸手扌支攵文斗斤方日曰月肉月木欠止歹殳母毋比毛氏气水氷氵火灬爫父片牛犬犭王礻耂

872

拠 ⑧ 一 十 扌 扌 扚 扚 拠 拠

音	拠	キョ	reliable; depend; base
		コ	
熟	拠点	キョテン	position; strong point base; foothold
¥	拠出金	キョシュツキン	contribution
	拠出制 国民年金	キョシュツセイ コクミンネンキン	national annuity through premium payment

873

拘 ⑧ 一 十 扌 扌 扚 扚 拘 拘

音	拘	コウ	arrest; detain; custody
熟	拘束	コウソク	restriction; restraint; constraint —v. restrict; restrain; constrain; bind; be binding
	拘置	コウチ	detention; confinement —v. detain; confine; keep a person in custody
	拘泥	コウデイ	adherence —vi. adhere/stick to
	拘留	コウリュウ	detention; custody; confinement —v. detain; keep a person in custody; lock a person up

874

招 ⑧ 一 十 扌 扗 扗 扷 招 招

音	招	ショウ	invite
熟	招集	ショウシュウ	call/invitation to a group of people —v. call/invite a group of people
	招待	ショウタイ	invitation —v. invite; get an invitation
	招待状	ショウタイジョウ	(letter of) invitation
	招聘	ショウヘイ	invitation/offer (of employment) —v. invite/offer (someone) a job
訓	招く	まねく	vt. call; beckon; invite

875

拙 ⑧ 一 十 扌 扎 扣 抖 拙 拙

| 音 | 拙 | セツ | clumsy; unskilled |

熟	拙者	セッシャ	*hum*. I
	拙宅	セッタク	*hum*. my house
	拙文	セツブン	*hum*. my writings; poor writings

876
拓⑧　一 　十　扌　扌　拓　拓　拓　拓

音	拓	タク	cultivate; print
熟	拓殖	タクショク	colonization; exploitation —*vi*. colonize; exploit; settle
	拓本	タクホン	rubbed copy; rubbing

877
担⑧　一　十　扌　扌　扣　扣　担　担

音	担	タン	shoulder; carry; bear
熟	担架	タンカ	stretcher; lifter
	担当	タントウ	charge; duty; person in charge —*v*. take charge; assume responsibility
	担任	タンニン	charge; duty; homeroom teacher —*v*. take charge; be in charge; be in charge of a homeroom class; be a class teacher
訓	担ぐ	かつぐ	*vt*. carry on one's shoulder; shoulder; bear
	担う	になう	*vt*. carry on one's shoulder; bear; shoulder responsibility
¥	担保	タンポ	collateral; mortgage; security; warranty
	担保権	タンポケン	security interest/right
	担保付社債	タンポつきシャサイ	secured debenture; collateral trust bonds

878
抽⑧　一　十　扌　扌　扣　抽　抽　抽

音	抽	チュウ	extract; abstract
熟	抽出	チュウシュツ	abstraction; extraction —*v*. abstract; extract
	抽象	チュウショウ	abstraction —*v*. abstract
	抽象画	チュウショウガ	abstract painting
	抽象的	チュウショウテキ	abstract; non-objective; metaphysical
	抽選	チュウセン	drawing lots; ballot; lottery; raffle —*vi*. draw lots; ballot

心 忄 小 戈 戸 手 扌 ● 支 攵 文 斗 斤 方 日 曰 月 肉 月 木 欠 止 歹 殳 母 毋 比 毛 氏 气 水 氺 氵 火 灬 爫 父 片 牛 犬 犭 王 礻 耂

4

心 忄 小 戈 戸 手 扌 支 攵 文 斗 斤 方 日 曰 月 肉 月 木 欠 止 歹 殳 母 毋 比 毛 氏 气 水 氺 氵 火 灬 爫 父 片 牛 犬 犭 王 礻 耂

抵 ⑧　一 十 扌 扌 扩 扩 折 抵 抵

音	抵	テイ	resist
熟	抵抗	テイコウ	resistance; opposition; defiance; struggle; drag —*v.* resist; offer resistance; put up a struggle; defy
	抵抗器	テイコウキ	resistor
	抵抗力	テイコウリョク	resistance; resistivity; resistibility
	抵触	テイショク	infringement; contradiction; conflict; collision —*v.* conflict; contradict; be incompatible/inconsistent
¥	抵抗線	テイコウセン	resistence level
	抵当	テイトウ	mortgage
	抵当権	テイトウケン	mortgage; hypothec
	抵当証券	テイトウショウケン	mortgage certificate
	抵当流れ	テイトウながれ	mortgage forfeit; foreclosure

拝 ⑧　一 十 扌 扌 扩 扩 挧 拝 拝

音	拝	ハイ	worship; pray; bow; look; witness; (prefix to make an expression humble)
熟	拝する	ハイする	*vt.* worship —*hon.* receive; see
	拝謁	ハイエツ	*hum.* audience (with a superior) —*v. hum.* be granted an audience
	拝観	ハイカン	*hum.* inspection; visit to a temple, etc. —*v. hum.* see; inspect; look at; view
	拝顔	ハイガン	*hum.* seeing/meeting (someone) —*v. hum.* see/meet (someone)
	拝啓	ハイケイ	(opening phrase in a letter)
	拝見	ハイケン	*hum.* looking; inspection —*v. hum.* have the honor of seeing; see; inspect
	拝察	ハイサツ	*hum.* guess
	拝借	ハイシャク	*hum.* borrowing; loan —*v. hum.* have a loan; borrow
	拝受	ハイジュ	*hum.* acceptance —*v. hum.* receive; accept
	拝聴	ハイチョウ	*hum.* listening; hearing —*v. hum.* listen; hear
	拝殿	ハイデン	front shrine; hall of worship
	拝読	ハイドク	*hum.* reading —*v. hum.* read; note
	拝復	ハイフク	*hum.* in reply to your letter

拝礼	ハイレイ	worship —*v.* worship
訓 拝む	おがむ	*vt.* ***hum.*** look; view; witness; worship; pray; bow; implore
拝み倒す	おがみたおす	*vt.* entreat (a person) into consent; win over by persuasive entreaty

---

881

�拍 ⑧ ＿ 扌 扌 扗 扩 拍 拍 拍

音 拍	ハク	clap one's hands
	（ヒョウ）	beat
熟 拍車	ハクシャ	spur
拍手	ハクシュ	hand clapping; applause —*vi.* clap one's hands; applaud
拍子	ヒョウシ	rhythm; chance; moment; time (in music)
拍子抜け	ヒョウシぬけ	disappointment —*vi.* be disappointed

882

披 ⑧ ＿ 扌 扌 扚 扩 护 抙 披

音 披	ヒ	open
熟 披露	ヒロウ	announcement; introduction; advertisement —*v.* announce; introduce; advertize
披露宴	ヒロウエン	wedding reception/dinner

883

抱 ⑧ ＿ 扌 扌 扌 扚 拘 拘 抱

音 抱	ホウ	embrace; hug; hold in one's arms
熟 抱懐	ホウカイ	cherishing; entertaining/harboring (an idea in one's heart) —*v.* cherish; entertain/harbor (an idea in one's heart)
抱負	ホウフ	ambition; aspiration
抱擁	ホウヨウ	embrace; hug —*vt.* embrace; hug
訓 抱く	だく	*vt.* embrace; hug; hold in one's arms
抱く	いだく	*vt.* embrace; hold; have; harbor (feelings)
抱える	かかえる	*vt.* carry in one's arms; hire; have (children)
お抱え	おかかえ	employing
抱え込む	かかえこむ	*vt.* hold/carry in one's arms; take in; take upon oneself

4

心忄小戈戸手扌支攴文斗斤方日曰月肉月木欠止歹殳母毋比毛氏气水氷氵火灬爪父片牛犬犭王礻耂

抱き合う　だきあう　*vt*. embrace/hold each other; cuddle
抱き込む　だきこむ　*vt*. win (someone) to your side; embrace; enfold
抱き締める　だきしめる　*vt*. embrace closely; cuddle; hug

884
抹 ⑧
一　十　扌　扩　扩　拝　抹　抹

音	抹	マツ	erase; expurge; rub; paint
熟	抹殺	マッサツ	denial; expurgement —*v*. deny; expurge; ignore
	抹消	マッショウ	erasing; crossing out —*v*. erase; cross out
	抹茶	マッチャ	powdered tea

885
括 ⑨
一　十　扌　扩　扩　扦　拝　括　括

音	括	カツ	tie
熟	括弧	カッコ	brackets; parentheses
訓	※括り	くくり	tying; fastening; knot; conclusion
	※括る	くくる	*vt*. tie; fasten; bundle

886
挟 ⑨
一　十　扌　扩　扩　护　挟　挟

音	挟	キョウ	get between; be caught in; be sandwiched; put between; insert; jam
熟	挟撃	キョウゲキ	attack from both sides
訓	挟まる	はさまる	*vi*. get between; be caught in; be sandwiched between
	挟む	はさむ	*vt*. put between; pinch; insert; put in

887
拷 ⑨
一　十　扌　扩　扩　拧　拷　拷

| 音 | 拷 | ゴウ | torture |
| 熟 | 拷問 | ゴウモン | torture; the rack —*v*. torture |

400

888

指 ⑨ 一 十 才 才 扩 指 指 指 指

音	指	シ	finger; point; indicate
熟	指圧	シアツ	*shiatsu* (form of massage) —*v.* give *shiatsu*
	指揮	シキ	command; direction —*v.* command; direct; lead; conduct an orchestra
	指揮者	シキシャ	conductor
	指示	シジ	instructions; indications; directions —*v.* indicate; instruct; direct
	指針	シシン	guide; indicator; pointer; compass needle
	指数	シスウ	*math.* index; exponent
	指定	シテイ	appointment; specification; designation —*v.* appoint; specify; designate; reserve
	指定席	シテイセキ	reserved seat
	指摘	シテキ	indication; pointing out —*v.* indicate; point out
	指導	シドウ	guidance; leadership; coaching —*v.* lead; guide; coach
	指導者	シドウシャ	leader; guide
	指導力	シドウリョク	leadership
	指南	シナン	instruction; teaching —*v.* teach; instruct; coach
	指標	シヒョウ	index
	指名	シメイ	nomination; designation —*v.* nominate; designate
	指紋	シモン	fingerprint
	指令	シレイ	order —*v.* order; instruct; give instructions
訓	指す	さす	*vt.* point to; indicate
	指図	さしず	direction; directions
	指	ゆび	finger; toe
	指折り	ゆびおり	leading; prominent
	指先	ゆびさき	fingertip
	指差す	ゆびさす	*vt.* point
	指輪	ゆびわ	ring

889

持 ⑨ 一 十 才 才 扌 扩 拌 持 持

音	持	ジ	have; hold
熟	持する	ジする	have; hold
	持久	ジキュウ	endurance; perserverance; tenacity —*vi.* endure; perservere

心 忄 小 戈 戸 手 扌 ● 支 攵 文 斗 斤 方 日 曰 月 肉 月 木 欠 止 歹 殳 母 毋 比 毛 氏 气 水 氺 氵 火 灬 爫 父 片 牛 犬 犭 王 礻 耂

心忄小戈戸手扌支攵文斗斤方日曰月肉月木欠止歹殳母毋比毛氏气水氷氵火灬一父片牛犬犭王礻耂

持久戦	ジキュウセン	protracted war
持久力	ジキュウリョク	tenacity; stamina; staying power
持参	ジサン	bringing; taking —*v.* bring; take
持参金	ジサンキン	dowry
持説	ジセツ	one's cherished opinion
持続	ジゾク	continuing; lasting —*v.* continue; last
持続性	ジゾクセイ	durability
持続的	ジゾクテキ	continuous; lasting
持病	ジビョウ	chronic disease
持論	ジロン	pet theory

訓	持つ	もつ	*v.* have; hold; take; carry; own; possess
	持ち	もち	durability; wear
	持ち上げる	もちあげる	*vt.* lift; raise; flatter
	持ち味	もちあじ	characteristic; peculiar flavor
	持ち合わせる	もちあわせる	*vt.* carry with oneself
	持ち家	もちいえ	one's own house
	持ち込む	もちこむ	*vt.* bring in
	持ち主	もちぬし	owner; proprietor
	持ち場	もちば	one's place/position/territory

| ¥ | 持ち株会社 | もちかぶガイシャ | holding company |
| | 持ち分法 | もちブンホウ | equity method |

890
拾 ⑨ 一 十 扌 扌 扮 扮 拾 拾 拾

音	拾	シュウ	pick up
熟	拾得	シュウトク	picking up from the ground; finding something that has been dropped —*v.* find/pick up something that has been dropped
	拾得物	シュウトクブツ	thing found (on the road); found article; find; windfall
訓	拾う	ひろう	*vt.* pick up; gather; find
	拾い読み	ひろいよみ	scanning —*vt.* scan; read here and there

891
挑 ⑨ 一 十 扌 扌 扮 扮 挑 挑 挑

| 音 | 挑 | チョウ | challenge |
| 熟 | 挑戦 | チョウセン | challenge; defiance; offer of combat —*vi.* challenge; defy; offer combat |

	挑発	チョウハツ	provocation; excitement; incitement —*v.* provoke; excite; stir up; arouse
訓	挑む	いどむ	*vi.* challenge; provoke

892
振 ⑩ 一 扌 扌 扩 扩 护 护 振 振 振

音	振	シン	swing
熟	振興	シンコウ	promotion; advancement —*v.* promote; advance
	振動	シンドウ	vibration —*v.* vibrate; swing; oscillate
	振幅	シンプク	amplitude
訓	振る	ふる	*v.* shake; wave; swing; sprinkle; abandon; desert
	振るう	ふるう	*v.* exercise; show off; demonstrate; display; sieve
	振替	ふりかえ	change; transfer
	振り返る	ふりかえる	*vt.* turn round; look back
	振り込む	ふりこむ	*vt.* transfer/pay into another's bank account
	振袖	ふりそで	long-sleeved kimono
	振り向く	ふりむく	*vi.* turn one's face; turn/look around
	振る舞い	ふるまい	behavior; conduct; entertainment; treat

893
捜 ⑩ 一 扌 扌 扌 护 护 押 押 捜 捜

音	捜	ソウ	search; look for
熟	捜査	ソウサ	investigation —*v.* investigate
	捜索	ソウサク	search —*v.* search
	捜索隊	ソウサクタイ	search party
訓	捜す	さがす	*vt.* search; look for

894
挿 ⑩ 一 扌 扌 扩 扩 扩 挿 挿 挿 挿

音	挿	ソウ	insert
熟	挿図	ソウズ	figure; illustration
	挿入	ソウニュウ	insertion —*v.* insert
	挿話	ソウワ	episode; anecdote
訓	挿す	さす	*vt.* insert; put in

895

捕 ⑩　　一　扌　扌　扩　扩　折　折　捐　捕　捕

音	捕	ホ	catch

熟	捕獲	ホカク	capture; seizure —*v.* catch; seize
	捕鯨	ホゲイ	whaling
	捕鯨船	ホゲイセン	whaling ship
	捕手	ホシュ	*bas.* catcher
	捕虫網	ホチュウあみ	insect net
	捕縛	ホバク	arrest; capture —*v.* arrest; capture
	捕虜	ホリョ	captive; prisoner of war

訓	捕まえる	つかまえる	*vt.* catch; capture; arrest; grab hold of; grasp
	捕まる	つかまる	*vi.* be caught/captured/arrested
	捕る	とる	*vt.* catch; capture; seize; grasp
	捕らえる	とらえる	*vt.* catch; capture; seize; grasp
	捕らわれる	とらわれる	*vi.* be caught/captured; be unable to think freely
	捕物	とりもの	capture; arrest

896

掛 ⑪　　一　扌　扌　扩　扩　扩　捞　挂　挂　掛　掛

音	掛	カイ	hang; suspend; multipy

訓	掛かる	かかる	*vi.* hang; set
	掛り	かかり	charge; duty; business; expenses; charges; tax; dependance; scale; bite; hold; relation; attack; anchorage
	掛かり合う	かかりあう	have relations with; be involved in
	掛ける	かける	*vt.* hang; multiply
	掛け算	かけザン	*math.* multiplication
	掛け軸	かけジク	hanging scroll; *kakemono*

¥	掛け値	かけね	overcharge; fancy price; two prices

897

掘 ⑪　　一　扌　扌　扩　护　护　折　押　掘　掘　掘

音	掘	クツ	dig; digging

熟	掘削	クッサク	digging; excavation
訓	掘る	ほる	*vt.* dig
	掘り下げる	ほりさげる	*vt.* dig down; investigate; delve

898

掲 ⑪
一 十 扌 扌 扌 护 护 护 护 掲 掲 掲

音	掲	ケイ	put up; display
熟	掲載	ケイサイ	publishing; carrying/running an article —*v.* publish; carry/run an article
	掲示	ケイジ	notice —*v.* put up; post
	掲示板	ケイジバン	bulletin board
	掲揚	ケイヨウ	hoisting/putting up a flag —*v.* hoist/put up a flag
訓	掲げる	かかげる	*vt.* put up; hoist; display

899

控 ⑪
一 十 扌 扌 扩 扩 控 控 控 控 控

音	控	コウ	note; write down; refrain; moderate; wait; deduct
熟	控訴	コウソ	intermediate appeal —*vi.* bring an intermediate appeal to court
訓	控え	ひかえ	note; memo; duplicate; copy; waiting; reserve
	控える	ひかえる	*vt.* hold back; refrain; desist; be moderate; note; write down; wait
	控え室	ひかえシツ	anteroom; waiting room
	控え目	ひかえめ	moderate; conservative
¥	控除	コウジョ	deduction; subtraction —*v.* deduct; subtract; take away; cut off

900

採 ⑪
一 十 扌 扌 扩 扩 扩 抨 抨 採 採

音	採	サイ	choose; take
熟	採掘	サイクツ	mining; digging —*v.* mine; dig
	採決	サイケツ	vote; parlimentary decision —*v.* vote; take a vote
	採血	サイケツ	*med.* blood sample/collection —*vi.* collect blood; take a blood sample

心忄小戈戸手扌支攵文斗斤方日曰月肉月木欠止歹殳母毋比毛氏气水氺氵火灬爫父片牛犬犭王礻耂

採光	サイコウ	lighting
採鉱	サイコウ	mining —*vi*. work a mine; mine
採取	サイシュ	collecting; extracting; collection; extract —*v*. gather; pick; collect; extract
採集	サイシュウ	collecting; gathering; hunting —*v*. collect; hunt; gather
採択	サイタク	adoption; selection —*v*. adopt; select; choose
採炭	サイタン	coal mining —*vi*. mine coal
採点	サイテン	marking papers; grading assignments —*v*. give marks; grade exams or papers
採否	サイヒ	adoption or rejection; employment and rejection; result; decision
採用	サイヨウ	adoption; employment; usage —*v*. adopt; employ; use; choose

訓 採る　とる　*vt*. adopt; employ; select; choose; prefer

¥ 採算　サイサン　commercial profit

採算買い	サイサンがい	buying on yield basis
採算価格	サイサンカカク	break-even price
採算分岐点	サイサンブンキテン	break-even point
採算割れ	サイサンわれ	below (prime) cost
採用条件	サイヨウジョウケン	employment conditions
採用通知	サイヨウツウチ	notification of employment

901

 捨 ⑪　一　十　扌　扌　扩　护　护　拎　拎　捨　捨

音 捨　シャ　throw away

訓
捨てる	すてる	*vt*. throw away; dump; abandon; desert
捨て金	すてがね	wasted money
捨て子	すてご	abandoned child; foundling
捨て値	すてね	dirt-cheap; giveaway price
捨て身	すてみ	wholeheartedly

902

 授 ⑪　一　十　扌　扌　扩　扩　扩　扩　护　授　授

音 授　ジュ　grant; give; teach

熟
| 授業 | ジュギョウ | lesson; lecture —*vi*. teach/give a lecture |
| 授産所 | ジュサンジョ | work center; labor exchange; place for the unemployed to find work |

授受	ジュジュ	transmission —*vt*. transfer
授賞	ジュショウ	prize-giving —*vi*. give/award a prize
授精	ジュセイ	fertillization; insemination; pollination
授乳	ジュニュウ	nursing (a baby); breast-feeding —*vi*. nurse (a baby); breastfeed
授与	ジュヨ	awarding; conferring —*v*. award; confer
訓 授かる	さずかる	*vi*. be given/granted/taught
授ける	さずける	*vt*. give; grant; teach; instruct

903

推 ⑪   一 亅 扌 扌 扌 扩 扩 扩 拃 拃 推 推

音 推	スイ	propel; recommend
熟 推移	スイイ	transition; change; progress —*vi*. change; undergo a change; shift; progress
推挙	スイキョ	proposal; recommendation —*v*. propose; recommend
推計	スイケイ	estimation —*v*. estimate
推敲	スイコウ	polish; elaboration —*v*. polish; elaborate; file; improve
推考	スイコウ	speculation —*v*. speculate
推察	スイサツ	conjecture; guess; inference; surmise —*v*. guess; conjecture; infer; surmise
推参	スイサン	univited visit —*vi*. barge in, crash a party
推奨	スイショウ	recommendation; commendation —*v*. recommend; commend
推進	スイシン	propulsion; drive —*v*. propel; drive forward; promote; further
推進力	スイシンリョク	thrust; impulse; driving force
推薦	スイセン	recommendation; proposal —*v*. recommend; propose
推測	スイソク	conjecture; surmise; supposition —*v*. conjecture; surmise; suppose
推定	スイテイ	presumption; assumption; inference —*v*. presume; assume; infer
推理	スイリ	reasoning; deduction; detection —*v*. reason; deduct; detect
推理小説	スイリショウセツ	detective story; mystery; thriller
推量	スイリョウ	guess; conjecture —*v*. guess; conjecture
推力	スイリョク	*phy*. thrust; driving force
推論	スイロン	reasoning; inference; induction; deduction —*v*. reason; infer; induce; deduce
訓 推す	おす	*vt*. infer; deduce; conclude; recommend; propose; nominate
推し量る (推し測る)	おしはかる	*vt*. guess; conjecture

407

心忄小戈戸手扌支攵文斗斤方日曰月肉月木欠止歹殳母毋比毛氏气水氺氵火灬爪父片牛犬犭王礻耂

904

据⑪ 一 十 扌 扌 扩 护 护 挧 捄 据 据

音	据	キョ	set; lay; fix; place
訓	据える	すえる	*vt.* set; lay; fix; place
	据え置き	すえおき	leaving something as it is; deferral of a payment
	据え膳	すえゼン	meal set before one
	据え付ける	すえつける	*vt.* install; set; fit; mount
	据わる	すわる	*vi.* sit; take a seat; set; be set

905

接⑪ 一 十 扌 扌 扩 扩 护 护 接 接 接

音	接	セツ	contact; join; near; touch
熟	接する	セッする	*v.* make contact; touch
	接角	セッカク	*math.* adjacent angles
	接近	セッキン	approaching; drawing near —*v.* approach; draw near
	接合	セツゴウ	joining; union —*v.* join; put together; unite
	接骨医	セッコツイ	bone setter; bonesetting —*v.* set bones
	接写	セッシャ	close-up photo —*v.* take close-up pictures
	接種	セッシュ	inoculation; vaccination —*v.* inoculate; vaccinate
	接収	セッシュウ	requisition; take over —*v.* requisite; take over
	接触	セッショク	contact; touch —*v.* make contact; touch
	接戦	セッセン	close combat/contest
	接線	セッセン	*math.* tangent
	接続	セツゾク	connection; joining —*v.* connect; join
	接続詞	セツゾクシ	*gram.* conjunction
	接待	セッタイ	reception; welcome; serving; offering —*v.* give a reception; welcome; serve; offer
	接着	セッチャク	adhesion —*v.* be adhesive; adhere to; stick
	接点	セッテン	point of tangency; contact
	接頭語	セットウゴ	*gram.* prefix
	接尾語	セツビゴ	*gram.* suffix
	接吻	セップン	kiss —*vi.* kiss
訓	接ぐ	つぐ	*vt.* join; piece
	接ぎめ	つぎめ	joint; seam

906

措 ⑪ ー 十 扌 扌 扩 扩 扩 拌 拌 措 措 措

音	措	ソ	put aside; leave as is; desist from; except
熟	措置	ソチ	measure; steps —v. take measures/steps
訓	措く	おく	v. put aside; desist from

907

掃 ⑪ ー 十 扌 扩 扩 扫 扫 扫 捽 掃 掃

音	掃	ソウ	sweep
熟	掃除	ソウジ	sweeping; cleaning —v. sweep; clean
	掃除機	ソウジキ	vacuum cleaner
訓	掃く	はく	vt. sweep

908

探 ⑪ ー 十 扌 扌 扩 扩 押 押 押 探 探

音	探	タン	search; inquire; investigate; explore
熟	探究	タンキュウ	research; investigation; inquiry; study —v. investigate; inquire into; explore; research into
	探求	タンキュウ	quest; search; pursuit —v. search for; pursue
	探検	タンケン	exploration; expedition; —v. explore; make an exploration; go on an expedition
	探索	タンサク	search —v. search/look for
	探知	タンチ	detection —v. detect; spy; trace
	探偵	タンテイ	detective work; espionage; detective; spy
	探訪	タンボウ	inquiry —v. make inquiries into; inquire into
訓	探す	さがす	vt. search/look for; trace; locate
	探る	さぐる	vt. search; look for; explore; spy
	探り	さぐり	spy; probe

909

排 ⑪ ー 十 扌 扌 扫 扫 扫 扫 排 排 排

| 音 | 排 | ハイ | drive away |

心 忄 小 戈 戸 手 扌 支 攵 文 斗 斤 方 日 曰 月 肉 月 木 欠 止 歹 殳 母 毋 比 毛 氏 气 水 氺 氵 火 灬 ⺗ 父 片 牛 犬 犭 王 ⺭ ⺹

心
忄
小
戈
戸
手
扌
● 攴
支
攵
文
斗
斤
方
日
曰
月
肉
月
木
欠
止
歹
殳
母
毋
比
毛
氏
气
水
氺
氵
火
灬
爪
父
片
牛
犬
犭
王
礻
耂

熟	排する	ハイする	*vt.* drive/push/keep away/aside; refuse; arrange; put in order
	排外思想	ハイガイシソウ	chauvinism; xenophobia
	排気	ハイキ	exhaust; exhalation —*vi.* exhaust; exhale
	排気ガス	ハイキガス	exhaust fumes (from a car, etc.)
	排撃	ハイゲキ	rejection; denunciation —*v.* reject; denounce; show strong dissapproval of
	排出	ハイシュツ	discharge; exhaust; excretion —*v.* discharge; exhaust; transpire
	排除	ハイジョ	exclusion; removal; elimination —*v.* exclude; remove; eliminate
	排水	ハイスイ	drainage; draining; displacement —*vi.* drain; pump; bail; displace
	排斥	ハイセキ	expulsion; rejection; exclusion —*v.* keep out; drive out; reject; eject
	排泄	ハイセツ	excretion; discharge; evacuation; dejection —*v.* excrete; purge; evacuate; discharge
	排泄物	ハイセツブツ	*med.* excreta
	排他	ハイタ	exclusion
	排日	ハイニチ	anti-Japanese
	排尿	ハイニョウ	urination —*vi.* urinate
	排卵	ハイラン	*med.* ovulation —*vi.* ovulate
	排列	ハイレツ	arrangement; grouping; configuration —*v.* arrange/group together

910

描 ⑪ 一 扌 扌 扩 扩 描 描 描 描 描 描

音	描	ビョウ	draw
熟	描写	ビョウシャ	description; portrayal; depiction —*v.* describe; portray; depict
訓	描く	えがく	*vt.* draw; paint; sketch; describe; depict; imagine

911

握 ⑫ 一 扌 扌 扩 护 护 护 捉 捉 握 握 握

音	握	アク	hold; grasp; seize; refuse to release
熟	握手	アクシュ	handshake —*vi.* shake hands
	握力	アクリョク	grip; grasping power
訓	握る	にぎる	*vt.* clasp; hold; grasp; grip; clutch; seize
	握り締める	にぎりしめる	*vt.* hold tight in one's hand; clasp; clench
	握り飯	にぎりめし	rice ball

912 援 ⑫

` ー 才 扌 扌 扩 扩 扩 护 抖 招 援 援 `

音	援	エン	aid; help; raise; pull out
熟	援軍	エングン	reinforcements
	援護	エンゴ	support; relief; protection —*v.* back up; support; protect
	援助	エンジョ	help; assistance; aid; support —*v.* help; assist; aid; support
	援用	エンヨウ	quotation —*v.* quote; invoke; claim

913 換 ⑫

` ー 才 扌 扌 扩 扩 护 护 換 換 換 換 `

音	換	カン	change
熟	換気	カンキ	ventilation —*v.* ventilate
	換言	カンゲン	in other words —*v.* say in other words; rephrase
訓	換える	かえる	*vt.* change; exchange
	換わる	かわる	*vi.* relieve; change
¥	換金	カンキン	realization (of securities/property); liquidation (of goods); cash —*v.* realize (one's securities, property); convert (goods) into money
	換金売り	カンキンうり	realization sales
	換算	カンサン	conversion from one unit into another —*v.* convert; change

914 揮 ⑫

` ー 才 扌 扌 扩 护 护 挿 挿 掃 揮 揮 `

音	揮	キ	wield; command
熟	揮発	キハツ	volatilization —*vi.* volatize
	揮発油	キハツユ	gasoline; benzine

915 提 ⑫

` ー 才 扌 扌 扩 护 护 押 捍 捍 提 提 `

音	提	テイ	present

心 忄 小 戈 戸 手 扌 • 支 攵 文 斗 斤 方 日 曰 月 肉 月 木 欠 止 歹 殳 母 毋 比 毛 氏 气 水 氺 氵 火 灬 爪 父 片 牛 犬 犭 王 礻 耂

心
忄
小
戈
戸
手
扌
●
支
攵
文
斗
斤
方
日
曰
月
肉
月
木
欠
止
歹
殳
母
毋
比
毛
氏
气
水
氺
氵
火
灬
爫
父
片
牛
犬
犭
王
礻
⺧

熟	提案	テイアン	proposal; offer; suggestion; overture —**v.** propose; suggest; make a proposal	
	提起	テイキ	institution; lodging —**v.** institute; lodge	
	提議	テイギ	proposal; proposition; suggestion —**v.** propose; make a proposition; suggest; recommend	
	提供	テイキョウ	offer; proffer; tender —**v.** offer; make an offer; produce evidence	
	提携	テイケイ	cooperation; coalition; concert —**v.** cooperate; act in concert	
	提示	テイジ	presentation —**v.** exhibit; present	
	提出	テイシュツ	presentation; introduction; exhibition; production —**v.** present; introduce; submit	
	提唱	テイショウ	advocacy; proposal —**v.** advocate; put forward; advance; lecture	
	提訴	テイソ	indictment —**v.** bring a case to court	
	提督	テイトク	admiral; commodore	
	提要	テイヨウ	summary; compendium	
訓	提げる	さげる	**vt.** carry in one's hand	
¥	提携	テイケイ	affiliation; cooperation; tie-up	
	提携会社	テイケイガイシャ	affiliated company	

916

搭 ⑫　一 十 扌 扩 扩 扩 护 扗 抉 抻 搭 搭

音	搭	トウ	board
熟	搭載	トウサイ	loading; embarkation —**v.** load; embark
	搭乗	トウジョウ	boarding an airplane or ship —**vi.** get on/board an airplane

917

揚 ⑫　一 十 扌 扌 扌 护 护 押 押 揚 揚 揚

音	揚	ヨウ	raise; elevate; praise
熟	揚言	ヨウゲン	profess; declare; assert; speak in a loud voice
	揚水	ヨウスイ	tap water —**v.** pump/draw water
	揚々	ヨウヨウ	in high spirits
	揚陸	ヨウリク	landing; arrival at port
	揚力	ヨウリョク	dynamic lift
訓	揚がる	あがる	**vi.** rise; be fried; fly high
	揚げる	あげる	**v.** raise; fry; fly (a kite)
	揚げ物	あげもの	deep-fried food

918

摇 ⑫ 一 十 扌 扩 扩 扩 护 押 捭 捽 摇 摇

音	揺	ヨウ	shake; sway; vibrate
熟	揺籃期	ヨウランキ	infancy
訓	揺れる	ゆれる	*vi.* shake; sway; vibrate
	揺らぐ	ゆらぐ	*vi.* shake
	揺るぐ	ゆるぐ	*vi.* shake; sway; vibrate
	揺さぶる	ゆさぶる	*vt.* shake; rock
	揺すぶる	ゆすぶる	*vt.* shake; rock
	揺する	ゆする	*vt.* shake

919

携 ⑬ 一 十 扌 扌 扩 扩 扞 揘 揘 摧 携

音	携	ケイ	carry; bring; accompany
熟	携行	ケイコウ	carrying; bringing —*v.* carry; bring
	携帯	ケイタイ	carrying; bringing —*v.* carry; bring
	携帯用	ケイタイヨウ	portable
訓	携える	たずさえる	*vt.* carry; accompany
	携わる	たずさわる	*vi.* participate; be involved in

920

搾 ⑬ 一 十 扌 扌 扩 扩 押 押 押 搾 搾 搾

音	搾	サク	squeeze; press
熟	搾取	サクシュ	exploitation —*v.* exploit
訓	搾る	しぼる	*vt.* squeeze; press; wring; limit; strain

921

摂 ⑬ 一 十 扌 扩 扩 扞 扡 揘 揖 摂 摂 摂

音	摂	セツ	adopt; act in place of; take
熟	摂氏	セッシ	Celsius; centigrade
	摂取	セッシュ	intake, adoption —*v.* ingest; take in
	摂政	セッショウ	regency; regent

413

| 摂生 | セッセイ | care of health —*vi.* take care of someone's health |
| 摂理 | セツリ | providence |

922 損 ⑬

十 扌 扌 扩 护 护 捐 捐 捐 捐 捐 損

音	損	ソン	loss; damage; disadvantage
熟	損壊	ソンカイ	destruction —*v.* destroy
	損害	ソンガイ	damage; loss; injury —*v.* damage; loss; injure
	損耗	ソンコウ	loss —*v.* suffer a loss
	損失	ソンシツ	loss —*v.* lose
	損傷	ソンショウ	damage; injury —*v.* damage; injure
	損得	ソントク	loss and gain; advantages and disadvantages
	損料	ソンリョウ	rental fee
訓	損なう	そこなう	*vt.* harm; spoil; hurt
	損ねる	そこねる	*vt.* injure; hurt; harm
¥	損益	ソンエキ	profit and loss
	損害	ソンガイ	damage; loss
	損害保険会社	ソンガイホケンガイシャ	non-life insurance company
	損失補填	ソンシツホテン	making up for a client's loss

923 搬 ⑬

十 扌 扌 扩 扌 扚 扚 捫 搟 搟 搬 搬

音	搬	ハン	convey
熟	搬出	ハンシュツ	taking; bringing —*v.* take/bring out
	搬入	ハンニュウ	carrying; bringing; sending; taking —*v.* carry in; bring/send/take in

924 摘 ⑭

扌 扌 扩 扩 扩 扩 拍 摘 摘 摘 摘

音	摘	テキ	pick; extract
熟	摘出	テキシュツ	extraction; exposure —*v.* pick/take out; extract; expose
	摘心	テキシン	pruning; plucking —*v.* prune
	摘発	テキハツ	exposure; disclosure —*v.* expose; disclose; unmask

摘要	テキヨウ	summary; synopsis
訓 摘む	つむ	***vt***. pick; pluck
摘み草	つみくさ	gathering young herbs

925

撡 ⑮　扌 扌 扩 护 押 押 押 押 押 揖 撮 撮

音 撮	サツ	photograph
熟 撮影	サツエイ	photography —***v***. photograph; take a picture
撮影所	サツエイジョ	photographic studio
訓 撮る	とる	***vt***. take (a picture/photograph)

926

撤 ⑮　扌 扩 扩 扩 扩 揹 揹 揹 揹 揹 撤 撤

音 撤	テツ	remove
熟 撤回	テッカイ	withdrawal; revocation; recantation; relinquishment —***v***. withdraw; revoke; take away; relinquish
撤去	テッキョ	removal; withdrawal; evacuation —***v***. remove; withdraw; evacuate
撤収	テッシュウ	withdrawal; removal —***v***. withdraw; remove
撤退	テッタイ	evacuation; withdrawal; pull-out; retreat —***vi***. withdraw; evacuate; pull out; retreat
撤廃	テッパイ	abolition; removal —***v***. abolish; remove; do away with; repeal
撤兵	テッペイ	withdrawal of troops; military withdrawal; disengagement —***vi***. withdraw/pull out troops

927

撲 ⑮　扌 扌' 扌" 扌" 扌" 扩 扩 揹 揹 撲 撲

音 撲	ボク	hit; strike
熟 撲殺	ボクサツ	clubbing to death; punching to death —***v***. club to death; punch to death
撲滅	ボクメツ	extermination; eradication —***v***. exterminate; eradicate
訓 撲る	なぐる	***vt***. hit; punch; club
※撲つ	うつ	***vt***. hit; strike

心 忄 小 戈 戸 手 扌 支 攵 文 斗 斤 方 日 曰 月 肉 月 木 欠 止 歹 殳 母 毋 比 毛 氏 气 水 氺 氵 火 灬 灬 父 片 牛 犬 犭 王 礻 耂

928 操 ⑯

一 扌 扌 扌 扌 护 护 揺 揺 揺 揺 操

音	操	ソウ	manipulate; operate
熟	操業	ソウギョウ	operation; work
	操業短縮	ソウギョウ タンシュク	curtailment of operations
	操行	ソウコウ	conduct; department
	操作	ソウサ	operation; handing; control —v. operate; handle; control
	操車	ソウシャ	operation (of trains)
	操縦	ソウジュウ	handling; manipulation; control —v. handle; manipulate; control; operate
	操練	ソウレン	military exercises; drill
訓	操る	あやつる	vt. manipulate; operate
	操	みさお	chastity; virginity; constancy; fidelity; honor

929 擁 ⑯

扌 扩 扩 扩 挕 挕 挕 挕 擁 擁 擁 擁

音	擁	ヨウ	embrace
熟	擁護	ヨウゴ	defense; protection —v. defend; protect
	擁護者	ヨウゴシャ	defender; supporter; advocate
	擁立	ヨウリツ	supporting/backing —v. support/back (one's lord, leader, etc.)

930 擬 ⑰

扌 扩 扗 扗 挼 挼 挼 挼 挼 擬 擬 擬

音	擬	ギ	imitate
熟	擬音	ギオン	imitation sound
	擬人法	ギジンホウ	personification; impersonation
	擬声	ギセイ	onomatopoeia
	擬声語	ギセイゴ	gram. onomatopoeic word
	擬装	ギソウ	camouflage —vt. camouflage; disguise
	擬態	ギタイ	mimesis; simulation
	擬態語	ギタイゴ	gram. mimesis; mimetic word
訓	※擬える	なぞらえる	vt. liken; compare; imitate

心 忄 小 戈 戸 手 扌 支 攵 文 斗 斤 方 日 曰 月 肉 月 木 欠 止 歹 殳 母 毋 比 毛 氏 气 水 氺 氵 火 灬 爫 父 片 牛 犬 犭 王 礻 耂

擦 ⑰

扌 扌゛ 扩 护 护 拗 拗 拗 摖 摖 擦 擦

音	擦	サツ	rub; graze; friction
熟	擦過傷	サッカショウ	*med.* abrasion; graze
訓	擦る	する	*vt.* rub; chafe; strike
	擦れる	すれる	*vi.* rustle; wear out; rub; be chafed; become shrewd

---

4 支 じゅうまた／しにょう／えだにょう branch

支 ④

一 十 ナ 支

音	支	シ	branch; separate; pay; support; prop up
熟	支援	シエン	support —*v.* support; help; back up
	支給	シキュウ	supply —*v.* provide; issue; supply
	支局	シキョク	branch office
	支持	シジ	support; backing —*v.* support; back; stand by
	支社	シシャ	branch office (of a company)
	支障	シショウ	hindrance; trouble
	支度	シタク	preparations; arrangements —*v.* prepare; arrange
	支柱	シチュウ	support; prop; mainstay
	支店	シテン	branch store/office
	支点	シテン	fulcrum
	支配	シハイ	rule; control; direction; management —*v.* rule; control; direct; manage
	支配人	シハイニン	manager (of hotels, restaurants, etc.)
	支払う	シはらう	*vt.* pay; make payments
	支部	シブ	branch/local office; chapter (of an organization)
	支離滅裂	シリメツレツ	inconsistent
	支流	シリュウ	branch (of a river or family); tributary; faction; splinter group
訓	支える	ささえる	*vt.* support; prop up; hold
¥	支出	シシュツ	expenditure; disbursements; expenses —*v.* pay out; spend; expend
	支払承諾	シはらいショウダク	acceptance and guarantee; bank's liabilities in account of guarantees

417

心 忄 小 戈 戸 手 扌 支 攵 文 斗 斤 方 日 曰 月 肉 月 木 欠 止 歹 殳 母 毋 比 毛 氏 气 水 氺 氵 火 灬 爫 父 片 牛 犬 犭 王 礻 耂

支払手形	シはらいてがた	notes payable-trade
支払利息	シはらいリソク	interest and discount expenses
割引料	わりびきリョウ	

---

4 攵 のぶん *no* (katakana); literature

933

改 ⑦ 　フ　コ　己　已　旦　改　改

音	改	カイ	improve; change; reform
熟	改悪	カイアク	change for the worse; deterioration —*v*. get worse; deteriorate
	改革	カイカク	reform; reformation —*v*. reform; reorganize
	改行	カイギョウ	new line/paragraph —*vi*. start a new line/paragraph
	改元	カイゲン	change of an imperial era —*v*. change an imperial era
	改作	カイサク	adaptation; recomposition —*v*. adapt; recompose; remodel
	改札	カイサツ	ticket inspection —*v*. inspect tickets
	改札口	カイサツぐち	ticket gate; wicket
	改宗	カイシュウ	conversion; proselytism —*vi*. be converted; change one's religion
	改修	カイシュウ	repair; improvement —*v*. repair; fix; improve
	改心	カイシン	reform; mending one's ways —*vi*. reform; mend one's ways
	改新	カイシン	renovation; reformation —*v*. renovate; reform
	改正	カイセイ	revision; amendment —*v*. revise; amend
	改選	カイセン	reelection —*v*. reelect
	改善	カイゼン	improvement —*v*. improve; make better
	改装	カイソウ	remodeling; refurbishing; modification —*v*. remodel; refurbish; modify
	改造	カイゾウ	reconstruction; reorganization —*v*. reconstruct; reorganize
	改築	カイチク	rebuilding; reconstruction —*v*. rebuild; reconstruct
	改定	カイテイ	reform; revision —*v*. reform; revise
	改訂	カイテイ	revision of (manuscript, etc.) —*v*. revise
	改名	カイメイ	name change —*vi*. change one's name
	改良	カイリョウ	improvement; reformation —*v*. improve; reform
訓	改まる	あらたまる	*vi*. be renewed
	改める	あらためる	*vt*. renew; improve; change

418

934 攻 ⑦

` 一 T エ ヱ ヹ 攻 攻 `

音	攻	コウ	attack; assault; assail
熟	攻撃	コウゲキ	attack; charge; assault; raid; drive —*v*. attack; assail; assault; charge; storm
	攻守	コウシュ	offense and defense
	攻勢	コウセイ	the offensive; aggression
	攻防	コウボウ	offense and defense
訓	攻める	せめる	*vt*. attack; assault; assail

935 放 ⑧

` 丶 亠 ラ 方 方 於 放 放 `

音	放	ホウ	let go; release; fire (a gun); emit
熟	放歌	ホウカ	loud singing —*vi*. sing loudly
	放火	ホウカ	arson —*vi*. deliberately set on fire
	放火狂	ホウカキョウ	pyromania; pyromaniac
	放火犯	ホウカハン	arson; arsonist
	放課後	ホウカゴ	after school
	放棄	ホウキ	abandonment; renouncement; waiver; forfeit —*v*. abandon; renounce; waive; forfeit
	放言	ホウゲン	unreserved talk; speaking without thinking —*v*. talk without reservations; speak without thinking
	放校	ホウコウ	expulsion from school —*v*. expel from school
	放散	ホウサン	radiation; diffusion; evaporation —*vi*. radiate; diffuse; evaporate
	放射	ホウシャ	radiation; emission; discharge —*v*. radiate; emit; discharge
	放射線	ホウシャセン	radiation
	放射線科	ホウシャセンカ	*med*. radiology
	放射能	ホウシャノウ	radioactivity; radiation
	放出	ホウシュツ	emittance; release; discharge —*v*. emit; release; discharge
	放心	ホウシン	absent-mindedness; uncertain psychological state —*vi*. be absent-minded; have one's mind on other things; relax; feel reassured
	放水	ホウスイ	drainage; pour water on a fire with a hose —*vi*. drain; be drained; put a fire out with a hose
	放送	ホウソウ	broadcasting; broadcast —*v*. broadcast

心 忄 小 戈 戸 手 扌 支 攵 文 斗 斤 方 日 曰 月 肉 月 木 欠 止 歹 殳 母 毋 比 毛 氏 气 水 氺 氵 火 灬 灬 父 片 牛 犬 犭 王 礻 耂

心
忄
小
戈
戸
手
扌
支
攵
文
斗
斤
方
日
曰
月
肉
月
木
欠
止
歹
殳
母
毋
比
毛
氏
气
水
氺
氵
火
灬
爪
父
片
牛
犬
犭
王
礻
耂

放送局	ホウソウキョク	broadcasting station
放題	ホウダイ	(verb suffix) all you can (eat, drink, sing, etc.)
放談	ホウダン	unreserved talk —*vi.* talk without any reservations
放置	ホウチ	leaving something as it is —*v.* leave as is; leave to chance; let alone
放逐	ホウチク	expulsion; banishment; exile —*v.* expel; banish; exile
放電	ホウデン	electric discharge —*vi.* discharge electricity
放蕩	ホウトウ	dissipation; fast living —*vi.* live fast
放尿	ホウニョウ	urination —*vi.* urinate
放任	ホウニン	nonintervention; indifference —*v.* do not intervene; be indifferent
放熱	ホウネツ	radiant heat —*vi.* radiate heat
放熱器	ホウネツキ	radiator
放念	ホウネン	relaxed mind —*vi.* feel at ease; relax; have no worries
放屁	ホウヒ	farting; breaking wind —*vi.* fart; break wind
放物線	ホウブツセン	*math.* parabola
放牧	ホウボク	grazing —*v.* let graze; put out to pasture
放牧地	ホウボクチ	grazing land; pasture
放漫	ホウマン	loose; lax; reckless
放免	ホウメン	release; acquittal —*v.* release; acquit
放流	ホウリュウ	stocking (rivers with fish); draining (a river)
放る	ホウる	*vt.* throw; leave as is
放浪	ホウロウ	wandering; roving —*v.* wander; rove
放浪者	ホウロウシャ	wanderer; vagabond; tramp; vagrant
放ったらかす	ホッたらかす	*vt.* neglect; lay aside; leave undone

訓
放す	はなす	*vt.* set free; release; let go
放つ	はなつ	*vt.* set free; release; fire (a gun); emit; set fire to; chase away
放れる	はなれる	get free; be released/fired (arrow/bullet, etc.)

936

一 十 十 古 古 古 古 故 故

⑨

音 故　コ　intentional; deliberate; willful; knowingly; (prefix) late; deceased

熟
故意	コイ	intentional; deliberate; wilful; knowingly
故郷	コキョウ	one's hometown
故国	ココク	one's homeland/native country

故事	コジ	historical fact; tradition; folklore
故実	コジツ	ancient practices/customs
故障	コショウ	hindrance; obstacle; trouble; breakdown; failure; damage —*v.* break down; fail; be out of order
故人	コジン	the deceased/departed
訓 故	ゆえ	reason; cause; meaning
※故郷	ふるさと	one's hometown; the town where one was born

937

政 ⑨　一　Ｔ　Ｆ　正　正　正　政　政

音 政	セイ	govern
	（ショウ）	government
熟 政界	セイカイ	political world/circles; politics
政教分離	セイキョウブンリ	religion and politics; Church and State
政局	セイキョク	political situation
政経	セイケイ	politics and economics
政見	セイケン	political views
政権	セイケン	political power; government; administration
政綱	セイコウ	political program/platform
政策	セイサク	policy
政治	セイジ	government; politics
政治家	セイジカ	statesman; politician; strategist
政情	セイジョウ	political situation
政争	セイソウ	political conflict
政敵	セイテキ	political enemy/opponent
政党	セイトウ	political party
政府	セイフ	government; administration
政変	セイヘン	political change; change in government; cabinet reshuffle
政務	セイム	State affairs; affairs of State
政略	セイリャク	political tactics/maneuvers
政令	セイレイ	government ordinance
訓 政	まつりごと	administration; government; politics
¥ 政策	セイサク	policy
政策運営	セイサクウンエイ	policy manoeuvre
政策目標	セイサクモクヒョウ	aim; goal; target; focus objective; purpose
政府保証債	セイフホショウサイ	government-guaranteed bond
政府補助金	セイフホジョキン	government subsidy

心忄小戈戸手扌支攵文斗斤方日曰月肉月木欠止歹殳母毌比毛氏气水氺氵火灬爫父片牛犬犭王礻

938

敏 ⑩ ノ ト 七 勾 勾 毎 毎 毎 敏 敏

音	敏	ビン	quick; agile; alert
熟	敏感	ビンカン	sensitivity; sensibility; susceptibility
	敏捷	ビンショウ	agile; nimble; quick; alert
	敏捷性	ビンショウセイ	agility; nimbleness; quickness
	敏速	ビンソク	prompt; quick; brisk
	敏腕	ビンワン	able; capable

939

救 ⑪ 一 十 寸 才 求 求 求 求 求 救 救

音	救	キュウ	assistance; help; aid
熟	救援	キュウエン	relief; rescue; deliverance
	救急	キュウキュウ	first aid
	救護	キュウゴ	relief; aid —*v.* relieve; help; aid
	救済	キュウサイ	relief; help; aid; redemption —*v.* relieve; help; aid; redeem
	救出	キュウシュツ	rescue; saving; relief —*v.* rescue; save; relieve
	救助	キュウジョ	rescue; relief —*v.* rescue; relieve
	救世主	キュウセイシュ	savior; Jesus Christ
	救命	キュウメイ	lifesaving
訓	救う	すくう	*vt.* rescue
¥	救済事業	キュウサイジギョウ	relief work
	救済資金	キュウサイシキン	relief funds

940

教 ⑪ 一 十 土 尹 考 考 考 孝 孝 教

音	教	キョウ	teach; instruction
熟	教育	キョウイク	education —*v.* educate
	教員	キョウイン	teacher; member of the teaching staff
	教化	キョウカ	culture; enlightenment; edification —*v.* culture; enlighten; edificate
	教科	キョウカ	subject; course of study; curriculum
	教科書	キョウカショ	textbook; school book
	教会	キョウカイ	Christian church

教官	キョウカン	teacher; instructor; faculty; teaching staff
教義	キョウギ	doctrine; dogma; tenet; creed
教訓	キョウクン	teachings; lesson; injunction
教材	キョウザイ	teaching materials
教師	キョウシ	schoolteacher; schoolmaster; schoolmistress
教示	キョウジ	instruction; teaching —*v.* instruct; teach
教室	キョウシツ	classroom
教授	キョウジュ	teachings; instruction; professor —*v.* teach; instruct
教習所	キョウシュウジョ	training school/institute
教書	キョウショ	message
教職	キョウショク	teaching profession
教祖	キョウソ	founder of a religion
教徒	キョウト	believer in a religion; convert
教養	キョウヨウ	culture; education
教理	キョウリ	principles; teachings; doctrine (of a religion)
訓 教える	おしえる	*vt.* teach; instruct; inform
教え子	おしえご	one's pupil
教わる	おそわる	*vt.* be taught/informed

941

敗 ⑪ 丨 冂 冂 月 目 貝 貝 貝 貯 財 敗

音 敗	ハイ	be defeated
熟 敗因	ハイイン	cause of defeat
敗軍	ハイグン	defeated army
敗者	ハイシャ	defeated person; the vanquished; loser
敗色	ハイショク	signs of defeat
敗戦	ハイセン	defeat; lost battle/war —*vi.* be defeated; lose the war
敗走	ハイソウ	flight; rout; debacle —*vi.* take to flight; be routed; flee
敗退	ハイタイ	defeat; setback —*vi.* retreat; be defeated
敗北	ハイボク	defeat; loss; setback —*vi.* be defeated/beaten; suffer a setback
訓 敗れる	やぶれる	*vi.* be beaten/defeated; lose

942

敢 ⑫ 一 丁 工 干 王 王 耳 亘 亘 彰 耴 耴 敢

| 音 敢 | カン | dare |

心
忄
小
戈
戸
手
扌
支
攵
文
斗
斤
方
日
曰
月
肉
月
木
欠
止
歹
殳
母
毋
比
毛
氏
气
水
氺
氵
火
灬
爪
父
片
牛
犬
犭
王
礻
耂

	敢行	カンコウ	daring/resolute action —*v.* take decisive action; carry out; execute
熟	敢然	カンゼン	boldly; resolutely; bravely; fearlessly
	敢闘	カントウ	courageous fight —*vi.* fight courageously
訓	*敢えて	あえて	boldly; resolutely; daringly

943

敬 ⑫   一 十 ㄠ ㅛ ㄕ 芍 苟 苟 苟 苟 苟 敬 敬

音	敬	ケイ	respect
熟	敬愛	ケイアイ	love and respect —*v.* love and respect
	敬意	ケイイ	respect; reverence; tribute
	敬遠	ケイエン	at a distance —*v.* keep at a distance
	敬具	ケイグ	Truly yours; Yours respectfully/faithfully (closing phrase of a letter)
	敬虔	ケイケン	piety; reverance
	敬語	ケイゴ	*gram.* honorific expression; term of respect
	敬称	ケイショウ	title of honor; courtesy title
	敬服	ケイフク	admiration; regard —*vi.* admire; have great regard for
	敬礼	ケイレイ	salute; bow —*vi.* salute; bow; greet
	敬老	ケイロウ	respect for the aged —*vi.* respect the aged
訓	敬う	うやまう	*vt.* respect; hold in high esteem; look up to

944

散 ⑫   一 十 ㅛ ㅛ 芏 芏 昔 昔 背 散 散 散

音	散	サン	scatter; spread; messy; powder
熟	散逸	サンイツ	scattered and lost —*vi.* be scattered and lost
	散会	サンカイ	adjournment —*vi.* adjourn; break up
	散開	サンカイ	deployment —*vi.* spread out; deploy
	散在	サンザイ	scattered; spread about —*vi.* be scattered; be spread about
	散財	サンザイ	squandering; waste of money —*vi.* squander; waste money
	散策	サンサク	walk —*vi.* take a walk
	散々	サンザン	severely; utterly; thoroughly
	散水	サンスイ	watering —*vi.* water; spray/sprinkle water
	散水機	サンスイキ	water sprinkler
	散発	サンパツ	scattering; occasional happenings —*v.* scatter; occur sporadically; happen occasionally

散髪	サンパツ	haircut —*vi.* have one's haircut
散布	サンプ	scattering; sprinkling; spraying —*v.* scatter; sprinkle; spray
散文	サンブン	prose
散歩	サンポ	walk; stroll —*vi.* take a walk; have a stroll; stroll
散漫	サンマン	vague; loose; careless
散乱	サンラン	scattered; littered —*vi.* be scattered about; diffuse; be littered

訓 散る	ちる	*vi.* fall; scatter; disperse; spread
散らす	ちらす	*vt.* scatter; shower; distract
散らかす	ちらかす	*vt.* scatter about; leave in disorder
散らかる	ちらかる	*vi.* be scattered; be all over the place; be in a mess

945

数 ⑬　｀　＼　゛　ユ　半　米　米　米　娄　娄　娄　数　数

音 数	スウ	number; count
	（ス）	number; count
熟 数回	スウカイ	several times
数学	スウガク	mathematics
数奇	スウキ	adverse fortune; hapless fate
数日	スウジツ	several days
数値	スウチ	numerical value; result
数量	スウリョウ	quantity; volume
訓 数	かず	number; figure
数々	かずかず	numerous; many; varied
数える	かぞえる	*vt.* count

946

敵 ⑮　｀　亠　广　产　产　产　商　商　商　商ノ　敵ノ　敵

音 敵	テキ	enemy; foe; opponent; adversary; rival; competitor
熟 敵する	テキする	*vi.* turn/fight against; antagonize
敵意	テキイ	enmity; hostility; animosity
敵愾心	テキガイシン	hostility; enmity; animosity
敵視	テキシ	enmity; hostility —*v.* be hostile; regard somone as an enemy
敵情	テキジョウ	enemy movements

心忄小戈戸手扌支攵文斗斤方日曰月肉月木欠止歹殳母毋比毛氏气水氷氵火灬 ⺍父片牛犬犭王礻耂

	敵陣	テキジン	enemy camp
	敵対	テキタイ	hostility; contention; antagonism —*v.* be hostile to; turn against
	敵地	テキチ	enemy country
訓	敵	かたき	enemy; foe; opponent
	敵討ち	かたきうち	revenge; vendetta

947

敷 ⑮

一 厂 厂 三 申 甫 甫 專 尃 敷 敷 敷

音	敷	フ	spread; lay; put down
熟	敷衍	フエン	amplification; extension; development —*v.* amplify; extend; develop
	敷設	フセツ	laying (railway tracks, etc.) building; construction —*v.* lay; build; construct
訓	敷く	しく	*v.* spread; lay; put down
	敷居	しきい	threshold
	敷石	しきいし	paving stone
	敷地	しきチ	site
	敷布	しきフ	sheet
	敷布団	しきブトン	floor mattress
	敷物	しきもの	carpet; rug
¥	敷金	しきキン	deposit

948

整 ⑯

一 丆 日 申 束 敕 敕 敕 整 整 整 整

音	整	セイ	arrange
熟	整形	セイケイ	*med.* orthopedics; orthopedic surgery; plastic/cosmetic surgery —*v.* have plastic surgery
	整形外科	セイケイゲカ	*med.* orthopedic surgery
	整形手術	セイケイシュジュツ	*med.* plastic/cosmetic surgery —*v.* undergo cosmetic surgery
	整合	セイゴウ	adjustment; coordination —*v.* adjust; coordinate
	整骨	セイコツ	*med.* bonesetting; osteopathy
	整数	セイスウ	*math.* integral number
	整然	セイゼン	orderly; regular; systematic
	整地	セイチ	ground leveling; soil preparation —*vi.* prepare the land for construction of a house
	整頓	セイトン	order —*v.* put in order; straighten up
	整備	セイビ	full equipment —*v.* be fully equipped;

		maintain; equip
整理	セイリ	arrangement; adjustment; reorganization —*v.* arrange; adjust; reorganize
整列	セイレツ	array; line up —*vi.* array; stand in a line; line up

訓

整う	ととのう	*vi.* be put in order/arranged/prepared
整える	ととのえる	*vt.* put in order; arrange; prepare

---

4 文　ぶん　literature

949

文 ④ 　、 一 ナ 文

音

文	ブン	writing; composition; sentence; text; style; literature
	モン	character; word; design; *mon* (former unit of currency); *mon* (unit of measurement, approx. 2.4cm)

熟

文案	ブンアン	draft; rough copy
文意	ブンイ	meaning of (a passage/sentence)
文化	ブンカ	culture
文化遺産	ブンカイサン	cultural heritage
文化勲章	ブンカクンショウ	Order of Cultural Merit
文化圏	ブンカケン	cultural sphere
文化交流	ブンカコウリュウ	cultural exchange
文化祭	ブンカサイ	cultural/school festival
文化財	ブンカザイ	cultural assets/properties
文化施設	ブンカシセツ	cultural facilities
文化人	ブンカジン	cultivated person; man of culture
文化人類学	ブンカジンルイガク	cultural anthoropology
文化水準	ブンカスイジュン	cultural level; level/standard of culture
文化生活	ブンカセイカツ	civilized life
文化的	ブンカテキ	cultural
文科	ブンカ	liberal arts
文学	ブンガク	literature
文官	ブンカン	civil servant; public official; civil service
文教	ブンキョウ	education
文具	ブング	stationery
文型	ブンケイ	*gram.* sentence pattern
文芸	ブンゲイ	literature and the arts; liberal arts; literature
文芸映画	ブンゲイエイガ	film based on a literary classic

427

心 忄 小 戈 戸 手 扌 支 攵 文 斗 斤 方 日 曰 月 肉 月 木 欠 止 歹 殳 母 毋 比 毛 氏 气 水 氺 氵 火 灬 ⺹ 父 片 牛 犬 犭 王 礻 ⺶

4

心
忄
小
戈
戸
手
扌
支
攵
● 文
斗
斤
方
日
曰
月
肉
月
木
欠
止
歹
殳
母
毋
比
毛
氏
気
水
氷
氵
火
灬
爪
父
片
牛
犬
犭
王
礻
耂

文芸家	ブンゲイカ	literary man; man of letters
文芸学	ブンゲイガク	study of literature
文芸批評	ブンゲイヒョウ	literary criticism
文献	ブンケン	literature; documents
文庫	ブンコ	library; collection of books; pocket-sized book
文庫本	ブンコボン	pocket-sized book
文語	ブンゴ	written/literary/classic language
文語体	ブンゴタイ	literary style (classical, etc.)
文豪	ブンゴウ	great/distinguished writer
文才	ブンサイ	literary talent; talent for writing
文士	ブンシ	writer; man of letters
文集	ブンシュウ	anthology; collection of works
文書	ブンショ	document; record; archives
文章	ブンショウ	sentence; writing; composition
文人	ブンジン	literary man; man of letters
文節	ブンセツ	*gram.* minimum division in a Japanese sentence
文選	ブンセン	typesetting —*v.* typeset
文体	ブンタイ	(writing) style
文題	ブンダイ	theme; subject (of an essay)
文壇	ブンダン	literary world/circles
文鎮	ブンチン	paperweight
文通	ブンツウ	correspondence —*vi.* write/exchange letters
文頭	ブントウ	beginning of a sentence; opening passage
文筆	ブンピツ	literary pursuits/career; writing
文武	ブンブ	civil and military affairs; the pen and the sword
文武両道	ブンブリョウドウ	literary and military arts
文法	ブンポウ	grammar
文房具	ブンボウグ	stationery; writing materials
文末	ブンマツ	end of a sentence; closing sentence
文脈	ブンミャク	context
文明	ブンメイ	civilization
文明国	ブンメイコク	civilized country/nation
文明社会	ブンメイシャカイ	civilized society
文面	ブンメン	contents of a letter
文楽	ブンラク	Bunraku (puppet show/performance)
分理	ブンリ	literature and science
文例	ブンレイ	model sentence; example sentence
文字	モジ	letter; writing; character
文句	モンク	words; expression; phrase; complaint; objection
文殊	モンジュ	Monju (Buddhist saint of wisdom)
文無し	モンなし	broke; penniless

	文盲	モンモウ	illiteracy
訓	文	ふみ	letter; note
※	文	あや	design; figure of speech; plan; plot
¥	文部省	モンブショウ	Ministry of Education
	文部大臣 (文相)	モンブダイジン (ブンショウ)	minister of education

---

4 斗 とます dots and cross

950

斗 ④ ` ´ ¬ 三 斗

音	斗	ト	*to* (unit of capacity, approx. 18ℓ); ladle; dipper; cluster of stars
熟	斗酒	トシュ	kegs of saké

951

料 ⑩ ` ´ ` ¬ 兰 半 米 米 米 料 料

音	料	リョウ	material; charge; fee
熟	料金	リョウキン	charge; fee; fare
	料簡	リョウケン	idea; forgive
	料亭	リョウテイ	Japanese restaurant
	料理	リョウリ	cooking; cuisine; dish; food —*v.* cook
	料理屋	リョウリや	restaurant

952

斜 ⑪ ノ ハ ᐱ 仝 彡 全 余 余 余 斜 斜

音	斜	シャ	slant
熟	斜視	シャシ	squint; cross-eyed
	斜線	シャセン	oblique/slanted line
	斜塔	シャトウ	leaning tower
	斜辺	シャヘン	*math*. hypotenuse; oblique side
	斜面	シャメン	slope
	斜陽	シャヨウ	setting sun; declining
訓	斜め	ななめ	slant; lean; slope; diagonal

心忄小戈戸手扌支攴文斗斤方日曰月肉月木欠止歹殳母毋比毛氏气水氷氵火灬爪父片牛犬犭王礻耂

429

4

心 忄 小 戈 戸 手 扌 支 攵 文 斗 斤 方 日 曰 月 肉 月 木 欠 歹 殳 母 毋 比 毛 氏 气 水 氺 氵 火 灬 爫 父 片 牛 犬 犭 王 礻 歩

---

4 斤　おのづくり　ax

953

斤 ④　　´ ̄ ℉ 斤

音 斤　　キン　　　*kin* (unit of mass, approx. 600g)

954

斥 ⑤　　´ ̄ ℉ 斤 斥

音 斥　　セキ　　　reject; repel; repulse; scout
熟 斥候　　セッコウ　　scout; patrol; spy
訓 斥ける　　しりぞける　　*vt*. repel; repulse; reject

955

断 ⑪　　丶 丷 ㇗ 半 米 米 幽 幽′ 㽕 断 断

音 断	ダン	decision; judgment; resolution; sever; refuse
熟 断じる	ダンじる	*vt*. decide; judge; resolve
断崖	ダンガイ	precipice; cliff; bluff
断言	ダンゲン	assertion; affirmation; declaration —*vi*. assert; affirm; declare
断固	ダンコ	firm; decisive; resolute
断交	ダンコウ	break in relations; rupture —*vi*. break off relations
断行	ダンコウ	decisive action; resolute enforcement —*v*. carry out; execute; effect; enforce
断食	ダンジキ	fast; fasting —*vi*. fast
断じて	ダンじて	definitely
断水	ダンスイ	suspension of water supply —*vi*. cut off the water supply
断絶	ダンゼツ	extinction; discontinuation; severance; rupture —*v*. become extinct; cease to exist; sever; cut off
断然	ダンゼン	positively; resolutely; absolutely; without hesitation
断層	ダンソウ	geological fault; throw; dislocation; shift; jump
断続	ダンゾク	intermittence —*vi*. be intermittent
断腸	ダンチョウ	heartbreak; broken heart

430

断定	ダンテイ	conclusion; decision —*v.* conclude; decide; come to a conclusion
断念	ダンネン	abandonment; relinquishment; despair —*v.* give up; abandon; forgo; relinquish
断片	ダンペン	piece; fragment; shred; scrap
断片的	ダンペンテキ	fragmentary; scrappy; piecemeal
断末魔	ダンマツマ	hour of death
断面	ダンメン	section; phase; profile
訓 断る	ことわる	*vt.* decline; ask to be excused; apologize; dismiss; prohibit
断つ	たつ	*vt.* sever; cut; chop/break off; abstain; exterminate

956

 新 ⑬　ㅗ ㅛ ㅛ 立 立 辛 亲 亲 亲 新 新 新

音 新	シン	new; novel; (prefix) neo-
熟 新案	シンアン	new device/design/idea
新入り	シンいり	newcomer
新鋭	シンエイ	new and powerful
新開地	シンカイチ	newly developed land
新型	シンガタ	new/latest style; new model
新館	シンカン	new building/wing
新刊	シンカン	new publication/book
新奇	シンキ	novel; latest
新規	シンキ	new; anew
新機軸	シンキジク	innovation; new departure/direction
新旧	シンキュウ	old and new
新居	シンキョ	new house/home
新教	シンキョウ	Protestantism
新劇	シンゲキ	*shingeki* (Western plays put on by Japanese players)
新月	シンゲツ	new moon
新香	シンコ	pickles
新語	シンゴ	new word; newly coined word
新興	シンコウ	newly risen; rising; burgeoning
新興国	シンコウコク	rising nation
新興宗教	シンコウ シュウキョウ	new religion
新興都市	シンコウトシ	new town
新婚	シンコン	newlyweds; newly married
新婚旅行	シンコンリョコウ	honeymoon

431

心 忄 小 戈 戸 手 扌 支 攵 文 斗 斤 方 日 曰 月 肉 月 木 欠 止 歹 殳 母 毋 比 毛 氏 气 水 氷 氵 火 灬 爫 父 片 牛 犬 犭 王 礻 耂

4

心
忄
小
戈
戸
手
扌
支
攵
文
斗
斤
●方
日
曰
月
肉
月
木
欠
止
歹
殳
母
毋
比
毛
氏
气
水
氺
氵
火
灬
爪
爪
父
片
牛
犬
犭
王
礻
耂

新作	シンサク	new work/composition
新参	シンザン	newcomer; new hand
新式	シンシキ	new type/style/method
新春	シンシュン	New Year
新進	シンシン	new face; up-and-coming
新進気鋭	シンシンキエイ	young and spirited
新人	シンジン	new member/figure/face
新人作家	シンジンサッカ	budding writer
新制	シンセイ	new system
新星	シンセイ	nova
新生	シンセイ	new birth; rebirth
新生児	シンセイジ	newborn infant
新設	シンセツ	newly established; new —v. found; establish; set up; organize
新説	シンセツ	new theory/view
新鮮	シンセン	freshness; fresh; new
新装	シンソウ	redecoration; refurbishment —v. redecorate; refurbish
新卒	シンソツ	new graduate
新大陸	シンタイリク	the New World
新築	シンチク	new house; newly built
新茶	シンチャ	first tea of the season
新着	シンチャク	new arrivals; newly imported
新調	シンチョウ	newly made; brand-new —v. make new (clothes, etc.)
新陳代謝	シンチンタイシャ	metabolism
新訂	シンテイ	new revision
新天地	シンテンチ	new world; new field of activity
新任	シンニン	newly appointed —v. appoint a new person
新年	シンネン	new year
新派	シンパ	new school
新品	シンピン	new article; brand-new; new
新婦	シンプ	bride
新風	シンプウ	new life; fresh current
新聞	シンブン	newspaper; the press
新聞記者	シンブンキシャ	newspaper reporter
新聞社	シンブンシャ	newspaper company
新聞発表	シンブンハッピョウ	press release —v. send out a press release
新米	シンマイ	new rice; first rice of the season *fig.* newcomer; beginner
新味	シンミ	novelty; fresh; novel; original
新芽	シンメ	sprout; shoot; bud

	新緑	シンリョク	fresh verdure; new green leaves
	新暦	シンレキ	solar/Western calendar
	新郎	シンロウ	bridegroom; groom
訓	新しい	あたらしい	new; novel; fresh; modern
	新た	あらた	new; renewed
	新手	あらて	new member/player; innovation
	新	にい	(prefix) new-
	新妻	にいづま	newly married woman
¥	新株引受権証書	シンカブヒキウケケンショウショ	warrant
	新興工業経済群	シンコウコウギョウケイザイグン	Newly Industrializing Economies
	新興工業国	シンコウコウギョウコク	newly industrializing countries

---

4 方 ほう／ほうへん direction; side

957

方 ④ `、一方方

音	方	ホウ	direction; side; square
熟	方位	ホウイ	direction; bearing (based on the four points of the compass)
	方円	ホウエン	round and/or square
	方角	ホウガク	direction; bearing
	方眼紙	ホウガンシ	graph paper
	方形	ホウケイ	square; regular quadrilateral
	方言	ホウゲン	dialect
	方向	ホウコウ	direction; destination —*fig*. one's aim
	方策	ホウサク	plan
	方式	ホウシキ	formula; method; system
	方丈	ホウジョウ	1 square *jo* (unit of area, approx. 3㎡) *Bud*. chief priest; chief priest's quarters
	方針	ホウシン	compass needle; course; policy
	方陣	ホウジン	square formation (of soldiers); phalanx; magic square (square of integers arranged so that the sum of each row, column or diagonal is always the same)
	方図	ホウズ	end; limit
	方錐形	ホウスイケイ	*math*. pyramid

心 忄 小 戈 戸 手 扌 支 攵 文 斗 斤 方 日 曰 月 肉 月 木 欠 止 歹 殳 母 毋 比 毛 氏 气 水 氷 氵 火 灬 宀 父 片 牛 犬 犭 王 礻 耂

心忄小戈戸手扌支攵文斗斤・方日曰月肉月木欠止歹殳母毋比毛氏气水氷氵火灬宀父片牛犬犭王礻耂

方寸	ホウスン	1 square *sun* (unit of area, approx. 3㎠); very small area; heart; mind; intention
方程式	ホウテイシキ	*math.* equation
方途	ホウト	way; means; method
方便	ホウベン	expedient; means; instrument
方法	ホウホウ	method; way; means
方法論	ホウホウロン	methodology
方々	ホウボウ	all directions; all over the place; everywhere
方面	ホウメン	general direction; district; standpoint
訓 方	かた	*hon.* person; direction; way; means; (mother's/father's) side of a family
～方	～がた	*hon.* plural suffix to denote people

958

 ⑨ ` ㇗ ㇇ 方 ㇰ 斺 斺 施

音 施	シ	install; do; perform
	セ	give; donate; provide
熟 施行	シコウ（セコウ）	enforcement —*v.* enforce; carry out
施策	シサク	policy; measure
施政	シセイ	administration
施設	シセツ	facilities; institution; establishment
施主	セシュ	donor to temple or priest; chief mourner
施肥	セヒ	fertilization —*vi.* fertilize; manure
訓 施す	ほどこす	*vt.* do; perform; provide; give
施し	ほどこし	almsgiving; charity
Ⓨ 施工	セコウ（シコウ）	construction —*v.* construct; carry out a construction project; put into operation; enforce

959

旅 ⑩ ` ㇗ ㇇ 方 ㇰ ㇰ 斺 斿 旅

音 旅	リョ	travel; trip journey
熟 旅客	リョカク リョキャク	traveler
旅館	リョカン	hotel; inn
旅券	リョケン	passport
旅行	リョコウ	journey; trip; travel —*vi.* make a trip; journey; travel
旅行案内	リョコウアンナイ	travel/tour guide

旅行記	リョコウキ	travel journal
旅愁	リョシュウ	loneliness on a journey
旅情	リョジョウ	one's mood while traveling
旅装	リョソウ	traveling clothes
旅団	リョダン	(military) brigade
旅程	リョテイ	itinerary; distance to be covered
旅費	リョヒ	traveling expenses

訓
旅	たび	travel; trip; journey
旅芸人	たびゲイニン	itinerant performer
旅心	たびごころ	one's mood while traveling
旅先	たびさき	destination
旅路	たびジ	journey
旅立つ	たびだつ	*vi*. start on a journey
旅人	たびびと	traveler; wayfarer; pilgrim

960

旋 ⑪ 　 ' 亠 ᅮ 方 方 方 旍 斿 斿 旋 旋

音 旋 　セン　rotate; revolve

熟
旋回	センカイ	revolution; turning — *vi*. revolve; turn; circle
旋盤	センバン	lathe
旋風	センプウ	whirlwind; tornado
旋律	センリツ	melody

961

族 ⑪ 　 ' 亠 ᅮ 方 方 方 方 斿 斿 族

音 族 　ゾク　family; tribe

962

旗 ⑭ 　 亠 ᅮ 方 方 方 旂 斿 旃 旆 旗 旗

音 旗 　キ　flag

熟 旗手 　キシュ　standard bearer; ensign

訓
旗	はた	flag
旗揚げ	はたあげ	opening — *vi*. start an enterprise/business
旗印	はたじるし	flag mark
旗日	はたび	national holiday

435

心忄小戈戸手扌支攵文斗斤方日曰月肉月木欠止歹殳母毋比毛氏气水氺氵火灬宀父片牛犬犭王礻耂

心忄小戈戸手扌支攵文斗斤方日曰月肉月木欠止歹殳母毋比毛氏气水氷氵火灬爪父片牛犬犭王礻耂

4 日 ひ／ひへん sun

963

日 ④ ｜ 冂 月 日

音	日	ニチ	sun; day; Japan
		ジツ	sun; day

熟	日伊	ニチイ	Italian-Japanese
	日印	ニチイン	Indo-Japanese
	日英	ニチエイ	Anglo-Japanese
	日豪	ニチゴウ	Japanese-Australian
	日時	ニチジ	date and time
	日常	ニチジョウ	usually; daily; everyday
	日常生活	ニチジョウセイカツ	everyday/daily life
	日舞 (日本舞踊)	ニチブ (ニホンブヨウ)	Japanese dancing
	日米	ニチベイ	Japanese-American
	日没	ニチボツ	sunset; sundown
	日夜	ニチヤ	day and night; constantly; around the clock
	日曜日	ニチヨウび	Sunday
	日用品	ニチヨウヒン	daily necessities
	日蓮宗	ニチレンシュウ	Nichiren sect of Buddhism
	日露	ニチロ	Russo-Japanese
	日課	ニッカ	daily work/schedule
	日刊	ニッカン	daily publication
	日韓	ニッカン	Japanese-Korean
	日記	ニッキ	diary; journal
	日給	ニッキュウ	daily wages
	日系	ニッケイ	Japanese (-related)
	日光	ニッコウ	sunlight
	日光浴	ニッコウヨク	sunbathing —*vi.* sunbathe
	日誌	ニッシ	diary; journal
	日射病	ニッシャビョウ	sunstroke
	日照	ニッショウ	sunshine
	日章旗	ニッショウキ	national flag of Japan; the Rising Sun
	日食	ニッショク	solar eclipse
	日進月歩	ニッシンゲッポ	ever-progressing; constantly advancing
	日赤 (日本 赤十字社)	ニッセキ (ニホン セキジュウジシャ)	Red Cross (Society)

日中	ニッチュウ	in the daytime; China and Japan; Sino-Japanese	
日直	ニッチョク	day duty	
日程	ニッテイ	day's program/schedule; agenda for the day	
日当	ニットウ	daily wages/allowance	
日本画	ニホンガ	Japanese painting	
日本語	ニホンゴ	the Japanese language	
日本	ニホン（ニッポン）	Japan	

訓
日	か	day
日	ひ	sun; sunshine; day; date
日帰り	ひがえり	day trip; excursion
日付	ひづけ	date; dating
日の出	ひので	sunrise
日焼け	ひやけ	sunburn; suntan —*vi*. tan
日和	ひより	weather; fine weather; perfect day

¥
日銀（日本銀行）	ニチギン（ニホンギンコウ）	Bank of Japan
日経連（日本経営者団体連盟）	ニッケイレン（ニホンケイエイシャダンタイレンメイ）	Japan Federation of Employer's Association; Nikkeiren

964

旧 ⑤ 　 I 　 II 　 Iⁿ 　 I�A 　 旧

音
旧	キュウ	old; previous; former; classic; old calendar

熟
旧家	キュウカ	old family
旧教	キュウキョウ	Roman Catholicism; Roman Catholic Church
旧交	キュウコウ	old/former relationship
旧式	キュウシキ	old type; old-fashioned; classic
旧姓	キュウセイ	maiden name
旧制度	キュウセイド	old/former system; ancient regime
旧跡	キュウセキ	historic site; place of historic interest
旧石器時代	キュウセッキジダイ	Stone Age; Paleolithic Period
旧知	キュウチ	old friend/acquaintance
旧道	キュウドウ	old road
旧年	キュウネン	the old year; last year
旧約聖書	キュウヤクセイショ	Old Testament
旧友	キュウユウ	old friend
旧暦	キュウレキ	old (lunar) calendar

¥
旧株	キュウカブ	old stock

心忄小戈戸手扌支攵文斗斤方日●日月肉月木欠止歹殳母毋比毛氏气水氺氵火灬宀父片牛犬犭王礻耂

心忄小戈戸手扌支攵文斗斤方 • 日曰月肉月木欠止歹殳母毋比毛氏气水氺氵火灬 爪父片牛犬犭王礻耂

965

旬 ⑥ ノ ク 勹 句 旬 旬

音	旬	ジュン	period of ten days; one-third of a month
熟	旬刊	ジュンカン	published every ten days
	旬日	ジュンジツ	period of ten days

966

早 ⑥ 丨 冂 日 日 旦 早

音	早	ソウ	swift; early; fast
		（サッ）	
熟	早期	ソウキ	early stage/phase
	早急	ソウキュウ	urgently; without delay
	早暁	ソウギョウ	dawn
	早計	ソウケイ	premature; hasty; rash (plan or idea)
	早婚	ソウコン	early marriage —*vi.* marry early
	早産	ソウザン	premature birth
	早熟	ソウジュク	precocious; maturing early
	早春	ソウシュン	early spring
	早々	ソウソウ	quickly; early; immediately
	早退	ソウタイ	leaving early —*vi.* leave earlier than usual
	早朝	ソウチョウ	early morning
	早天	ソウテン	sky at dawn
	早稲	ソウトウ わせ	early ripening rice
	早晩	ソウバン	sooner or later
	※早速	サッソク	immediately; at once
訓	早い	はやい	quick; early; fast
	早合点	はやガテン （はやガッテン）	jumping to a conclusion —*vi.* jump to a conclusion
	早口	はやくち	speaking fast
	早瀬	はやせ	swift current; rapids
	早まる	はやまる	*vi.* be hasty/in a hurry
	早道	はやみち	shortcut
	早見表	はやみヒョウ	chart; table
	早耳	はやみみ	quick-eared; in the know
	早目	はやめ	a little early
	早める	はやめる	*vt.* hasten; accelerate
¥	早耳	はやみみ	tip

438

4

心忄小戈戸手扌支攵文斗斤方日 • 日月肉月木欠止歹殳母毌比毛氏气水氺氵火灬爫父片牛犬犭王礻耂

967

易 ⑧　ノ 口 日 日 戸 号 易 易

音	易	イ	easy; simple
		エキ	trade; divination
熟	易々	イイ	easy; easily
	易者	エキシャ	fortuneteller
訓	易しい	やさしい	easy; simple; soft

968

昆 ⑧　ノ 口 日 日 目 目 昆 昆

音	昆	コン	insect
熟	昆虫	コンチュウ	insect; bug
	昆布	コンブ	kelp

969

昇 ⑧　ノ 口 日 日 尸 尸 尹 昇

音	昇	ショウ	rise; advance
熟	昇華	ショウカ	sublimation —*vi.* sublimate; sublime
	昇格	ショウカク	promotion —*vi.* be promoted
	昇級	ショウキュウ	promotion —*vi.* be promoted
	昇給	ショウキュウ	raise in salary; rise —*vi.* have one's salary raised; get a raise
	昇降	ショウコウ	elevating —*vi.* go up and down; rise and fall
	昇進	ショウシン	promotion —*vi.* be promoted
	昇天	ショウテン	ascension; death —*vi.* die; pass away
訓	昇る	のぼる	*vi.* rise; climb; ascend; go up; advance

970

昔 ⑧　一 十 廾 井 芦 苦 昔 昔

音	昔	セキ	old times
		(シャク)	
熟	昔日	セキジツ	old times; formerly; in the past
訓	昔	むかし	long ago; formerly; in the past

439

971

春⑨ 一 二 三 声 夫 夫 春 春 春

音	春	シュン	spring
熟	春夏秋冬	シュンカシュウトウ	the four seasons; all year around
	春季	シュンキ	springtime; spring
	春期	シュンキ	spring
	春秋	シュンジュウ	spring and fall; year; years; age
	春風	シュンプウ	spring breeze
	春分	シュンブン	vernal/spring equinox
	春眠	シュンミン	sleeping on a spring night
訓	春	はる	spring; springtime of life; prime; puberty
	春先	はるさき	early spring
	春雨	はるさめ	spring rain; sticks of bean jelly
	春巻き	はるまき	spring roll
	春めく	はるめく	*vi*. become spring/springlike
¥	春闘 (春期闘争)	シュントウ (シュンキトウソウ)	the spring labor offensive

972

是⑨ 丨 冂 冂 日 旦 早 早 昻 是

音	是	ゼ	right; approve
熟	是正	ゼセイ	correction —*v*. correct; rectify
	是々非々	ゼゼヒヒ	free and unbiased; free and just
	是認	ゼニン	approval; approbation; admission —*v*. approve of; approbate; warrant; endorse
	是非	ゼヒ	right or wrong; by all means; without fail

973

星⑨ 丨 冂 冂 日 戸 戸 早 星 星

音	星	セイ (ショウ)	star
熟	星雲	セイウン	nebula
	星座	セイザ	constellation

星団	セイダン	star cluster

訓 星 ほし star; spot; mark; asterisk; aim
星占い ほしうらない astrology
星影 ほしかげ starlight
星空 ほしぞら starry sky

974

昼 ⑨ 　一 コ コ 尸 尺 尺 尽 昼 昼 昼

音 昼 チュウ daytime; noon; lunch
熟 昼食 チュウショク lunch; luncheon
昼夜 チュウヤ day and night
昼夜兼行 チュウヤケンコウ around the clock
訓 昼 ひる daytime; noon
昼下がり ひるさがり early afternoon
昼過ぎ ひるすぎ early afternoon
昼寝 ひるね afternoon nap; siesta —*vi.* take an afternoon nap
昼間 ひるま day; daytime
昼飯 ひるめし lunch
昼休み ひるやすみ lunchbreak

975

景 ⑫ 　丶 冂 冂 日 日 旦 早 昇 昊 景 景 景

音 景 ケイ scenery; appearance; looks
熟 景観 ケイカン scenery
景勝 ケイショウ picturesque scenery; scenic beauty
景品 ケイヒン gift; premium
訓 ※景色 けしき scenery; landscape
¥ 景気 ケイキ business conditions

976

暑 ⑫ 　丶 冂 冂 日 旦 早 星 昇 昇 暑 暑 暑

音 暑 ショ hot; summer
熟 暑中 ショチュウ hot season; height of summer
暑中見舞 ショチュウみまい summer greeting card

441

4

心 忄 小 戈 戸 手 扌 支 攵 文 斗 斤 方 日 曰 月 肉 月 木 欠 止 歹 殳 母 毋 比 毛 氏 气 水 氺 氵 火 灬 爫 父 片 牛 犬 犭 王 礻 耂

4

訓 暑い　　あつい　　hot; warm

977
晶 ⑫　　｜　冂　月　日　日　日　日　日　畠　晶　晶　晶

音 晶　　ショウ　　crystal

978
普 ⑫　　丶　ソ　ソ　ソ　並　並　並　普　普　普　普

音 普　　フ　　general; common

熟 普及　　フキュウ　　diffusion; wide use; popularization —v. spread; diffuse; propagate; become widespread; popularize

　　普請　　フシン　　building; construction —v. build; construct
　　普段　　フダン　　usual; ordinary; constant
　　普通　　フツウ　　common; usual; ordinary
　　普遍　　フヘン　　universal; general

¥ 普通銀行　　フツウギンコウ　　ordinary bank
　　普通預金　　フツウヨキン　　ordinary deposit

979
暮 ⑭　　艹　艹　苧　苎　莒　苜　莫　莫　莫　幕　幕　暮

音 暮　　ボ　　get dark; come to an end

熟 暮雨　　ボウ　　evening rain
　　暮景　　ボケイ　　evening scenery
　　暮愁　　ボシュウ　　evening melancholy
　　暮秋　　ボシュウ　　late fall/autumn
　　暮春　　ボシュン　　late spring
　　暮色　　ボショク　　evening twilight
　　暮夜　　ボヤ　　evening; night

訓 暮れ　　くれ　　nightfall; year-end; end of a season
　　暮れる　　くれる　　*vi.* get dark; become night; come to the end of (a day, year)
　　暮らす　　くらす　　*vi.* live; dwell
　　暮らし　　くらし　　(daily) living
　　暮らし向き　　くらしむき　　(financial) circumstances; livelihood

心 忄 小 戈 戸 手 扌 支 攵 文 斗 斤 方 日 曰 月 肉 月 木 欠 止 歹 殳 母 毋 比 毛 氏 气 水 氷 氵 火 灬 爫 父 片 牛 犬 犭 王 礻 爿

442

980

暦 ⑭　一 厂 厂 厅 厉 厉 厤 厤 厤 麻 暦 暦

音	暦	レキ	calendar
熟	暦年	レキネン	calendar year; time
	暦法	レキホウ	calendar making
訓	暦	こよみ	calendar

981

暫 ⑮　一 冖 盲 盲 旦 車 車′ 斬 斬 斬 暫

音	暫	ザン	short time
熟	暫時	ザンジ	short while/time
	暫定的	ザンテイテキ	temporary; provisional; tentative; interim
訓	※暫く	しばらく	short while; a few minutes; for the time being
¥	暫定予算	ザンテイヨサン	provisional budget

982

暴 ⑮　口 日 旦 旦 早 昃 昗 昇 昦 暴 暴 暴 暴

音	暴	ボウ	violence; sudden
		（バク）	expose; reveal
熟	暴露	バクロ	exposure —*v.* expose; be exposed; bring to light
	暴飲	ボウイン	heavy excessive drinking —*vi.* drink to excess
	暴漢	ボウカン	ruffian; goon; thug
	暴挙	ボウキョ	violence; recklessness; riot
	暴君	ボウクン	tyrant; despot
	暴言	ボウゲン	violent/abusive language
	暴行	ボウコウ	violence; rape; assault —*vi.* use violence/force; rape; assault
	暴食	ボウショク	gluttony; gorging oneself —*vi.* be gluttonous; gorge oneself; eat too much
	暴政	ボウセイ	tyranny; oppressive rule
	暴走	ボウソウ	wild; (running) out of control; joyride —*vi.* run wild/out of control; take a car for a joyride
	暴走族	ボウソウゾク	motorbike gang; bikers
	暴徒	ボウト	mob; rioters

443

心 忄 小 戈 戸 手 扌 支 攵 文 斗 斤 方 日 曰 月 肉 月 木 欠 止 歹 殳 母 毋 比 毛 氏 气 水 氺 氵 火 灬 爪 父 片 牛 犬 犭 王 礻 耂

4

心忄小戈戸手扌支攵文斗斤方日曰月肉月木欠止歹殳母毋比毛氏气水氺氵火灬爪父片牛犬犭王礻耂

	暴動	ボウドウ	riot; disturbance; uprising
	暴発	ボウハツ	sudden/spontaneous occurrence; accidental firing of a gun —*vi.* occur suddenly/spontaneously; go off accidentally (pistols, guns, etc.)
	暴風	ボウフウ	wind storm; high winds
	暴風雨	ボウフウウ	rainstorm
	暴風圏	ボウフウケン	storm zone/area
	暴利	ボウリ	profiteering; excessive profits; illegal profit
	暴力	ボウリョク	violence; force
	暴力団	ボウリョクダン	gangster organization
	暴論	ボウロン	irrational/wild argument
訓	暴く	あばく	*vt.* disclose; expose; bring to light; dig up
	暴れる	あばれる	*vi.* act violently; rage; rampage
¥	暴騰	ボウトウ	sudden rise (in prices); sharp rise; skyrocketing; abnormal rise —*vi.* rise suddenly (prices)
	暴落	ボウラク	break; crash; heavy fall

983

曇 ⑯

口　日　目　戸　串　昌　帛　昴　果　曼　曇　曇　曇

音	曇	ドン	cloudy
熟	曇天	ドンテン	cloudy/overcast sky
訓	曇り	くもり	cloudiness; cloudy weather; shadow; cloud; dimness; dullness
	曇る	くもる	*vi.* become cloudy/dim

984

明 ⑧

丨　冂　月　日　明　明　明　明

音	明	ミョウ	light; next; following
		メイ	light
		（ミン）	Ming dynasty
熟	明春	ミョウシュン	next spring
	明星	ミョウジョウ	the morning star; the planet Venus
	明神	ミョウジン	gracious god
	明朝	ミョウチョウ	tomorrow morning
	明日	ミョウニチ	tomorrow; next/following day
	明年	ミョウネン	next year
	明晩	ミョウバン	tomorrow evening

明暗	メイアン	light and dark; shading; happiness and sadness
明快	メイカイ	clear; lucid
明解	メイカイ	clear
明確	メイカク	clear; distinct; well-defined
明記	メイキ	clearly written/stated —*v.* stipulate; specify (in writing)
明君	メイクン	wise ruler
明月	メイゲツ	bright/full moon
明言	メイゲン	declaration; assertation —*v.* declare; assert
明細	メイサイ	details; particulars
明示	メイジ	clear statement/indication —*v.* state/indicate clearly
明治	メイジ	*hist.* Meiji (period/emperor 1868-1912)
明度	メイド	brightness; luminosity
明答	メイトウ	definite answer
明白	メイハク	clear; unmistakable
明敏	メイビン	intelligent; discerning
明朗	メイロウ	cheerful; clear; open

訓
明かす	あかす	*vt.* pass; spend the night; confide; divulge
明らむ	あからむ	*vi.* become light
明かり	あかり	light; clearness
明るい	あかるい	bright; cheerful; knowledgeable
明るむ	あかるむ	*vi.* become light
明らか	あきらか	clear; definite
明く	あく	*vi.* be open; be visible
明くる	あくる	next; following
明ける	あける	*vi.* dawn; (a new year) begin; expire (a term of office) *vt.* open (up)
※明日	あす	tomorrow; next/following day

985

 映 ⑨　｜ Π Ħ 日 日¹ 日¹⁷ 日⁷ 映 映

音 映　エイ　project; reflect

熟
映画	エイガ	motion picture; movie; film
映画館	エイガカン	movie theater; cinema
映画俳優	エイガハイユウ	movie actor
映写	エイシャ	projection —*v.* project an image onto a screen
映像	エイゾウ	reflection; image; video

訓
| 映す | うつす | *vt.* reflect |
| 映る | うつる | *vi.* reflect; match; harmonize |

心忄小戈戸手扌支攵文斗斤方
● 日曰月肉月木欠止歹殳母毋比毛氏气水氺氵火灬宀父片牛犬犭王礻耂

986

昨 ⑨　ノ　�　日　日′　旷　旷　昨　昨

音	昨	サク	yesterday
熟	昨日	サクジツ	yesterday
	昨年	サクネン	last year
	昨晩	サクバン	last night
	昨夜	サクヤ	last night
	昨今	サッコン	these days; lately; recently
訓	※昨日	きのう	yesterday

987

昭 ⑨　丨　冂　日　日　日㇆　明　昭　昭　昭

| 音 | 昭 | ショウ | clear |
| 熟 | 昭和 | ショウワ | Showa (period/emperor 1925-1988) |

988

時 ⑩　丨　冂　日　日　旷　旷　哇　時　時

音	時	ジ	time; hour; opportunity
熟	時間	ジカン	time; hour
	時期	ジキ	time; timing; season
	時機	ジキ	opportunity; chance
	時給	ジキュウ	payment by the hour
	時局	ジキョク	situation; current state of affairs
	時限	ジゲン	closing time; time limit; deadline
	時効	ジコウ	prescription (in the legal sense); statute of limitations
	時候	ジコウ	seasonal weather
	時刻	ジコク	time; the hour; appointed time
	時差	ジサ	time difference
	時事	ジジ	current events
	時々刻々	ジジコクコク	every moment; hour to hour; moment to moment
	時制	ジセイ	*gram.* tense
	時勢	ジセイ	trend of the times; the times

時世	ジセイ	the times; the day; the age
時節	ジセツ	the season; the times; the occasion; the moment; good opportunity
時速	ジソク	speed per hour
時代	ジダイ	the times; era; age; antiquity
時代遅れ	ジダイおくれ	old-fashioned
時代錯誤	ジダイサクゴ	anachronism
時点	ジテン	point in time; instant
時分	ジブン	time; season; opportunity
時報	ジホウ	time signal; current news
訓 時	とき	time; hour; case; opportunity; then; the times; the season
時折	ときおり	sometimes; occasionally
時々	ときどき	sometimes
時めく	ときめく	*vi.* prosper; flourish
時計	とケイ	watch; clock
¥ 時価	ジカ	current price; market value; today's price
時価総額	ジカソウガク	aggregate market value
時価発行	ジカハッコウ	public offering of new shares at market prices; issue at market price
時系列	ジケイレツ	time series
時差出勤	ジサシュッキン	staggered office hours
時差相関	ジサソウカン	timing relationship; leadlag correlation

989

暁 ⑫   ⌒ 冂 月 日 日⁻ 日⁺ 日ᵗ 日ᵗ 時ᵗ 暁 暁 暁

音 暁	ギョウ	dawn; daybreak; understand
熟 暁天	ギョウテン	dawn
訓 暁	あかつき	dawn; daybreak

990

晴 ⑫   ⌒ 冂 月 日 日⁻ 日⁺ 日ᵗ 日ᵗ 晴 晴 晴

音 晴	セイ	clear
熟 晴雨	セイウ	rain or shine; weather
晴耕雨読	セイコウウドク	plowing on fine days and reading on wet days; free life-style
晴天	セイテン	fine weather; blue sky
訓 晴れる	はれる	*vi.* clear; be dispelled

心 忄 小 戈 戸 手 扌 支 攵 文 斗 斤 方 日 曰 月 肉 月 木 欠 止 歹 殳 母 毋 比 毛 氏 气 水 氺 氵 火 灬 爪 父 片 牛 犬 犭 王 礻 耂

447

心
忄
小
戈
戸
手
扌
支
攴
文
斗
斤
方
● 日
日
月
肉
月
木
欠
止
歹
殳
母
毋
比
毛
氏
气
水
氷
氵
火
灬
爪
父
片
牛
犬
犭
王
礻
耂

晴れ	はれ	sunny/fine weather; clear skies
晴れ着	はれぎ	one's best clothes; one's Sunday best
晴れやか	はれやか	radiant; beaming; cheerful
晴らす	はらす	*vt.* clear oneself; avenge oneself; dispel; remove (doubts, etc.)

991

晩 ⑫ ｜ 丨 冂 日 日´ 日゛ 日゛ 昈 昈 晄 晚 晚

音	晩	バン	evening; late
熟	晩夏	バンカ	late summer; latter part of summer
	晩学	バンガク	learning late in life; late education
	晩婚	バンコン	marrying late in life
	晩餐	バンサン	dinner; supper
	晩酌	バンシャク	drinking with one's evening meal —*vi.* have a drink at dinner
	晩秋	バンシュウ	late autumn; latter part of autumn
	晩春	バンシュン	late spring; latter part of spring
	晩冬	バントウ	late winter; latter part of winter
	晩年	バンネン	one's closing years; last part of one's life

992

暗 ⑬ ｜ 丨 日 日´ 旷 旷 旷 晬 晬 晤 暗 暗

音	暗	アン	dark; dull; secret; hidden; learn by heart; foolish
熟	暗雲	アンウン	dark clouds
	暗影	アンエイ	shadow; gloom; penumbra
	暗記	アンキ	memorizing; learning by heart —*v.* memorize; learn by heart
	暗号	アンゴウ	code; cipher; cryptograph; passsword
	暗黒	アンコク	darkness; blackness
	暗殺	アンサツ	assassination —*v.* assassinate
	暗算	アンザン	***math.*** mental arithmetic —*v.* do sums in one's head
	暗示	アンジ	hint; suggestion; reminder —*v.* hint; suggest; remind
	暗唱	アンショウ	recital; recitation —*v.* recite
	暗礁	アンショウ	reef; rock; deadlock
	暗然	アンゼン	tearful; doleful; gloomy
	暗中模索	アンチュウモサク	groping in the dark —*vi.* grope in the dark
	暗幕	アンマク	blackout curtain

暗黙	アンモク	tacit
暗夜	アンヤ	dark night
暗躍	アンヤク	secret maneuvers; furtive activities —*vi.* be active behind the scenes
暗涙	アンルイ	gloomy tears; crying alone
訓 暗い	くらい	dark; black
暗闇	くらやみ	darkness; blackness

993

暗 ⑬   丨 冂 日 日゛ 日゜ 即 即 即 即゛ 即゜ 暇 暇

音 暇	カ	spare time
熟 暇日	カジツ	holiday
訓 暇	ひま	spare time; leisure
暇	いとま	leave-taking; leave of absence; dismissal

994

暖 ⑬   丨 冂 日 日゛ 日゜ 日゛ 日゜ 日゜ 暚 暚 暖 暖

音 暖	ダン	warmth; heat
音 暖気	ダンキ	warmth; warm weather
暖色	ダンショク	warm colors
暖帯	ダンタイ	subtropical zone
暖地	ダンチ	warm region
暖冬	ダントウ	mild winter
暖房	ダンボウ	heating
暖流	ダンリュウ	warm sea current
暖炉	ダンロ	fireplace
訓 暖か	あたたか	warmly; kindly
暖かい	あたたかい	warm; mild; kind; friendly
暖まる	あたたまる	*vi.* warm oneself; get warm
暖める	あたためる	*vt.* warm; heat; heat up

995

曜 ⑱   冂 日 日゜ 日゛ 日゜ 日゛゛ 暚゛ 暚゜ 暚 暚 曜 曜

| 音 曜 | ヨウ | day of the week |
| 熟 曜日 | ヨウび | day of the week |

心 忄 小 戈 戸 手 扌 支 攵 文 斗 斤 方 日 曰 月 肉 月 木 欠 止 歹 殳 母 毋 比 毛 氏 气 水 氺 氵 火 灬 ハ 父 片 牛 犬 犭 王 礻 耂

449

心忄小戈戸手扌支攵文斗斤方日曰月肉月木欠止歹殳母毋比毛氏气水氺氵火灬宀父片牛犬犭王礻歩

996

曲 ⑥　丨 冂 冂 冊 冊 曲

音	曲	キョク	bend; wrong; detail; unusual; song; play
熟	曲芸	キョクゲイ	acrobatics; trick; stunt
	曲折	キョクセツ	winding; meandering; bending —*vi.* wind; meander; bend
	曲線	キョクセン	curved line; curve
	曲目	キョクモク	musical program; one's repertoire; musical number
	曲解	キョッカイ	perversion; distortion —*v.* pervert; distort
訓	曲がる	まがる	*vi.* bend; twist; turn; wind
	曲げる	まげる	*vt.* bend; twist; turn; wind
	※曲者	くせもの	scoundrel; rascal

997

更 ⑦　一 ㄏ 冂 � 百 更 更

音	更	コウ	change; revise; reform; alter
熟	更衣	コウイ	changing one's clothes —*v.* change one's clothes
	更衣室	コウイシツ	dressing/locker/changing room
	更改	コウカイ	rennovation; renewal; change; alteration —*v.* rennovate; renew; change; alter
	更新	コウシン	renewal; replacement; rennovation —*v.* renew; replace; rennovate
	更生	コウセイ	regeneration; rebirth; revival —*v.* be born again; revive; ressurect
	更正	コウセイ	correction; revision; rectification —*v.* correct; revise; rectify
	更訂	コウテイ	revision; ammendment —*v.* revise; ammend; edit
	更迭	コウテツ	change in job; switch of position; reshuffle; shake-up —*v.* change someone's position; make a switch; reshuffle
	更年期	コウネンキ	menopause
訓	更	さら	new; fresh; again; furthermore; moreover; further; more
	更かす	ふかす	*vt.* stay up till late
	更ける	ふける	*vi.* grow late; be late

450

書 ⑩ ⁊ ⁊ ⁊ ⊐ ⊐ 聿 聿 書 書 書 書

音	書	ショ	write; letter; book
熟	書架	ショカ	bookshelf
	書画	ショガ	paintings and calligraphic works
	書簡	ショカン	letter; correspondence; note
	書記	ショキ	clerk; secretary
	書記長	ショキチョウ	secretary-general (of the UN, Japanese Communist Party, etc.)
	書庫	ショコ	library
	書斎	ショサイ	study; private library
	書式	ショシキ	set way of writing or filling out (forms, etc.)
	書写	ショシャ	transcription
	書状	ショジョウ	letter
	書生	ショセイ	student; houseboy
	書籍	ショセキ	book
	書体	ショタイ	style of handwriting/type
	書店	ショテン	bookstore; bookshop; publisher
	書道	ショドウ	calligraphy
	書評	ショヒョウ	book review
	書風	ショフウ	style of calligraphy
	書名	ショメイ	title of a book
	書面	ショメン	letter; writing; document
	書物	ショモツ	book
	書類	ショルイ	documents; papers
訓	書く	かく	*vt.* write; spell; compose
	書き入れる	かきいれる	*vt.* enter; fill out (a form)
	書き置き	かきおき	note left behind; memo; message
	書き初め	かきぞめ	first calligraphy of the New Year (Japanese custom)
	書留	かきとめ	registered mail
¥	書き換え	かきかえ	rewriting; renewal; transfer

曹 ⑪ ⁊ ⁊ ⁊ 帀 帀 曲 曹 曹 曹 曹

音	曹	ソウ	friend; comrade; officer
熟	曹長	ソウチョウ	sergeant major; master sergeant

心 忄 小 戈 戸 手 扌 支 攵 文 斗 方 日 曰 月 肉 月 木 欠 止 歹 殳 母 毋 比 毛 氏 气 水 氺 氵 火 灬 爫 父 片 牛 犬 犭 王 礻 耂

1000

最 ⑫ ⟍ 冂 冂 日 冒 早 昱 昻 昰 昱 最 最

心忄小戈戸手扌支攵文斗斤方日曰月肉月木欠止歹殳母毌比毛氏气水氺氵火灬爫父片牛犬犭王礻艹

音	最	サイ	utmost; the most
熟	最愛	サイアイ	one's dearest/closest
	最悪	サイアク	worst
	最下位	サイカイ	lowest rank; last place; bottom
	最強	サイキョウ	strongest
	最近	サイキン	lately; recently
	最敬礼	サイケイレイ	most respectful bow —*vi.* bow most respectfully
	最古	サイコ	oldest
	最後	サイゴ	last; end; final; in conclusion
	最後通牒	サイゴツウチョウ	ultimatum
	最期	サイゴ	one's death/last moment
	最高	サイコウ	highest; best; maximum
	最高裁判所	サイコウサイバンショ	Supreme Court
	最高潮	サイコウチョウ	climax; peak; the height
	最高峰	サイコウホウ	highest peak; most prominent; greatest authority
	最終	サイシュウ	last; final
	最終駅	サイシュウエキ	terminal station; last station
	最初	サイショ	first; beginning; start; initial
	最小	サイショウ	smallest; minimum
	最少	サイショウ	least; smallest; lowest
	最上	サイジョウ	best; finest; highest
	最新	サイシン	latest; newest; most up to date
	最盛期	サイセイキ	golden age; heyday
	最前	サイゼン	foremost; forefront
	最善	サイゼン	best; ideal
	最多	サイタ	most
	最大	サイダイ	maximum; largest; biggest
	最短	サイタン	shortest
	最中	サイチュウ	in the middle; while
	最長	サイチョウ	longest
	最低	サイテイ	lowest; minimum
	最適	サイテキ	best; most suitable; perfect; optimum
	最年少	サイネンショウ	youngest
	最年長	サイネンチョウ	oldest
	最良	サイリョウ	best; ideal
訓	最も	もっとも	most

※最寄り　　もより　　　　　nearest; nearby

1001

替 ⑫　一　二　声　夫　夫一　夫二　夫夫　夫夫　夫夫　替　替　替

音	替	タイ	be replaced
訓	替える	かえる	*vt.* change; alter; reverse; shift; convert
	替わり	かわり	substitute; change
	替わる	かわる	*vi.* take the place of; relieve; be substituted

4　月　つき／つきへん　moon　　　　**月**（にくづき）⇨p.458

1002

月 ④　丿　几　月　月

音	月	ゲツ	month; moon
		ガツ	month; moon
熟	月刊	ゲッカン	monthly issue
	月光	ゲッコウ	moonlight; moonshine
	月謝	ゲッシャ	monthly tuition/fee
	月食	ゲッショク	lunar eclipse
	月曜日	ゲツヨウび	Monday
	月例	ゲツレイ	monthly
訓	月	つき	moon; month
	月並み	つきなみ	conventional; commonplace; hackneyed
	月日	つきひ	time; days; years
¥	月額	ゲツガク	monthly sum
	月給	ゲッキュウ	salary
	月産	ゲッサン	monthly output
	月収	ゲッシュウ	monthly income
	月賦	ゲップ	monthly payment

1003

有 ⑥　丿　ナ　才　冇　有　有

| 音 | 有 | ユウ | possession |
| | | ウ | existence; being |

453

心忄小戈戸手扌支攵文斗斤方日曰・月・肉月木欠止歹殳母毋比毛氏气水氷氵火灬亠父片牛犬犭王礻耂

4

心忄小戈戸手扌支攵文斗斤方日曰月肉月木欠止歹殳母毋比毛氏气水氷氵火灬爪父片牛犬犭王礻爿

熟	有する	ユウする	*vt*. have; possess; own
	有象無象	ウゾウムゾウ	rabble; riff-raff
	有頂天	ウチョウテン	exaltation; rapture; ecstacy
	有無	ウム	existence; presence; yes or no
	有為	ユウイ	promising; capable; efficient
	有意義	ユウイギ	significant
	有益	ユウエキ	beneficial; profitable; instructive; edifying
	有害	ユウガイ	harmful; noxious; destructive
	有閑	ユウカン	leisure
	有機	ユウキ	organic
	有給	ユウキュウ	salaried
	有形	ユウケイ	concrete; material; visible
	有限	ユウゲン	limited; finite
	有権者	ユウケンシャ	qualified person; electorate
	有効	ユウコウ	validity; efficiency; effectiveness
	有罪	ユウザイ	guilt; criminality
	有志	ユウシ	volunteer; interest; sympathy
	有史以来	ユウシイライ	since the dawn of history
	有識者	ユウシキシャ	intellectual person
	有刺鉄線	ユウシテッセン	barbed wire
	有終	ユウシュウ	perfection; fine conclusion
	有色人種	ユウショクジンシュ	colored race
	有数	ユウスウ	leading; prominent; distinguished
	有線	ユウセン	cable; wire
	有段者	ユウダンシャ	grade holder (of Japanese go, shōgi or martial arts)
	有毒	ユウドク	poisonous; toxic
	有能	ユウノウ	able; capable; efficient
	有望	ユウボウ	promising; good prospects
	有名	ユウメイ	famous; well-known; notorious; proverbial
	有名無実	ユウメイムジツ	nominal; titular
	有用	ユウヨウ	useful; available; serviceable
	有利	ユウリ	profitable; advantageous
	有料	ユウリョウ	charge; toll
	有力	ユウリョク	influential; powerful
訓	有る	ある	*vi*. be; have; exist; occur; be located; consist of
	有り様	ありさま	situation; circumstances; sight; the naked truth
¥	有価証券	ユウカショウケン	negotiable/marketable securities
	有給休暇	ユウキュウキュウカ	paid vacation/holiday
	有形固定資産	ユウケイコテイシサン	tangible/fixed assets

有形財産	ユウケイザイサン	tangible property/assets
有限会社	ユウゲンガイシャ	limited company
有効求人	ユウコウキュウジン	ratio of effective labor demand to effective
倍数	バイスウ	supply

1004

服 ⑧

丿 几 月 月 月 肝 肌 服 服

音	服	フク	clothes; dress; dose; obey; serve; admit to
熟	服する	フクする	*v.* obey; submit; serve; drink; wear; put on
	服役	フクエキ	penal servitude; military service —*vi.* serve a prison sentence; do military service
	服罪	フクザイ	pleading guilty; acceptance of punishment —*vi.* plead guilty; admit one's crime and accept punishment
	服地	フクジ	cloth; fabric; material
	服従	フクジュウ	obedience; submission —*vi.* obey; submit to
	服飾	フクショク	clothing and accessories; attire
	服装	フクソウ	dress; attire
	服毒	フクドク	taking poison —*vi.* take poison
	服務	フクム	service; duties —*vi.* serve; be on duty
	服喪	フクモ	mourning —*vi.* mourn
	服薬	フクヤク	taking medicine —*vi.* take medicine
	服用	フクヨウ	taking (medicine) —*vi.* take (medicine)

1005

朕 ⑩

丿 几 月 月 月 月 肝 肸 朕 朕

| 音 | 朕 | チン | I (used now only by the emperor) |

1006

朗 ⑩

, ﾕ ﾖ ﾖ 自 良 良 朗 朗 朗

音	朗	ロウ	clear; bright; cheerful
熟	朗詠	ロウエイ	recitation —*v.* recite
	朗読	ロウドク	recitation —*v.* read aloud
	朗報	ロウホウ	good news; glad tidings
	朗々	ロウロウ	clear; sonorous
訓	朗らか	ほがらか	clear; bright; cheerful

心 忄 小 戈 戸 手 扌 支 攵 文 斗 斤 方 日 曰 月 肉 月 木 欠 止 歹 殳 母 毋 比 毛 氏 气 水 氺 氵 火 灬 ナ 父 片 牛 犬 犭 王 礻 耂

心忄小戈戸手扌支攵文斗斤方日曰月
●
肉月木欠止歹殳母毋比毛氏气水氺氵火灬爫父片牛犬犭王礻耂

1007 望 ⑪

丶　亠　と　と　切　切　胡　胡　契　望　望

音	望	ボウ	hope; desire; look into the distance; full moon
		モウ	
熟	望遠鏡	ボウエンキョウ	telescope
	望外	ボウガイ	unexpected; not even dreamed of
	望郷	ボウキョウ	nostalgia; homesickness
	望見	ボウケン	watching from afar —*v.* watch from afar
	望楼	ボウロウ	watchtower
訓	望む	のぞむ	*vt.* desire; hope for; look into the distance; look up; long for
	望み通り	のぞみどおり	as desired

1008 期 ⑫

一　十　廿　甘　甘　其　其　其　期　期　期　期

音	期	キ	time; period
		（ゴ）	time; period
熟	期間	キカン	period; time
	期限	キゲン	time limit; term; deadline
	期日	キジツ	fixed date
	期待	キタイ	expectation —*v.* expect; hope
	期末	キマツ	end of a term
¥	期日指定定期	キジツシテイテイキ	maturity-designated time deposit
	期首	キシュ	beginning of a period/term

1009 朝 ⑫

一　十　古　古　古　直　卓　車　朝　朝　朝　朝

音	朝	チョウ	morning; court; dynasty; reign; regime; period; era
熟	朝会	チョウカイ	morning assembly
	朝刊	チョウカン	morning edition/newspaper
	朝食	チョウショク	breakfast
	朝夕	チョウセキ	morning and evening; day and night; always; usually
	朝廷	チョウテイ	imperial court

朝礼	チョウレイ	morning assembly/gathering; morning meetings (at school or a company)

朝	あさ	morning
朝露	あさつゆ	morning dew
朝寝	あさね	getting up late —*vi.* get up late; sleep late into the morning
朝寝坊	あさねボウ	person who sleeps late —*vi.* oversleep
朝晩	あさバン	morning and evening
朝日	あさひ	morning sun
朝風呂	あさブロ	morning bath

---

6 肉 にく meat   月 (p.458)

1010

肉 ⑥   丿 冂 冂 内 肉 肉

音 肉	ニク	flesh; muscles; meat
熟 肉眼	ニクガン	naked eye
肉食	ニクショク	meat diet; meat-eating; flesh-eating —*vi.* eat meat; live on a meat diet
肉親	ニクシン	blood relation; flesh and blood
肉声	ニクセイ	natural/human voice
肉体	ニクタイ	body; flesh
肉団子	ニクダンご	meat dumpling/ball
肉薄	ニクハク	bitter/hand-to-hand fighting —*vi.* press hard; close in
肉筆	ニクヒツ	autograph; one's own handwriting
肉太	ニクぶと	full-faced; bold-faced; thick type
肉片	ニクヘン	piece of meat
肉欲	ニクヨク	lust; animal passions; carnal desire; sexual appetite

1011

 腐 ⑭   丶 广 广 庁 庁 府 府 府 腐 腐 腐 腐 腐

音 腐	フ	rot; decay
熟 腐食	フショク	corrosion —*v.* corrode; erode; eat away
腐心	フシン	great pains/trouble/worry —*vi.* worry; take pains; be intent
腐肉	フニク	tainted meat; carrion; gangrene

心 忄 小 戈 戸 手 扌 支 攵 文 斗 斤 方 日 曰 月 肉 月 木 欠 止 歹 殳 母 毋 比 毛 氏 气 水 氷 氵 火 灬 ⺹ 父 片 牛 犬 犭 王 礻 耂

	腐敗	フハイ	decomposition; corruption —*vi.* decay; rot; perish; decompose; grow corrupt
	腐乱	フラン	decomposition; decay —*vi.* decompose; decay
訓	腐る	くさる	*vi.* rot; decay
	腐らす	くさらす	*vt.* let rot/spoil; corrode
	腐れる	くされる	*vi.* rot; decay
	腐れ縁	くされえん	unfortunate but inescapable relationship; fatal bond

---

4 月　にくづき　meat; body　　　月（つきへん）⇨P.453

1012
肖 ⑦　ノ ⼩ ⺌ ⼩ 片 肖 肖

音	肖	ショウ	resemble
熟	肖像	ショウゾウ	portrait

1013
育 ⑧　ㇾ 一 亠 云 产 产 育 育

音	育	イク	bring up; grow up; breed; train
熟	育英	イクエイ	cultivation of young talent; education and scholarship
	育児	イクジ	child/baby care; infant rearing
	育成	イクセイ	rearing; upbringing —*v.* bring up; rear; raise; foster
訓	育つ	そだつ	*vi.* grow up; be brought up; be bred
	育てる	そだてる	*vt.* bring up; rear; raise; nurture
	育む	はぐくむ	*vt.* bring up; nurse; foster; cultivate

1014
肩 ⑧　一 ㇡ ㇕ 戸 戸 肩 肩 肩

音	肩	ケン	shoulder
熟	肩章	ケンショウ	epaulet
訓	肩	かた	shoulder
	肩書	かたがき	title; honor; degree

458

肩掛け	かたかけ	shawl
肩身	かたみ	face; attitude towards other people
¥ 肩書	かたがき	title
肩代わり	かたがわり	*v.* take over a business; substitute

1015

肯 ⑧ 丶 亠 屮 止 止 肯 肯 肯

| 音 | 肯 | コウ | agree; affirm |
| 熟 | 肯定 | コウテイ | affirmation; affirmative —*v.* affirm; acknowledge |

1016

胃 ⑨ 丶 冂 冖 田 田 胃 胃 胃 胃

音	胃	イ	stomach
熟	胃液	イエキ	*med.* gastric juice
	胃潰瘍	イカイヨウ	*med.* stomach ulcer
	胃癌	イガン	*med.* stomach cancer
	胃散	イサン	stomach powder
	胃腸	イチョウ	*med.* stomach and intestines; gastrointestinal tract; digestive organs
	胃腸科	イチョウカ	gastrointestinal medicine; hospital department for diseases of the gastrointestinal tract
	胃袋	イぶくろ	stomach

1017

背 ⑨ 一 丬 ユ 屮 北 北 背 背 背

音	背	ハイ	back; height; rebel
熟	背泳	ハイエイ	backstroke
	背教	ハイキョウ	renegation; apostasy
	背景	ハイケイ	background; scenery; setting
	背後	ハイゴ	back; rear
	背信	ハイシン	betrayal; infidelity —*v.* betray a person's confidence
	背水の陣	ハイスイのジン	with one's back to the wall
	背徳	ハイトク	immorality; corruption
	背任	ハイニン	breach of trust; malpractice
	背反	ハイハン	rebellion; revolt —*vi.* rebel; revolt

459

4

心 忄 小 戈 戸 手 扌 支 攵 文 斗 斤 方 日 曰 月 肉 月 ● 木 欠 止 歹 殳 母 毋 比 毛 氏 气 水 氺 氵 火 灬 爫 父 片 牛 犬 犭 王 礻 耂

4

心忄小戈戸手扌支攵文斗斤方日曰月肉月木欠止歹殳母毋比毛氏气水氺氵火灬爪父片牛犬犭王礻爿

| 背面 | ハイメン | rear; back |
| 背理 | ハイリ | irrationality; absurdity; preposterous |

訓
背	せ	back; stature; height; ridge
背	せい	stature; height
背負う	せおう	*vt.* carry (a burden) on one's back; shoulder (a burden)
背泳ぎ	せおよぎ	backstroke
背筋	せすじ	line of the backbone; seam of the back
背丈	せたけ	height; stature
背伸び	せのび	straightening one's back —*vi.* straighten one's back
背広	せびろ	gentleman's suit
背骨	せぼね	backbone; spine; spinal column
背く	そむく	*v.* go against; be contrary; disobey; violate; rebel; revolt
背ける	そむける	*vt.* turn one's face away; look away

1018

能 ⑩ ㄥ ㄠ ㄏ 佁 台 台 肖 能 能 能

音
| 能 | ノウ | talent; faculty; ability; Noh drama |

熟
能楽	ノウガク	Noh drama
能動	ノウドウ	activity
能動的	ノウドウテキ	active
能筆	ノウヒツ	good writing/writer
能弁	ノウベン	eloquence; oratory
能面	ノウメン	Noh mask
能率	ノウリツ	efficiency
能力	ノウリョク	ability; capacity; capability

1019

脅 ⑩ マ カ 夯 劧 肋 肋 胁 脅 脅 脅

音
| 脅 | キョウ | threaten; menance |

熟
脅威	キョウイ	menance; threat; danger to
脅喝	キョウカツ	threat; menace; blackmail; intimidation —*vt.* threaten; intimidate; blackmail
脅迫	キョウハク	threat; menance —*v.* intimidate

訓
| 脅かす | おどかす | *vt.* threaten; menance; frighten; scare |
| 脅す | おどす | *vt.* threaten; menance; intimidate |

脅かす　おびやかす　*vt*. threaten; menance; intimidate

1020

膚 ⑮　　丶　ㅏ　�　广　产　卢　庐　庐　庐　庐　膚　膚

音　膚　　フ　　　　skin
訓※膚　　はだ　　　skin

1021

肌 ⑥　　丿　几　月　月　刖　肌

音　肌　　キ　　　　skin
訓　肌　　はだ　　　skin; body; grain; character; nature; surface
　　肌合い　　はだあい　　disposition
　　肌色　　はだいろ　　skin/flesh color
　　肌着　　はだぎ　　underwear
　　肌寒い　　はだざむい　chilly
　　肌身　　はだみ　　body

1022

肝 ⑦　　丿　几　月　月　肝　肝　肝

音　肝　　カン　　　liver; heart
熟　肝心　　カンジン　essential; main; important
　　肝腎　　カンジン　important
　　肝臓　　カンゾウ　*med*. liver
　　肝胆　　カンタン　one's true heart
　　肝銘　　カンメイ　profound impression — *vi*. be etched into
　　　　　　　　　　one's memory
　　肝油　　カンユ　　cod-liver oil
　　肝要　　カンヨウ　vital; important
訓　肝　　きも　　　liver; heart

1023

肢 ⑧　　丿　几　月　月　肝　肤　肢　肢

音　肢　　シ　　　　limbs
熟　肢体　　シタイ　　body and limbs; arms and legs

461

心忄小戈戸手扌支攵文斗斤方日曰月肉月木欠止歹殳母毋比毛氏气水氺氵火灬宀父片牛犬犭王礻耂

心忄小戈戸手扌支攵文斗斤方日曰月肉月木欠止歹殳母毋比毛氏气水氺氵火灬亠父片牛犬犭王礻耂

1024

肥 ⑧

) 刀 月 月 月⁻ 月⁻ 月⁻ 肥

音	肥	ヒ	grow fat/fertile
熟	肥育	ヒイク	fattening —*v.* fatten
	肥大	ヒダイ	fleshiness; corpulence *med.* hypertrophy —*vi.* get fat; become corpulent/fleshy; swell
	肥満	ヒマン	fatness; corpulence; obesity —*vi.* grow corpulent/stout; become fat
	肥沃	ヒヨク	fertility/richness (of soil)
	肥料	ヒリョウ	fertilizer; manure
訓	肥	こえ	manure; night soil
	肥える	こえる	*vi.* grow fat/fertile; gain experience
	肥やし	こやし	manure; fertilizer
	肥やす	こやす	*vt.* fertilize; fatten (livestock); enrich
	肥る	ふとる	*vi.* get fat

1025

肪 ⑧

) 刀 月 月 月' 肝 肪 肪

音	肪	ボウ	(animal) fat

1026

胎 ⑨

) 刀 月 月 肝 肝 胎 胎 胎

音	胎	タイ	womb; embryo; conception
熟	胎教	タイキョウ	prenatal care
	胎児	タイジ	*med.* embryo
	胎動	タイドウ	fetal movement; signs; indications —*vi.* quicken in the womb
	胎内	タイナイ	inside the womb

1027

胆 ⑨

) 刀 月 月 肝 肝 胆 胆 胆

音	胆	タン	gallbladder; liver; spirit; courage; pluck; grit; nerves
熟	胆汁	タンジュウ	*med.* bile; gall

胆石	タンセキ	*med*. gallstone
胆嚢	タンノウ	*med*. gall; gallbladder; cholecyst
訓 胆	きも	liver

1028

肺 ⑨　) 刀 月 月 月' 肝 肝 肺 肺

音 肺	ハイ	lung
熟 肺炎	ハイエン	*med*. pneumonia; inflammation of the lung
肺活量	ハイカツリョウ	*med*. breathing/lung capacity
肺結核	ハイケッカク	*med*. tuberculosis
肺臓	ハイゾウ	*med*. lungs
肺病	ハイビョウ	*med*. lung disease

1029

胞 ⑨　) 刀 月 月 月' 肑 肑 胞 胞

| 音 胞 | ホウ | sac; sheath; placenta; afterbirth |
| 熟 胞子 | ホウシ | spore |

1030

胸 ⑩　) 刀 月 月 月' 肑 肑 胸 胸 胸

音 胸	キョウ	chest; bosom; heart
熟 胸囲	キョウイ	chest measurement; girth of the chest
胸像	キョウゾウ	bust
胸中	キョウチュウ	feelings; thoughts; intent
訓 胸	むね	chest; bosom; heart
胸	むな	(prefix) chest; bosom; heart; feelings
胸騒ぎ	むなさわぎ	uneasiness; vague apprehension; presentiment
胸算用	むなザンヨウ	mental arithmetic; expectation; anticipation
胸元	むなもと	pit of the stomach; bosom; breast

1031

脂 ⑩　) 刀 月 月 月' 肥 肥 脂 脂 脂

| 音 脂 | シ | fat; resin |

心忄小戈戸手扌支攵文斗斤方日曰月肉月
•月木欠止歹殳母毋比毛氏气水氺氵火灬爫父片牛犬犭王礻耂

熟	脂肪	シボウ	fat; grease; lard; blubber
訓	脂	あぶら	fat

¹⁰³²
胴 ⑩) 丿 刀 月 月 月 肋 肌 胴 胴 胴

音	胴	ドウ	trunk
熟	胴着	ドウぎ	vest
	胴体	ドウタイ	trunk; body; torso
	胴欲	ドウヨク	greedy; cruel

¹⁰³³
脈 ⑩) 丿 刀 月 月 肝 肵 肵 胁 脈 脈

音	脈	ミャク	blood vessel; pulse; vein
熟	脈打つ	ミャクうつ	*vi*. pulsate; beat
	脈管	ミャクカン	*med*. blood vessel; duct
	脈動	ミャクドウ	*med*. pulsation —*vi*. pulsate; beat
	脈搏	ミャクハク	*med*. pulse (rate)
	脈拍	ミャクハク	*med*. pulse (rate)
	脈々	ミャクミャク	continuous; unbroken
	脈絡	ミャクラク	logical connection; coherence

¹⁰³⁴
脚 ⑪) 丿 刀 月 月 肝 肚 胠 胠 脚 脚

音	脚	キャク （キャ）	leg; walking; base; position
熟	脚色	キャクショク	dramatization —*v*. dramatize
	脚線美	キャクセンビ	beauty of leg lines; leggy
	脚注	キャクチュウ	footnote
	脚本	キャクホン	play; drama; script; scenario
	脚力	キャクリョク	strength of one's legs
	脚立	キャたつ	stepladder
	脚下	キャッカ	at one's feet
	脚光	キャッコウ	footlights
	※脚気	カッケ	*med*. beriberi
訓	脚	あし	leg; legs

脱 ⑪ ノ 几 月 月 月 月゛ 月゛ 肝 胪 胪 脱

音	脱	ダツ	take off; remove; withdraw; escape
熟	脱する	ダッする	v. withdraw; leave
	脱衣	ダツイ	divestiture; divestment; undressing —vi. undress; take off one's clothes
	脱会	ダッカイ	withdrawal from a group; leaving an organization —vi. withdraw; give up; break away; leave (a group)
	脱却	ダッキャク	break away —v. get rid of; free oneself of; emerge from
	脱臼	ダッキュウ	med. dislocation of a joint —vi. dislocate; put out of joint
	脱穀	ダッコク	threshing; thrashing —vi. thresh; thrash
	脱獄	ダツゴク	prison break; escaping from jail —vi. escape from prison; break jail
	脱字	ダツジ	omission; missing letter
	脱脂綿	ダッシメン	absorbent cotton; cotton wool
	脱臭	ダッシュウ	deodorization —vi. deodorize
	脱出	ダッシュツ	escape; prolapse —vi. escape; extricate; fall down; prolapse
	脱水	ダッスイ	dehydration; desiccation; evaporation —vi. dehydrate; dessicate; dry; evaporate
	脱線	ダッセン	derailment; deviation; digression —v. be derailed; derail; deviate; digress
	脱走	ダッソウ	flight; escape; breakout; desertion —v. flee; escape; abscond; break away
	脱退	ダッタイ	withdrawal; secession —v. withdraw; secede
	脱皮	ダッピ	ecdysis; casting off; self-renewal —v. cast off a skin; shed; emerge
	脱帽	ダツボウ	taking off one's hat (to) —v. take off one's hat (to)
	脱落	ダツラク	omission; being unable to keep up —v. omit; be unable to keep up
訓	脱ぐ	ぬぐ	vt. take off; strip; remove; undress
	脱げる	ぬげる	vi. come off; slip off/down
¥	脱税	ダツゼイ	tax evasion —vi. evade/dodge taxes

脳 ⑪ ノ 几 月 月 月 厂゛ 厈゛ 肵 脳 脳

音	脳	ノウ	brain

心 艹 小 戈 戸 手 扌 支 攵 文 斗 斤 方 日 曰 月 肉 月 木 欠 止 歹 殳 母 毋 比 毛 氏 气 水 氺 氵 火 灬 爪 父 片 牛 犬 犭 王 礻 耂

熟	脳外科	ノウゲカ	*med*. brain surgery
	脳出血	ノウシュッケツ	*med*. cerebral hemorrhage
	脳髄	ノウズイ	brain; brains
	脳天	ノウテン	pate; crown
	脳貧血	ノウヒンケツ	*med*. cerebral anemia
	脳味噌	ノウミソ	brain; brains
	脳裏	ノウリ	one's mind/memory

1037

脹 ⑫ 　) 丿 月 月 月' 刖 肝 胩 胜 胀 胀 脹

音	脹	チョウ	expand
訓	脹れる	ふくれる	*vi*. swell; bulge; expand

1038

腕 ⑫ 　) 丿 月 月 月' 刖' 肵 肵 胶 胶 腕 腕

音	腕	ワン	arm; skill
熟	腕章	ワンショウ	armband
	腕白	ワンパク	naughty; mischievous
	腕力	ワンリョク	physical strength; strength in one's arms
訓	腕	うで	arm; ability; skill
	腕木	うでぎ	roof truss; bracket
	腕利き	うできき	skilled; able
	腕自慢	うでジマン	pride in one's own ability
	腕っ節	うでっぷし	great strength
	腕前	うでまえ	ability; skill
	腕輪	うでわ	bracelet
	※腕	かいな	arm
¥	腕力相場	ワンリョクソウば	forced market

1039

腸 ⑬ 　) 丿 月 月' 刖 刖 胛 胛 胛 腸 腸 腸

音	腸	チョウ	intestines; entrails; gut
熟	腸捻転	チョウネンテン	*med*. volvulus; twist in the intestines
訓	腸	はらわた	bowels; intestines; entrails; gut

1040

腹 ⑬) 刀 月 月 扩 扩 肵 肵 肺 胪 腹 腹

音	腹	フク	belly; stomach; heart; mind
熟	腹案	フクアン	(secret) plan; forethought
	腹式呼吸	フクシキコキュウ	abdominal breathing
	腹心	フクシン	confidant; trusted associate
	腹痛	フクツウ	*med.* stomachache; abdominal pain
	腹部	フクブ	*med.* abdomen; belly
	腹膜	フクマク	*med.* peritoneum
	腹話術	フクワジュツ	ventriloquism
	腹筋	フッキン	*med.* abdominal muscles
訓	腹	はら	belly; stomach; heart; mind
	腹切	はらきり	suicide by disembowlment; hara-kiri
	腹立つ	はらだつ	*vi.* get angry
	腹八分	はらハチブ	moderate eating
	腹巻	はらまき	stomach wrapper

1041

腰 ⑬) 刀 月 扩 扩 肵 肵 睡 睡 腰 腰 腰

音	腰	ヨウ	waist; pelvic region; loins; hips; small of the back
熟	腰部	ヨウブ	waist; hips; loins
訓	腰	こし	waist; loins; hips; small of the back
	腰掛ける	こしかける	sit down (on a chair)
	腰元	こしもと	*clas.* lady's maid

1042

膜 ⑭) 刀 月 扩 扩 扩 肪 肪 膜 膣 膜 膜

音	膜	マク	membrane; film

1043

膨 ⑯ 刀 月 扩 扩 肰 胖 胖 肤 腜 腜 膨

音	膨	ボウ	expand; swell

心
忄
小
戈
戸
手
扌
支
攵
文
斗
斤
方
日
曰
月
肉
月
•
木
欠
止
歹
殳
母
毋
比
毛
氏
气
水
氺
氵
火
灬
灬
父
片
牛
犬
犭
王
礻
耂

熟	膨大	ボウダイ	swelling; large; enormous
	膨張	ボウチョウ	expansion; swelling —*vi.* swell; expand
訓	膨らむ	ふくらむ	*vi.* swell; expand
	膨れる	ふくれる	*vi.* swell; expand; sulk

1044

臓 ⑲ 　月　月　月　月　月　月　月　脏　臓　臓　臓

音	臓	ゾウ	entrails; internal organs
熟	臓器	ゾウキ	*med.* internal organs; viscera
	臓器移植	ゾウキイショク	*med.* organ transplant
	臓腑	ゾウフ	*med.* entrails; viscera
	臓物	ゾウモツ	entrails; giblets

4　木　き／きへん　tree

1045

木 ④ 　一　十　オ　木

音	木	ボク	tree; wood
		モク	tree; wood
熟	木刀	ボクトウ	wooden sword
	木訥	ボクトツ	simple; straightforward; honest
	木魚	モクギョ	wooden temple drum
	木材	モクザイ	wood; lumber
	木質	モクシツ	ligneous
	木製	モクセイ	wooden; made of wood
	木星	モクセイ	the planet Jupiter
	木造	モクゾウ	wooden; made of wood
	木像	モクゾウ	wooden image
	木炭	モクタン	charcoal
	木彫	モクチョウ	wood carving
	木馬	モクバ	wooden/rocking/carousel/vaulting horse
	木版	モクハン	woodblock printing/print
	木片	モクヘン	block/chip/splinter of wood
	木目	モクめ	wood grain
	木曜日	モクヨウび	Thursday
	木琴	モッキン	xylophone

木工	モッコウ	carpenter; woodworker; carpentry; woodworking	
木綿	モメン	cotton (cloth)	

訓
木	き	tree; wood
木屑	きくず	wood shavings/chips
木戸	きど	gate; wicket; entrance; castle gate
木	こ	(prefix) wood; tree
木立	こだち	grove; thicket
木霊	こだま	spirit of a tree; echo

1046

本 ⑤ 一 十 才 木 本

音
本	ホン	book; this; main; origin; (counter for long objects)

熟
本意	ホンイ	one's real intention
本院	ホンイン	main institution; this institution
本営	ホンエイ	(military) headquarters
本懐	ホンカイ	long-cherished desire
本格的	ホンカクテキ	full-scale; genuine; in earnest
本官	ホンカン	one's permanent/principal function; I (used by officials); the present official
本気	ホンキ	serious; in earnest
本義	ホンギ	true meaning; basic principle
本決まり	ホンぎまり	final decision
本給	ホンキュウ	basic/regular salary
本拠	ホンキョ	military headquarters; base
本業	ホンギョウ	one's main occupation
本家	ホンケ	main family; originator
本校	ホンコウ	this school
本国	ホンゴク	one's own country
本腰	ホンごし	earnest effort
本山	ホンザン	head temple; this temple
本紙	ホンシ	this newspaper
本誌	ホンシ	this magazine
本旨	ホンシ	main purpose
本式	ホンシキ	regular; orthodox
本質	ホンシツ	essence
本日	ホンジツ	today
本社	ホンシャ	head office; main shrine; this shrine
本州	ホンシュウ	Honshu

心 忄 小 戈 戸 手 扌 支 攵 文 斗 斤 方 日 曰 月 肉 月 木 ● 欠 止 歹 殳 母 毋 比 毛 氏 气 水 氷 氵 火 灬 ⺌ 宀 父 片 牛 犬 犭 王 礻 耂

469

4

心
忄
小
戈
戸
手
扌
支
攵
文
斗
斤
方
日
曰
月
肉
月
● 木
欠
止
歹
殳
母
毋
比
毛
氏
气
水
氺
氵
火
灬
爫
父
片
牛
犬
犭
王
礻
爻

本性	ホンショウ	true nature/character
本職	ホンショク	one's regular occupation; expert
本心	ホンシン	one's right mind/senses; real intention/motive; conscience
本陣	ホンジン	troop headquarters; daimyo's inn; stronghold
本筋	ホンすじ	plot (of a story)
本姓	ホンセイ	real/original surname
本籍	ホンセキ	one's legal domicile
本線	ホンセン	main (railway) line
本尊	ホンゾン	*Bud*. main image (of worship); idol
本体	ホンタイ	true form
本隊	ホンタイ	main body (of troops)
本題	ホンダイ	main (this) issue/subject/problem
本宅	ホンタク	principal residence
本棚	ホンだな	bookshelf
本調子	ホンチョウシ	proper key (of an instrument); regular form
本邸	ホンテイ	principal residence
本店	ホンテン	head office; main store; this store
本殿	ホンデン	main/inner Shinto shrine
本土	ホンド	mainland
本当	ホントウ	true; real
本島	ホントウ	main island; this island
本堂	ホンドウ	main temple building
本人	ホンニン	the person himself; the said person; the principal figure
本音	ホンね	real intention; underlying motive
本年	ホンネン	this year
本能	ホンノウ	instinct
本場	ホンば	the best place for (a product); the place where something is produced (food, etc.)
本箱	ホンばこ	bookcase
本番	ホンバン	actual performance (not a rehearsal)
本文	ホンブン	main text; body of a letter
本分	ホンブン	duty (as a student, soldier, etc.)
本俸	ホンポウ	basic/regular salary
本末転倒	ホンマツテントウ	getting things backward
本丸	ホンまる	castle proper; donjon; keep
本名	ホンミョウ	one's real name
本務	ホンム	duty (as a student, soldier, etc.)
本命	ホンメイ	probable winner; favorite (to win)
本望	ホンモウ	satisfaction; long cherished desire
本物	ホンもの	real thing; genuine article
本屋	ホンや	bookstore; bookshop

	本来	ホンライ	in essence; naturally; originally; primarily	**4**
	本流	ホンリュウ	mainstream	
	本領	ホンリョウ	characteristic; nature; true ability	
	本塁	ホンルイ	base; stronghold *bas.* homeplate	
	本塁打	ホンルイダ	*bas.* home run	
	本論	ホンロン	main subject/discussion; this subject	
訓	本	もと	the origin; former	
¥	本部	ホンブ	head office; headquarters	

1047

末 ⑤ 一 二 キ オ 末

音	末	マツ	end; powder
		バツ	
熟	末裔	マツエイ	descendant
	末期	マッキ	last/closing years; last stage
	末期	マツゴ	one's last dying moments
	末座	マツザ	lowest-ranking seats
	末日	マツジツ	last day
	末子	マッシ (バッシ)	youngest child
	末世	マッセ	future ages —*Bud.* last days of the world
	末席	マッセキ	lowest-ranking seats
	末代	マツダイ	all ages to come; eternity; the next world; future ages
	末端	マッタン	tip; end; terminal
	末尾	マツビ	end; last; final
	末筆	マッピツ	closing written remarks
	末葉	マツヨウ	close; end of an era
	末流	マツリュウ	descendants; lower reaches of a river
	末路	マツロ	last days; end; end of one's life; old age
訓	末	すえ	end; future; descendant; youngest child; trivialities
	末恐ろしい	すえおそろしい	potential to do something terrible in the future
	末っ子	すえっこ	youngest child

1048

未 ⑤ 一 二 キ オ 未

音	未	ミ	not yet; (prefix) un-
熟	未開	ミカイ	uncivilized; barbarous; undeveloped

心 忄 小 戈 戸 手 扌 支 攵 文 斗 斤 方 日 曰 月 肉 月 ● 木 欠 止 歹 殳 母 毋 比 毛 氏 气 水 氺 氵 火 灬 灬 爪 父 片 牛 犬 犭 王 礻 耂

	未開拓	ミカイタク	undeveloped
	未開発	ミカイハツ	undeveloped
	未解決	ミカイケツ	unsolved; unsettled
	未刊	ミカン	unpublished
	未完	ミカン	incomplete; unfinished
	未完成	ミカンセイ	incomplete; unfinished
	未決	ミケツ	undecided; pending; unsettled
	未見	ミケン	unacquainted; unknown
	未婚	ミコン	single; unmarried
	未済	ミサイ	unpaid; unsettled; outstanding
	未熟	ミジュク	unripe; inexperienced; premature; immature
	未遂	ミスイ	attempt
	未成年	ミセイネン	underage; minority; minor
	未然	ミゼン	before it happens; beforehand
	未曽有	ミゾウユウ	unprecedented
	未知	ミチ	unknown; strange
	未知数	ミチスウ	unknown quantity
	未着	ミチャク	not yet arrived
	未定	ミテイ	undecided; pending
	未到	ミトウ	untrodden; unexplored
	未踏	ミトウ	untrodden; unexplored; as yet unachieved (record, etc.)
	未納	ミノウ	nonpayment; default; arrears
	未亡人	ミボウジン	widow
	未満	ミマン	less than; below
	未明	ミメイ	early dawn before sunrise
	未聞	ミモン	unheard of; unknown
	未来	ミライ	future *gram.* future tense
	未了	ミリョウ	unfinished
	未練	ミレン	regret; lingering affection
訓	＊未だ	まだ	still; not yet
	＊未だ	いまだ	still; as yet; to this day; ever
	＊未	ひつじ	the sheep (eighth sign of the Chinese zodiac)
¥	未完成工事	ミカンセイコウジ	long-term construction in progress
	未決	ミケツ	pending
	未実現損益	ミジツゲンソンエキ	unrealized profit and loss
	未収収益	ミシュウシュウエキ	accrued revenue (income)
	未収入金	ミシュウニュウキン	uncollected balance
	未払い金	みばらいキン	account payable
	未払い費用	みばらいヒヨウ	accrued expenses

4

1049
朱 ⑥   ノ �ー 二 牛 牛 朱

音	朱	シュ	vermilion
熟	朱肉	シュニク	vermilion inkpad
	朱筆	シュヒツ	correcting a manuscript

1050
条 ⑦   ノ ク タ 冬 夅 条 条

音	条	ジョウ	branch; reason
熟	条件	ジョウケン	condition; prerequisite; terms; requirement
	条項	ジョウコウ	article; clause; provision
	条文	ジョウブン	provision; the text; notes
	条約国	ジョウヤクコク	treaty power/nation
	条理	ジョウリ	reason
	条例	ジョウレイ	ordinance; rules; regulation
訓	※条	えだ	branch
¥	条約	ジョウヤク	convention; pact; treaty

1051
束 ⑦   一 ㄷ 一 曰 申 束 束

音	束	ソク	bundle; sheaf; ream
熟	束縛	ソクバク	restraint; constraint; shackles
	束髪	ソクハツ	bun hairdo
訓	束	たば	bundle; bunch; sheaf
	束ねる	たばねる	*vt*. bundle; govern; manage; control
	束	つか	handbreadth; span; brief time; thickness
	束ねる	つかねる	*vt*. tie in bundles; fold (one's arms)

1052
果 ⑧   丶 冂 冂 曰 旦 甲 畀 果

音	果	カ	fruit; effect; complete
熟	果敢	カカン	daring; boldness

心 忄 小 戈 戸 手 扌 支 攵 文 斗 斤 方 日 曰 月 肉 月 木 ● 欠 止 歹 殳 母 毋 比 毛 氏 气 水 氺 氵 火 灬 爫 父 片 牛 犬 犭 王 礻 耂

473

心忄小戈戸手扌支攵文斗斤方日曰月肉月木欠止歹殳母毋比毛氏气水氺氵火灬牛父片牛犬犭王礻耂

果実	カジツ	fruit
果樹	カジュ	fruit tree
果汁	カジュウ	fruit juice
果然	カゼン	as expected; sure enough
果報	カホウ	good fortune; luck; reward

訓

果たして	はたして	as expected; sure enough
果たす	はたす	*vt*. carry out; accomplish; finish; complete; effect
果て	はて	limits; end; outcome
果てる	はてる	*vi*. terminate; end; die
※果物	くだもの	fruit

1053

東 ⑧　一 　二 　三 　三 　亘 　車 　東 　東

音

東	トウ	east

熟

東亜	トウア	eastern Asia
東欧	トウオウ	Eastern Europe
東海道	トウカイドウ	Tokaido (route between Kyoto and Tokyo)
東京	トウキョウ	Tokyo
東宮	トウグウ	crown prince
東経	トウケイ	east longitude
東国	トウゴク	eastern country; Kanto provinces
東奔西走	トウホンセイソウ	on the move —*vi*. be on the move; move around busily
東洋	トウヨウ	Orient

訓

東	ひがし	east
※東	あずま	east

1054

栄 ⑨　丶 　丷 　丷 　丷 　ヴ 　学 　栄 　栄

音

栄	エイ	prosper; thrive; glory

熟

栄華	エイガ	prosperity; glory; splendor; luxury
栄冠	エイカン	honor; the crown
栄枯	エイコ	prosperity and decline; rise and fall
栄光	エイコウ	glory; honor
栄転	エイテン	promotion; transference —*vi*. be promoted; be transferred to another post
栄誉	エイヨ	honor; glory

474

栄養	エイヨウ	nutrition
栄養価	エイヨウカ	nutritive value

訓

栄える	さかえる	*vi*. prosper; be prosperous; flourish
栄え	はえ	glory
栄える	はえる	*vi*. shine; be brilliant

1055

架 ⑨ 　 つ カ か 加 加 加 架 架 架

音

架	カ	frame; lay

熟

架橋	カキョウ	bridge construction —*vi*. build bridges
架空	カクウ	aerial; overhead; imaginary; fanciful
架設	カセツ	erection; installation —*v*. erect; put up; install
架線	カセン	wiring; aerial line

訓

架かる	かかる	*vi*. be built/constructed/laid
架ける	かける	*vt*. construct; build; lay; install; span

1056

査 ⑨ 　 一 十 オ 木 木 杏 杏 査 査

音

査	サ	investigation; inquiry

熟

査察	ササツ	inspection —*v*. inspect
査察官	ササツカン	inspector
査証	サショウ	visa —*v*. grant a visa
査定	サテイ	assessment —*v*. assess; make an assessment
査問	サモン	inquiry —*v*. inquire

訓 ＊査べる　しらべる　*vt*. investigate; inspect; inquire

¥

査定価格	サテイカカク	assessed price
査定額	サテイガク	assessed value
査定機関	サテイキカン	assessing agency

1057

柔 ⑨ 　 フ マ 歹 予 矛 柔 柔 柔 柔

音

柔	ジュウ	soft; gentle; soften
	ニュウ	tender; weak

熟

柔順	ジュウジュン	gentleness; obedience; submission
柔道	ジュウドウ	judo

475

心 忄 小 戈 戸 手 扌 支 攵 文 斗 斤 方 日 曰 月 肉 月 木 欠 止 歹 殳 母 毋 比 毛 氏 气 水 氺 氵 火 灬 爫 父 片 牛 犬 犭 王 礻 耂

	柔軟	ジュウナン	soft; supple; flexible; pliant; pliable
	柔弱	ニュウジャク	weakness
	柔和	ニュウワ	gentle; mild; tender; sweet
訓	柔らかい	やわらかい	soft; gentle; mild; tender
	柔らげる	やわらげる	*vt*. soften; moderate; ease; lessen; relieve; appease; pacify

---

1058

染 ⑨   丶 冫 氵 汄 汍 洂 染 染 染

音	染	セン	dye; color
熟	染色	センショク	dyeing; staining —*v*. dye; stain
	染料	センリョウ	dyestuff
訓	染み	しみ	stain; blot; smudge
	染みる	しみる	*vi*. be influenced/infected; hurt
	染まる	そまる	*vi*. be dyed/imbued with
	染める	そめる	*vt*. dye; color

1059

某 ⑨   一 十 廿 甘 甘 甘 莒 苴 某 某

音	某	ボウ	certain; one
熟	某氏	ボウシ	somebody; certain person
	某所	ボウショ	somewhere; certain place
	某地	ボウチ	certain place
訓	※某	それがし	certain person; I
	※某	なにがし	certain person/amount/place/thing

1060

案 ⑩   丶 宀 宀 亇 安 安 安 案 案 案

音	案	アン	desk; investigate; idea; plan; proposal; draft
熟	案じる	アンじる	*vt*. worry over; be anxious; be concerned; devise; consider
	案	アン	plan; draft; idea
	案外	アンガイ	contrary to expectations; unexpectedly; unforeseen
	案内	アンナイ	guidance; conduct; lead; information —*v*. guide; conduct; lead; notify; inform

| | 案内状 | アンナイジョウ | letter of invitation; advice note |
| ¥ | 案件 | アンケン | matter; item on the agenda |

1061

栽 ⑩　　一　十　丰　丰　丰　丰　未　栽　栽　栽

音	栽	サイ	plant; grow; cultivate
熟	栽培	サイバイ	cultivation; culture —v. cultivate; grow; raise
訓	※栽える	うえる	vt. plant; grow

1062

桑 ⑩　　フ　ヌ　ヌ　圣　叒　叒　叒　桑　桑　桑

音	桑	ソウ	mulberry
熟	桑田	ソウデン	mulberry field
訓	桑	くわ	mulberry

1063

森 ⑫　　一　十　オ　木　木　杢　杏　杏　杏　森　森　森

音	森	シン	forest
熟	森閑	シンカン	stillness; quiet; silence
	森林	シンリン	forest
訓	森	もり	wood; forest

1064

楽 ⑬　　′　′　ſ　白　白　白　泊　泊　泊　泊　楽　楽

音	楽	ガク	music
		ラク	pleasure; ease; comfort; relief
熟	楽聖	ガクセイ	celebrated musician
	楽隊	ガクタイ	band; orchestra
	楽団	ガクダン	band; orchestra
	楽壇	ガクダン	musical circles
	楽典	ガクテン	rules of musical composition
	楽譜	ガクフ	musical notation/score; sheet music

心忄小戈戸手扌支攵文斗斤方日曰月肉月木●欠止歹殳母毋比毛氏气水氺氵火灬宀父片牛犬犭王礻耂

心忄小戈戸手扌支攴文斗斤方日曰月肉月木欠止歹殳母毋比毛氏气水氺氵火灬爪爻父片牛犬犭王礻耂

	楽屋	ガクや	dressing room; backstage; behind the scenes; secret
	楽器	ガッキ	musical instrument
	楽園	ラクエン	paradise
	楽勝	ラクショウ	easy victory —*vi.* win an easy victory
	楽天	ラクテン	optimism
	楽天家	ラクテンカ	optimist
	楽天的	ラクテンテキ	optimistic; cheerful
	楽々	ラクラク	comfortably; with great ease
	楽観	ラッカン	optimism —*v.* be optimistic; look on the bright side
	楽観的	ラッカンテキ	optimistic; hopeful
訓	楽しい	たのしい	fun; enjoyable; pleasant
	楽しむ	たのしむ	*vt.* enjoy
	楽しみ	たのしみ	pleasure; enjoyment; delight; happiness

1065
棄 ⑬ 　、　一　亡　亡　亠　产　产　产　峹　峹　車　棄

音	棄	キ	abandon; cast away
熟	棄却	キキャク	dismissal; abandon; rejection —*v.* dismiss; abandon; reject
	棄権	キケン	abstention from voting —*v.* abstain from voting
訓	※棄てる	すてる	*vt.* abandon; reject

1066
業 ⑬ 　、　〃　〃〃　〃〃〃　〟　芣　芣　芣　芣　芈　業

音	業	ギョウ ゴウ	work; duty; enterprise; achievement; karma
訓	業	わざ	work; deed; act
¥	業界	ギョウカイ	business world; industry; trade
	業況	ギョウキョウ	business activity/conditions
	業況調査	ギョウキョウ チョウサ	business research/survey
	業者	ギョウシャ	traders; makers
	業種	ギョウシュ	type of business/industry; industrial branch/sector
	業種別分類	ギョウシュベツ ブンルイ	classification by industry; industry-by-industry breakdown
	業績	ギョウセキ	business results; achievements

業績報告	ギョウセキ ホウコク	business report
業態	ギョウタイ	business conditions
業務	ギョウム	business; service
業務管理	ギョウムカンリ	business management

1067

札 ⑤ 一 十 才 木 札

音	札	サツ	card; ticket; bill; bank note
訓	札	ふだ	card; ticket
	札所	ふだショ	*Bud*. temple from which amulets may be obtained
	札付き	ふだつき	price label/ticket; (person with) bad reputation

1068

机 ⑥ 一 十 才 木 朾 机

音	机	キ	desk
熟	机下	キカ	in front of you; your desk
	机上	キジョウ	on the desk; on top of a desk
	机上の空論	キジョウの クウロン	unrealistic/impractical idea
訓	机	つくえ	desk; table

1069

朽 ⑥ 一 十 才 木 朽 朽

音	朽	キュウ	rot; decay; cumble
熟	朽木	キュウボク	*vi*. decayed/rotted wood
訓	朽ちる	くちる	rot; decay; molder; crumble
	朽木	くちき	decayed tree; rotted wood
	朽葉	くちば	dead leaves

1070

朴 ⑥ 一 十 才 木 朴 朴

| 音 | 朴 | ボク | simple; plain |

479

心忄小戈戸手扌支攵文斗斤方日曰月肉月木欠止歹殳母毋比毛氏气水氺氵火灬☲父片牛犬犭王礻耂

1071

材 ⑦　一 十 才 木 朴 村 材

音	材	ザイ	material; talent
熟	材木	ザイモク	lumber; wood; timber
	材料	ザイリョウ	materials; raw materials; data; factor; ingredients

1072

杉 ⑦　一 十 才 木 杉 杉 杉

| 音 | 杉 | サン | cedar (tree) |
| 訓 | 杉 | すぎ | cedar (tree) |

1073

村 ⑦　一 十 才 木 朴 村 村

音	村	ムラ	village
熟	村議会	ソンギカイ	village assembly
	村長	ソンチョウ	village mayor
	村民	ソンミン	villagers
	村落	ソンラク	village; hamlet
	村立	ソンリツ	established by the village
訓	村	むら	village
	村雨	むらさめ	passing shower
	村八分	むらハチブ	social ostracism
	村人	むらびと	villager

1074

枝 ⑧　一 十 才 木 朴 枝 枝 枝

音	枝	シ	branch
熟	枝葉	ショウ（えだは）	branches and leaves *fig*. minor details
	枝葉末節	ショウマッセツ	trivia; minor details
訓	枝	えだ	branch
	枝豆	えだまめ	green soybeans

1075

松 ⑧　一　十　オ　オ　オ　オ　松　松　松

音	松	ショウ	pine
熟	松竹梅	ショウチクバイ	pine, bamboo, and plum
訓	松	まつ	pine tree
	松飾り	まつかざり	New Year pine decorations
	松葉杖	まつばづえ	crutches
	※松明	たいまつ	torch

1076

枢 ⑧　一　十　オ　オ　杆　杆　枢　枢

音	枢	スウ	pivot
熟	枢機	スウキ	cardinal; most important
	枢要	スウヨウ	important; principal; cardinal; responsible
¥	枢密院	スウミツイン	Privy Council

1077

析 ⑧　一　十　オ　オ　オ　析　析　析

| 音 | 析 | セキ | analyze |
| 熟 | 析出 | セキシュツ | eduction; extract —v. educe; extract |

1078

杯 ⑧　一　十　オ　オ　オ　杆　杯　杯

| 音 | 杯 | ハイ | winecup; (counter for cups) |
| 訓 | 杯 | さかずき | saké cup |

1079

板 ⑧　一　十　オ　オ　オ　板　板

| 音 | 板 | バン | board |
| | | ハン | |

4

心 忄 小 戈 戸 手 扌 支 攵 文 斗 斤 方 日 曰 月 肉 月 木 ● 欠 止 歹 殳 母 毋 比 毛 氏 气 水 氺 氵 火 灬 爫 父 片 牛 犬 犭 王 礻 耂

481

心 忄 小 戈 戸 手 扌 支 攵 文 斗 斤 方 日 曰 月 肉 月 • 木 欠 止 歹 殳 母 毋 比 毛 氏 气 水 氺 氵 火 灬 灬 父 片 牛 犬 犭 王 礻 耂

熟	板金	バンキン	sheet metal
	板書	バンショ	writing on a blackboard —v. write on the blackboard
訓	板	いた	board; plank; plate; the stage
	板紙	いたがみ	paper covering a board on which food is served; cardboard
	板塀	いたベイ	fence; wooden wall
	板前	いたまえ	cook/chef (who prepares Japanese food)
	板目	いため	wood grain of a plank

1080

枚 ⑧ 一 十 才 木 朴 朾 枚 枚

音	枚	マイ	sheet; (counter for flat, thin objects)
熟	枚挙	マイキョ	enumeration; list —v. enumerate; list; count
	枚数	マイスウ	number of sheets

1081

林 ⑧ 一 十 才 木 杧 村 材 林

音	林	リン	forest; wood
熟	林間学校	リンカンガッコウ	camp; outdoor school
	林業	リンギョウ	forestry
	林産物	リンサンブツ	forest products
	林地	リンチ	forest region
	林道	リンドウ	forest road/trail
	林野	リンヤ	forests and fields; woodlands
	林立	リンリツ	standing close together —vi. stand close together
訓	林	はやし	wood; forest
¥	林野庁	リンヤチョウ	Forestry Agency

1082

枠 ⑧ 一 十 才 木 朾 朾 枠 枠

訓	枠	わく	frame; restriction; framework; limit
	枠外	わくガイ	beyond the limits
	枠組み	わくぐみ	frame; framework; framing; scope
	枠内	わくナイ	within the limits

1083

枯 ⑨ 一 十 才 木 杧 杧 枯 枯

音	枯	コ	wither; die
熟	枯渇	コカツ	exhausted; drained —*v.* dry up; run dry; be exhausted/drained
	枯死	コシ	withering; blight —*v.* wither and die; be blighted
	枯淡	コタン	simple but refined
訓	枯らす	からす	*vt.* let die; blight; season (wood)
	枯れる	かれる	*vi.* die; wither; season; mature
	枯れ木	かれき	dead/bare tree
	枯れ野	かれの	desolate field

1084

柱 ⑨ 一 十 才 木 杧 杧 杧 柱 柱

音	柱	チュウ	pillar; cylinder
熟	柱石	チュウセキ	mainstay; pillar; prop; support
訓	柱	はしら	pillar; support

1085

柄 ⑨ 一 十 才 木 杧 杧 枛 柄 柄

音	柄	ヘイ	handle; grip; hilt
訓	柄	え	handle; grip; hilt
	柄	がら	pattern; design; build; physique; character; nature
	※柄	つか	handle; grip; hilt
	※柄杓	ひシャク	ladle; dipper; scoop

1086

柳 ⑨ 一 十 才 木 杧 杧 柳 柳 柳

音	柳	リュウ	willow tree
熟	柳眉	リュウビ	beautiful eyebrows
訓	柳	やなぎ	willow tree

柳腰　　　やなぎごし　　slender graceful hips

心忄小戈戸手扌支攵文斗斤方日曰月肉月●木欠止歹殳母毋比毛氏气水氺氵火灬宀父片牛犬犭王礻耂

1087 桜 ⑩

一 十 才 オ 木 ギ 栌 柕 桜 桜

音	桜	オウ	cherry tree; cherry
熟	桜花	オウカ	cherry blossoms
	桜桃	オウトウ	cherry
訓	桜	さくら	cherry tree
	桜色	さくらいろ	pink; cerise
	桜肉	さくらニク	horsemeat

1088 格 ⑩

一 十 才 オ 木 ギ 柗 杦 柊 格 格

音	格	カク	character; syntactic case; rank
		（コウ）	
熟	格言	カクゲン	maxim; proverb; adage; saying
	格式	カクシキ	formality; social status
	格段	カクダン	special; marked difference
	格調	カクチョウ	style and tone of poetry
	格闘	カクトウ	hand-to-hand fighting — *vi.* fight hand-to-hand; grapple
	格納庫	カクノウコ	aircraft hangar
	格好	カッコウ	shape; form; appearance; dress; style
	格子	コウシ	lattice; latticework
¥	格上げ	カクあげ	raise the status; upgrade
	格差	カクサ	gap; differential; difference in quality
	格付け	カクづけ	ranking; rating; grading; classification
	格付け機関	カクづけキカン	bond-rating agency; rating agency
	格安	カクやす	inexpensive; moderate in price

1089 核 ⑩

一 十 才 オ 木 ギ 栌 杦 柂 核

音	核	カク	nucleus; fruit stone
熟	核心	カクシン	core; kernel
	核爆発	カクバクハツ	nuclear explosion

核分裂	カクブンレツ	(nuclear) fission; nuclear division —*vi*. fission; undergo fission
核兵器	カクヘイキ	nuclear weapons
訓 ※核	さね	stone; kernel; core

1090 株 ⑩

一 十 オ オ オ 术 村 杵 株 株

音	株	（シュ）	stump; root; share; stocks
¥	株	かぶ	stump; root; share; stocks
	株価	かぶカ	stock prices
	株券	かぶケン	stock certificate
	株式	かぶシキ	stocks; shares
	株式会社	かぶシキガイシャ	corporation; joint-stock company
	株式償却	かぶシキ ショウキャク	retirement of shares; cancellation of shares
	株式配当	かぶシキハイトウ	stock dividend
	株式分割	かぶシキブンカツ	stock split; split-ups
	株式分布	かぶシキブンプ	distribution of stocks
	株主	かぶぬし	stockholder
	株主総会	かぶぬしソウカイ	stockholders meeting

1091 校 ⑩

一 十 オ オ オ 术 栌 栌 柼 校

音	校	コウ	school; correct; compare
熟	校医	コウイ	school doctor
	校閲	コウエツ	revision; supervision —*v*. revise; supervise
	校旗	コウキ	school banner/flag
	校訓	コウクン	school precepts/motto
	校舎	コウシャ	school house/building
	校正	コウセイ	proofreading —*v*. proofread; correct
	校則	コウソク	school regulations/rules
	校長	コウチョウ	principal; headmaster
	校庭	コウテイ	school grounds; schoolyard; campus
	校風	コウフウ	school spirit/tradition
	校友	コウユウ	schoolmate
訓	※校倉作り	あぜくらづくり	style of architecture in which the sides of the building are made by placing triangularly cut logs across each other

心 忄 小 戈 戸 手 扌 支 攵 文 斗 斤 方 日 曰 月 肉 月 木 • 欠 止 歹 殳 母 毋 比 毛 氏 气 水 氺 氵 火 灬 ⺌ 父 片 牛 犬 犭 王 礻 耂

4

1092

根 ⑩ 一 十 十 オ 木 杆 杆 杆 柤 柤 根

音	根	コン	root; foundation; basis
熟	根幹	コンカン	basis; root; nucleus
	根気	コンキ	patience; perseverance; endurance; stamina
	根拠	コンキョ	ground; basis; foundation
	根拠地	コンキョチ	headquarters; stronghold
	根源	コンゲン	origin; root; source
	根治	コンジ（コンチ）	radical/permanent cure —*v.* cure permanently/radically
	根性	コンジョウ	nature; disposition; spirit; mind; willpower
	根絶	コンゼツ	extermination; eradication —*v.* exterminate; eradicate
	根底	コンテイ	root; bottom; foundation
	根本	コンポン	root; source; origin; foundation; basis
	根本的	コンポンテキ	fundamental; cardinal; basic
	根負け	コンまけ	losing stamina/patience —*vi.* have one's patience exhausted
訓	根	ね	root; origin; nature
	根深い	ねぶかい	deep-rooted; ingrained; incurable
	根掘り 葉掘り	ねほりはほり	inquisitively
	根元	ねもと	root; base

1093

桟 ⑩ 一 十 十 オ 木 杙 杉 栈 栈 栈

音	桟	サン	temporary bridge; plank bridge; plank
熟	桟道	サンドウ	bridge between two cliffs; road along a mountainside
	桟橋	サンばし	pier; jetty
	※桟敷	さじき	box; the stands; dress circle
訓	※桟	かけはし	temporary/makeshift bridge

1094

栓 ⑩ 一 十 十 オ 术 栌 栌 栓 栓 栓

音	栓	セン	cork

486

1095

桃 ⑩ 　一 十 オ 才 木 村 村 材 机 桃 桃

音	桃	トウ	peach
熟	桃源郷	トウゲンキョウ	Shangri-La; earthly paradise
訓	桃	もも	peach
	桃色	ももいろ	pink; rosy; sexual affair
	桃尻	ももじり	poor at riding horses
	桃太郎	ももタロウ	Momotarō (Japanese fairy tale character)
	桃の節句	もものセック	girl's day; Doll's Festival

1096

梅 ⑩ 　一 十 オ 才 木 栌 柠 栴 梅 梅

音	梅	バイ	plum tree
熟	梅雨	バイウ	rain in the wet/rainy season
	梅園	バイエン	plum tree garden
	梅毒	バイドク	*med*. syphillis
	梅林	バイリン	plum orchard/grove
訓	梅	うめ	plum; plum tree
	梅酒	うめシュ	plum wine
	梅干し	うめぼし	pickled plum
	※梅雨	つゆ	rainy/wet season

1097

械 ⑪ 　一 十 オ 才 木 杵 栌 栝 械 械 械

| 音 | 械 | カイ | device; apparatus |
| 訓 | 械 | かせ | shackles; handcuffs |

1098

棺 ⑫ 　一 十 オ 才 木 栌 栌 栌 栌 栌 棺 棺

音	棺	カン	coffin; casket
熟	棺桶	カンおけ	coffin; casket
訓	※棺	ひつぎ	coffin; casket

心 忄 小 戈 戸 手 扌 支 攵 文 斗 斤 方 日 曰 月 肉 月 木 欠 止 歹 殳 母 毋 比 毛 氏 气 水 氷 氵 火 灬 爫 父 片 牛 犬 犭 王 礻 耂

心忄小戈戸手扌支攵文斗斤方日曰月肉月•木欠止歹殳母毋比毛氏气水氺氵火灬冖父片牛犬犭王礻耂

1099 棋 ⑫

一 十 才 木 朮 村 柑 柑 柑 棋 棋 棋

| 音 | 棋 | キ | game of go or shōgi |
| 熟 | 棋士 | キシ | professional go player |

1100 極 ⑫

一 十 才 木 朮 朾 柯 柯 柯 極 極 極

音	極	キョク	go to extremes; the end; the poles; magnetic/electrical poles
		ゴク	
熟	極言	キョクゲン	so far as to say —v. go so far as to say; go to the length of saying
	極限	キョクゲン	utmost limits; bounds
	極端	キョクタン	extreme; extremity
	極致	キョクチ	culmination; acme; height
	極地	キョクチ	polar region; wilderness
	極度	キョクド	highest degree; utmost
	極東	キョクトウ	far east
	極力	キョクリョク	to the utmost; to the best of one's ability
	極論	キョクロン	carrying logic to extremes —v. carry logic to extremes
	極悪	ゴクアク	atrocity; brutality; villainy
	極意	ゴクイ	the secret; the mystery; the essence
	極彩色	ゴクサイシキ	rich coloring; full color
	極上	ゴクジョウ	first rate; premier quality
	極道	ゴクドウ	wicked; dissipated
	極秘	ゴクヒ	top secret
	極楽	ゴクラク	paradise; heaven
訓	極まる	きわまる	vi. end; terminate; be at an end; reach an extreme
	極める	きわめる	vt. go to the end; go to the extremes
	極み	きわみ	height; apex; end; limit

1101 検 ⑫

一 十 才 木 朮 朾 杦 杦 枌 枱 椧 検

| 音 | 検 | ケン | investigate; examine; test; inspect |

熟	検疫	ケンエキ	quarantine —*v*. quarantine; inspect
	検閲	ケンエツ	censorship; inspection —*v*. inspect; examine; censor
	検眼	ケンガン	eye test —*vi*. examine a person's eyes
	検挙	ケンキョ	arresting —*v*. arrest
	検挙者	ケンキョシャ	person in custody/under arrest
	検査	ケンサ	test; inspection; examination; audit —*v*. inspect; examine; check; test; audit
	検索	ケンサク	reference; retrieval —*v*. look up; refer to
	検察	ケンサツ	investigation; examination; prosecution
	検察側	ケンサツがわ	the prosecution
	検察庁	ケンサツチョウ	Public Prosecutor's Office
	検算	ケンザン	verification of accounts —*v*. check/verify the accounts
	検事	ケンジ	public prosecutor; the prosecution
	検出	ケンシュツ	detection —*v*. detect; find
	検証	ケンショウ	verification; inspection —*v*. verify; inspect
	検診	ケンシン	medical examination —*v*. examine (a person's) body
	検針	ケンシン	meter inspection —*v*. read a meter
	検定	ケンテイ	official approval —*v*. give official approval; sanction; authorize
	検討	ケントウ	examination; investigation; consideration —*v*. examine; investigate; consider; discuss
	検分	ケンブン	survey; inspection; examination —*v*. inspect; examine
	検便	ケンベン	stool test —*vi*. examine a stool sample
	検問	ケンモン	check; inspection —*v*. check; inspect; examine

1102

植 ⑫　一 十 オ 木 朾 朾 朾 枯 柿 植 植 植

音	植	ショク	plant; cultivate; set type
熟	植字	ショクジ	typesetting —*vi*. set type
	植樹	ショクジュ	tree planting —*vi*. plant a tree
	植物	ショクブツ	plant; vegetation
	植物園	ショクブツエン	botanical garden
	植物学	ショクブツガク	botany
	植民	ショクミン	colonization; settler; colonial —*vi*. colonize
	植民地	ショクミンチ	colony
	植林	ショクリン	afforestation —*vi*. plant trees
訓	植える	うえる	*vt*. plant; grow
	植わる	うわる	*vi*. be planted

心 忄 小 戈 戸 手 扌 支 攵 文 斗 斤 方 日 曰 月 肉 月 木 ● 欠 止 歹 殳 母 毋 比 毛 氏 气 水 氺 氵 火 灬 爫 父 片 牛 犬 犭 王 礻 耂

植木　　　うえき　　garden plant

1103 棚 ⑫

一 十 才 才 才 机 机 棚 棚 棚 棚 棚 棚

音	棚	ホウ	shelf
訓	棚	たな	shelf
	棚上げ	たなあげ	sheltering; pigeonhole —v. shelve; put something into pigeonhole
	棚卸し	たなおろし	stocktaking; inventory —v. take an inventory

1104 棟 ⑫

一 十 才 才 杧 杧 杧 栌 栖 棟 棟 棟

音	棟	トウ	ridge of a roof
熟	棟梁	トウリョウ	pillar/chief support/master carpenter/builder (of a country, family, etc.)
訓	棟	むな	(prefix) roof; ridge
	棟	むね	ridge of a roof
	棟上げ式	むねあげしき	framework raising ceremony

1105 棒 ⑫

一 十 才 才 杧 杧 栌 梼 梼 梼 棒 棒

音	棒	ボウ	stick; pole
熟	棒暗記	ボウアンキ	indiscriminate memorization; memorization without understanding —v. memorize indiscriminately; memorize without understanding
	棒組	ボウぐみ	typesetting
	棒縞	ボウじま	wide stripes
	棒術	ボウジュツ	(martial art using long staffs)
	棒状	ボウジョウ	cylindrical; stick
	棒高跳び	ボウたかとび	pole vault
	棒立ち	ボウだち	frozen in an upright position with shock
	棒読み	ボウよみ	monotone reading
¥	棒上げ	ボウあげ	straight climb
	棒下げ	ボウさげ	straight fall
	棒引き	ボウびき	cancellation of a debt; writing off (a debt); drawing a line

1106

楼 ⑬ 一 十 ォ ォ ォ゙ ォ゙ 柠 柠 柙 楼 楼 楼 楼

音	楼	ロウ	tower; turret; lookout
熟	楼閣	ロウカク	tower; castle
	楼門	ロウモン	two-story gate

1107

概 ⑭ 十 十 ォ ォ゙ 杓 杓 柑 根 柑 柑 柑 椢 概

音	概	ガイ	rough; general
熟	概括	ガイカツ	summary; generalization —*v*. summarize; sum up; generalize
	概観	ガイカン	general view; overview; summary
	概況	ガイキョウ	general condition/situation
	概算	ガイサン	rough estimate —*v*. make a rough estimate
	概数	ガイスウ	round figures; approximation
	概説	ガイセツ	general statement —*v*. give an outline/overview
	概念	ガイネン	concept; general idea; notion
	概要	ガイヨウ	outline; summary; synopsis
	概して	ガイして	generally; in general; on the whole
訓	※概ね	おおむね	generally speaking; in general; for the most part

1108

構 ⑭ 十 ォ ォ゙ ォ゙ 柑゙ 椎 椎 椪 椪 構 構 構

音	構	コウ	structure; attitude; concern
熟	構外	コウガイ	outside the premises
	構図	コウズ	composition; plot
	構成	コウセイ	composition; organization; construction —*v*. make; compose; organize; construct
	構想	コウソウ	plan; plot; conception; idea —*v*. plan; plot; conceive an idea
	構造	コウゾウ	structure; construction; framework; organization
	構築	コウチク	construction; structure —*v*. build; construct; erect
	構内	コウナイ	premises; precincts; grounds
訓	構う	かまう	*vi*. mind; care about; be concerned; meddle; interfere; entertain

4

心忄小戈戸手扌支攵文斗斤方日曰月肉月•木欠止歹殳母毋比毛氏气水氺氵火灬爫父片牛犬犭王礻耂

| 構える | かまえる | *vt.* keep; set up; build; pose; feign; pretend |
| 構え | かまえ | structure; construction; posture; position; attitude |

1109

模 ⑭ 一 十 オ 木 朾 朾 栉 栉 栉 档 档 模 模

音	模	ボ	model; copy; imitation
		モ	model; copy; imitation
熟	模する	モする	*vt.* model; copy; imitate
	模擬	モギ	imitation; mock; dry-run
	模型	モケイ	model; mold
	模索	モサク	fumbling; grope —*v.* fumble; grope
	模写	モシャ	copy; replica —*v.* copy; make a replica
	模造	モゾウ	imitation —*v.* imitate; copy
	模範	モハン	model; exemplar
	模倣	モホウ	imitation; copy —*v.* imitate; copy
	模様	モヨウ	pattern; design; appearance; situation
¥	模様	モヨウ	pattern; sign; looks; condition; state of affairs
	模様眺め	モヨウながめ	wait and see; watch and wait

1110

様 ⑭ 一 十 オ 木 术 栏 栏 栏 样 样 様 様 様

音	様	ヨウ	way; manner; similar; like; condition
熟	様式	ヨウシキ	mode; form; style
	様子	ヨウス	situation; appearance; aspect
	様相	ヨウソウ	phase; aspect; condition
	様態	ヨウタイ	situation; condition
訓	様	さま	appearance
	様々	さまざま	various; varied

1111

横 ⑮ 一 十 オ 木 朾 朾 栏 栟 栟 横 横 横

音	横	オウ	side; direction; dishonesty
熟	横臥	オウガ	lying down on one's side —*vi.* lie down on one's side
	横隔膜	オウカクマク	*med.* diaphragm; midriff

492

	横行	オウコウ	swaggering; walking sideways —*vi.* overrun; swagger; walk sideways
	横隊	オウタイ	rank; line
	横断	オウダン	crossing; intersection —*v.* cross; intersect
	横断歩道	オウダンホドウ	pedestrian/zebra crossing
	横着	オウチャク	cunning; wayward; dishonest —*vi.* be cunning/wayward/dishonest
	横転	オウテン	turning sideways; rolling —*vi.* turn sideways; roll
	横暴	オウボウ	oppression; tyranny; violence
	横領	オウリョウ	usurpation; embezzlement; misappropriation —*v.* usurp; embezzle; misappropriate
訓	横	よこ	width; side; wicked; dishonest
	横顔	よこがお	face in profile; profile
	横書き	よこがき	horizontal writing
	横切る	よこぎる	*vi.* go across; cross
	横滑り	よこすべり	sideslip —*v.* slip sideways
	横たえる	よこたえる	*vt.* lay
	横たわる	よこたわる	*vi.* lie
	横町	よこチョウ	alleyway; alley
	横綱	よこづな	*yokozuna* (grand champion sumo wrestler)
	横取り	よこどり	snatching; stealing —*v.* take away
	横腹	よこばら	side; flank
	横笛	よこぶえ	flute
	横道	よこみち	byroad; sidetrack
	横文字	よこモジ	Western language/alphabet
¥	横這い	よこばい	leveling-out; leveling-off —*vi.* hold level; remain flat; change little

---

1112

権⑮　十 才 才 疒 疒 疒 桙 桙 栌 桙 権 権

音	権	ケン	authority
		ゴン	secondary
熟	権威	ケンイ	authority
	権威主義	ケンイシュギ	authoritarianism
	権限	ケンゲン	authority; power
	権謀術数	ケンボウジュッスウ	trickery; scheming; Machiavellianism
	権利	ケンリ	right; rights; claim
	権力	ケンリョク	power; authority
	権化	ゴンゲ	incarnation; embodiment; personification
¥	権利落ち	ケンリおち	ex rights; ex warrants

493

心忄小戈戸手扌支攴文斗斤方日曰月肉月
•木欠止歹殳母毋比毛氏气水氷氵火灬爫父片牛犬犭王礻耂

1113

槽 ⑮ 十 才 木 杧 柿 柿 槽 槽 槽 槽 槽

| 音 | 槽 | ソウ | trough |

1114

標 ⑮ 十 才 木 栏 栌 柿 栖 桿 樗 標 標 標

音	標	ヒョウ	mark; sign
熟	標記	ヒョウキ	mark; heading —*vt.* mark
	標語	ヒョウゴ	slogan; motto
	標高	ヒョウコウ	above sea level
	標識	ヒョウシキ	mark; sign; beacon
	標準	ヒョウジュン	standard; criterion; level; average; normal
	標準語	ヒョウジュンゴ	standard language
	標準時	ヒョウジュンジ	standard time
	標的	ヒョウテキ	target
	標榜	ヒョウボウ	advocation; self-profession —*v.* profess (oneself to be); advocate; stand for
	標本	ヒョウホン	sample; specimen

1115

機 ⑯ 十 才 木 杉 桦 楔 栈 栈 桜 機 機 機

音	機	キ	mechanism; loom; machine; chance
熟	機運	キウン	fortune; opportunity; chance
	機会	キカイ	opportunity; chance
	機械	キカイ	machine; machinery
	機械化	キカイカ	mechanization —*v.* mechanize; introduce machinery
	機械的	キカイテキ	mechanical
	機関	キカン	engine; organ; agency; institution
	機器	キキ	machinery; tools; apparatus
	機嫌	キゲン	mood; temper; disposition
	機構	キコウ	mechanism; system; organization; structure
	機首	キシュ	nose of a plane
	機種	キシュ	type of airplane
	機上	キジョウ	aboard an aircraft; in flight
	機知	キチ	wit

	機長	キチョウ	captain; chief pilot
	機転	キテン	wit; tact
	機能	キノウ	function; faculty —v. function; work; operate
	機敏	キビン	smart; keen; astute
	機密	キミツ	secret; secrecy
訓	機	はた	loom
¥	機関	キカン	organization; institution; agency
	機関投資家	キカントウシカ	institutional investor
	機動性	キドウセイ	mobility

1116

橋 ⑯　十　十　才　术　栌　栌　栌　杯　柝　栫　橋　橋　橋

音	橋	キョウ	bridge
熟	橋脚	キョウキャク	pier
訓	橋	はし	bridge
	橋渡し	はしわたし	mediation; good offices —v. mediate (between); act as intermediary

---

1117

樹 ⑯　十　十　才　术　栌　栌　桔　桔　桔　植　椪　樹　樹

音	樹	ジュ	tree; establish
熟	樹下	ジュカ	beneath the trees
	樹海	ジュカイ	sea of trees; broad expanse of dense woodland
	樹脂	ジュシ	resin
	樹氷	ジュヒョウ	rime on trees; coat of ice of tree branches
	樹木	ジュモク	trees
	樹立	ジュリツ	establishment; founding —v. establish; found
	樹林	ジュリン	forest; lignosae (woody plants)
	樹齢	ジュレイ	age of a tree

1118

欄 ⑳　木　朷　朳　榴　椚　欄　椚　椚　欄　欄　欄　欄

音	欄	ラン	newspaper column; blank; space; railing
熟	欄外	ランガイ	margin
	欄干	ランカン	railing; banister

心忄小戈戸手扌支攵文斗斤方日曰月肉月木欠止歹殳母毋比毛氏气水氷氵火灬爫父片牛犬犭王礻耂

心忄小戈戸手扌支攵文斗斤方日曰月肉月木 • 欠止歹殳母毋比毛氏气水氺氵火灬爪父片牛犬犭王礻疒

4 欠 かける／あくび　yawning

1119

 欠　④　ノ　ケ　ア　欠

音	欠	ケツ	lack
熟	欠員	ケツイン	vacancy
	欠陥	ケッカン	defect; flaw; deficiency
	欠勤	ケッキン	absence —*vi*. be absent from work
	欠航	ケッコウ	flight/ship cancellation —*vi*. cancel a sailing/a flight
	欠如	ケツジョ	lack; want; shortage —*vi*. want; lack; be wanting
	欠場	ケツジョウ	failure to make an appearance —*vi*. fail to appear; cancel an appearance
	欠席	ケッセキ	absence —*vi*. be absent
	欠損	ケッソン	loss; deficit —*vi*. lose
	欠点	ケッテン	defect; fault; shortcoming; drawback
	欠番	ケツバン	missing number
	欠乏	ケツボウ	want; shortage —*vi*. want; lack; be wanting; run short of
	欠落	ケツラク	lack —*v*. lack
訓	欠く	かく	*vt*. break; chip; lack; be wanting in; fail to carry out
	欠ける	かける	*vi*. break/chip off; wane; lack; miss; be short
	欠け	かけ	fragment; broken piece
	欠かす	かかす	lack; be deficient

1120

次　⑥　丶　冫　冫　ゲ　ヶ　次

音	次	ジ	next; order
		シ	order
熟	次回	ジカイ	next time
	次官	ジカン	vice-minister; undersecretary
	次期	ジキ	next period/term/session
	次元	ジゲン	dimension; sphere
	次席	ジセキ	second position/place; deputy of a bureau/department

次第	シダイ	order; process; reason; circumstances	
次第に	シダイに	gradually	
次点	ジテン	second-best mark	
次男	ジナン	second son	
訓 次	つぎ	next; following; adjoining	
次ぐ	つぐ	*vi*. rank next to; follow	
次々	つぎつぎ	one after another; in rapid succession	

1121

欧 ⑧　一 フ ヌ 区 区 欧 欧 欧

音 欧	オウ	Europe	
熟 欧亜	オウア	Europe and Asia	
欧州	オウシュウ	Europe	
欧文	オウブン	European writing	
¥ 欧州共同体	オウシュウ キョウドウタイ	the European Community (EC)	
欧米	オウベイ	Europe and America; the West	

1122

欲 ⑪　丶 ハ グ 父 𡗗 谷 谷 谷 𲁑 𲁒 欲

音 欲	ヨク	desire	
熟 欲情	ヨクジョウ	passions; desires	
欲得	ヨクトク	selfishness; self-interest	
欲念	ヨクネン	desires; wishes; passions	
欲張り	ヨクばり	greed; covetousness	
欲望	ヨクボウ	desire; craving	
欲目	ヨクめ	favorable view; partiality; favoritism	
欲求	ヨッキュウ	desires; wants —*v*. desire; want	
欲求不満	ヨッキュウフマン	frustration	
訓 欲しい	ほしい	want	
欲する	ほっする	*vt*. want	

1123

款 ⑫　一 十 士 圭 圭 寺 青 青 款 款 款 款

音 款	カン	sincere	

497

4

| 熟 | 款待 | カンタイ | hospitality; warm reception —*v.* be hospitable; give a warm reception |
| 訓 | ※款 | まこと | sincerity; honesty; devotion |

1124

欺 ⑫ 一 十 卄 井 甘 其 其 其 其 欺 欺 欺

| 音 | 欺 | ギ | deceive |
| 訓 | 欺く | あざむく | *vt.* deceive; cheat |

1125

歌 ⑭ 一 亓 亓 可 可 哥 哥 哥 哥 歌 歌 歌

音	歌	カ	song; sing; poem
熟	歌曲	カキョク	song
	歌劇	カゲキ	opera
	歌詞	カシ	lyrics
	歌手	カシュ	singer
	歌集	カシュウ	collection of *tanka* poems; collection of odes
	歌人	カジン	*tanka* poet
	歌道	カドウ	the art of *waka* poetry; poetry
	歌風	カフウ	poetical style
	歌舞伎	カブキ	Kabuki (classical Japanese drama)
	歌謡	カヨウ	song; ballad
	歌謡曲	カヨウキョク	Japanese popular song
訓	歌	うた	*tanka* poem; song
	歌う	うたう	*vt.* sing
	歌声	うたごえ	singing voice

1126

歓 ⑮ 亠 二 夕 � 幷 幷 幷 雈 雈 雚 歓 歓

音	歓	カン	joy; delight
熟	歓喜	カンキ	delight; joy; gladness —*vi.* rejoice; be glad/delighted
	歓迎	カンゲイ	welcome —*v.* welcome
	歓呼	カンコ	ovation; cheer —*vi.* cheer; applaud
	歓声	カンセイ	shout of joy
	歓送	カンソウ	send-off —*v.* give a send-off

歓待	カンタイ	warm reception; hospitality; entertainment —*v.* entertain; welcome; be hospitable
歓談	カンダン	pleasant talk —*vi.* have a pleasant chat
歓楽街	カンラクガイ	pleasure haunt; amusement quarter
訓 ＊歓ぶ	よろこぶ	*vi.* rejoice; be pleased

---

4 止 とめる stop

1127

止 ④ 丨 ト 止 止

音	止	シ	stop
熟	止血	シケツ	*med.* hemostasis —*v.* stop the bleeding
訓	止まる	とまる	*vi.* stop; come to an end
	止める	とめる	*vt.* stop; put an end to; check

1128

正 ⑤ 一 丅 下 正 正

音	正	ショウ	right; just
		セイ	just; correct; formal
熟	正気	ショウキ	sanity; soberness; consciousness
	正午	ショウゴ	noon; noontime; midday
	正直	ショウジキ	honest; upright; square
	正真正銘	ショウシン ショウメイ	real; true; genuine; authentic
	正体	ショウタイ	true character/form; consciousness
	正札	ショウフダ	price mark/tag
	正味	ショウミ	net; clear; the actual amount
	正面	ショウメン	front; facade
	正課	セイカ	regular subject/curriculum; compulsory subject
	正解	セイカイ	right answer; correct interpretation —*v.* interpret correctly; give a right answer
	正確	セイカク	accuracy; precision; exactness; correctness
	正規	セイキ	regularity; formality; rule
	正義	セイギ	justice; right; righteousness; correct meaning
	正誤	セイゴ	correction
	正攻法	セイコウホウ	frontal attack

499

心忄小戈戸手扌支攵文斗斤方日曰月肉月木欠
●止歹殳母毋比毛氏气水氺氵火灬爪父片牛犬犭王礻耂

正座	セイザ	*seiza* (formal kneeling position) —*vi.* sit upright; sit square; sit in the correct manner; kneel in the Japanese manner	
正視	セイシ	looking straight at —*v.* look in the face; face up to	
正式	セイシキ	formal; proper; regular; official	
正常	セイジョウ	normal; regular	
正数	セイスウ	**math.** positive number	
正々堂々	セイセイドウドウ	fair and square; open and above board	
正装	セイソウ	full/formal dress —*vi.* dress up; be in full uniform	
正当	セイトウ	just; justifiable; warrantable; right; rightful	
正当防衛	セイトウボウエイ	legal defense; legitimate self-defense	
正統	セイトウ	legitimacy; orthodoxy; direct line; lineal descent	
正道	セイドウ	right track; path of righteousness	
正反対	セイハンタイ	exact opposite/reverse	
正否	セイヒ	right or wrong	
正比例	セイヒレイ	direct proportion —*vi.* be in direct proportion	
正方形	セイホウケイ	square; four-square; quadrate	
正論	セイロン	just argument	

訓

正しい	ただしい	right; just; correct; formal
正す	ただす	*vt.* correct; rectify; put right; redress
正	まさ	right; exact; true
正に	まさに	just; exactly; precisely; surely; certainly
正夢	まさゆめ	dream that comes true; prophetic dream

1129

 ⑧　一 一 〒 干 干 圧 正 武 武

音

武	ブ	military
	ム	

熟

武器	ブキ	arms; weapon
武家	ブケ	samurai
武芸	ブゲイ	martial arts
武骨	ブコツ	boorish; uncouth; rude
武士	ブシ	samurai; warrior
武士道	ブシドウ	samurai code of chivalry
武術	ブジュツ	martial arts
武将	ブショウ	military commander
武装	ブソウ	arming for war —*vi.* arm oneself; militarize
武道	ブドウ	martial arts
武門	ブモン	military family; samurai family

武勇	ブユウ	valor; bravery
武力	ブリョク	military force
武者	ムシャ	warrior; samurai

1130

歩 ⑧ 　 丨 　 ト 　 ⺊ 　 止 　 屮 　 歩 　 步 　 歩

音	歩	ホ	walk; step; pace
		ブ	rate; one percent; *bu* (unit of area, approx. 3.3㎡)
		（フ）	pawn (in shogi)
熟	歩行	ホコウ	walking; ambulatory —*vi*. walk
	歩行者	ホコウシャ	pedestrian
	歩測	ホソク	measurement by paces —*v*. measure off a distance by pacing
	歩調	ホチョウ	pace; step
	歩道	ホドウ	sidewalk; footpath; pavement
	歩道橋	ホドウキョウ	pedestrian overpass
	歩幅	ホはば	length of a pace/step/stride
	歩兵	ホヘイ	infantry; foot soldier
訓	歩く	あるく	*vi*. walk
	歩む	あゆむ	*vi*. walk; progress step-by-step; tread
	歩み	あゆみ	step; pace; walking; progress
	歩み寄る	あゆみよる	*vi*. walk towards; converge on; compromise
¥	歩合	ブあい	rate; percentage; commission
	歩引き	ブびき	discount
	歩割り	ブわり	proportion; commission

1131

歳 ⑬ 　 丨 　 ト 　 ⺊ 　 屮 　 广 　 产 　 芦 　 芦 　 岸 　 岸 　 歳 　 歳 　 歳

音	歳	サイ	time; age
		（セイ）	year
熟	歳月	サイゲツ	time; years
	歳末	サイマツ	year-end
	お歳暮	おセイボ	year-end gift
¥	歳出	サイシュツ	annual expenditure
	歳入	サイニュウ	revenue; annual income
	歳費	サイヒ	annual expenditure/salary

心
忄
小
戈
戸
手
扌
支
攵
文
斗
斤
方
日
曰
月
肉
月
木
欠
止
歹
殳
母
毋
比
毛
氏
气
水
氺
氵
火
灬
爪
父
片
牛
犬
犭
王
礻
耂

1132

歴 ⑭　一　厂　厂　厂　厂　厂　厖　厤　厤　厤　歴　歴

音	歴	レキ	continuation; passage of time; successive; clear
熟	歴史	レキシ	history
	歴然	レキゼン	clear; unmistakable
	歴代	レキダイ	successive generations
	歴任	レキニン	successively holding various posts —*v.* hold various post in succession
	歴訪	レキホウ	round of calls/visits —*v.* make a round of calls/visits

4　歹　いちたへん／かばねへん　death

1133

死 ⑥　一　ア　ヌ　歹　歺　死

音	死	シ	die; death; inactivity
熟	死因	シイン	cause of death
	死骸	シガイ	corpse; dead body; carcass
	死角	シカク	blind spot; dark corner
	死火山	シカザン	extinct/dead volcano
	死活問題	シカツモンダイ	matter of life and death
	死期	シキ	hour/time of death
	死球	シキュウ	*bas.* dead ball
	死去	シキョ	death —*vi.* die
	死刑	シケイ	death penalty; capital punishment
	死後	シゴ	after one's death; posthumously
	死語	シゴ	dead language
	死罪	シザイ	capital punishment/crime
	死産	シザン	*med.* stillbirth —*vi.* give birth to a stillborn baby
	死屍	シシ	dead body; corpse
	死者	シシャ	dead person; the dead; the deceased
	死守	シシュ	defense to the death/last —*v.* defend to the death/last
	死傷	シショウ	casualities
	死相	シソウ	look like a dead person; shadow of death; face of a dead person

死蔵	シゾウ	shutting/locking up; storing away —*v.* shut/lock up; store away
死体	シタイ	dead body; corpse; cadaver
死地	シチ	jaws of death; death trap; place to die
死闘	シトウ	desperate struggle; fight —*vi.* put up a desperate struggle; fight
死人	シニン	dead person
死病	シビョウ	fatal disease
死別	シベツ	bereavement —*vi.* be bereaved; lose someone close
死亡	シボウ	death —*vi.* die
死亡率	シボウリツ	death rate
死滅	シメツ	extinction —*vi.* become extinct; perish; die out
死力	シリョク	desperate efforts

訓
死ぬ	しぬ	*vi.* die; pass away; be lifeless; be unusable
死なす	しなす	*vt.* let die; kill
死に顔	しにがお	face of a dead person
死に絶える	しにたえる	*vi.* die out; become extinct
死に目	しにめ	the moment a person dies
死に物狂い	しにものぐるい	desperately; madly; very hard

1134

残 ⑩

一 ア 歹 歹 歹 歹 歼 残 残 残

音
| 残 | ザン | remain; survive; cruel; brutal |

熟
残骸	ザンガイ	wreck; dead body; remains; ruins
残額	ザンガク	account balance
残虐	ザンギャク	cruelty; atrocity
残業	ザンギョウ	overtime work —*vi.* work overtime
残酷	ザンコク	cruelty; brutality
残暑	ザンショ	lingering summer heat
残照	ザンショウ	twilight; traces; vestiges
残雪	ザンセツ	remaining/unmelted snow
残像	ザンゾウ	afterimage; lingering impression
残存	ザンゾン	survival —*vi.* survive; remain; be extant
残忍	ザンニン	brutality; cruelty
残念	ザンネン	regrettable; disappointing; vexing; pity
残飯	ザンパン	leftover rice; leftover food; leftovers
残部	ザンブ	remainder; the rest
残余	ザンヨ	the rest; residue
残留	ザンリュウ	remaining; stay behind —*vi.* remain; stay behind

心 忄 小 戈 戸 手 扌 支 攵 文 斗 斤 方 日 曰 月 肉 月 木 欠 止 歹 殳 母 毋 比 毛 氏 气 水 氺 氵 火 灬 爪 父 片 牛 犬 犭 王 礻 耂

4

訓	残る	のこる	*vi*. be left; remain; stay; remain; survive
	残す	のこす	*vt*. leave; save
	残り	のこり	remainder; the rest
	残り物	のこりもの	leftovers
¥	残金	ザンキン	balance; remainder
	残高	ザンだか	balance
	残高表	ザンだかヒョウ	balance sheet
	残品	ザンピン	remaining stock
	残余額	ザンヨガク	balance

1135

殊 ⑩   一 ア 歹 歹 歹 歹 歹 殊 殊 殊

音	殊	シュ	unusually
熟	殊勲	シュクン	distinguished services
	殊勝	シュショウ	praiseworthy; admirable; commendable
訓	殊	こと	in particular; especially; moreover
	殊更	ことさら	especially; on purpose; deliberately

1136

殉 ⑩   一 ア 歹 歹 歹 歹 殉 殉 殉 殉

音	殉	ジュン	follow one's lord to the grave
熟	殉教	ジュンキョウ	martyrdom — *vi*. become a martyr
	殉死	ジュンシ	following one's lord to the grave — *vi*. follow one's lord to the grave
	殉職	ジュンショク	dying at one's post of duty — *vi*. die at one's post of duty
	殉難	ジュンナン	self-sacrifice; martyrdom

1137

殖 ⑫   一 ア 歹 歹 歹 歹 殖 殖 殖 殖 殖

音	殖	ショク	increase
熟	殖財	ショクザイ	moneymaking
	殖産	ショクサン	promotion of industry
訓	殖える	ふえる	*vi*. increase; multiply
	殖やす	ふやす	*vt*. increase; add to; enlarge

504

4 殳 るまた windy again

1138

殳⑧ 一 フ ヌ 区 区 区 殴 殴

音	殴	オウ	beating; battering
熟	殴殺	オウサツ	beating to death —v. beat to death
	殴打	オウダ	assault; blow; thrashing —v. beat; strike; hit; batter
訓	殴る	なぐる	vt. beat; hit; knock
	殴り合い	なぐりあい	fight
	殴り込む	なぐりこむ	vt. attack; raid

1139

段⑨ ´ ʹ ʹ ʹ 自 自 郎 郎 段

音	段	ダン	steps; stairs; column; grade; degree; extent
熟	段階	ダンカイ	steps; grade; rank
	段丘	ダンキュウ	natural terrace/bench
	段々	ダンダン	gradually; increasingly; growingly; more and more
	段々畑	ダンダンばたけ	terraced farm/fields; field in terraces
	段取り	ダンどり	program; plan; arrangements
	段落	ダンラク	end of a paragraph; conclusion; ending
¥	段階的移行	ダンカイテキイコウ	step-by-step transition; gradual transition
	段階的引下げ	ダンカイテキひきさげ	step-by-step reduction; gradual reduction; reduction by degrees

---

1140

殺⑩ ノ メ ㄨ 乎 矛 杀 杀 殺 殺 殺

音	殺	サツ	kill; get rid of
		(サイ)	lessen
		(セツ)	
熟	殺意	サツイ	murderous intent; urge to kill
	殺気	サッキ	thirst for blood; stormy atmosphere

505

4

心 忄 小 戈 戸 手 扌 支 攵 文 斗 斤 方 日 曰 月 肉 月 木 欠 止 歹 殳 母 毋 比 毛 氏 气 水 氷 氵 火 灬 爫 父 片 牛 犬 犭 王 礻 歩

殺菌	サッキン	sterilization; pasteurization —v. sterilize; pasteurize
殺傷	サッショウ	killing and wounding; blood shedding —v. kill and wound; shed blood
殺陣	サツジン たて	fight scene in film/play
殺人	サツジン	murder; manslaughter; homicide
殺人罪	サツジンザイ	murder; homicide
殺人的	サツジンテキ	deadly
殺人犯人	サツジンハンニン	murderer
殺虫剤	サッチュウザイ	insecticide; pesticide
殺到	サットウ	rush; flood —vi. rush in; throng; flood; pour into
殺伐	サツバツ	bloody; savage; fierce; brutal
殺風景	サップウケイ	desolate; bleak; dreary; drab; prosaic; matter-of-fact; unimaginative
殺生	セッショウ	slaughter; cruelty —v. kill; take life
訓 殺す	ころす	vt. kill; murder; surpress; restrain
殺し文句	ころしモンク	clincher; killing expression

1141

殻 ⑪ 　 一 十 土 士 士 声 声 壳 壳 壳 殼 殼 殼

| 音 殻 | カク | shell |
| 訓 殻 | から | shell; slough; husk; corpse |

1142

殿 ⑬ 　 一 コ 尸 尸 尸 尺 屄 屄 屄 殿 殿 殿

音 殿	デン テン	hall; palace
熟 殿下	デンカ	Your (Imperial) Highness; His/Her (Imperial) Highness
殿舎	デンシャ	palace
殿中	デンチュウ	within the palace
殿堂	デンドウ	palace; hall; shrine
訓 殿	との	lord; mansion; palace
殿	どの	Mr./Ms. (used in official documents, etc.)
殿方	とのがた	gentlemen
殿御	とのゴ	man; gentleman; husband
殿様	とのさま	lord; prince; feudal lord

4 母 ははのかん／なかれ mother 母 はは mother

1143

母 ⑤ 〈 ㄅ ㄅ ㄅ 母

音	母	ボ	mother
熟	母音	ボイン	vowel
	母系	ボケイ	maternal line (of a family)
	母系制度	ボケイセイド	matriarchal system
	母校	ボコウ	*alma mater*
	母国	ボコク	mother/native country
	母国語	ボコクゴ	mother/native tongue
	母子	ボシ	mother
	母性	ボセイ	motherhood; maternity
	母船	ボセン	mother ship
	母胎	ボタイ	***med***. womb; uterus
	母体	ボタイ	mother's body; parent organization
	母堂	ボドウ	**hon**. mother
	母乳	ボニュウ	mother's milk
訓	母	はは	one's mother
	母上	ははうえ	**hon**. mother
	母親	ははおや	mother
	母君	ははぎみ	**hon**. mother
	母屋(母家)	おもや	main building/house
	※お母さん	おかあさん	mom **hon**. mother

1144

毎 ⑥ ノ ー ヒ 与 与 毎

音	毎	マイ	every; each
熟	毎回	マイカイ	every time
	毎号	マイゴウ	every issue
	毎時	マイジ	per hour; every hour
	毎週	マイシュウ	every week; weekly
	毎食	マイショク	each meal; at mealtime
	毎月	マイつき	every month; monthly
	毎度	マイド	each time; frequently; always
	毎日	マイニチ	every day; daily

507

心忄小戈戸手扌支攵文斗斤方日曰月肉月木欠止歹殳母毋比毛氏气水氺氵火灬爫父片牛犬犭王礻耂

毎年	マイネン （マイとし）	every year; annually
毎秒	マイビョウ	every second

1145

毒 ⑧　一　十　キ　主　丰　青　青　毒

音	毒	ドク	poison; toxicant; virus; germ; harm
熟	毒する	ドクする	*vt.* poison; corrupt; contaminate
	毒気	ドクケ	poisonous character; virulence; malice; spite
	毒殺	ドクサツ	death by poisoning —*v.* poison; kill by poison
	毒舌	ドクゼツ	spiteful/malicious tongue
	毒素	ドクソ	toxin; poisonous matter
	毒々しい	ドクドクしい	poisonous-looking
	毒物	ドクブツ	poisonous substance; poison; toxicant
	毒味（毒見）	ドクミ（ドクみ）	tasting for poison
	毒虫	ドクむし	poisonous insect
	毒矢	ドクヤ	poison arrow/dart
	毒薬	ドクヤク	poisonous drug; poison

4　比　くらべる／ならびひ　comparing

1146

比 ④　一　上　上　比

音	比	ヒ	compare; ratio; the Philippines
熟	比する	ヒする	*vt.* compare
	比較	ヒカク	comparison —*v.* compare
	比較的	ヒカクテキ	comparatively; relatively
	比肩	ヒケン	comparable —*vi.* be comparable to; rank with
	比重	ヒジュウ	*phy.* specific gravity
	比熱	ヒネツ	*phy.* specific heat
	比喩	ヒユ	simile; metaphor; allegory
	比率	ヒリツ	percentage; rate; ratio
	比類	ヒルイ	parallel; equal
	比例	ヒレイ	proportion; ratio —*vi.* be proportioned/proportionate
訓	比べる	くらべる	*vt.* compare

4 毛 け hair; fur

1147
毛 ④ 一 二 三 毛

音	毛	モウ	hair; tiny amount; 1/10,000 yen
熟	毛細血管	モウサイケッカン	capillary
	毛頭	モウトウ	person with uncropped hair; acolyte; young samurai
	毛頭ない	モウトウない	by no means; not at all
	毛髪	モウハツ	hair (on the head)
	毛布	モウフ	blanket
訓	毛	け	hair; fur; wool
	毛孔	けあな	pores
	毛糸	けいと	woolen yarn; worsted
	毛色	けいろ	color of hair; nature; type; kind
	毛織物	けおりもの	woolen goods
	毛皮	けがわ	fur; skin; pelt
	毛嫌い	けぎらい	prejudice; dislike; antipathy —*v.* be prejudiced; dislike; have an antipathy
	毛並み	けなみ	lie of the hair *fig.* social standing/status of a family; birth; stock
	毛虫	けむし	caterpillar

4 氏 うじ clan

1148
氏 ④ ´ ㇄ ㇄ 氏

音	氏	シ	clan; family; Mr.
熟	氏族	シゾク	family; clan
	氏族制度	シゾクセイド	family system
	氏名	シメイ	one's full name
訓	氏	うじ	family name; birth; lineage
	氏神	うじがみ	tutelary deity; patron god
	氏子	うじこ	local residents under the protection of the same guardian deity

心
忄
小
戈
戸
手
扌
支
攵
文
斗
斤
方
日
曰
月
肉
月
木
欠
止
歹
殳
母
毋
比
毛
• 氏
气
水
氷
氵
火
灬
宀
父
片
牛
犬
犭
王
礻
耂

1149

民 ⁻ ⁻ 尸 尸 民
⑤

音	民	ミン	the people
熟	民家	ミンカ	private house
	民間	ミンカン	private (not public)
	民芸	ミンゲイ	folk art/craft
	民権	ミンケン	civil rights
	民事	ミンジ	civil affairs; civil
	民主	ミンシュ	democratic
	民主主義	ミンシュシュギ	democracy
	民主的	ミンシュテキ	democratic
	民衆	ミンシュウ	the people; populace; the masses
	民宿	ミンシュク	lodging house
	民情	ミンジョウ	public sentiment
	民心	ミンシン	popular sentiment; the people's feelings
	民生委員	ミンセイイイン	district welfare officer
	民俗	ミンゾク	folk customs; ethnic
	民俗学	ミンゾクガク	folklore
	民族	ミンゾク	race; a people
	民度	ミンド	level of popular sophistication
	民兵	ミンペイ	militia
	民法	ミンポウ	the civil law/code
	民有	ミンユウ	privately owned
	民謡	ミンヨウ	folk song
	民力	ミンリョク	national strength
	民話	ミンワ	folk tale; folklore
訓	民	たみ	the people
	民草	たみぐさ	the people; the populace
¥	民営	ミンエイ	private management
	民営化	ミンエイカ	privatization —v. privatize
	民活 (民間活力)	ミンカツ (ミンカンカツリョク)	vitality of private industry
	民間	ミンカン	private; nongovernmental
	民間外資	ミンカンガイシ	private foreign capital
	民間企業	ミンカンキギョウ	private enterprise
	民間消費	ミンカンショウヒ	private consumption
	民社党	ミンシャトウ	the Japan Democratic Social Party (DSP)
	民主党	ミンシュトウ	(US) Democratic Party

1150

気 ⑥ 　 ノ　ハ　ヒ　气　気　気

音	気	キ	air; weather; feeling
		ケ	sign; appearance
熟	気圧	キアツ	atmospheric pressure
	気圧配置	キアツハイチ	distribution of atmospheric pressure
	気運	キウン	tendency
	気鋭	キエイ	spiritedness
	気後れ	キおくれ	diffidence; self-distrust; timidity —*vi*. be timid/diffident
	気温	キオン	temperature
	気化	キカ	evaporation; vaporization —*vi*. evaporate; vaporize
	気概	キガイ	mettle; backbone; pluck
	気兼ね	キがね	constraint; scruples —*vi*. feel constraint; have scruples
	気構え	キがまえ	expectation; preparedness
	気軽	キがる	lighthearted; cheerful
	気管	キカン	*med*. trachea; windpipe
	気管支	キカンシ	*med*. bronchial tubes
	気球	キキュウ	balloon
	気苦労	キグロウ	worries; care; anxiety
	気候	キコウ	climate
	気質	キシツ	temperament; disposition
	気性	キショウ	temper; nature; disposition
	気象	キショウ	atmospheric phenomena; meteorology
	気色	キショク	countenance; feeling
	気勢	キセイ	spirit; ardor
	気絶	キゼツ	fainting —*vi*. faint; pass out; black out
	気体	キタイ	gas; vapor
	気違い	キちがい	*derog*. madness; insanity; mania; madman; fan; crazy
	気疲れ	キづかれ	mental fatigue; worry; boredom —*vi*. be mentally tired; worry; be bored
	気付	キつけ	encouragement; resurrection
	気の毒	キのドク	pitiable; regrettable; feeling sorry for
	気乗り	キのり	interest; inclination —*vi*. be interested in; feel inclined

511

心 忄 小 戈 戸 手 扌 支 攵 文 斗 斤 方 日 曰 月 肉 月 木 欠 止 歹 殳 母 毋 比 毛 氏 气 水 氺 氵 火 灬 ⺋ 父 片 牛 犬 犭 王 礻 老

心 忄 小 戈 戸 手 扌 支 攵 文 斗 斤 方 日 曰 月 肉 月 木 欠 止 歹 殳 母 毋 比 毛 氏 气 ● 水 氺 氵 火 灬 ⺌ 父 片 牛 犬 犭 王 礻 ⺹

気迫	キハク	spirit; vigor
気晴らし	キばらし	diversion; recreation
気品	キヒン	nobility; dignity; grace
気風	キフウ	character; disposition; temper
気分	キブン	feeling; mood; atmosphere
気前	キまえ	generosity; liberality
気味	キミ	feeling; sensation; touch of; tinge
気短か	キみじか	short-tempered; rash; impatient
気持ち	キもち	feeling; sensation; mood
気休め	キやすめ	relieving one's conscience
気楽	キラク	feeling at ease; carefree; easygoing
気流	キリュウ	air current/steam
気力	キリョク	spirit; guts; vitality
気色	ケシキ	appearance; countenance
気配	ケハイ	sign; indication
¥ 気配	キハイ	quotes; quotation; tone of the market

---

4 水 みず water   氺 (p.515) 氵 (p.516)

1151

水④   ⌉ ⌿ 水 水

音 水	スイ	water; river; Wednesday
熟 水圧	スイアツ	water/hydraulic pressure
水位	スイイ	water level
水域	スイイキ	water area
水運	スイウン	water transport; transportation by water
水泳	スイエイ	swimming; bathing —*vi.* swim; bathe; have a swim
水煙	スイエン	(clouds) of spray
水温	スイオン	water temperature
水化	スイカ	hydration —*v.* hydrate
水化物	スイカブツ	hydrate
水害	スイガイ	flood disaster/damage
水銀	スイギン	*chem.* mercury; quicksilver
水源	スイゲン	riverhead; fountain head; source of water supply; reservoir
水郷	スイゴウ	riverside/lakeside district
水彩画	スイサイガ	watercolor (painting)

512

水産	スイサン	fishing
水死	スイシ	drowning
水質	スイシツ	water quality
水車	スイシャ	water mill/wheel
水準	スイジュン	level; standard; water level
水準器	スイジュンキ	level
水晶	スイショウ	crystal; crystallized quartz
水蒸気	スイジョウキ	steam; water vapor
水深	スイシン	depth of water
水星	スイセイ	the planet Mercury
水勢	スイセイ	force of water; current
水生動物	スイセイドウブツ	aquatic animal
水洗	スイセン	flushing; washing; rinsing
水素	スイソ	*chem*. hydrogen
水族館	スイゾクカン	aquarium
水中	スイチュウ	in the water; underwater
水滴	スイテキ	water drop; drop of water
水田	スイデン	rice paddy
水筒	スイトウ	canteen; flask; water bottle
水道	スイドウ	water works/supply/way
水難	スイナン	drowning; disaster at sea; shipwreck
水爆	スイバク	hydrogen/fusion bomb
水盤	スイバン	basin
水分	スイブン	water; moisture; humidity; juice; sap
水兵	スイヘイ	seaman; sailor
水平	スイヘイ	horizontally
水平線	スイヘイセン	horizon; horizontal line
水泡	スイホウ	bubble; foam
水防	スイボウ	flood control/prevention
水墨画	スイボクガ	India ink painting; black-and-white drawing
水面	スイメン	water surface
水門	スイモン	floodgate; sluice gate
水薬	スイヤク	liquid medicine
水溶液	スイヨウエキ	*chem*. solution
水曜日	スイヨウび	Wednesday
水浴	スイヨク	bathing —*vi*. bathe
水利	スイリ	water facility/supply; irrigation; navigability
水量	スイリョウ	water volume; quantity of water
水量計	スイリョウケイ	water gauge
水力	スイリョク	water/hydraulic power
水力学	スイリョクガク	hydraulics; hydrodynamics
水路	スイロ	waterway; water course/conduit

心忄小戈戸手扌支攵文斗斤方日曰月肉月木欠止歹殳母毋比毛氏气 • 水氺氵火灬 冖 父片牛犬犭王礻爿

訓	水	みず	water; flood; inundation
	水足	みずあし	speed of flowing water
	水鏡	みずかがみ	reflective surface of water
	水瓶座	みずがめザ	Aquarius, the water carrier
	水着	みずぎ	swimsuit; bathing costume
	水煙	みずけむり	(clouds) of spray
	水先案内	みずさきアンナイ	pilot; pilotage; piloting
	水商売	みずショウバイ	night-time entertainment business such as bars, clubs

1152
永 ⑤ 　 ` 亅 刁 永 永

音	永	エイ	long; eternal; forever
熟	永遠	エイエン	eternity; perpetuity; infinity; permanence; immortality
	永久	エイキュウ	permanence; eternity; perpetuity
	永久歯	エイキュウシ	permanent/second teeth
	永住	エイジュウ	domiciliation; permanent residence —*vi.* settle down; take up permanent residence
	永世中立	エイセイチュウリツ	permanent neutrality
	永続	エイゾク	permanence; perpetuity; perpetuation —*vi.* last long; endure; remain; perpetuate
	永年	エイネン	many years; eternity; a long time
	永眠	エイミン	passing away; eternal sleep; death —*vi.* pass away; die
訓	永い	ながい	long; lengthy

1153
氷 ⑤ 　] 丁 丬 氷 氷

音	氷	ヒョウ	ice
		（ヒ）	
熟	氷河	ヒョウガ	glacier
	氷河時代	ヒョウガジダイ	ice age
	氷海	ヒョウカイ	frozen sea
	氷塊	ヒョウカイ	block of ice; ice floe
	氷解	ヒョウカイ	cleared away; dispelled —*vi.* be cleared (of suspision, etc.); be dispelled
	氷結	ヒョウケツ	frozen over; icebound —*vi.* freeze
	氷原	ヒョウゲン	ice field

氷山	ヒョウザン	iceberg
氷室	ヒョウシツ	icehouse; ice room
氷人	ヒョウジン	go-between; matchmaker
氷雪	ヒョウセツ	ice and snow
氷柱	ヒョウチュウ	icicle; ice pillar placed in a room in summer
氷点	ヒョウテン	*chem.* freezing point
訓 氷	こおり	ice
※氷る	こおる	*vi.* freeze (up)

1154

泉 ⑨　＇ ′ ′ 勹 白 白 皃 皁 皁 泉

音 泉	セン	spring
熟 泉下	センカ	underworld
泉水	センスイ	ornamental pond; pond of spring water
訓 泉	いずみ	spring

---

5 氷　したみず　water at bottom

1155

求 ⑦　一 寸 寸 寸 求 求 求

音 求	キュウ	request; search; want; desire; demand
熟 求愛	キュウアイ	amorous advances —*vi.* court; woo
求刑	キュウケイ	sentence desired by the prosecution
求婚	キュウコン	marriage proposal; courtship; wooing —*vi.* propose marriage (to a girl)
求心力	キュウシンリョク	centripetal force
訓 求める	もとめる	*vt.* want; wish for; desire; request; demand; pursue
¥ 求償	キュウショウ	barter
求償貿易	キュウショウボウエキ	barter trade
求職	キュウショク	job hunting; looking for a job —*vi.* hunt/look for a job
求職者	キュウショクシャ	job appliant; people seeking work
求人	キュウジン	situation vacant; job offer
求人市場	キュウジンシジョウ	job market

心忄小戈戸手扌支攵文斗斤方日曰月肉月木欠止歹殳母毋比毛氏气水氺氵火灬爪爫父片牛犬犭王礻耂

1156

泰 ⑩

一 二 三 声 夫 泰 泰 泰 泰 泰

音	泰	タイ	tranquil; peace; large; very
熟	泰然	タイゼン	composed; collected; calm; cool
	泰平	タイヘイ	peace; tranquillity; quiet

3 氵 さんずい water at left

1157

汁 ⑤

丶 �ː ⼡ ⼡ ⼡ ⼡ ⼡ 汁

音	汁	ジュウ	juice
訓	汁	しる	soup; sap
	汁粉	しるこ	*shiruko* (sweet red-bean soup with rice cake)

1158

汚 ⑥

丶 ⼡ 氵 汚 汚 汚

音	汚	オ	dirty; stain; defile; pollute; wrong; not right
熟	汚辱	オジョク	disgrace; dishonor; slander —*v.* disgrace; dishonor
	汚水	オスイ	dirty/foul water; sewage
	汚染	オセン	pollution; contamination —*v.* pollute; contaminate
	汚損	オソン	stain; corruption —*v.* stain; soil; spoil
	汚濁	オダク	corruption; decadence —*vi.* be corrupt/decadent
	汚点	オテン	stain; dirty spot; blot
	汚物	オブツ	filth; dirt; muck; impurities; feces
	汚名	オメイ	disgrace; bad name; slur
訓	汚い	きたない	dirty; mean; base
	汚す	けがす	*vt.* stain; soil; pollute; contaminate; disgrace
	汚らわしい	けがらわしい	dirty; odious; foul; nasty; disgusting
	汚れる	けがれる	*vi.* get dirty; become soiled; be polluted/contaminated
	汚す	よごす	*vt.* soil; stain; defile; foul; slur
	汚れ	よごれ	dirt; soil; spot; stain

| 汚れる | よごれる | *vi*. become dirty; be stained/blemished |
| ¥ 汚職 | オショク | official corruption; bribery |

1159

汗 ⑥ 　 ﹅ 丶 冫 汁 汗 汗

音 汗	カン	sweat
熟 汗腺	カンセン	*med*. sweat glands
訓 汗	あせ	sweat

1160

江 ⑥ 　 ﹅ 丶 氵 汀 汀 江 江

音 江	コウ	inlet; large river; creek
熟 江河	コウガ	Yangtze and Yellow rivers; big rivers
江湖	コウコ	the public; the world
訓 江	え	inlet
江戸	えど	Edo (the former name of Tokyo)
江戸時代	えどジダイ	*hist*. Edo period (1603-1867)

1161

池 ⑥ 　 ﹅ 丶 氵 汀 池 池

音 池	チ	pond; lake
熟 池畔	チハン	pondside
訓 池	いけ	pond; lake

1162

汽 ⑦ 　 ﹅ 丶 氵 汽 汽 汽 汽

音 汽	キ	steam; vapor
熟 汽圧	キアツ	steam pressure
汽缶	キカン	boiler
汽車	キシャ	(steam) train
汽船	キセン	steam ship
汽笛	キテキ	steam whistle

心 忄 小 戈 戸 手 扌 支 攵 文 斗 斤 方 日 曰 月 肉 月 木 欠 止 歹 殳 母 毌 比 毛 氏 气 水 氺 氵 火 灬 爫 父 片 牛 犬 犭 王 礻 耂

心 忄 小 戈 戸 手 扌 支 攵 文 斗 斤 方 日 曰 月 肉 月 木 欠 止 歹 殳 母 毋 比 毛 氏 气 水 氺 氵 ● 火 灬 爫 父 片 牛 犬 犭 王 礻 耂

1163

決⑦　丶　冫　氵　沪　沪　決決

音	決	ケツ	fix; settle; decide, collapse
熟	決する	ケッする	fix; settle; decide
	決壊	ケッカイ	collapse —*v.* collapse; break down
	決起	ケッキ	going into action —*vi.* rise and go into action
	決行	ケッコウ	execution —*v.* carry out; go ahead
	決裁	ケッサイ	sanction; approval —*v.* sanction; approve
	決死	ケッシ	desperate; ready to die
	決勝	ケッショウ	finals (of a competition)
	決心	ケッシン	determination; resolution —*vi.* determine; be determined; make up one's mind; resolve
	決戦	ケッセン	decisive battle
	決然	ケツゼン	determinedly; decisively; resolutely
	決断	ケツダン	decision; determination —*vi.* decide; make a decision
	決着	ケッチャク	conclusion; the end; settlement —*vi.* conclude; end; settle
	決定	ケッテイ	decision; conclusion; determination —*v.* decide; determine; set; fix
	決闘	ケットウ	duel —*vi.* fight a duel
	決裂	ケツレツ	break down; rupture —*vi.* breakdown; come to a rupture
訓	決まる	きまる	*vi.* be decided/settled
	決める	きめる	*vt.* decide; fix; settle; determine
¥	決意	ケツイ	resolution; determination —*vi.* determine; make up one's mind
	決議	ケツギ	resolution; vote; decision —*v.* pass a resolution; resolve
	決済	ケッサイ	settlement; payment —*v.* settle an account; pay up
	決算	ケッサン	settlement of accounts —*v.* settle/balance an account
	決算期	ケッサンキ	settlement term; accounting period

1164

沢⑦　丶　冫　氵　沪　沪　沪沢

音	沢	タク	swamp; marsh; bog
熟	沢庵	タクアン	*takuan* (type of pickled radish)
	沢山	タクサン	many; much; a lot of

訓	沢	さわ	swamp; marsh; bog; pond

1165

沖 ⑦　` ` ⌋ シ シ 汀 沪 沖

音	沖	チュウ	offing; open sea; rise to heaven
熟	沖天	チュウテン	ascendant; rising skyward
訓	沖	おき	offing; open sea

1166

沈 ⑦　` ` ⌋ シ シ 汀 沙 沈

音	沈	チン	sink
熟	沈下	チンカ	subsidence; sinking; settlement —*vi*. subside; sink; settle
	沈思	チンシ	meditation; contemplation; deep thought —*vi*. meditate; contemplate
	沈静	チンセイ	stillness; quietness; tranquillity —*vi*. be still/quiet/tranquil
	沈滞	チンタイ	dullness; slackness; stagnation; inactivity —*vi*. stagnate; become inactive
	沈着	チンチャク	composure; self-possession; presence of mind
	沈痛	チンツウ	grave; serious; pathetic; sad
	沈澱	チンデン	precipitation; sedimentation; subsidence —*vi*. settle; be precipitated/deposited
	沈没	チンボツ	sinking; submersion; foundering —*vi*. sink; go down; be submerged; founder
	沈黙	チンモク	silence; taciturnity; reticence —*vi*. become/fall silent
訓	沈む	しずむ	*vi*. sink; be submerged; go down; mope; be downcast
	沈める	しずめる	*vt*. sink; send to the bottom; submerge

1167

没 ⑦　` ` ⌋ シ シ 沪 汐 没

音	没	ボツ	sink; lose; die
熟	没する	ボッする	*v*. sink; go down; hide; disappear; die
	没却	ボッキャク	ignoring; forgetting —*v*. ignore; forget
	没後	ボツゴ	after one's death; posthumous
	没収	ボッシュウ	confiscation —*v*. confiscate

心忄小戈戸手扌支攵文斗斤方日曰月肉月木欠止歹殳母毋比毛氏气水氺氵火灬爪父片牛犬犭王礻耂

没頭	ボットウ	absorption; engrossment —*vi.* be absorbed/engrossed
没入	ボツニュウ	absorption; immersion —*vi.* be absorbed/immersed in
没年	ボツネン	one's age at death; year of death
没落	ボツラク	downfall; ruin; bankruptcy —*vi.* be ruined/bankrupt

1168
泳 ⑧ ` ⸱ ⸲ ⸲ 氵 汀 汈 沪 泳

音	泳	エイ	swimming
熟	泳者	エイシャ	swimmer
訓	泳ぎ	およぎ	swimming; swim
	泳ぐ	およぐ	*vi.* swim

1169
沿 ⑧ ` ⸱ ⸲ 氵 氿 沿 沿 沿

音	沿	エン	lie along; go along; run parallel
熟	沿海	エンカイ	coast
	沿革	エンカク	history; chronicle; development; changes
	沿岸	エンガン	coast; shore
	沿線	エンセン	along a railroad
	沿道	エンドウ	roadside; route; course
訓	沿う	そう	*vi.* go/lie along; run parallel

1170
河 ⑧ ` ⸱ 氵 沪 沪 沪 沪 河

音	河	カ	river; Yellow River
熟	河岸	カガン	riverbank
	河口	カコウ	mouth of a river; river mouth
	河川	カセン	rivers
	河川敷	カセンしき	riverside
	河豚	カトン ふぐ	blowfish
訓	河	かわ	river
	河原	かわら	dry riverbed; river beach

1171

泣 ⑧　　`　`　氵　氵　氵　汁　汁　泣　泣

音	泣	キュウ	crying; weeping
熟	泣訴	キュウソ	tearful supplication/appeal —*v.* implore/supplicate/appeal with tears in one's eyes
訓	泣く	なく	*vi.* cry; weep
	泣き声	なきごえ	tearful voice; whine
	泣き言	なきごと	complaint; grieviance; whimper
	泣き上戸	なきジョウゴ	sentimental drinker; crying drunk
	泣きっ面	なきっつら	tearstained face
	泣き虫	なきむし	crybaby

1172

況 ⑧　　`　`　氵　氵　氵　氵　氵　況

音	況	キョウ	condition; state of things

1173

沼 ⑧　　`　`　氵　氵　氵　氵　沼　沼

音	沼	ショウ	marsh
熟	沼沢	ショウタク	marsh
訓	沼	ぬま	marsh; swamp; bog
	沼地	ぬまチ	marshland; swampland

1174

治 ⑧　　`　`　氵　汁　氵　治　治　治

音	治	チ ジ	govern; rule; cure; heal; remedy; recover
熟	治安	チアン	public peace and order
	治外法権	チガイホウケン	extraterritoriality; extraterritorial rights
	治水	チスイ	flood control; river improvement —*vi.* carry out flood control work

心 忄 小 戈 戸 手 扌 支 攵 文 斗 斤 方 日 曰 月 肉 月 木 欠 止 歹 殳 母 毋 比 毛 氏 气 水 氺 氵 火 灬 爪 父 片 牛 犬 犭 王 礻 耂

心 ⺖ 小 戈 戸 手 扌 支 攵 文 斗 斤 方 日 曰 月 肉 月 木 欠 止 歹 殳 母 毋 比 毛 氏 气 水 氺 氵 火 灬 爪 父 片 牛 犬 犭 王 礻 耂

	治癒	チユ	healing; curing; recovery —*vi.* cure; heal; recover; be cured
	治療	チリョウ	medical treatment; remedy —*v.* treat; doctor; cure; remedy
訓	治まる	おさまる	*vi.* be at peace; be tranquil; calm down
	治める	おさめる	*vt.* rule; govern; administer; manage; put down; suppress
	治す	なおす	*vt.* mend; repair; put in order; reform; correct; cure; heal; remedy
	治る	なおる	*vi.* get well/better; recover; be cured

1175

注 ⑧ ` ⼂ シ ヅ 汀 汁 洼 注

	注	チュウ	annotation; notes; comments; flow into; pour
音			
熟	注意	チュウイ	attention; observation; note; notice; care; caution —*vi.* pay attention; give heed; observe; take note; be cautious
	注意人物	チュウイジンブツ	dangerous person; suspicious character
	注意力	チュウイリョク	attentiveness
	注記	チュウキ	note; entry —*v.* note; make entries; write down
	注視	チュウシ	gaze; close observation; scrutiny —*v.* watch carefully; contemplate; scrutinize
	注射	チュウシャ	injection; shot; inoculation —*v.* inject; syringe; inoculate
	注射器	チュウシャキ	injector; syringe
	注釈	チュウシャク	commentary; notes; comments —*v.* annotate; comment; expound
	注水	チュウスイ	watering; pouring water —*vi.* pour water; water
	注入	チュウニュウ	injection; infusion; infiltration —*v.* pour into; inject; impregnate; infuse; implant
	注目	チュウモク	attention; observation; notice; remark —*v.* pay attention; observe; remark; notice
	注文	チュウモン	order; commission; request; demand; wish; desire —*v.* order; request; demand; desire; wish
	注油	チュウユ	oiling; lubrication —*v.* oil; lubricate
訓	注ぐ	そそぐ	*v.* pour into; irrigate; flow into; drain

1176

泥 ⑧ ` ⼂ シ 沪 沪 沪 沪 泥

	泥	デイ	mud
音			
熟	泥水	デイスイ	muddy water

泥酔	デイスイ	extreme drunkeness —*vi*. get dead drunk	
泥炭	デイタン	peat; turf	
訓 泥	どろ	mud; mire; dirt	
泥仕合	どろジあい	mud slinging	
泥縄	どろなわ	thief; robber	
泥沼	どろぬま	bog; swamp	
泥棒	どろボウ	thief; crook; robber —*v*. steal; rob	

1177

波 ⑧ 丶 丶 氵 氵 沪 沪 波 波

音 波	ハ	wave
熟 波及	ハキュウ	influence —*vi*. extend/spread to; influence; affect
波状	ハジョウ	wave; undulation
波長	ハチョウ	wavelength
波動	ハドウ	undulation; fluctuation —*vi*. undulate; fluctuate; wave
波紋	ハモン	ripple; water ring
波乱	ハラン	trouble; disturbance; commotion; storm
波浪	ハロウ	waves; billow; surge
※波止場	ハとば	pier; wharf; quay; jetty
訓 波	なみ	wave; sea; billow; surge
波風	なみかぜ	wind and waves; trouble; discord; quarrel
波立つ	なみだつ	*vi*. be choppy; run high; billow

1178

泊 ⑧ 丶 丶 氵 氵 氿 泊 泊 泊

音 泊	ハク	berth
訓 泊まる	とまる	*vi*. stop; lodge; stay; lie at anchor
泊める	とめる	*vt*. lodge; shelter; accommodate

1179

泌 ⑧ 丶 丶 氵 氵 汃 泌 泌 泌

音 泌	ヒ	secrete; flow
	ヒツ	secrete; flow
熟 泌尿器	ヒニョウキ	*med*. urinary organs
泌尿器科	ヒニョウキカ	*med*. urology department (in a hospital)

心 忄 小 戈 戸 手 扌 支 攵 文 斗 斤 方 日 曰 月 肉 月 木 欠 止 歹 殳 母 毋 比 毛 氏 气 水 氺 氵 火 灬 爫 父 片 牛 犬 犭 王 礻 耂

心忄小戈戸手扌支攵文斗斤方日日月肉月木欠止歹殳母毋比毛氏气水氺氵火灬爫父片牛犬犭王礻爻

1180

沸⑧ 　｀　｀　氵　氵　氵　沪　沸　沸

音	沸	フツ	boil
熟	沸点	フッテン	boiling point
	沸騰	フットウ	boiling; excitement; agitation —*vi.* boil up; be excited/agitated
訓	沸かす	わかす	*vt.* boil; heat up
	沸く	わく	*vi.* boil; seethe
	沸き返る	わきかえる	*vi.* boil hard; seethe; be in an uproar; be furious
	沸き立つ	わきたつ	*vi.* come to a boil; seethe; be in an uproar

1181

法⑧ 　｀　｀　氵　氵　汁　泔　法　法

音	法	ホウ	law; method; religion
		（ホ）	
		（ハ）	
熟	法度	ハット	ban; law; prohibition
	法衣	ホウイ	*Bud.* vestments; priestly robes
	法医学	ホウイガク	forensic medicine
	法王	ホウオウ	Pope
	法皇	ホウオウ	ex-emperor who has become a monk
	法貨	ホウカ	legal tender
	法外	ホウガイ	unreasonable; preposterous
	法学	ホウガク	law; jurisprudence
	法官	ホウカン	judicial officer; judge
	法規	ホウキ	laws and regulations
	法権	ホウケン	legal right
	法号	ホウゴウ	(priest's or posthumous) Buddhist name
	法師	ホウシ	*Bud.* priest
	法事	ホウジ	*Bud.* memorial service
	法式	ホウシキ	regulation; rite; rule
	法制	ホウセイ	legislation; laws
	法曹	ホウソウ	legal profession
	法則	ホウソク	law; rule
	法治国	ホウチコク	constitutional state
	法廷	ホウテイ	(law) court; courtroom
	法定	ホウテイ	legal; prescribed by law

法典	ホウテン	law code
法名	ホウミョウ	(priest's or posthumous) Buddhist name
法要	ホウヨウ	***Bud***. memorial service
法力	ホウリキ	merits/powers of Buddhism
法律	ホウリツ	law
法律上	ホウリツジョウ	legally
法令	ホウレイ	laws and (cabinet or ministerial) orders
法華経	ホケキョウ	Lotus Sutra
¥ 法案	ホウアン	(legislative) bill/measure
法人	ホウジン	corporation; juridical person; legal entity
法人株主	ホウジンかぶぬし	institutional stockholder
法人税	ホウジンゼイ	corporate (income) tax
法定準備金	ホウテイ ジュンビキン	legal reserve
法務省	ホウムショウ	Ministry of Justice

1182

泡⑧ 　丶 　ヽ　氵　氵　汋　泃　泡　泡

音	泡	ホウ	foam; bubble; froth; suds
訓	泡	あわ	foam; bubble; froth; suds
	泡立つ	あわだつ	***vi***. froth; lather
	泡立てる	あわだてる	***vt***. beat; whip

1183

油⑧ 　丶 　ヽ　氵　氿　汕　沖　油　油

音	油	ユ	oil
熟	油煙	ユエン	soot
	油脂	ユシ	oils and fats; fats
	油井	ユセイ	oil well
	油断	ユダン	carelessness; inattentiveness
	油田	ユデン	oil field
訓	油	あぶら	oil
	油絵	あぶらエ	oil painting
	油ぎる	あぶらぎる	***vi***. be oily/fatty; glisten with oil
	油っこい	あぶらっこい	oily; fatty

心 忄 小 戈 戸 手 扌 支 攵 文 斗 斤 方 日 曰 月 肉 月 木 欠 止 歹 殳 母 毋 比 毛 氏 气 水 氺 氵 火 灬 爫 父 片 牛 犬 犭 王 礻 耂

心 忄 小 戈 戸 手 扌 支 攵 文 斗 斤 方 日 曰 月 肉 月 木 欠 止 歹 殳 母 毋 比 毛 氏 气 水 氷 氵 火 灬 爪 父 片 牛 犬 犭 王 礻 耂

1184

海 ⑨   ` ` 氵 氵 汒 洨 海 海 海

音	海	カイ	sea
熟	海王星	カイオウセイ	the planet Neptune
	海外	カイガイ	abroad; overseas; foreign countries
	海岸	カイガン	seaside
	海峡	カイキョウ	strait; channel
	海軍	カイグン	the navy
	海国	カイコク	maritime country/power
	海産物	カイサンブツ	marine products
	海図	カイズ	nautical chart
	海水	カイスイ	sea water
	海水浴	カイスイヨク	swimming at the beach
	海藻	カイソウ	seaweed
	海賊	カイゾク	pirate
	海抜	カイバツ	above sea level
	海浜	カイヒン	beach; seaside
	海風	カイフウ	sea wind/breeze
	海綿	カイメン	sponge
	海洋	カイヨウ	ocean
	海里	カイリ	nautical mile; knot
	海流	カイリュウ	ocean current
	海路	カイロ	sea route
訓	海	うみ	sea; lake; well of an inkstone
¥	海運	カイウン	marine transportation; shipping
	海上保険	カイジョウホケン	marine insurance

1185

活 ⑨   ` ` 氵 氵 汗 汗 汗 活 活

音	活	カツ	vivid; live; life
熟	活火山	カッカザン	active/live volcano
	活気	カッキ	vigor; liveliness; activity
	活況	カッキョウ	activity; animated appearance; briskness
	活字	カツジ	printing type
	活字体	カツジタイ	typeface
	活動	カツドウ	activity; action —*vi.* be active; lead an active life; play an active part

活発	カッパツ	lively; brisk; active
活版	カッパン	typography; letterpress
活躍	カツヤク	activity; action —*vi.* be active; take an active part in
活用	カツヨウ	practical use; application —*v.* apply; utilize; put to practical use
活力	カツリョク	vitality; vigor
活路	カツロ	means of escape; way out
訓 活き	いき	freshness
活きる	いきる	*vi.* live; be alive
活ける	いける	*vt.* arrange flowers
¥ 活性化	カッセイカ	activation

1186

洪 ⑨   ` ヽ 氵 沪 汫 汫 洪 洪 洪

| 音 洪 | コウ | flood |
| 熟 洪水 | コウズイ | flood; deluge |

1187

浄 ⑨   ` ヽ 氵 氵 沪 沪 浄 浄 浄

音 浄	ジョウ	pure
熟 浄化	ジョウカ	purification; purge; clean-up —*v.* purify; purge; clean up
浄化設備	ジョウカセツビ	sanitation facilities
浄財	ジョウザイ	offertory; donation
浄書	ジョウショ	block copy; block copy artist
浄水	ジョウスイ	clean water
浄水場	ジョウスイジョウ	water purification plant
浄水池	ジョウスイチ	pure-water reservoir
浄土	ジョウド	promised land; Pure Land
浄土宗	ジョウドシュウ	Jōdo sect of Buddhism; Pure Land Buddhism

1188

津 ⑨   ` ヽ 氵 沪 沪 沪 津 津 津

| 音 津 | シン | harbor; port; ferry |
| 熟 津々 | シンシン | absorbing; deep; profound |

527

心忄小戈戸手扌支攵文斗斤方日曰月肉月木欠止歹殳母毋比毛氏气水氷氵●火灬爫父片牛犬犭王礻耂

訓	津	つ	harbor; port; ferry
	津々浦々	つつうらうら	all over the country
	津波	つなみ	tsunami; tidal wave

1189

洗 ⑨ 　`　ミ　氵　氵　氵　汄　洪　洣　洗

音	洗	セン	wash
熟	洗眼	センガン	eyewashing
	洗顔	センガン	washing one's face —*vi.* wash one's face
	洗剤	センザイ	detergent
	洗車	センシャ	car wash —*vi.* wash the car
	洗浄	センジョウ	washing; rinsing; cleansing —*v.* wash; rinse; clean
	洗濯	センタク	washing; laundering —*v.* wash; launder
	洗濯機	センタクキ	washing machine
	洗濯物	センタクもの	the wash; laundry
	洗脳	センノウ	brainwashing —*v.* brainwash
	洗面	センメン	washing one's face —*vi.* wash one's face
	洗面台	センメンダイ	wash basin
	洗礼	センレイ	baptism
	洗練	センレン	refinement; polishing —*v.* refine; polish
訓	洗う	あらう	*vt.* wash; probe

1190

浅 ⑨ 　`　ミ　氵　氵　氵　氵　浅　浅　浅

音	浅	セン	shallow
熟	浅学	センガク	shallow learning; superficial knowledge
	浅薄	センパク	shallow/superficial (knowledge, beliefs); flimsy
訓	浅い	あさい	shallow
	浅瀬	あさせ	shoal; shallows; ford
	浅ましい	あさましい	shameful; mean

1191

洞 ⑨ 　`　ミ　氵　汩　洞　洞　洞　洞　洞

音	洞	ドウ	cave

熟	洞窟	ドウクツ	cave
	洞察	ドウサツ	discernment; penetration; insight —v. discern; penetrate; see through
訓	洞	ほら	cave
	洞穴	ほらあな	cave

1192 派 ⑨

`丶 冫 氵 氵 汀 沪 沪 沪 派 派`

音	派	ハ	group; school; sect; denomination
熟	派遣	ハケン	dispatch; detachment —v. dispatch; detach; send; detail
	派出	ハシュツ	dispatch —v. send out; dispatch; detach
	派出所	ハシュツジョ	branch office; police office/box
	派生	ハセイ	derivation —vi. derive; be derived from; originate
	派手	ハで	showy; gaudy; flashy; vain
	派閥	ハバツ	clique; faction; coterie
	派兵	ハヘイ	dispatch of troops —vi. dispatch troops

1193 洋 ⑨

`丶 冫 氵 氵 氵 沣 洋 洋 洋`

音	洋	ヨウ	ocean; foreign; western
熟	洋画	ヨウガ	Western picture/movie
	洋学	ヨウガク	Western learning
	洋楽	ヨウガク	Western music
	洋菓子	ヨウガシ	Western cakes
	洋館	ヨウカン	Western-style building
	洋行	ヨウコウ	travels to the US or Europe —vi. go to the US or Europe
	洋裁	ヨウサイ	Western-style dressmaking
	洋式	ヨウシキ	Western-style
	洋室	ヨウシツ	Western-style room; non-*tatami* room
	洋酒	ヨウシュ	Western liquors
	洋書	ヨウショ	foreign/Western book
	洋上	ヨウジョウ	on the sea; seagoing
	洋食	ヨウショク	Western food
	洋装	ヨウソウ	Western dress —v. wear Western dress
	洋品店	ヨウヒンテン	haberdashery; hosier
	洋風	ヨウフウ	Western-style

心
忄
小
戈
戸
手
扌
支
攵
文
斗
斤
方
日
曰
月
肉
月
木
欠
止
歹
殳
母
毋
比
毛
氏
气
水
氺
氵
• 火
灬
爪
父
片
牛
犬
犭
王
礻
耂

洋服	ヨウフク	(Western-type) clothes
洋間	ヨウま	Western-style room
洋々たる	ようようたる	wide; broad; vast

1194

消 ⑩ 　 ` ゛ シ ジ ゙ジ ジ シ゛ 氵 消 消 消

音	消	ショウ	vanish; extinguish; consume
熟	消火	ショウカ	fire extinguisher —*vi*. extinguish a fire
	消化	ショウカ	digestion; consumption; absorption —*v*. digest; consume; absorb
	消却	ショウキャク	spending; consumption —*v*. spend; consume; use up
	消極的	ショウキョクテキ	negative; passive; half-hearted
	消失	ショウシツ	disappearance; vanishing —*vi*. disappear; vanish
	消息	ショウソク	news; information
	消灯	ショウトウ	lights off —*vi*. put out/turn off the lights
	消毒	ショウドク	disinfection; sterilization; fumigation —*v*. disinfect; sterilize; fumigate
	消費	ショウヒ	consumption; expenditure —*v*. consume; use up
	消防	ショウボウ	fire fighting —*v*. fight a fire
	消耗	ショウモウ	waste; consumption; exhaustion —*v*. waste; consume; exhaust; wear out
訓	消える	きえる	*vi*. go out; die; disappear; go/fade away
	消す	けす	*vt*. put out; extinguish; switch/turn off; erase; liquidate
	消印	けしイン	postmark
	消しゴム	けしゴム	pencil eraser
	消し止める	けしとめる	*vt*. put out; extinguish
¥	消費財	ショウヒザイ	consumption goods
	消費者	ショウヒシャ	consumer
	消費税	ショウヒゼイ	consumption tax

1195

浸 ⑩ 　 ` ` 氵 氵 氵 氵 氵 浸 浸 浸

音	浸	シン	soak
熟	浸食	シンショク	erosion; corrosion —*v*. erode; corrode
	浸水	シンスイ	inundation; flooding —*v*. be flooded/inundated
	浸透	シントウ	infiltration; penetration; permeation —*v*. penetrate; infiltrate; permeate

	浸入	シンニュウ	permeation; penetration; infiltration —v. permeate; penetrate; infitrate	**4**
訓	浸す	ひたす	**vt.** soak; moisten	
	浸る	ひたる	**vi.** be flooded/immersed/soaked; wallow in	

1196

浜 ⑩ ` ⺀ ⺀ ⻐ ⻐ ⻐ ⻐ ⻐ ⻐ 浜

音	浜	ヒン	beach; seashore
訓	浜	はま	beach; seashore
	浜辺	はまべ	beach; sands; shore

1197

浮 ⑩ ` ⺀ ⺀ ⻐ ⻐ ⻐ ⻐ ⻐ 浮 浮

音	浮	フ	float
熟	浮説	フセツ	rumor
	浮沈	フチン	ups and downs; rise and fall; ebb and flow
	浮動	フドウ	wafting; floating —**vi.** waft; float
	浮薄	フハク	fickle; frivolous; insincere; shallow
	浮標	フヒョウ	buoy; float (for a fishing net, etc.)
	浮遊	フユウ	floating; wafting; suspension —**vi.** float; waft; be suspended
	浮力	フリョク	buoyancy; lift
	浮浪児	フロウジ	juvenile vagrant
	浮浪者	フロウシャ	street bum; tramp; hobo
訓	浮く	うく	**vi.** float; rise to the surface; feel buoyant/lighthearted
	浮かぶ	うかぶ	**vi.** float; rise to the surface; think of; be revealed; appear
	浮かべる	うかべる	**vt.** set afloat; show; reveal
	浮かれる	うかれる	**vi.** be in high spirits; be excited
	浮いた	ういた	cheerful; buoyant; frivolous
	浮き	うき	float
	浮き立つ	うきたつ	**vi.** be enlivened/exhilarated/buoyant
	浮名	うきな	rumor; gossip; gossip about a love affair
	浮世	うきよ	this transitory world
	浮世絵	うきよエ	ukiyoe woodblock print
	※浮つく	うわつく	**vi.** be fickle/flippant/restless
	※浮気	うわキ	marital infidelity; love affair

¥ 浮動株　フドウかぶ　floating stock

1198

浦 ⑩　 丶 氵 氵 汀 汀 沪 浧 浦 浦

| 音 | 浦 | ホ | inlet; shore; bay |
| 訓 | 浦 | うら | inlet; shore; bay |

1199

浴 ⑩　 丶 氵 氵 氵 浴 浴 浴 浴 浴

音	浴	ヨク	bathe; bath
熟	浴室	ヨクシツ	bathroom
	浴場	ヨクジョウ	bathroom; bath house
	浴槽	ヨクソウ	bathtub
	※浴衣	ゆかた	*yukata* (light cotton kimono)
訓	浴びる	あびる	*vt*. pour over oneself; bathe in
	浴びせる	あびせる	*vt*. pour on; shower upon

1200

流 ⑩　 丶 氵 氵 氵 浐 浐 浐 浐 流 流

音	流	リュウ （ル）	flow; wander; style; school; rank; class
熟	流域	リュウイキ	river basin/valley
	流会	リュウカイ	adjournment —*vi*. be adjourned/called off
	流感	リュウカン	influenza; flu
	流儀	リュウギ	style; system; method
	流刑	リュウケイ	deportation, exile; banishment
	流血	リュウケツ	bloodshed
	流言	リュウゲン	false rumor
	流行	リュウコウ	fashionable; popular; prevalent —*vi*. be in fashion; be popular/prevalent/epidemic
	流行性感冒	リュウコウセイ カンボウ	influenza
	流行病	リュウコウビョウ	epidemic
	流産	リュウザン	miscarriage —*v*. suffer a miscarriage
	流失	リュウシツ	washed away —*vi*. be washed away
	流出	リュウシュツ	outflow —*vi*. outflow; flow out
	流星	リュウセイ	shooting star; meteor

流説	リュウセツ	rumor; idle talk
流線型	リュウセンケイ	streamline
流体	リュウタイ	*phy*. fluid
流暢	リュウチョウ	fluent
流通	リュウツウ	circulation; distribution —*vi*. circulate; distribute
流動	リュウドウ	flowing; liquid (assets); current —*vi*. flow; be liquid/current
流動体	リュウドウタイ	fluid
流入	リュウニュウ	influx —*vi*. flow in
流派	リュウハ	school (of thought/art)
流氷	リュウヒョウ	drift ice; ice floe
流木	リュウボク	driftwood
流民	リュウミン	refugees
流用	リュウヨウ	multipurpose —*v*. use for other purposes
流量	リュウリョウ	*phy*. volume of floating fluid
流罪	ルザイ	banishment; exile
流転	ルテン	constant change; wandering; vagrancy; reincarnation —*vi*. change constantly; wander
流布	ルフ	circulation; dissemination —*vi*. circulate; spread; disseminate
流浪	ルロウ	wandering; roaming —*vi*. wander about; roam
訓 流す	ながす	*vt*. let flow
流し	ながし	sink
流れる	ながれる	*vi*. flow
流れ	ながれ	stream
¥ 流通機構	リュウツウキコウ	distribution/marketing system
流通市場	リュウツウシジョウ	secondary/trading market
流動資産	リュウドウシサン	current/liquid assets
流動負債	リュウドウフサイ	current/liquid liabilities

1201

涙 ⑩ 丶 冫 氵 氵 沪 沪 沪 沪 涙 涙

音 涙	ルイ	tear; sympathy
熟 涙腺	ルイセン	*med*. lachrymal/tear glands
訓 涙	なみだ	tear; sympathy
涙顔	なみだがお	tearful face
涙金	なみだキン	consolation money
涙声	なみだごえ	tearful voice
涙もろい	なみだもろい	given to weeping

心忄小戈戸手扌支攵文斗斤方日曰月肉月木欠止歹殳母毌比毛氏气水氺氵火灬亠父片牛犬犭王礻老

心忄小戈戸手扌支攵文斗斤方日曰月肉月木欠止歹殳母毋比毛氏气水氵・火灬爫父片牛犬犭王礻耂

1202 浪 ⑩

` ＼ ゝ シ ジ ジ シ̀ シ̄ 泊 浪 浪

音	浪	ロウ	waves; wander
熟	浪人	ロウニン	masterless samurai; student who has failed the university entrance examinations and will resit them the following year —*v*. be forced to resit university examinations
	浪費	ロウヒ	waste; squander —*v*. waste; squander
	浪漫主義	ロウマンシュギ	romanticism
	浪浪	ロウロウ	flowing; wandering

1203 液 ⑪

` ＼ ゝ シ ジ 氵 汸 汸 汸 液 液 液

音	液	エキ	liquid; fluid; juice; sap
熟	液化	エキカ	liquefaction —*v*. be liquefied
	液剤	エキザイ	liquid medicine
	液状	エキジョウ	liquid form
	液体	エキタイ	liquid substance; fluid
	液肥	エキヒ	liquid fertilizer

1204 涯 ⑪

` ＼ ゝ シ 汀 汀 汒 涯 涯 涯 涯

| 音 | 涯 | ガイ | horizon; shore; end |

1205 渇 ⑪

` ＼ ゝ シ 汀 沪 沪 沪 渇 渇 渇

音	渇	カツ	thirsty; yearn for
熟	渇する	カッする	*vi*. be/feel thirsty
	渇水	カッスイ	shortage of water; drought
	渇望	カツボウ	craving; earnest desire —*v*. crave/yearn for; be thirsty for
訓	渇く	かわく	*vi*. dry up; feel thirsty

1206

渓 ⑪ ` ` ⺡ ⺡ ⺡ ⺡ ⺡ 渓 渓 渓 渓

音	渓	ケイ	valley; canyon; gorge; ravine; river valley
熟	渓谷	ケイコク	gorge; ravine
	渓流	ケイリュウ	mountain torrent/stream
訓	※渓	たに	valley; ravine; gorge

1207

混 ⑪ ` ` ⺡ ⺡ ⺡ 沪 沪 沪 混 混 混

音	混	コン	mix
熟	混血児	コンケツジ	half-breed; child of mixed blood
	混合	コンゴウ	mixture —*v.* mix; mingle; blend; compound
	混雑	コンザツ	congestion; confusion; disorder —*vi.* be congested/confused; be in disorder
	混戦	コンセン	confused/free fight —*vi.* fight in confusion
	混線	コンセン	cross; contact; entanglement —*vi.* be crossed; be mixed up; be entangled
	混同	コンドウ	mixing; confusion; merger —*v.* confuse; confound; mix-up
	混沌	コントン	chaos; nebulosity; confusion
	混入	コンニュウ	mixing; mixture; blending —*v.* mix; mingle; blend
	混紡	コンボウ	mixed spinning
	混用	コンヨウ	composite —*v.* mingle; use together
	混乱	コンラン	confusion; disorder; chaos —*vi.* be confused/chaotic; be mixed up
訓	混ざる	まざる	*vi.* be mixed/blended
	混じる	まじる	*vi.* mix; mingle; blend
	混ぜる	まぜる	*vt.* blend; mix

1208

済 ⑪ ` ` ⺡ ⺡ 沪 沪 済 済 済 済 済

音	済	サイ	relieve; help; end; finish; repay
熟	済度	サイド	*Bud.* salvation; redemption —*v. Bud.* save; redeem
訓	済ます	すます	*vt.* finish; repay; payback; make do; manage; settle; solve

心 忄 小 戈 戸 手 扌 支 攵 文 斗 斤 方 日 曰 月 肉 月 木 欠 止 歹 殳 母 毋 比 毛 氏 气 水 氺 ⺡ 火 灬 爫 父 片 牛 犬 犭 王 礻 耂

済む	すむ	*vi.* be over; finish; be paid; settle; complete; manage
済みません	すみません	excuse me; pardon; sorry; thank you

心忄小戈戸手扌支攵文斗斤方日曰月肉月木欠止歹殳母毋比毛氏气水氺氵火灬爫父片牛犬犭王礻爿

1209

渋 ⑪ ` ` 氵 氵 汁 汁 沪 沪 渋 渋 渋

音	渋	ジュウ	astringent; hesitate
熟	渋滞	ジュウタイ	delay; congestion; traffic jam —*vi.* be delayed/held up/congested
	渋面	ジュウメン	frown; grimace
訓	渋	しぶ	persimmon tannin
	渋い	しぶい	astringent; quiet; tasteful; glum; sullen
	渋る	しぶる	*v.* hesitate; be reluctant; stick; be constipated
	渋々	しぶしぶ	unwillingly; reluctantly
	渋味	しぶミ	astringency

1210

淑 ⑪ ` ` 氵 氵 汁 汁 沫 沫 淑 淑

音	淑	シュク	graceful
熟	淑女	シュクジョ	lady

1211

渉 ⑪ ` ` 氵 氵 汁 沪 沪 沸 渉 渉

音	渉	ショウ	ford; cross over
熟	渉外	ショウガイ	public relations; liason

1212

深 ⑪ ` ` 氵 氵 汀 汀 泙 泙 深 深 深

音	深	シン	deep
熟	深遠	シンエン	profound; deep
	深淵	シンエン	abyss; the depths
	深海	シンカイ	deep sea
	深紅	シンク	deep red
	深呼吸	シンコキュウ	deep breathing —*vi.* breathe deeply

深刻	シンコク	serious; grave; critical
深山	シンザン	deep mountains
深謝	シンシャ	hearty thanks; sincere apology —v. express one's gratitude; make a sincere apology
深窓	シンソウ	tender care; happy family circumstances
深層	シンソウ	the depths
深長	シンチョウ	profound; deep
深度	シンド	depth
深部	シンブ	depth
深夜	シンヤ	midnight; dead of night
深緑	シンリョク	dark green
訓 深い	ふかい	deep; profound; late; serious
深まる	ふかまる	*vi*. become deep; deepen
深める	ふかめる	*vt*. make deep; deepen
深入り	ふかいり	deeply involved —*vi*. be deeply involved

1213

清 ⑪ 　 ` 冫 氵 汁 汁 沣 清 清 清 清

音 清	セイ (ショウ)	pure; clear; clean
熟 清閑	セイカン	quiet; secluded
清教徒	セイキョウト	Puritan
清潔	セイケツ	clean; untainted
清算	セイサン	liquidation; settlement; clearance —v. settle; clear; liquidate
清酒	セイシュ	refined saké
清純	セイジュン	purity; innocence
清書	セイショ	fair/clean copy —v. write a clean copy
清浄	セイジョウ	purity; innocence
清々	セイセイ	relief —*vi*. feel relieved
清楚	セイソ	neat and clear
清掃	セイソウ	cleaning —v. clean
清掃車	セイソウシャ	garbage truck; dustcart
清聴	セイチョウ	paying attention; listening quietly
清貧	セイヒン	honest poverty
清流	セイリュウ	limpid/clear stream
清涼	セイリョウ	cool; refreshing
清涼飲料水	セイリョウインリョウスイ	cooling/refreshing/soft drinks
清廉	セイレン	integrity; upright; honest

右欄（部首索引）：心 忄 小 戈 戸 手 扌 支 攵 文 斗 斤 方 日 曰 月 肉 月 木 欠 止 歹 殳 母 毋 比 毛 氏 气 水 氺 氵 火 灬 爪 父 片 牛 犬 犭 王 礻 歩

心忄小戈戸手扌支攴文斗斤方日曰月肉月木欠止歹殳母毋比毛氏气水氷氵●火灬 ﬦ 父片牛犬犭王礻⺹

訓	清い	きよい	clean; clear; pure
	清まる	きよまる	*vi*. become clean; be purified
	清める	きよめる	*vt*. cleanse; make clean; purify; purge
	※清水	しみず	clean/pure water; springwater

1214 淡 ⑪

` 丶 氵 氵 氵 氵 氵 氵 淡 淡 淡 淡 淡

音	淡	タン	light; plain; simple
熟	淡水	タンスイ	fresh water
	淡々	タンタン	indifference; being unconcerned; plainness; lightness
	淡泊(淡白)	タンパク	lightness; plainness; simplicity; candidness; frankness; indifference
訓	淡い	あわい	light; faint; pale
	淡雪	あわゆき	light snow

1215 添 ⑪

` 丶 氵 氵 氵 氵 沃 泝 添 添 添 添

音	添	テン	add
熟	添加	テンカ	annexing; addition —*v*. annex; append; affix; add
	添加物	テンカブツ	annex; appendix; addition; additive
	添削	テンサク	correction; editing —*v*. correct; look over; touch up
	添付	テンプ	appending; annexing —*v*. append; annex; attach
訓	添う	そう	*vi*. accompany; go with; marry; be married to
	添える	そえる	*vt*. add/attach to; affix; append; annex
	添え書き	そえがき	legend; postscript
	添状	そえジョウ	accompanying letter
	添え物	そえもの	addition; premium; giveaway; supplement

1216 涼 ⑪

` 丶 氵 氵 氵 氵 泸 泸 涼 涼 涼 涼

音	涼	リョウ	cool
熟	涼気	リョウキ	cool air
	涼風	リョウフウ	cool breeze

涼味	リョウミ	the cool; coolness
訓 涼しい	すずしい	cool; refreshing
涼む	すずむ	*vi.* cool off

1217

温 ⑫　 丶 〻 氵 沪 沪 沪 沪 沪 沪 渭 温 温 温

音 温	オン	warmth; temperature; gentle
熟 温顔	オンガン	warm expression
温厚	オンコウ	gentle; courteous
温室	オンシツ	hothouse; greenhouse
温室効果	オンシツコウカ	greenhouse effect
温順	オンジュン	obedient; gentle; submissive; docile
温床	オンショウ	hotbed; bed of soil enclosed in glass used for raising seedlings —*fig.* environment that favors rapid growth or development
温情	オンジョウ	warm; cordial; kind
温泉	オンセン	hot spring; spa
温存	オンゾン	preservation; maintainence —*v.* preserve; retain; keep
温帯	オンタイ	temperate zone
温暖	オンダン	mild; warm; temperate
温度	オンド	temperature
温良	オンリョウ	gentle; amiable
温和	オンワ	pleasantly mild; gentle hearted
訓 温かい	あたたかい	warm; mild; genial; kind
温か	あたたか	warm; mild
温かみ	あたたかみ	warmth
温まる	あたたまる	*vi.* get warm
温める	あたためる	*vt.* warm; heat; keep

1218

渦 ⑫　 丶 〻 氵 沪 沪 沪 沪 沪 渦 渦 渦 渦

音 渦	カ	whirlpool
熟 渦中	カチュウ	eddy; whirlpool; vortex
渦紋	カモン	scroll; scroll pattern
訓 渦	うず	eddy; whirlpool; vortex
渦潮	うずしお	swirling sea water
渦巻き	うずまき	eddy; whirlpool; vortex

心忄小戈戸手扌支攵文斗斤方日曰月肉月木欠止歹殳母毋比毛氏气水氺氵火灬罒父片牛犬犭王礻老

心
忄
小
戈
戸
手
扌
支
攵
文
斗
斤
方
日
曰
月
肉
月
木
欠
止
歹
殳
母
毋
比
毛
氏
气
水
氺
氵
火
灬
爫
爻
父
片
牛
犬
犭
王
礻
耂

1219 減 ⑫

`丶 丶 冫 氵 氵 汀 汻 汻 泂 泂 減 減 減`

音	減	ゲン	decrease; reduce
熟	減額	ゲンガク	reduction; cut —*v.* reduce; cut
	減収	ゲンシュウ	decrease in income; drop in revenue
	減少	ゲンショウ	decrease; diminution —*v.* fall off; go down; drop; diminish; be decreased/reduced
	減食	ゲンショク	diet —*vi.* eat less; cut down; diet
	減水	ゲンスイ	fall in water level —*v.* drop; fall; reduce
	減速	ゲンソク	speed reduction; deceleration —*v.* reduce speed; decelerate; slow down
	減退	ゲンタイ	decline —*vi.* decline; fall off; weaken; fail
	減点	ゲンテン	demerit marks; deducted points
	減量	ゲンリョウ	weight loss; losing weight —*v.* lose weight
訓	減る	へる	*vi.* decrease; diminish; run short; dwindle; drop; lose
	減らす	へらす	*vt.* reduce; decrease; cut down; take away
¥	減益	ゲンエキ	decrease of profit
	減産	ゲンサン	reduction/decrease in production/output; decreased production —*v.* decrease/reduce output/production
	減資	ゲンシ	capital reduction
	減税	ゲンゼイ	tax reduction/cut —*v.* reduce/cut/lower taxes
	減俸	ゲンポウ	salary reduction —*v.* reduce salaries

1220 湖 ⑫

`丶 丶 冫 氵 汁 汁 汰 汰 油 湖 湖 湖`

音	湖	コ	lake
熟	湖水	コスイ	lake
	湖畔	コハン	lakeside
訓	湖	みずうみ	lake

1221 港 ⑫

`丶 丶 冫 氵 汁 汁 洪 港 洪 洪 港 港`

音	港	コウ	port; harbor
熟	港口	コウコウ	harbor entrance

| 港湾 | コウワン | harbor |
| 訓 港 | みなと | port; harbor |

1222

滋 ⑫　丶　ヽ　冫　ジ　ジ　氵　氵　汴　滋　滋　滋　滋

音 滋	ジ	rich; luxurious
熟 滋味	ジミ	savoriness; tastiness; delicious; delicacy; rich food
滋養	ジョウ	nourishment; nutrition

1223

湿 ⑫　丶　ヽ　冫　氵　汀　汨　汨　汨　涅　湿　湿　湿

音 湿	シツ	moisten; damp; humid
熟 湿気	シッケ	moisture; humidity; damp
湿原	シツゲン	damp plain
湿潤	シツジュン	wet; damp; moist; humid
湿疹	シッシン	eczema
湿地	シッチ	damp ground
湿度	シツド	humidity
湿布	シップ	compress —*v.* compress
訓 湿る	しめる	*vi.* become damp; moist
湿す	しめす	*vt.* moisten; wet; make wet

1224

測 ⑫　丶　ヽ　氵　氵　汀　沪　泪　泪　泪　測　測　測

音 測	ソク	measure
熟 測算	ソクサン	measuring and calculating
測地	ソクチ	land surveying; geodetic
測定	ソクテイ	measurement —*v.* measure
測度	ソクド	measurement; gauging
測量	ソクリョウ	survey; measurement —*v.* survey; measure
測距儀	ソッキョギ	range finder
測候所	ソッコウジョ	weather station
訓 測る	はかる	*vt.* measure; estimate

4

心 忄 小 戈 戸 手 扌 支 攵 文 斗 斤 方 日 曰 月 肉 月 木 欠 止 歹 殳 母 毋 比 毛 氏 气 水 氺 氵 火 灬 爫 父 片 牛 犬 犭 王 礻 耂

1225 渡 ⑫
` ＇ ⺀ ⺀ 氵 沪 泸 泸 泸 泸 渡 渡

音	渡	ト	cross
熟	渡航	トコウ	voyage; passage; sailing; crossing —*vi*. make a passage; set sail for
	渡米	トベイ	going to America; visit to America —*vi*. go/visit/America; emigrate to America
	渡来	トライ	visit; introduction; importation; influx —*vi*. come over the sea; make an overseas visit; be introduced/brought over
訓	渡す	わたす	*vt*. pass over; carry across; hand over; transfer
	渡し	わたし	ferry crossing; delivery
	渡し船	わたしぶね	ferryboat; ferry *fig*. help
	渡る	わたる	*vi*. go over; cross; traverse; be imported; migrate
	渡り	わたり	passage; transit; negotiations
	渡り歩く	わたりあるく	*vi*. wander; go from one place to another

1226 湯 ⑫
` ＇ ⺀ 氵 沪 沪 浔 湨 湨 湯 湯 湯

音	湯	トウ	hot water
熟	湯治	トウジ	hot-spring cure; taking the baths —*v*. take the baths/waters
訓	湯	ゆ	hot water/bath; public bath
	湯気	ゆゲ	steam; vapor
	湯呑み	ゆのみ	teacup; cup; mug
	湯元	ゆもと	source of a hot spring

1227 満 ⑫
` ＇ ⺀ 氵 汁 汁 浐 浐 満 満 満 満

音	満	マン	full; abundant; Manchuria
熟	満員	マンイン	no vacancy; full
	満悦	マンエツ	great delight; rapture; satisfaction
	満開	マンカイ	in full bloom
	満期	マンキ	expiration
	満喫	マンキツ	enough; full —*v*. have enough; have one's fill of; enjoy to the full

542

満月	マンゲツ	full moon	**4**
満座	マンザ	the whole company; everyone present	
満載	マンサイ	full load —*v.* be fully loaded	
満州	マンシュウ	Manchuria	
満場	マンジョウ	the whole company/hall	
満場一致	マンジョウイッチ	unanimous	
満身	マンシン	the whole body	
満水	マンスイ	filled to the brim with water —*vi.* be filled to the brim with water	
満足	マンゾク	satisfaction; contentment —*vi.* be satisfied/contented with	
満潮	マンチョウ	high tide	
満天	マンテン	the whole sky	
満点	マンテン	full marks; perfect score	
満腹	マンプク	full stomach/belly	
満々	マンマン	full of; brimming with	
満面	マンメン	the whole face	
満了	マンリョウ	expiration	
満塁	マンルイ	*bas.* full base	

訓	満たす	みたす	*vt.* fill; satisfy; fulfill
	満ちる	みちる	*vi.* be full; (tide) come in; expire; be fulfilled
	満ち潮	みちしお	high tide

| ¥ | 満期 | マンキ | maturity |
| | 満期日 | マンキび | due date; date of maturity |

1228

湾 ⑫ 、 ⼆ ⼆ ⼆ ⼆ ⼆ ⼆ ⼆ ⼆ ⼆ 湾 湾

音	湾	ワン	bay; gulf
熟	湾岸	ワンガン	the Persian Gulf area; bay area
	湾岸戦争	ワンガンセンソウ	*hist.* Gulf War (1991)
	湾曲	ワンキョク	curve; curvature; bend —*vi.* curve; bend; be curved/bent
	湾内	ワンナイ	inside the bay
	湾流	ワンリュウ	Gulf Stream

1229

滑 ⑬ 、 ⼆ ⼆ ⼆ ⼆ ⼆ ⼆ ⼆ ⼆ 滑 滑 滑

| 音 | 滑 | カツ | slide; smooth |

543

心
忄
小
戈
戸
手
扌
支
攵
文
斗
斤
方
日
曰
月
肉
月
木
欠
止
歹
殳
母
毋
比
毛
氏
气
水
氷
氵
火
灬
爫
父
片
牛
犬
犭
王
礻
耂

心 忄 小 戈 戸 手 扌 支 攵 文 斗 斤 方 日 曰 月 肉 月 木 欠 止 歹 殳 母 毋 比 毛 氏 气 水 氺 氵 火 灬 爫 父 片 牛 犬 犭 王 礻 歺

熟	滑空機	カックウキ	glider
	滑降	カッコウ	downhill; descent —*vi.* descend a slope
	滑車	カッシャ	pulley
	滑走	カッソウ	gliding —*vi.* glide; plane; taxi
	滑稽	コッケイ	comic; amusing
訓	滑る	すべる	*vi.* slide; slip
	滑らか	なめらか	smooth

1230

漢 ⑬　丶 氵 氵 汁 汁 芦 芦 芦 芦 莫 漢 漢

音	漢	カン	Han dynasty; fellow
熟	漢学	カンガク	study of Chinese classics
	漢語	カンゴ	Chinese word
	漢詩	カンシ	Chinese poetry
	漢字	カンジ	*kanji* (Chinese character)
	漢数字	カンスウジ	Chinese numerals
	漢文	カンブン	Chinese classics
	漢方薬	カンポウヤク	medicinal herb
	漢民族	カンミンゾク	the Han race; the Chinese
	漢和辞典	カンワジテン	Chinese-character dictionary with Japanese definitions; *kanji* dictionary

1231

源 ⑬　丶 氵 氵 汀 沥 沥 沥 沥 沥 沥 源 源 源

音	源	ゲン	source
熟	源泉	ゲンセン	source; origin
	源流	ゲンリュウ	source; origin
訓	源	みなもと	source; origin
¥	源泉徴収	ゲンセン チョウシュウ	taxation at source

1232

溝 ⑬　丶 氵 氵 汁 汁 洪 洪 溝 溝 溝 溝 溝

| 音 | 溝 | コウ | ditch |
| 訓 | 溝 | みぞ | ditch; gutter; drain; groove; gap |

1233

準 ⑬ ニ ニ ゝ シ゚ ジ ジ シ冫 シ产 冫隹 淮 進 準

音	準	ジュン	rule; standard; measure
熟	準じる	ジュンじる	*vi.* follow; conform
	準急	ジュンキュウ	local express
	準拠	ジュンキョ	based on; following — *vi.* be based on; follow
	準決勝	ジュンケッショウ	semi-final
	準備	ジュンビ	preparations — *v.* prepare; make preparations; get ready
	準用	ジュンヨウ	corresponding application — *vt.* apply correspondingly
¥	準備金	ジュンビキン	reserve fund

1234

滞 ⑬ ニ ニ 氵 汁 汁 滞 滞 滞 滞 滞 滞 滞 滞

音	滞	タイ	stagnate; stay
熟	滞貨	タイカ	freight congestion; backlog; stockpiles
	滞空	タイクウ	staying in the air; flying — *vi.* stay airborne; fly
	滞在	タイザイ	stay; stop; sojourn — *vi.* stay; stop; sojourn
	滞日	タイニチ	staying in Japan — *vi.* stay in Japan
	滞納	タイノウ	nonpayment; default; failure to pay — *v.* default on payments; fail to keep up payments
	滞留	タイリュウ	stay; visit; sojourn — *vi.* stay; visit; sojourn
訓	滞る	とどこおる	*vi.* stagnate; be stagnant; be left undone; fall into arrears

1235

滝 ⑬ ニ ニ ゞ 氵 汁 汁 浐 浐 潅 潅 潅 滝

訓	滝	たき	waterfall
	滝壷	たきつぼ	basin of a waterfall

1236

漠 ⑬ ニ ニ 氵 汁 汁 沽 沽 洁 洁 渲 淔 漠 漠

音	漠	バク	vast; boundless; vague; obscure
熟	漠然	バクゼン	vague; obscure; ambiguous

4

心忄小戈戸手扌支攴文斗斤方日曰月肉月木欠止歹殳母毋比毛氏气水氺氵火灬爫父片牛犬犭王礻耂

1237

滅 ⑬　ミ　ミ　氵　汦　汀　汀　汀　涀　涀　滅　滅　滅

音	滅	メツ	ruin; perish; die out
熟	滅茶苦茶	メチャクチャ	incoherent; preposterous; mess; wreck; ruin
	滅却	メッキャク	destruction —*v.* extinguish; destroy
	滅多	メッタ	seldom; rarely
	滅亡	メツボウ	destruction —*vi.* be destroyed/wasted/exhausted
	滅裂	メツレツ	in chaos; incoherent
※	滅入る	めいる	*vi.* discouraged; shattered; let down
訓	滅びる	ほろびる	*vi.* perish; fall into ruin; die out
	滅ぼす	ほろぼす	*vt.* ruin; destroy; overthrow; annihilate

1238

溶 ⑬　ミ　氵　氵ˊ　氵ˊ　汸　汸　汸　浐　浐　浐　溶　溶

音	溶	ヨウ	dissolve; melt
熟	溶液	ヨウエキ	solution
	溶解	ヨウカイ	solution; melting —*v.* melt; dissolve
	溶岩	ヨウガン	lava
	溶鉱炉	ヨウコウロ	blast furnace
	溶剤	ヨウザイ	solvent
	溶性	ヨウセイ	soluble
	溶接	ヨウセツ	welding —*v.* weld
	溶媒	ヨウバイ	solvent
	溶融	ヨウユウ	molten —*vi.* fuse; melt
訓	溶かす	とかす	*vt.* melt; dissolve
	溶く	とく	*vt.* dissolve; melt
	溶ける	とける	*vi.* dissolve; thaw; melt

1239

演 ⑭　ミ　氵ˊ　氵ˊ　汢　汢　汢　洰　洰　演　演　演　演

音	演	エン	state; act; apply
熟	演じる	エンじる	perform; play act; act
	演技	エンギ	acting; performance —*vi.* act; perform
	演芸	エンゲイ	performance; dramatic art

演劇	エンゲキ	play; drama
演算	エンザン	***math.*** operation —***v.*** operate; calculate; cipher; figure out
演習	エンシュウ	seminar; practice; exercise —***vi.*** practice; carry out exercises
演出	エンシュツ	production —***v.*** produce; stage; present
演説	エンゼツ	public speech; oration; address —***v.*** make a speech; address
演奏	エンソウ	musical performance —***v.*** give a musical performance
演壇	エンダン	platform; rostrum

1240

漁⑭ シ ミ デ ジ 沪 沪 渔 渔 渔 渔 渔 渔

音	漁	ギョ リョウ	fishing; angling
熟	漁獲	ギョカク	fishery; fishing; haul; catch
	漁業	ギョギョウ	fishery; the fishing industry
	漁具	ギョグ	fishing tackle
	漁港	ギョコウ	fishing harbor
	漁場	ギョジョウ	fishing ground
	漁村	ギョソン	fishing village/community
	漁夫	ギョフ	fisherman; fisher
	漁民	ギョミン	fishermen; fishing people
	漁師	リョウシ	fishermen
訓	※漁火	いさりび	fisherman's fire

1241

漆⑭ シ ミ ニ 汁 汁 沐 沐 漆 漆 漆 漆 漆

音	漆	シツ	Japanese lacquer
熟	漆器	シッキ	lacquerware
	漆黒	シッコク	jet-black
訓	漆	うるし	lacquer

1242

漸⑭ シ ミ ニ 汀 沪 沪 泻 渐 渐 渐 漸 漸

| 音 | 漸 | ゼン | gradually |

心 忄 小 戈 戸 手 扌 支 攵 文 斗 斤 方 日 曰 月 肉 月 木 欠 止 歹 殳 母 毋 比 毛 氏 气 水 氺 氵 火 灬 ⺈ 父 片 牛 犬 犭 王 礻 ⺹

心 忄 小 戈 戸 手 扌 支 攵 文 斗 斤 方 日 曰 月 肉 月 木 欠 止 歹 殳 母 毋 比 毛 氏 气 水 氺 氵 火 灬 爫 父 片 牛 犬 犭 王 礻 耂

熟	漸減	ゼンゲン	diminution; gradual decrease —*v.* diminish; decrease gradually
	漸次	ゼンジ	gradually
	漸進	ゼンシン	gradual procession —*vi.* proceed gradually
	漸増	ゼンゾウ	gradual increase —*v.* increase gradually

1243

漬 ⑭ ⅰ ⅰ⁻ ⅰ⁺ ⅰ⁺ 汢 清 清 清 清 清 漬

音	漬	（シ）	soak; pickle
訓	漬ける	つける	*vt.* soak; salt; pickle; preserve
	漬物	つけもの	*tsukemono* (Japanese pickles)
	漬かる	つかる	*vi.* soak; be soaked in/seasoned

1244

滴 ⑭ ⅰ ⅰ ⅰ⁻ 泸 泸 泸 滴 滴 滴 滴 滴

音	滴	テキ	drop
訓	滴	しずく	drop
	滴る	したたる	*vi.* drip; drop; dribble
	滴り	したたり	dripping; drop; trickle; dribble

1245

漂 ⑭ ⅰ ⅰ⁻ 沪 沪 沪 浬 浬 浬 潭 漂 漂

音	漂	ヒョウ	drift; float
熟	漂着	ヒョウチャク	drifting ashore —*vi.* drift ashore; be washed/cast ashore
	漂白	ヒョウハク	bleach —*v.* bleach
	漂泊	ヒョウハク	wandering; roaming; drifting —*vi.* wander; roam; drift
	漂流	ヒョウリュウ	drifting —*vi.* drift
訓	漂う	ただよう	drift; float

1246

漫 ⑭ ⅰ ⅰ 沪 沪 沪 沪 浬 浬 浬 漫 漫

| 音 | 漫 | マン | rambling; aimless; involuntarily |

熟	漫画	マンガ	cartoon; comic book/strip
	漫才	マンザイ	comic dialog
	漫然	マンゼン	random; rambling; careless
	漫談	マンダン	idle chat —vi. chat idly
	漫読	マンドク	light reading —vi. do some light reading
	漫筆	マンピツ	notes; random thoughts; jottings
	漫歩	マンポ	stroll; walk; rambling —vi. stroll; walk; ramble
	漫遊	マンユウ	tour; trip; travel —vi. make a tour/trip; travel
訓	※漫ろ	そぞろ	involuntarily; in spite of oneself; somehow

1247

漏 ⑭ シ 汀 沪 沪 沪 沪 渭 漏 漏 漏 漏 漏

音	漏	ロウ	leak; be disclosed
熟	漏洩	ロウエイ	leakage; disclosure —v. leak out; be let out/revealed
	漏出	ロウシュツ	leaking out; escape —v. leak out; escape
	漏水	ロウスイ	water leakage —vi. leak
	漏電	ロウデン	short circuit —vi. short circuit
	漏斗	ロウト	funnel
訓	漏らす	もらす	vt. reveal; divulge
	漏る	もる	vi. leak; be disclosed
	漏れる	もれる	vi. leak; be disclosed

1248

潟 ⑮ ゝ 氵 氵 氵 氵 沪 沪 沪 沪 潟 潟 潟

音	潟	セキ	lagoon; inlet; beach
訓	潟	かた	lagoon; inlet; beach

1249

潔 ⑮ シ 氵 汁 津 津 潔 潔 潔 潔 潔 潔

音	潔	ケツ	pure
熟	潔白	ケッパク	innocence; purity
	潔癖	ケッペキ	clean; fastidious; punctilious
訓	潔い	いさぎよい	manly; frank; honorable; brave

心忄小戈戸手扌支攵文斗斤方日曰月肉月木欠止歹殳母毋比毛氏气水氺氵火灬爪父片牛犬犭王礻耂

心 忄 小 戈 戸 手 扌 支 攵 文 斗 斤 方 日 曰 月 肉 月 木 欠 止 歹 殳 母 毋 比 毛 氏 气 水 氷 氵 火 灬 爪 父 片 牛 犬 犭 王 礻 耂

1250

潤 ⑮　シ シ 沪 沪 沪 沪 沪 沪 沪 潤 潤 潤

音	潤	ジュン	be moistened
熟	潤滑	ジュンカツ	lubrication
	潤滑油	ジュンカツユ	lubricating oil
	潤色	ジュンショク	embellishment —*v.* embellish; color
	潤沢	ジュンタク	abundance
訓	潤う	うるおう	*vi.* be moistened; benefit; enrich; help
	潤す	うるおす	*vt.* wet; water; moisten; benefit (someone); enrich (someone)
	潤む	うるむ	*vi.* be wet/emotional
	潤い	うるおい	moisture

1251

潜 ⑮　シ シ 氵 浐 浐 浐 浐 浐 浐 潜 潜 潜

音	潜	セン	dive; hide
熟	潜行	センコウ	undercover activity; incognito —*vi.* travel incognito; go underground
	潜航	センコウ	submarine voyage —*vi.* cruise underwater; be submerged
	潜在	センザイ	latent; hidden; potential —*vi.* be latent/hidden; have potential
	潜水	センスイ	diving; submerging —*vi.* dive; submerge
	潜水艦	センスイカン	submarine
	潜水服	センスイフク	diving suit
	潜入	センニュウ	infiltration —*vi.* infiltrate
	潜伏	センプク	latency; dormancy —*vi.* hide; be hidden/dormant/latent
	潜望鏡	センボウキョウ	periscope
訓	潜む	ひそむ	*v.* lurk; lie hidden
	潜める	ひそめる	*vt.* conceal; hide
	潜る	もぐる	*vi.* dive; crawl into; crawl under; intiltrate

1252

潮 ⑮　シ シ 氵 汁 沽 沽 沽 渣 渣 潮 潮 潮

音	潮	チョウ	tide; salt water

550

熟	潮流	チョウリュウ	tide; current; trend; tendency
訓	潮	しお	tide; current; sea water; brine; opportunity; chance
	潮風	しおかぜ	sea breeze
	潮騒	しおさい	sound of the waves/sea
	潮時	しおどき	tidal hour; opportunity; chance
	潮干狩り	しおひがり	gathering sea shells (at low tide)

1253

澄 ⑮　氵 氵 氵 氵 浐 浐 浐 浐 浐 澄 澄 澄

音	澄	チョウ	clear
訓	澄ます	すます	*vt*. clear; make clear; clarify; look demure/prim
	澄む	すむ	*vi*. become clear; clear; clarify

1254

激 ⑯　氵 氵 氵 沪 沪 浄 渭 渭 渭 激 激 激

音	激	ゲキ	violent; acute; sharp; sudden; excite; encourage
熟	激する	ゲキする	*v*. get excited; be agitated
	激化	ゲキカ	intensification —*vi*. become intense; intensify
	激減	ゲキゲン	sharp/marked decrease —*vi*. fall sharply; drop sharply
	激震	ゲキシン	severe earthquake
	激戦	ゲキセン	fierce battle
	激増	ゲキゾウ	sharp increase; sudden rise —*vi*. increase sharply; show a sudden increase
	激痛	ゲキツウ	acute/sharp pain
	激怒	ゲキド	wrath; rage; fury —*vi*. be enraged by; be infuriated at; fly into a rage
	激動	ゲキドウ	violent shaking/shock; excitement; turbulence —*vi*. shake violently; be excited/turbulent
	激突	ゲキトツ	crash —*vi*. crash; smash into
	激変	ゲキヘン	violent/sudden change —*vi*. undergo a violent/sudden/rapid change
	激務	ゲキム	hard work; demanding job; pressing duties
	激流	ゲキリュウ	rapids; torrent; swift current
	激励	ゲキレイ	encouragement —*v*. encourage; cheer up
	激烈	ゲキレツ	violence
	激論	ゲキロン	hot argument; heated discussion

訓 激しい　はげしい　　　violent; extreme; severe; intense

左側縦書き部首リスト：
心 忄 小 戈 戸 手 扌 支 攵 文 斗 斤 方 日 曰 月 肉 月 木 欠 止 歹 殳 母 毋 比 毛 氏 气 水 氺 氵 火 灬 ⺗ 父 片 牛 犬 犭 王 礻 耂

1255

濁 ⑯　氵 氵 氵 氵 氵 氵 氵 氵 氵 濁 濁 濁 濁

音　濁　　ダク　　　become muddy

熟　濁音　　ダクオン　　sonant; voiced sound

　　濁点　　ダクテン　　symbol used to indicate a voiced sound in written Japanese (゛)

　　濁流　　ダクリュウ　　muddy stream

訓　濁す　　にごす　　*vt.* make muddy/cloudy; speak ambiguously

　　濁る　　にごる　　*vi.* become muddy; have a voiced sound; be vague

　　濁り　　にごり　　muddiness; turbidity; voiced sound

1256

濃 ⑯　氵 氵 氵 氵 氵 氵 濃 濃 濃 濃 濃 濃 濃

音　濃　　ノウ　　　thick

熟　濃厚　　ノウコウ　　thickness; density; deepening

　　濃縮　　ノウシュク　　concentration; enrichment; graduation —*v.* concentrate; enrich; graduate

　　濃淡　　ノウタン　　light and shade

　　濃度　　ノウド　　density; thickness; concentration

　　濃霧　　ノウム　　dense fog

訓　濃い　　こい　　dark; deep; thick; heavy; strong (coffee, etc.); close; intimate

---

1257

濯 ⑰　氵 氵 氵 氵 濯 濯 濯 濯 濯 濯 濯 濯

音　濯　　タク　　　wash

1258

濫 ⑱　氵 氵 氵 氵 氵 氵 氵 濫 濫 濫 濫 濫

音　濫　　ラン　　　overflow; excessive; indiscriminate

熟　濫造　　ランゾウ　　overproduction; careless manufacture —*v.* overproduce; manufacture carelessly

552

濫読	ランドク	indiscriminate/random reading —*v.* read indiscriminately/randomly
濫費	ランピ	waste; extravagance —*v.* waste; dissipate; lavish; squander
濫用	ランヨウ	abuse; misuse; misappropriation —*v.* abuse; misuse; missappropriate

1259

瀬 ⑲　氵　氵　尸　戸　沪　沪　沪　沪　瀬　瀬　瀬

訓	瀬	せ	rapids; torrent; current; shallows; shoal
	瀬戸際	せとぎわ	critical moment; crisis
	瀬戸物	せともの	porcelain; china; earthenware; crockery

---

4 火　ひ／ひへん　fire　ハ丶丶 (p.558)

1260

火 ④　丶　丶ヽ　少　火

音	火	カ	fire; flame; light
熟	火炎	カエン	flames; blaze
	火気	カキ	fire; heat of fire
	火器	カキ	firearms
	火口	カコウ	(volcano) crater; muzzle (of a gun)
	火災	カサイ	fire; conflagration; large disastrous fire
	火山	カザン	volcano
	火事	カジ	fire; conflagration; disastrous fire
	火星	カセイ	the planet Mars
	火勢	カセイ	force of the flames
	火葬	カソウ	cremation —*v.* cremate
	火薬	カヤク	gunpowder; explosives
	火曜日	カヨウび	Tuesday
	火力	カリョク	heat; calorific force; thermal power
訓	火	ひ	fire; flame; light
	火加減	ひカゲン	how well/poorly a fire is burning
	火箸	ひばし	tongs
	火柱	ひばしら	pillar of fire
	火鉢	ひばち	charcoal brazier
	火花	ひばな	sparks; hot glowing particles heated by friction

心
忄
小
戈
戸
手
扌
支
攵
文
斗
斤
方
日
曰
月
肉
月
木
欠
止
歹
殳
母
毋
比
毛
氏
气
水
氺
氵
火
灬
爫
父
片
牛
犬
犭
王
礻
耂

火蓋	ひぶた	cover（of a gun barrel）
火元	ひもと	origin of a fire
火	ほ	fire
火影	ほかげ	firelight; flickering light
※火傷	やけど	burn; injury resulting from exposure to fire/heat —*vi.* be/get burnt; have/suffer a burn

1261

灰 ⑥　　一 厂 厂 灰 灰 灰

音	灰	カイ	ash
熟	灰塵	カイジン	ashes
訓	灰	はい	ash
	灰色	はいいろ	gray *fig.* hopelessness; uncertain attitude
	灰神楽	はいかぐら	cloud of ashes
	灰皿	はいざら	ashtray

1262

灯 ⑥　　丶 丷 少 火 灯 灯

音	灯	トウ	light
熟	灯火	トウカ	light/lamplight
	灯下	トウカ	by lamplight
	灯心	トウシン	lampwick
	灯台	トウダイ	lighthouse/light/beacon
	灯油	トウユ	lamp oil; kerosene
	灯篭	トウロウ	garden/hanging lantern
訓	灯	ひ	light

1263

災 ⑦　　く くく くくく くくく くくく 巛 災

音	災	サイ	calamity; disaster; misforture
熟	災禍	サイカ	disaster; calamity
	災害	サイガイ	disaster; calamity
	災難	サイナン	misfortune; disaster; accident
	災厄	サイヤク	disaster; misfortune; catastrophe
訓	災い	わざわい	disaster; misfortune; calamity

1264

炎 ⑧ 　 丶 　 丶 　 丷 　 火 　 火 　 炏 　 炏 　 炎

音	炎	エン	flame; hot; heat; inflammation
熟	炎々	エンエン	flaming; blazing
	炎暑	エンショ	intense heat
	炎症	エンショウ	*med.* inflammation
	炎上	エンジョウ	in flames; destruction by fire —*vi.* be destroyed by fire; be burnt down
訓	炎	ほのお	flame

1265

炊 ⑧ 　 丶 　 丶 　 丷 　 火 　 火 　 炉 　 炒 　 炊

音	炊	スイ	boil
熟	炊事	スイジ	cooking; kitchen work —*vi.* cook; do the cooking
	炊事場	スイジば	kitchen; cookery; cookhouse
	炊飯	スイハン	cooking rice
	炊飯器	スイハンキ	rice cooker
訓	炊く	たく	*vt.* boil; cook

1266

炉 ⑧ 　 丶 　 丶 　 丷 　 火 　 炉 　 炉 　 炉 　 炉

音	炉	ロ	hearth; furnace
熟	炉だな	ロだな	mantelpiece
	炉端	ロばた	fireside; hearth
	炉辺	ロヘン	fireside; hearth

1267

炭 ⑨ 　 丶 　 屮 　 屮 　 屵 　 戸 　 岸 　 岸 　 岸 　 炭

音	炭	タン	charcoal; coal
熟	炭坑	タンコウ	coal mine
	炭鉱	タンコウ	coal mine
	炭酸	タンサン	*chem.* carbonic acid

555

4

心 忄 小 戈 戸 手 扌 支 攵 文 斗 斤 方 日 曰 月 肉 月 木 欠 止 歹 殳 母 毋 比 毛 氏 气 水 氺 氵 火 灬 宀 父 片 牛 犬 犭 王 礻 耂

心忄小戈戸手扌支攵文斗斤方日曰月肉月木欠止歹殳母毋比毛氏气水氺氵火灬爫父片牛犬犭王礻耂

炭酸水	タンサンスイ	*chem.* carbonated water
炭水化物	タンスイカブツ	carbohydrate
炭素	タンソ	carbon
炭田	タンデン	coal field
訓 炭	すみ	charcoal

1268

焼 ⑫ 丶 丷 丷 火 灯 灯 炸 炸 烒 焼 焼 焼

音	焼	ショウ	burn
熟	焼却	ショウキャク	burning; incineration —*v.* burn up; incinerate
	焼却炉	ショウキャクロ	incinerator
	焼香	ショウコウ	incense offering —*vi.* burn incense
	焼死	ショウシ	death by fire —*vi.* be burned to death
	焼失	ショウシツ	destruction by fire —*vi.* be burned down; be destroyed by fire
	焼酎	ショウチュウ	*shōchū* (white distilled liquor)
訓	焼く	やく	*v.* burn; heat; bake; grill; boil; roast
	焼ける	やける	*vi.* be burned/grilled/sun-tanned
	焼き餅	やきもち	toasted rice cake *fig.* jealousy
	焼き物	やきもの	ceramic ware; pottery; porcelain; china

1269

煙 ⑬ 丶 丷 火 灯 灯 炉 炉 炉 炉 煙 煙 煙

音	煙	エン	smoke; smoking
熟	煙雨	エンウ	drizzling rain; drizzle
	煙害	エンガイ	smoke pollution
	煙毒	エンドク	smoke pollution
	煙突	エントツ	chimney; smokestack
	煙幕	エンマク	smoke screen
	煙霧	エンム	smoke and fog; smog
訓	煙	けむり	smoke; fumes
	煙る	けむる	*vi.* smoke; smoulder
	煙い	けむい	smoky
	煙たい	けむたい	smoky; feeling awkward
	煙たがる	けむたがる	*vi.* be sensitive to smoke; feel awkward; keep away from (a person)
	※煙管	きせる	long-stemmed pipe
	※煙草	たばこ	tobacco; cigarette

1270

煩 ⑬ 　 丶 丷 火 灯 灯 炉 炉 炉 煩 煩 煩 煩

音	煩	ハン（ボン）	troublesome
熟	煩雑	ハンザツ	trouble; agony; worry
	煩悶	ハンモン	agony; anguish; worry; qualm —*vi.* be in agony; fret; worry; be troubled
	煩悩	ボンノウ	evil/worldly passions; lust; carnal desire
訓	煩う	わずらう	*v.* be ill/sick; suffer from; be afflicted with
	煩わしい	わずらわしい	troublesome; onerous; annoying; cumbersome
	煩わす	わずらわす	*vt.* trouble; bother; keep busy; annoy; plague; pester

1271

燃 ⑯ 　 丶 丷 火 火 灯 灼 炒 炒 燃 燃 燃 燃

音	燃	ネン	burn
熟	燃焼	ネンショウ	combustion; burning; ignition —*vi.* combust; burn; ignite
	燃料	ネンリョウ	fuel
訓	燃える	もえる	*vi.* burn; blaze; be in flames
	燃す	もす	*vt.* burn; light; kindle; ignite
	燃やす	もやす	*vt.* burn; kindle; ignite

1272

燥 ⑰ 　 丶 火 火 灯 炉 炉 炉 焯 焯 燥 燥

音	燥	ソウ	dry

1273

爆 ⑲ 　 丶 火 灯 炉 炉 焊 焊 爆 爆 爆 爆

音	爆	バク	explode; bomb
熟	爆音	バクオン	roaring; explosion; detonation
	爆撃	バクゲキ	bombing; bombardment from the air —*v.* bomb; drop bombs; make a bombing raid

557

心 忄 小 戈 戸 手 扌 支 攵 文 斗 斤 方 日 曰 月 肉 月 木 欠 止 歹 殳 母 毋 比 毛 氏 气 水 氷 氵 火 灬 爫 父 片 牛 犬 犭 王 礻 耂

心忄小戈戸手扌支攵文斗斤方日曰月肉月欠止歹殳母毋比毛氏气水氺氵●火灬爫父片牛犬犭王礻耂

爆死	バクシ	death from bombing —*vi.* bomb to death; be killed by bombing
爆笑	バクショウ	burst/roar of laughter —*vi.* burst out laughing
爆弾	バクダン	bomb
爆沈	バクチン	sinking by explosion; blowing up and sinking —*v.* blow up and sink
爆破	バクハ	blasting; blowing up; explosion —*v.* blast; blow up; explode
爆発	バクハツ	explosion; detonation; blowing up —*vi.* explode; detonate; blow up
爆風	バクフウ	bombshell blast; blast from an explosion
爆薬	バクヤク	explosive compound; detonator; blasting powder

---

4 ハ丶 よつてん/れっか fire in a row; four dots

1274

⑨

丶 ソ ゾ 尹 为 为 為 為 為 為

音	為	イ	do; for
熟	為政者	イセイシャ	ruler; governor; statesman; administrator
訓	為	ため	benefit; interests; sake; advantage; profit
	為す	なす	*vt.* do; perform; commit; practice; carry out
¥	※為替	かわせ	money order; exchange; transfer
	※為替裁定	かわせサイテイ	arbitration of exchange
	※為替差益	かわせサえき	(foreign) exchange profit/gain
	※為替差損	かわせサソン	(foreign) exchange loss; loss from currency fluctuation
	※為替相場	かわせソウば	foreign exchange rate
	※為替手形	かわせてがた	bill of exchange
	※為替取組	かわせとりくみ	negotiation of export bills
	※為替予約	かわせヨヤク	exchange contract

1275

⑨

丨 卜 ┝ 占 占 占 点 点 点

| 音 | 点 | テン | dot; spot; mark; grades; points; score; fault; defect; item; piece |
| 熟 | 点火 | テンカ | ignition; lighting —*vi.* ignite; light; kindle; set off; fire |

点眼	テンガン	dropping eyedrops in the eyes —*v.* apply eyewash; drop eyedrops in the eyes
点検	テンケン	inspection; examination; checking; muster —*v.* inspect; examine; scrutinize; check
点呼	テンコ	roll call; calling of the roll —*v.* call the roll
点在	テンザイ	scattered —*vi.* be dotted with; be scattered
点字	テンジ	braille type; braille; raised letters
点心	テンジン	sweets served with tea
点数	テンスウ	marks; points; score; number of articles
点線	テンセン	dotted/perforated line
点滴	テンテキ	falling drop of water; raindrops; intravenous drip
点々	テンテン	here and there; sporadically; in drops
点灯	テントウ	lighting —*vi.* light; light up; turn on a light
点描	テンビョウ	sketch
点滅	テンメツ	on/off —*v.* switch on and off
訓 点ける	つける	*vt.* light; put a match to; turn/switch on

1276

 烈 ⑩　一　ア　歹　歹　歹　列　列　烈　烈　烈

音 烈	レツ	violent; intense
熟 烈火	レッカ	raging fire
烈日	レツジツ	blazing sun
烈震	レッシン	violent earthquake
烈風	レップウ	gale
烈々	レツレツ	ardent; fierce; fervent
訓 ※烈しい	はげしい	violent; intense

1277

 煮 ⑫　一　十　土　耂　耂　者　者　者　者　者　煮　煮

音 煮	シャ	boil
熟 煮沸	シャフツ	boiling —*v.* boil
訓 煮る	にる	*vt.* boil; simmer; stew
煮える	にえる	*vi.* be cooked; cook
煮込む	にこむ	*vt.* boil well; cook together
煮立つ	にたつ	*vi.* boil briskly
煮物	にもの	cooking
煮やす	にやす	*v.* be cooked; cook

559

心忄小戈戸手扌支攵文斗斤方日曰月肉月木欠止歹殳母毋比毛氏气水氷氵火灬●⺍父片牛犬犭王礻耂

1278

焦 ⑫ ノ イ イ′ 广 什 仹 隹 隹 焦 焦 焦 焦

音	焦	ショウ	scorch; burn; impatience
熟	焦燥	ショウソウ	fretfulness; impatience
	焦点	ショウテン	focus; center; crucial point
	焦土	ショウド	scorched land
	焦慮	ショウリョ	impatience; worry; anguish —*vi.* be impatient; worry; feel anxious
訓	焦る	あせる	*vi.* be in a hurry; be impatient/anxious
	焦がす	こがす	*vt.* burn; scorch
	焦げる	こげる	*vi.* be burned/charred/scorched
	焦がれる	こがれる	*vi.* crave; yearn; be ardently in love

1279

然 ⑫ ノ ク タ タ タ゛ 矴 殊 然 然 然 然 然

音	然	ゼン	yes
		ネン	nature

1280

無 ⑫ ノ ′ ⌐ ⌐ 仁 仨 無 無 無 無 無 無 無

音	無	ム	nothing; without; (prefix) -less, -free, un-
		ブ	
熟	無愛想	ブアイソウ	unsociable; curt
	無遠慮	ブエンリョ	unreserved; forward; impertinent
	無気味	ブキミ	ominous; eerie; uncanny
	無器用	ブキヨウ	unskillful; clumsy
	無骨	ブコツ	boorish; uncouth
	無細工	ブサイク	clumsy; plain; ugly
	無作法	ブサホウ	bad manners; rudeness
	無事	ブジ	safe and sound
	無精	ブショウ	idle; lazy
	無勢	ブゼイ	numerical inferiority
	無難	ブナン	safe; not dangerous; acceptable
	無用心	ブヨウジン	carelessness
	無礼	ブレイ	rudeness; discourtesy

無意義	ムイギ	meaningless; not significant
無意識	ムイシキ	unconscious; involuntary
無意味	ムイミ	meaningless; pointless
無医村	ムイソン	doctorless village
無一物	ムイチモツ	penniless; possessionless
無一文	ムイチモン	penniless
無益	ムエキ	useless; futile
無縁	ムエン	unrelated; with no surviving relatives
無価	ムカ	priceless
無我	ムガ	selflessness; self-forgetfulness
無我夢中	ムガムチュウ	total absorption; being totally involved in; forgetting oneself
無害	ムガイ	harmless
無学	ムガク	uneducated; ignorant
無学文盲	ムガクモンモウ	uneducated and illiterate
無価値	ムカチ	worthless
無関心	ムカンシン	indifference; unconcern; apathy
無期	ムキ	indefinite (period of time)
無機	ムキ	inorganic
無傷	ムきず	undamaged; unblemished; unhurt
無軌道	ムキドウ	trackless; erratic; aberrant
無記名	ムキメイ	unregistered
無休	ムキュウ	no holidays; always open
無給	ムキュウ	unpaid; non-salaried
無気力	ムキリョク	spiritless; flabby; gutless
無口	むくち	reticent; taciturn; laconic
無下	ムゲ	(refuse) flatly/roundly
無形	ムケイ	intangible
無形文化財	ムケイブンカザイ	intangible cultural assets (the skills of art, music and drama)
無欠	ムケツ	flawless; faultless
無限	ムゲン	infinite
無効	ムコウ	invalid; null; void; ineffective
無根	ムコン	groundless; unfounded
無言	ムゴン	silent; mute
無罪	ムザイ	innocent; not guilty
無差別	ムサベツ	indiscriminate
無産	ムサン	without property
無産者	ムサンシャ	proletariat
無残	ムザン	cruel; ruthless; pitiful
無私	ムシ	unselfish; disinterested
無視	ムシ	disregard —v. ignore; disregard

心 忄 小 戈 戸 手 扌 支 攵 文 斗 斤 方 日 曰 月 肉 月 木 欠 止 歹 殳 母 毋 比 毛 氏 气 水 氷 氵 火 灬 ● 爫 父 片 牛 犬 犭 王 礻 耂

心忄小戈戸手扌支攵文斗斤方日曰月肉月木欠止歹殳母毋比毛氏气水氺氵火灬☰爻父片牛犬犭王礻歺

無地	ムジ	solid color; patternless
無実	ムジツ	false; unfounded; innocent
無慈悲	ムジヒ	merciless; ruthless
無邪気	ムジャキ	innocent; ingenuous
無償	ムショウ	free of charge; gratuitous
無上	ムジョウ	supreme; greatest; highest
無情	ムジョウ	unfeeling; callous; cruel
無常	ムジョウ	transitory; mutable; uncertain
無条件	ムジョウケン	unconditional
無色	ムショク	colorless; achromatic
無職	ムショク	no occupation; unemployed
無所属	ムショゾク	independent; unaffiliated
無心	ムシン	not thinking of anything
無神経	ムシンケイ	dull; insensitive; unfeeling
無尽蔵	ムジンゾウ	inexhaustible supply
無人地帯	ムジンチタイ	no man's land
無人島	ムジントウ	uninhabited island
無数	ムスウ	innumerable; countless
無声	ムセイ	silent; mute; voiceless; noiseless
無税	ムゼイ	duty-free; tax-free
無制限	ムセイゲン	unlimited; unrestricted
無生物	ムセイブツ	inanimate object
無責任	ムセキニン	irresponsibility
無線	ムセン	wireless; radio
無銭	ムセン	without money; penniless
無造作	ムゾウサ	with ease; simple; artless
無駄	ムダ	futile; useless; wasteful
無断	ムダン	unannounced; unauthorized
無知	ムチ	ignorance
無恥	ムチ	shameless; brazen
無茶	ムチャ	absurd; rash; excessive
無茶苦茶	ムチャクチャ	mixed up; confused; nonsensical; reckless
無賃	ムチン	free of charge
無敵	ムテキ	invincible; unrivaled
無鉄砲	ムテッポウ	reckless; rash
無二	ムニ	peerless; unequaled
無念	ムネン	regret; resentment; vexation
無能	ムノウ	incompetent; ineffective
無比	ムヒ	matchless; incomparable; unrivaled
無病	ムビョウ	well; healthy
無風	ムフウ	windless; dead calm
無分別	ムフンベツ	indiscrete; imprudent; thoughtless; rash

無法	ムホウ	outrageous; unlawful; unjust
無謀	ムボウ	reckless; incautious
無味乾燥	ムミカンソウ	dry as dust; uninteresting
無名	ムメイ	nameless; unknown; anonymous
無用	ムヨウ	unnecessary; useless; prohibited
無欲	ムヨク	unselfish; free from avarice
無理	ムリ	unreasonable; impossible; beyond one's power; too difficult; by force; against one's will
無理解	ムリカイ	lack of understanding
無理算段	ムリサンダン	scraping together —*v.* scrape together
無理難題	ムリナンダイ	unreasonable demand
無理矢理	ムリやリ	forcibly; under compulsion
無料	ムリョウ	free of charge; free
無量	ムリョウ	beyond measure; immense
無力	ムリョク	powerless; ineffectual; feeble; incompetent
無類	ムルイ	finest; choicest
無論	ムロン	of course; naturally

訓
無い	ない	not; no
無くす	なくす	*vt.* lose; get rid of
無くなる	なくなる	*vi.* be gone/lost; run out of; die; pass away

¥
無形固定資産	ムケイコテイシサン	intangible fixed assets
無形財産	ムケイザイサン	intangible property
無償交付	ムショウコウフ	free share distribution

1281

照 ⑬   ㇐ ㇆ 日 日㇆ 日㇀ 昭㇀ 昭 昭 照 照 照 照

音
| 照 | ショウ | shine; check |

熟
照応	ショウオウ	correspondence; agreement; accordance —*vi.* correspond; agree; accord
照会	ショウカイ	inquiry; reference —*v.* refer; inquire; make inquiries
照会状	ショウカイジョウ	letter of inquiry
照合	ショウゴウ	check; collation —*v.* check; collate
照準	ショウジュン	aim; aiming
照度	ショウド	illumination
照明	ショウメイ	illumination; lighting —*v.* illuminate; light up

訓
| 照らす | てらす | *vt.* shine; light up; flash; consult; refer |
| 照らし合わせる | てらしあわせる | *vt.* check; confirm |

心 忄 小 戈 戸 手 扌 支 攵 文 斗 斤 方 日 曰 月 肉 月 木 欠 止 歹 殳 母 毋 比 毛 氏 气 水 氺 氵 火 灬 • 宀 父 片 牛 犬 犭 王 礻 耂

心 忄 小 戈 戸 手 扌 支 攵 文 斗 斤 方 日 曰 月 肉 月 木 欠 止 歹 殳 母 毋 比 毛 氏 气 水 氺 氵 火 ●灬 爪 父 片 牛 犬 犭 王 礻 尗

照る	てる	*vi.* shine; illuminate
照れる	てれる	*vi.* feel self-conscious/shy; be embarrassed
照れ屋	てれや	bashful person; person who blushes easily
照り	てり	sunshine; glaze; glare
照り焼き	てりやき	teriyaki (broiling meat/fish that has been soaked in soy sauce)

1282

熟 ⑮　一 亠 六 亠 亯 亨 享 孰 孰 孰 孰 熟

音	熟	ジュク	ripen; mature; thorough
熟	熟する	ジュクする	*vi.* ripen; mature
	熟語	ジュクゴ	phrase; idiom; compound
	熟視	ジュクシ	intense stare
	熟睡	ジュクスイ	sound sleep —*vi.* sleep soundly/well
	熟成	ジュクセイ	ripe; mature —*vi.* ripen; mature; age
	熟達	ジュクタツ	mastering —*vi.* master; become proficient in
	熟知	ジュクチ	well-known; well-informed; familiar —*v.* know well; be familiar with; be well informed
	熟読	ジュクドク	careful reading —*v.* read carefully
	熟年	ジュクネン	middle-aged
	熟練	ジュクレン	skill; mastery —*vi.* be skilled/expert in
	熟考	ジュッコウ	consideration; deliberation —*v.* consider; deliberate
訓	熟れる	うれる	*vi.* ripen

1283

熱 ⑮　一 十 土 圥 夫 耂 坴 刻 埶 埶 執 熱

音	熱	ネツ	hot; heat; zeal; ardor; enthusiasm
熱	熱する	ネッする	*vt.* heat up *vi.* become hot/excited
	熱愛	ネツアイ	passionate love; devotion —*v.* love passionately/fervently; be madly in love
	熱意	ネツイ	zeal; ardor; enthusiasm
	熱演	ネツエン	ardent/impassioned performance —*v.* give an impassioned performance
	熱気	ネッキ	heat; ardor; hot air; heated atmosphere; feverishness
	熱狂	ネッキョウ	frenzy; fanaticism; mania; excitement —*vi.* be wildly excited/mad/frantic
	熱狂的	ネッキョウテキ	enthusiastic; wild; mad; frantic; manic
	熱血	ネッケツ	zeal; hot blood; enthusiasm; ardor

熱源	ネツゲン	heat source
熱効率	ネツコウリツ	*phy.* thermal efficiency
熱射病	ネッシャビョウ	heatstroke
熱情	ネツジョウ	fervor; ardor; passion; warmth; ardent love
熱処理	ネツショリ	heat treatment
熱心	ネッシン	enthusiasm; zeal; fervor; ardor; earnestness
熱誠	ネッセイ	feverish; earnest; devoted; sincere; enthusiastic
熱戦	ネッセン	hot contest; hard fight
熱帯	ネッタイ	torrid zone; tropics
熱中	ネッチュウ	absorption; enthusiasm; zeal —*vi.* become enthusiastic; have a mania for
熱伝導	ネツデンドウ	*phy.* thermal conduction
熱湯	ネットウ	boiling water
熱病	ネツビョウ	fever
熱風	ネップウ	hot wind; blast of hot air; hot blast
熱弁	ネツベン	fervent speech
熱望	ネツボウ	ardent wish; eager desire —*v.* desire earnestly; be anxious for
熱量	ネツリョウ	*phy.* heat capacity; calorific value
熱烈	ネツレツ	ardent; passionate; fervent; fiery
訓 熱い	あつい	hot; heated; be madly in love
熱さ	あつさ	heat; warmth

1284 ⑮ 一 一 仨 亖 旨 車 車 重 動 動 勳 勲

音 勲	クン	award; medal
熟 勲功	クンコウ	distinguished services; merits
勲章	クンショウ	decoration; order; medal
勲等	クントウ	medals for merit

4 爫 つめ／つめかんむり nail

1285 ⑰ 一 ⺈ ⺤ 爫 爫 爭 爭 爵 爵 爵 爵

| 音 爵 | シャク | peerage; Baron |
| 熟 爵位 | シャクイ | peerage |

565

心
忄
小
戈
戸
手
扌
支
攵
文
斗
斤
方
日
曰
月
肉
月
木
欠
止
歹
殳
母
毋
比
毛
氏
气
水
氷
氵
火
灬
爪
● 父
● 片
牛
犬
犭
王
礻
耂

4 父 ちち father

1286

父 ④　`ノ ハ グ 父`

音	父　フ	father
熟	父兄　フケイ	father and elder brother; guardians or parents of children
	父母　フボ	father and mother; parents
訓	父　ちち	one's father
	父親　ちちおや	father
※	お父さん　おとうさん	father

4 片 かたへん right side

1287

片 ④　`ノ ᐟ ア 片`

音	片　ヘン	one half of a whole; one side; fragment; piece; pence (unit of British currency)
熟	片影　ヘンエイ	shadow; sign; glimpse; partial view of a figure
	片々　ヘンペン	in pieces; in small fragments
	片鱗　ヘンリン	very tiny fragment; indication; partial glimpse
訓	片　かた	one (of two); one side; single
	片足　かたあし	one leg/foot
	片意地　かたイジ	stubborn; bigoted
	片一方　かたイッポウ	one side/party; other side/party
	片田舎　かたいなか	remote village in the country
	片腕　かたうで	one arm; righthand man
	片思い　かたおもい	unrequited love
	片親　かたおや	one parent
	片仮名　かたかな	*katakana* (the non-cursive syllabary)
	片側　かたがわ	one side
	片側通行　かたがわツウコウ	One Way (traffic)
	片言　かたこと	baby talk; broken (English); few words
	片隅　かたすみ	corner; nook; cranny
	片便り　かただより	one-way correspondence

片付く	かたづく	*vi*. be tidied up; be put away; be settled; be disposed of; be married off
片付ける	かたづける	*vt*. tidy up; put away; settle; dispose of; marry off
片手間	かたてま	in one's spare time; on the side
片時	かたとき	a moment; instant
片刃	かたは	single-edge blade
片端	かたはし	edge; end; side
片腹痛い	かたはらいたい	ridiculous; absurd; laughable
片方	かたホウ	one side/party; other side/party
片身	かたみ	one side of the body
片道	かたみち	one-way (trip/ticket)
片目	かため	one eye; one-eyed
片面	かたメン	one side/aspect
片寄る	かたよる	*vi*. lean to one side; be unfair
片割れ	かたわれ	fragment; member of a group/gang (of criminals)
¥ 片貿易	かたボウエキ	one-sided trade

1288

版 ⑧　丿　ノ　Ｐ　Ｆ　Ｆ　片　斤　版　版

音	版	ハン	plate
熟	版画	ハンガ	print
	版権	ハンケン	copyright

4　**牛**　うし／うしへん　cow

1289

牛 ④　丿　ｆ　二　牛

音	牛	ギュウ	cow; ox; beef; dairy
熟	牛飲馬食	ギュウインバショク	heavy eating and drinking; immoderation in eating and drinking —*vi*. eat and drink heavily
	牛舎	ギュウシャ	cattle stall; cow barn
	牛耳る	ギュウジる	*vt*. take the lead; control
	牛肉	ギュウニク	beef
	牛乳	ギュウニュウ	cow's milk
訓	牛	うし	cow; ox; bull

567

心忄小戈戸手扌支攴文斗斤方日曰月肉月木欠止歹殳母毋比毛氏气水氺氵火灬宀父片牛犬犭王礻爿

1290

物 ⑧ ` �'′ 丬 牛 牜 牞 物 物 物

音	物	ブツ	thing; object
		モツ	thing; object
熟	物議	ブツギ	public criticism/discussion
	物件	ブッケン	thing; article; object
	物故	ブッコ	death —*vi*. die; pass away
	物故者	ブッコシャ	the deceased
	物産	ブッサン	product; produce; commodity
	物資	ブッシ	goods; resources
	物質	ブッシツ	matter; substance
	物質的	ブッシツテキ	material; physical
	物色	ブッショク	ransacking; rummaging; looking for —*v*. ransack; rummage; look/search for; select
	物騒	ブッソウ	unsettled; troubled; dangerous
	物体	ブッタイ	body; object; substance
	物的	ブッテキ	material; physical
	物品	ブッピン	goods; article; commodity
	物欲	ブツヨク	worldly desires/ambition
	物理	ブツリ	law of nature; physics
	物理学	ブツリガク	physics
	物理療法	ブツリリョウホウ	physiotherapy
訓	物	もの	thing; object
	物入り	ものいり	expenses
	物語	ものがたり	story; narrative
	物乞い	ものごい	begging; begger
	物心	ものごころ	discretion; judgment
	物腰	ものごし	manner; demeanor
	物事	ものごと	things; matters
	物好き	ものずき	curious; whimsical; eccentric
	物足りない	ものたりない	unsatisfying; something missing
	物干し	ものほし	(frame for) drying clothes
	物見	ものみ	sightseeing; watchtower; scout; patrol
	物見遊山	ものみユサン	pleasure trip; sightseeing tour
	物々しい	ものものしい	showy; imposing; elaborate; overdone; excessive
	物分かり	ものわかり	understanding
	物忘れ	ものわすれ	forgetfulness
¥	物価	ブッカ	prices (of commodities)

物価指数	ブッカシスウ	price index
物色買い	ブッショクがい	selective buying
物々交換	ブツブツコウカン	barter —*vi.* do business by barter
物流	ブツリュウ	distribution of goods
物別れ	ものわかれ	reaching no agreement; being broken off

1291

牧 ⑧　ノ ′ ⺧ 牛 牛 牛 牜 牧 牧

音	牧	ボク	pasture
熟	牧牛	ボクギュウ	grazing/pasturing cattle
	牧師	ボクシ	pastor; minister
	牧舎	ボクシャ	cattleshed
	牧場	ボクジョウ	ranch; (cattle/sheep) farm
	牧神	ボクシン	Pan
	牧草	ボクソウ	grass; pasturage; meadow
	牧畜	ボクチク	livestock raising
	牧畜業	ボクチクギョウ	stock farming; ranching
	牧童	ボクドウ	cowboy; shepherd boy
訓	牧	まき	ranch; (cattle/sheep) farm
	牧場	まきば	ranch; (cattle/sheep) farm

1292

牲 ⑨　ノ ′ ⺧ 牛 牛 牜 牪 牪 牲

| 音 | 牲 | セイ | sacrifice |

1293

特 ⑩　ノ ′ ⺧ 牛 牛 牜 牜 牜 特 特

音	特	トク	special; specific; particular
熟	特異	トクイ	unique; singular
	特技	トクギ	specialty; special talent/ability
	特産	トクサン	special product; specialty
	特使	トクシ	special envoy/express messenger
	特質	トクシツ	characteristic; property; special quality
	特赦	トクシャ	amnesty
	特殊	トクシュ	special; specific; particular; peculiar; distinct; typical

569

心 忄 小 戈 戸 手 扌 支 攵 文 斗 斤 方 日 曰 月 肉 月 木 欠 止 歹 殳 母 毋 毌 比 毛 氏 气 水 氺 氵 火 灬 爪 父 片 牛 犬 犭 王 礻 耂

心
忄
小
戈
戸
手
扌
支
攵
文
斗
斤
方
日
曰
月
肉
月
木
欠
止
歹
殳
母
毋
比
毛
氏
气
水
氷
氵
火
灬
爪
父
片
牛
犬
犭
王
礻
歩

特需	トクジュ	special/emergency demand
特集	トクシュウ	special edition (of a newspaper, magazine, etc.) —v. bring out a special edition
特賞	トクショウ	special prize
特色	トクショク	character; feature; distinguishing mark; idiosyncrasy
特性	トクセイ	special quality; characteristic; distinguishing mark
特製	トクセイ	special make/manufacture
特設	トクセツ	special establishment/installment/accomodation
特選	トクセン	special selection/approval; recognition
特大	トクダイ	outsize
特種	トクだね	scoop; exclusive news
特長	トクチョウ	merit; forte; strong point
特徴	トクチョウ	feature; characteristic; distinctive feature
特定	トクテイ	specific —v. specify
特典	トクテン	privilege; special favor; benefit
特電	トクデン	special telegram
特等	トクトウ	special/top grade
特派	トクハ	special dispatch —v. send a special dispatch; send; detail
特売	トクバイ	bargain/special sale; sale at a special price —v. sell at a special/reduced prices
特筆	トクヒツ	special mention —v. make a special mention/feature of
特別	トクベツ	special; extraordinary
特報	トクホウ	news flash —v. give a news flash
特約	トクヤク	special contract/agreement —v. make/come to a special agreement
特有	トクユウ	peculiar; characteristic; special
特例	トクレイ	special case/treatment; exception
特価	トッカ	special/bargain price
特急	トッキュウ	limited/super express
特許	トッキョ	patent; charter; license; special permission
特権	トッケン	privilege; special right; charter; option
特効薬	トッコウヤク	specific remedy
¥ 特定金銭信託	トクテイキンセンシンタク	designated money in trust
特定引当金	トクテイひきあてキン	specific reserve
特定銘柄	トクテイメイがら	specified stock
特別積立金	トクベツつみたてキン	special retained earnings
特約店	トクヤクテン	specified agent
特約取引	トクヤクとりひき	seller's option

特許	トッキョ	patent
特許庁	トッキョチョウ	Patent Office
特許品	トッキョヒン	patented article; patent

1294

犠 ⑰　牛　犬゛　犬゛　犬゛　犬゛　犬゛　犬゛　犬゛　犬゛　犠　犠　犠

音	犠	ギ	sacrifice; victim
熟	犠牲	ギセイ	sacrifice
訓	※犠	いけにえ	sacrifice; scapegoat

---

4 犬 いぬ dog; animal 犭 (p.572)

1295

犬 ④　一　ナ　大　犬

音	犬	ケン	dog
熟	犬猿の仲	ケンエンのなか	dog and monkey *fig.* bitter enmity; on bad terms
	犬歯	ケンシ	canine teeth
訓	犬	いぬ	dog
	犬死に	いぬじに	unrewarded death —*vi.* die for nothing

1296

状 ⑦　丨　丬　丬　爿　爿　状　状

音	状	ジョウ	condition; letter
熟	状況	ジョウキョウ	conditions; situation; state of affairs; circumstances
	状勢	ジョウセイ	situation; state of affairs; conditions
	状態	ジョウタイ	state; condition

1297

献 ⑬　一　十　广　广　肯　肯　南　南　南一　献一　献　献

| 音 | 献 | ケン | give; present; offer; contribute; dedicate |

心 忄 小 戈 戸 手 扌 支 攵 文 斗 斤 方 日 曰 月 肉 月 木 欠 止 歹 殳 母 毋 比 毛 氏 気 水 氺 氵 火 灬 爫 父 片 牛 犬 犭 王 礻 耂

献	（コン）	fine dishes; good food
熟 献じる	ケンじる	*vt*. present; make a present of; offer; dedicate
献金	ケンキン	contribution; donation; collection —*v*. contribute; donate
献血	ケンケツ	blood donation —*vi*. donate/give blood
献上	ケンジョウ	presentation —*v*. present; offer
献身	ケンシン	devotion; unselfish aid —*vi*. devote oneself to helping others
献身的	ケンシンテキ	devotedly; unselfishly
献呈	ケンテイ	dedication —*v*. dedicate
献立	コンだて	menu; bill of fare

1298

獣 ⑯　" `` 丷 䒑 䒑 単 単 兽 兽 獣 獣 獣

音 獣	ジュウ	beast
熟 獣医	ジュウイ	veterinary surgeon; vet
訓 獣	けもの	animal; beast

3 犭 けものへん animal

1299

犯 ⑤　ノ 丿 犭 犭 犯 犯

音 犯	ハン	offense
熟 犯行	ハンコウ	crime; offense; criminal act
犯罪	ハンザイ	crime; offense
犯人	ハンニン	criminal; offender
訓 犯す	おかす	*vt*. commit an offense; violate; attack; assault; rape

1300

狂 ⑦　ノ 丿 犭 犭 犭 狂 狂

音 狂	キョウ	mad; insane
熟 狂気	キョウキ	insanity; madness
狂喜	キョウキ	ecstasy; rapture —*vi*. be in ecstasy; go into raptures

572

狂言	キョウゲン	*Kyogen* (Japanese comic play)
狂人	キョウジン	lunatic; madman
狂暴	キョウボウ	range; frenzy; fury
訓 狂う	くるう	*vi.* go mad; get out of order; go wrong; be upset
狂おしい	くるおしい	mad/crazy (with grief, etc.)

1301

狭 ⑨　ノ　イ　オ　犭　犭　犲　犲　狭　狭

音 狭	キョウ	narrow; tight
熟 狭義	キョウギ	narrow sense/meaning
狭量	キョウリョウ	narrow mindedness; intolerance
訓 狭まる	せばまる	*vi.* become narrow; contract
狭める	せばめる	*vt.* narrow; contract; reduce (the width)
狭い	せまい	narrow; tight

1302

狩 ⑨　ノ　イ　オ　犭'　犭'　犲　犲　狩　狩

音 狩	シュ	hunting
熟 狩猟	シュリョウ	hunting; shooting
訓 狩り	かり	hunting
狩人	かりうど（かりゅうど）	huntsman; hunter
狩る	かる	*vt.* hunt

1303

独 ⑨　ノ　イ　オ　犭　犯　犯　独　独　独

音 独	ドク	alone; by oneself; Germany
熟 独逸	ドイツ	Germany
独演	ドクエン	recital; single; solo performance —*v.* give a solo performance/recital
独学	ドクガク	self-education; self-instruction —*v.* teach/educate oneself
独語	ドクゴ	the German language
独裁	ドクサイ	dictatorship; despotism; autocracy —*vi.* dictate; hold a country under despotic rule
独裁者	ドクサイシャ	dictator

心忄小戈戸手扌支攵文斗斤方日曰月肉月木欠止歹殳母毋比毛氏气水氺氵火灬爫父片牛犬犭王礻耂

4

心
忄
小
戈
戸
手
扌
支
攵
文
斗
斤
方
日
曰
月
肉
月
木
欠
止
歹
殳
母
毋
比
毛
氏
気
水
氺
氵
火
灬
爫
父
片
牛
犬
犭
王
礻
爿

独裁主義	ドクサイシュギ	dictatorship
独裁的	ドクサイテキ	dictatorial; despotic; autocratic
独自	ドクジ	original; peculiar; individual; oneself
独習	ドクシュウ	self-teaching; self-study —v. teach oneself; study without a teacher
独唱	ドクショウ	vocal solo; recital —v. sing a solo
独身	ドクシン	single life; single; celibacy; bachelorhood
独占	ドクセン	monopoly; exclusive possession —v. monopolize; keep a thing to oneself
独善	ドクゼン	self-righteousness
独走	ドクソウ	running alone; runaway; walkover —vi. run away; walkover
独奏	ドクソウ	solo; recital —v. play a solo/alone
独創	ドクソウ	originality
独断	ドクダン	arbitrary decision; dogmatism
独特	ドクトク	unique; peculiar; special; original
独房	ドクボウ	cell; prison cell
独立	ドクリツ	independence; self-help; self-reliance; freedom; self-support —vi. become independent/free/isolated
独立心	ドクリツシン	independent spirit
独立独歩	ドクリツドッポ	independence; self-reliance; self-help
独力	ドクリョク	one's own efforts; single-handed

訓

独り	ひとり	alone; by oneself
独り言	ひとりごと	monolog; soliloquy

¥

独占禁止法 （独禁法）	ドクセン キンシホウ （ドクキンホウ）	Antimonopoly (Antitrust) Law

1304

猫 ⑪　ノ　丬　犭　犭　犷　犲　犵　狺　猫　猫　猫

音	猫	ビョウ	cat
訓	猫	ねこ	cat
	猫舌	ねこじた	tongue that is sensitive to heat
	猫背	ねこぜ	stoop; round shoulders
	猫ばば	ねこばば	embezzlement; misappropriation

1305

猛 ⑪　ノ　丬　犭　犭　犷　犴　狩　猛　猛　猛　猛

音	猛	モウ	fierce; strong; intense

熟	猛威	モウイ	ferocity; vehemence
	猛火	モウカ	raging flames; conflagration
	猛犬	モウケン	fierce/vicious dog
	猛攻	モウコウ	heavy blow/attack —*v.* mount a heavy attack
	猛獣	モウジュウ	ferocious animal
	猛進	モウシン	rushing/plunging ahead —*vi.* rush forward; plunge ahead
	猛然	モウゼン	violently; fiercely; resolutely
	猛打	モウダ	heavy hit/blow (sports)
	猛毒	モウドク	deadly/virulent poison
	猛烈	モウレツ	violent; fierce; intense
	※猛者	モサ	stalwart; veteran; man of courage
訓	※猛る	たける	*vi.* rush; rage; rave
	※猛々しい	たけだけしい	fierce; ferocious; audacious

1306

猎 ⑪　ノ　犭　犭　犭　犭　犭″　犭″　犷　猎　猎　猎

音	猟	リョウ	hunting
熟	猟期	リョウキ	hunting season
	猟犬	リョウケン	hound; hunting dog
	猟師	リョウシ	hunter
	猟銃	リョウジュウ	hunting gun; shotgun
	猟場	リョウば	game preserve; hunting ground

1307

猶 ⑫　ノ　ノ　犭　犭　犭′　犷　犷　犷　犹　猶　猶　猶

音	猶	ユウ	delay; still; still more
熟	猶予	ユウヨ	postponement; deferment; hesitation —*vi.* reprieve; postpone; defer; hesitate
¥	猶予期間	ユウヨキカン	grace period

1308

猿 ⑬　ノ　犭　犭　犭′　犭⁺　犷　猜　猜　猗　猿　猿　猿

音	猿	エン	monkey; ape
訓	猿	さる	monkey
	猿芝居	さるしばい	monkey show; shallow-minded trick

猿真似　　さるまね　　blind imitation
猿回し　　さるまわし　　monkey showman

左側の縦書き部首一覧：
心 忄 小 戈 戸 手 扌 支 攵 文 斗 斤 方 日 曰 月 肉 月 木 欠 止 歹 殳 母 毋 比 毛 氏 气 水 氺 氵 火 灬 爫 父 片 牛 犬 犭

● 犭
● 王 礻
● 耂

1309

獄 ⑭　ノ　丿　犭　犭　犭　狾　狺　狺　狺　獄　獄　獄

音　獄　　ゴク　　prison; punishment; judgment; hell

1310

獲 ⑯　ノ　丿　犭　犭犬　犭犬　犭犬　犭犬　犭犬　獲　獲　獲　獲

音　獲　　カク　　catch; gain
熟　獲得　　カクトク　　gain; acquisition —*v.* get; acquire; obtain
訓　獲る　　える　　*vt.* capture
　　獲物　　えもの　　wild game

4　王　see ⇨p.578

4　礻　see ⇨p.623

4　耂　see ⇨p.684

5 玄 げん dark

1311

玄 ⑤   ` 亠 ナ 玄 玄

音	玄	ゲン	black; dark; deep
熟	玄関	ゲンカン	entrance; hallway
	玄米	ゲンマイ	*genmai* (unpolished/brown rice)
訓	※玄人	くろうと	professional

1312

率 ⑪   ` 亠 ナ 玄 玄 玄 泫 泫 浓 滐 率

音	率	ソツ	lead; all; light; easy
		リツ	proportion; percentage; rate
熟	率先	ソッセン	taking the lead —*vi*. take the lead; be the first
	率然	ソツゼン	suddenly; unexpectedly
	率直	ソッチョク	frank; straightforward
訓	率いる	ひきいる	*vt*. lead; be in command of

5 玉 たま jewel   王 (p.578)

1313

玉 ⑤   一 丁 干 王 玉

音	玉	ギョク	jewel; pearl; jewel like
熟	玉石混交	ギョクセキコンコウ	good and bad
訓	玉	たま	jewel; gem

1314

璽 ⑲   一 宀 宀 宀 帘 帘 帘 爾 爾 璽 璽 璽 璽

音	璽	ジ	Privy Seal; imperial seal

玄玉王瓦甘生用田疋疒癶白皮皿目矛矢石示礻禾穴立罒旡母水氺礻

4 王 おう／たまへん／おうへん king

1315

王④ 一 Ｔ 王 王

音	王	オウ	king; prince; lord
熟	王位	オウイ	the throne; the crown
	王冠	オウカン	crown; bottle top
	王宮	オウキュウ	king's palace; royal palace
	王侯	オウコウ	king and his feudal lords
	王国	オウコク	kingdom
	王座	オウザ	the throne
	王様	オウさま	king
	王子	オウジ	prince
	王室	オウシツ	royal family
	王者	オウシャ (オウジャ)	king; monarch; ruler
	王女	オウジョ	princess
	王政	オウセイ	imperial rule
	王政復古	オウセイフッコ	*hist.* restoration of imperial rule (1867)
	王族	オウゾク	royal family
	王朝	オウチョウ	dynasty
	王手	オウて	checkmate; *ote* (shogi)
	王妃	オウヒ	queen; empress

1316

珍⑨ 一 Ｔ 王 王 王 珍 珍 珍

音	珍	チン	curious; strange; odd; rare; remarkable
熟	珍奇	チンキ	rarity; novelty; curiosity
	珍客	チンキャク	rare visitor; welcome guest
	珍事	チンジ	rare event; unexpected occurrence
	珍重	チンチョウ	something that one values —*v.* treasure; value; esteem; prize
	珍品	チンピン	rarity; curio; curiosity
	珍味	チンミ	delicacy; unusual taste
	珍妙	チンミョウ	queer; odd
訓	珍しい	めずらしい	rare; odd; queer; remarkable

1317

珠 ⑩ 　 一　丁　チ　王　ヨ　チ　珍　珍　珠　珠

音	珠	シュ	pearl; bead
熟	珠玉	シュギョク	pearls and jewels; precious object; literary gem
	珠算	シュザン	calculation on the abacus
訓	※珠	たま	bead; jewel; gem

1318

班 ⑩ 　 一　丁　チ　王　玊　到　玔　班　班

音	班	ハン	group
熟	班長	ハンチョウ	squad/section/group leader

1319

球 ⑪ 　 一　丁　チ　王　王　玏　珒　对　球　球　球

音	球	キュウ	ball; sphere; spherical; baseball
熟	球技	キュウギ	ball game
	球根	キュウコン	bulb
	球状	キュウジョウ	spherical shape; globe
	球場	キュウジョウ	baseball ground; ballpark
	球審	キュウシン	*bas*. plate/chief umpire
	球速	キュウソク	*bas*. (pitcher's) pace; speed of a pitcher's ball
訓	球	たま	ball

1320

現 ⑪ 　 一　丁　チ　王　玎　玑　玥　珇　珇　現　現

音	現	ゲン	appear; now; current; present
熟	現役	ゲンエキ	active service/duty
	現金	ゲンキン	cash; ready money *adj*. mercenary; calculating; selfish
	現行	ゲンコウ	current; present; existing
	現行犯	ゲンコウハン	flagrant offense; red-handed
	現在	ゲンザイ	now; the present; existing; current —*v*. exist; be current

玄
玉
• 王
瓦
甘
生
用
田
疋
疒
癶
白
皮
皿
目
矛
矢
石
示
礻
禾
穴
立
罒
罘
母
水
礻

現実	ゲンジツ	reality; actuality; hard fact
現実化	ゲンジツカ	realization —v. realize; be realized; put into effect
現実主義	ゲンジツシュギ	realism
現住所	ゲンジュウショ	present address
現出	ゲンシュツ	appearance; emergence; revelation —v. appear; emerge; come out; reveal
現象	ゲンショウ	phenomenon; happening; phase; aspect
現状	ゲンジョウ	present state; actual situation; status quo
現職	ゲンショク	one's present post/office
現世	ゲンセ	this world/life; worldly; earthy; temporal; secular
現像	ゲンゾウ	film development —v. develop (a film)
現存	ゲンゾン	existence —vi. exist; be extant
現代	ゲンダイ	today; modern; the present age; contemporary
現地	ゲンチ	on the spot; locality; the field; the actual place
現地時間	ゲンチジカン	local time
現場	ゲンば	the spot; the field; the actual place
現品	ゲンピン	goods; the actual article

訓
| 現す | あらわす | vt. express; show; reveal |
| 現れる | あらわれる | vi. come out; appear; emerge |

¥
現先取引	ゲンさきとりひき	repurchase agreement (transaction)
現地法人	ゲンチホウジン	local affiliated firm (overseas)
現物	ゲンブツ	spot goods; actuals
現渡し	ゲンわたし	actual delivery of stock sold

1321

理 ⑪ 　一　丁　王　王　玗　珂　珥　珇　理　理　理

音 理	リ	reason; justice; truth; principle
熟 理科	リカ	science
理解	リカイ	understanding; comprehension —v. understand; comprehend
理化学	リカガク	physics and chemistry
理屈	リクツ	reason; logic; theory; argument; pretext
理事	リジ	director; trustee
理性	リセイ	reason; reasoning power
理想	リソウ	ideal
理想郷	リソウキョウ	utopia; ideal land; Shangri-La
理想的	リソウテキ	ideal
理知	リチ	intellect; intelligence
理念	リネン	idea; doctrine; ideology

理髪	リハツ	haircutting
理髪師	リハツシ	barber; hairdresser
理非	リヒ	rights and wrongs; relative merits
理不尽	リフジン	unreasonable; inconceivable; preposterous
理法	リホウ	law
理由	リユウ	reason; cause
理容	リヨウ	hairdressing
理路整然	リロセイゼン	logical; well-argued; cogent
理論	リロン	theory

1322

琴 ⑫　一 T チ 王 玗 珇 珏 玨 玽 珡 珡 琴

音	琴	キン	harp; zither
熟	琴線	キンセン	heartstrings; one's innermost feelings
訓	琴	こと	*koto* (Japanese zither)

1323

環 ⑰　T 王 玕 玗 珇 玾 玾 珋 環 環 環 環

音	環	カン	ring; enclose
熟	環境	カンキョウ	environment
	環礁	カンショウ	atoll
	環状線	カンジョウセン	loop line
	環流	カンリュウ	back flow; circulation
訓	※環	わ	ring; circle; loop

5 瓦 かわら tile

1324

瓶 ⑪　丶 ソ ユ 兰 羊 并 并 瓶 瓶 瓶

音	瓶	ビン	bottle; jar
熟	瓶詰	ビンづめ	bottled (beer, etc.)

玄
玉
王 •
瓦 •
甘
生
用
田
疋
疒
癶
白
皮
皿
目
矛
矢
石
示
礻
禾
穴
立
罒
罖
母
水
衤

玄玉王瓦甘生用田疋疒癶白皮皿目矛矢石示礻禾穴立罒罙母水氺

5 甘 あまい sweet

1325

甘 ⑤ 一 十 廿 甘 甘

音	甘	カン	sweet
熟	甘言	カンゲン	flattery
	甘受	カンジュ	submission; resignation —*v*. submit (tamely) to; be resigned to (one's fate)
	甘味料	カンミリョウ	sweetening
訓	甘い	あまい	sweet; sugary; flattering; indulgent
	甘える	あまえる	*vi*. behave like a spoiled child; be indulgent; take advantage of
	甘やかす	あまやかす	*vt*. indulge; pamper; overindulge; spoil
	甘口	あまくち	light; sweet
	甘酒	あまざけ	sweet alcoholic drink made from saké
	甘党	あまトウ	person with a sweet tooth

1326

甚 ⑨ 一 十 廿 甘 甘 甚 其 甚 甚

音	甚	ジン	greatly
熟	甚大	ジンダイ	serious; great; enormous
訓	甚だ	はなはだ	very; much; greatly
	甚だしい	はなはだしい	extreme; enormous; blatant; outrageous

---

5 生 うまれる life; birth

1327

生 ⑤ ノ ╱ ┝ 牛 生

音	生	ショウ	live; life
		セイ	life; living; birth; produce; grow
熟	生じる	ショウじる	*v*. develop; accrue; come about; engender
	生姜	ショウが	ginger
	生涯	ショウガイ	life; career; working life

生国	ショウゴク (ショウコク)	country/province of one's birth
生育	セイイク	growth; development —*v*. grow; raise; be born and bred; vegetate
生家	セイカ	one's parents' house; house one was born in
生花	セイカ	real flower; flower arrangement
生活	セイカツ	life; existence; livelihood —*vi*. live; exist; make a living
生活水準	セイカツスイジュン	standard of living
生活費	セイカツヒ	living expenses
生還	セイカン	surviving —*vi*. come back alive; survive
生気	セイキ	vitality; life; animation; vigor; spirit
生計	セイケイ	living; livelihood
生彩	セイサイ	vividness; luster; brilliance; live
生産	セイサン	production —*v*. produce; make; turn/put out
生産高	セイサンだか	output; yield
生産地	セイサンチ	producing center
生死	セイシ	life or death; safety; fate
生殖	セイショク	generation; reproduction; procreation
生殖器	セイショクキ	*med*. sexual/reproductive organs; genitals
生成	セイセイ	creation; formulation; generation —*vi*. be created/formed
生鮮	セイセン	fresh; perishable
生前	セイゼン	while alive; during one's lifetime; before one's death
生息	セイソク	inhabited —*vi*. inhabit; live
生存	セイゾン	existence; being; life —*vi*. exist; live; survive; outlive
生存競争	セイゾンキョウソウ	struggle for existence
生存者	セイゾンシャ	survivor
生態	セイタイ	mode of life; ecology
生態学	セイタイガク	ecology
生誕	セイタン	birth; nativity —*vi*. be born
生地	セイチ	birthplace/home
生年	セイネン	year of birth; age
生年月日	セイネンガッぴ	date of birth
生物	セイブツ	living thing; organism; creature; life
生物学	セイブツガク	biology
生別	セイベツ	eternal/lifelong separation —*v*. never meet again
生命	セイメイ	life; the soul
生来	セイライ	by nature; naturally; by birth
生理	セイリ	physiology; menstruation
訓 生きる	いきる	*vi*. live; exist; survive
生かす	いかす	*vi*. revive; resuscitate; bring to life; give life to

玄玉王瓦生 •
用田疋广癶
白皮皿目矛
矢石示ネ禾
穴立罒疒
母氷ネ

玄
玉
王
瓦
甘
● 生
用
田
疋
广
ᐧᐟ
白
皮
皿
目
矢
石
示
ネ
禾
穴
立
皿
无
母
水
ネ

生ける	いける	*vt.* arrange flowers
生まれる	うまれる	*vi.* be born
生む	うむ	*vt.* bear; give birth to; produce
生う	おう	*v.* grow; come out
生える	はえる	*vi.* grow; come out
生やす	はやす	*vt.* grow; cultivate
生	き	pure; raw
生一本	きイッポン	pure; neat; straight; straightforward; honest
生糸	きいと	raw silk
生地	きジ	cloth
生真面目	きまじめ	honest; earnest; sincere
生	なま	raw; uncooked; rare; draft
生意気	なまイキ	conceit; self-conceit; selfishness
生演奏	なまエンソウ	live performance
生傷	なまきず	fresh wound
生々しい	なまなましい	fresh; green; vivid; graphic
生返事	なまヘンジ	vague answer; noncommittal reply
生放送	なまホウソウ	live broadcast
¥ 生産財	セイサンザイ	production goods
生産性	セイサンセイ	productivity
生産費	セイサンヒ	costs of production; production costs
生産目標	セイサンモクヒョウ	production target
生産力	セイサンリョク	production capacity
生命保険	セイメイホケン	life insurance

1328
産 ⑪ 　 ' ㅗ ㅗ ㅗ 立 产 产 产 产 産 産

音 産	サン	give birth to; produce; output
熟 産院	サンイン	maternity hospital
産科	サンカ	*med.* obstetrics; the obstetrical department
産気	サンケ	feeling that a baby is about to be born
産児制限	サンジセイゲン	birth control —*vi.* practice birth control
産地	サンチ	producing area/center
産婦人科	サンフジンカ	*med.* gynecology
産物	サンブツ	products; produce
産卵	サンラン	laying eggs; spawning —*vi.* lay eggs; spawn
訓 産む	うむ	*vt.* have a baby; bear; give birth to; produce
産まれる	うまれる	*vi.* be born; be established; be started
産	うぶ	naive; innocent; unsophisticated

産毛	うぶげ	downy hair
¥ 産休	サンキュウ	maternity leave
産業	サンギョウ	industry
産業化	サンギョウカ	industrialization —v. industrialize
産業革命	サンギョウ カクメイ	industrial revolution
産業資本	サンギョウシホン	industrial capital
産出	サンシュツ	production —v. produce; yield; output
産油国	サンユコク	oil producing nation

---

5 用　もちいる　using

1329

用 ⑤ 　ノ 刀 月 月 用

音 用	ヨウ	business; errand; use
熟 用意	ヨウイ	preparations; arrangements
用意周到	ヨウイシュウトウ	thoroughly prepared; well arranged
用器	ヨウキ	instrument; tool
用具	ヨウグ	equipment; kit
用件	ヨウケン	business; things to be done
用語	ヨウゴ	term; terminology
用材	ヨウザイ	lumber; materials
用紙	ヨウシ	(application) form; stationery
用字	ヨウジ	use of characters
用事	ヨウジ	business; errand; things to be done
用心	ヨウジン	caution; care —vi. take care of; pay attention to
用心棒	ヨウジンボウ	bodyguard
用水	ヨウスイ	city/irrigation water
用談	ヨウダン	business talk —vi. have an important business talk
用地	ヨウチ	lot; site; land for some use
用途	ヨウト	use; purpose
用品	ヨウヒン	supplies
用便	ヨウベン	going to the toilet —v. go to the toilet
用法	ヨウホウ	how to use; directions
用務	ヨウム	business
用務員	ヨウムイン	janitor; custodian
用命	ヨウメイ	command; order

	用例	ヨウレイ	example; illustration
訓	用いる	もちいる	*vt*. use

---

5 田　た／たへん　rice field

1330

田　丨　冂　冊　丗　田　⑤

音	田	デン	field
熟	田園	デンエン	fields and gardens; the country; rural districts
	田園生活	デンエンセイカツ	country life; life in the country
	田園都市	デンエントシ	rural city
	田楽	デンガク	*dengaku* (ritual music and dancing performed in Shinto shrines)
	田地	デンジ	rice paddies; state of mind; female genitals
	田畑	デンばた	cultivated fields
	田野	デンヤ	cultivated fields
訓	田	た	rice field
	田植え	たうえ	rice planting
	田畑	たはた	rice field; farmland; fields
	田圃	たんボ	rice field
	※田舎	いなか	the country; countryside

1331

甲　丨　冂　日　日　甲　⑤

音	甲	コウ	grade A; the first in a series; crust; shell; carapace
		カン	
熟	甲斐	カイ	use; effect; result *hist*. former name of Yamanashi prefecture (until the Meiji period)
	甲高い	カンだかい	high-pitched; shrill
	甲板	カンパン	ship's deck
	甲乙	コウオツ	A and B; difference (between A and B)
	甲殻	コウカク	crust; shell; carapace
	甲殻類	コウカクルイ	crustacea
	甲虫	コウチュウ	beetle
	甲羅	コウラ	shell; carapace

1332

申 ⑤ 丨 口 曰 曰 申

音	申	シン	state; say; report; declare
熟	申告	シンコク	report; return; declaration —*v.* report; declare
	申告書	シンコクショ	report; declaration
	申請	シンセイ	application; petition —*v.* apply; make an application
	申請書	シンセイショ	application form
訓	申す	もうす	***hum. vt.*** say; speak; mention
	申し上げる	もうしあげる	***hum. vt.*** tell; inform
	申し込む	もうしこむ	***vt.*** propose; request; apply; reserve; subscript
	申し訳ない	もうしわけない	sorry; excuse me; thank you
	※申	さる	the monkey (ninth sign of the Chinese zodiac)

1333

由 ⑤ 丨 口 巾 由 由

音	由	ユ	reason; cause; significance; means; way
		ユウ	
		（ユイ）	
熟	由緒	ユイショ	history; lineage; origin
	由々しい	ユユしい	grave; serious
	由来	ユライ	origin; derivation; originally; by nature —*vi.* date back to; originate
訓	由	よし	reason; cause; significance; means; way

1334

男 ⑦ 丨 口 皿 甲 田 里 男

音	男	ダン	man; male; baron
		ナン	man
熟	男子	ダンシ	male; man; boy; son
	男児	ダンジ	boy
	男女	ダンジョ	man and woman; couple
	男性	ダンセイ	male sex; man; masculinity; manliness
	男性的	ダンセイテキ	manly; masculine
	男尊女卑	ダンソンジョヒ	predominance of men over women; male supremacy

訓 男　　　　おとこ　　　　man; boy

玄玉王瓦甘生用
・田疋疒癶白皮皿
目矛矢石示衤禾
穴立罒无母氺衤

1335

町 ⑦　　１　冂　冂　用　田　田一　町

音 町　　　　チョウ　　　　town; street; block
熟 町家　　　チョウカ　　　town house
　　町会　　　チョウカイ　　town block association; town assembly
　　町村　　　チョウソン　　towns and villages; municipalities
　　町長　　　チョウチョウ　town headman/manager
　　町内　　　チョウナイ　　town; streets; neighborhood
　　町人　　　チョウニン　　townsman; merchant
　　町民　　　チョウミン　　town resident
訓 町　　　　まち　　　　　town; city; street
　　町中　　　まちなか　　　the streets; the middle of the town
　　町並み　　まちなみ　　　row of stores and houses on a street
　　町外れ　　まちはずれ　　outskirts of a town
　　町役場　　まちやくば　　town hall/office

1336

界 ⑨　　１　冂　冂　用　田　里　畀　界　界

音 界　　　　カイ　　　　　border; circles; scope
熟 界隈　　　カイワイ　　　neighborhood; vicinity
訓 界　　　　さかい　　　　border; limit

1337

畑 ⑨　　丶　丷　少　火　灯　灯　畑　畑　畑

訓 畑　　　　はた　　　　　plowed field; farm; plantation
　　畑　　　　はたけ　　　　plowed field; farm; plantation *fig.* specialty;
　　　　　　　　　　　　　　one's field

1338

畝 ⑩　　丶　亠　广　亩　亩　亩　畝　畝　畝　畝

訓 畝　　　　うね　　　　　ridge; furrow; groove
　　畝　　　　せ　　　　　　*se* (unit of area, approx. 0.991 a)

1339

畜 ⑩ 　`ー亠玄玄产斉斋斋畜

音	畜	チク	breed; raise; beast; cattle
熟	畜産	チクサン	stock raising/breeding
	畜生	チクショウ	beast *col.* Damn it!; Shit!

1340

畔 ⑩ 　丿冂冂田田田田丷田丷畔畔

| 音 | 畔 | ハン | side |
| 訓 | ※畔 | あぜ | ridge between rice fields |

1341

留 ⑩ 　丶丿㇉卬卬卬留留留留

音	留	リュウ （ル）	stop; hold; fast; detain; keep
熟	留意	リュウイ	attention; mindful —*vi.* pay attention to; give head to; be mindful of
	留任	リュウニン	remaining in office —*vi.* remain in office
	留学	リュウガク	studying abroad —*vi.* study abroad
	留置	リュウチ	detention; custody —*v.* detain; lockup; hold in custody
	留保	リュウホ	reservation; withholding —*v.* reserve; withhold
	留守	ルス	absence; being away from home; neglecting
	留守番	ルスバン	looking after the house (while the owner is away); someone who looks after a house (while the owner in away)
	留守番電話	ルスバンデンワ	answering machine
訓	留まる	とまる	*vi.* stop; be fixed in one position
	留める	とめる	*vt.* stop; detain; fix in one position
	留め立て	とめだて	dissuasion

1342

異 ⑪ 　丶冂田田田里異異異異異

| 音 | 異 | イ | different; unusual; curious; peculiar; uncommon |

玄玉王瓦甘生用田疋广𠂤白皮皿目矛矢石示礻禾穴立罒𠘨母水氺

熟	異義	イギ	different/another meaning
	異議	イギ	objection; complaint
	異郷	イキョウ	strange/foreign land
	異境	イキョウ	foreign country/land
	異口同音	イクドウオン	with one voice/accord; unanimously
	異国	イコク	foreign land/country
	異彩	イサイ	striking/conspicuous color
	異質	イシツ	heterogeneity
	異種	イシュ	different species/kind; variety
	異状	イジョウ	something wrong; accident; change; disorder
	異常	イジョウ	unusual; abnormal; extraordinary
	異色	イショク	different color
	異人	イジン	foreigner; stranger; alien
	異性	イセイ	the opposite sex
	異説	イセツ	different view/theory; conflicting views
	異存	イゾン	objection
	異端	イタン	heresy; heterodoxy
	異同	イドウ	difference
	異動	イドウ	change; reshuffle
	異物	イブツ	foreign matter
	異変	イヘン	accident; mishap
	異邦人	イホウジン	foreigner; alien; outsider
	異名	イミョウ	nickname; another name; alias
	異様	イヨウ	strange; outlandish; fantastic; grotesque
	異例	イレイ	exception; singular case
	異論	イロン	different opinion; objection; controversial opinion
訓	異なる	ことなる	*vi.* differ; be different/dissimilar/unlike

1343

略 ⑪ ⎯ ⎯ ⎯ ⎯ 田 田 略 略 略 略 略

音	略	リャク	omission; abridgement; abbreviation
熟	略する	リャクする	*vt.* omit; abbreviate; abridge; shorten
	略画	リャクガ	rough sketch
	略言	リャクゲン	abbreviated statement —*vi.* state briefly
	略語	リャクゴ	abbreviation
	略号	リャクゴウ	cable address
	略字	リャクジ	simplified Chinese character
	略式	リャクシキ	informal; summary
	略述	リャクジュツ	brief account; outline —*v.* give a brief account; outline

略称	リャクショウ	abbreviation —*v.* abbreviate
略図	リャクズ	rough sketch; outline map
略装	リャクソウ	everyday clothes; informal wear
略奪	リャクダツ	plunder; pillage; looting —*v.* plunder; pillage; loot
略伝	リャクデン	brief account; short history
略筆	リャクヒツ	abbreviated —*vt.* leave out formalities (in a letter)
略歴	リャクレキ	brief personal history; résumé
略記	リャッキ	brief account; outline —*v.* give a brief account; outline

1344

畳 ⑫ 　丶 口 田 用 甲 甲 畾 畾 畾 畳 畳

音	畳	ジョウ	fold; *jō* (counter for *tatami* mats)
熟	畳語	ジョウゴ	reduplication; repetitive use of the same word or root
訓	畳	たたみ	*tatami* (straw mat layed on the floors of Japanese homes)
	畳む	たたむ	*vt.* fold up; close/shut down

1345

番 ⑫ 　丿 丶 丷 丷 平 平 来 来 番 番 番 番

音	番	バン	watch; vigil; guard; turn; number
熟	番外	バンガイ	extra; outsize
	番傘	バンがさ	coarse oil-paper umbrella
	番組	バンぐみ	program billing (of performers)
	番狂わせ	バンくるわせ	upsetting of arrangements
	番犬	バンケン	watchdog; housedog
	番号	バンゴウ	number
	番台	バンダイ	watch stand; raised platform for a ticket seller, etc.
	番地	バンチ	lot/house number; address
	番茶	バンチャ	*bancha* (coarse green tea)
	番付	バンづけ	program; list; ranking list
	番頭	バントウ	clerk; secretary
	番人	バンニン	guard; watchman
	番兵	バンペイ	sentry; guard

玄 玉 王 瓦 甘 生 用 田 疋 疒 癶 白 皮 皿 目 矛 矢 石 示 礻 禾 穴 立 罒 毋 水 氵

玄玉王瓦甘生用田●疋疒癶白皮皿目矛矢石示ネ禾穴立罒旡母水ネ

5 疋　ひき　animal counter

1346

疎 ⑫　丁 丁 下 疋 疋 疋 疋 距 距 跭 跭 疎

音	疎	ソ	sparse; estrangement; shun; neglect
熟	疎遠	ソエン	estrangement; long separation
	疎開	ソカイ	evacuation; removal; dispersal —*vi.* evacuate; remove; dispense
	疎外	ソガイ	alienation; estrangement —*v.* shun; alienate; estrange
	疎忽	ソコツ	carelessness; heedlessness; thoughtlessness; rashness
	疎食	ソショク	coarse food; plain/simple diet; poor meal
	疎水	ソスイ	drainage; canal
	疎通	ソツウ	mutual understanding —*vi.* understand one another
	疎放	ソホウ	inattentive; careless
	疎密	ソミツ	roughness and fineness
	疎略	ソリャク	coarse; crude
	疎漏	ソロウ	carelessness; negligence
訓	疎い	うとい	little known; unfamiliar; distant; estranged
	疎む	うとむ	*vt.* neglect; shun; estrange
	※疎ましい	うとましい	negligent; remiss
	※疎か	おろそか	disagreeable

1347

疑 ⑭　ヒ ヒ 匕 と 矣 矣 矣 矣 疑 疑 疑 疑 疑

音	疑	ギ	doubt
熟	疑獄	ギゴク	scandal; criminal case; graft case
	疑似	ギジ	looking very alike
	疑点	ギテン	doubtful point; doubt
	疑念	ギネン	doubt; suspicion
	疑問	ギモン	question; problem; doubt
	疑惑	ギワク	distrust; doubt; suspicion
訓	疑い	うたがい	doubt; suspicion
	疑う	うたがう	*vt.* doubt; suspect; distrust
	疑わしい	うたがわしい	doubtful; questionable

5 疒 やまいだれ sickness

1348

疒⑨ 　`　一　广　广　疒　疒　疒　疒　疫

音	疫	エキ	epidemic
		（ヤク）	plague
熟	疫病	エキビョウ	*med*. epidemic
	疫痢	エキリ	*med*. infant dysentery

1349

疾⑩ 　`　一　广　广　疒　疒　疒　疒　疾　疾

音	疾	シツ	disease; speedy
熟	疾患	シッカン	disease; ailment
	疾駆	シック	fast driving/riding —*vi*. ride/drive at high speed
	疾走	シッソウ	speed —*vi*. run at full speed; make a dash
	疾風	シップウ	gale; strong wind
	疾病	シッペイ	disease; illness

1350

症⑩ 　`　一　广　广　疒　疒　疒　疒　症　症

| 音 | 症 | ショウ | condition of an illness |
| 熟 | 症状 | ショウジョウ | *med*. symptom; condition |

1351

疲⑩ 　`　一　广　广　疒　疒　疒　疒　疲　疲

音	疲	ヒ	get tired
熟	疲弊	ヒヘイ	impoverishment; ruin; exhaustion —*vi*. become impoverished; fall into ruin; exhaust oneself
	疲労	ヒロウ	fatigue; weariness; exhaustion —*vi*. tire; exhaust oneself
訓	疲れる	つかれる	*vi*. get tired
	疲れ果てる	つかれはてる	*vi*. get tired out; be exhausted

玄玉王瓦甘生用田疋
疒癶白皮皿目矛矢石示礻禾穴立罒罓母水礻

1352

病 ⑩　　`ー 广 广 广 疒 疒 疒 病 病 病

音	病	ビョウ （ヘイ）	disease; illness; sickness
熟	病院	ビョウイン	hospital; clinic; infirmary; doctor's office/surgery
	病臥	ビョウガ	bedridden —*vi.* be bedridden/ill in bed
	病気	ビョウキ	disease; illness; sickness *fig.* failing; weakness —*vi.* be ill/sick
	病苦	ビョウク	pain/suffering caused by illness
	病欠	ビョウケツ	sick leave —*vi.* be absent because of sickness
	病原菌	ビョウゲンキン	*med.* pathogenic bacteria/fungi; bacillus
	病後	ビョウゴ	convalescence; after-care
	病根	ビョウコン	cause of a disease; root of an evil
	病死	ビョウシ	death from disease —*vi.* die from a disease
	病室	ビョウシツ	sickroom; sick bay; infirmary
	病弱	ビョウジャク	weak; sickly; weak constitution
	病床	ビョウショウ	sickbed; bedridden; laid up
	病状	ビョウジョウ	condition of a disease; (patient's) condition
	病身	ビョウシン	ill/poor health; sickly; susceptible to illness
	病中	ビョウチュウ	during illness/sickness
	病的	ビョウテキ	morbid; abnormal
	病毒	ビョウドク	*med.* disease-causing virus; pathogen
	病人	ビョウニン	sick person; invalid; patient; the sick
	病没	ビョウボツ	death from disease —*vi.* die from disease/illness
	病魔	ビョウマ	disease
	病理学	ビョウリガク	pathology
訓	病	やまい	sickness; illness; disease; bad habit; weakness
	病む	やむ	be ill; get sick; suffer from
	病み上がり	やみあがり	convalescence
	病み付き	やみつき	addicted to; hooked on; unable to give up

1353

痛 ⑫　　`ー 广 广 疒 疒 疒 疒 痞 痞 痛 痛

音	痛	ツウ	ache
熟	痛快	ツウカイ	keen pleasure; thrill
	痛感	ツウカン	strong/intense feeling; intuition —*v.* feel strongly; take to heart; fully realize

痛撃	ツウゲキ	severe blow/attack —*v.* attack severely
痛切	ツウセツ	keen; poignant; acute
痛風	ツウフウ	*med.* gout
痛烈	ツウレツ	severe; fierce; sharp; bitter; biting
訓 痛い	いたい	painful; sore; ache
痛む	いたむ	*vi.* feel/suffer pain; be wounded/injured
痛める	いためる	*vt.* hurt; injure; ache
痛手	いたで	serious wound; heavy blow

1354

痘 ⑫ ＇ 一 广 广 疒 疒 疒 疖 疖 疴 痘 痘

| 音 痘 | トウ | smallpox |
| 熟 痘苗 | トウビョウ | vaccine |

1355

痢 ⑫ ＇ 一 广 广 疒 疒 疒 疒 疜 痁 痢 痢 痢

| 音 痢 | リ | diarrhea |

1356

痴 ⑬ ＇ 一 广 疒 疒 疒 痄 疢 疾 病 痴 痴

音 痴	チ	fool
熟 痴漢	チカン	molester of women; pervert —*vi.* molest; be a pervert
痴人	チジン	simpleton; idiot; fool
痴呆	チホウ	imbecility; dementia

1357

療 ⑰ 广 疒 疒 疒 疒 疒 疒 痄 痦 痦 瘂 療 療

音 療	リョウ	cure; heal
熟 療治	リョウジ	medical treatment; remedy —*v.* treat an illness
療法	リョウホウ	remedy; therapy; medical treatment
療養	リョウヨウ	medical treatment/care —*vi.* receive medical treatment/care
療養所	リョウヨウジョ	sanitarium

1358

癖 ⑱

广 疒 疒 疒 疒 疒 疒 疒 疒 疒 癖 癖

| 音 | 癖 | ヘキ | (bad) habit; fault |
| 訓 | 癖 | くせ | (bad) habit; fault; bad point; cowlick |

1359

癒 ⑱

广 疒 疒 疒 疒 疥 疥 瘉 瘉 癒 癒 癒

音	癒	ユ	heal; cure; satisfy; soothe
熟	癒合	ユゴウ	*med*. agglutination; adhesion —*vi*. agglutinate; adhere
	癒着	ユチャク	adhesion; healing up —*vi*. adhere; heal up
訓	※癒える	いえる	*vi*. be healed; recover
	※癒す	いやす	*vt*. heal; cure; satisfy; soothe

---

5 癶 はつがしら departing head

1360

発 ⑨

フ ㇇ ㇆ 癶 癶 癶 癶 癶 発

音	発	ハツ	discharge; break out; disclose; start
		ホツ	occur
熟	発する	ハッする	*vi*. discharge; fire; issue; publish; cry out; start off; leave
	発案	ハツアン	proposition; suggestion; motion —*v*. propose; suggest; move
	発育	ハツイク	growth; development —*vi*. grow; develop
	発音	ハツオン	pronunciation; articulation —*v*. pronounce; articulate
	発芽	ハツガ	germination; sprouting; budding —*vi*. germinate; sprout; bud
	発会	ハッカイ	first club meeting —*vi*. have the first club meeting
	発覚	ハッカク	revelation; detection; discovery; disclosure; exposure —*vi*. be revealed/detected/discovered/exposed
	発刊	ハッカン	publication; issue —*v*. publish; issue; bring out; start; launch

発汗	ハッカン	sweating; perspiration —*vi*. sweat; perspire
発揮	ハッキ	manifestation; exhibition; demonstration; display —*v*. make manifest; exhibit; demonstrate; display; show
発狂	ハッキョウ	madness; craziness; insanity —*vi*. go mad/crazy/out of one's mind
発禁	ハッキン	prohibition of sale or publication
発掘	ハックツ	excavation; exhumation; digs; find —*v*. excavate; exhume; dig up; unearth
発見	ハッケン	discovery; revelation; detection —*v*. discover; detect; spot
発言	ハツゲン	utterance; speaking; speech; opinion —*vi*. speak; utter; open one's mouth; give an opinion
発光	ハッコウ	radiation; luminescence —*vi*. radiate; emit light; luminate
発行	ハッコウ	issue; publication; flotation —*v*. issue; publish; float
発効	ハッコウ	effectuation; coming in to effect —*v*. become effective; come/put into effect
発酵	ハッコウ	fermentation —*v*. ferment
発散	ハッサン	exhalation; radiation; diffusion; evaporation; divergence —*v*. exhale; emit; radiate; evaporate
発車	ハッシャ	departure (of a train, car, etc.) —*vi*. start; leave; depart
発射	ハッシャ	firing; shooting; lift-off —*v*. discharge firearms; fire; shoot
発祥	ハッショウ	beginning —*vi*. begin; start off; originate
発信	ハッシン	dispatch of a letter, telegram, etc. —*vi*. send/dispatch a letter; telegraph; cable
発進	ハッシン	start; departure; take-off; launch —*vi*. start; depart; take-off; launch
発疹	ハッシン (ホッシン)	eruption; rash —*vi*. break out into a rash
発生	ハッセイ	occurrence; outbreak; appearance; birth; creation —*v*. occur; happen; come into existence
発声	ハッセイ	utterance —*vi*. utter; speak out; exclaim
発送	ハッソウ	sending; forwarding; shipping; dispatch —*v*. send out; forward; ship; dispatch
発想	ハッソウ	expression; conception; idea —*v*. conceive/come up with an idea
発達	ハッタツ	development; growth; progress —*vi*. develop; grow; make progress
発着	ハッチャク	departure and arrival —*vi*. depart and arrive
発注	ハッチュウ	ordering —*v*. order; give an order
発展	ハッテン	expansion; extension; progress; prosperity; dissipation —*vi*. expand; extend; develop; grow
発電	ハツデン	electricity generation; sending a telegram —*vi*. generate electricity; send a telegram; wire

玄玉王瓦甘生用田疋疒癶 ● 白皮皿目矛矢石示礻禾穴立罒罒母氺礻

玄
玉
王
瓦
甘
生
用
田
疋
疒
● 癶
白
皮
皿
目
矛
矢
石
示
礻
禾
穴
立
罒
罓
母
水
礻

発電所	ハツデンショ	power station/plant
発動	ハツドウ	motion; activity; exercise —*v*. move; put in motion; exercise
発熱	ハツネツ	fever; generation of heat ***phy***. calorification —*vi*. break out into a fever ***phy***. generate heat
発表	ハッピョウ	announcement; publication; statement —*v*. announce; publish; make public
発病	ハツビョウ	outbreak of a disease —*vi*. contract a disease; fall sick
発布	ハップ	promulgation; proclamation; issue —*v*. promulgate; proclaim; issue
発奮	ハップン	inspiration; stimulation —*vi*. be inspired/stimulated
発砲	ハッポウ	gunfire —*vi*. fire; open fire; discharge firearms
発明	ハツメイ	invention; contrivance; cleverness; brightness —*v*. invent; devise; contrive
発令	ハツレイ	official announcement; proclamation —*v*. announce; proclaim
発露	ハツロ	manifestation; expression; exhibition —*vi*. manifest; express; exhibit
発起	ホッキ	proposal; suggestion —*v*. project; propose; suggest
発句	ホック	haiku poetry; first line of a *renga*
発作	ホッサ	spasm; fit
発作的	ホッサテキ	spasmodic; fitful
発足	ホッソク	starting; inauguration —*vi*. start; make a start; be inaugurated
発端	ホッタン	origin; genesis; beginning
¥ 発券	ハッケン	issue of banknotes/securities; note issuing —*vt*. issue banknotes/securities
発行者 利回り	ハッコウシャ りまわり	issuer's cost
発展途上国	ハッテン トジョウコク	developing countries
発売	ハツバイ	sale —*v*. sell; put on the market
発売中	ハツバイチュウ	now on sale

1361

 ⑫ 　フ　ヲ　プ　癶　癶　癶　癶　癶　癶　登　登　登

音 登	ト トウ	climb; attendance
熟 登記	トウキ	registration; registry —*v*. register; get on the register
登校	トウコウ	school attendance; attending school

	—*vi*. go to/attend school
登場	トウジョウ	entry; advent —*vi*. make an entrance; enter upon the stage; appear; show up
登頂	トウチョウ	reaching the summit —*vi*. reach/climb to the summit
登板	トウバン	*bas*. going up to the mound —*vi*. *bas*. take the plate; go to the mound
登用	トウヨウ	appointment; assignment; elevation; promotion; advancement —*v*. appoint; assign; designate; promote
登竜門	トウリュウモン	gateway to success
登録	トウロク	registration; record; entry —*v*. register; enter on a register; enroll
登山	トザン	mountaineering; mountain climbing —*vi*. go up/climb/scale a mountain
訓 登る	のぼる	*vi*. climb; scale; go up; ascend; rise
¥ 登録商標	トウロク ショウヒョウ	registered trademark

---

5 白 しろい white

1362

白 ⑤ ノ イ 白 白 白

音 白	ハク	white; clean; clear
	ビャク	white
熟 白衣	ハクイ	white robe
白眼視	ハクガンシ	cold/indifferent look; frown —*v*. look coldly; frown upon; look with indifference
白銀	ハクギン	silver
白紙	ハクシ	blank paper; clean sheet of paper
白日	ハクジツ	daytime; broad daylight; bright day
白書	ハクショ	white paper; economic white paper
白状	ハクジョウ	confession; avowal —*v*. confess; avow; own up to; admit to
白色人種	ハクショクジンシュ	white race
白人	ハクジン	white person
白痴	ハクチ	*derog*. idiot
白昼	ハクチュウ	daytime; broad daylight
白昼夢	ハクチュウム	day dream
白鳥	ハクチョウ	swan
白銅	ハクドウ	nickel

599

玄玉王瓦甘生用田疋广癶白皮皿目矛矢石示礻禾穴立罒歹母氷礻

白熱	ハクネツ	climax; white heat; incandescence —*vi*. grow excited; climax; become white hot; be incandescent
白髪	ハクハツ	white/gray hair
白票	ハクヒョウ	white/blank vote
白米	ハクマイ	polished/cleaned rice
白金	ハッキン	platinum
白血病	ハッケツビョウ	*med.* leukemia
白夜	ビャクヤ	nights with the midnight sun

訓

白	しろ	white
白い	しろい	white; fair; blank; spotless; immaculate; clean
白身	しろみ	white meat/fish; white of an egg; albumen
白	（しら）	white
白髪	しらが	gray/white hair
白樺	しらかば	white birch
白壁	しらかべ	whitewashed wall
白木	しらき	plain/unpainted wood
白ける	しらける	*vi.* become chilled/spoiled
白々しい	しらじらしい	tense; awkward
白む	しらむ	*vi.* grow light

1363

 百 ⑥ 一 ア 丆 万 百 百

音

| 百 | ヒャク | hundred; numerous; many |

熟

百害	ヒャクガイ	many evils; much harm
百獣	ヒャクジュウ	all beasts; all kinds of animals
百姓	ヒャクショウ	farmer; farm laborer
百戦錬磨	ヒャクセンレンマ	veteran; old-timer
百点	ヒャクテン	perfect score; full marks
百人一首	ヒャクニンイッシュ	*hyakuninisshu* (Hundred Poems by One Hundred Poets)
百年	ヒャクネン	one hundred years; century
百聞	ヒャクブン	hearing many things
百分	ヒャクブン	one hundred parts —*v.* divide into one hundred parts
百分率	ヒャクブンリツ	percentage
百万	ヒャクマン	million
百万長者	ヒャクマンチョウジャ	millionnaire
百面相	ヒャクメンソウ	all kinds of comic faces; many facial expressions

百科事典	ヒャッカジテン	encyclopedia
百貨店	ヒャッカテン	department store
百発百中	ヒャッパツ ヒャクチュウ	never fail to hit the mark; all correct; right on target
訓 ※百合	ゆり	lily

1364

的 ⑧ ′ ′ ′ 竹 白 白 白 的 的

音 的	テキ	target; exact
熟 的確	テキカク	exact; precise; accurate
的中	テキチュウ	hit —*vi.* hit the bull's eye
訓 的	まと	target

1365

皆 ⑨ ー ヒ ヒ' 比 比 比' 毕 毕 皆

音 皆	カイ	all
熟 皆既食	カイキショク	total eclipse
皆勤	カイキン	perfect attendance; nonabsence —*vi.* attend regularly
皆無	カイム	nothing
訓 皆	みな	everybody; all

1366

皇 ⑨ ′ ′ 竹 白 白 自 阜 阜 皇

音 皇	オウ	emperor; imperial
	コウ	emperor; lord; imperial
熟 皇子	オウジ	prince
皇女	オウジョ	princess
皇位	コウイ	the throne
皇居	コウキョ	imperial palace
皇后	コウゴウ	empress; queen; empress/queen consort
皇室	コウシツ	imperial household; royal family
皇族	コウゾク	imperial/royal family
皇太后	コウタイゴウ	queen
皇太子	コウタイシ	crown prince

玄玉王瓦甘生用田疋广癶白皮皿目矛矢石示礻禾穴立罒罘母水氵

601

玄玉王瓦甘生用田疋疒癶
● 白
● 皮
● 皿目矛矢石示礻禾穴立罒罓母水礻

5 皮　ひのかわ／けがわ　leather; skin

1367

皮 ⑤　丿 厂 广 皮 皮

音	皮	ヒ	skin; hide; leather; bark
熟	皮下	ヒカ	under the skin; subcutaneous
	皮下注射	ヒカチュウシャ	*med.* hypodermic injection
	皮革	ヒカク	hide; skin; leather
	皮相	ヒソウ	superficial; outward
	皮肉	ヒにく	irony; sarcasm
	皮膚	ヒフ	skin
	皮膚科	ヒフカ	*med.* dermatology
	皮膚病	ヒフビョウ	*med.* skin disease
	皮膜	ヒマク	*med.* membrane
訓	皮	かわ	skin
	皮切り	かわきり	beginning; start
	皮算用	かわザンヨウ	count one's chickens before they are hatched

5 皿　さら　dish; plate

1368

皿 ⑤　丨 冂 冊 皿 皿

訓	皿	さら	dish; plate

1369

盆 ⑨　丿 八 今 分 分 盆 盆 盆 盆

音	盆	ボン	the Bon/Lantern Festival; Festival of the Dead; tray
熟	盆栽	ボンサイ	bonsai; potted dwarf tree
	盆石	ボンセキ	miniature landscape arranged on a tray

盆地　　　ボンチ　　　basin; round valley

1370

益 ⑩　　丶　丷　丷　ゲ　兴　犬　谷　谷　益　益

音	益	エキ	profit; gain; use; benefit
		（ヤク）	use; benefit
熟	益する	エキする	*vt.* be beneficial/useful
	益虫	エキチュウ	useful/beneficial insect
	益鳥	エキチョウ	useful/beneficial bird
	益金	エッキン	profit; gain
訓	益す	ます	increase; multiply; augment
	益々	ますます	increasingly; more and more

1371

盛 ⑪　　ノ　厂　厃　成　成　成　成　盛　盛　盛　盛

音	盛	セイ	prosperous
		（ジョウ）	
熟	盛夏	セイカ	midsummer; height of summer
	盛会	セイカイ	successful meeting
	盛況	セイキョウ	prosperity; flourishing
	盛業	セイギョウ	thriving business; success in business
	盛衰	セイスイ	rise and fall; ups and downs; vicissitudes
	盛装	セイソウ	formal dress —*vi.* dress formally
	盛大	セイダイ	grand; magnificent; lavish
訓	盛る	さかる	*vi.* thrive; prosper; flourish; be popular
	盛ん	さかん	prospering; flourishing; popular; enthusiastic
	盛る	もる	*vt.* heap; pile up; serve; fill; poison
	盛り上がる	もりあがる	*vi.* swell; rise; arise; surge
	盛り沢山	もりダクサン	various; colorful; full

1372

盗 ⑪　　丶　丷　ソ　ゾ　沙　次　次　咨　浴　盗　盗

音	盗	トウ	steal
熟	盗作	トウサク	plagiarism; literary/artistic theft —*vi.* plagiarize
	盗賊	トウゾク	thief; robber; burglar

玄玉王瓦甘生用田疋疒癶白皮皿目矛矢石示礻禾穴立罒旡母水衤

	盗聴	トウチョウ	wiretapping; wire tap —v. wiretap; listen in; eavesdrop
	盗難	トウナン	robbery; theft; burglary
	盗品	トウヒン	stolen article/goods; loot; hot goods
	盗品売買	トウヒンバイバイ	dealing in stolen goods; fencing
	盗癖	トウヘキ	kleptomania
	盗用	トウヨウ	appropriation; embezzlement; plagiarism —v. appropriate; embezzle
	盗塁	トウルイ	*bas.* stealing a base —*vi.bas.* steal a base
訓	盗み	ぬすみ	theft; stealing; larceny
	盗む	ぬすむ	*vt*. steal; rob; pilfer
	盗人	ぬすびと	robber; thief; burglar

1373

盟 ⑬ 　 亅 冂 日 日 日 明 明 明 明 明 盟 盟

音	盟	メイ	pledge; oath; alliance
熟	盟邦	メイホウ	allied nation
	盟約	メイヤク	pledge; pact; alliance
	盟友	メイユウ	comrade; sworn friend; staunch ally

1374

監 ⑮ 　 亅 厂 厂 戶 戶 戶 臣 臣ノ 臣仁 臣仁 監 監

音	監	カン	watch; lookout
熟	監禁	カンキン	confinement; imprisonment; detention in custody —v. imprison; confine
	監獄	カンゴク	prison
	監査	カンサ	inspection; superintendence —v. inspect; superintend
	監察	カンサツ	inspection —*vt*. inspect
	監視	カンシ	watch; surveillance —v. watch; keep watch; be on the lookout
	監修	カンシュウ	editorial supervision —v. supervise the editing (of an anthology, dictionary, etc.)
	監督	カントク	supervisor; superintendent; director —v. supervise; direct
	監房	カンボウ	prison cell/block
¥	監査	カンサ	audit
	監査法人	カンサホウジン	audit corporation
	監査役	カンサヤク	auditor

盤 ⑮ ＇ 丿 刀 舟 舟 舟 舟 舟 船 般 磐 盤 盤

| 音 | 盤 | バン | plate; board; disk |
| 熟 | 盤石 | バンジャク | huge rock; firmness |

---

5 目　め／めへん　eye

1376

目 ⑤ 丨 冂 冃 月 目

音	目	モク （ボク）	eye; classification; order
熟	目撃	モクゲキ	witnessing; observation —*v.* witness; observe
	目撃者	モクゲキシャ	witness
	目算	モクサン	expectation; estimate; plan —*v.* expect; estimate; plan
	目次	モクジ	table of contents
	目前	モクゼン	before one's eyes
	目測	モクソク	measuring by eye —*v.* measure by eye
	目的	モクテキ	purpose; object; aim
	目標	モクヒョウ	aim; target; goal; objective
	目礼	モクレイ	eye greeting —*v.* greet by eye
	目録	モクロク	contents; catalog; list; inventory
	目下	モッカ	at present; now
訓	目	め （ま）	eye; look; judgment; pip; grain
	目当て	めあて	guide; aim
	目上	めうえ	one's superior/senior
	目移り	めうつり	waivering —*vi.* waiver/be at a loss what to choose
	目方	めかた	weight
	目先	めさき	before one's eyes; the near future; foresight
	目指す	めざす	*vt.* aim at/for
	目覚し時計	めざましどケイ	alarm clock
	目覚める	めざめる	*vi.* wake up; awaken
	目下	めした	one's inferior/subordinate/junior
	目印	めじるし	mark; sign

玄玉王瓦甘生用田疋疒癶白皮皿目矛矢石示礻禾穴立罒无母氺礻

目立つ	めだつ	*vi*. be conspicuous; stand out
目玉	めだま	eyeball
目付き	めつき	look; expression
目鼻	めはな	eyes and nose
目分量	めブンリョウ	by eye measure; by sight
目星	めぼし	aim; object
目盛り	めもり	graduation; scale
目安	めやす	standard; yardstick
¥ 目先	めさき	near future
目先筋	めさきすじ	day-to-day trader
目玉	めだま	eyeball; striking point
目玉商品	めだまショウヒン	leader; loss leader
目論見書	モクロみショ	prospectus

1377

 直 ⑧ 一 ナ ナ 广 市 市 首 首 直

音 直	ジキ	direct; at once; soon
	チョク	straight; directly; upright; frank
熟 直々	ジキジキ	personal; direct
直筆	ジキヒツ	one's own handwriting; autograph
直営	チョクエイ	direct management/control/operation —*v*. manage/control directly
直撃	チョクゲキ	direct hit —*v*. score a direct hit
直言	チョクゲン	plain speaking; straight talking —*v*. speak plainly; speak without reserve; speak one's mind
直後	チョクゴ	just/soon after
直視	チョクシ	looking in the face —*v*. look a person directly in the face
直射	チョクシャ	direct rays/fire —*v*. fire point-blank/directly
直進	チョクシン	straight on —*vi*. go straight on; make straight for
直接	チョクセツ	directly
直線	チョクセン	straight line
直前	チョクゼン	just before
直送	チョクソウ	direct delivery —*v*. send directly
直属	チョクゾク	under the direct control of —*v*. be under the direct control of
直腸	チョクチョウ	*med*. rectum
直通	チョクツウ	direct service/communication —*vi*. be in direct communication
直配	チョクハイ	direct distribution —*v*. distribute directly

直売	チョクバイ	direct sales —v. sell directly
直面	チョクメン	confrontation —vi. confront; face; be up against
直訳	チョクヤク	literal translation —v. translate/render literally
直喩	チョクユ	simile
直輸入	チョクユニュウ	direct import —v. import directly
直立	チョクリツ	erectness —vi. stand erect; rise perpendicularly
直立不動	チョクリツフドウ	standing at attention
直流	チョクリュウ	direct current (DC)
直下	チョッカ	directly/right under —vi. fall perpendicularly/down
直角	チョッカク	*math*. right angle
直轄	チョッカツ	direct control; immediate supervision —v. have the direct control of
直感	チョッカン	intuition; hunch —v. know by intuition; have a hunch
直観	チョッカン	intuition —v. know by intuition
直系	チョッケイ	direct line of family descent
直径	チョッケイ	*math*. diameter
直結	チョッケツ	direct connection —v. connect/link directly
直行	チョッコウ	going straight; uprightness —vi. go straight/direct

訓	直す	なおす	*vt*. mend; repair; do over again
	直る	なおる	*vi*. be mended; get better; recover; be corrected
	直ちに	ただちに	at once; directly; immediately

¥	直物市場	ジキものシジョウ	spot market
	直接税	チョクセツゼイ	direct tax
	直接投資	チョクセツトウシ	direct investment

1378

盲 ⑧ ` 亠 亡 产 亡 育 育 盲

音	盲	モウ	blind
熟	盲学校	モウガッコウ	school for the blind
	盲従	モウジュウ	blind obedience —vi. be very obedient
	盲信	モウシン	blind acceptance; credulity —v. accept blindly
	盲人	モウジン	blind person
	盲腸	モウチョウ	*med*. appendix
	盲点	モウテン	blind spot
	盲導犬	モウドウケン	guide dog
	盲目	モウモク	blindness
	盲目的	モウモクテキ	blind; reckless

玄玉王瓦甘生用田疋疒癶白皮皿目矛矢石示衤禾穴立罒罘母水衤

1379

看 ⑨ 　一 二 三 チ 牟 看 看 看 看

音	看	カン	care; watch
熟	看過	カンカ	connivance (at wrong doing) —v. overlook an error
	看護	カンゴ	caring; nursing —v. nurse; care for the sick
	看護婦	カンゴフ	nurse
	看守	カンシュ	guard; warder; jailer
	看取	カンシュ	discernment; perception —v. discern; perceive; notice; detect
	看破	カンパ	penetration —v. penetrate; see through
	看板	カンバン	signboard; sign
	看病	カンビョウ	nursing the sick —v. nurse; tend; care for a sick person
訓	※看る	みる	*vt*. see

1380

県 ⑨ 　1 口 曰 月 目 眉 冒 県 県

音	県	ケン	prefecture
熟	県営	ケンエイ	prefectural administration
	県下	ケンカ	within a prefecture
	県議会	ケンギカイ	prefectural assembly
	県政	ケンセイ	prefectural government
	県税	ケンゼイ	prefectural taxes
	県知事	ケンチジ	prefectural governor
	県庁	ケンチョウ	prefectural office
	県道	ケンドウ	prefectural road
	県立	ケンリツ	prefectural (school, hospital, etc.)

1381

盾 ⑨ 　一 厂 厂 厂 厔 厔 盾 盾 盾

音	盾	ジュン	shield
訓	盾	たて	shield
	盾突く	たてつく	*vi*. oppose; rebel against

1382

省 ⑨   亅 丷 小 少 少 省 省 省 省

音	省	ショウ	omit
		セイ	review; consider
熟	省略	ショウリャク	omission; abbreviation —v. omit; abbreviate
訓	省みる	かえりみる	vt. consider; think of; reflect on; worry about
	省く	はぶく	vt. omit; leave out; cut down; save

1383

相 ⑨   一 十 才 木 机 机 相 相 相

音	相	ソウ	each other; reciprocal; aspect; phase; physiognomy
		ショウ	minister
熟	相伴	ショウバン	accompaniment —vi. accompany
	相違	ソウイ	difference; discrepancy —vi. be different; have a discrepancy
	相応	ソウオウ	suitable; fitting —vi. be suitable/fitting
	相関	ソウカン	correlation —vi. correlate
	相関関係	ソウカンカンケイ	correlation; relation; relationship
	相関的	ソウカンテキ	interrelated
	相互	ソウゴ	mutual; reciprocal
	相殺	ソウサイ	offset; counteraction; compensation —v. offset; countervail
	相似	ソウジ	similarity; resemblance; analogy —vi. be similar/analogous; resemble
	相続	ソウゾク	inheritance; succession —v. inherit; succeed
	相続人	ソウゾクニン	heir; heiress; successor
	相対	ソウタイ	relativity
	相対的	ソウタイテキ	relative
	相談	ソウダン	consultation; discussion —v. consult; confer; discuss
	相当	ソウトウ	fit; suitable; appropriate; equivalent —vi. be equivalent/correspond to
	相等	ソウトウ	equality; equivalence
訓	相	あい	together; fellow; each other
	相変わらず	あいかわらず	as usual
	相性	あいショウ	affinity; compatibility
	相対する	あいタイする	vi. facing each other directly
	相次ぐ	あいつぐ	vi. follow in succession

玄玉王瓦甘生用田疋广癶白皮皿目矛矢石示礻禾穴立罒罖母水氵

相手	あいて	the other party; partner; opponent
※相撲	すもう	sumo wrestling
¥ 相対取引 （売買）	あいタイとりひき （バイバイ）	negotiated transaction
相関係数	ソウカンケイスウ	coefficient of correlation
相互援助	ソウゴエンジョ	mutual aid
相互銀行 （相銀）	ソウゴギンコウ （ソウギン）	mutual savings and loan bank
相続財産	ソウゾクザイサン	inheritance; inherited property
相続税	ソウゾクゼイ	inheritance (sucession) tax
相場	ソウば	current/market price; speculation; estimation; the market

1384 冒 ⑨　丶 冂 冂 冃 冃 冐 冒 冒 冒

音	冒	ボウ	brave; risk; defy; dare
熟	冒険	ボウケン	adventure —*vi.* have an adventure
	冒頭	ボウトウ	opening; beginning; start
	冒瀆	ボウトク	blasphemy; sacrilege; desecration —*v.* blaspheme; desecrate
訓	冒す	おかす	*vt.* risk; brave; defy; dare; challenge; (a disease) attack

1385 真 ⑩　一 十 广 方 方 肯 直 直 真 真

音	真	シン	truth; genuine; real
熟	真意	シンイ	one's real mind; real intention; true meaning
	真因	シンイン	true cause/motive
	真打ち	シンうち	star performer; headliner
	真価	シンカ	real value; true worth
	真偽	シンギ	true or false; authenticity
	真紅	シンク	crimson
	真空	シンクウ	vacuum; evacuated
	真空包装	シンクウホウソウ	vacuum packing
	真剣	シンケン	sword; true; honest
	真摯	シンシ	sincere
	真実	シンジツ	truth; true; real; truly; really
	真珠	シンジュ	pearl

真珠湾	シンジュワン	Pearl Harbor
真情	シンジョウ	true feelings
真髄	シンズイ	essence; quintessence; soul
真性	シンセイ	genuine
真正	シンセイ	genuine; true
真善美	シンゼンビ	truth, good, and beauty
真相	シンソウ	the truth; fact
真底	シンテイ	bottom of one's heart; very bottom
真否	シンピ	truth or falsehood; the truth
真理	シンリ	truth

訓

真	ま	truth; sincerity
真新しい	まあたらしい	brand-new
真顔	まがお	serious look/face
真心	まごころ	sincerity
真四角	まシカク	perfect square
真面目	まじめ	serious; earnest; honest; reliable
真っ赤	まっか	deep red
真っ青	まっさお	azure; deep blue; white as a sheet; pale
真っ盛り	まっさかり	at their best
真っ白	まっしろ	pure white; snow-white
真っ直ぐ	まっすぐ	straight; in a straight line; in a beeline
真夏	まなつ	midsummer
真似	まね	imitation; mimicry; aping; copying; action; behavior —v. imitate; mimic; copy
真似る	まねる	vt. imitate; mimic; copy; follow
真昼	まひる	midday; high noon
真冬	まふゆ	midwinter
真水	まみず	fresh water
真夜中	まよなか	middle of the night; at midnight
※真	まこと	true; real

1386

眠 ⑩ 丨 冂 冃 冃 目 盯 盯 肌 眠 眠

音 眠　ミン　sleep

訓
眠い	ねむい	sleepy; drowsy; tired
眠る	ねむる	vi. sleep
眠たい	ねむたい	sleepy; drowsy; tired
眠り薬	ねむりぐすり	sleeping pills
眠気	ねむケ	sleepiness; drowsiness

玄
玉
王
瓦
甘
生
用
田
疋
广
犭
白
皮
皿
目 •
矛
矢
石
示
衤
禾
穴
立
罒
罘
母
氺
衤

玄玉王瓦甘生用田疋疒癶白皮皿目矛矢石示礻禾穴立罒罒母氺礻

1387

眼 ⑪ 丨 冂 冂 冃 月 目 目⌐ 目⌐ 目⌐ 眼 眼 眼

音	眼	ガン	eye; point
		（ゲン）	
熟	眼下	ガンカ	under one's eyes
	眼科	ガンカ	*med*. ophthalmology
	眼球	ガンキュウ	eyeball
	眼光	ガンコウ	glitter of one's eyes; discernment; insight
	眼中	ガンチュウ	in one's eyes; consideration
	眼目	ガンモク	main point; gist; essence
	眼力	ガンリキ	insight; penetration; perception
訓	眼	まなこ	eye; eyeball
	※眼	め	eye; optics
	※眼鏡	めがね	glasses; spectacles

1388

眺 ⑪ 丨 冂 冃 月 目 目] 目] 目] 眺 眺 眺

音	眺	チョウ	look
熟	眺望	チョウボウ	view; prospect; lookout —*v*. view; look out
訓	眺め	ながめ	view; scene; outlook; prospect
	眺める	ながめる	*vt*. look; stare; gaze

1389

睡 ⑬ 丨 冂 月 目 目⌐ 目⌐ 旷 旷 睗 睡 睡

音	睡	スイ	sleep
熟	睡魔	スイマ	Morpheus (god of sleep)
	睡眠	スイミン	sleep; slumber —*vi*. sleep; slumber
訓	※睡る	ねむる	*vi*. sleep

1390

督 ⑬ 丿 ト 上 十 朿 朿 叔 叔 叔 督 督

| 音 | 督 | トク | control |

熟	督促	トクソク	urge; demand; pressing —v. urge; press
	督励	トクレイ	encouragement —v. encourage; urge

1391

瞬 ⑱　丨 月 目 目 旷 旷 瞬 瞬 瞬 瞬 瞬 瞬 瞬

音	瞬	シュン	moment
熟	瞬間	シュンカン	moment
	瞬時	シュンジ	moment; instant
訓	瞬く	またたく	*vi*. wink; blink
	瞬き	またたき	blink; twinkle

5 矛 ほこ spear

1392

矛 ⑤　フ マ ユ 予 矛

音	矛	ム	halberd; spear; lance
熟	矛盾	ムジュン	contradiction —*vi*. be contradictory
訓	矛	ほこ	halberd
	矛先	ほこさき	spearhead; point of a spear

5 矢 や／やへん arrow

1393

矢 ⑤　丿 ㇒ ㇗ 生 矢

音	矢	シ	arrow
訓	矢	や	arrow
	矢先	やさき	arrowhead; moment; point; in time
	矢印	やじるし	arrow-shaped mark
	矢玉	やだま	arrows and bullets
	矢庭に	やにわに	on the spot; suddenly
	矢来	やライ	temporary bamboo and log fence

玄玉王瓦甘生用田疋疒癶白皮皿目矛矢石示礻禾穴立罒毋水礻

1394

知 ⑧ ノ ㇒ ⇂ 牛 矢 知 知 知

音	知	チ	knowledge; wisdom; intellect; acquaintance
熟	知恵	チエ	wisdom; sense; wits; brains
	知覚	チカク	perception; sensation; feeling —v. perceive; sense; feel
	知己	チキ	acquaintance; intimate friend
	知事	チジ	governor (of a prefecture)
	知識	チシキ	knowledge; information; know-how; learning; understanding
	知識階級	チシキカイキュウ	intelligentsia
	知人	チジン	acquaintance; friend
	知性	チセイ	intellect; intelligence
	知的	チテキ	intellectual; mental
	知能	チノウ	intellect; intelligence; mental faculties
	知名	チメイ	noted; distinguished; famous; well-known
訓	知る	しる	vt. know; be aware of; learn; understand; recognize; realize; feel
	知らせ	しらせ	information; notice; report; news
	知らせる	しらせる	vt. inform; advise; notify; report
	知らん顔	しらんかお	feigned ignorance; indifference; nonchalance
	知り合い	しりあい	friend; acquaintance
¥	知的所有権	チテキ ショユウケン	intellectual property

1395

短 ⑫ ノ ㇒ ⇂ 牛 矢 矢 矢 知 矢 矢 短 短

音	短	タン	short; brief; close
熟	短歌	タンカ	tanka (31-syllable Japanese poem)
	短気	タンキ	quick/short temper
	短期	タンキ	short term
	短縮	タンシュク	shortening; contraction; curtailment —v. shorten; contract; curtail
	短所	タンショ	defect; fault; demerit; failing; shortcoming
	短針	タンシン	the short hand (of a clock)
	短調	タンチョウ	minor key (in music)
	短波	タンパ	shortwave
	短編	タンペン	short piece/story; sketch

	短命	タンメイ	short life
訓	短い	みじかい	short; brief; abbreviated
¥	短期借入金	タンキ かりいれキン	short-term loans repayable

1396

矯 ⑰　　ノ　ト　ケ　失　矢　矢　矢　矫　矫　矫　矯　矯

音	矯	キョウ	rectify; correct; train
熟	矯正	キョウセイ	reform; rectification; correction —*v.* reform; rectify; correct
訓	矯める	ためる	*vt.* reform; correct; rectify

5　石　いし／いしへん　stone

1397

石 ⑤　　一　ア　不　石　石

音	石	セキ	stone; jewel
		（コク）	*koku* (unit of volume, approx. 0.18 *ml*)
		（シャク）	
熟	石像	セキゾウ	stone image; statue
	石炭	セキタン	coal
	石碑	セキヒ	stone monument; tombstone
	石仏	セキブツ	stone image of Buddha
	石墨	セキボク	graphite
	石油	セキユ	oil; petroleum; kerosene
	石灰	セッカイ	lime
	石器	セッキ	prehistoric/Stone Age tools
	石器時代	セッキジダイ	Stone Age
	石鹸	セッケン	soap
訓	石	いし	stone
	石頭	いしあたま	bigot
	石垣	いしがき	stone wall
	石畳	いしだたみ	stone pavement
	石橋	いしばし	stone bridge
¥	石油	セキユ	oil; petroleum
	石油化学	セキユカガク	petrochemistry

玄玉王瓦甘生用田疋疒癶白皮皿目矛矢●石示礻禾穴立皿旡母水氺

1398

研 ⑨　一　ァ　�　石　石　石　研　研　研

音	研	ケン	polish; research
熟	研究	ケンキュウ	research; study; investigation; inquiry —*v*. study; make a study of; do research in; investigate
	研究員	ケンキュウイン	research worker
	研究科	ケンキュウカ	post-graduate course
	研究開発	ケンキュウカイハツ	R & D; (Research and Development)
	研修	ケンシュウ	study and training —*v*. study; be trained
	研磨	ケンマ	polishing; grinding —*v*. polish; grind
	研磨機	ケンマキ	grinder; abrader; polishing machine
	研磨材	ケンマザイ	abradant; abrasive
	研磨紙	ケンマシ	sandpaper; emery cloth; glass paper
訓	研ぐ	とぐ	*vt*. grind; sharpen; whet

1399

砂 ⑨　一　ァ　ㇵ　石　石　石丿　砂丿　砂小　砂

音	砂	サ	sand
		シャ	sand
熟	砂丘	サキュウ	sand hill; dune
	砂金	サキン	gold dust
	砂州	サス	sand reef
	砂鉄	サテツ	iron sand
	砂糖	サトウ	sugar
	砂漠	サバク	desert
	砂利	ジャリ	gravel
訓	砂	すな	sand; dune
	砂時計	すなどケイ	hourglass
	砂場	すなば	sand pit
	砂浜	すなはま	sandy beach; sands

1400

砕 ⑨　一　ァ　ㇵ　石　石　砂丿　砕ノ　砕　砕

音	砕	サイ	crush; break; smash

熟	砕石	サイセキ	rubble; smashed rock; macadam —*vi*. macadamize
訓	砕く	くだく	*vt*. break; smash; crush
	砕ける	くだける	*vi*. break; be broken; be simple; be informal

1401

破 ⑩   一 ７ ７ 石 石 石 矿 矿 矿 破 破

音	破	ハ	destroy; break; demolish
熟	破戒	ハカイ	apostasy; breaking a Buddhist commandment
	破壊	ハカイ	destruction; demolition; breakdown —*v*. destroy; break; ruin; wreck; demolish
	破格	ハカク	exception
	破顔	ハガン	smiling face —*vi*. smile broadly
	破棄	ハキ	destruction; annulment; cancellation —*v*. destroy; annul; cancel
	破局	ハキョク	catastrophe; collapse
	破獄	ハゴク	jail breaking —*vi*. escape from prison
	破砕	ハサイ	demolishing; crushing —*v*. demolish; crush
	破傷風	ハショウフウ	*med*. tetanus; lockjaw
	破損	ハソン	damage; injury; breakdown; dilapidation —*v*. be damaged; breakdown; be dilapidated/ destroyed
	破綻	ハタン	failure; rupture; breaking —*vi*. fail; rupture; break
	破談	ハダン	cancellation; rupture; breaking off; rejection
	破天荒	ハテンコウ	unprecedented
	破片	ハヘン	fragment; splinter; broken piece
	破滅	ハメツ	destruction; wreck; ruin; collapse —*vi*. destroy; wreck; ruin; collapse
	破門	ハモン	expulsion; excommunication —*v*. expel; excommunicate
	破約	ハヤク	breach of promise/contract —*v*. break a promise; breach a contract
	破裂	ハレツ	burst; rupture; explosion; eruption —*v*. burst; be ruptured; explode; erupt
	破廉恥	ハレンチ	shamelessness; infamy; ignominy
	ご破算	ごハサン	new calculation
訓	破る	やぶる	*v*. tear; rip; break; destroy; violate; infringe
	破れる	やぶれる	*vi*. be torn/ripped/broken/destroyed
	破れ	やぶれ	rupture; breach; failure; ruin; breakdown; collapse
¥	破産	ハサン	bankruptcy; insolvency; financial failure —*v*. go bankrupt; fail; be ruined

玄玉王瓦甘生用田疋疒癶白皮皿目矛矢石示礻禾穴立罒无母水氵

1402

砲 ⑩ 一 厂 メ 石 石 石 矽 矽 砲 砲

音	砲	ホウ	cannon; gun
熟	砲煙	ホウエン	cannon smoke; gunsmoke
	砲火	ホウカ	gunfire; shellfire
	砲架	ホウカ	gun carriage
	砲艦	ホウカン	gunboat
	砲丸	ホウガン	cannonball; shot (as in shot put)
	砲丸投げ	ホウガンなげ	shot put
	砲撃	ホウゲキ	bombardment; shelling —v. bombard; shell
	砲口	ホウコウ	muzzle (of a gun); caliber
	砲座	ホウザ	gun platform
	砲手	ホウシュ	gunner; artilleryman
	砲術	ホウジュツ	gunnery
	砲身	ホウシン	gun barrel
	砲声	ホウセイ	sound of firing/shelling
	砲戦	ホウセン	artillery engagement
	砲台	ホウダイ	gun battery
	砲弾	ホウダン	shell; cannonball
	砲塔	ホウトウ	gun (turret)
	砲兵	ホウヘイ	artillerist; artilleryman; gunner
	砲門	ホウモン	muzzle (of a gun); gunport
	砲列	ホウレツ	artillery battery
訓	砲	つつ	gun

1403

硬 ⑫ 一 厂 メ 石 石 石 砳 砳 硬 硬 硬 硬

音	硬	コウ	hard; stiff; firm; strong
熟	硬化	コウカ	hardening; vulcanization; stiffening; development —vi. stiffen; harden; metallize; ossify
	硬質	コウシツ	hard
	硬水	コウスイ	hard water
	硬直	コウチョク	stiffness; rigidity —vi. stiffen; become rigid
	硬度	コウド	hardness; solidity
訓	硬い	かたい	hard; stiff; firm
¥	硬貨	コウカ	hard currency; coin

1404

硝 ⑫ 一 厂 ナ 石 石 石' 石" 石" 矿 硝 硝 硝

音	硝	ショウ	saltpeter
熟	硝煙	ショウエン	powder smoke
	硝石	ショウセキ	*chem*. saltpeter
	※硝子	がらす	glass

1405

硫 ⑫ 一 厂 ナ 石 石 石' 矿 硫 硫 硫 硫 硫

音	硫	リュウ	sulfur
熟	硫安	リュウアン	*chem*. ammonium sulfate
	硫酸	リュウサン	*chem*. sulfuric acid
	硫酸紙	リュウサンシ	parchment paper
	※硫黄	いおう	*chem*. sulfur

1406

碁 ⑬ 一 十 廾 廾 甘 甘 其 其 其 其 碁 碁

音	碁	ゴ	the game of go
熟	碁石	ゴいし	black and white stones for go
	碁盤	ゴバン	go board

1407

磁 ⑭ 一 厂 石 石 石" 矿 砭 磁 磁 磁 磁 磁

音	磁	ジ	magnet; pottery; ceramics
熟	磁気	ジキ	magnetism
	磁器	ジキ	porcelain; china; chinaware
	磁極	ジキョク	magnetic pole
	磁石	ジシャク	magnet; magnetite; compass
	磁針	ジシン	magnetic/compass needle
	磁性	ジセイ	magnetism
	磁場	ジば	magnetic field
	磁力	ジリョク	magnetic force

玄玉王瓦甘生用田疋疒癶白皮皿目矛矢
● 石示礻禾穴立罒罒母水礻

1408

碑 ⑭   一 ｢ 石 石 石′ 矿 矿 砷 硬 碑 碑 碑

音	碑	ヒ	stone monument; tombstone
熟	碑文	ヒブン	inscription (on a stone monument); epitaph
	碑銘	ヒメイ	epitaph
訓	碑	いしぶみ	(inscribed) stone monument

1409

確 ⑮   一 ｢ 石 石 矿 矿 矿 矿 砗 砗 碏 確

音	確	カク	certainty; steady; sure
熟	確実	カクジツ	certainty; reliability
	確証	カクショウ	corroboration; confirmation; positive proof
	確信	カクシン	conviction; firm belief; confidence —v. convince oneself; believe firmly; be confident
	確定	カクテイ	final settlement; decision —v. decide; settle; fix; confirm
	確認	カクニン	confirmation; validation —v. confirm; ascertain; validate
	確保	カクホ	guarantee; security —v. guarantee; secure
	確約	カクヤク	definite promise —v. give one's word; commit oneself to
	確立	カクリツ	establishment —v. establish; build up
	確率	カクリツ	probability
	確固	カッコ	firm; steady
訓	確か	たしか	sound; right; perhaps; firm; certain; probable
	確かめる	たしかめる	vt. ascertain
¥	確定申告	カクテイシンコク	final tax return
	確定利付き証券	カクテイリづきショウケン	fixed interest-bearing securities

1410

磨 ⑯   一 广 广 庁 庆 床 麻 麻 麻 麼 磨 磨

音	磨	マ	polish; brush
熟	磨耗	マモウ	wear and tear; abrasion
訓	磨く	みがく	vt. polish/brush (one's teeth); shine (shoes, etc.)

※磨る　　　　する　　　**vt**. rub; chafe; file

1411
礁 ⑰　　一　厂　石　石　石′　石″　石″　砕′　碓　碓　碓　礁

|音| 礁　　ショウ　　reef

1412
礎 ⑱　　一　厂　石　石　石′　石″　石林　砕　碑　碎　礎　礎

|音| 礎　　ソ　　foundation; stone; cornerstone
|熟| 礎材　ソザイ　foundation materials
　　礎石　ソセキ　footstone; foundation stone
|訓| 礎　　いしずえ　foundation stone; cornerstone

5　示　しめす　show　　　　ネ　(p.623)

1413
示 ⑤　　一　二　テ　示　示

|音| 示　　シ　　show; display; express; teaching
　　　　　ジ
|熟| 示威　ジイ　demonstration —**v**. demonstrate
　　示唆　シサ　suggestion; hint —**v**. suggest
　　示談　ジダン　private settlement; settlement out of court
　　　　　　　　—**v**. settle out of court
|訓| 示す　しめす　**vt**. show; display; reveal; indicate; prove
　　示し　しめし　display; revelation; example; indication; proof
　　示し合わ　しめしあわせる　**vt**. prearrange; conspire
　　せる

1414
祭 ⑪　　ノ　ク　タ　夕　夘　タメ　タメ　祭　祭　祭　祭

|音| 祭　　サイ　　festival; feast; deify; worship

621

玄玉王瓦甘生用田疋疒癶白皮皿目矛石示ネ禾穴立罒罖母水ネ

5

玄玉王瓦甘生用田疋广癶白皮皿目矛矢石 • 示ネ禾穴立罒疒母氺衤

	祭日	サイジツ	national holiday; festival day
熟	祭壇	サイダン	altar
	祭典	サイテン	festival
	祭礼	サイレイ	festival
訓	祭り	まつり	feast; festival
	祭る	まつる	*vt*. deify; worship

1415

票 ⑪

一 亠 丆 帀 襾 西 覀 覀 覀 票 票

音	票	ヒョウ	slip of paper; ballot; vote
熟	票決	ヒョウケツ	voting; vote —*v*. vote

1416

禁 ⑬

一 十 才 木 朩 朴 林 林 埜 枼 禁 禁 禁

音	禁	キン	forbid; prohibit
熟	禁じる	キンじる	*vt*. forbid; prohibit
	禁煙	キンエン	no smoking —*vi*. forbid/prohibit smoking
	禁忌	キンキ	taboo
	禁固	キンコ	imprisonment; incarceration; confinement
	禁止	キンシ	prohibition; embargo; ban —*v*. forbid; prohibit; embargo; ban
	禁酒	キンシュ	temperance —*vi*. be temperant; prohibit/forbid alcohol
	禁制	キンセイ	prohibition; taboo; embargo; ban
	禁足	キンソク	confinement —*vt*. confine
	禁断	キンダン	prohibition; withdrawal
	禁治産	キンチサン	incompetence; diminished responsibility
	禁鳥	キンチョウ	protected bird
	禁物	キンモツ	taboo; prohibited object
	禁欲	キンヨク	obstinence; ascetism —*vi*. practice abstinence
	禁猟	キンリョウ	closed season
	禁漁	キンリョウ	no fishing
	禁令	キンレイ	prohibitory decree; prohibition; ban
¥	禁輸	キンユ	ban (no export or import); embargo
	禁輸商品	キンユショウヒン	embargo goods
	禁輸品	キンユヒン	article under the embargo; contraband

礻 しめすへん　show to the left

1417

礼 ⑤　　丶 ラ ネ ネ 礼

音	礼	レイ	courtesy; politeness; salutation; bow
		ライ	
熟	礼讃	ライサン	*Bud.* adore; worship; glorify
	礼拝	ライハイ	Buddhist worship/services —*v.* worhship Buddha
	礼儀	レイギ	manners; courtesy; politeness
	礼金	レイキン	honorarium; fee
	礼式	レイシキ	etiquette
	礼状	レイジョウ	letter of thanks
	礼節	レイセツ	decorum; propriety; politeness
	礼装	レイソウ	formal/ceremonial dress; full dress
	礼典	レイテン	ceremony; ritual; rites
	礼拝	レイハイ	Christian worship/services —*v.* worship God
	礼服	レイフク	formal dress

1418

社 ⑦　　丶 ラ ネ ネ ネ一 衦 社

音	社	シャ	shrine; company; society
熟	社会	シャカイ	society; community; class; world
	社会運動	シャカイウンドウ	social movement
	社会科	シャカイカ	social studies
	社会学	シャカイガク	sociology
	社会主義	シャカイシュギ	socialism
	社会人	シャカイジン	public person; working adult
	社会的	シャカイテキ	social
	社会奉仕	シャカイホウシ	social service
	社会面	シャカイメン	general news page of a newspaper
	社会問題	シャカイモンダイ	social problem
	社訓	シャクン	company motto
	社交	シャコウ	social intercourse/contact; society
	社交家	シャコウカ	sociable person
	社交界	シャコウカイ	the fashionable world; high society
	社交性	シャコウセイ	sociability; outgoing; extrovert

玄玉王瓦甘生用田疋广癶白皮皿目矛矢石示ネ禾穴立罒疒母水ネ

	社主	シャシュ	company owner
	社説	シャセツ	editorial; leading article
	社宅	シャタク	company house/housing
	社団	シャダン	association; corporation
	社長	シャチョウ	company president
	社殿	シャデン	main hall of a shrine
	社務所	シャムショ	shrine office
訓	社	やしろ	Shinto shrine
¥	社会党	シャカイトウ	the Socialist Party
	社会福祉	シャカイフクシ	social welfare
	社会保障	シャカイホショウ	social security
	社債	シャサイ	corporate bond; debenture; (company) bond; debenture
	社債券	シャサイケン	debenture bond
	社費	シャヒ	company expenses
	社有	シャユウ	company owned
	社用	シャヨウ	company business

1419

祈 ⑧ 　 丶 ラ ネ ネ ネ ネ 祈 祈

音	祈	キ	pray
熟	祈願	キガン	prayer —v. pray
	祈禱	キトウ	prayer —v. pray
	祈念	キネン	prayer —v. pray
訓	祈る	いのる	vt. pray; say a prayer

1420

祉 ⑧ 　 丶 ラ ネ ネ ネ 衤 衤 祉

音	祉	シ	welfare

1421

祝 ⑨ 　 丶 ラ ネ ネ ネ 衤 衤 祝

音	祝	シュク（シュウ）	celebrate
熟	祝する	シュクする	vt. congratulate; celebrate

祝儀	シュウギ	celebration; ceremony; tip; gratuity
祝宴	シュクエン	banquet; feast
祝賀	シュクガ	celebration; congratulations
祝祭日	シュクサイジツ	public/national holiday
祝辞	シュクジ	congratulatory address/speeches
祝日	シュクジツ	public/national holday
祝典	シュクテン	festival; celebration; jubilee
祝電	シュクデン	congratulatory telegram
祝杯	シュクハイ	toast
祝福	シュクフク	blessing —*v.* bless
祝砲	シュクホウ	salute of guns

| 訓 | 祝う | いわう | *vt.* congratulate; celebrate; observe an anniversary, etc. |
| | ※祝詞 | のりと | Shinto prayer |

1422

神 ⑨ 　ラ ネ ネ ネ 初 初 袖 神

音	神	シン	god
		ジン	god
熟	神学	シンガク	theology
	神格化	シンカクカ	deification —*v.* deify
	神官	シンカン	Shinto priest
	神宮	ジングウ	major Shinto shrine
	神経	シンケイ	nerve; nervous; nerves
	神経科	シンケイカ	neurology; department of neurology
	神経質	シンケイシツ	nervous temperament; nervousness
	神経症	シンケイショウ	*med.* neurosis
	神権	シンケン	divine right
	神社	ジンジャ	Shinto shrine
	神出鬼没	シンシュツキボツ	elusiveness; be everywhere at once; appearing and disappearing
	神聖	シンセイ	holiness; sacredness; sanctity
	神代	ジンダイ	mythological age; age of the gods
	神通力	ジンツウリキ	magical power
	神殿	シンデン	shrine
	神道	シントウ	Shintoism; Shinto
	神秘	シンピ	mystery
	神秘主義	シンピシュギ	mysticism
	神秘的	シンピテキ	mystic; mysterious
	神父	シンプ	Roman Catholic priest; Father

玄
玉
王
瓦
甘
生
用
田
疋
广
癶
白
皮
皿
目
矛
矢
石
示
ネ
禾
穴
立
罒
罙
母
水
ネ

玄玉王瓦甘生用田疋疒癶白皮皿目矛矢石示礻禾穴立罒旡母水氺

神仏	シンブツ	gods and Buddhas; Shintoism and Buddhism
神妙	シンミョウ	docile; meek; gentle; unresisting
神話	シンワ	myth; mythology

訓

神	かみ	god; deity
神風	かみかぜ	kamikaze
神棚	かみだな	household Shinto altar
神業	かみわざ	act of God; divine work; miracle
神	（かん）	(prefix) Shinto
神主	かんぬし	Shinto priest
神	（こう）	divine; sublime
神々しい	こうごうしい	divine; sublime
＊お神酒	おみき	sacred saké; libation
神様	かみさま	god; deity
＊神楽	かぐら	*kagura* (sacred mucic and dancing)

1423

祖 ⑨ 、 ラ ネ ネ 礻 袒 袒 祖 祖

音 祖　ソ　ancestor

熟

祖国	ソコク	homeland; fatherland
祖先	ソセン	ancestor; forefathers
祖父	ソフ	grandfather
祖父母	ソフボ	grandparents
祖母	ソボ	grandmother

1424

祥 ⑩ 、 ラ ネ ネ ネ ネ゛ 衤 衤 祥 祥

音 祥　ショウ　good omen/sign

1425

禍 ⑬ 、 ラ ネ ネ 礻 袒 袒 祒 袒 禍 禍 禍

音 禍　カ　misfortune; disaster; trouble

熟

| 禍根 | カコン | the root of evil; the source of trouble |
| 禍福 | カフク | fortune and misfortune |

訓 禍　わざわい　trouble; evil; disaster —*vi.* bring trouble on; inflict evil

626

1426

禅 ⑬ 丶 ラ ネ ネ ネ ネ ネ ネ 衤 衵 衵 禅

音	禅	ゼン	silent meditation; Zen
熟	禅師	ゼンシ	***Bud***. the Reverend
	禅宗	ゼンシュウ	Zen sect of Buddhism

1427

福 ⑬ 丶 ラ ネ ネ ネ 衤 衤 衵 福 福 福 福

音	福	フク	fortune; happiness; welfare; wealth
熟	福音	フクイン	the gospel; good news
	福運	フクウン	happiness and good fortune
	福祉	フクシ	welfare
	福利	フクリ	welfare; well-being
	福利厚生	フクリコウセイ	welfare program

---

5 禾 のぎへん *no* (katakana) + tree

1428

私 ⑦ 一 二 千 禾 禾 私 私

音	私	シ	I; private
熟	私案	シアン	one's private plan
	私意	シイ	personal opinion; selfish motive
	私益	シエキ	personal interest/gain
	私怨	シエン	personal enmity; grudge; grievance
	私学	シガク	private school/college/university
	私企業	シキギョウ	private enterprise; privately-owned company
	私見	シケン	personal view/opinion
	私語	シゴ	whisper; whispering
	私恨	シコン	personal grudge
	私財	シザイ	private property
	私事	シジ	personal affairs; private matter
	私室	シシツ	private room
	私書	シショ	private document; personal letter

玄玉王瓦甘生用田疋疒癶白皮皿目矛矢石示礻
●禾穴立罒禸母氺衤

私書箱	シショばこ	post office box
私情	シジョウ	personal feelings
私小説	シショウセツ	"I" novel; novel based on the author's own life
私心	シシン	selfishness; one's own idea
私信	シシン	private letter/message
私生活	シセイカツ	one's private life
私生児	シセイジ	illegitimate child; love child
私設	シセツ	private establishment
私蔵	シゾウ	private ownership — *v.* own privately
私的	シテキ	private
私鉄	シテツ	privately-owned railway
私道	シドウ	private road; driveway; drive
私費	シヒ	one's own expense
私服	シフク	plain clothes; civillian clothes
私腹	シフク	one's own pockets; one's own profit or estate
私物	シブツ	private property; personal effects
私憤	シフン	personal grudge
私文書	シブンショ	personal writings; private documents
私有	シユウ	private ownership; —*v.* own privately
私用	シヨウ	private use/business
私欲	シヨク	self-interest; selfish desire
私利	シリ	self-interest; one's own interest
私立	シリツ	private; non-governmental
訓 私	わたし	I; me
私	わたくし	I; me; private
私事	わたくしごと	private matters
¥ 私営	シエイ	private management/enterprise
私法人	シホウジン	private corporation
私募債	シボサイ	bonds offered through private placement

1429

⑦

一 二 チ 禾 禾 禿 秀

音 秀	シュウ	eminent
熟 秀逸	シュウイツ	excellence; superb
秀才	シュウサイ	talented man; brilliant person
秀作	シュウサク	excellent work
秀麗	シュウレイ	graceful; beautiful
訓 秀でる	ひいでる	*vi.* be superior/prominent; excel

1430 科 ⑨
一 ニ 千 千 千 禾 禾 禾 科

音	科	カ	course of study; offense
熟	科学	カガク	science; natural science
	科目	カモク	academic subject; curriculum; items
	科料	カリョウ	minor fine
訓	※科	しな	items
	※科	とが	fault; blame; offense

1431 秋 ⑨
一 ニ 千 千 千 禾 禾 秒 秋

音	秋	シュウ	fall; autumn
熟	秋季	シュウキ	fall; autumn
	秋期	シュウキ	fall season; autumn
	秋分	シュウブン	autumnal equinox
訓	秋	あき	fall; autumn
	秋風	あきかぜ	autumn breeze
	秋晴れ	あきばれ	fine autumn day
	秋雨	あきさめ	autumn rain
	※秋刀魚	さんま	saury

1432 秒 ⑨
一 ニ 千 千 禾 禾 利 利 秒 秒

音	秒	ビョウ	second (of time/arc)
熟	秒針	ビョウシン	second hand (of a watch/clock)
	秒速	ビョウソク	velocity per second
	秒読み	ビョウよみ	countdown —*vi.* count down

1433 称 ⑩
一 ニ 千 千 禾 禾 秒 秒 秒 称

音	称	ショウ	name; praise
熟	称する	ショウする	*vt.* call; name; claim; pretend; feign

629

玄玉王瓦甘生用田疋疒癶白皮皿目矛矢石示礻禾穴立罒旡母水礻

| 称号 | ショウゴウ | title; degree |
| 称賛 | ショウサン | praise; admiration; applause —*v.* praise; admire; applaud |

1434

租 ⑩　ノ ニ 千 チ 禾 利 和 和 租 租

音	租	ソ	tribute; crop tax
¥	租界	ソカイ	(foreign) settlement; concession
	租借	ソシャク	leasing a foreign territory —*v.* hold a foreign territory by lease
	租借権	ソシャクケン	lease; leasehold
	租税	ソゼイ	taxes

1435

秩 ⑩　ノ ニ 千 チ 禾 禾 秆 秆 秩 秩

| 音 | 秩 | チツ | order; discipline; stipend |
| 熟 | 秩序 | チツジョ | order; discipline; system; method |

1436

秘 ⑩　ノ ニ 千 チ 禾 禾 秖 秘 秘 秘

音	秘	ヒ	secret
熟	秘する	ヒする	*vt.* keep secret; conceal
	秘境	ヒキョウ	unexplored territory; land of mystery
	秘訣	ヒケツ	the secret/key to
	秘策	ヒサク	secret plot/plan/measures
	秘史	ヒシ	hidden history; historical secrets; unknown historical facts
	秘事	ヒジ	secret; mystery
	秘術	ヒジュツ	secret art; secrets/mysteries of
	秘書	ヒショ	(private) secretary
	秘書課	ヒショカ	secretariat; secretarial section
	秘書官	ヒショカン	minister's secretary
	秘蔵	ヒゾウ	treasuring —*v.* treasure; prize; cherish; keep (a thing) under lock and key
	秘伝	ヒデン	secret/esoteric mysteries; the secret/mystery of
	秘匿	ヒトク	concealment —*v.* conceal; keep secret
	秘宝	ヒホウ	hidden treasure

秘法	ヒホウ	secret method/formula
秘本	ヒホン	treasured book; secret/hidden/forbidden book
秘密	ヒミツ	secret; confidential; private
秘薬	ヒヤク	secret medicine/remedy
秘録	ヒロク	confidential notes; private papers
秘話	ヒワ	secret story

訓
秘か	ひそか	secret
秘める	ひめる	*vt*. conceal; keep secret

1437

移 ⑪　一　ニ　千　千　禾　禾　移　移　移　移　移

音
移	イ	move; shift; change

熟
移管	イカン	moving; transfer —*vt*. move; transfer
移行	イコウ	uniform motion of a body in a straight line —*vi*. move; transfer; shift; switch
移住	イジュウ	migration; emigration; transmigration —*vi*. migrate; emigrate; transmigrate; settle
移出	イシュツ	export; shipment; clearance —*v*. export; ship out
移植	イショク	transplantation; implantation; naturalization —*v*. transplant; implant; naturalize
移転	イテン	moving; removal; transfer —*v*. move house; transfer
移動	イドウ	movement; motion; locomotion; transfer —*v*. move; get around; be mobile
移入	イニュウ	import; shipping in; introduction —*v*. import; ship in; introduce
移民	イミン	emigration; immigration; settlement —*vi*. emigrate; immigrate; settle

訓
移す	うつす	*vt*. move; transfer; change; divert; turn; direct
移り気	うつりギ	wandering mind; inability to concentrate
移る	うつる	*vi*. move; remove; change; swift; be infected; spread

1438

税 ⑫　一　ニ　千　千　禾　禾　税　税　税　税　税

音
税	ゼイ	tax

¥
税額控除	ゼイガクコウジョ	tax credit; tax exemption; tax reduction
税関	ゼイカン	customhouse; customs
税金	ゼイキン	tax
税込み	ゼイこみ	including tax

玄玉王瓦甘生用田疋疒癶白皮皿目矛矢石示礻禾穴立罒无母水衤

税収	ゼイシュウ	tax revenues/yields
税制	ゼイセイ	tax system
税引き	ゼイびき	after tax
税引き前 当期利益	ゼイびきまえ トウキリエキ	net profit before tax
税法	ゼイホウ	tax law; method of taxation
税務署	ゼイムショ	tax office
税吏	ゼイリ	customs officer
税率	ゼイリツ	tax rates

1439

程 ⑫ 　 ノ ニ 千 禾 禾 禾 禾 秆 秆 秆 秆 程

音	程	テイ	degree
熟	程度	テイド	degree; extent; measure; proportion
訓	程	ほど	extent; limit; time; distance
	程々	ほどほど	moderate; within bounds

1440

稚 ⑬ 　 ノ ニ 千 禾 禾 利 利 秆 秆 稚 稚 稚

音	稚	チ	infant
熟	稚魚	チギョ	fry
	稚児	チゴ	infant; boy; child in a Buddhist procession
	稚拙	チセツ	crudeness; artlessness

1441

穀 ⑭ 　 一 十 士 声 声 声 幸 素 素 穀 穀 穀

音	穀	コク	grain
熟	穀倉	コクソウ	granary
	穀物	コクモツ	grain; cereal; corn

1442

種 ⑭ 　 ニ 千 禾 禾 禾 禾 稆 稆 稆 種 種 種

音	種	シュ	seed; kind; type; variety

熟	種子	シュシ	seed; stone; pip
	種々	シュジュ	various; variety; all kinds
	種族	シュゾク	race; tribe
	種痘	シュトウ	*med.* vaccination
	種別	シュベツ	classification; class; kind —*v.* classify
	種目	シュモク	item; event
	種類	シュルイ	kind; sort; species
訓	種	たね	seed; stone; kernel; breed; stock; topic
	種明かし	たねあかし	revealing the secret (of magic, etc.)
	種油	たねあぶら	seed/rape oil
	種馬	たねうま	stud horse; stallion
	種切れ	たねぎれ	short of topics
	種本	たねホン	source of a written work, etc.
	種蒔	たねまき	sowing; seeding —*vi.* sow; seed

1443

稲 ⑭ 二 千 禾 禾 禾 禾 禾 稻 稻 稲 稲 稲

音	稲	トウ	rice plant
訓	稲	いな	(prefix) rice plant; lightning
	稲作	いなさく	rice crop
	稲妻	いなづま	flash of lightning
	稲光	いなびかり	lightning; flash of lightning
	稲荷	いなり	*inari* (god of harvests, fox deity)
	稲	いね	rice plant; paddy

1444

稼 ⑮ 二 千 禾 禾 秆 秆 秆 秆 稉 稼 稼 稼

音	稼	カ	earn
熟	稼業	カギョウ	occupation; work; trade; business
	稼働	カドウ	work; operation —*v.* work; operate
訓	稼ぐ	かせぐ	*vi.* work; earn a living; earn money

1445

稿 ⑮ 二 千 禾 禾 秆 秆 秆 秆 稿 稿 稿 稿

| 音 | 稿 | コウ | manuscript; straw; straw-paper |

633

玄玉王瓦甘生用田疋疒癶白皮皿目矛矢石示礻禾•穴立罒旡母水氺

玄玉王瓦甘生用田疋疒癶白皮皿目矛矢石示礻禾穴立罒疋母水衤

| 熟 | 稿料 | コウリョウ | copy money; manuscript fee |
| 訓 | ※稿 | わら | straw; straw-paper |

1446

穂 ⑮ ⼆ 千 禾 禾 秆 秆 秆 秬 秬 穂 穂

音	穂	スイ	head
訓	穂	ほ	ear; spearhead
	穂先	ほさき	tip of an ear; head; spearhead
	穂波	ほなみ	waving heads

1447

穏 ⑯ ⼆ 千 禾 秆 秆 秆 秆 稍 穏 穏 穏 穏

音	穏	オン	gentle; calm; mild
熟	穏健	オンケン	moderate
	穏当	オントウ	proper; just; right
	穏便	オンビン	gentle; quiet; amicable
	穏和	オンワ	moderate
訓	穏やか	おだやか	calm; mild; tranquil; gentle

1448

積 ⑯ ⼆ 千 禾 秆 秈 秲 秲 秲 積 積 積 積

音	積	セキ	accumulate; product; size; area; volume
熟	積載	セキサイ	loading —v. load
	積載量	セキサイリョウ	carrying capacity; load
	積雪	セキセツ	fallen snow
	積分	セキブン	*math*. integral calculus
	積極的	セッキョクテキ	positive; active
訓	積む	つむ	*vt*. heap; load
	積もる	つもる	*vi*. accumulate; pile up; estimate
	積み上げる	つみあげる	*vt*. pile/heap up
	積み立てる	つみたてる	*vt*. save; lay aside; put by
¥	積金	つみキン	installment; installment savings
	積立金	つみたてキン	surplus reserve; reserve fund
	積荷保険	つみにホケン	cargo insurance

玄玉王瓦甘生用田疋广癶白皮皿目矛矢石示礻禾穴立罒禸母水氵

1449

�稜 ㉘ 二 千 禾 禾 禾 秄 秄 秄 秭 稚 稜 稜

| 音 | 穫 | カク | harvest |

---

5 穴　あな／あなかんむり　hole

1450

穴 ⑤ 丶 宀 宀 宀 穴

音	穴	ケツ	hole
熟	穴居	ケッキョ	cave dwelling —*vi.* live in a cave
訓	穴	あな	hole
	穴場	あなば	excellent but little known place
¥	穴埋め	あなうめ	fill a blank; cover (a deficit); make up (a loss)

1451

究 ⑦ 丶 宀 宀 宀 究 究 究

音	究	キュウ	go to the end of; investigate thoroughly; end; terminate; reach an extreme
熟	究極	キュウキョク	extreme; ultimate
	究明	キュウメイ	study; investigation; inquiry —*v.* study; investigate; inquire into
訓	究める	きわめる	*vt.* go to the end of; master; go to extremes

1452

空 ⑧ 丶 宀 宀 宀 空 空 空 空

音	空	クウ	empty; useless; the sky; the heavens; aircraft
熟	空間	クウカン	space; the infinite
	空気	クウキ	air; atmosphere
	空虚	クウキョ	emptiness; void; vacuum
	空軍	クウグン	air force
	空港	クウコウ	airport

5

玄
玉
王
瓦
甘
生
用
田
疋
疒
癶
白
皮
皿
目
矛
矢
石
示
礻
禾
穴
立
罒
无
母
水
氵

空車	クウシャ	empty car; For Hire; taxi for hire
空襲	クウシュウ	air raid/attack —v. launch an air raid/attack
空席	クウセキ	empty/vacant seat
空前	クウゼン	unprecedented; unheard of
空前絶後	クウゼンゼツゴ	the first and probably the last
空想	クウソウ	daydream; fantasy —v. daydream; fantasize
空中	クウチュウ	air; sky; space; midair
空洞	クウドウ	cave; cavern; cavity
空白	クウハク	blank; space; vacuum; void
空費	クウヒ	waste —v. waste
空腹	クウフク	empty stomach
空輸	クウユ	air/aerial transport —v. transport by air
空路	クウロ	air route/way
空論	クウロン	empty theory

訓

空く	あく	*vi.* open; be opened
空ける	あける	*vt.* open (something)
空	から	empty
空回り	からまわり	skidding; racing; ineffective business activity; fruitless effort —*vi.* skid; race; prove/turn out ineffective
空	そら	sky

1453

突 ⑧ 　 ＇ ㇒ 宀 宀 空 空 穷 突

音

| 突 | トツ | thrust |

熟

突貫	トッカン	charge; rush
突起	トッキ	projection; prominence; protuberance —*vi.* project; protrude; rise
突撃	トツゲキ	charge; rush; onrush; dash; assault —*vi.* charge; rush; make a dash; assault
突出	トッシュツ	projection; protrusion; prominence —*vi.* project; protrude; jut/stick out
突如	トツジョ	suddenly
突進	トッシン	rush; onrush; dash; charge —*vi.* rush; dash; push ahead
突然	トツゼン	suddenly; abruptly; all at once
突端	トッタン	tip; point
突入	トツニュウ	inrush; thrust —*vi.* rush; dash; charge; crush
突破	トッパ	breakthrough; breaking through; breakout —*v.* break/smash through; breach
突発	トッパツ	outbreak; sudden occurrence —*vi.* occur suddenly

	突風	トップウ	gust; strong blast	
訓	突く	つく	*vt*. thrust; pierce; transfix; push; strike; attack; rush	
	突き刺す	つきさす	*vt*. stick; stab; thrust	

1454 窃 ⑨

` ` ' 宀 宀 宀 空 空 窃 窃

音	窃	セツ	steal
熟	窃取	セッシュ	intake; adoption; theft —*v*. take in; adopt; steal
	窃盗	セットウ	theft —*v*. steal; commit theft

1455 窓 ⑪

` ` ' 宀 宀 宀 空 空 空 窓 窓 窓

音	窓	ソウ	window
熟	窓外	ソウガイ	outside the window
訓	窓	まど	window
	窓際	まどぎわ	windowside; by the window
	窓口	まどぐち	(ticket) window
¥	窓口販売	まどぐちハンバイ	over-the-counter sale/selling

1456 窒 ⑪

` ` ' 宀 宀 宀 空 空 空 窄 窒

音	窒	チツ	suffocation; nitrogen
熟	窒素	チッソ	*chem*. nitrogen
	窒息	チッソク	suffocation; asphyxiation —*v*. be suffocated/choked/asphyxiated

1457 窮 ⑮

` 宀 宀 宀 宀 窄 窄 窄 窮 窮 窮 窮

音	窮	キュウ	investigate thoroughly; reach an extreme; reach its limits
熟	窮する	キュウする	*vi*. be in need; be destitute; be in a dilemma
	窮極	キュウキョク	the extreme/ultimate

玄玉王瓦生用田疋广癶白皮皿目矛矢石示礻禾穴立罒罓母氷礻

玄玉王瓦甘生用田疋广癶白皮皿目矛矢石示礻禾穴立罒旡母水礻

窮屈	キュウクツ	narrowness; tightness
窮状	キュウジョウ	distress; sorry plight
窮地	キュウチ	predicament; difficult situation
窮乏	キュウボウ	want; destitution; poverty
訓 窮まる	きわまる	*vi*. reach an extreme; come to an end
窮める	きわめる	*vt*. carry to extremes; bring to an end

1458

窯 ⑮   ` 宀 宀 穸 穸 穸 空 窣 窣 窒 窰 窯

音 窯	ヨウ	kiln
熟 窯業	ヨウギョウ	ceramics
訓 窯	かま	kiln

5 立 たつ standing

1459

立 ⑤   ` 亠 立 立 立

音 立	リツ	stand; rise
	（リュウ）	
熟 立案	リツアン	plan; devise; draft —*v*. make/form a plan; devise; design
立夏	リッカ	first day of summer
立脚	リッキャク	based on —*vi*. be based on
立憲	リッケン	adopting a constitution
立憲政治	リッケンセイジ	constitutional government
立候補	リッコウホ	candidacy; running for office —*vi*. stand/run for office
立国	リッコク	founding of a state
立志伝	リッシデン	success story
立秋	リッシュウ	first day of autumn
立春	リッシュン	first day of spring
立証	リッショウ	proof —*v*. prove; establish
立身出世	リッシンシュッセ	success in life —*v*. succeed in life
立像	リツゾウ	statue of someone standing
立体	リッタイ	solid; three-dimensional
立体感	リッタイカン	sense of depth

立体交差	リッタイコウサ	grade separation
立体的	リッタイテキ	three-dimensional
立地	リッチ	location; siting
立地条件	リッチジョウケン	geographical conditions
立冬	リットウ	first day of winter
立派	リッパ	splendid; fine; magnificient
立腹	リップク	anger; offense —*vi.* get angry; lose one's temper
立方	リッポウ	cubic; cube
立方体	リッポウタイ	cube
立法	リッポウ	legislation; law making
立礼	リツレイ	standing and bowing
立論	リツロン	argument —*vi.* put forth an argument

訓

立つ	たつ	*vi.* erect; rise; stand
立ち会う	たちあう	*vi.* attend; witness
立ち上がる	たちあがる	*vi.* stand up
立ち入る	たちいる	*vi.* enter; interfere; go into (an issue)
立ち往生	たちオウジョウ	*vi.* standing death —*vi.* come to a standstill; be in a dilemma
立ち退く	たちのく	*vi.* leave
立場	たちば	standpoint; viewpoint; position
立ち回る	たちまわる	*vt.* act
立ち向かう	たちむかう	*vi.* confront; fight; stand against
立てる	たてる	*vt.* erect; set up; raise
立て替える	たてかえる	*vt.* pay in advance; pay (for another)
立行司	たてギョウジ	head sumo referee
立札	たてふだ	signboard

¥

| 立会い | たちあい | session |

1460

章 ⑪ ` 亠 产 产 音 音 音 章 章

音	章	ショウ	chapter; passage; writing
熟	章句	ショウク	passage of writing
	章節	ショウセツ	chapters and sections (of a thesis, etc.)

1461

童 ⑫ ` 亠 产 产 音 音 音 童 童 童

| 音 | 童 | ドウ | child |

玄玉王瓦甘生用田疋广癶白皮皿目矛矢石示礻禾穴立罒罘母水氵

熟	童顔	ドウガン	child's face; childlike face
	童心	ドウシン	child's mind; childlike heart
	童貞	ドウテイ	virginity; chastity
	童謡	ドウヨウ	nursery song/rhyme
	童話	ドウワ	nursery tale; children's story
訓	童	わらべ	child

1462

端⑭　　亠　亡　立　立'　䇦　䇦　䇦　䇦　䇦　端　端　端　端

音	端	タン	end; tip; edge; margin; beginning
熟	端午	タンゴ	Boys' Festival
	端子	タンシ	terminal
	端緒	タンショ	clue; beginning; start
	端正	タンセイ	correct; right; just
	端的	タンテキ	plain; direct; pointblank
	端麗	タンレイ	grace; elegance; beauty
訓	端	は	edge; margin
	端	はし	end; tip; edge; margin; beginning
	端数	はスウ	*math.* fraction; odd sum; fragment; scrap
	端	はた	edge; bank; side
¥	端株	はかぶ	odd-lot (broken-lot) stocks

1463

競⑳　　亠　亡　立　音　产　竟　竟　竞　竞　䶂　䶂　競

音	競	キョウ ケイ	rival; compete; dispute; quarrel
熟	競泳	キョウエイ	swimming race/competition —*v.* compete in a swimming race
	競演	キョウエン	contest —*v.* contest; enter a competition
	競技	キョウギ	match; contest; competition —*v.* contest; compete
	競争	キョウソウ	competition; contest; rivalry —*vi.* compete; contest; be rivals
	競走	キョウソウ	race; running race —*vi.* run in a race
	競馬	ケイバ	horse race
	競輪	ケイリン	bicycle race
訓	競う	きそう	*vi.* compete; rival
	競る	せる	*vt.* compete with

¥	競合	キョウゴウ	competition; rivalry
	競争市場	キョウソウ シジョウ	competitive market place
	競争品	キョウソウヒン	competitor
	競争力	キョウソウリョク	competitiveness
	競売	キョウバイ (ケイバイ)	(public) auction; auction sale —*v.* auction; sell by auction

---

5 罒 あみがしら net

1464

罪 ⑬ 　 丶 冖 ⼕ 冖 罒 罒 罪 罪 罪 罪 罪 罪

音	罪	ザイ	crime; sin
熟	罪悪	ザイアク	vice; crime
	罪人	ザイニン	criminal; offender; convict
	罪名	ザイメイ	offence; charge
訓	罪	つみ	sin; crime; act of wrong doing

1465

署 ⑬ 　 丶 冖 ⼕ 罒 罒 罒 署 罗 罗 署 署 署

音	署	ショ	divide; office
熟	署長	ショチョウ	chief of police
	署名	ショメイ	signature —*vi.* sign

1466

置 ⑬ 　 丶 冖 ⼕ 罒 罒 罒 罗 罗 罗 置 置 置

音	置	チ	put; place; positon
訓	置き換える	おきかえる	*vt.* replace; substitute; transpose
	置き去り にする	おきざりにする	*vt.* leave (a person) in the lurch
	置場	おきば	yard; garage; shed; storage space
	置物	おきもの	ornament
	置き忘れる	おきわすれる	*vt.* mislay; misplace
	置く	おく	*vt.* put; place; position; leave; allow; let; keep; hold

玄玉王瓦甘生用田疋广癶白皮皿目矛矢石示ネ禾穴立罒
● 旡母水氵

1467 罰 ⑭

一　冖　罒　罒　罒　罰　罰　罰　罰　罰　罰　罰　罰　罰

音	罰	バチ	punishment
		バツ	punishment
熟	罰金	バッキン	fine
	罰則	バッソク	penal regulations

1468 罷 ⑮

一　冖　罒　罒　罒　罒　罷　罷　罷　罷　罷　罷　罷

音	罷	ヒ	stop; end; discontinue
訓	※罷り通る	まかりとおる	*vi.* pass; go unchallenged
	※罷る	まかる	*vt.* leave; withdraw
	※罷む	やむ	*vi.* end; discontinue; stop
	※罷める	やめる	*vt.* end; discontinue; stop
¥	罷業	ヒギョウ	strike; walkout
	罷免	ヒメン	dismissal; discharge (from a job)—*v.* dismiss; discharge; relieve (a person) of his post; fire (someone)

1469 羅 ⑲

一　冖　罒　罒　罒　罒　罒　羅　羅　羅　羅　羅　羅

音	羅	ラ	net; silk gauze; thin silk
熟	羅漢	ラカン	arhat (person who attains Nirvana)
	羅針盤	ラシンバン	(magnetic) compass
	羅列	ラレツ	list; enumeration —*v.* list; enumerate

5 旡 むにょう crooked heaven

1470 既 ⑩

一　ヨ　ヨ　ヨ　艮　艮　既　既　既　既

音	既	キ	already
熟	既往症	キオウショウ	medical history; anamnesis

642

既刊	キカン	previous publication; backlist book
既婚	キコン	married
既製	キセイ	ready-made; ready to wear
既成	キセイ	completed; accomplished; established
既知	キチ	known; established
既定	キテイ	fixed; predetermined; established
訓 既に	すでに	already; previously; before
¥ 既発債	キハッサイ	outstanding bond

---

5 母 see ⇨p.507

---

5 氷 see ⇨p.515

---

5 衤 see ⇨p.708

5

玄
玉
王
瓦
甘
生
用
田
疋
疒
癶
白
皮
皿
目
矛
矢
石
示
礻
禾
穴
立
罒
　　•
　　•
　　•
无　•
母
氷
礻

643

竹 米 糸 缶 羊 羽 老 耂 而 耒 耳 肉 自 至 舌 舟 色 虍 虫 血 行 衣 衤 西 艮

6 竹 たけ／たけかんむり bamboo

1471

竹 ⑥ ノ ノ ⺮ ⺮ ⺮ 竹

音	竹	チク	bamboo
熟	竹馬の友	チクバのとも	childhood friend
	竹林	チクリン	bamboo forest
訓	竹	たけ	bamboo
	竹の子	たけのこ	bamboo shoot
	竹薮	たけやぶ	bamboo grove
	※竹刀	しない	*shinai* (bamboo sword for kendo practice)

1472

笑 ⑩ ノ ノ ⺮ ⺮ ⺮ ⺮ ⺮ 竺 竺 竿 笑

音	笑	ショウ	laugh
訓	笑う	わらう	*v.* laugh; smile; chuckle; giggle
	笑い	わらい	laugh; smile
	笑話	わらいばなし	humorous/amusing story
	笑む	えむ	*vi.* come out; open; bloom; smile
	※笑顔	えがお	smiling face; smile

1473

第 ⑪ ノ ノ ⺮ ⺮ ⺮ ⺮ 竺 竺 笋 第 第

音	第	ダイ	(ordinal prefix)
熟	第一	ダイイチ	first; number one; foremost; primary
	第一印象	ダイイチインショウ	first impressions
	第一人者	ダイイチニンシャ	first man; most talented person (in a group etc.)
	第一人称	ダイイチニンショウ	*gram.* first person
	第一線	ダイイッセン	first line; front line; front
	第三者	ダイサンシャ	third party
	第六感	ダイロクカン	sixth sense
¥	第一次産業	ダイイチジサンギョウ	primary industry

1474

笛 ⑪ 　ノ ト ﾑ ﾑ' 竹 竹 竹 竺 笛 笛 笛

| 音 | 笛 | テキ | pipe |
| 訓 | 笛 | ふえ | flute; whistle |

1475

符 ⑪ 　ノ ト ﾑ ﾑ' 竹 竹 竹 竻 竻 符 符

音	符	フ	tally; sign; mark
熟	符号	フゴウ	mark; symbol; code *math*. plus or minus sign (＋/−)
	符合	フゴウ	coincidence; agreement; correspondence —*vi*. agree; correspond

---

1476

筋 ⑫ 　ノ ト ﾑ ﾑ' 竹 竹 竹 筋 筋 筋 筋

音	筋	キン	muscle; sinew
熟	筋骨	キンコツ	muscular; hard-muscled; well-built
	筋肉	キンニク	muscle
	筋力	キンリョク	ability; capacity; strength
訓	筋	すじ	muscle; sinew; blood vessel; line; stripe; streak; logic; coherence; plot (of a story); source (of information)
	筋書き	すじがき	synopsis; outline; plan
	筋金	すじがね	metal reinforcement
	筋違い	すじちがい	sprain; unreasonable; absurd
	筋道	すじみち	reason; logic; coherence
	筋目	すじめ	fold; crease; pedigree

1477

策 ⑫ 　ノ ト ﾑ ﾑ' 竹 竹 笁 竿 笞 第 第 策

音	策	サク	plan; plot; whip stick
熟	策する	サクする	*vt*. plan; plot; scheme
	策謀	サクボウ	plot; scheme; intrigue —*v*. plot; scheme
	策略	サクリャク	plot; stratagem; trick

645

竹
米
糸
缶
羊
羽
老
耂
而
耒
耳
肉
自
至
舌
舟
色
虍
虫
血
行
衣
衤
西
艮

1478

答 　 ノ　ノ　ヶ　ヶ　ヶ　竹　竹　ク　タ　タ　タ　答　答 ⑫

音	答	トウ	answer
熟	答案	トウアン	written answers; examination paper
	答辞	トウジ	formal reply
	答申	トウシン	report; reply (to one's superior) —v. report; submit a report (to a superior)
	答弁	トウベン	reply; answer; account; explanation —v. reply; answer; say something in self-defense
	答礼	トウレイ	return salute
訓	答え	こたえ	answer; reply; response
	答える	こたえる	vt. answer; reply; respond

1479

等 　 ノ　ノ　ヶ　ヶ　ヶ　竹　竹　竿　竿　笙　笙　等　等 ⑫

音	等	トウ	equal
熟	等圧	トウアツ	uniform pressure
	等圧線	トウアツセン	isobar
	等価	トウカ	equivalence; parity
	等外	トウガイ	failure; also-ran
	等級	トウキュウ	grade; class; order; rank
	等号	トウゴウ	equal sign (=)
	等式	トウシキ	math. equality
	等時性	トウジセイ	phy. isochronism
	等質	トウシツ	homogeneity
	等身	トウシン	life size
	等分	トウブン	division into equal parts —v. divide into equal parts
訓	等しい	ひとしい	equal; similar; like

1480

筒 　 ノ　ノ　ヶ　ヶ　ヶ　竹　竹　ヶ　竺　笌　笌　筒　筒 ⑫

音	筒	トウ	tube
訓	筒	つつ	pipe; tube; case; cylinder; gun; canon
	筒抜け	つつぬけ	leaving out entirely

1481

筆 ⑫　ノ　ト　ヶ　ゲ　ゲ　ゲ　竹　竺　等　等　筆

音	筆	ヒツ	writing brush
熟	筆記	ヒッキ	note-taking; notes —*v.* take notes
	筆記体	ヒッキタイ	longhand (writing)
	筆耕	ヒッコウ	copying; copyist —*v.* copy
	筆算	ヒッサン	calculations on paper —*v.* do sums on a piece of paper
	筆写	ヒッシャ	copying; transcription —*v.* copy; transcribe
	筆者	ヒッシャ	author; writer
	筆順	ヒツジュン	stroke order (of Chinese characters)
	筆跡	ヒッセキ	penmanship; handwriting; written letters
	筆舌し難い	ヒツゼツしがたい	beyond description
	筆談	ヒツダン	written communication —*vi.* communicate in writing
	筆頭	ヒットウ	tip of a writing brush; first on the list
	筆頭者	ヒットウシャ	head of a family (as recorded in a family register)
	筆答	ヒットウ	written answer —*vi.* answer in writing
	筆法	ヒッポウ	manner of using a writing brush *fig.* method; way of thinking
	筆名	ヒツメイ	pen name; pseudonym
	筆力	ヒツリョク	power of the brush stroke/pen; powerful writing
訓	筆	ふで	writing brush
	筆入れ	ふでいれ	pencil case
	筆箱	ふでばこ	pencil box
	筆無精（筆不精）	ふでブショウ	poor correspondent
	筆まめ	ふでまめ	ready pen; (someone who) likes writing letters, etc.

1482

節 ⑬　ノ　ト　ヶ　ゲ　ゲ　竹　竿　笁　笳　節　節

音	節	セツ	season; occasion; section; paragraph; verse; joint; knot
		（セチ）	
熟	節句	セック	annual festivals
	節減	セツゲン	curtailment —*v.* curtail

竹
米
糸
缶
羊
羽
老耂
而
耒
耳
肉
自
至
舌
舟
色
虍
虫
血
行
衣衤
西覀

6

竹米糸缶羊羽老耂而耒耳肉自至舌舟色虍虫血行衣衤西艮

	節制	セッセイ	moderation; temperance —*v.* moderate one's lifestyle
	節操	セッソウ	constancy; fidelity; integrity; chastity
	節度	セツド	moderation; rule; standard
	節分	セツブン	last day of winter
	節約	セツヤク	economy; saving; thrift —*v.* economize; save
訓	節	ふし	knot; joint; tune; point; item
¥	節税	セツゼイ	tax avoidance —*vi.* avold paying high taxes

1483

箇 ⑭　ノ　ト　ケ　竹　竹　竻　笱　简　简　简　箇

音	箇	カ	piece
熟	箇所	カショ	place; part; point
	箇条	カジョウ	article; provision; clause
	箇条書き	カジョウがき	itemization

1484

管 ⑭　ノ　ト　ケ　竹　竹　竻　竻　竺　竺　管　管

音	管	カン	pipe; administer
熟	管轄	カンカツ	jurisdiction; control —*vt.* have jurisdiction/control over
	管楽器	カンガッキ	wind instrument
	管弦楽	カンゲンガク	orchestra
	管内	カンナイ	within the jurisdiction
	管理	カンリ	control; administration; supervision —*v.* control; administrate; supervise
訓	管	くだ	tube; pipe
¥	管理職	カンリショク	administrator; management
	管理費	カンリヒ	administrative expenses; maintenance fee

1485

算 ⑭　ノ　ト　ケ　竹　竹　笞　笞　管　箅　算　算

音	算	サン	count; calculation; reckoning; counting sticks
熟	算出	サンシュツ	calculation; computation —*v.* calculate; compute
	算数	サンスウ	arithmetic; calculation
	算段	サンダン	contrivance; thinking —*v.* contrive/think of a good way

算定	サンテイ	computation; calculation; estimate; estimation —*v.* calculate; estimate; appraise
算入	サンニュウ	item in an calculation —*v.* include in a calculation
算用数字	サンヨウスウジ	Arabic figures/numerals
訓 ※算盤	そろばん	abacus

1486

箱 ⑮
ノ ノ ⺈ ⺮ 竺 竺 笁 笁 笴 筣 箝 箱 箱

訓 箱	はこ	box; case; casket
箱入り娘	はこいりむすめ	innocent/over-protected girl
箱庭	はこにわ	miniature garden

1487

範 ⑮
ノ ノ ⺈ ⺮ 竺 竻 笁 筥 筥 篁 篂 範 範

音 範	ハン	model
熟 範囲	ハンイ	extent; scope; sphere; range; limits
範例	ハンレイ	model; epitome; basis

1488

築 ⑯
ノ ノ ⺈ ⺮ 竺 竻 竻 笁 筑 筑 篫 築

音 築	チク	construct; build
熟 築城	チクジョウ	construction of a castle; fortification —*vi.* fortify; build a castle
築造	チクゾウ	construction
訓 築く	きずく	*vt.* build; make; construct; erect

1489

篤 ⑯
ノ ノ ⺈ ⺮ 竹 笁 笁 笡 篙 篤 篤 篤

音 篤	トク	hospitable
熟 篤学	トクガク	love of learning; devotion to one's studies
篤志	トクシ	benevolence; charity
篤志家	トクシカ	volunteer; supporter
篤実	トクジツ	sincerity; faithfulness

1490

簡 ⑱ ` ´ ⺮ ⺮ ⺮ ⺮ ⺮ ⺮ ⺮ ⺮ 簡 簡 簡

音	簡	カン	letter; brevity
熟	簡易	カンイ	simplicity; ease; easiness
	簡潔	カンケツ	brevity; conciseness
	簡素	カンソ	simplicity
	簡単	カンタン	simplicity; simple; ease; easy
	簡便	カンベン	handiness; expediency; convenience; simplicity
	簡明	カンメイ	conciseness; brevity
	簡略	カンリャク	simplicity; conciseness

1491

簿 ⑲ ` ´ ⺮ ⺮ ⺮ 笁 笁 簿 簿 薄 簿 簿

音	簿	ボ	record book; ledger; register; list
¥	簿価	ボカ	book value
	簿記	ボキ	bookkeeping

1492

籍 ⑳ ` ´ ⺮ 竺 筆 筆 筆 籍 籍 籍 籍 籍

音	籍	セキ	writing; membership; books; record

---

6 米 こめ／こめへん rice

1493

米 ⑥ ` 丶 丷 � 半 半 米

音	米	ベイ	rice; eighty-eight years of age; America; meter (unit of measurement)
		マイ	rice
熟	米国	ベイコク	the United States
	米穀	ベイコク	rice; grain
	米作	ベイサク	rice cultivation/crop
	米寿	ベイジュ	one's eighty-eighth birthday

米収	ベイシュウ	rice crop/harvest
米食	ベイショク	diet with rice as the staple
米人	ベイジン	American person
米兵	ベイヘイ	US soldier/sailor
訓 米	こめ	(uncooked) rice
米所	こめどころ	rice-producing area
米間屋	こめどんや	rice wholesaler
米屋	こめや	rice dealer
※米	メートル	meter (unit of measurement)
※米	よね	rice; eighty-eighth birthday
¥ 米価	ベイカ	price of rice (set by the govermnent)

1494 粋 ⑩

` 、 ` ` ` ` ` ` ⺌ 艹 米 米 米 籵 籵 粹 粋

音	粋	スイ	pure; smart
熟	粋狂	スイキョウ	whimsical; freakish; capricious; eccentric
	粋人	スイジン	man of refined tastes/the world
訓	※粋	いき	smart; stylish

1495 粉 ⑩

` 、 ` ` ` ` ` ` ⺌ 艹 米 米 米 籵 粉 粉

音	粉	フン	flour; powder
熟	粉骨	フンコツ	assidiousness —*vi*. be assidious
	粉骨砕身	フンコツサイシン	one's best/utmost —*vi*. do one's best/utmost
	粉砕	フンサイ	crushed; pulverized —*v*. crush; pulverize; smash/break into pieces
	粉飾	フンショク	embellishment; window dressing —*v*. embellish; window-dress
	粉炭	フンタン	powdered coal
	粉本	フンポン	copy (for a painting/writing); rough sketch
	粉末	フンマツ	powder
訓	粉	こ	powder
	粉	こな	flour; powder
	粉薬	こなぐすり	powdered medicine
	粉々	こなごな	pieces; dust
	粉状	こなジョウ	powder form; powdered
	粉微塵	こなミジン	tiny fragments; pieces; smithereens

竹
米
糸
缶
羊
羽
老耂
而
耒
耳
肉
自
至
舌
舟
色
虍
虫
血
行
衣衤
西覀
艮

1496

粗⑪ 、 丶 ⹁ 半 米 米 米 籵 粐 粗 粗

音	粗	ソ	coarse; rough
熟	粗悪	ソアク	coarse; crude; inferior
	粗雑	ソザツ	coarse; crude
	粗品	ソしな	small gift
	粗食	ソショク	coarse food; plain diet
	粗製	ソセイ	crudely made; inferior make
	粗相	ソソウ	carelessness; blunder —*vi.* be careless; blunder
	粗大	ソダイ	big and coarse; large and rough
	粗茶	ソチャ	(coarse) tea
	粗暴	ソボウ	wild; rough; violent
	粗末	ソマツ	coarse; plain; crude; rough; rude
	粗野	ソヤ	rude; rustic; loutish; vulgar
訓	粗い	あらい	coarse; rough

1497

粘⑪ 、 丶 ⹁ 半 米 米 籵 粐 粘 粘

音	粘	ネン	stick
熟	粘液	ネンエキ	*med.* mucus; phlegm
	粘性	ネンセイ	viscosity
	粘着	ネンチャク	adhesion; viscosity —*vi.* stick/adhere to
	粘土	ネンド	clay; plasticene
	粘膜	ネンマク	*med.* mucosa membrane
訓	粘る	ねばる	*vi.* be sticky/glutinous/adhesive
	粘り気	ねばりケ	sticky
	粘り強い	ねばりづよい	perservering; tenacious

1498

粒⑪ 、 丶 ⹁ 半 米 米 籵 籵 粒 粒

音	粒	リュウ	grain; drop(let)
熟	粒子	リュウシ	(atomic) particle; grain
	粒状	リュウジョウ	granular; granulated

訓	粒	つぶ	grain; drop(let)
	粒揃い	つぶぞろい	uniformly excellent
	粒々	つぶつぶ	lumps; grains
	粒選り	つぶより	the best; picked; choice

1499

粧 ⑫ 、 ` ` ` ‍ 丷 半 米 米 米′ 米ナ 米† 粒 粧

| 音 | 粧 | ショウ | dress |

1500

精 ⑭ ` ` ‍ 丷 半 米 米′ 米ナ 米† 精 精 精 精

音	精	セイ	spirit; energy; vitality; semen; precise
		（ショウ）	
熟	精進	ショウジン	devotion; diligence; purification —*vi.* abstain from meat or fish
	精進料理	ショウジンリョウリ	vegetarian cooking/cuisine
	精霊	ショウリョウ	spirit of a dead person
	精一杯	セイイッパイ	with all one's strength; as hard as possible
	精鋭	セイエイ	elite; crack; the best
	精液	セイエキ	semen
	精確	セイカク	accurate; precise; exact
	精巧	セイコウ	exquisite; detailed; delicate
	精根	セイコン	energy; vitality
	精魂	セイコン	spirit; energy; vitality
	精彩	セイサイ	luster; vitality
	精算	セイサン	exact calculation; settling of accounts —*v.* settle accounts
	精子	セイシ	sperm
	精神	セイシン	mind; spirit
	精神科	セイシンカ	psychiatry
	精神病	セイシンビョウ	mental disorder
	精製	セイセイ	refining; careful manufacture —*v.* refine
	精選	セイセン	careful/choice selection —*v.* choose/select carefully
	精通	セイツウ	well-informed; familiarity —*vi.* be familiar/well versed in
	精度	セイド	precision; accuracy
	精読	セイドク	careful reading —*v.* read carefully

竹 米 糸 缶 羊 羽 老 耂 而 耒 耳 肉 自 至 舌 舟 色 虍 虫 血 行 衣 衤 西 艮

精分	セイブン	nourishment; vitality
精米	セイマイ	polished rice —*v.* polish rice
精密	セイミツ	precision
精油	セイユ	refined/perfume oil —*vi.* refine oil
精力	セイリョク	energy; vigor; vitality
精励	セイレイ	diligence —*vi.* be diligent; work hard
精霊	セイレイ	spirit; soul
精錬	セイレン	refining; smelting —*v.* refine; smelt
¥ 精密機械	セイミツキカイ	precision machine

1501

糖 ⑯ ⸜ ⸝ ¥ 米 籵 粐 粐 粐 粐 糖 糖 糖

音 糖	トウ	sugar; sweetened carbohydrate
熟 糖尿病	トウニョウビョウ	*med.* diabetes
糖分	トウブン	sugar (content)
糖類	トウルイ	saccharide

1502

糧 ⑱ ⸜ ⸝ ¥ 米 籵 粐 粐 糧 糧 糧 糧 糧

音 糧	リョウ （ロウ）	food; provisions
熟 糧食	リョウショク	food; provisions
糧道	リョウドウ	road for supplying; provisions to troops
訓 糧	かて	food; provisions

---

6 糸 いと／いとへん thread

1503

糸 ⑥ ⸜ 乡 幺 糸 糸 糸

音 糸	シ	thread
訓 糸	いと	thread; string; line
糸口	いとぐち	end of a thread *fig.* first step; beginning; lead; clue
糸切り歯	いときりば	canine tooth

1504

系 ⑦　一　ㄥ　至　玄　至　系　系

音	系	ケイ	system; descent
熟	系図	ケイズ	genealogy; lineage
	系統	ケイトウ	system; lineage; genealogy; school; party
	系統的	ケイトウテキ	systematically; methodically
	系譜	ケイフ	genealogy; lineage
	系列	ケイレツ	order; series
訓	系ぐ	つなぐ	*vt.* connect; join
¥	系列会社	ケイレツガイシャ	affiliated company

1505

索 ⑩　一　十　ㅗ　ㄇ　虍　宇　宷　宷　索

音	索	サク	seek; cord
熟	索引	サクイン	index

1506

素 ⑩　一　十　キ　丰　圭　丰　圭　素　素

音	素	ス	naked; uncovered; simple
		ソ	element; beginning
熟	素足	スあし	barefoot
	素顔	スがお	unpainted face; face without makeup
	素性	スジョウ	birth; lineage; identity
	素手	スで	bare hands
	素敵	ステキ	splendid; marvelous; great; beautiful; nice
	素直	スなお	frank; gentle; meek; docile; honest
	素肌	スはだ	bare skin
	素晴らしい	スばらしい	splendid; magnificent
	素因	ソイン	contributing factor; cause
	素行	ソコウ	behavior; conduct
	素材	ソザイ	material; subject matter
	素地	ソジ	groundwork; the makings of
	素質	ソシツ	quality; nature; makeup
	素数	ソスウ	*math.* prime number

竹米糸缶羊羽老耂而耒耳肉自至舌舟色虍虫血行衣衤西艮

竹
米
糸
缶
羊
羽
老
聿
而
耒
耳
肉
自
至
舌
舟
色
虍
虫
血
行
衣
衤
西
艮

素読	ソドク	reading aloud without making any effort to understand what is written —*v.* read aloud without making any effort to understand what is written
素描	ソビョウ	rough sketch —*v.* make a rough sketch
素振り	ソぶり	manner; behavior; attitude; air; look
素封家	ソホウカ	wealthy person
素朴	ソボク	simple; artless; ingenuous
素養	ソヨウ	culture; one's knowledge; attainments
訓 ＊素	もと	beginning; base
＊素人	しろうと	amateur; layman

1507

紫 ⑫　　ﾉ　ﾄ　止　止　止　此　此　紫　紫　紫　紫　紫

音 紫	シ	purple
熟 紫煙	シエン	violet/tobacco smoke
紫外線	シガイセン	ultraviolet rays
紫紺	シコン	purple blue
訓 紫	むらさき	purple; gromwell

1508

累 ⑪　　ﾉ　冂　冊　冊　田　甲　里　罘　罘　累　累

音 累	ルイ	accumulate; pile up; encumber; incessantly
熟 累加	ルイカ	acceleration; progressive increase —*v.* accelerate; increase progressively
累計	ルイケイ	total; sum
累減	ルイゲン	regression; progressive decrease —*v.* regress; decrease progressively
累次	ルイジ	successive; repeated
累進	ルイシン	successive promotions; progressive; graduated —*vi.* be successively promoted; progress; graduate
累積	ルイセキ	accumulation —*v.* accumulate
累々	ルイルイ	in heaps; piled up

1509

緊 ⑮　　ﾉ　厂　厂　臣　臣　臣　臤　臤　堅　堅　緊

| 音 緊 | キン | strict; tight; severe |

熟	緊急	キンキュウ	emergency; urgency
	緊縮	キンシュク	shrinkage; contraction —*v.* shrink; contract
	緊張	キンチョウ	strain; tension —*vi.* be strained/tense
	緊迫	キンパク	tension; strain; under pressure —*vi.* be tense/under pressure
	緊密	キンミツ	close; tight; tightly knit

1510

繁 ⑯ ノ ト ケ 每 每 每 每 每 敏 敏 繁 繁 繁

音	繁	ハン	prosper
熟	繁栄	ハンエイ	prosperity —*vi.* prosper; thrive; flourish
	繁華街	ハンカガイ	shopping mall/parade; busy street
	繁雑	ハンザツ	complicated; complex; intricate; troublesome
	繁盛	ハンジョウ	prosperity; success —*vi.* prosper; flourish; thrive; be successful
	繁殖	ハンショク	breeding; reproduction; propagation; multiplication —*vi.* breed; reproduce; propagate; multiply
	繁茂	ハンモ	luxuriant growth; rankness —*vi.* grow thick; exuberate; flourish

---

1511

繭 ⑱ 艹 芌 艹 芌 芌 荊 蓄 繭 繭 繭 繭

| 音 | 繭 | ケン | cocoon |
| 熟 | 繭 | まゆ | cocoon |

1512

紀 ⑨ く 乡 乡 幺 糸 糸 紀 紀 紀

音	紀	キ	account; writing; era; year
熟	紀元	キゲン	era; epoch
	紀行	キコウ	travelogue

1513

級 ⑨ く 乡 乡 幺 糸 糸 紗 級 級

| 音 | 級 | キュウ | class; grade; position; symbol; group |

竹米糸缶羊羽老耂而耒耳肉自至舌舟色虍虫血行衣衤西艮

竹
米
• 糸
缶
羊
羽
老
耂
而
耒
耳
肉
自
至
舌
舟
色
虍
虫
血
行
衣
衤
西
艮

熟	級数	キュウスウ	*math*. series; progression
	級長	キュウチョウ	president of a class; homeroom president
	級友	キュウユウ	classmate

1514
糾 ⑨

く ㄠ ㄠ ㄠ ≶ 糸 糸 糸' 糾 糾

音	糾	キュウ	twist; intertwine; collect together; tangle; entangle; correct; rectify
熟	糾合	キュウゴウ	rally; muster —*v*. rally; muster
	糾弾	キュウダン	impeachment —*v*. impeach
	糾明	キュウメイ	searching examination —*v*. examine (a matter) closely

1515
紅 ⑨

く ㄠ ㄠ ㄠ ≶ 糸 糸 糸' 紅 紅

音	紅	コウ	crimson; rouge; red
		（ク）	
熟	紅一点	コウイッテン	only woman in a group
	紅顔	コウガン	rosy face; ruddy cheeks
	紅茶	コウチャ	tea
	紅潮	コウチョウ	blush; flush —*vi*. blush; flush; turn red/rosy
	紅白	コウハク	red and white
	紅葉	コウヨウ	autumnal leaves —*vi*. turn red/yellow
訓	紅	くれない	deep red; crimson
	紅	べに	rouge; deep red; crimson
※	紅葉	もみじ	maple tree

1516
約 ⑨

く ㄠ ㄠ ㄠ ≶ 糸 糸 糸' 約 約

音	約	ヤク	promise; appproximately; curtail
熟	約する	ヤクする	*vt*. promise; reduce; abbreviate
	約言	ヤクゲン	contraction; summary
	約定	ヤクジョウ	promise; agreement; contract —*vi*. promise; make a contract; agree
	約数	ヤクスウ	*math*. divisor; factor
	約束	ヤクソク	promise; appointment —*v*. make a promise/appointment

	約諾	ヤクダク	promise; commitment —*vt.* promise; commit
	約分	ヤクブン	***math.*** reduction of a factor to its lowest terms —*v.* ***math.*** reduce a fraction to its lowest terms
	約款	ヤッカン	agreement; stipulation
¥	約束手形	ヤクソクてがた	promissory note

1517 紙 ⑩
く ⼇ ⼇ ⼇ 糸 糸 糽 紅 紙 紙

音	紙	シ	paper; newspaper
熟	紙型	シケイ	paper mold/mat (used to make a printing plate)
	紙質	シシツ	paper quality
	紙上	シジョウ	in the press; in the papers; on paper
	紙幣	シヘイ	paper money; bill; note
	紙片	シヘン	piece/strip/slip of paper
	紙面	シメン	the papers; the press
訓	紙	かみ	paper
	紙切れ	かみきれ	piece of paper
	紙屑	かみくず	wastepaper
	紙一重	かみひとえ	very fine line

1518 純 ⑩
く ⼇ ⼇ ⼇ 糸 糸 糸 純

音	純	ジュン	pure; naive; genuine; authentic
熟	純愛	ジュンアイ	pure/true love
	純化	ジュンカ	purification —*v.* purify
	純金	ジュンキン	pure gold
	純銀	ジュンギン	pure silver
	純潔	ジュンケツ	purity; chastity
	純血	ジュンケツ	pure-blooded; thoroughbred
	純情	ジュンジョウ	pure heart; naivete; innocence
	純真	ジュンシン	pure heart; purity; naiveté
	純粋	ジュンスイ	purity
	純正	ジュンセイ	pure; genuine
	純然	ジュンゼン	pure; sheer; utter; absolute
	純度	ジュンド	purity
	純白	ジュンパク	snow-white
	純文学	ジュンブンガク	serious literature

竹米糸缶羊羽老耂而耒耳肉自至舌舟色虍虫血行衣衤西艮

純朴	ジュンボク	simple; naive
純綿	ジュンメン	pure cotton
純毛	ジュンモウ	pure wool
純良	ジュンリョウ	pure and good; grade A
¥ 純益	ジュンエキ	net profit
純資産	ジュンシサン	net assets (worth)
純増	ジュンゾウ	net increase
純投資	ジュントウシ	portfolio investment
純利益	ジュンリエキ	net profit/income

1519

納 ⑩ 　 く 幺 幺 幺 糸 糸 糸 糸 紃 納 納

音 納	ノウ	offer; accept
	（トウ）	
	（ナッ）	
	（ナン）	put away
熟 納豆	ナットウ	*natto* (fermented soybeans)
納得	ナットク	understanding; consent; assent; compliance —*v*. understand; assent; give consent; agree
納屋	なや	barn
納戸	ナンド	closet; wardrobe; storeroom
納会	ノウカイ	last meeting of the year
納棺	ノウカン	laying a body in a coffin
納期	ノウキ	time of delivery; payment date
納骨	ノウコツ	laying a person's ashes to rest —*vi*. lay a person's ashes to rest
納税	ノウゼイ	payment of taxes —*vi*. pay one's taxes
納税者	ノウゼイシャ	taxpayer
納入	ノウニュウ	delivery; payment —*v*. deliver; pay; supply
納品	ノウヒン	delivery of goods —*v*. deliver; supply
納品書	ノウヒンショ	statement of delivery
納付	ノウフ	delivery; payment —*v*. deliver; supply; pay
納涼	ノウリョウ	enjoying the cool of the evening —*vi*. enjoy the cool of the evening
訓 納まる	おさまる	*vi*. stay; be contented; be paid; settle down
納める	おさめる	*vt*. obtain; gain; acquire; deliver; supply
¥ 納税準備預金	ノウゼイジュンビヨキン	deposit for tax; deposit earmarked for tax payment

1520

紛 ⑩　く　幺　幺　乡　糸　糸　糸　糹　紛　紛

音	紛	フン	be mistaken for; be hardly distinguishable; get mixed
熟	紛議	フンギ	controversy; dissension —*vi.* be controversial
	紛糾	フンキュウ	complication; entanglement —*vi.* be complicated/entangled
	紛失	フンシツ	loss —*v.* lose
	紛然	フンゼン	confused; in a jumble
	紛争	フンソウ	trouble; dispute; strife; disturbance —*vi.* cause trouble/strife; dispute
	紛々	フンプン	divided; mixed; in confusion; conflicting
訓	紛れる	まぎれる	*vi.* be mistaken for; get mixed up; disappear (in the midst of); be diverted/distracted
	紛らす	まぎらす	*vt.* divert; distract; conceal; evade
	紛らわしい	まぎらわしい	ambiguous; misleading; confusing
	紛らわす	まぎらわす	*vt.* divert; distract; conceal; evade
	紛れ込む	まぎれこむ	*vi.* be lost/disappear among
	紛れもない	まぎれもない	unmistakable; obvious
	※紛う	まがう	*vi.* be mistaken for; be confused with; be mixed together; be mixed up

1521

紡 ⑩　く　幺　幺　乡　糸　糸　糹　紵　紡　紡

音	紡	ボウ	spin; make yarn
熟	紡糸	ボウシ	spinning; yarn
	紡織	ボウショク	spinning and weaving
	紡錘	ボウスイ	spindle
	紡績	ボウセキ	spinning
	紡績工	ボウセキコウ	spinner
訓	紡ぐ	つむぐ	*vt.* spin; make yarn

1522

紋 ⑩　く　幺　幺　乡　糸　糸　糹　紵　紡　紋

音	紋	モン	family crest; textile pattern
熟	紋切り型	モンきりがた	crest pattern; conventional; stereotyped

竹米糸缶羊羽老耂而未耳肉自至舌舟色虍虫血行衣衤西艮

| 紋章 | モンショウ | crest; coat of arms |
| 紋所 | モンどころ | family crest |

1523

経 ⑪ ⟨ 幺 幺 彳 纟 糸 糸 紆 紇 経 経 経

音	経	ケイ	elapse; pass; go through; normal; usual
		キョウ	sutra; mantra
熟	経文	キョウモン	sutra; text of a sutra
	経緯	ケイイ	longitude and latitude; warp and woof; details
	経営	ケイエイ	management —*v.* manage; run; operate
	経過	ケイカ	progress; development; passage —*vi.* pass; elapse
	経験	ケイケン	experience —*v.* experience; go through; undergo
	経済	ケイザイ	economy; husbandry; the economy; finances
	経済的	ケイザイテキ	economical; frugal; thrifty
	経線	ケイセン	meridian
	経典	ケイテン	Scriptures; classics; literary works by the sages
	経度	ケイド	longitude
	経由	ケイユ	via; by way of; through —*vi.* go via/by way of/through
	経歴	ケイレキ	personal history; background; career
	経路	ケイロ	course; route; process
訓	経る	へる	*vi.* pass; elapse; go/pass through; experience
¥	経営難	ケイエイナン	financial difficulty
	経済活動	ケイザイカツドウ	economic activity
	経済企画庁	ケイザイキカクチョウ	Economic Planning Agency
	経済成長	ケイザイセイチョウ	economic growth
	経常収支	ケイジョウシュウシ	current account balance
	経常費	ケイジョウヒ	working expenses; operating costs
	経常利益	ケイジョウリエキ	recurring profit
	経費	ケイヒ	expenses(s); cost(s); expenditure
	経理	ケイリ	accounting
	経理士	ケイリシ	public accountant

1524

紺 ⑪ ⟨ 幺 幺 彳 纟 糸 糸 紆 紺 紺 紺

| 音 | 紺 | コン | dark blue |

6

竹米糸 •
缶羊羽
老耂而
耒耳肉
自至舌
舟色虍
虫血行
衣衤西艮

熟	紺色	コンいろ	dark/navy blue
	紺青	コンジョウ	deep/Prussian blue
	紺碧	コンペキ	dark/deep blue
	紺屋	コンや（コウや）	dyer; dyer's shop

1525

細 ⑪ 　 〈　 纟　 纟　 纟　 糸　 糸　 糸　 糽　 細　 細　 細

音	細	サイ	narrow; thin; fine; minute; detail
熟	細菌	サイキン	germ; microbe; bacteria
	細工	サイク	workmanship; handiwork; trick —*v.* use tricks; play tricks
	細事	サイジ	trifle
	細心	サイシン	very careful; scrupulous; meticulous
	細則	サイソク	bylaws
	細大	サイダイ	minutest detail; detailed; full
	細部	サイブ	details; particulars
	細分	サイブン	subdivision; segmentation —*v.* subdivide; segment
	細別	サイベツ	subdivision —*v.* subdivide
	細胞	サイボウ	cell
	細密	サイミツ	fine; close; minute
	細目	サイモク	details; particulars; specifications
訓	細かい	こまかい	small; fine; close; minute; delicate; subtle
	細か	こまか	small; fine; delicate; subtle
	細々	こまごま	in detail; minutely
	細る	ほそる	*vi.* become thin; slim down
	細い	ほそい	fine; thin; narrow; slender
	細面	ほそおもて	slender face
	細長い	ほそながい	slender; long and narrow
	細道	ほそみち	narrow lane

1526

終 ⑪ 　 〈　 纟　 纟　 纟　 糸　 糸　 糸　 紒　 終　 終　 終

音	終	シュウ	finish; last; complete
熟	終演	シュウエン	end of a performance
	終業	シュウギョウ	close of work/school —*vi.* close; break-up
	終曲	シュウキョク	finale; last song of a musical
	終極	シュウキョク	ultimate

663

終局	シュウキョク	end; close
終結	シュウケツ	conclusion; end —*vi.* end; be concluded
終始	シュウシ	throughout; unchanged from beginning to end —*vi.* remain unchanged throughout
終始一貫	シュウシイッカン	consistency
終止	シュウシ	end; stop; termination —*vi.* stop; terminate; end; come to end
終止符	シュウシフ	period; full stop
終日	シュウジツ	all day long; from morning to night; throughout the day
終身刑	シュウシンケイ	life imprisonment
終生	シュウセイ	all one's life; life-long
終戦	シュウセン	end of a war
終着駅	シュウチャクエキ	terminal train station; terminus
終点	シュウテン	terminal train station; end of the line; last stop
終電	シュウデン	last train
終幕	シュウマク	final scene; end of the performance
終末	シュウマツ	end; conclusion
終夜	シュウヤ	all night
終夜営業	シュウヤエイギョウ	stay open all night
終了	シュウリョウ	close; end —*v.* come to an end; be completed; finish
訓 終える	おえる	*vt.* finish; complete; go through with
終わる	おわる	*vi.* end; be over; finish; be finished; come to an end
¥ 終業時間	シュウギョウジカン	closing time
終身雇用	シュウシンコヨウ	lifetime employment

1527

紹 ⑪   く 幺 幺 幺 糸 糸 糸 糸 約 紹 紹 紹

音 紹	ショウ	introduce
熟 紹介	ショウカイ	introduction; presentation —*v.* introduce; present; report; review

1528

紳 ⑪   く 幺 幺 幺 糸 糸 糸 糸 約 紳 組 紳

音 紳	シン	gentleman
熟 紳士	シンシ	gentleman

1529

組 ⑪ ⸜ ⸌ ⠆ ⸱ ⸱ 糸 糸 紅 紅 組 組

音	組	ソ	set; association; group; class; company
熟	組閣	ソカク	Cabinet formation —***vi***. form a Cabinet
	組織	ソシキ	organization; setup —***v***. organize; set up
	組織的	ソシキテキ	systematic
	組成	ソセイ	composition; makeup —***v***. compose; constitute; make up
訓	組	くみ	class; set; group; company
	組む	くむ	***v***. put together; assemble; cross one's legs; form; group
¥	組合	くみあい	(trade) union association; (labor) union; society
	組み合わせる	くみあわせる	***vt***. combine; assemble; match
	組み曲	くみキョク	musical suite
	組み立てる	くみたてる	***vt***. fabricate; assemble

1530

絵 ⑫ ⸜ ⸌ ⠆ ⸱ ⸱ 糸 紅 紅 絵 絵 絵

音	絵	エ	picture
		カイ	picture
熟	絵図	エズ	graphic drawing; scale sketch
	絵の具	エのグ	water colors
	絵葉書	エはがき	picture postcard
	絵筆	エふで	paintbrush; drawing pen
	絵本	エホン	picture/illustrated book
	絵巻物	エまきもの	picture scroll
	絵文字	エモジ	pictorial symbol
	絵画	カイガ	pictures and paintings collectively

1531

給 ⑫ ⸜ ⸌ ⠆ ⸱ ⸱ 糸 紅 紅 給 給 給

音	給	キュウ	give; allowance; salary; be enough/sufficient; serve; provide
熟	給仕	キュウジ	waiter; waitress; steward —***vi***. wait on; serve

竹米糸缶羊羽老耂而耒耳肉自至舌舟色虍虫血行衣衤西艮

給食	キュウショク	provision of meals (at schools, etc.) —*vi*. provide/serve meals
給水	キュウスイ	water supply/service —*vi*. supply water
給付	キュウフ	presentation; delivery; benefit —*v*. make a presentation; deliver; pay
給付金	キュウフキン	benefit
給油	キュウユ	oil supply —*vi*. lubricate; refuel
給与	キュウヨ	allowance; grant; supplies —*v*. grant; supply
給料	キュウリョウ	wages; salary
¥ 給与水準	キュウヨスイジュン	pay level
給与体系	キュウヨタイケイ	pay structure
給料日	キュウリョウび	payday

1532

結 ⑫　〵　纟　纟　纟　糸　糸　糸一　糸十　糸土　結　結　結

音 結	ケツ（ケッ）	tie; join; union; conclusion
熟 結果	ケッカ	result; effect; outcome; consequence
結核	ケッカク	*med*. tuberculosis (T.B.)
結局	ケッキョク	after all; finally; ultimately; eventually
結構	ケッコウ	fine; enough; sufficient
結合	ケツゴウ	union; combination —*v*. unite; combine
結婚	ケッコン	marriage —*vi*. marry; get married
結実	ケツジツ	fruition —*vi*. bear fruit; realize
結晶	ケッショウ	crystal; crystallization —*vi*. crystalize
結審	ケッシン	conclusion of a trial
結成	ケッセイ	formation; organization —*v*. form; organize
結石	ケッセキ	*med*. stones (in the liver; gall bladder etc.)
結束	ケッソク	unity; union —*v*. unite; stand together
結託	ケッタク	collusion; conspiracy —*vi*. conspire with
結末	ケツマツ	the end; conclusion; outcome
結論	ケツロン	conclusion —*vi*. come to/reach a conclusion
訓 結ぶ	むすぶ	*v*. tie; join; connect; link; conclude; bear (fruit)
結び	むすび	bow; end; conclusion
結び目	むすびめ	knot
結う	ゆう	*vt*. tie an *obi*; dress; put one's hair up in a traditional Japanese hairstyle
結納	ゆいノウ	betrothal gifts
結わえる	ゆわえる	*vt*. bind; fasten; tie

絞 ⑫ 〈 纟 纟 纟 纟 糸 糸 糸' 紶 紵 紵 絞

音	絞	コウ	strangle; press; squeeze; wring
熟	絞殺	コウサツ	strangulation; hanging —*v.* strangle; hang; suffocate
	絞首刑	コウシュケイ	execution by hanging
訓	絞る	しぼる	*vt.* wring; squeeze; press; extort; exploit
	絞まる	しまる	*vi.* tighten; become tight
	絞める	しめる	*vt.* tie up; tighten bind; strangle; press; squeeze

絶 ⑫ 〈 纟 纟 纟 纟 糸 糸 糸 紵 紷 紷 紵 絶

音	絶	ゼツ / ゼッ	die out; end; fail
熟	絶する	ゼッする	*v.* die out; end; fail
	絶縁体	ゼツエンタイ	insulator; non-conductor
	絶海	ゼッカイ	distant seas
	絶叫	ゼッキョウ	scream —*vi.* scream; cry out; shout
	絶景	ゼッケイ	splendid view
	絶交	ゼッコウ	severance of relations; rupture —*vi.* sever one's relationship with
	絶好	ゼッコウ	splendid; first rate
	絶賛	ゼッサン	great admiration/praise —*v.* admire/praise greatly
	絶食	ゼッショク	fasting; —*vt.* fast
	絶世	ゼッセイ	peerless; unequaled
	絶対	ゼッタイ	absolute; definite
	絶体絶命	ゼッタイゼツメイ	desperate situation
	絶大	ゼツダイ	immense; great
	絶頂	ゼッチョウ	summit; peak; climax
	絶版	ゼッパン	out-of-print —*v.* cease publication
	絶筆	ゼッピツ	last piece of writing (before giving up, dying, etc.)
	絶品	ゼッピン	superb article; masterpiece
	絶壁	ゼッペキ	precipice; cliff
	絶望	ゼツボウ	despair —*vi.* despair; be full of despair
	絶命	ゼツメイ	death —*vi.* die
	絶滅	ゼツメツ	extermination; extinction —*v.* exterminate; eradicate; become extinct

竹
米
糸
缶
羊
羽
老
耂
而
耒
耳
肉
自
至
舌
舟
色
虍
虫
血
行
衣
衤
西
艮

訓	絶える	たえる	**vi.** cease; die out
	絶つ	たつ	**vt.** cut off
	絶やす	たやす	**vt.** exterminate

1535

統 ⑫ 　 く 　 纟 　 纟 　 糸 　 糸 　 糸 　 糸 　 糸´ 　 紵 　 紵 　 紵 　 統

音	統	トウ	control
熟	統一	トウイツ	unity; unification; uniformity; consolidation —**v.** unify; standardize; coordinate
	統括	トウカツ	generalization —**v.** generalize
	統御	トウギョ	control; rule; management —**v.** rule; govern; control; manage
	統計	トウケイ	statistics; figures; numerical statement —**v.** show statistically/numerically
	統合	トウゴウ	integration; unification; combination; consolidation —**v.** integrate; unify; combine; consolidate
	統制	トウセイ	control; regulation —**v.** control; regulate; govern
	統率	トウソツ	command; generalship; leadership —**v.** command; take the lead; lead; direct
	統率力	トウソツリョク	leadership
	統治	トウチ	rule; reign; government; administration —**v.** rule; govern; administer
訓	統べる	すべる	**vt.** generalize

1536

絡 ⑫ 　 く 　 纟 　 纟 　 糸 　 糸 　 糸 　 糸´ 　 紹 　 終 　 終 　 絡 　 絡

音	絡	ラク	get entangled
訓	絡む	からむ	**vi.** twine around; complicate matters on purpose
	絡める	からめる	**vt.** entwine; twine around
	絡ます	からます	**vt.** entwine; twine around
	絡まる	からまる	**vi.** twine around
	絡み付く	からみつく	**vi.** coil around; cling to

1537

継 ⑬ 　 く 　 纟 　 纟 　 糸 　 糸 　 糸 　 糸´´ 　 紒 　 絆 　 絆 　 絆 　 継

音	継	ケイ	inherit; heir; succeed; continue

熟	継承	ケイショウ	succession —*v.* succeed to; inherit
	継続	ケイゾク	continuation —*v.* continue; go on; keep on; renew
	継父	ケイフ (ままちち)	stepfather
	継母	ケイボ (ままはは)	stepmother
訓	継ぐ	つぐ	*vt.* follow; continue; succeed
	継ぎ	つぎ	patch

1538

絹 ⑬ く ㄠ ㄠ ㄠ 幺 糸 糸 糹 糹 糹 絹 絹 絹

音	絹	ケン	silk
訓	絹	きぬ	silk
	絹糸	きぬいと	silk thread

1539

続 ⑬ く ㄠ ㄠ ㄠ 糸 糸 糹 紀 結 結 続 続

音	続	ゾク	continue
熟	続出	ゾクシュツ	successive appearances —*v.* occur in succession; appear one after another
	続々	ゾクゾク	successively; one after another
	続発	ゾクハツ	successive occurences —*v.* occur in succession/one after another
	続編	ゾクヘン	sequel
	続行	ゾッコウ	continuation —*v.* continue
訓	続く	つづく	*vi.* continue
	続き柄	つづきがら	family relations; kinship
	続ける	つづける	*vt.* continue

1540

維 ⑭ く ㄠ 幺 糸 糸 糸 糹 糹 紳 絆 維 維

音	維	イ	cord; maintenance; hold
熟	維持	イジ	maintenance; upkeep; preservation; support; conservation —*v.* maintain; keep; preserve; support; sustain
	維新	イシン	*hist.* Meiji Imperial Restoration (1867); revolution

竹 米 糸 缶 羊 羽 老 耂 而 耒 耳 肉 自 至 舌 舟 色 虍 虫 血 行 衣 衤 西 艮

竹米糸缶羊羽老耂而耒耳肉自至舌舟色虍虫血行衣衤西艮

1541

綱 ⑭ 〈 幺 乡 糸 糸 糸 糽 綱 綱 網 網 綱 綱

音	綱	コウ	hawser; rope; outline; summary
熟	綱目	コウモク	main points; gist; outline
	綱要	コウヨウ	elements; essentials; outline; summary
	綱領	コウリョウ	general plan/principles; outline; epitome
訓	綱	つな	rope; hawser; cord; string

1542

緒 ⑭ 〈 幺 乡 糸 糸 糸 絆 紵 絆 緒 緒 緒

音	緒	ショ	beginning
		（チョ）	beginning
熟	緒戦	ショセン	first fighting; beginning of war
訓	緒	お	cord; string; rope

1543

総 ⑭ 〈 幺 乡 糸 糸 糽 �“ 絵 絵 総 総 総

音	総	ソウ	general; overall
熟	総意	ソウイ	consensus
	総員	ソウイン	all hands; in full force
	総会	ソウカイ	general meeting; plenary session
	総画	ソウカク	the total stroke-count (of a Chinese character)
	総括	ソウカツ	summarization —*v.* summarize; generalize
	総監	ソウカン	superintendent-general
	総計	ソウケイ	total
	総合	ソウゴウ	synthesis; comprehensive —*v.* synthesize; integrate; put together
	総攻撃	ソウコウゲキ	general/all-out offensive —*v.* launch an all-out offensive; attack the enemy in full force
	総裁	ソウサイ	president; governor
	総菜	ソウザイ	everyday food; side dish
	総辞職	ソウジショク	mass resignation
	総称	ソウショウ	general/generic term —*v.* give a general name; name generically
	総数	ソウスウ	total number
	総勢	ソウゼイ	the whole army/group

総選挙	ソウセンキョ	general election
総体	ソウタイ	on the whole
総代	ソウダイ	representative; delegate
総長	ソウチョウ	president; chancellor
総出	ソウで	in full force; all together
総動員	ソウドウイン	general mobilization
総督	ソウトク	governor-general; viceroy
総本山	ソウホンザン	head temple
総本店	ソウホンテン	head office
総務	ソウム	manager; general affairs
総理	ソウリ	prime minister
総量	ソウリョウ	gross weight
総領	ソウリョウ	heir; eldest child
総領事	ソウリョウジ	consul general
総力	ソウリョク	the whole strength; all one's might
総和	ソウワ	(sum) total
¥ 総会	ソウカイ	general meeting
総額	ソウガク	sum total; total/gross amount
総決算	ソウケッサン	complete financial statement
総合課税	ソウゴウカゼイ	taxation of an aggregate income
総合銀行	ソウゴウギンコウ	universal bank
総合口座	ソウゴウコウザ	general account
総資産	ソウシサン	total assets
総資本	ソウシホン	total liabilities and net worth; gross capital
総評	ソウヒョウ	(abbreviation for General Council of Trade Unions of Japan)
総理大臣	ソウリダイジン	prime minister

1544

綿 ⟨ 纟 纟 糸 糸′ 糹 紵 紵 紵 綿 綿 綿 ⑭

音 綿	メン	cotton
熟 綿織物	メンおりもの	cotton fabrics
綿花	メンカ	raw cotton
綿糸	メンシ	cotton yarn/thread
綿製品	メンセイヒン	cotton goods
綿布	メンプ	cotton (cloth)
綿密	メンミツ	minute; meticulous; detailed
綿々	メンメン	continuous; endless; unabating
綿羊	メンヨウ	sheep
訓 綿	わた	cotton

竹米糸缶羊羽老耂而耒耳肉自至舌舟色虍虫血行衣⻂西艮

1545

網 ⑭

く 幺 幺 糸 糸 糸 糽 糽 網 網 網 網

音	網	モウ	net
熟	網膜	モウマク	*med*. retina
	網羅	モウラ	inclusion —*v*. include; comprise; be comprehensive
訓	網	あみ	net
	網戸	あみど	wire door
	網元	あみもと	head of a fishing crew

1546

緑 ⑭

く 幺 幺 糸 糽 糽 紓 紓 紓 緑 緑

音	緑	リョク	green
		（ロク）	green
熟	緑陰	リョクイン	shade of trees
	緑化	リョクカ	tree planting —*v*. plant trees
	緑酒	リョクシュ	fine saké
	緑樹	リョクジュ	greenery; lush, green tree
	緑地	リョクチ	green track of land
	緑地帯	リョクチタイ	green belt
	緑茶	リョクチャ	green tea
	緑青	ロクショウ	verdigris; green/copper rust
訓	緑	みどり	green

1547

練 ⑭

く 幺 幺 糸 糸 糽 糽 紓 綀 緤 練 練

音	練	レン	train
熟	練習	レンシュウ	practice; exercise —*v*. practice; exercise
	練達	レンタツ	skill; dexterity
	練乳	レンニュウ	condensed milk
	練磨	レンマ	training; practice —*v*. train; practice; drill
訓	練る	ねる	*v*. knead; train; polish
	練れる	ねれる	*vi*. be mellowed; be matured (of a personality, character)
	練り物	ねりもの	paste; procession; parade float

1548

縁 ⑮ 〈 幺 幺 糸 糸 糽 糿 紌 紾 緑 緑 縁

音	縁	エン	edge; relation; veranda
熟	縁側	エンがわ	veranda; porch; balcony
	縁起	エンギ	story; origin (of a temple or shrine); omen
	縁組	エンぐみ	marriage; adoption
	縁故	エンコ	relation; connection; relative
	縁者	エンジャ	blood relative
	縁台	エンダイ	bench
	縁談	エンダン	marriage talk/proposal
	縁日	エンニチ	fête day of a local deity
訓	縁	ふち	edge; brim
¥	縁故募集	エンコボシュウ	private subscription

1549

緩 ⑮ 〈 幺 幺 糸 糸 糽 紒 紵 絟 絻 緲 緩

音	緩	カン	loose
熟	緩急	カンキュウ	fast and slow; urgency; emergency
	緩行	カンコウ	going/moving slowly —*vi.* go/move slowly
	緩衝	カンショウ	buffer
	緩慢	カンマン	slackness; slowness; dullness; inactivity
	緩和	カンワ	relief; easing; relaxation —*v.* relieve; ease; relax
訓	緩い	ゆるい	loose; generous; lenient
	緩む	ゆるむ	*vi.* become slack; be careless
	緩める	ゆるめる	*vt.* loosen; relax
	緩やか	ゆるやか	gentle; easy; slack

1550

縄 ⑮ 〈 幺 幺 糸 糸 糽 紒 絽 絹 絹 絹 縄

音	縄	ジョウ	rope
熟	縄文時代	ジョウモンジダイ	*hist.* Jōmon period (10,000BC-300BC)
訓	縄	なわ	rope; cord
	縄飛び	なわとび	skipping
	縄張り	なわばり	roped-off; territory; sphere of influence

竹米糸缶羊羽老耂而耒耳肉自至舌舟色虍虫血行衣衤西艮

1551

線 ⑮ ⟨ 幺 乡 幺 糸 糹 紅 紣 線 線 線 線

音	線	セン	line
熟	線	セン	line
	線画	センガ	line drawing
	線香	センコウ	joss/incense stick
	線路	センロ	railway track

1552

締 ⑮ ⟨ 幺 乡 幺 糸 糹 紣 紵 締 締 締 締

音	締	テイ	settle
熟	締結	テイケツ	conclusion —*v.* conclude; contract
	締約	テイヤク	completion of contract/treaty
訓	締まる	しまる	*vi.* be shut/closed/locked/tightened; become sober; be frugal
	締まり	しまり	tightness; firmness; steadiness
	締まり屋	しまりや	thrifty person
	締める	しめる	*vt.* tie up; tighten; strangle; shut; close; add; sum up; economize
	締め	しめ	bundle
	締切り	しめきり	deadline; closing down

1553

編 ⑮ ⟨ 幺 乡 幺 糸 糸 紵 糽 紵 絹 絹 編

音	編	ヘン	knit; compile; edit
熟	編曲	ヘンキョク	(musical) arrangement —*v.* arrange (a piece of music)
	編纂	ヘンサン	compilation; editing —*v.* compile; edit
	編者	ヘンシャ (ヘンジャ)	editor; compiler
	編修	ヘンシュウ	compilation/editing (of books) —*v.* compile; edit
	編集	ヘンシュウ	compilation; editing —*v.* compile; edit
	編集者	ヘンシュウシャ	editor
	編集長	ヘンシュウチョウ	editor-in-chief

編成	ヘンセイ	organization; putting into a systematic/logical form —*v.* organize
編隊	ヘンタイ	formation flying
編入	ヘンニュウ	entry; incorporation; transfer —*v.* enter; incorporate; transfer (to a new school, university department)

訓
編む	あむ	*vt.* knit; braid; compile; edit
編み上げ	あみあげ	laceup (shoes, boots, etc.)
編み出す	あみだす	*vt.* work out; think up; devise
編み戸	あみど	(bamboo/wood) braided door
編み針	あみばり	knitting needle; crochet hook
編み棒	あみボウ	knitting needle/pin
編み物	あみもの	knitting

1554

緯 ⑯ ⟨ 幺 糸 糸 糸 紆 紆 結 結 緯 緯 緯

音	緯	イ	woof; latitude
熟	緯線	イセン	parallel of latitude
	緯度	イド	degree of latitude

1555

縛 ⑯ ⟨ 幺 糸 糸 紆 紆 紳 紳 縛 縛 縛

| **音** | 縛 | バク | tie |
| **訓** | 縛る | しばる | *vt.* bind; tie; fasten; restrict; restrain; chain |

1556

縦 ⑯ ⟨ 幺 糸 糸 終 終 紣 紣 絆 絆 縦 縦

音	縦	ジュウ	length
熟	縦横無尽	ジュウオウムジン	free; without opposition; in all directions
	縦貫	ジュウカン	vertically; from north to south
	縦線	ジュウセン	vertical line
	縦断	ジュウダン	cutting vertically; running through
	縦列	ジュウレツ	column; file
訓	縦	たて	length; height; vertical; perpendicular
	縦書き	たてがき	vertical writing
	縦横	たてよこ	length and breadth; lengthwise and crosswise

竹米糸缶羊羽老耂而耒耳肉自至舌舟色虍虫血行衣衤西艮

1557

縫 ⑯ 〈 幺 糸 糸 糸 糹 終 紳 縫 縫 縫 縫

音	縫	ホウ	sew
熟	縫製	ホウセイ	sewing
	縫製品	ホウセイヒン	machine-sewn/hand-sewn goods
訓	縫う	ぬう	*vt*. sew
	縫い上げる	ぬいあげる	*vt*. tuck a child's kimono (so that it can be let out later)
	縫糸	ぬいいと	sewing thread
	縫い代	ぬいしろ	margin left for the seam; seam allowance
	縫い取り	ぬいとり	embroidery
	縫い箔	ぬいハク	embroidery; silver and gold embroidery
	縫針	ぬいばり	sewing needle
	縫い目	ぬいめ	seam; stitch
	縫物	ぬいもの	sewing; needlework

1558

縮 ⑰ 〈 幺 糸 糸 糸 紵 紵 絟 綗 縮 縮 縮

音	縮	シュク	shrink; shorten; contract; reduce
熟	縮減	シュクゲン	reduction; cut back —*v*. reduce; cut back
	縮写	シュクシャ	reduced/miniature copy —*v*. make a reduced copy
	縮尺	シュクシャク	reduced scale —*v*. reduce the scale of; make smaller
	縮小	シュクショウ	reduction; curtailment —*v*. reduce; curtail; cut back
	縮図	シュクズ	reduced drawing; miniature copy
訓	縮む	ちぢむ	*vi*. shrink; contract; crinkle
	縮まる	ちぢまる	*vi*. shrink; contract
	縮み	ちぢみ	shrinkage
	縮める	ちぢめる	*vt*. shorten; cut down; reduce; condense
	縮れる	ちぢれる	*vi*. crinkle; be frizzled/curly

1559

績 ⑰ 〈 幺 糸 糸 糹 紵 絟 緒 緒 績 績

音	績	セキ	spin; achievements

1560

繊 ⑰ 　ㄑ　ㄠ　ㄠ　糸　糸′　糸土　糸圭　糸丰　絣　絾　繊　繊

音	繊	セン	fine; fiber
熟	繊維	センイ	fiber
	繊細	センサイ	delicacy

1561

織 ⑱ 　ㄑ　ㄠ　ㄠ　糸　糸′　糸刀　糸立　糸音　縮　織　織　織

音	織	シキ	organize
		ショク	weave; textiles
熟	織機	ショッキ	weaving machine; loom
訓	織る	おる	*vt.* weave; work at the loom
	織り地	おりジ	texture of woven fabric
	織物	おりもの	textiles; fabrics; woven cloth
	織物業	おりものギョウ	textile trade/business

1562

繕 ⑱ 　ㄑ　ㄠ　ㄠ　糸　糸′　糸ソ　糸半　絆′　絆′　繕　繕　繕

| 音 | 繕 | ゼン | repair |
| 訓 | 繕う | つくろう | *vt.* repair; trim |

1563

繰 ⑲ 　ㄑ　ㄠ　ㄠ　糸　糸′　糸刀　糸刀　紹　綽　綽′　繰

音	繰	（ソウ）	reel; gin; count
訓	繰る	くる	*vt.* reel; wind
	繰り上げる	くりあげる	*vt.* advance; move/carry up
	繰り返す	くりかえす	*vt.* repeat; reiterate; echo
	繰り下げる	くりさげる	*vt.* carry/move/take down; put off; postpone
¥	繰り上げ償還	くりあげショウカン	pre-maturity redemption
	繰越金	くりこしキン	sum of money carried over to next account
	繰延資金	ソウエンシキン	deferred assets

竹
米
糸
● 缶
● 羊
羽
老
耂
而
耒
耳
肉
自
至
舌
舟
色
虍
虫
血
行
衣
衤
西
艮

6 缶 ほどき jar

1564 缶 ⑥ ／ ㇑ ㇠ 午 缶 缶

音	缶	カン	can; boiler
熟	缶詰	カンづめ	canned foodstuffs

6 羊 ひつじ sheep

1565 羊 ⑥ 丶 ㇜ 丷 䒑 兰 羊

音	羊	ヨウ	sheep
熟	羊皮	ヨウヒ	sheepskin
	羊皮紙	ヨウヒシ	parchment
	羊毛	ヨウモウ	wool
訓	羊	ひつじ	sheep
	羊飼い	ひつじかい	shepherd

1566 美 ⑨ 丶 丷 丷 䒑 䒑 半 羊 兰 美 美

音	美	ビ	beauty
熟	美化	ビカ	beautification; glorification; idealization —*v.* beautify (a city); glorify; idealize
	美学	ビガク	aesthetics
	美観	ビカン	fine view; beautiful scenery
	美妓	ビギ	beautiful/brilliant performance; (sports) good play
	美形	ビケイ	beautiful; handsome
	美酒	ビシュ	delicious saké
	美術	ビジュツ	fine arts; art
	美術館	ビジュツカン	art gallery
	美女	ビジョ	beautiful/lovely woman; pretty girl
	美少年	ビショウネン	handsome youth; pretty boy

美食	ビショク	delicious food —*vi*. live on/eat fancy food
美食家	ビショクカ	gourmet; epicure
美人	ビジン	beautiful woman
美声	ビセイ	beautiful voice
美談	ビダン	fine anecdote/story
美的	ビテキ	aesthetic
美点	ビテン	merit; virtue; good point
美徳	ビトク	virtue; noble attribute
美男	ビナン	handsome man
美男子	ビナンシ	handsome man
美風	ビフウ	fine/good custom
美文	ビブン	flowery/elegant prose
美文調	ビブンチョウ	ornate style
美貌	ビボウ	beauty; beautiful face
美味	ビミ	delicious; good; tasting
美名	ビメイ	good/reputable name
美容	ビヨウ	beautiful face; beautification of face or form
美容院	ビヨウイン	beauty parlor; hairdresser
美容外科	ビヨウゲカ	*med*. cosmetic surgery
美容師	ビヨウシ	beautician; hairdresser
美容整形	ビヨウセイケイ	cosmetic surgery
訓 美しい	うつくしい	beautiful
※美味しい	おいしい	good-tasting; delicious

1567

着 ⑫

、　ゝ　ツ　ヅ　ヸ　羊　芦　羊　养　着　着　着

音 着	チャク (ジャク)	put on; wear; clothe; arrive; reach
熟 着衣	チャクイ	one's clothes
着眼	チャクガン	attention; notice; perception —*vi*. pay attention; notice; perceive
着眼点	チャクガンテン	point of view
着実	チャクジツ	steadiness; honesty
着手	チャクシュ	start; commencement; outset —*vi*. start; commence; begin
着順	チャクジュン	order of arrival
着色	チャクショク	coloration; coloring —*vi*. color; paint
着水	チャクスイ	alighting on the water; splashdown —*vi*. alight on the water; splashdown
着席	チャクセキ	taking a seat; sitting down —*vi*. take a seat; sit down

竹
米
糸
缶
羊
羽
老耂
而
耒
耳
肉
自
至
舌
舟
色
虍
虫
血
行
衣衤
西覀

竹
米
糸
缶
• 羊
羽
老
耂
而
耒
耳
肉
自
至
舌
舟
色
虍
虫
血
行
衣
礻
西
艮

着想	チャクソウ	idea; conception
着地	チャクチ	landing —*vi.* land
着々	チャクチャク	steadily; step by step
着任	チャクニン	arrival at one's post —*vi.* arrive at one's post
着服	チャクフク	getting dressed; embezzlement; misappropriation —*v.* get dressed; misappropriate; embezzle
着目	チャクモク	attention; notice —*vi.* pay attention to; take notice of
着用	チャクヨウ	wearing (clothes) —*v.* wear (clothes)
着陸	チャクリク	landing; touchdown —*vi.* land; touchdown
着工	チャッコウ	commencement of construction work —*vi.* start construction work

訓

着る	きる	*vt.* put on; wear
着せる	きせる	*vt.* dress someone; clothe; put on; plate; coat; cover
着替える	きがえる	*vi.* change clothes
着付け	きつけ	dressing; fitting
着物	きもの	kimono
着く	つく	*vi.* arrive at; reach; come to hand
着ける	つける	*vt.* put on; wear

1568

⑬ 　 ヽ　ソ　ッ　⺍　⺌　尐　羊　羊　羊　義　義　義

音 義　ギ　justice; meaning

熟

義援金	ギエンキン	contribution; subscription; donation
義眼	ギガン	artificial/glass eye
義挙	ギキョ	righteous act; heroic deed
義兄弟	ギキョウダイ	brothers-in-law; blood brothers
義兄	ギケイ	(older) brother-in-law
義姉	ギシ	(older) sister-in-law
義歯	ギシ	false tooth/teeth
義手	ギシュ	artificial arm
義足	ギソク	artificial leg
義弟	ギテイ	(younger) brother-in-law
義父	ギフ	stepfather; father-in-law
義憤	ギフン	indignation; outrage
義母	ギボ	stepmother; mother-in-law
義妹	ギマイ	(younger) sister-in-law
義務	ギム	duty; obligation
義務教育	ギムキョウイク	compulsory education
義理	ギリ	obligation; justice; duty

1569

群 ⑬　　フ　ヨ　ヨ　尹　尹　君　君　君゛　君゛　群゛　群゛　群

音	群	グン	gather; collect; many
熟	群居	グンキョ	living together in large numbers
	群衆	グンシュウ	large group of people
	群集	グンシュウ	crowd; multitude; throng
	群集心理	グンシュウシンリ	group psychology
	群小	グンショウ	insignificant; minor; petty
	群生	グンセイ	gregarious —*vi*. be gregarious
	群島	グントウ	group of islands
	群落	グンラク	group of villages; plant community
訓	群	(むら)	group; crowd; cluster; clump
	群がる	むらがる	*vi*. crowd (together); herd; flock; pack
	群れ	むれ	group; troop; crowd; herd; flock; pack
	群れる	むれる	*vi*. crowd (together); throng; flock together

 6 羽　はね feather

1570

羽 ⑥　　フ　ヲ　ヨ　羽　羽　羽

音	羽	ウ	feather; wing
熟	羽化	ウカ	emergence —*vi*. emerge; grow wings
	羽毛	ウモウ	feather; plume; feathering; plummage
訓	羽	はね	feather; wing
	羽	は	feather; wing; (counter for birds and rabbits)
	羽織	はおり	*haori* (Japanese overgarment)
	羽衣	はごろも	robe of feathers; winged jacket worn by angels
	羽振り	はぶり	position/status in life

1571

 翁 ⑩　　ノ　八　公　公　公　弅　弅　翁　翁　翁

| 音 | 翁 | オウ | old man |
| 訓 | ※翁 | おきな | old man |

竹米糸缶羊羽老耂而耒耳肉自至舌舟色虍虫血行衣衤西艮

竹
米
糸
缶
羊
● 羽
老耂
而
耒
耳
肉
自
至
舌
舟
色
虍
虫
血
行
衣衤
西�覀
艮

1572

習 ⑪ 　ㄱ　ㄱ　ㅋ　ㅋㄱ　ㅋㄱ　ㅋㅋ　ㅋㅋ　羽羽　習羽　習習

音	習	シュウ	study; custom
熟	習慣	シュウカン	custom; habit; practice
	習作	シュウサク	study (in art, music, etc.)
	習字	シュウジ	penmanship; calligraphy
	習熟	シュウジュク	mastering (a skill, etc.) —*vi*. master; become proficient
	習性	シュウセイ	habit; behavior; nature
	習俗	シュウゾク	manners and customs; usage; folkways; conventions
	習得	シュウトク	learning; acquiring skills —*v*. learn; acquire a skill; master
	習癖	シュウヘキ	habit
訓	習う	ならう	*vt*. learn; train; take lessons
	習わし	ならわし	practice; custom; way; tradition

1573

翌 ⑪ 　ㄱ　ㄱ　ㅋ　ㅋㄱ　ㅋㄱ　ㅋㅋ　翌翌　翌翌　翌翌　翌

音	翌	ヨク	next/following
熟	翌月	ヨクゲツ	following month
	翌日	ヨクジツ	next/following day
	翌朝	ヨクチョウ	next morning
	翌年	ヨクネン	next/following year

1574

翼 ⑰ 　ㄱ　ㄱ　ㅋ　ㅋㄱ　ㅋㅋ　翌羽　翌羽　翌羽　翼翼　翼翼　翼翼　翼

音	翼	ヨク	wing; help
熟	翼状	ヨクジョウ	wing-shaped
訓	翼	つばさ	wing (of a bird or plane)

1575

翻 ⑱ 　ノ　ㅇ　㠯　乎　釆　希　希　番　翻　翻　翻　翻

音	翻	ホン	change; turn over; flutter/swirl (in a breeze)

熟	翻案	ホンアン	adaptation —*v.* adapt (a novel, etc.)
	翻意	ホンイ	change of mind —*vi.* change one's mind
	翻刻	ホンコク	reprint —*v.* reprint
	翻然	ホンゼン	all of a sudden
	翻訳	ホンヤク	translation —*v.* translate
	翻弄	ホンロウ	trifling with —*v.* trifle/play with
訓	翻す	ひるがえす	*vt.* turn over; change suddenly (one's opinion, belief); flutter/swirl (in a breeze)
	翻る	ひるがえる	*vi.* turn over; change suddenly; flutter/swirl (in a breeze)
	※翻す	こぼす	overturn; spill

---

6 老 おいがしら／おいかんむり old man 耂 (p.684)

1576

老 ⑥ 一 十 土 耂 耂 老

音	老	ロウ	old age
熟	老眼	ロウガン	presbyopia
	老朽	ロウキュウ	age; decrepitude —*vi.* get old; become decrepit
	老後	ロウゴ	in one's old age
	老巧	ロウコウ	veteran; experienced
	老骨	ロウコツ	one's old bones; old person's body
	老死	ロウシ	death by old age —*vi.* die of old age
	老中	ロウジュウ	*hist.* member of the shogun's council of elders
	老熟	ロウジュク	experienced; mature —*vi.* be experienced/mature
	老女	ロウジョ	old woman
	老人	ロウジン	old man; the elderly
	老衰	ロウスイ	senility —*vi.* be senile
	老体	ロウタイ	old body; elderly person
	老大家	ロウタイカ	veteran; authority
	老若	ロウニャク	young and old; young or old
	老年	ロウネン	old age; elderly person
	老婆	ロウバ	old woman
	老婆心	ロウバシン	old-womanish solicitude
	老舗	ロウホ ※(しにせ)	long-established shop or store
	老齢	ロウレイ	old age
	老練	ロウレン	experienced; veteran
訓	老いる	おいる	*vi.* grow old

683

竹米糸缶羊羽
● 老耂
● 耂而
耒耳肉自至
舌舟色虍虫
血行衣衤西艮

老い	おい	old age
老いらく	おいらく	old age
老ける	ふける	*vi*. grow old

---

4 耂 おいがしら／おいかんむり old man

1577

考 ⑥ 一 十 土 耂 耂 考

音	考	コウ	consider; reflect; think; contemplate; test; examine
熟	考案	コウアン	conception; idea; plan; device; project —*v*. conceive; plan; design; devise; originate
	考課	コウカ	examination of personal records
	考究	コウキュウ	investigation —*vt*. investigate
	考古学	コウコガク	archaeology
	考査	コウサ	examination; test; consideration —*v*. test; examine; quiz; consider
	考察	コウサツ	contemplation; consideration; examination; study; inquiry —*v*. contemplate; consider; examine; study
	考試	コウシ	examination
	考証	コウショウ	historical research/investigation —*v*. carry out historical research
	考慮	コウリョ	consideration; deliberation; reflection; thinking —*v*. consider; think; ponder; deliberate; reflect
訓	考える	かんがえる	*vt*. think; consider; take a view; be of an opinion; regard
	考え	かんがえ	thinking; thought; ideas; conception; opinion
	考え方	かんがえかた	line of thought; point of view; solution
	考え事	かんがえごと	concern; worry

1578

者 ⑧ 一 十 土 耂 耂 者 者 者

| 音 | 者 | シャ | person |
| 訓 | 者 | もの | *hum*. person |

684

6 而 しこうして rake

1579
耐 ⑨ 一 ア 丆 丂 而 而 而一 耐丨 耐

音	耐	タイ	endure; bear; stand; withstand; hold out
熟	耐火	タイカ	fireproof
	耐寒	タイカン	coldproof; resistance against the cold
	耐久	タイキュウ	endurance; persistance; permanence; durability
	耐暑	タイショ	heat-resistant
	耐震	タイシン	earthquakeproof
	耐水	タイスイ	waterproof
	耐性	タイセイ	tolerance
	耐熱	タイネツ	heat-resistant
	耐乏	タイボウ	withstanding poverty —*vi*. withstand poverty
訓	耐える	たえる	*vi*. endure; bear; support; withstand; be fit for

6 耒 すきへん plow

1580
耕 ⑩ 一 二 三 丰 丰 耒 耒 耒一 耒二 耕

音	耕	コウ	till; plow; cultivate
熟	耕具	コウグ	farm implements
	耕作	コウサク	cultivation; farming; tillage —*v*. cultivate; farm; till
	耕地	コウチ	arable/cultivated/plowed land
訓	耕す	たがやす	*vt*. till; plow; cultivate

1581
耗 ⑩ 一 二 三 丰 丰 耒 耒 耒 耗 耗

音	耗	モウ	consume; decrease
		(コウ)	

685

竹米糸缶羊羽老耂而耒
• 耳肉自至舌舟色虍虫血行衣衤西艮

6 耳　みみ／みみへん　ear

1582

耳 ⑥　一　ㄒ　下　下　手　耳

音	耳	ジ	ear
熟	耳鼻咽喉科	ジビインコウカ	**med.** otorhinolaryngology; ear, nose, and throat department
	耳目	ジモク	seeing and hearing; eyes and ears
訓	耳	みみ	ear; hearing; (bread) crust
	耳垢	みみあか	ear wax
	耳打ち	みみうち	whispering —**vi.** whisper
	耳搔き	みみかき	ear pick
	耳学問	みみガクモン	hearsay
	耳寄りな話	みみよりなはなし	welcome news
	耳輪	みみわ	earring

1583

聖 ⑬　一　ㄒ　下　手　耳　耵　耴　耵　耵　聖　聖

音	聖	セイ	saint; holy; sacred; sage
熟	聖域	セイイキ	sacred precincts
	聖火	セイカ	sacred flame; Olympic Flame
	聖者	セイジャ	saint; holy man
	聖書	セイショ	Bible
	聖人	セイジン	sage; saint; holy man
	聖地	セイチ	sacred land; Holy Land
	聖典	セイテン	holy book; scriptures
	聖母	セイボ	Holy Mother
	聖夜	セイヤ	Christmas Eve

1584

聞 ⑭　l　ㄇ　ㄇ　門　門　門　門　門　門　聞　聞

音	聞	ブン	hear; listen to; heed; ask
		モン	

訓	聞く	きく	*vt.* hear; listen to; heed; ask
	聞こえる	きこえる	*vi.* hear; be heard/audible; be able to hear
	聞き入る	ききいる	*vi.* listen attentively
	聞き入れる	ききいれる	*vt.* accede to; comply with
	聞き納め	ききおさめ	last time to hear (somebody say something)
	聞き落とす	ききおとす	*vt.* not hear; miss
	聞き覚え	ききおぼえ	learning by ear; heard before
	聞き返す	ききかえす	*vt.* ask back/again
	聞き書き	ききがき	taking notes (from a talk/lecture)
	聞き苦しい	ききぐるしい	offensive to the ear
	聞き込む	ききこむ	*vt.* hear about; listen; ask about; investigate (by asking)
	聞き上手	ききジョウズ	good listener
	聞き出す	ききだす	*vt.* ask about; begin to listen/ask
	聞き付ける	ききつける	*vt.* hear; learn of; be used to hearing
	聞き伝え	ききづたえ	hearsay
	聞き手	ききて	listener
	聞き取る	ききとる	*vt.* hear and understand; catch; follow
	聞き流す	ききながす	*vt.* pay no attention to
	聞き耳	ききみみ	attentive ears; listening carefully
	聞き漏らす	ききもらす	*vt.* not hear/catch
	聞き役	ききヤク	one who hears people's complaints
	聞き分ける	ききわける	*vt.* distinguish between (sounds, stories, etc.); listen to reason; listen to and accept

1585

 聴 ⑰　一 丆 耳 耳 耳 耵 聍 聴 聴 聴 聴 聴

音	聴	チョウ	listen
熟	聴音機	チョウオンキ	audio tracer; sound locator
	聴覚	チョウカク	*med.* auditory sense; hearing
	聴講	チョウコウ	attendance at a lecture —*v.* attend/listen to a lecture
	聴取	チョウシュ	listening; hearing; audition —*v.* listen; hear; give audience to
	聴衆	チョウシュウ	audience
	聴診	チョウシン	*med.* ausculation; stethoscopy —*vi.* examine (a patient) with a stethoscope
	聴診器	チョウシンキ	*med.* stethoscope
	聴神経	チョウシンケイ	*med.* acoustic nerve
	聴力	チョウリョク	*med.* hearing; hearing ability
訓	聴く	きく	*vt.* listen; hear

竹米糸缶羊羽老耂而耒耳肉自至舌舟色虍虫血行衣衤西艮

竹
米
糸
缶
羊
羽
老⺹
而
未
耳
● 肉
● 自
至
舌
舟
色
虍
虫
血
行
衣衤
西覀
艮

1586

職 ⑱

一 丁 丆 耳 耵 耵 聍 聸 睅 聵 職 職 職

音	職	ショク	job; work; occupation
熟	職域	ショクイキ	one's job/occupation/area of responsibility
	職員	ショクイン	staff; personnel; member of staff
	職業	ショクギョウ	occupation; trade; profession
	職責	ショクセキ	one's work responsibility; duties
	職人	ショクニン	craftsman; workman; artisan
	職能	ショクノウ	professional ability; occupational function
	職場	ショクば	workshop; workplace; the office
	職務	ショクム	work duties
	職名	ショクメイ	official title
	職権	ショッケン	official authority
	職工	ショッコウ	worker; factory hand
¥	職種	ショクシュ	type of occupation/job; job classification
	職制	ショクセイ	office organization; managerial post; executive
	職場研修	ショクばケンシュウ	on-the-job training
	職歴	ショクレキ	work record/experience; career record; job history

6 肉 see ⇨p.457

6 自 みずから dotted eye

1587

自 ⑥

丶 丿 冂 自 自 自

音	自	ジ	oneself
		シ	natural; nature
熟	自愛	ジアイ	self-love; self-indulgence —*vi.* take care of oneself
	自衛	ジエイ	self-defense; self-protection —*vi.* defend oneself
	自衛隊	ジエイタイ	the Self-Defense Force (SDF)
	自我	ジガ	the self/ego

自戒	ジカイ	self-discipline —*v.* exercize self-discipline
自害	ジガイ	suicide —*vi.* commit suicide
自覚	ジカク	consciousness; self-awareness —*v.* be aware/conscious
自画自賛	ジガジサン	self-praise —*vi.* sing one's own praises; praise oneself
自画像	ジガゾウ	self-portrait
自家製	ジカセイ	homemade
自家用	ジカヨウ	for private use
自活	ジカツ	self-support —*vi.* support oneself
自虐	ジギャク	masochism; self-torture
自給	ジキュウ	self-support; self-sustenance —*v.* provide for oneself
自給自足	ジキュウジソク	self-sufficiency —*vi.* be self-sufficient
自供	ジキョウ	confession —*v.* confession
自決	ジケツ	self-determination; suicide —*vi.* determine/decide for oneself; commit suicide; kill oneself
自己	ジコ	self; oneself
自己暗示	ジコアンジ	autosuggestion
自己紹介	ジコショウカイ	self-introduction —*vi.* introduce oneself
自己中心	ジコチュウシン	egocentricity
自己流	ジコリュウ	one's own way of doing something
自業自得	ジゴウジトク	natural consequence of one's evil deed; asking for it; deserving what one gets
自国	ジコク	one's own country/homeland
自国語	ジコクゴ	native language; mother tongue
自在	ジザイ	at will; freely
自作	ジサク	one's own work; made by oneself —*v.* make something by oneself
自作農	ジサクノウ	landed farmer
自殺	ジサツ	suicide —*vi.* commit suicide; kill oneself
自賛	ジサン	self-praise; narcissism —*vi.* praise oneself
自首	ジシュ	surrendering —*vi.* give oneself up; surrender
自習	ジシュウ	self-study; learning by oneself —*vi.* teach oneself; study by oneself
自粛	ジシュク	self-control; self-restraint —*vi.* exercise self-control; restrain oneself
自主的	ジシュテキ	independent; autonomous
自称	ジショウ	self-styled; self-professed —*vi.* call oneself; praise oneself
自叙伝	ジジョデン	autobiography
自身	ジシン	oneself; personally; in person
自信	ジシン	self-confidence; confidence
自炊	ジスイ	cooking one's own meals —*vi.* cook one's own meals

竹米糸缶羊羽老耂而耒耳肉 • 自至舌舟色虍虫血行衣衤西艮

自制	ジセイ	self-control —*v*. control one's emotions
自省	ジセイ	reflection; self-examination —*vi*. examine oneself
自責	ジセキ	self-reproach —*vi*. reproach oneself; have a guilty conscious
自説	ジセツ	one's own view/opinion
自然	シゼン	nature; natural; spontaneous; automatic
自然界	シゼンカイ	nature; the natural world
自然科学	シゼンカガク	natural science
自然現象	シゼンゲンショウ	natural phenomenon
自然主義	シゼンシュギ	naturalism
自然林	シゼンリン	natural/virgin forest
自尊心	ジソンシン	pride; self-respect
自他	ジタ	oneself and others; other people and oneself
自体	ジタイ	itself; the thing itself; one's own body
自宅	ジタク	one's house/home
自治	ジチ	self-government; autonomy
自治会	ジチカイ	student/town council
自治体	ジチタイ	self-governing body
自治領	ジチリョウ	dominion
自重	ジチョウ	self-respect; self-love —*vi*. be prudent
自邸	ジテイ	one's private residence/home
自転	ジテン	rotation —*vi*. rotate; revolve
自転車	ジテンシャ	bicycle
自伝	ジデン	autobiography
自動	ジドウ	automatic; mechanical
自動車	ジドウシャ	car; automobile; motorcar
自動的	ジドウテキ	automatically; mechanically
自認	ジニン	acknowledgement —*v*. acknowledge
自白	ジハク	confession —*v*. confess; make a confession
自発的	ジハツテキ	voluntarily; of one's own volition
自費	ジヒ	one's own expense
自筆	ジヒツ	one's own handwriting
自負	ジフ	self-confidence —*vi*. be self-confident
自分	ジブン	oneself; myself; me; I
自分自身	ジブンジシン	oneself; I; myself
自弁	ジベン	at one's own expenses —*v*. pay one's own way
自暴自棄	ジボウジキ	despair; desperation
自慢	ジマン	boasting; bragging; pride —*v*. be proud of; brag; boast
自明	ジメイ	self-evidence; truism
自滅	ジメツ	self-destruction —*vi*. ruin oneself; destroy oneself

自問自答	ジモンジトウ	questioning oneself; monolog —*vi.* talk to oneself
自由	ジユウ	freedom; liberty
自力	ジリキ	self-effort; one's own efforts
自立	ジリツ	independence —*vi.* become independent; stand on one's feet
自律	ジリツ	autonomy —*vi.* be autonomous
訓 自ら	みずから	oneself
¥ 自己資本	ジコシホン	owned capital; net worth; equity capital
自己資本比率	ジコシホンヒリツ	ratio of net worth to total liabilities; net worth ratio
自主規制	ジシュキセイ	voluntary restriction
自治省	ジチショウ	Ministry of Home Affairs
自治大臣	ジチダイジン	minister of home affairs
自民党（自由民主党）	ジミントウ（ジユウミンシュトウ）	Liberal Democratic Party (LDP)
自由化	ジユウカ	liberalization —*v.* liberalize

1588
臭 ⑨ ′ ′′ 宀 宀 自 自 皀 臭 臭

音 臭	シュウ	smell
熟 臭覚	シュウカク	sense of smell
臭気	シュウキ	bad/offensive smell; stench
訓 臭い	くさい	foul/bad smelling; stink; smell; be suspicious
臭味	くさミ	bad smell; offensive odor; stench

6 至 いたる arriving

1589
至 ⑥ 一 乙 云 云 至 至

音 至	シ	arrive; reach; extend
熟 至急	シキュウ	emergency; urgent; prompt
至近	シキン	point-blank; close range
至芸	シゲイ	unrivaled performance
至言	シゲン	wise saying

竹米糸缶羊羽老耂而耒耳肉自
●至
●舌舟色虍虫血行衣衤西艮

至高	シコウ	supremacy; highest; tallest
至極	シゴク	very; extremely
至上	シジョウ	supreme; urgent
至誠	シセイ	true sincerity; great devotion
至当	シトウ	highly appropriate; proper; right
至難	シナン	most difficult; almost impossible
至福	シフク	supreme bliss
至便	シベン	most convenient
至宝	シホウ	great treasure; valuable asset
訓 至る	いたる	*vi.* reach; arrive; come; extend; result in
至る所	いたるところ	everywhere; all over; throughout

1590

致 ⑩ 一 ㄥ ㄥ 云 至 至 至 致 致 致

音 致	チ	do; bring about; cause
熟 致死	チシ	fatal; mortal; lethal; deadly —*v.* be fatal/mortal/lethal/deadly
致死量	チシリョウ	lethal dose
致命傷	チメイショウ	fatal wound; mortal injury
致命的	チメイテキ	fatal; mortal; deadly; lethal
訓 致す	いたす	*vt. hon.* do; bring about; cause; incur; render; exert

6　舌　した　tongue

1591

舌 ⑥ 一 二 千 千 舌 舌

音 舌	ゼツ	tongue
熟 舌禍	ゼッカ	unfortunate slip of the tongue
舌戦	ゼッセン	verbal contest; war of words; quarrel
舌頭	ゼットウ	tip of the tongue
訓 舌	した	tongue; language
舌打ち	したうち	clicking one's tongue —*vi.* click one's tongue
舌先	したさき	tip of the tongue
舌足らず	したたらず	unclear/mumbled speech
舌鼓	したつづみ	eating with gusto

6

1592

舟 ⑥　`'` `「` `ナ` `冇` `舟` `舟`

音	舟	シュウ	boat
熟	舟運	シュウウン	transportation by ship
	舟行	シュウコウ	boat movement/speed
	舟航	シュウコウ	going by boat
	舟艇	シュウテイ	small boat
訓	舟	ふね	ship; boat
	舟	ふな	ship; boat
	舟歌	ふなうた	sailor's song; sea chantey
	舟乗り	ふなのり	seaman; sailor
	舟人	ふなびと	sailor; ferryman

1593

航 ⑩　`'` `「` `ナ` `冇` `舟` `舟` `舟'` `舟广` `舟广` `航`

音	航	コウ	cross; sail; navigate; fly; ship; airplane
熟	航海	コウカイ	voyage; navigation; sailing; crossing; passage —*vi.* sail; make a voyage/crossing; navigate; take a passage
	航空	コウクウ	aviation; flying; flight; air traffic
	航空機	コウクウキ	aircraft; airplane
	航空書簡	コウクウショカン	aerogram
	航空便	コウクウビン	airmail
	航空母艦	コウクウボカン	aircraft carrier
	航行	コウコウ	navigation; sailing; cruise —*vi.* navigate; sail; cruise
	航程	コウテイ	distance covered; passage; flight; lap
	航路	コウロ	course; sea route; line; service; run

1594

般 ⑩　`'` `「` `ナ` `冇` `舟` `舟` `舟'` `舟广` `船` `般`

音	般	ハン	kind
熟	般若	ハンニャ	wisdom; female demon; hag

竹米糸缶羊羽老耂而耒耳肉自至舌 • 舟色虍虫血行衣衤西艮

1595

船 ⑪ 　 ′ 丿 丫 丬 舟 舟 舟 舟ヘ 舟ヘ 船 船

音	船	セン	vessel; ship
熟	船医	センイ	ship doctor
	船員	センイン	crewman; seaman
	船客	センキャク	ship's passenger
	船号	センゴウ	ship's name
	船室	センシツ	cabin
	船主	センシュ	shipowner
	船首	センシュ	bow; prow
	船体	センタイ	hull; ship
	船団	センダン	fleet; convoy
	船長	センチョウ	captain
	船底	センテイ	bottom of a ship
	船頭	センドウ	boatman
	船舶	センパク	ship; vessel; shipping
	船尾	センビ	stern
	船腹	センプク	tonnage; counter for ships; hold; bottoms
訓	船	ふね	ship; boat
	船	ふな	ship; boat
	船歌	ふなうた	chantey; song
	船賃	ふなチン	ship fare
	船出	ふなで	sailing —*vi*. set sail; put out to sea
	船乗り	ふなのり	sailor
	船人	ふなびと	seaman
	船酔い	ふなよい	seasickness —*vi*. be seasick

1596

舶 ⑪ 　 ′ 丿 丬 丬 舟 舟 舟′ 舟′ 舶 舶

音	舶	ハク	large ship
熟	舶来	ハクライ	foreign/imported goods

1597

艇 ⑬ 　 ′ 丿 丬 舟 舟 舟ˊ 舟ˊ 舟ˉ 舟主 舟主 艇 艇

音	艇	テイ	boat

熟	艇身	テイシン	length of a boat

1598

艦 ㉑　刀　角　舟　舟'　舟'' 　舟''' 　舟''''　舟'''''　舟''''''　舮　艦　艦

音	艦	カン	warship
熟	艦隊	カンタイ	fleet of warships

---

6 色　いろ　color

1599

色 ⑥　ノ　ク　ク　名　名　色

音	色	シキ	color; looks; sexual love
		ショク	color; aspect
熟	色感	シキカン	sense of color
	色彩	シキサイ	color; coloring; hue; tint
	色紙	シキシ	square piece of fancy paper
	色弱	シキジャク	partial color blindness
	色情	シキジョウ	sexual desire
	色素	シキソ	pigment
	色調	シキチョウ	tone of color; hue
	色盲	シキモウ	color blindness
	色欲	シキヨク	lust; sexual desire
訓	色	いろ	color; complexion; expression; love affair
	色合い	いろあい	shade; hue
	色々	いろいろ	various; many kinds
	色男	いろおとこ	handsome man; ladykiller
	色女	いろおんな	mistress; beautiful woman
	色香	いろか	feminine charms; color and fragrance
	色紙	いろがみ	colored paper
	色気	いろケ	sex appeal; sexual passion; inclination; ambitions
	色づく	いろづく	*vi.* color; turn (red, yellow, etc.); become sexy/attractive
	色っぽい	いろっぽい	sexy; attractive
	色眼鏡	いろめがね	colored/rose-tinted spectacles
	色物	いろもの	colored clothes/fabrics; variety entertainment; variety show

竹米糸缶羊羽老耂而耒耳肉自至舌舟色卢虫血行衣衤西艮

6 虍 とらかんむり／とらがしら tiger

1600

虐 ⑨ ｀ ｨ ﾄ ﾄﾞ 广 声 虍 虍 虐 虐

音	虐	ギャク	cruel; savage; tyrannical; oppressive
熟	虐殺	ギャクサツ	slaughter; carnage; massacre; butchery —v. slaughter; massacre; butcher
	虐待	ギャクタイ	cruel/ill treatment; abuse —v. treat cruelly; abuse
訓	虐げる	しいたげる	vt. oppress; persecute; tyrannize over

1601

虚 ⑪ ｀ ｨ ﾄ ﾄﾞ 广 声 虍 虍 虍 虚 虚 虚

音	虚	キョ	emptiness; nothingness; hollow; lie; falsehood; weak; vain
		（コ）	
熟	虚栄	キョエイ	vanity; vainglory
	虚偽	キョギ	falsehood; lie; fallacy
	虚弱	キョジャク	weekness; feebleness; infirmity
	虚勢	キョセイ	bluff
	虚脱感	キョダツカン	lethargy; absentmindedness
	虚無主義	キョムシュギ	Nihilism
	虚礼	キョレイ	empty formalities; meaningless politeness
	虚空	コクウ	air; space; sky

1602

虞 ⑬ ｀ ｨ ﾄ ﾄﾞ 广 声 声 虍 虍 虞 虞 虞 虞

音	虞	グ	fear; anxiety
訓	虞	おそれ	fear; anxiety

1603

虜 ⑬ ｀ ｨ ﾄ ﾄﾞ 广 声 声 虍 虍 庿 庿 虜 虜

音	虜	リョ	captive; prisoner of war; barbarian

訓 ※虜　　とりこ　　capture; slave; captive

---

6 虫　むし　insect

1604

虫 ⑥　　ヽ ロ ロ 中 虫 虫

音	虫	チュウ	insect
熟	虫害	チュウガイ	damage done by insects; blight
	虫垂	チュウスイ	*med.* vermiform appendix
訓	虫	むし	insect; bug; worm; feeling
	虫食い	むしくい	vermiculation; damage by worms
	虫歯	むしば	decayed tooth
	虫眼鏡	むしめがね	magnifying glass

1605

蚊 ⑩　　ヽ ロ ロ 中 虫 虫 虫' 虻 蚋 蚊

訓	蚊	か	mosquito
	蚊取線香	かとりセンコウ	mosquito-repellent incense
	蚊屋 （蚊帳）	かや	mosquito net

1606

蚕 ⑩　　一 二 チ 天 天 呑 呑 香 蚕 蚕

音	蚕	サン	silkworm
熟	蚕糸	サンシ	silkwork
	蚕食	サンショク	encroachment; aggression —*v.* encroach on; make inroads; eat into
訓	蚕	かいこ	silkworm

1607

蛍 ⑪　　ヽ ゛ ゛゛ ゛゛゛ 営 営 営 営 常 蛍 蛍

音	蛍	ケイ	firefly

697

竹米糸缶羊羽老耂而耒耳肉自至舌舟色虍虫血行衣衤西艮

竹米糸缶羊羽老耂而耒耳肉自至舌舟色虍虫血行衣衤西艮

熟	蛍光	ケイコウ	fluorescence
	蛍光灯	ケイコウトウ	fluorescent lamp
	蛍光塗料	ケイコウトリョウ	fluorescent paint
訓	蛍	ほたる	firefly

1608

蛇 ⑪　 丶 口 口 虫 虫 虫 虫' 虫' 虻 蚨 蛇

音	蛇	ジャ	snake
		ダ	snake
熟	蛇口	ジャぐち	faucet; tap
	蛇行	ダコウ	winding; meandering —*vi.* wind; meander
	蛇足	ダソク	superfluous
訓	蛇	へび	snake; serpent

1609

蛮 ⑫　 丶 亠 亠 方 亦 亦 亦 䜌 䜌 帝 蛮 蛮

音	蛮	バン	barbarian; savage
熟	蛮行	バンコウ	act of barbarity; atrocity; brutality
	蛮人	バンジン	barbarian; savage
	蛮勇	バンユウ	brute courage

1610

融 ⑯　 一 一 弓 弓 弓 鬲 鬲 鬲 融 融 融

音	融	ユウ	dissolve; melt
熟	融解	ユウカイ	melting; dissolution; fusion —*v.* melt; dissolve; fuse
	融合	ユウゴウ	fusion; merger —*vi.* fuse; merge
	融点	ユウテン	melting point
	融和	ユウワ	harmony —*vi.* get along well with
訓	※融ける	とける	*vi.* melt; dissolve
¥	融資	ユウシ	finance; loan
	融資会社	ユウシガイシャ	financing corporation
	融通	ユウズウ	accomodation; loan; finance —*vi.* finance (an enterprise)
	融通証券	ユウズウショウケン	treasury accomodation bill

融通手形　ユウズウてがた　accomodation bill
融通手形　ユウズウテガタ　kite-flier
　振出人　ふりだしニン

6 血　ち　blood

1611

 　 ﾉ 　ㇷ 　ㅁ 　血 　血 　血

⑥

音	血	ケツ	blood
熟	血圧	ケツアツ	*med.* blood pressure
	血液	ケツエキ	*med.* blood
	血液型	ケツエキがた	*med.* blood type/group
	血液銀行	ケツエキギンコウ	*med.* blood bank
	血液検査	ケツエキケンサ	blood test
	血縁	ケツエン	blood relative
	血管	ケッカン	*med.* blood vessel
	血気	ケッキ	vigor; hotbloodedness; youthfulness
	血球	ケッキュウ	*med.* blood corpuscle
	血行	ケッコウ	*med.* circulation of the blood
	血痕	ケッコン	*med.* blood stain
	血小板	ケッショウバン	*med.* (blood) platelet
	血色	ケッショク	complexion
	血清	ケッセイ	*med.* serum
	血税	ケツゼイ	heavy taxes
	血戦	ケッセン	bloody battle
	血相	ケッソウ	expression
	血族	ケツゾク	blood relative
	血沈	ケッチン	*med.* sedimentation of blood
	血糖値	ケットウチ	*med.* blood sugar level
	血統付き	ケットウつき	pedigreed
	血肉	ケツニク	blood and flesh; living things
	血尿	ケツニョウ	*med.* bloody urine
	血便	ケツベン	*med.* bloody excrement
	血脈	ケツミャク	*med.* blood vessel
訓	血	ち	blood
	血潮	ちしお	blood
	血筋	ちすじ	lineage; blood relationship
	血走る	ちばしる	be bloodshot
	血眼	ちまなこ	bloodshot eyes

竹米糸缶羊羽老耂而耒耳肉自至舌舟色虍虫血行衣衤西民

1612

衆 ⑫

ノ ` ⼧ ⾎ 血 血 卑 卑 卑 卑 衆 衆

音 衆　シュウ　　many; multitude; the people; the masses
　　　（シュ）　many

熟 衆議　　シュウギ　　general consultation
　　衆議院　シュウギイン　the House of Representatives
　　衆愚　　シュウグ　　vulgar masses
　　衆愚政治　シュウグセイジ　mob rule
　　衆人　　シュウジン　the people/public
　　衆人環視　シュウジンカンシ　public attention
　　衆目　　シュウモク　public attention
　　衆生　　シュジョウ　***Bud.*** living things

---

6 行　ぎょうがまえ　going

1613

行 ⑥

ノ ⼃ ⼻ 彳 行 行

音 行　ギョウ　　stroke; line
　　　コウ　　go; going; do; exercise; conduct; line
　　　（アン）　walking tour; pilgrimage

熟 行脚　　アンギャ　　pilgrimage —***vi.*** make a pilgrimage
　　行間　　ギョウカン　between the lines
　　行儀　　ギョウギ　　manners; behavior; deportment
　　行司　　ギョウジ　　*gyōji* (referee in sumo wrestling)
　　行事　　ギョウジ　　event; function
　　行書　　ギョウショ　semicursive style of writing *kanji*
　　行商　　ギョウショウ　peddling; hawking —***v.*** peddle; hawk
　　行状　　ギョウジョウ　behavior; conduct; demeanor
　　行水　　ギョウズイ　ablution —***vi.*** wash oneself
　　行列　　ギョウレツ　line; queue —***vi.*** line up; queue up
　　行為　　コウイ　　deed; act; action; behavior; conduct
　　行軍　　コウグン　march; marching
　　行使　　コウシ　　exercise; use (of one's authority, etc.) —***v.*** use; make use of; employ; exercise
　　行進　　コウシン　march; parade —***vi.*** march; parade; proceed
　　行進曲　コウシンキョク　parade; musical march

行程	コウテイ	journey; distance; itinery
行動	コウドウ	action; act; conduct; behavior —*vi*. act; behave; conduct; move
行楽	コウラク	pleasure trip; excursion; picnic; outing

訓 行く　　　いく　　　　　*vi*. go; walk; depart

行う	おこなう	*vt*. do; perform; conduct; carry out
行き違い	ゆきちがい	crossing; misunderstanding; disagreement
行き詰まる	ゆきづまる	*vi*. come to a deadlock; be at a standstill
行く	ゆく	*vi*. go; pass
行方	ゆくえ	destination; whereabouts
行く先	ゆくさき	whereabouts
行く末	ゆくすえ	future; forthcoming happening
行手	ゆくて	destination

¥ 行政改革　ギョウセイカイカク　administrative reform

1614

術⑪　　ノ　ク　彳　彳　什　彳十　彳木　彳木　彳木　彳木　術

音	術	ジュツ	means; art; skill
熟	術語	ジュツゴ	technical term; terminology
	術策	ジュッサク	stratagem; trick; artifice
	術中	ジュッチュウ	trick; trap

1615

街⑫　　ノ　ク　彳　彳　彳十　彳土　彳圭　彳圭　街　街　街　街

音	街	ガイ	street
		（カイ）	street; highway
熟	街道	カイドウ	highway; high road
	街頭	ガイトウ	street
	街灯	ガイトウ	street lamp
	街路樹	ガイロジュ	roadside tree; trees lining a street
訓	街	まち	street; downtown

1616

衝⑮　　彳　彳　彳　彳　彳　彳　衛　衛　衝　衝　衝　衝

音	衝	ショウ	collide; shock

竹
米
糸
缶
羊
羽
老耂
而
耒
耳
肉
自
至
舌
舟
色
虍
虫
血
行 ●
衣衤
西覀
艮

701

竹
米
糸
缶
羊
羽
老
耂
而
耒
耳
肉
自
至
舌
舟
色
虍
虫
血
行
衣
衤
西
艮

熟 衝撃　ショウゲキ　shock; impact
衝撃的　ショウゲキテキ　shocking
衝動　ショウドウ　impulse; urge
衝動買い　ショウドウがい　impulse buying —*v.* buy on impulse
衝動的　ショウドウテキ　impulsive
衝突　ショウトツ　collision; conflict; clash —*vi.* collide; conflict; clash

---

1617

衛⑯　イ　イ　イ　イ　イ　イ　イ　イ　イ　イ　イ　衛

音 衛　エイ　defend; guard
熟 衛視　エイシ　Diet guard
衛生　エイセイ　hygiene; sanitation
衛星　エイセイ　satellite
衛星放送　エイセイホウソウ　satellite broadcasting
衛兵　エイヘイ　sentry; guard
訓 ※衛る　まもる　*vt.* protect; guard; defend

1618

衡⑯　イ　イ　イ　イ　イ　イ　イ　衡

音 衡　コウ　balance; equilibrium
熟 衡器　コウキ　balance; scales; weighing machine

---

6 衣　ころも　clothes　　衤 (p.708)

1619

衣⑥　、　亠　ナ　亠　衣　衣

音 衣　イ　clothes; clothing; garments; robes
熟 衣装　イショウ　costume; apparel; dress
衣食　イショク　food and clothes
衣食住　イショクジュウ　food, clothing, and shelter; living
衣服　イフク　clothing; clothes
衣料　イリョウ　clothing; clothes
衣類　イルイ　clothes; garments

訓	衣	きぬ	clothes
	衣	ころも	robes; garments

1620

表 ⑧　一 十 キ 圭 乒 表 表 表

音	表	ヒョウ	table; chart; surface; express
熟	表する	ヒョウする	express/show (respect, regret, congratulations, etc.)
	表意文字	ヒョウイモジ	ideograph; ideogram
	表音文字	ヒョウオンモジ	phonetic symbol; phonogram
	表記	ヒョウキ	written on the face/outside —*v.* write; transcribe; show
	表敬訪問	ヒョウケイ ホウモン	courtesy call
	表決	ヒョウケツ	vote; voting —*v.* make a decision by vote; vote
	表現	ヒョウゲン	expression; representation —*v.* express; represent
	表現主義	ヒョウゲンシュギ	expressionism (art, literature, etc.)
	表札	ヒョウサツ	nameplate (on a door, gate, etc.)
	表紙	ヒョウシ	cover/binding (of a book)
	表示	ヒョウジ	indication; sign; expression —*v.* indicate; express; show on a chart; tabulate
	表出	ヒョウシュツ	expression —*v.* express (one's feelings)
	表彰	ヒョウショウ	(official) commendation —*v.* commend; make public recognition of
	表象	ヒョウショウ	symbol; emblem; image; idea —*v.* symbolize
	表情	ヒョウジョウ	expression
	表題	ヒョウダイ	title (of a book, play, etc.); heading; caption
	表土	ヒョウド	topsoil
	表皮	ヒョウヒ	*med.* cuticle; epidermis
	表明	ヒョウメイ	demonstration; manifestation; expression —*v.* demonstrate; show; manifest; express
	表面	ヒョウメン	surface; face *fig.* superficial; appearances; pretext
	表面化	ヒョウメンカ	coming to the surface —*vi.* come to the surface; attract public attention
	表面積	ヒョウメンセキ	surface area
	表裏	ヒョウリ	front and back; both sides *fig.* two faced; double-dealer
	表裏一体	ヒョウリイッタイ	one and indivisible
訓	表す	あらわす	*vt.* express; show; reveal; manifest
	表れる	あらわれる	*vi.* come out; appear; come in sight; show itself; be expressed

竹
米
糸
缶
羊
羽
老
耂
而
耒
耳
肉
自
至
舌
舟
色
虍
虫
血
行
衣
衤 •
西
艮

竹米糸缶羊羽老耂而耒耳肉自至舌舟色虍虫血行衣衤西艮

表	おもて	surface; right side; public; outside a house **bas**. top of an inning
表沙汰	おもてザタ	make public
表立つ	おもてだつ	**vi**. become public; be made public
表向き	おもてむき	openly; publicly; ostensibly; officially
¥ 表記価格	ヒョウキカカク	declared/insured value
表紙手形	ヒョウシてがた	consolidated bill
表面金利	ヒョウメンキンリ	nominal interest rate; coupon rate
表面預金	ヒョウメンヨキン	nominal deposit

1621

衷 ⑨ 一 冖 冂 冃 吉 声 吏 吏 衷

音 衷	チュウ	in one's heart
熟 衷情	チュウジョウ	one's inmost feelings/true heart
衷心	チュウシン	one's inmost feelings/true heart

1622

衰 ⑩ ` 一 亠 亠 亠 亩 声 声 声 衰

音 衰	スイ	decline
熟 衰弱	スイジャク	weakness; prostration; breakdown; collapse —**vi**. weaken; become feeble; be worn out
衰退	スイタイ	degeneration; atrophy —**vi**. degenerate
衰微	スイビ	decline; wane; decadence —**vi**. decline; decay; wane; fall into decay
衰亡	スイボウ	decline; decay; ruin; fall; downfall —**vi**. go to ruin; be ruined; fall; decay; decline
訓 衰える	おとろえる	**vi**. become weak; lose vigor; waste away
衰え	おとろえ	weakening; emaciation; decline

1623

袋 ⑪ ノ 亻 亻 代 代 代 伐 伐 袋 袋 袋

音 袋	タイ	bag
訓 袋	ふくろ	bag; sack
袋小路	ふくろコウジ	blind alley
袋物	ふくろもの	bags

1624 裁 ⑫

一 十 土 キ 土 歩 圭 圭 表 表 裁 裁 裁

音	裁	サイ	cut; judge
熟	裁決	サイケツ	decision; verdict —v. decide; reach a verdict; judge
	裁断	サイダン	cutting; judgment; decision —v. cut; decide; judge; pass judgment
	裁定	サイテイ	decision; arbitration —vt. decide; judge
	裁判	サイバン	trial; suit —v. try; judge; put to the courts to decide
	裁判官	サイバンカン	judge
	裁判権	サイバンケン	jurisdiction
	裁判所	サイバンショ	court; law court
	裁縫	サイホウ	sewing; needlework —vi. sew; do needlework
	裁量	サイリョウ	discretion —v. use one's discretion
訓	裁く	さばく	vt. judge; sit in judgment; decide; pass verdict; punish
	裁き	さばき	judgment
	裁つ	たつ	vt. cut; cut out
¥	裁定取引	サイテイとりひき	arbitrage transaction

1625 装 ⑫

丨 丬 爿 爿 壮 壮 壮 壮 壮 壮 装 装 装 装

音	装	ソウ	wear; feigh; pretend
		ショウ	
熟	装束	ショウゾク	dress; attire
	装具	ソウグ	equipment
	装甲	ソウコウ	armor; armor plating
	装甲車	ソウコウシャ	armored car
	装飾	ソウショク	ornament; decoration
	装身具	ソウシング	personal accessories
	装置	ソウチ	apparatus; device; equipment
	装着	ソウチャク	equipped; installed; fitted with —v. equip; instal; fit with
	装丁	ソウテイ	binding
	装備	ソウビ	equipment
訓	装う	よそおう	vt. wear; feigh; pretend

竹 米 糸 缶 羊 羽 老 耂 而 耒 耳 肉 自 至 舌 舟 色 虍 虫 血 行 衣 ⻂ 西 艮

竹米糸缶羊羽老耂而耒耳肉自至舌舟色虍虫血行
● 衣衤西艮

1626 裂 ⑫

一 ナ テ 歹 歹ﾞ 列 列 列 列 裂 裂 裂

音	裂	レツ	tear; split; rip; burst
熟	裂傷	レッショウ	*med*. laceration
訓	裂く	さく	*vt*. tear; split; burst
	裂ける	さける	*vi*. tear; split; rip; burst
	裂け目	さけめ	rip; split; crack; fissure

1627 裏 ⑬

一 亠 亠ﾞ 亠 亩 审 审 审 审 亩 裏 裏

音	裏	リ	back; reverse side; opposite; rear
熟	裏面	リメン	back; reverse side; background
訓	裏	うら	back; reverse side
	裏表	うらおもて	both sides; reverse; inside out; two-faced
	裏方	うらかた	lady consort; stagehand
	裏側	うらがわ	back; reverse side; far side (of the moon)
	裏切る	うらぎる	*vt*. betray
	裏口	うらぐち	back door; rear entrance
	裏声	うらごえ	falsetto
	裏地	うらジ	lining
	裏付ける	うらづける	*vt*. support; endorse
	裏手	うらて	at the back; rear
	裏話	うらばなし	inside story
	裏腹	うらはら	reverse; opposite
	裏町	うらまち	backstreet
¥	裏書き	うらがき	endorsement
	裏書譲渡	うらがきジョウト	transfer by endorsement

1628 製 ⑭

ノ 亠 丄 午 告 告 制 制ﾞ 制ﾞ 製 製 製

音	製	セイ	manufacture; make
熟	製する	セイする	*vt*. manufacture; make
	製材	セイザイ	lumber; sawing
	製作	セイサク	work; manufacturing; production —*v*. work; product; make

製図	セイズ	draftsmanship; drawing; cartography —*v.* draw; draft
製造	セイゾウ	manufacturing —*v.* manufacture
製鉄	セイテツ	iron manufacture
製糖	セイトウ	sugar manufacture —*vi.* produce sugar
製版	セイハン	(printing) plate making/engraving
製品	セイヒン	product; manufactured goods
製粉	セイフン	flour milling
製法	セイホウ	manufacturing process; recipe
製本	セイホン	bookbinding —*v.* bind books
製薬	セイヤク	pharmacy; manufacturing drugs
製油	セイユ	refining/processing oil
製錬	セイレン	refining; smelting —*v.* refine; smelt
¥ 製造業	セイゾウギョウ	manufacturing industry

1629 褒 ⑮

一 亠 ㇒ 疒 㥁 㥁 㦩 㦩 褎 褒 褒 褒

音	褒	ホウ	praise
熟	褒章	ホウショウ	medal
	褒賞	ホウショウ	prize; reward; praise
	褒状	ホウジョウ	certificate of merit; commendation
	褒美	ホウビ	reward; prize
訓	褒める	ほめる	*vt.* praise highly
	褒めちぎる	ほめちぎる	*vt.* praise highly

1630 襲 ㉒

亠 立 㡀 肯 音 龷 青 竜 龍 龍 襲 襲

音	襲	シュウ	attack; succeed
熟	襲撃	シュウゲキ	surprise attack; sudden assault —*v.* raid; attack; assault
	襲名	シュウメイ	succession to another's name; assumption of one's parents' name —*v.* succeed to (a person's) stage name; inherit one's father's name
	襲来	シュウライ	raid; invasion —*v.* attack; make a raid
訓	襲う	おそう	*vt.* attack; fall on; raid

竹
米
糸
缶
羊
羽
老耂
而
未
耳
肉
自
至
舌
舟
色
虍
虫
血
行
衣
衤
西
艮

5 衤　ころもへん　clothes at the left

1631

被 ⟨16 31⟩　丶　ラ　ァ　ネ　ネ　ネ　衤　初　衫　祛　被

音	被	ヒ	suffer; incur; receive; (prefix) -ed; -ee
熟	被害	ヒガイ	damage; harm; injury; casualties
	被害者	ヒガイシャ	victim; the injured (party)
	被疑者	ヒギシャ	suspect; person suspected of committing a crime
	被告	ヒコク	accused; defendant
	被告人	ヒコクニン	defendant
	被災	ヒサイ	suffering —vi. suffer from; fall victim to; be hit by (a natural disaster/fire)
	被災者	ヒサイシャ	victim (of a natural disaster/fire)
	被選挙権	ヒセンキョケン	electoral eligibility
	被選挙人	ヒセンキョニン	individual eligible for elective office
	被爆	ヒバク	being bombed (in particular, nuclear or hydrogen bomb) —vi. be bombed
	被爆者	ヒバクシャ	hibakusha (atomic bomb victim)
	被曝	ヒバク	exposure to radiation —vi. be exposed to radiation
	被曝者	ヒバクシャ	hibakusha (radiation exposure victim)
	被服	ヒフク	clothing
	被覆	ヒフク	covering —v. cover; coat
訓	被る	こうむる	vt. suffer; incur; receive
	被う	おおう	vt. cover
	被さる	かぶさる	vi. get covered; hang over
	被せる	かぶせる	vt. place/pour on top of; cover
	被る	かぶる	vt. wear/put on (one's head); take the blame
¥	被保険者	ヒホケンシャ	the insured
	被保険物	ヒホケンブツ	insured article/property

1632

補 ⑫　丶　ラ　ァ　ネ　ネ　衤　初　袻　袻　袻　補　補

音	補	ホ	assist; supplement
熟	補する	ホする	vt. appoint; assign
	補角	ホカク	math. supplementary angle

補完	ホカン	complement; supplement —*v*. complement; supplement
補記	ホキ	appendage/addition (to an article) —*v*. add/append
補給	ホキュウ	supply; replenishment —*v*. supply; replenish
補強	ホキョウ	reinforcement —*v*. reinforce
補欠	ホケツ	filling a vacancy; substitute; spare
補血	ホケツ	*med*. blood replenishment —*vi*. replenish one's blood
補語	ホゴ	*gram*. complement
補佐	ホサ	assistant; aide; adviser; assistance; aid —*v*. assist; aid; help; advise
補修	ホシュウ	repair —*v*. repair; fix; mend
補習	ホシュウ	supplementary lessons; extracurricular education
補充	ホジュウ	supplement; replacement —*v*. supplement; replace
補助	ホジョ	aid; assistance; supplement; subsidy —*v*. help; assist; supplement; subsidize
補色	ホショク	complementary color
補正	ホセイ	correction; revision —*v*. correct; revise
補則	ホソク	supplementary rules
補足	ホソク	supplement; supply; replenishment —*v*. supplement; supply; replenish
補聴器	ホチョウキ	hearing aid
補填	ホテン	filling/supplying (a deficiency); compensation —*v*. fill/supply (a deficiency); compensate
補導	ホドウ	guidance; advice —*v*. guide; lead; advise
補任	ホニン	appointment (to a post, vacancy) —*v*. appoint
訓 補う	おぎなう	*vt*. supply; make up/compensate for
¥ 補欠選挙	ホケツセンキョ	by-election
補償	ホショウ	compensation; indemnification —*v*. compensate; indemnify
補償金	ホショウキン	indemnity; compensation (money)
補助金	ホジョキン	subsidy; grant-in-aid
補正予算	ホセイヨサン	revived budget

1633

裕 ⑫ 　` ラ ネ ネ ネ ネ ネ 衿 衿 衿 裕 裕

音 裕	ユウ	rich; abundant; fruitful; fertile
熟 裕福	ユウフク	prosperity; affluence
訓 ※裕	ゆたか	abundant; rich

竹米糸缶羊羽老耂而耒耳肉自至舌舟色虍虫血行衣衤西艮

1634

褐 ⑬ ﹅ ラ ネ ネ ネ 初 袒 袒 衵 褐 褐 褐

音	褐	カツ	brown
熟	褐色	カッショク	brown

1635

裸 ⑬ ﹅ ラ ネ ネ ネ 初 袒 袒 裎 裸 裸 裸

音	裸	ラ	nude; naked
熟	裸眼	ラガン	the naked eye
	裸身	ラシン	nakedness
	裸体	ラタイ	naked body; nudity
	裸婦	ラフ	nude woman
訓	裸	はだか	naked body; nakedness; nudity
	裸ん坊	はだかんボウ	naked person/child
	※裸足	はだし	barefoot; barefooted

1636

複 ⑭ ﹅ ラ ネ ネ ネ ネ 初 衤 袒 複 複 複

音	複	フク	double; multiple; composite
熟	複眼	フクガン	compound eye (of an insect)
	複合	フクゴウ	composite; compound; complex —v. compound; pound together
	複合語	フクゴウゴ	*gram.* compound (word)
	複雑	フクザツ	complicated; complex
	複式	フクシキ	double-entry (bookkeeping)
	複写	フクシャ	copying; duplication; facsimile —vi. copy; duplicate
	複数	フクスウ	*gram.* plural
	複製	フクセイ	reproduction; duplication —v. reproduce; duplicate
	複線	フクセン	double track
	複葉	フクヨウ	compound leaf
¥	複利	フクリ	compound interest

1637

襟 ⑱
ラ ミ ネ ネ ネ 衤 衤 衤 裄 襟 襟 襟

音	襟	キン	collar; heart
訓	襟	えり	collar; neck; lapel
	襟足	えりあし	hairline above the nape
	襟元	えりもと	front of the neck

---

6 西 にし west

1638

西 ⑥
一 丆 丆 丙 西 西

音	西	セイ	west
		サイ	
熟	西方	サイホウ	the West; Buddhist paradise
	西経	セイケイ	west longitude
	西方	セイホウ	(the) west; western
	西洋	セイヨウ	Western countries; the West; western; occidental
	西洋化	セイヨウカ	westernization; Europeanization —v. become westernized
	西暦	セイレキ	Christian Era; Anno Domini (AD)
訓	西	にし	west; western
	※西瓜	すいか	watermelon

1639

要 ⑨
一 丆 丆 襾 襾 覀 要 要 要

音	要	ヨウ	main point; principal; necessary; essential; important
熟	要する	ヨウする	require; need
	要因	ヨウイン	chief factor; principal cause
	要員	ヨウイン	essential personnel
	要求	ヨウキュウ	demand; requirement —v. demand; require
	要件	ヨウケン	requisite; essentials
	要港	ヨウコウ	important/strategic port

要項	ヨウコウ	essential point(s)
要綱	ヨウコウ	summary; outline
要塞	ヨウサイ	fortress; stronghold
要旨	ヨウシ	gist; purport; substance
要式	ヨウシキ	formal
要所	ヨウショ	important/strategic place
要職	ヨウショク	responsible position; important job
要人	ヨウジン	leading figure; important person
要請	ヨウセイ	request; requirement; demand —*v*. request; demand; ask; call for
要素	ヨウソ	element; factor
要地	ヨウチ	important strategic place
要注意	ヨウチュウイ	requiring care/caution
要点	ヨウテン	main point(s)
要部	ヨウブ	principal/essential part
要望	ヨウボウ	demand —*v*. demand
要務	ヨウム	important business
要目	ヨウモク	principal items
要約	ヨウヤク	summary —*v*. summarize
要領	ヨウリョウ	gist; purport; synopsis
訓 要る	いる	*vi*. need; cost
¥ 要求払い	ヨウキュウばらい	payable on demand

1640

覆 ⑱　一　宀　襾　襾　严　覀　覂　覂　覆　覆　覆　覆

音 覆	フク	overturn; cover
熟 覆面	フクメン	(cloth) mask
訓 覆う	おおう	*vt*. cover; conceal; spread over
覆す	くつがえす	*vt*. overturn; overthrow
覆る	くつがえる	*vi*. be overturned/overthrown

1641

覇 ⑲　一　宀　襾　襾　覀　覀　覀　覇　覇　覇　覇　覇

音 覇	ハ	supremacy; leadership; domination
熟 覇気	ハキ	ambition; aspiration
覇権	ハケン	supremacy; leadership; domination
覇者	ハシャ	supreme ruler; champion

712

1642

良 ⑦ ` ゥ ゥ ヨ 白 良 良

音	良	リョウ	good
熟	良好	リョウコウ	good; favorable; satisfactory
	良妻	リョウサイ	good wife
	良識	リョウシキ	good sense
	良質	リョウシツ	superior quality
	良種	リョウシュ	good breed; thoroughbred
	良書	リョウショ	good book
	良心	リョウシン	conscience
	良心的	リョウシンテキ	conscientious
	良知	リョウチ	intuition
	良否	リョウヒ	good or bad
	良品	リョウヒン	superior quality goods
	良民	リョウミン	good citizens
	良薬	リョウヤク	effective medicine
訓	良い	よい	good
	良し悪し	よしあし	good or evil; right or wrong; merits and demerits

7 見　みる　seeing

1643

見 ⑦　｜ 冂 冂 闩 月 目 貝 見

音	見	ケン	see; view; meet; show
熟	見解	ケンカイ	opinion; view; outlook
	見学	ケンガク	observation; tour (for educational purposes) —v. inspect; observe
	見学者	ケンガクシャ	visitor
	見識	ケンシキ	pride; self-respect; judgment; discernment; insight
	見地	ケンチ	standpoint; viewpoint; point of view
	見当	ケントウ	aim; direction; estimate; guess; about; approximately
	見物	ケンブツ	sightseeing —v. go sightseeing; see the sights
	見聞	ケンブン	information; experience; observation —v. go sightseeing
訓	見る	みる	vt. see; watch; look
	見える	みえる	vi. be seen; can see; seem to; visit; come; arrive
	見せる	みせる	vt. show; display; allow to be watched
	見合い	みあい	small party to introduce two prospective marriage candidates —vi. meet each other with a view to marriage
	見送る	みおくる	vt. see off one's guest
	見苦しい	みぐるしい	dishonorable; disgraceful; ugly; shabby
	見事	みごと	excellent; fine; splendid; superb; admirable
	見込む	みこむ	vt. expect; anticipate; count on; trust; estimate
	見殺し	みごろし	leaving someone to his fate
	見境	みさかい	distinction
	見世物	みせもの	show; sideshow
	見所	みどころ	promise; good points; the point; highlight
	見習う	みならう	vt. follow a person's example; learn
	見本	みホン	sample; specimen; example; model
	見舞い	みまい	inquiry; expression of one's sympathy; visit to a sick person
¥	見返り	みかえり	incentive goods; collateral expert goods; collateral goods
	見出し	みだし	index; contents (of a book); title; headline; heading; readline; caption
	見積り	みつもり	estimate

714

見積書	みつもりショ	written estimate
見通し	みとおし	outlook; forecast; prospect
見本市	みホンいち	(sample) trade fair

1644

規 ⑪　一　ニ　ナ　夫　丸　刔　刔　邦　規　規　規

音	規	キ	regulation; rule
熟	規格	キカク	standard; norm
	規準	キジュン	criterion
	規正	キセイ	readjustment; correction; rectification
	規制	キセイ	regulation; control —v. regulate; control
	規則	キソク	rule; regulation
	規則的	キソクテキ	regular; systematic
	規定	キテイ	rule; regulations; stipulations; prescriptions —v. prescribe; ordain; stipulate
	規範	キハン	model; example
	規模	キボ	scale; scope
	規約	キヤク	rules; bylaws
	規律	キリツ	discipline; regulation; order; rules

1645

視 ⑪　丶　ラ　ネ　ネ　礻　初　礽　祁　祁　祁　視

音	視	シ	watch; regard
熟	視界	シカイ	field of vision; visibility; sight
	視覚	シカク	sense of sight
	視覚的	シカクテキ	visual; visually
	視察	シサツ	inspection; observation —v. inspection; make an inspection
	視察員	シサツイン	observer
	視線	シセン	one's gaze; one's line of vision
	視聴	シチョウ	looking and listening; attention —v. look and listen; be attentive
	視聴覚	シチョウカク	senses of seeing and hearing
	視聴者	シチョウシャ	audience; the viewers
	視聴率	シチョウリツ	audience rating
	視点	シテン	point of view; viewpoint
	視野	シヤ	field of vision; range of view; one's view
	視力	シリョク	sight; eyesight; vision

視力検査　シリョクケンサ　eye test

訓 ※視る　　みる　　**vt**. see

1646

覚 ⑫　｀　″　″′　′″　⺍　⺌　⺍′　常　常　営　賞　覚

音 覚　　カク　　sense; feel; comprehend

熟 覚悟　カクゴ　resolution; resignation —**v**. be prepared for; be resigned to; be determined

覚醒　カクセイ　awakening; disillusionment —**v**. awake; wake up; arouse; be awakened; be disillusioned

覚醒剤　カクセイザイ　stimulant drug

訓 覚える　おぼえる　**vi**. feel; remember; learn

覚ます　さます　**vt**. awake; wake up

覚める　さめる　**vi**. wake up; become sober; be enlightened

1647

親 ⑯　亠　立　立　立　辛　辛　亲　亲′　新′　新′　親′　親

音 親　　シン　　parent; intimate

熟 親愛　シンアイ　affection; love

親衛隊　シンエイタイ　bodyguards

親近感　シンキンカン　sense of closeness

親権　シンケン　parental authority

親交　シンコウ　intimacy; friendship

親戚　シンセキ　relative; relation

親切　シンセツ　kind; kindhearted; good; nice

親善　シンゼン　friendship; goodwill

親族　シンゾク　relative; relation

親展　シンテン　confidential; personal

親等　シントウ　degree of kinship

親睦　シンボク　friendship

親身　シンミ　kind; warm; tender; blood relation

親密　シンミツ　intimacy; close friendship

親友　シンユウ　bosom/close/good friend

親類　シンルイ　relative; relation

親和　シンワ　friendship; affinity

訓 親　　おや　　parent

親方　おやかた　boss; foreman; master; home; parents

親孝行　おやコウコウ　filial devotion/piety

親心	おやごころ	parental love
親父	おやじ	father; old man; the boss
親潮	おやしお	Kurile Current
親馬鹿	おやバカ	doting/indulgent parent
親分	おやブン	gang leader; boss
親元	おやもと	one's parents/home
親指	おやゆび	thumb; big toe
親しい	したしい	intimate; close; friendy; familiar
親しむ	したしむ	*vi.* become familiar with; get to know; make friends with
¥ 親会社	おやガイシャ	parent company

1648

覧 ⑰　ㅣ　厂　厂　戸　臣　臥　臥　斦　斦　暫　覧　覧

音	覧	ラン	inspect; see; look at

1649

観 ⑱　ト　レ　ケ　ヶ　ヶ　产　弁　隹　観　観　観　観

音	観	カン	observe; view; see; look
熟	観客	カンキャク	spectators
	観劇	カンゲキ	theatergoing —*v.* go to the theater; see a play
	観光	カンコウ	sightseeing; tourism —*v.* go sightseeing
	観光客	カンコウキャク	tourist
	観察	カンサツ	observation —*v.* observe; view; make observations
	観衆	カンシュウ	spectators; audience
	観賞	カンショウ	enjoyment; admiration —*v.* enjoy; admire
	観戦	カンセン	watch a battle/competition/contest
	観測	カンソク	observation; survey —*v.* observe; make an observation; survey
	観点	カンテン	standpoint; viewpoint; point of view
	観念	カンネン	idea; conception; notion
	観念的	カンネンテキ	ideal; ideological
	観音	カンノン	Kwannon, Avalokitesvara (Buddhist goddess of mercy)
	観望	カンボウ	sightseeing
	観覧	カンラン	viewing; inspection —*v.* view; inspect
訓	※観る	みる	*vt.* view; watch; observe

7 角 つの horn

1650

角 ⑦　ノ　ク　ク　ヶ　勺　角　角

音	角	カク	horn; angle; corner
熟	角界	カクカイ（カッカイ）	sumo wrestling world
	角材	カクザイ	square lumber
	角柱	カクチュウ	square pillar; prism
	角度	カクド	*math.* geometric angle
	角張る	カクばる	*vi.* be angular/square/sharp; become formal/ceremonious
訓	角	かど	corner; angle
	角	つの	animal's horn

1651

解 ⑬　ノ　ク　ク　ヶ　角　角　角　角ノ　解ノ　解ノ　解ノ　解ノ　解

音	解	カイ	solve; untie; melt; understand; explain
		ゲ	realize; untie; melt
熟	解する	カイする	*vt.* interpret; understand
	解決	カイケツ	solution; settlement; conclusion —*v.* solve; settle; conclude
	解雇	カイコ	discharge; dismissal; firing —*v.* discharge; dismiss; fire
	解散	カイサン	breakup; dispersion —*v.* break up; disperse
	解釈	カイシャク	interpretation; explanation —*v.* interpret; explain
	解除	カイジョ	release; cancellation; removal —*v.* release; cancel; remove
	解消	カイショウ	dissolution; cancellation; liquidation —*v.* dissolve; cancel; liquidate
	解説	カイセツ	commentary; explanation —*v.* make a commentary; explain
	解答	カイトウ	solution; answer —*vi.* solve; answer
	解読	カイドク	deciphering; decoding —*v.* decipher; decode
	解放	カイホウ	release; emancipation; liberation —*v.* release; emancipate; liberate
	解剖	カイボウ	dissection; autopsy; vivisection —*v.* dissect; vivisect; cut up

解明	カイメイ	elucidation; solution —*v.* elucidate; solve
解せない	ゲせない	incomprehensible
解毒剤	ゲドクザイ	*med.* antidote
解熱剤	ゲネツザイ	*med.* antipyretic

訓
解く	とく	*vt.* untie; relieve; answer; construe
解かす	とかす	*vt.* melt
解ける	とける	*vi.* loose; be dispelled; be relieved; melt
解く	ほどく	*vt.* untie; undo; unfasten; loosen
※解る	わかる	*vi.* understand; comprehend

¥
解禁	カイキン	removal of a ban/embargo —*v.* lift a ban/embargo
解任	カイニン	dismissal; firing —*v.* displace (a person) from (his or her) position; dismiss
解約	カイヤク	cancellation of a contract/agreement —*v.* cancel a contract; call off (an agreement)
解け合い	とけあい	liquidation by compromise

1652

触 ⑬ 　ク　ゲ　角　角　角　角　角　角　角　触　触　触

音
| 触 | ショク | touch; feel |

熟
触手	ショクシュ	tentacle; feeler
触媒	ショクバイ	catalyst
触発	ショクハツ	touched off; started —*v.* touch off; start
触角	ショッカク	antenna; feeler
触覚	ショッカク	sense of touch

訓
| 触る | さわる | *vi.* touch; feel |
| 触れる | ふれる | *v.* touch; feel; stroke; perceive; incur |

7 　言　げん／ごんべん　word

1653

言 ⑦ 　丶　一　二　三　言　言　言

音
| 言 | ゲン | say; speak; word; language |
| | ゴン | word |

熟
| 言外 | ゲンガイ | implied; hinted |
| 言及 | ゲンキュウ | mention; reference to —*vi.* mention; refer to; touch upon |

見
角
● 言
谷
豆
豕
貝
赤
走
足
跫
身
車
辛
辰
酉
釆
里
臣
舛

言語	ゲンゴ	language; speech
言語学	ゲンゴガク	linguistics
言行	ゲンコウ	words and deeds; speech and behavior
言行一致	ゲンコウイッチ	consistency of speech and action
言質	ゲンシツ	pledge; promise
言上	ゲンジョウ	statement —*vt.* state; convey
言動	ゲンドウ	speech and action; p's and q's
言明	ゲンメイ	declaration; assertion; positive statement —*v.* declare; assert; make a positive statement
言論	ゲンロン	expression of one's opinion through speech or writing
言論界	ゲンロンカイ	press; media
言論機関	ゲンロンキカン	organ of public opinion
言語道断	ゴンゴドウダン	outrageous; unspeakable; abominable; shocking
言い返す	いいかえす	*vt.* talk back; retort
言い方	いいかた	expression; how to speak; one's words
言い張る	いいはる	*vt.* insist on
言い回し	いいまわし	(mode of) expression
言い訳	いいわけ	explanation; excuse; apology
言う	いう	*vt.* speak; say; mention; talk
言	こと	word
言伝て	ことづて	message
言葉	ことば	word; language; speech; phrase; statement

1654

誉 ⑬

` ` `` ``` ``` `` ``` ``` ``` ``` 誉 誉 誉 誉

音	誉	ヨ	praise; honor
熟	誉望	ヨボウ	glory; honor; fame
訓	誉れ	ほまれ	honor; glory

1655

誓 ⑭

一 十 才 扌 扩 扩 折 哲 誓 誓 誓 誓

音	誓	セイ	oath
熟	誓約	セイヤク	vow; oath; promise —*v.* avowal; make an oath; promise
訓	誓う	ちかう	*vt.* swear; promise; make an oath
	誓い	ちかい	oath; promise

1656

謄 ⑰ ノ 几 月 月 月` 𦜝 𦜝 𦜝 𦜝 𦜝 謄 謄

音	謄	トウ	copy
熟	謄写	トウシャ	copy; transcription; reproduction —v. copy; transcribe; reproduce
	謄写版	トウシャバン	mimeographed copy
	謄本	トウホン	copy; transcript; duplicate

1657

警 ⑲ 一 ⺍ ⺊ 芍 苟 苟 苟 敬 敬 警 警 警

音	警	ケイ	warn; guard; vigilance; caution
熟	警戒	ケイカイ	vigilance; caution; precaution —v. be on one's guard; be cautious; be on guard; watch out for
	警句	ケイク	aphorism; epigram
	警護	ケイゴ	guard —v. guard
	警告	ケイコク	warning; caution —v. warn; caution; advise
	警察	ケイサツ	police
	警察官	ケイサツカン	policeman
	警察署	ケイサツショ	police station
	警察庁	ケイサツチョウ	National Police Agency
	警笛	ケイテキ	horn; alarm whistle; foghorn
	警備	ケイビ	guard; defense —v. guard; defend; keep guard
	警備員	ケイビイン	security guard
	警報	ケイホウ	alarm; warning
訓	※警める	いましめる	vt. admonish; caution; warn

1658

計 ⑨ 丶 ニ 言 言 言 言 言 言 計

音	計	ケイ	count; measure; plan; estimate; gauge
熟	計画	ケイカク	plan; project; scheme —v. plan; project; scheme
	計画的	ケイカクテキ	planned; scheduled; premeditated
	計器	ケイキ	meter; gauge
	計算	ケイサン	calculation; computation —v. calculate; compute; figure out; reckon
	計算機	ケイサンキ	computer; calculator

見
角言谷豆豕貝赤走足趾身車辛辰酉釆里臣舛

	計上	ケイジョウ	summing/adding up; aggregate —v. sum/add up; appropriate
	計略	ケイリャク	stratagem; scheme; trick; plot
	計量	ケイリョウ	weighing; measuring; gauging —v. weigh; measure; gauge
	計量器	ケイリョウキ	gauge; scales
訓	計る	はかる	vt. time; measure; judge; estimate; guess
	計り	はかり	measure; weight; scales
	計らう	はからう	vt. take care; settle; handle

1659

訂 ⑨　` ㇔ ㇒ 言 言 言 言 訂 訂

音	訂	テイ	correct
熟	訂正	テイセイ	correction; rectification; revision —v. correct; rectify; revise

1660

記 ⑩　` ㇔ ㇒ 言 言 言 言 訂 訂 記

音	記	キ	write down; record; note; remember
熟	記憶	キオク	memory; recollection —v. remember; commit to memory; memorize
	記号	キゴウ	mark; sign; symbol
	記載	キサイ	description; statement —v. state; describe; mention
	記事	キジ	news story/article
	記者	キシャ	reporter; writer
	記述	キジュツ	description; account —v. describe; give an account of
	記帳	キチョウ	record; entry —vt. record; enter; register
	記入	キニュウ	recording; entering —v. enter; make an entry; record; fill in
	記念	キネン	commemoration; remembrance —v. commemorate; honor the memory of
	記念日	キネンび	anniversary
	記名	キメイ	signature —v. sign one's name
	記録	キロク	record; document; archives —v. record; register; write down
	記録的	キロクテキ	record-breaking
訓	記す	しるす	vt. write down; record; note

7

見角言谷豆豕貝赤走足身車辛辰酉釆里臣舛

1661

訓 ⑩ ` ゛ ゠ ゠ 言 言 言 訂 訓 訓

音	訓	クン	teaching; lead; guide
熟	訓戒	クンカイ	admonition; exhortation; lecture
	訓示	クンジ	instruction —*vi.* instruct
	訓辞	クンジ	admonitory speech —*v.* give an admonitory speech
	訓令	クンレイ	instructions; order; directive —*vi.* instruct; order; direct
	訓練	クンレン	training; drill; practice —*v.* train; drill; practice
	訓話	クンワ	moral discourse —*vi.* discuss morals

1662

託 ⑩ ` ゛ ゠ ゠ 言 言 言 訂 訐 託

音	託	タク	entrust
熟	託する	タクする	*vt.* entrust; trust; commit
	託児所	タクジショ	day nursery; crèche
	託送	タクソウ	consignment —*v.* consign; send

1663

討 ⑩ ` ゛ ゠ ゠ 言 言 言 討 討

音	討	トウ	attack
熟	討議	トウギ	discussion; debate; deliberation —*v.* discuss; deliberate; debate; hold a discussion
	討伐	トウバツ	subjugation; suppression —*v.* subjugate; suppress; subdue; put down
	討論	トウロン	debate; discussion; talk —*v.* debate; discuss; talk
	討論会	トウロンカイ	forum; discussion
訓	討つ	うつ	*vt.* strike; hit; attack; subjugate; conquer

1664

許 ⑪ ` ゛ ゠ ゠ 言 言 言 言 許 許 許

音	許	キョ	forgive; permit; allow

723

見角言谷豆豕貝赤走足趾身車辛辰酉釆里臣舛

熟	許可	キョカ	permission; license —*v.* permit; license; sanction
	許諾	キョダク	consent; assent; approval —*v.* consent; assent; approve
	許容	キョヨウ	permission; allowance; permit —*v.* permit; allow
訓	許す	ゆるす	*vt.* forgive; allow; permit; approve
¥	許可制	キョカセイ	license system; licensing
	許容限度	キョヨウゲンド	tolerance limits; allowable maximum

1665

訟 ⑪　　` ` ⼆ ⼆ ⾔ ⾔ ⾔ ⾔ ⾔ 訟 訟

| 音 | 訟 | ショウ | sue |

1666

設 ⑪　　` ` ⼆ ⼆ ⾔ ⾔ ⾔ ⾔ 設 設 設

音	設	セツ	set up; establish; provide; prepare
熟	設営	セツエイ	construction; preparations —*v.* put up (a tent, etc.)
	設計	セッケイ	design; planning —*v.* design; plan
	設置	セッチ	establishment; founding; institution —*v.* establish; found
	設定	セッテイ	fixation; establishment; creation —*v.* fix; establish; create
	設備	セツビ	facilities; equipment; accommodations —*v.* facilitate; equip; accommodate
	設問	セツモン	question —*vi.* ask questions; question
	設立	セツリツ	founding; establishment —*v.* found; establish
訓	設ける	もうける	*vt.* prepare; provide; establish; set up
¥	設備	セツビ	equipment; provision
	設備投資	セツビトウシ	capital investment; investment in plant and equipment

1667

訪 ⑪　　` ` ⼆ ⼆ ⾔ ⾔ ⾔ ⾔ 訪 訪 訪

音	訪	ホウ	visit
熟	訪客	ホウキャク	visitor; guest
	訪日	ホウニチ	visiting Japan

	訪問	ホウモン	visiting; visit —*v*. visit
訓	訪れる	おとずれる	*vi*. visit
	訪ねる	たずねる	*vt*. visit

1668

訳 ⑪

` ⊃ ⋛ ⋚ 言 言 言 訂 訳 訳 訳

音	訳	ヤク	translation
熟	訳する	ヤクする	*vt*. translate
	訳語	ヤクゴ	*gram*. translated term; equivalent
	訳者	ヤクシャ	translator
	訳文	ヤクブン	translation; translated literature
訓	訳	わけ	meaning; reason; cause; meaning; circumstances; the case
	訳無い	わけない	easy; simple

1669

詠 ⑫

` ⊃ ⋛ ⋚ 言 言 言 訂 訽 詠 詠

音	詠	エイ	recite/compose poetry
熟	詠歌	エイカ	poetry composition
	詠嘆	エイタン	exclamation; admiration —*vi*. exclaim; admire
訓	詠む	よむ	*vt*. recite/compose poetry

1670

詐 ⑫

` ⊃ ⋛ ⋚ 言 言 訂 訏 訐 詐 詐

音	詐	サ	lie; deceive; cheat; swindle
熟	詐欺	サギ	cheat; fraud; swindling; swindle
	詐欺師	サギシ	swindler; con man; fraud
	詐取	サシュ	swindle; fraud —*v*. defraud; swindle; cheat

1671

詞 ⑫

` ⊃ ⋛ ⋚ 言 言 訂 訂 訽 詞 詞

音	詞	シ	word; writing
訓	※詞	ことば	word; writing

見
角
言
谷
豆
豕
貝
赤
走
足
𧿹
身
車
辛
辰
酉
釆
里
臣
舛

1672

証 ⑫ ` ⺀ ⺀ ⺀ 宁 言 言 訂 訂 訝 証 証

音	証	ショウ	proof
熟	証する	ショウする	*vt.* prove; guarantee; supply evidence
	証言	ショウゲン	testimony —*v.* testify; give evidence
	証拠	ショウコ	evidence; proof
	証書	ショウショ	bond; deed; certificate
	証人	ショウニン	witness; guarantor
	証明	ショウメイ	proof; evidence; testimony; demonstration —*v.* prove; testify; certify; demonstrate
	証明書	ショウメイショ	certificate
	証文	ショウモン	bond; deed
¥	証券	ショウケン	(valuable) securities; bond; bill
	証券化	ショウケンカ	converting into securities
	証券会社	ショウケンガイシャ	securities company; stockbroking firm
	証券取引所	ショウケンとりひきジョ	securities/stock exchange
	証券取引法	ショウケンとりひきホウ	Securities and Exchange Law
	証書	ショウショ	certificate; bond; bill

1673

詔 ⑫ ` ⺀ ⺀ 宁 言 言 言 訂 訊 訂 詔 詔

音	詔	ショウ	imperial rescript
熟	詔書	ショウショ	imperial edict
	詔勅	ショウチョク	imperial edict
訓	詔	みことのり	imperial edict

1674

診 ⑫ ` ⺀ ⺀ 宁 言 言 言 診 診 診 診 診

音	診	シン	examine
熟	診察	シンサツ	medical examination; consultation —*v.* examine (a patient)
	診察券	シンサツケン	patient's registration card
	診察時間	シンサツジカン	consultation hours

診察室	シンサツシツ	consultation room
診断	シンダン	diagnosis; examination —*v*. examine (a patient); make a diagnosis
診断書	シンダンショ	medical certificate
診療	シンリョウ	medical examination and treatment —*v*. give medical examinations and treatment
診療所	シンリョウジョ	clinic
訓 診る	みる	*vt*. examine

1675

訴 ⑫   ` ㇒ ㇗ ㇗ 言 言 言 訁 訃 訢 訴 訴

音 訴	ソ	sue; complain of; appeal to
熟 訴訟	ソショウ	lawsuit; litigation —*vi*. file a lawsuit; litigate
訴状	ソジョウ	petition; written complaint
訴追	ソツイ	prosecution; indictment —*v*. prosecute; indict
訴人	ソニン	suer; plaintiff
訓 訴える	うったえる	*v*. appeal; sue; complain

1676

評 ⑫   ` ㇗ ㇗ 言 言 言 言 訁 訐 評 評

音 評	ヒョウ	criticism; comment
熟 評する	ヒョウする	*vt*. criticize; comment on; speak of (a person) as
評価	ヒョウカ	valuation; estimate; assessment; evaluation; appraisal —*v*. value; estimate; assess; evaluate; appraise
評議	ヒョウギ	conference; discussion; council; meeting —*v*. hold a conference/council/meeting; discuss
評決	ヒョウケツ	verdict (of guilty/not guilty) —*v*. pronounce a verdict; sentence
評者	ヒョウシャ	critic; reviewer
評釈	ヒョウシャク	annotation —*v*. annotate
評注	ヒョウチュウ	annotation; (critical) notes —*v*. annotate
評定	ヒョウテイ	evaluation; rating —*v*. evaluate; rate
評点	ヒョウテン	(examination) marks/grades
評判	ヒョウバン	(public) estimation; reputation; popularity; rumor; gossip; fame
評論	ヒョウロン	criticism; review; comment —*v*. review; comment
評論家	ヒョウロンカ	critic; reviewer; commentator; publicist

見
角
言
谷
豆
豕
貝
赤
走
足
⻊
身
車
辛
辰
酉
釆
里
臣
舛

1677

該 ⑬

` ⊃ ヨ 言 言 言 言 計 訪 訪 該

| 音 | 該 | ガイ | that; correspond |
| 熟 | 該当 | ガイトウ | relevent; applicable —*vi.* come under; be applicable |

1678

詰 ⑬

` ⊃ ヨ 言 言 言 計 計 詰 詰 詰

音	詰	キツ	blame; rebuke; reprimand; pack; stuff
熟	詰問	キツモン	cross-examination; interrogation —*v.* cross-examine; cross-question
訓	詰まる	つまる	*vi.* be stuffed/full/packed/blocked
	詰める	つめる	*vt.* stuff; cram; pack into
	詰め込む	つめこむ	cram; load; squeeze into
	詰め物	つめもの	packing; stuffing; filling
	詰む	つむ	*vi.* be stuffed/full/packed/blocked

1679

誇 ⑬

` ⊃ ヨ 言 言 言 計 許 誇 誇 誇

熟	誇示	コジ	ostentation; showing off —*v.* show off; flaunt
	誇大	コダイ	exaggeration
	誇張	コチョウ	exaggeration; overstatement —*v.* exaggerate; overstate
訓	誇る	ほこる	*vi.* boast; brag; show off
	誇り	ほこり	pride; haughtiness

1680

試 ⑬

` ⊃ ヨ 言 言 言 計 訂 試 試 試

音	試	シ	try
熟	試合	シあい	match; game; tournament —*vi.* play/have a match/game; have a tournament
	試案	シアン	tentative plan; proposal
	試運転	シウンテン	test/trial run —*v.* make a test/trial run; run a trial
	試金石	シキンセキ	touchstone; test; test case

試験	シケン	examination; test; experiment —*v.* experiment; put a thing to the test; test	
試験管	シケンカン	test tube	
試験的	シケンテキ	experimental; tentative	
試作	シサク	trial manufacture/production —*v.* make (a machine) on an experimental basis	
試作品	シサクヒン	trial product	
試写	シシャ	preview —*v.* give/hold a preview of	
試乗	シジョウ	test ride/drive —*v.* test drive a car	
試食	シショク	tasting; sampling —*v.* taste; sample; try	
試着	シチャク	trying clothes on —*v.* try on	
試着室	シチャクシツ	fitting room	
試用	シヨウ	trial —*v.* try; make a trial	
試練	シレン	ordeal; trial	

訓 試みる　こころみる　*vt.* try; attempt
　　試み　　こころみ　　trial; test; experiment; temptation (biblical sense)
　　試す　　ためす　　　*vt.* test; try

1681

⑬　　` ゝ ゜ ゠ 言 言 言 計 計 詰 詩 詩

音　詩　　シ　　　　　poetry; verse; Chinese poem
熟　詩歌　シイカ　　　poetry; verse
　　詩吟　シギン　　　recitation of a Chinese poem —*vi.* recite a Chinese poem
　　詩作　シサク　　　writing poetry —*vi.* write poetry
　　詩集　シシュウ　　collection of poems; poetry anthology
　　詩情　シジョウ　　poetic sentiment
　　詩人　シジン　　　poet
　　詩的　シテキ　　　poetic
訓　※詩　うた　　　　poetry; verse; Chinese poem

1682

⑬　　` ゝ ゜ ゠ 言 言 言 言゛ 詳 詳 詳 詳

音　詳　　ショウ　　　　minute; fine; details
熟　詳細　ショウサイ　　details; detailed; minute
　　詳述　ショウジュツ　detailed explanation —*v.* make a detailed explanation; explain in detail

729

	詳説	ショウセツ	detailed explanation —*v.* make a detailed explanation; explain in detail
	詳報	ショウホウ	full information; detailed report
訓	詳しい	くわしい	detailed; precise; in detail; familiar

1683

誠 ⑬　　` 亠 訁 訁 言 言 訁 訂 訢 訹 誠 誠

音	誠	セイ	sincerity; fidelity; truth
熟	誠意	セイイ	sincerity; good faith
	誠実	セイジツ	sincere; faithful; loyal
訓	誠	まこと	sincerity; fidelity; truth

1684

話 ⑬　　` 亠 訁 訁 言 言 訁 訁 計 訐 話 話

音	話	ワ	story; conversation; talk
熟	話術	ワジュツ	storytelling
	話題	ワダイ	topic; subject (of a story/discussion)
	話法	ワホウ	speech; parlance
訓	話	はなし	talk; conversation; story
	話す	はなす	*vt.* talk; speak
	話し中	はなしチュウ	while speaking; (phone is) busy/engaged
	話し手	はなして	speaker

1685

語 ⑭　　亠 訁 訁 言 言 訁 訂 訏 語 語 語 語 語

音	語	ゴ	speak; word; language
熟	語意	ゴイ	meaning of a word
	語彙	ゴイ	vocabulary
	語学	ゴガク	linguistics; language study
	語感	ゴカン	nuance; shade of meaning
	語気	ゴキ	tone of voice
	語義	ゴギ	mearing of a word
	語句	ゴク	words and phrases
	語源	ゴゲン	etymology
	語順	ゴジュン	*gram.* word order

語調	ゴチョウ	tone of voice
語尾	ゴビ	*gram*. word ending; inflexion
語弊	ゴヘイ	wrong word; misleading expression
語法	ゴホウ	diction; usage; expression; wording
語録	ゴロク	analects; collection of sayings
訓 語る	かたる	*vt*. talk; recite; narrate
語らう	かたらう	*vt*. talk over

1686

誤 ⑭ ゛ ゛ ゛ 言 言 言 訓 訓 評 評 誤 誤 誤

音 誤	ゴ	mistake; error
熟 誤解	ゴカイ	misunderstanding —*v*. misunderstand
誤差	ゴサ	error; difference; margin of error; tolerance
誤算	ゴサン	miscalculation —*vi*. miscalculate
誤字	ゴジ	wrong letter; erratum; misprint
誤診	ゴシン	incorrect diagnosis —*vi*. make an incorrect diagnosis; make an error in diagnosis
誤報	ゴホウ	false report; misinformation
誤訳	ゴヤク	mistranslation —*v*. mistranslate; make an error in translation
誤用	ゴヨウ	misuse —*v*. misuse; use improperly
訓 誤る	あやまる	*v*. err; make a mistake
誤り	あやまり	mistake; error

1687

誌 ⑭ ゛ ゛ ゛ 言 言 言 計 計 計 註 誌 誌

音 誌	シ	record; magazine
熟 誌上	シジョウ	in a magazine
誌面	シメン	in a magazine

1688

説 ⑭ ゛ ゛ ゛ 言 言 言 計 訓 説 説 説 説

音 説	セツ	explain; view; theory; opinion
	（ゼイ）	explain; persuade
熟 説教	セッキョウ	preaching; sermon —*vi*. preach; sermonize
説得	セットク	persuasion —*v*. persuade

見角言谷豆豕貝赤走足身車辛辰酉釆里臣舛

説明	セツメイ	explanation —*v.* explain
説明文	セツメイブン	written explanation
説話	セツワ	legend; tale; narrative
訓 説く	とく	*v.* explain; persuade

1689

読 ⑭ ` ` ` ` ` ` ` ` ` ` ` ` 読

音 読	ドク	read
	トク	read
	（トウ）	
熟 読点	トウテン	comma
読経	ドキョウ	sutra-chanting —*vi.* chant sutras
読者	ドクシャ	reader (of books)
読書	ドクショ	reading —*vi.* read books
読破	ドクハ	reading through a book —*v.* read/go through a book
読本	トクホン	reader; reading book
読了	ドクリョウ	end of reading —*vt.* finish reading
訓 読む	よむ	*vt.* read; peruse; chant; recite
読み	よみ	reading; judgment; calculation
読み書き	よみかき	reading and writing
読み方	よみかた	reading; pronunciation
読み切る	よみきる	*vt.* read through; finish reading
読み物	よみもの	reading; reading matter; literature

1690

認 ⑭ ` ` ` ` ` ` ` ` ` ` ` ` 認

音 認	ニン	recognize; approve; consent
熟 認可	ニンカ	sanction; approval; authorization; license; permission —*v.* approve; authorize; permit
認識	ニンシキ	recognition; cognition; perception; knowledge; understanding —*v.* recognize; cognize; perceive; know; understand
認証	ニンショウ	authentication; certification; validation; confirmation —*v.* certify; atest; authenticate; confirm
認知	ニンチ	recognition; acknowledgment —*v.* recognize; acknowledge
認定	ニンテイ	recognition; acknowledgment; identity —*v.* admit; recognize; find; deem

	認容	ニンヨウ	admission; acknowledgment —*v*. admit; acknowledge; accept
訓	認める	みとめる	*vt*. see; witness; recognize; approve; accept; judge; conclude

1691

誘 ⑭

⟍ ⟍ 言 言 言 言 訁 訁 誘 誘 誘

音	誘	ユウ	invite; induce; entice; lure
熟	誘引	ユウイン	enticement; inducement; attraction —*v*. entice; induce; attract
	誘因	ユウイン	enticement; inducement —*v*. entice; induce; bring about; cause
	誘拐	ユウカイ	abduction; kidnapping —*v*. abduct; kidnap
	誘致	ユウチ	attraction; lure; enticement —*v*. attract; lure; entice
	誘導	ユウドウ	guidance; induction; incitement —*v*. guide; induce; incite
	誘発	ユウハツ	cause; inducement —*v*. cause; induce; give rise to
	誘惑	ユウワク	temptation; seduction —*v*. tempt; seduce
訓	誘う	さそう	*vt*. tempt; entice; lure; invite
※	誘う	いざなう	*vt*. invite; lead; entice
※	誘く	おびく	*vt*. lure; entice

1692

謁 ⑮

⟍ ⟍ 言 言 言 訒 訐 訐 訐 謁 謁 謁

音	謁	エツ	audience with (someone of importance)
熟	謁見	エッケン	audience with (someone in authority) —*vi*. have an audience with; be presented to

1693

課 ⑮

⟍ ⟍ 言 言 訒 訒 訐 訐 評 課 課

音	課	カ	allot; section; impose
熟	課外	カガイ	extracurricular
	課業	カギョウ	class lesson
	課題	カダイ	subject; theme; problem; task; assignment
	課長	カチョウ	section chief
	課程	カテイ	curriculum

見角言谷豆豕貝赤走足跙身車辛辰酉釆里臣舛

	課目	カモク	subject
訓	課す	かす	*vt.* impose; assign
¥	課税	カゼイ	imposition of taxes —*vi.* impose taxes
	課徴金	カチョウキン	surcharge

1694

諸 ⑮ 　 二 三 言 言 言 計 計 訣 訣 諸 諸 諸

音	諸	ショ	various
熟	諸行無常	ショギョウムジョウ	all things pass; everything is transient
	諸君	ショクン	Gentlemen!; Ladies and gentlemen!; Boys and girls!; Boys!
	諸芸	ショゲイ	accomplishments
	諸国	ショコク	various countries
	諸説	ショセツ	various views
	諸説紛々	ショセツフンプン	divided opinion on a subject
	諸島	ショトウ	archipelago; group of islands
訓	※諸々	もろもろ	various; all kinds/sorts; all

1695

請 ⑮ 　 二 三 言 言 言 計 計 詰 詰 請 請 請

音	請	セイ （シン）	ask; request; invite
熟	請願	セイガン	petition; application —*v.* petition; apply
	請求	セイキュウ	claiming; demand; request —*v.* claim; demand; request
訓	請ける	うける	*vt.* receive; undertake; pay and take receipt of
	請け負い	うけおい	contracting
	請け書	うけショ	written acknowledgment
	請う	こう	*vt.* ask for
¥	請求書	セイキュウショ	bill; written claim

1696

諾 ⑮ 　 二 三 言 言 言 計 計 評 評 諾 諾 諾

音	諾	ダク	consent
熟	諾否	ダクヒ	acceptance or refusal

見角言谷豆豕貝赤走足趾身車辛辰酉釆里臣舛

1697

誕 ⑮

〻 ニ ゠ 言 言 訁´ 訮 訷 誕 誕 誕 誕 誕

音	誕	タン	be born
熟	誕生	タンジョウ	birth; nativity —*vi.* be born; come into the world
	誕生日	タンジョウび	birthday

1698

談 ⑮

〻 ニ ゠ 言 言 言´ 訟 談 談 談 談 談

音	談	ダン	talk; conversation; story; tale
熟	談じる	ダンじる	*vt.* talk
	談合	ダンゴウ	consultation; conference —*vi.* consult; confer
	談笑	ダンショウ	chat; intimate conversation —*vi.* chat
	談判	ダンパン	negotiation; bargaining —*vi.* negotiate; bargain
	談話	ダンワ	talk; conversation —*vi.* talk; chat; converse

1699

調 ⑮

〻 ゠ 言 言 訁 訂 訂 訊 調 調 調 調

音	調	チョウ	inspect; survey; examine; tune; tone; pitch
熟	調印	チョウイン	signing; signature; sealing —*vi.* sign; seal
	調教	チョウキョウ	horse training/breaking; train a wild animal —*v.* break in a horse; train a wild animal
	調貢	チョウコウ	offering; tribute
	調合	チョウゴウ	compounding; mixing; preparation; concoction —*v.* compound; mix; prepare; concoct
	調査	チョウサ	examination; investigation; inquiry; survey; research —*v.* investigate; inquire; survey
	調子	チョウシ	tune; tone; key; way; manner; style; condition; order
	調子者	チョウシもの	person who is easily carried away
	調書	チョウショ	protocol; written evidence; record
	調整	チョウセイ	regulation; adjustment; correction; modulation; tuning —*v.* regulate; adjust; rectify; govern; control
	調節	チョウセツ	regulation; adjustment; control; governing —*v.* regulate; adjust; control; govern

見
角
言
谷
豆
豕
赤
走
足
⻊
身
車
辛
辰
酉
釆
里
臣
舛

調達	チョウタツ	supply; procurement; provision —*v.* supply; provide; furnish; purvey; procure
調停	チョウテイ	mediation; arbitration; intercession —*v.* mediate; arbitrate; intercede; intervene
調度品	チョウドヒン	personal/household effects; furniture
調髪	チョウハツ	hair dressing —*vi.* cut/style hair
調味	チョウミ	seasoning; flavoring —*v.* season; flavor; spice
調味料	チョウミリョウ	seasoning; flavoring
調理	チョウリ	cooking; cookery —*v.* cook; arrange; organize
調理師	チョウリシ	cook; chef
調律	チョウリツ	tuning (a musical instrument) —*v.* tune (a musical instrument)
調律師	チョウリツシ	piano tuner
調和	チョウワ	harmony; accord; agreement —*v.* harmonize; match; agree; fit in well

訓

調べる	しらべる	*vt.* investigate; examine; survey; inspect; check
調べ	しらべ	melody
調う	ととのう	*vi.* be prepared/arranged/settled/concluded
調える	ととのえる	*vt.* prepare; make ready; arrange; settle; conclude

1700

論 ⑮ 丶 ㇐ 言 言 言 訃 訟 訟 諭 論 論 論

音

| 論 | ロン | argument; discussion; thesis |

熟

論じる	ロンじる	*vt.* discuss; argue; dispute; debate
論外	ロンガイ	out of the question; irrelevant
論客	ロンカク (ロンキャク)	disputant; polemicist
論議	ロンギ	discussion; argument —*v.* discuss; argue
論及	ロンキュウ	reference —*vi.* refer to; mention
論拠	ロンキョ	the grounds; basis (of a discussion)
論告	ロンコク	prosecutor's summation —*v.* address (the court) for the last time
論旨	ロンシ	point of an argument
論述	ロンジュツ	statement; enunciation —*v.* set forth; enunciate; state
論証	ロンショウ	proof/demonstration (by argument) —*v.* proof/demonstrate (by argument)
論説	ロンセツ	editorial; dissertation
論戦	ロンセン	verbal battle; war of words —*vi.* have a verbal battle; exchange views
論争	ロンソウ	argument; dispute; controversy —*v.* argue; dispute

論点	ロンテン	point at issue
論破	ロンパ	refutation —*v.* refute
論評	ロンピョウ	criticism; comment; review —*v.* criticize; comment; review
論文	ロンブン	thesis; essay
論弁	ロンベン	argument —*vi.* argue
論法	ロンポウ	argument; reasoning; logic
論理	ロンリ	logic
論理的	ロンリテキ	logical

1701

諮 ⑯　　一　二　言　言　言　言　診　診　診　診　諮　諮

音	諮	シ	consult
熟	諮問	シモン	inquiry; request for an inferior's opinion —*v.* consult; refer a problem to an inferior
	諮問機関	シモンキカン	advisory organ/body
訓	諮る	はかる	*vt.* consult; ask for advice

1702

謀 ⑯　　一　二　言　言　計　計　詳　詳　詳　詳　謀　謀

音	謀	ボウ (ム)	plan; plot; devise; deceive
熟	謀議	ボウギ	conspiracy —*vi.* conspire
	謀殺	ボウサツ	premeditated murder —*v.* commit willful murder
	謀略	ボウリャク	plot; scheme
	謀反	ムホン	rebellion; insurrection
	謀反人	ムホンニン	rebel; conspirator
訓	謀る	はかる	*vt.* plan; plot; devise; deceive

1703

諭 ⑯　　一　二　言　言　諭　諭　諭　諭　諭　諭　諭　諭

音	諭	ユ	admonish; remonstrate; warn; counsel
熟	諭告	ユコク	counsel; admonition —*vi.* advise; admonish
	諭旨	ユシ	admonition; instructions; explanation
訓	諭す	さとす	*vt.* admonish; remonstrate; warn; counsel; explain

見角言谷豆豸貝赤走足跫身車辛辰酉釆里臣舛

1704

謠 ⑯ ニ　ミ　言　言　言　訁　訁　訡　謠　謠　謠

音	謠	ヨウ	song; Noh chanting
熟	謠曲	ヨウキョク	Noh song/chant
訓	謠	うたい	Noh chanting
	謠う	うたう	*vt*. sing without accompaniment; chant

1705

謹 ⑰ ニ　言　言　言　訁　訃　詳　詳　謹　謹　謹

音	謹	キン	discretion; prudence; modesty
熟	謹賀新年	キンガシンネン	Happy New Year
	謹慎	キンシン	good behavior —*v*. conduct oneself well
	謹製	キンセイ	carefully produced
訓	謹む	つつしむ	*vt*. be discrete/prudent/modest

1706

謙 ⑰ ニ　言　言　言　訁　訊　謙　謙　謙　謙　謙

音	謙	ケン	modesty; humility
熟	謙虚	ケンキョ	modesty; humility
	謙譲	ケンジョウ	modesty; humility
	謙遜	ケンソン	modesty; humility —*vi*. be modest/humble

1707

講 ⑰ ニ　言　言　言　計　詳　詳　詳　講　講　講

音	講	コウ	lecture; speech; interpretation; training
熟	講じる	コウじる	*vt*. lecture; give a speech; read out aloud; devise; workout
	講演	コウエン	lecture; address; discourse; talk —*vi*. give a lecture; address; lecture
	講義	コウギ	lecture; exposition; explanation —*v*. lecture on; give a lecture
	講師	コウシ	lecturer; speaker; reader; instructor
	講釈	コウシャク	storytelling; lecture —*v*. lecture; explain

講習	コウシュウ	short course; class
講壇	コウダン	podium; lectern
講談	コウダン	storytelling; narration
講堂	コウドウ	auditorium; lecture hall/theater
講読	コウドク	exigesis/study of sutras
講評	コウヒョウ	criticism; commentary; review —*v*. criticize; comment on; review
講和	コウワ	peace; reconciliation —*vi*. make peace; bury the hatchet
講話	コウワ	lecture; discourse; address —*vi*. lecture; deliver a lecture; address

1708

謝 ⑰　丶　亠　言　言　言　訂　訝　誚　謝　謝　謝　謝

音	謝	シャ	thanks; apologize; decline; refuse
熟	謝する	しゃする	*vt*. thank a person for their help; apologize; decline; refuse
	謝意	シャイ	gratitude; thanks; apology
	謝恩	シャオン	expression of gratitude; appreciation
	謝金	シャキン	honorarium
	謝罪	シャザイ	apology —*vi*. apologize; beg a person's forgiveness
	謝罪状	シャザイジョウ	written apology
	謝辞	シャジ	address of gratitude; a few words of thanks; apology
	謝状	シャジョウ	letter of thanks/apology
	謝絶	シャゼツ	refusal —*v*. refuse; decline
	謝肉祭	シャニクサイ	carnival
	謝礼	シャレイ	thanks; reward; renumeration
訓	謝る	あやまる	*v*. apologize

1709

識 ⑲　丶　亠　言　言　訁　訡　識　識　識　識　識　識

音	識	シキ	discern; sight; consciousness
熟	識見	シキケン	discernment; judgment; insight; view; opinion
	識者	シキシャ	intellectual; person of intelligence; intelligentsia
	識別	シキベツ	discrimination —*v*. discriminate; distinguish; tell apart

見
角
言
谷
豆
豕
貝
赤
走
足
跙
身
車
辛
辰
酉
釆
里
臣
舛

見
角
言
谷
豆
豕
貝
赤
走
足
跙
身
車
辛
辰
酉
釆
里
臣
舛

1710

譜 ⑲   ニ ミ 言 言 言 計 詳 詳 詳 詳 詳 譜 譜

音	譜	フ	music; note; staff; score
熟	譜代	フダイ	successive generations (of vassals)
	譜面	フメン	sheet music

1711

議 ⑳   ニ ミ 言 言 計 計 詳 詳 議 議 議 議

音	議	ギ	talk over; consultation
熟	議する	ギする	*vt.* talk over; consult
	議案	ギアン	bill; measure; proposal for discussion
	議員	ギイン	elected representative; Diet member
	議院	ギイン	houses of parliament; lower and upper houses
	議会	ギカイ	assembly; national assembly; Diet
	議決	ギケツ	decision; resolution —*v.* decide; resolve; pass a vote
	議事	ギジ	proceedings; agenda
	議事堂	ギジドウ	Diet building
	議席	ギセキ	parlimentary seat
	議題	ギダイ	subject for discussion; agenda; program
	議長	ギチョウ	chairperson; president; speaker
	議論	ギロン	argument; discussion; debate; dispute —*v.* argue; discuss; debate; dispute
訓	議る	はかる	*vt.* consult; confer; deliberate
¥	議決権	ギケツケン	right to vote at a meeting; voting power (right)
	議決権信託証書	ギケツケン シンタクショウショ	voting trust certificate

1712

譲 ⑳   ニ ミ 言 言 訁 許 諱 諱 諱 諱 譲 譲

音	譲	ジョウ	transfer
熟	譲渡	ジョウト	conveyance; negotiation; assignment; transfer —*v.* hand over; transfer; assign
	譲歩	ジョウホ	compromise; concession —*vi.* compromise; concede; make a concession

740

訓	譲る	ゆずる	*vt.* hand over; transfer; sell; give; concede; save for later
	譲り	ゆずり	inheritance
	譲り合う	ゆずりあう	*vi.* make mutual concessions; compromise
	譲り受ける	ゆずりうける	*vt.* take over; obtain by transfer; inherit; buy
¥	譲渡制限	ジョウトセイゲン	restriction of transfer
	譲渡性預金	ジョウトセイヨキン	certificate of deposit (CD); negotiable deposit

---

1713

護 ⑳　　二 三 言 訂 評 許 評 謹 謹 謹 護 護

音	護	ゴ	protect; guard
熟	護衛	ゴエイ	bodyguard; escort —*v.* guard; escort
	護身	ゴシン	self-protection/-defense
	護送	ゴソウ	escort —*v.* escort; send under guard
訓	護る	まもる	*vt.* protect; guard

---

7 谷　たに valley

1714

谷 ⑦　　ノ ハ グ 父 父 谷 谷

音	谷	コク	valley; river valley; ravine
訓	谷	たに	valley
	谷底	たにぞこ	the bottom of ravine; valley floor
	谷間	たにま	ravine; gorge; chasm; valley

---

7 豆　まめ bean

1715

豆 ⑦　　一 厂 戸 呂 戸 豈 豆

| 音 | 豆 | トウ（ズ） | bean |

741

見
角
言
谷
● 豆
● 豕
貝
赤
走
足
⻊
身
車
辛
辰
酉
釆
里
臣
舛

熟	豆乳	トウニュウ	soya milk
	豆腐	トウフ	tofu
訓	豆	まめ	bean; pea; soybean
	豆知識	まめチシキ	bits of knowledge/information
	豆鉄砲	まめデッポウ	popgun
	豆電球	まめデンキュウ	miniature/small bulb

1716

豊 ⑬　　丶 一 曲 曲 曲 典 豊 豊 豊 豊 豊 豊

音	豊	ホウ	abundant; rich
熟	豊艶	ホウエン	voluptuous; plentiful
	豊凶	ホウキョウ	rich or poor harvest; good or bad year
	豊作	ホウサク	good/abundant harvest
	豊熟	ホウジュク	ripening of crops —*vi*. (crops) ripen abundantly
	豊潤	ホウジュン	rich; abundant
	豊饒	ホウジョウ	fertile; productive
	豊年	ホウネン	fruitful/good year
	豊富	ホウフ	abundance; affluence
	豊満	ホウマン	plump; corpulent; full-figured
	豊漁	ホウリョウ	big/abundant catch (of fish)
訓	豊か	ゆたか	abundant; rich

7 豕　ぶた／いのこ　pig

1717

豚 ⑪　　丿 刀 月 月 肝 肵 肵 肵 肵 豚 豚

音	豚	トン	pig
熟	豚児	トンジ	*hum*. my son
訓	豚	ぶた	pig; swine

1718

象 ⑫　　丿 ⺈ ⺄ ⺌ 台 色 兔 兔 兔 象 象

| 音 | 象 | ショウ | shape |

742

象	ゾウ	elephant

熟
象形	ショウケイ	hieroglyph
象形文字	ショウケイモジ	hieroglyphic
象徴	ショウチョウ	symbol —*v.* symbolize
象徴的	ショウチョウテキ	symbolic
象牙	ゾウゲ	ivory

1719

豪 ⑭ 一 亠 亠 吉 亯 亯 亨 亨 豪 豪 豪 豪

音
豪	ゴウ	mighty; splendor; grand; Australia

熟
豪雨	ゴウウ	heavy rain
豪華	ゴウカ	gorgeousness; splendor; pomp; luxury
豪傑	ゴウケツ	hero; great man
豪語	ゴウゴ	boasting; big talk; bragging —*vi.* boast; talk big; brag
豪州	ゴウシュウ	Australia
豪勢	ゴウセイ	grand; great; magnificent
豪壮	ゴウソウ	magnificence; splendor; grandeur
豪遊	ゴウユウ	extravagant merry-making; orgy —*vi.* indulge in extravagant merry-making; go on a spree

---

7 貝 かい／かいへん shell

1720

貝 ⑦ 丨 冂 冂 月 月 目 貝 貝

音
貝	（バイ）	shellfish; shell

訓
貝	かい	shellfish; shell
貝殻	かいがら	seashell
貝細工	かいザイク	shellwork
貝塚	かいづか	shell mound

1721

貞 ⑨ ' 亠 ㅏ 广 卢 卢 卢 貞 貞

音
貞	テイ	chastity

743

見
角
言
谷
豆
豕
• 貝
赤
走
足
⻊
身
車
辛
辰
西
采
里
臣
舛

熟	貞淑	テイシュク	chastity; female virtue
	貞女	テイジョ	chaste woman; woman of good virtue; faithful wife
	貞節	テイセツ	chastity; fidelity; faithfulness
	貞操	テイソウ	chastity; honor; virginity

1722

負 ⑨　ノ � ⺈ イ 乍 乍 角 有 負 負

音	負	フ	bear; suffer; sustain; lose; be defeated
熟	負荷	フカ	bearing a burden; taking over a company
	負傷	フショウ	wound; injury —*vi.* be wounded; get injured
	負数	フスウ	*math.* minus/negative number
	負担	フタン	charge; responsibilty; burden; onus —*v.* bear; stand; shoulder; carry
訓	負ける	まける	*vi.* be defeated/beaten/overcome/daunted *vt.* make something cheap
	負かす	まかす	*vt.* beat; defeat; vanquish; get the better of
	負う	おう	*vt.* bear; carry; be charged/accused of; suffer; sustain
¥	負債	フサイ	debt; liabilities; dues

1723

貢 ⑩　一 T 工 干 于 吉 吉 吉 貢 貢

音	貢	コウ (ク)	tribute; contribution; service
熟	貢献	コウケン	contribution; services —*vi.* contribute to; make a contribution to
訓	貢ぐ	みつぐ	*vt.* supply with money; finance

1724

貨 ⑪　ノ イ 仁 化 化 伜 貨 貨 貨 貨

音	貨	カ	goods; coin
熟	貨客船	カキャクセン	cargo-passenger ship
	貨車	カシャ	freight car; goods wagon
¥	貨幣	カヘイ	money; coin; bill
	貨物	カモツ	goods; freight; cargo

1725

貫 ⑪　　　レ ロ 皿 毌 毌 冊 冊 冊 冊 貫 貫

音	貫	カン	penetrate
熟	貫通	カンツウ	piercing; penetration —v. pierce; penetrate; pass through
	貫徹	カンテツ	accomplishment; achievement; attainment —v. accomplish; achieve; attain
	貫流	カンリュウ	flowing/running through —vi. flow/run through (a city)
	貫禄	カンロク	dignity; importance
訓	貫く	つらぬく	vt. pierce; penetrate; pass through; accomplish; attain
	貫	ぬき	brace

1726

責 ⑪　　　一 十 キ 主 青 青 青 青 青 責 責

音	責	セキ	condemn; censure; torture
熟	責任	セキニン	responsibility; liability
	責任感	セキニンカン	sense of responsibility
	責務	セキム	duty; obligation
訓	責める	せめる	vt. duty

1727

貧 ⑪　　　ノ 八 分 分 介 糸 糸 糸 糸 貧 貧

音	貧	ヒン	poverty
		ビン	poor
熟	貧窮	ヒンキュウ	poverty; poverty-stricken
	貧苦	ヒンク	poverty; hardship of poverty
	貧血	ヒンケツ	med. anemia —vi. be anemic; suffer from anemia
	貧困	ヒンコン	poverty fig. lack (of proper government, ideas, etc.)
	貧者	ヒンジャ	poor person; the poor
	貧弱	ヒンジャク	poverty; poor; weak; shabby; feeble; scanty; meager
	貧相	ヒンソウ	poor appearance; poor-looking
	貧富	ヒンプ	wealth and poverty; rich and poor

見角言谷豆豕
● 貝赤走足跫身車辛辰酉釆里臣舛

	貧乏	ビンボウ	poverty; poor —*vi*. be poor/badly off
	貧民	ヒンミン	the poor/needy
訓	貧しい	まずしい	poor

1728

賀 ⑫　　フ カ か 加 加 加 智 智 智 智 賀 賀

音	賀	ガ	congratulations
熟	賀春	ガシュン	spring greetings
	賀正	ガショウ	A Happy New Year!; New Year's greetings
	賀状	ガジョウ	greeting card; New Year's card

1729

貴 ⑫　　、 ⊓ コ 中 虫 虫 串 串 毒 書 貴 貴

音	貴	キ	noble; precious; high
熟	貴金属	キキンゾク	precious metals
	貴族	キゾク	nobility; aristocracy
	貴重	キチョウ	valuable; precious
	貴重品	キチョウヒン	valuables
	貴賓	キヒン	honored guest
	貴婦人	キフジン	lady
訓	貴い	たっとい	noble; precious; exalted; valuable
	貴ぶ	たっとぶ	*vt*. respect; honor; value; esteem
	貴い	とうとい	noble; precious
	貴ぶ	とうとぶ	*vt*. respect; honor; value; esteem

1730

貸 ⑫　　ノ イ 亻 代 代 代 伐 侪 侪 借 貸 貸

音	貸	タイ	lend
熟	貸借	タイシャク	debit and credit; lending and borrowing; loan —*v*. lend and borrow; debt and credit
	貸与	タイヨ	loan; lending —*v*. lend; lease; loan
訓	貸切	かしきり	reserved; chartered
	貸す	かす	*vt*. lend; give credit
¥	貸方勘定	かしかたカンジョウ	credit account

貸倒引当金	かしだおれ ひきあてキン	bad-debt reserve
貸出	かしだし	loan; advance
貸し付ける	かしつける	*vt.* lend
賃貸対照表	チンタイ タイショウヒョウ	balance sheet

1731

買 ⑫　丶 冂 冂 罒 罒 罒 胃 胃 胃 胃 買 買

音	買	バイ	buy
訓	買う	かう	*vt.* buy; purchase
	買い物	かいもの	purchases; shopping; bargain
¥	買い入れる	かいいれる	*vt.* buy (in); purchase
	買掛金	かいかけキン	accounts payable
	買い方	かいかた	buyer; purchaser; bulls; longs
	買い気配	かいキハイ （かいケハイ）	bid/bidding quotation
	買い越し	かいこし	on-balance buying
	買い支え	かいささえ	support buying/operation
	買い占める	かいしめる	*vt.* corner a market; buy up (all the goods)
	買いつなぎ	かいつなぎ	hedge-buying; hedging by buying
	買い手	かいて	buyer; purchaser; customer
	買い時	かいどき	best time to buy
	買い取り	かいとり	compulsory purchase; buy up
	買い主	かいぬし	buyer; purchaser
	買値	かいね	purchase/bid price
	買い場	かいば	buying opportunity
	買い控え	かいびかえ	hesitating; restrained purchasing
	買い戻し	かいもどし	redemption; repurchase; covering/short covering
	買価	バイカ	buying/purchase price
	買収	バイシュウ	acquisition; purchase; buying up; corruption; bribery —*v.* purchase; buy up; take over; corrupt; bribe

---

1732

費 ⑫　フ 弓 弔 弗 弗 弗 弗 弗 費 費 費

音	費	ヒ	expenses; cost
熟	費用	ヒヨウ	expenses; cost
訓	費やす	ついやす	*vt.* spend; waste; use up

7

見角言谷豆豕貝赤走足身車辛辰酉采里臣舛

| 費える | ついえる | *vi*. be wasted/used up |
| ¥ 費目 | ヒモク | item of expense |

1733
貿 ⑫ 　 ' ⺊ ⺀ ⺹ ⺤ ⺤ 留 留 留 貿 貿

音 貿	ボウ	trade; exchange
熟 貿易風	ボウエキフウ	trade wind
¥ 貿易	ボウエキ	trade; commerce —*vi*. trade; do business with
貿易会社	ボウエキガイシャ	trading company
貿易業	ボウエキギョウ	trading business; commerce
貿易商	ボウエキショウ	trader
貿易場	ボウエキジョウ	foreign market
貿易摩擦	ボウエキマサツ	trade friction

1734
資 ⑬ 　 ` ⺀ ⺀ ⺾ ⺿ 次 次 咨 咨 咨 資 資

音 資	シ	fund; nature; resources
熟 資格	シカク	qualification
資源	シゲン	resources
資材	シザイ	materials
資質	シシツ	nature; one's nature
資料	シリョウ	data; materials
資力	シリョク	means; funds; money
¥ 資金	シキン	funds; money
資金運用	シキンウンヨウ	application of funds
資金源	シキンゲン	source of funds
資金調達	シキンチョウタツ	raising of funds
資源	シゲン	resources
資産	シサン	assets; property; means
資産株	シサンかぶ	income stocks
資産再評価	シサンサイヒョウカ	assets revaluation
資産負債表	シサンフサイヒョウ	financial statement; statement of assets and liabilities
資本	シホン	capital; funds; stockholder's equity
資本家	シホンカ	capitalist
資本回転率	シホンカイテンリツ	turnover of capital

748

資本金	シホンキン	capital
資本合計	シホンゴウケイ	total stockholder's equity
資本財	シホンザイ	capital goods
資本集約的産業	シホンシュウヤクテキサンギョウ	capital-intensive industry
資本主義	シホンシュギ	capitalism
資本準備金	シホンジュンビキン	legal capital surplus

1735

賃 ⑬ ／ イ イ 仁 仟 任 侄 侉 賃 賃 賃 賃

音	賃	チン	price; fare; fee; hire; wages; rent
熟	賃銀	チンギン	compensation; remuneration
	賃借	チンシャク	hire; hiring; lease —*v.* hire; lease; rent
	賃貸	チンタイ	lease; hiring out —*v.* lease; hire out
¥	賃上げ	チンあげ	wage increase —*vi.* increase/raise wages
	賃金	チンギン	wages; pay
	賃貸借	チンタイシャク	lease; charter
	賃貸住宅	チンタイジュウタク	house to let; rental house
	賃貸料	チンタイリョウ	leasing charge; rent

1736

賛 ⑮ 一 ㄱ ㅋ 夫 夫= 夫ㄱ 夫夫 㚈 替 替 賛

音	賛	サン	praise; dedication; inscription; tribute; help; support; agree
熟	賛意	サンイ	one's approval/assent
	賛歌	サンカ	song of praise; paean
	賛辞	サンジ	praise; tribute
	賛助	サンジョ	support; patronage —*v.* support; patronize
	賛成	サンセイ	approval; agreement —*vi.* approve; agree; support; favor
	賛同	サンドウ	approval; support; endorsement —*vi.* approve; support; endorse
	賛美	サンビ	praise; glorification —*v.* praise; glorify
	賛美歌	サンビカ	hymn
	賛否	サンピ	approval and disapproval; yes or no

見角言谷豆豕貝 • 赤走足身車辛辰酉釆里臣舛

1737

質 ⑮   ` ｱ ｦ ｦ ｦ 斤 斦 斦 斦 斦 質 質 質

音	質	シチ	pawn
		シツ	nature; disposition; temperament; matter; quality
		（チ）	
熟	質屋	シチや	pawnshop; pawnbroker
	質疑応答	シツギオウトウ	questions and answers —*vi.* have a question-and-answer session
	質実剛健	シツジツゴウケン	rough-hewn and robust
	質素	シッソ	simple; plain; modest
	質的	シツテキ	qualitative
	質点	シツテン	*phy.* particle
	質問	シツモン	question —*v.* question; ask questions
	質量	シツリョウ	mass; quality and quantity
訓	※質	たち	nature; disposition; temperament

1738

賞 ⑮   ` ` ⺌ ⺌ 尚 尚 尚 尚 尚 賞 賞

音	賞	ショウ	prize; reward
熟	賞金	ショウキン	prize money; prize; reward
	賞賛	ショウサン	praise; admiration —*v.* praise; admire; applaud
	賞状	ショウジョウ	certificate of merit; honorary certificate
	賞罰	ショウバツ	reward and punishment
	賞品	ショウヒン	prize; award
	賞味	ショウミ	relishment/enjoyment of food —*v.* relish; enjoy food
	賞与	ショウヨ	bonus; reward
訓	※賞める	ほめる	*vt.* praise; admire

1739

賓 ⑮   ` 宀 宀 宁 宁 宀 宀 宾 審 賓 賓

音	賓	ヒン	guest
熟	賓客	ヒンキャク （ヒンカク）	guest of honor; honored/distinguished guest; company

1740

賢 ⑯　１ 厂 厂 戸 臣 臣ノ 臤ヌ 臤ヌ 臤又 賢 賢 賢 賢

音	賢	ケン	wise
熟	賢察	ケンサツ	*hon.* consideration; understanding
	賢人	ケンジン	wise man; sage
	賢母	ケンボ	wise mother
	賢明	ケンメイ	wise; advisable
訓	賢い	かしこい	clever; wise; smart

1741

財 ⑩　１ 冂 冂 日 目 目 貝 貝 財 財

音	財	ザイ	property; finance; business
		（サイ）	
熟	財貨	ザイカ	wealth
	財界人	ザイカイジン	big businessman; financier
	財布	サイフ	purse; pocketbook; wallet
	財宝	ザイホウ	treasures; riches
	財力	ザイリョク	financial power
¥	財界	ザイカイ	financial world/circles
	財形貯蓄	ザイケイチョチク	workers property accumulation savings
	財源	ザイゲン	source of revenue; financial resources
	財産	ザイサン	estate; property; fortune
	財政	ザイセイ	public finance; finances
	財団	ザイダン	foundation
	財団法人	ザイダンホウジン	foundation; nonprofit corporation
	財テク	ザイテク	financial technique/technology
	財閥	ザイバツ	*zaibatsu* (financial conglomerate)
	財務諸表	ザイムショヒョウ	financial statements

1742

販 ⑪　１ 冂 冂 日 目 貝 貝 貝 販 販 販

音	販	ハン	deal
¥	販売	ハンバイ	sale; selling; marketing —*v.* sell; market; deal in; handle
	販路	ハンロ	market (for goods); outlet

見角言谷豆豕
•貝赤走足跫身車辛辰酉釆里臣舛

1743

貯 ⑫ 丨 冂 冂 冃 目 貝 貝 貝' 貝' 貯 貯 貯

音	貯	チョ	store; stock; save; savings
熟	貯金	チョキン	savings; deposit —*vi.* save money; put money by
	貯水	チョスイ	storage of water; impoundment; reservoir water
	貯水池	チョスイチ	reservoir
	貯蔵	チョゾウ	storage; storing; preservation —*v.* store; put aside; conserve; preserve
	貯蓄	チョチク	saving; storing up; savings —*v.* save; store; put aside
訓	貯える	たくわえる	*vt.* save; store; conserve
	貯める	ためる	*vt.* save; store

1744

賊 ⑬ 丨 冂 冂 冃 貝 貝 貝 賊 賊 賊 賊 賊

音	賊	ゾク	rebel; robber
熟	賊軍	ゾクグン	rebel army; rebels
	賊子	ゾクシ	rebel; traitor
	賊徒	ゾクト	rebels; traitors

1745

賄 ⑬ 丨 冂 冂 目 貝 貝 貝' 貯 財 賄 賄 賄

音	賄	ワイ	pay; cover
熟	賄賂	ワイロ	bribe; bribery
訓	賄う	まかなう	*vt.* obtain; provide (food); carry out (household chores)

1746

賜 ⑮ 丨 冂 目 貝 貝 貝' 賏 賏 賏 賜 賜 賜

音	賜	シ	gift
熟	賜暇	シカ	leave; leave of absence
訓	賜る	たまわる	*vt. hum.* receive; get
	賜物	たまもの	*hum.* gift received

1747

賠 ⑮
丨 冂 目 貝 貝 貝ˋ 貯 貯 賉 賠 賠 賠 賠

音	賠	バイ	indemnify
熟	賠償	バイショウ	reparation; indemnity; compensation —*v.* indemnify; compensate

1748

賦 ⑮
丨 冂 目 貝 貝ˋ 貯 貯ˇ 賦 賦 賦 賦 賦

音	賦	フ	tribute; payment; installment
熟	賦課	フカ	levy; assessment; imposition —*v.* levy; assess; impose
	賦与	フヨ	innate; endowed; blessed —*v.* grant; give

1749

購 ⑰
丨 冂 目 貝 貝ˋ 貝ˇ 購ˇ 購ˇ 購 購 購 購 購

音	購	コウ	purchase; buy; procure
熟	購読	コウドク	subscription —*v.* subscribe; take a newspaper, etc.
	購入	コウニュウ	purchase; buying —*v.* purchase; buy; procure
	購買	コウバイ	purchase; buying —*v.* purchase; buy; procure
訓	※購う	あがなう	*vt.* purchase; buy

1750

贈 ⑱
丨 冂 目 貝 貝ˋ 貝ˇ 貯 貯ˇ 贈ˇ 贈 贈 贈ˉ 贈

音	贈	ゾウ	present; give; bestow
		（ソウ）	present
熟	贈収賄	ゾウシュウワイ	bribery
	贈呈	ゾウテイ	presentation; gift —*v.* make a presentation; offer a gift
	贈答	ゾウトウ	exchange of gifts —*v.* exchange gifts
	贈与	ゾウヨ	donation; gift —*v.* donate; make a gift
	贈賄	ゾウワイ	bribery —*v.* bribe
訓	贈る	おくる	*vt.* present; give; bestow
	贈り物	おくりもの	gift; present

753

見
角
言
谷
豆
豕
貝
● 赤
走
足
趴
身
車
辛
辰
酉
釆
里
臣
舛

7 赤 あかい red

1751

赤 ⑦　一　十　土　ナ　赤　赤　赤

音	赤	セキ	red
		（シャク）	
熟	赤銅	シャクドウ	gold-copper alloy
	赤外線	セキガイセン	infrared rays
	赤軍	セキグン	Red Army
	赤十字	セキジュウジ	Red Cross
	赤心	セキシン	sincerity; true heart
	赤道	セキドウ	equator
	赤飯	セキハン	rice with red beans
	赤貧	セキヒン	dire poverty
	赤面	セキメン	blush —*vi*. blush; go red in the cheeks
	赤裸々	セキララ	frank; outspoken; stark naked
	赤痢	セキリ	dysentery
	赤化	セッカ	making Communist —*v*. make Communist
	赤血球	セッケッキュウ	red corpuscles
訓	赤	あか	red
	赤字	あかジ	deficit; in the red
	赤ちゃん	あかちゃん	baby
	赤帽	あかボウ	redcap; luggage porter
	赤い	あかい	red
	赤らむ	あからむ	*vi*. become red; blush
	赤らめる	あからめる	*vt*. make red
¥	赤字	あかジ	deficit; balance (figure) in the red; loss
	赤字国債	あかジコクサイ	bond issued for deficit financing; deficit bond
	赤字財政	あかジザイセイ	deficit spending (by the government); deficit finance

1752

赦 ⑪　一　十　土　ナ　赤　赤　赤　赤　赦　赦　赦

| 音 | 赦 | シャ | pardon |
| 熟 | 赦免 | シャメン | pardon —*v*. pardon; remit |

7 走 はしる／そうにょう running

1753

走⑦ 一 十 土 キ キ 赤 走

音	走	ソウ	run; run away
熟	走者	ソウシャ	runner
	走破	ソウハ	running the whole distance —*vi*. run the whole distance
	走法	ソウホウ	form of running; running style
	走馬灯	ソウまトウ	revolving lantern
	走路	ソウロ	running track/course
訓	走る	はしる	*vi*. run; run away
	走り書き	はしりがき	scribbling —*v*. scribble; write hurriedly

1754

赴⑨ 一 十 土 キ キ 赤 走 走 起 赴

音	赴	フ	go
熟	赴任	フニン	one's place of appointment; one's new post —*vi*. start one's new post
訓	赴く	おもむく	*vi*. go; proceed towards; get; become

1755

起⑩ 一 十 土 キ キ 赤 走 走 起 起 起

音	起	キ	get up; be stirred up; happen
熟	起案	キアン	draft; charter; plan
	起因	キイン	origin; cause; attribute —*vi*. originate in; be caused by; be attributable to
	起源	キゲン	origin; beginning; source
	起工	キコウ	start of construction work —*vi*. begin construction
	起床	キショウ	rising in the morning; getting up —*vi*. rise; get up
	起訴	キソ	prosecution; indictment; litigation —*v*. prosecute; indict
	起草	キソウ	drafting —*v*. draft; draw up
	起点	キテン	starting point

見角言谷豆豕貝赤走足趸身車辛辰酉釆里臣舛

| 起用 | キヨウ | appointment; employment —*v*. appoint; employ |
| 起立 | キリツ | rising; standing up —*vi*. rise; stand up |

訓
起きる	おきる	*vi*. get up; rise
起こす	おこす	*vt*. raise up; awake; bring about; wake up
起こる	おこる	*vi*. happen; come to pass

¥
| 起債 | キサイ | issue of bonds |
| 起債市場 | キサイシジョウ | bond issuance market |

1756

越 ⑫ 一 十 土 キ キ 走 走 走 起 起 越 越 越

音
| 越 | エツ | cross; go to excess; pass over; exceed |

熟
越境	エッキョウ	violation of a border; border jumping —*vi*. jump/violate a border
越権	エッケン	exceeding one's authority; abuse of power
越冬	エットウ	spending the winter —*vi*. pass the winter; winter
越年	エツネン	seeing the old year out —*vi*. see the old year out

訓
| 越える | こえる | *vi*. cross; go across; pass; go over; exceed |
| 越す | こす | *vt*. cross; go over; exceed; pass; surpass |

1757

超 ⑫ 一 十 土 キ キ 走 走 起 起 超 超 超

音
| 超 | チョウ | exceed; excel; (prefix) super-; ultra- |

熟
超越	チョウエツ	transcendence; transcendancy —*vi*. transcend; rise above; be superior
超音速	チョウオンソク	supersonic speed
超音波	チョウオンパ	supersonic waves
超過	チョウカ	excess; surplus —*v*. exceed; be over
超自然	チョウシゼン	supernaturalness
超人	チョウジン	superman
超然	チョウゼン	unworldliness
超大国	チョウタイコク	superpower
超特急	チョウトッキュウ	super express (train)
超満員	チョウマンイン	overflowing with people; filled beyond capacity

訓
| 超える | こえる | *vi*. cross; go across; exceed; pass; go over |
| 超す | こす | *vt*. cross; go over; pass; spend; tide over; pass; exceed; surpass |

1758

趣 ⑮ 一 十 キ キ 走 走 走 起 起 趄 趣 趣

音	趣	シュ	taste
熟	趣意	シュイ	purpose; aim; point; purport
	趣意書	シュイショ	prospectus
	趣向	シュコウ	idea; plan
	趣旨	シュシ	purpose; aim
	趣味	シュミ	taste; liking; hobby
訓	趣	おもむき	import; effect; contents; air; looks; appearances; taste; elegance

---

7 足 足 あし／あしへん leg

1759

足 ⑦ 丶 ロ ロ 尸 尸 尺 足

音	足	ソク	foot; leg; suffice; add
熟	足下	ソッカ	at one's foot; you
	足跡	ソクセキ（あしあと）	footprint
	足労	ソクロウ	trouble of coming
訓	足	あし	leg; foot
	足音	あしおと	sound of footsteps
	足首	あしくび	ankle
	足場	あしば	foothold; scaffold
	足元	あしもと	at one's feet
	足す	たす	*vt*. add; supply
	足りる	たりる	*vi*. be enough; suffice
	足る	たる	*vi*. be enough; suffice
	※足袋	たび	*tabi* (Japanese socks)

1760

距 ⑫ 丶 ロ ロ 尸 尸 尹 足 趴 距 距 距 距

音	距	キョ	distance; interval; space
熟	距離	キョリ	distance; interval; space between two places

757

見角言谷豆豕貝赤走足
•足身車辛辰酉釆里臣舛

1761 跡 ⑬
ㄇ �口 ㄆ ㄇ 足 足 足' 跙 跙 跡 跡 跡

音	跡	セキ	footprint
訓	跡	あと	trace; ruins; remains
	跡始末	あとシマツ	dealing with the aftermath
	跡継ぎ	あとつぎ	inheritor; heir; successor
	跡取り	あととり	inheritor; heir; successor

1762 践 ⑬
ㄇ �口 ㄆ ㄇ 足 足 足 跂 跓 践 践 践

| 音 | 践 | セン | do |

1763 跳 ⑬
ㄇ �口 ㄆ ㄇ 足 足 趴 趴 趴 跳 跳 跳

音	跳	チョウ	leap
熟	跳躍	チョウヤク	jump; spring; skip —vi. spring; jump; leap; skip; prance
訓	跳ぶ	とぶ	vi. leap; jump; skip
	跳ねる	はねる	vi. leap; skip; jump

1764 路 ⑬
ㄇ ㄖ ㄆ ㄇ 足 足 跙 跁 跄 路 路 路

音	路	ロ	road; path; way
熟	路肩	ロかた	edge of a road
	路地	ロジ	alley; lane; path
	路上	ロジョウ	on the road
	路線	ロセン	route; line; alignment
	路頭	ロトウ	road side; wayside
	路傍	ロボウ	roadside; wayside
	路面	ロメン	road surface
訓	路	じ	road; path; way
	※路	みち	road; path; way

1765

踊 ⑭ ⌐ ⌐ ⼞ ⼞ ⼞ ⼞ 跙 跀 跀 踊 踊 踊

音	踊	ヨウ	dance
訓	踊る	おどる	*vi*. dance
	踊り	おどり	dance; dancing
	踊り子	おどりこ	dancer; dancing girl
	踊り場	おどりば	dance hall/floor; landing; halfpace

1766

踏 ⑮ ⌐ ⌐ ⼞ ⼞ ⼞ 足 跙 跀 跀 踍 踏 踏

音	踏	トウ	step
熟	踏査	トウサ	survey; exploration; investigation —*v*. survey; explore; investigate
	踏襲	トウシュウ	following; continuing; carrying on with —*v*. follow in someone's footsteps
	踏破	トウハ	traveling on foot —*v*. traverse; travel on foot; hike; travel all over
訓	踏む	ふむ	*vt*. step; trample; tread; value; experience
	踏まえる	ふまえる	*vt*. step/stand on; be based on
	踏み絵	ふみエ	*fumie* (copper tablet with a religious image on it to be trodden on to prove oneself a non-Christian) *fig*. loyalty test
	踏切	ふみきり	railway crossing
	踏み台	ふみダイ	step; stool; footstool
	踏み段	ふみダン	step; stair
¥	踏み	ふみ	short covering at a loss

1767

躍 ㉑ ⌐ ⼞ ⼞ ⼞ 足 跀 跙 踛 踊 躍 躍 躍

音	躍	ヤク	jump; leap; hop
熟	躍如	ヤクジョ	vivid; lifelike
	躍進	ヤクシン	advance by leaps and bounds —*vi*. rush; make a dash
	躍動	ヤクドウ	lively motion —*vi*. move lively/actively
	躍起	ヤッキ	excitement; enthusiasm
訓	躍る	おどる	*vi*. leap; hop

7 身 み body

1768

身 ⑦ ＇ ｒ ｒ 冎 冎 身 身

音	身	シン	body
熟	身上	シンジョウ	personal reasons; merit; asset
	身上書	シンジョウショ	personal information form
	身上持ち	シンショウもち	fortune; wealthy person; housekeeper; handling the household budget
	身心	シンシン	body and mind
	身体	シンタイ	body; physical; bodily
	身体検査	シンタイケンサ	physical examination; medical check-up; search; frisking —*vi*. have a check-up; be searched/frisked
	身体障害者	シンタイ ショウガイシャ	physically handicapped/disabled person
	身代	シンダイ	total estate; being wealthy
	身長	シンチョウ	height; stature
	身辺	シンペン	personal
訓	身	み	body; position; place; status
	身内	みうち	relative; family; fellow; all over the body
	身重	みおも	pregnant; expecting; with child
	身勝手	みがって	selfish
	身構え	みがまえ	posture; attitude
	身柄	みがら	person; one's social position
	身軽	みがる	light; agile; nimble
	身代わり	みがわり	subsitution; substitute
	身近	みぢか	near/close to oneself
	身投げ	みなげ	suicide by drowning or jumping —*vi*. drown oneself; throw oneself from a high place
	身の上	みのうえ	history; personal circumstances
	身振り	みぶり	gesture; motion
	身震い	みぶるい	shudder; shiver; trembling —*vi*. shudder; shiver; tremble
	身分	みブン	social position; rank; means; circumstances; birth
	身元	みもと	one's identity; background
	身元引受人	みもと ひきうけニン	surety; guarantor; guarantee

760

7 車 くるま／くるまへん car

1769

車⑦　一 厂 厅 戸 百 亘 車

音	車	シャ	car; vehicle
熟	車間距離	シャカンキョリ	the distance between two cars
	車検	シャケン	car inspection; safety check on a motor vehicle
	車庫	シャコ	garage; car port; bus depot
	車軸	シャジク	wheel axle
	車種	シャシュ	type/model of car
	車掌	シャショウ	conductor (on a bus or train)
	車線	シャセン	traffic lane
	車窓	シャソウ	car/train window
	車体	シャタイ	the body of a car; bicycle frame
	車中	シャチュウ	in a train/car
	車道	シャドウ	roadway; road
	車内	シャナイ	in a car/train
	車両	シャリョウ	cars; vehicles; rolling stock; coach; car; carriage
	車輪	シャリン	wheel
訓	車	くるま	wheel; vehicle; car
	車椅子	くるまイス	wheelchair
	車座	くるまざ	sitting in a circle
	車酔い	くるまよい	carsickness

1770

軌⑨　一 厂 厅 戸 百 亘 車 軋 軌

音	軌	キ	track; rule; railway line; norm
熟	軌跡	キセキ	locus (in geometry)
	軌道	キドウ	orbit; railway track

1771

軍⑨　' 冖 冖 ワ 冐 冐 冒 宣 軍

音	軍	グン	military; army; soldiers

熟

軍医	グンイ	military physician; army doctor; medic
軍艦	グンカン	warship; battleship
軍港	グンコウ	naval station
軍国主義	グンコクシュギ	militarism
軍事	グンジ	naval and military; military
軍資金	グンシキン	war/campaign funds
軍縮	グンシュク	arms reduction —*vi.* reduce arms/military expenditure
軍人	グンジン	soldier; serviceman; service woman
軍隊	グンタイ	troops; forces; army
軍配	グンバイ	stratagem; tactics
軍備	グンビ	armaments; military preparation

1772

軒 ⑩   一 ㄏ 戸 戸 亘 車 車 軒 軒 軒

音 軒	ケン	eaves
訓 軒	のき	eaves; edge of the roof
軒先	のきさき	along the eaves; in front of the houses
軒下	のきした	under the eaves

1773

転 ⑪   一 ㄏ 戸 戸 亘 車 車 軒 転 転

音 転	テン	roll; tumble; move
熟 転じる	テンじる	*v.* turn round; revolve; rotate; shift; alter; convert; remove
転位	テンイ	transposition; dislocation; displacement
転移	テンイ	change; transition; transfer —*v.* change; transfer
転化	テンカ	change; transformation; inversion; conversion —*vi.* change; be transformed/inverted
転回	テンカイ	revolution; rotation; evolution —*v.* revolve; rotate; evolve
転換	テンカン	conversion; switch; turnabout; diversion —*v.* convert; switch to; divert; turn
転換期	テンカンキ	turning point
転記	テンキ	copying information into another (family) register —*v.* copy information into another (family) register
転機	テンキ	turning point; point of change

転居	テンキョ	moving; change of address —*vi.* move; change one's address
転業	テンギョウ	change of trade; change of occupation —*vi.* change one's employment/trade
転勤	テンキン	transferal (to another city, etc.) —*vi.* be transferred (to another city, etc.)
転向	テンコウ	conversion; turn; turning —*vi.* turn; be converted; abandon an idea
転校	テンコウ	change of schools —*vi.* change one's school
転載	テンサイ	reproduction; reprinting —*v.* reproduce; reprint
転写	テンシャ	transference; copying; transcription —*v.* transfer; copy; transcribe
転出	テンシュツ	transfer out; moving out —*vi.* be transferred out; move out
転職	テンショク	change of occupation —*vi.* change one's occupation
転身	テンシン	turnover; complete change —*vi.* change over; change completely
転成	テンセイ	transformation; transmutation —*vi.* be transformed; change into
転送	テンソウ	transmission; forwarding —*v.* transmit; forward; send on
転地	テンチ	moving away for a change of air; trying a change of climate —*vt.* go somewhere for a change of air; try a change of air
転調	テンチョウ	modulation (music); transition —*vi.* modulate
転々	テンテン	from one place to another; from hand to hand —*vi.* go from one place to another; pass from hand-to-hand
転倒	テントウ	violent fall; inversion; reversal; upset —*v.* fall down; invert; reverse; lose one's head
転入	テンニュウ	transference in; moving in —*vi.* be transfered in; move into
転任	テンニン	transferal (to another city, etc.) —*vi.* be transferred (to another city, etc.)
転変	テンペン	mutation; change
転用	テンヨウ	diversion —*v.* divert; convert
転落	テンラク	fall; degradation —*vi.* fall; have a fall; degrade
訓 転がす	ころがす	*vt.* roll; trundle
転がる	ころがる	*vi.* roll; tumble; fall; lie down
転げる	ころげる	*vi.* roll; tumble; fall
転ばす	ころばす	*vt.* roll over; knock down
転ぶ	ころぶ	*vi.* roll; tumble; fall over
¥ 転換社債	テンカンシャサイ	convertible bond (CB)
転借	テンシャク	sublease
転貸	テンタイ	sublease
転売	テンバイ	resale —*v.* resell

見角言谷豆豕貝赤走足𧾷身車辛辰酉釆里臣舛

1774 軟 ⑪

一 厂 🗖 𠃌 𢆥 𠃍 車 車 軒 軟 軟

音	軟	ナン	soft
熟	軟化	ナンカ	soften; mollification —v. soften; tone down; be mollified
	軟球	ナンキュウ	soft ball
	軟膏	ナンコウ	ointment; salve
	軟骨	ナンコツ	cartilage; gristle
	軟弱	ナンジャク	weakness; effeminacy
	軟水	ナンスイ	soft water
	軟派	ナンパ	moderate party; light/erotic literature; playing around with women —v. play around with women
訓	軟らかい	やわらかい	soft; tender; limp; plastic
	軟らか	やわらか	soft; tender

1775 軽 ⑫

一 厂 🗖 𠃌 𢆥 𠃍 車 軒 軒 軽 軽 軽

音	軽	ケイ	light; light-hearted; slight; easy; casual
熟	軽音楽	ケイオンガク	light/easy-listening music
	軽快	ケイカイ	light; cheerful; casual
	軽金属	ケイキンゾク	light metals
	軽減	ケイゲン	reduction; commutation; alleviation —v. reduce; commute; lighten; alleviate; relieve; ease
	軽視	ケイシ	making light of; slighting; belittling —v. make light of; slight; belittle
	軽傷	ケイショウ	slight injury/wound
	軽症	ケイショウ	slight illness; mild case
	軽少	ケイショウ	slight; trifling
	軽食	ケイショク	light meal; snack
	軽震	ケイシン	light earthquake; earth tremor
	軽装	ケイソウ	light/casual dress —vi. be lightly/casually dressed
	軽卒	ケイソツ	rashness; haste; carelessness; imprudence
	軽度	ケイド	slight
	軽薄	ケイハク	thoughtlessness; frivolity; flippancy; imprudence
	軽蔑	ケイベツ	contempt; scorn; disdain —v. contempt; scorn
	軽妙	ケイミョウ	smart; witty
訓	軽い	かるい	light; agile; slight; mild; easy

軽やか	かろやか	lightly
軽んじる	かろんじる	*vt*. look down upon; make light of
¥ 軽工業	ケイコウギョウ	light industry
軽油	ケイユ	light oil

1776

軸 ⑫　　一　　厂　　冎　　冎　　百　　亘　　車　　車　　軕　　軸　　軸　　軸

| 音 | 軸 | ジク | spindle; axle; pivot; scroll; holder |

1777

較 ⑬　　一　　厂　　冎　　百　　亘　　車　　車'　　軒　　軒　　軒　　軗　　較

| 音 | 較 | カク | compare |
| 訓 | ※較べる | くらべる | *vt*. compare; contrast |

1778

載 ⑬　　一　　十　　土　　去　　吉　　吉　　吉　　亩　　車　　載　　載　　載

音	載	サイ	load; write
訓	載せる	のせる	*vt*. put on; place; load; publish; carry (an article in a newspaper)
	載る	のる	*vi*. appear; be printed/carried (in a newspaper)

1779

輝 ⑮　　ノ　　ヽ　　ル　　ヽ　　光　　光'　　光ˊ　　炉　　炉　　焜　　煇　　輝

音	輝	キ	shine; glitter; brilliant
訓	輝かしい	かがやかしい	bright; brilliant; shiny
	輝かす	かがやかす	*vt*. light up; brighten; glorify
	輝き	かがやき	brilliancy; radiance; brightness; glow
	輝く	かがやく	*vi*. shine; sparkle; gleam; be brilliant

1780

輩 ⑮　　ノ　　ヽ　　ヨ　　ヨ　　ヨ非　　ヨ非　　非　　非　　背　　輩　　輩

| 音 | 輩 | ハイ | fellow; people |

7

見角言谷豆豕貝赤走足⻊身車辛辰酉釆里臣舛

●

熟	輩出	ハイシュツ	in succession; in great numbers —*vi.* appear in succession/one after another

1781

輪 ⑮ 一 ⼆ ⼾ 日 車 車 車 軒 軔 軩 軩 輪 輪

音	輪	リン	wheel; circle; rotate; (counter for flowers/wheels)
熟	輪禍	リンカ	traffic accident
	輪郭	リンカク	outline; facial features; contours
	輪姦	リンカン	gang rape; gangbang —*v.* gangrape; gangbang
	輪作	リンサク	crop rotation
	輪唱	リンショウ	canon (in music); round —*v.* sing a canon
	輪状	リンジョウ	circular; ring-shaped
	輪転	リンテン	rotation; revolution
	輪転機	リンテンキ	rotary press
	輪読	リンドク	reading a book in turns —*v.* take turns reading a book
	輪廻	リンネ	transmigration of souls
	輪番	リンバン	rotation; taking turns
訓	輪	わ	ring; wheel; circle; hoop; loop
	輪切り	わぎり	round slices

1782

輸 ⑯ 一 ⼆ ⼾ 日 車 車 車 軒 軩 輪 輪 輸

音	輸	ユ	transport; send
熟	輸血	ユケツ	blood transfusion —*vi.* give a blood transfusion
	輸出	ユシュツ	exports —*v.* export
	輸送	ユソウ	transport —*v.* transport; convey; carry; forward
	輸入	ユニュウ	imports —*v.* import
¥	輸出入銀行	ユシュツニュウギンコウ	export-import bank

1783

轄 ⑰ 一 ⼆ 日 車 車 車 軒 軒 軒 軒 轄 轄

音	轄	カツ	jurisdiction
訓	轄	くさび	wedge; tie

7 辛 からい bitter

1784

辛 ⑦   ` 亠 立 立 立 辛 辛

音	辛	シン	pungent; bitter
熟	辛苦	シンク	hardship; trials; pains
	辛酸	シンサン	hardships; trials and tribulations
	辛勝	シンショウ	narrow victory; close margin —*vi*. win by a close margin
	辛抱	シンボウ	endurance; patience; staying power —*vi*. endure; be patient; perservere; bear; stand; hold out
	辛辣	シンラツ	biting; caustic; sharp; scathing; severe
訓	辛い	からい	hot; pungent; salty; spicy
	辛口	からくち	dry; hot
	辛子	からシ	mustard
	辛味	からミ	sharp/salty taste

1785

辞 ⑬   一 二 千 千 舌 舌 舌 舌 舌 辞 辞 辞

音	辞	ジ	word; address; resign; give up
熟	辞する	ジする	*vi*. resign; give up (one's post)
	辞意	ジイ	intention to resign
	辞去	ジキョ	departing —*vi*. take one's leave
	辞書	ジショ	dictionary; lexicon; thesaurus
	辞職	ジショク	resignation; giving up one's job —*vi*. resign one's post; hand in one's notice; give up work
	辞世	ジセイ	one's dying poem; one's death
	辞退	ジタイ	declination; refusal —*v*. refuse; decline; turn down
	辞典	ジテン	dictionary
	辞任	ジニン	resignation; notice —*v*. resign; hand in one's resignation
	辞表	ジヒョウ	one's resignation
	辞令	ジレイ	written appointment to a position
訓	辞める	やめる	*vi*. resign; retire; give up
	※辞	ことば	word; phrase

767

見角言谷豆豕貝赤走足⻊身車辛辰酉釆里臣舛

7 辰　しんのたつ　small dragon

1786

辱 ⑩　一　厂　厂　厃　戸　戸　辰　辰　辱　辱

音	辱	ジョク	humiliation
訓	辱める	はずかしめる	*vt.* humiliate; insult; disgrace someone; bring disrepute; violate; rape
	辱め	はずかしめ	humiliation; disgrace

1787

農 ⑬　丶　冂　冂　曲　曲　曲　芦　芦　芦　農　農　農

音	農	ノウ	cultivate; farming; agriculture
熟	農園	ノウエン	farm; plantation
	農家	ノウカ	farmhouse; farming family
	農閑期	ノウカンキ	farmer's slack season
	農機具	ノウキグ	agricultural implement
	農業	ノウギョウ	farming; agriculture
	農業国	ノウギョウコク	farming country
	農具	ノウグ	farm implements
	農耕	ノウコウ	farming; agriculture
	農作	ノウサク	cultivation of land; tillage of soil; farming
	農作物	ノウサクモツ（ノウサクブツ）	crops; farm produce
	農産物	ノウサンブツ	farm produce; agricultural products
	農場	ノウジョウ	farm
	農村	ノウソン	farm village; rural community
	農地	ノウチ	farm/agricultural land
	農地改革	ノウチカイカク	farmland/agrarian reform
	農繁期	ノウハンキ	farming season
	農夫	ノウフ	farmer
	農民	ノウミン	farmers
	農薬	ノウヤク	agricultural chemicals
	農林	ノウリン	agriculture and forestry
¥	農協（農業協同組合）	ノウキョウ（ノウギョウキョウドウくみあい）	agricultural cooperative

| 農相 | ノウショウ | minister of agriculture, forestery, and fisheries |
| 農林水産省 | ノウリンスイサンショウ | Ministry of Agriculture, Forestery, and Fisheries |

7 酉 さけづくり／とりへん　liquor; sake

1788

酌 ⑩　一　厂　厅　丙　丙　酉　酉　酌′　酌

音	酌	シャク	serve saké
熟	酌量	シャクリョウ	consideration; allowance —v. take into consideration; make allowance for
訓	酌む	くむ	*vt.* pour out wine

1789

酒 ⑩　丶　氵　氵　汀　汀　沔　沔　沔　酒　酒

音	酒	シュ	saké; wine; liquor
熟	酒宴	シュエン	feast; banquet
	酒気	シュキ	smell of alcohol
	酒豪	シュゴウ	heavy drinker
	酒色	シュショク	wine and women
	酒精	シュセイ	alcohol
	酒席	シュセキ	banquet; drinking party
	酒造	シュゾウ	saké brewing; wine making; distilling
	酒乱	シュラン	drunken fit; ugly drunk
訓	酒	さけ	rice wine; saké; liquor
	酒癖	さけぐせ	one's behavior when drunk
	酒飲み	さけのみ	drinker
	酒	さか	rice wine; saké; liguor
	酒蔵	さかぐら	room for storing saké
	酒代	さかダイ	beer money; money for drinks
	酒樽	さかだる	wine casket; beer barrel
	酒場	さかば	bar; pub
	酒盛り	さかもり	drinking party
	酒屋	さかや	wine shop; liquor store

7

1790

配 ⑩　一　厂　厂　厏　酉　酉　酉　酉´　酉´´　配

音	配	ハイ	distribute
熟	配する	ハイする	*vt.* allot; arrange; match; exile; place under
	配下	ハイカ	followers; subordinates
	配管	ハイカン	installment of gas/water pipes
	配給	ハイキュウ	distribution; supply; rationing —*v.* distribute; supply; deal out; ration
	配偶者	ハイグウシャ	spouse
	配合	ハイゴウ	combination; harmony; match; mixture; blending —*v.* combine; distribute; arrange; match; tone
	配車	ハイシャ	car allocation —*v.* alllocate cars
	配色	ハイショク	color scheme
	配水	ハイスイ	water supply —*vi.* supply/distribute water
	配線	ハイセン	electric wiring —*vi.* wire (a house) for electricity
	配属	ハイゾク	assignment; job allocation —*v.* assign (a person to a position)
	配達	ハイタツ	delivery —*v.* deliver
	配置	ハイチ	arrangement; disposition; posting; placement —*v.* arrange; distribute; post; station; detail
	配電	ハイデン	supply of electric power; power distribution —*vi.* supply electricity; distribute power
	配備	ハイビ	(troop) positioning —*vt.* position (troops)
	配布	ハイフ	distribution —*v.* distribute
	配付	ハイフ	distribution; division; handing out —*v.* distribute; give/hand out
	配分	ハイブン	distribution; division; allotment; allocation —*v.* distribute; divide; share; allot; allocate
	配本	ハイホン	book delivery to subscribers
	配役	ハイヤク	the cast; casting
	配慮	ハイリョ	consideration; attention; care; concern; anxiety; trouble —*v.* give consideration/attention to; be concerned/troubled
	配列	ハイレツ	arrangement; disposal; grouping —*v.* arrange; dispose; put in order; array
訓	配る	くばる	*vt.* distribute; deliver; hand out
¥	配当	ハイトウ	allotment; share; cut; dividend —*v.* allocate dividends
	配当率	ハイトウリツ	dividend rate

見角言谷豆豕貝赤走足⻊身車辛辰●西釆里臣舛

1791

酔 ⑪ 　一　厂　厅　丙　西　西　酉　酉′　酉九　酉卆　酔

音	酔	スイ	get drunk
熟	酔客	スイカク	drunkard
	酔漢	スイカン	drunkard
	酔狂	スイキョウ	whimsical; freakish; capricious; eccentric
	酔態	スイタイ	drunkenness; intoxication; tipsiness
訓	酔う	よう	*vi*. get drunk; become intoxicated; feel sick; be poisoned
	酔っ払い	よっぱらい	drunkard; boozer
	酔っ払う	よっぱらう	*vi*. get drunk/tipsy/intoxicated

1792

酢 ⑫ 　一　厂　厅　丙　西　西　酉　酉′　酉乍　酉乍　酢　酢

音	酢	サク	vinegar
熟	酢酸	サクサン	*chem*. acetic acid
訓	酢	す	vinegar

1793

酬 ⑬ 　一　厅　丙　西　西　酉　酉　酉丿　酉丿丿　酉川　酉川　酉川

音	酬	シュウ	reward

1794

酪 ⑬ 　一　厅　丙　西　西　酉　酉′　酉クノ　酉クン　酪　酪

音	酪	ラク	whey
熟	酪酸	ラクサン	*chem*. butyric acid
	酪農	ラクノウ	dairy farming

1795

酵 ⑭ 　一　厅　丙　西　酉　酉′　酉十　酉士　酉尹　酉耂　酵　酵

音	酵	コウ	yeast; ferment

見角言谷豆豕貝赤走足跫身車辛辰酉釆里臣舛

熟 酵素　　コウソ　　*chem*. enzyme
　　酵母　　コウボ　　yeast

1796
酷 ⑭　一　厂　西　西　酉　酉'　酉⸍　酉⸌　酉⸝　酉⸡　酷　酷

音 酷　　コク　　harsh; bitter; intense
熟 酷使　　コクシ　　forced labor —*v*. work to death; make someone work hard
　　酷似　　コクジ　　close resemblance; striking likeness —*vi*. be very much like; be similar
　　酷暑　　コクショ　　intense heat
　　酷薄　　コクハク　　cruel and heartless
　　酷評　　コクヒョウ　　severe criticism; cruel remark —*v*. speak bitterly; offer harsh criticism
　　酷寒　　コッカン　　intense cold

1797
酸 ⑭　一　厂　西　西　酉　酉'　酉⸍　酉⸌　酉⸝　酉⸡　酸　酸

音 酸　　サン　　sour; acid
熟 酸化　　サンカ　　*chem*. oxidation —*vi*. be oxidized
　　酸性　　サンセイ　　*chem*. acidity
　　酸性雨　　サンセイウ　　acid rain
　　酸素　　サンソ　　*chem*. oxygen
　　酸味　　サンミ　　sourness; sour taste; acidity
訓 酸い　　すい　　sour; acidic; vinegary
　　酸っぱい　　すっぱい　　sour; acidic; vinegary

1798
醜 ⑰　一　厂　西　西　酉　酉'　酉⸍　酉⸌　酉⸝　酉⸡　醜　醜

音 醜　　シュウ　　ugly
熟 醜悪　　シュウアク　　ugly; mean
　　醜行　　シュウコウ　　disgraceful conduct
　　醜態　　シュウタイ　　disgraceful behavior
　　醜聞　　シュウブン　　scandal; bad reputation
訓 醜い　　みにくい　　ugly; bad-looking; plain

1799

醸 ⑳ 　一　丆　西　酉　酉⁺　酉⁺　酉⁺　酉⁺　醀　醀　醀　醸

音	醸	ジョウ	brew
熟	醸成	ジョウセイ	brewing; fermenting —v. brew; ferment
	醸造	ジョウゾウ	brewing —v. brew
訓	醸す	かもす	vt. brew; cause; bring out; arouse
	醸し出す	かもしだす	vt. brew; cause; bring out; arouse

---

7 釆 のごめ topped rie

1800

釈 ⑪ 　一　′　′′　′′′′　平　乎　釆　釈′　釈′　釈′　釈

音	釈	シャク	explain; Buddhism
熟	釈迦	シャカ	Shakyamuni; Gautama; Buddha
	釈然	シャクゼン	mind relieved of all doubt, anxiety, and ill feeling; clear and free mind
	釈放	シャクホウ	release —v. release; set a person free
	釈明	シャクメイ	explanation; vindication —v. explain; vindicate

---

7 里 さと/さとへん village

1801

里 ⑦ 　丶　口　日　日　甲　里　里

音	里	リ	village; ri (unit of length, approx. 3.9 km)
熟	里程	リテイ	distance; milage
	里程標	リテイヒョウ	milepost; milestone
訓	里	さと	village; the country; hometown
	里親	さとおや	foster parents
	里帰り	さとがえり	bride's first call at her old (parent's) house
	里子	さとご	foster child
	里心	さとごころ	homesickness; nostalgia

見
角
言
谷
豆
豕
貝
赤
走
足
⻊
身
車
辛
辰
酉
釆
里
舛

●
●
●

1802

重 ⑨   一 二 广 声 声 盲 盲 重 重 重

音	重	ジュウ	heavy; steady; pile up; important
		チョウ	heavy
熟	重圧	ジュウアツ	strong pressure
	重圧感	ジュウアツカン	oppressive feeling
	重刑	ジュウケイ	severe sentence
	重厚	ジュウコウ	solid; dignified
	重婚	ジュウコン	bigamy
	重罪	ジュウザイ	felony; grave offense/crime
	重視	ジュウシ	attaching greater importance —*v.* attach greater importance; take seriously
	重々	ジュウジュウ	very; well; fully
	重症	ジュウショウ	serious illness
	重傷	ジュウショウ	serious wound/injury
	重心	ジュウシン	center of gravity/mass
	重責	ジュウセキ	heavy responsibility; important mission
	重体	ジュウタイ	serious condition; critically ill
	重大	ジュウダイ	serious; grave; critical; important
	重点	ジュウテン	important point; great importance; emphasis; priority
	重罰	ジュウバツ	severe punishment
	重病	ジュウビョウ	serious illness
	重油	ジュウユ	heavy oil
	重要	ジュウヨウ	importance; essential; key; vital
	重量	ジュウリョウ	weight
	重力	ジュウリョク	gravity
	重労働	ジュウロウドウ	hard/heavy labor
	重複	チョウフク	duplication; repetition; redundancy —*vi.* duplicate; repeat; make redundant
	重宝	チョウホウ	convenient; handy; useful —*v.* be convenient/handy to use
訓	重	え	fold
	重い	おもい	heavy; important; serious
	重々しい	おもおもしい	solemn; grave; dignified
	重さ	おもさ	weight; emphasis; importance
	重たい	おもたい	heavy
	重んじる	おもんじる	*vt.* regard highly; hold in high esteem
	重荷	おもに	heavy load; burden
	重なる	かさなる	*vi.* be on top of; be piled up; come in succession

重ねる	かさねる	*vt*. pile/stack up
重ね重ね	かさねがさね	repeatedly; over and over again
¥ 重工業	ジュウコウギョウ	heavy industry
重商主義	ジュウショウ シュギ	mercantilism
重税	ジュウゼイ	heavy tax/taxation
重電機 （重電器）	ジュウデンキ	heavy electric apparatus/equipment
重役	ジュウヤク	director; executive; board of directors

1803

野 ⑪　丶 丷 口 日 日 甲 甲 里 野 野 野 野

音	野	ヤ	field; the opposition; rustic; wild
熟	野営	ヤエイ	camp; bivouac —*vi*. camp out; make camp
	野外	ヤガイ	the open air; outdoor
	野球	ヤキュウ	baseball
	野犬	ヤケン	stray dog
	野菜	ヤサイ	vegetables
	野次	ヤジ	hooting; jeering
	野次馬	ヤジうま	curious crowd
	野趣	ヤシュ	rural beauty; rustic air
	野獣	ヤジュウ	wild animal/beast
	野心	ヤシン	ambition
	野人	ヤジン	rustic; bumpkin; uncouth person
	野性	ヤセイ	wild nature; uncouthness; wild (animal, beast, etc.)
	野戦病院	ヤセンビョウイン	field hospital
	野鳥	ヤチョウ	wild fowl/birds
	野党	ヤトウ	the Opposition; opposition party
	野蛮	ヤバン	savage; barbarous
	野卑	ヤヒ	vulgar; coarse; boorish
	野暮	ヤボ	senseless; booric
	野望	ヤボウ	ambition
	野郎	ヤロウ	*col*. fellow; guy; bastard
訓	野	の	field
	野宿	のジュク	camping out —*vi*. spend the night outdoors; sleep in the open
	野天	のテン	open air
	野中	のなか	in a field
	野原	のはら	field; plain

見角言谷豆豕貝赤走足身車辛辰酉釆里臣舛

野火	のび	burning off grass and weeds
野武士	のブシ	*hist*. marauding samurai and groups of farmers who stole armor, etc., from defeated samurai
野山	のやま	hills and fields
野良	のら	wild; stray; outdoors

1804

量 ⑫ ⟨ ⟨ ⟨ ⟨ ⟨ ⟨ ⟨ ⟨ ⟨ ⟨ ⟨ 量

音	量	リョウ	quantity
熟	量感	リョウカン	volume; bulk; massiveness
	量産	リョウサン	mass production —*v*. produce in large quantities
	量的	リョウテキ	quantitative
	量目	リョウめ	weight
訓	量る	はかる	*vt*. weigh; measure

7 臣 しん minister

1805

臣 ⑦

音	臣	シン	subject
		ジン	
熟	臣下	シンカ	subject; retainer
	臣民	シンミン	subject

1806

臨 ⑱

音	臨	リン	be present at; look out over; go to; copy; rule
熟	臨海	リンカイ	seaside; coastal; marine
	臨機応変	リンキオウヘン	adaptation to circumstances
	臨月	リンゲツ	the last month of pregnancy
	臨時	リンジ	extra; temporary; provisional
	臨終	リンジュウ	one's last moment
	臨床	リンショウ	clinical; attending a patient
	臨席	リンセキ	attendance; presence —*vi*. attend; be present

	臨地	リンチ	on-site
訓	臨む	のぞむ	*vt.* face; attend; be present

---

7 舛 まいあし dancing legs

1807

舞 ⑮   ノ ⼆ ⼆ 冊 無 無 舞 舞 舞 舞 舞 舞

音	舞	ブ	dance
熟	舞台	ブタイ	stage
	舞踏	ブトウ	dancing
	舞踊	ブヨウ	dance; dancing
訓	舞	まい	dance
	舞子	まいこ	(Japanese) dancing girl
	舞い込む	まいこむ	*vi.* stray in; wander in; flutter in; be blown in (unexpectedly)
	舞う	まう	dance; twirl around; flutter

8 金　かね／かねへん　metal; money

1808

金 ⑧　ノ　ㅅ　ㅅ　合　全　余　金　金

音	金	キン	gold; currency; metal; coin
		（コン）	gold
熟	金一封	キンイップウ	gift of money (in an envelope)
	金貨	キンカ	gold coin/currency
	金科玉条	キンカギョクジョウ	golden rule
	金言	キンゲン	wise saying; watchword
	金庫	キンコ	safe
	金鉱	キンコウ	gold mine
	金策	キンサク	raising money; getting a loan —*vi.* raise money; get a loan
	金星	キンセイ	the planet Venus
	金銭	キンセン	money
	金属	キンゾク	metal; metallic
	金箔	キンパク	gold leaf; gilt
	金髪	キンパツ	blonde/fair hair
	金品	キンピン	money and other valuables
	金曜日	キンヨウび	Friday
	金利	キンリ	interest
	金色	コンジキ	gold color
訓	金	かね	metal; money
	金目	かねめ	(monetary) value
	金持ち	かねもち	rich; having a lot of money
	金	かな	(prefix) metal; money
	金具	かなグ	metal fittings; metallic parts
¥	金塊	キンカイ	gold ingot/bullion
	金額	キンガク	amount/sum of money
	金為替	キンかわせ	gold exchange
	金地金	キンジがね	gold bullion
	金銭債権	キンセンサイケン	money alarm
	金銭出納	キンセンスイトウ	receipts and expenses
	金融	キンユウ	finance
	金融機関	キンユウキカン	financial institution
	金融恐慌	キンユウキョウコウ	financial crisis

金長門隶隹雨青非斉食

金融公庫	キンユウコウコ	financial cooperation
金融債	キンユウサイ	bank debenture
金融資産	キンユウシサン	financial asset/portfolio
金融市場	キンユウシジョウ	financial market; money and capital market
金融政策	キンユウセイサク	monetary policy
金融操作	キンユウソウサ	monetary operation
金融調節	キンユウチョウセツ	monetary and credit control
金融手形	キンユウてがた	bill; note for finance
金利	キンリ	interest
金利機構	キンリキコウ	interest rate mechanism
金利差	キンリサ	interest rate discrepancy (spread)
金利裁定取引	キンリサイテイとりひき	interest arbitrage (transaction)

1809

 ⑩ ノ 𠆢 𠂤 𠂤 午 𡨄 余 金 金 針

音	針	シン	needle
熟	針小棒大	シンショウボウダイ	exaggeration; making a mountain out of a mole hill
	針葉樹	シンヨウジュ	coniferous tree
	針路	シンロ	course
訓	針	はり	needle; hook; pin
	針金	はりがね	wire
	針仕事	はりシごと	needlework

1810

 ⑪ ノ 𠆢 𠂤 𠂤 午 𡨄 余 金 釘 釣 釣

音	釣	チョウ	fish; angle
熟	釣魚	チョウギョ	angling; fishing
訓	釣り	つり	angling; fishing; change (from shopping, etc.)
	釣り合い	つりあい	balance; equilibrium; poise
	釣り上げる	つりあげる	*vt.* fish/hook up; raise by manipulation
	釣り糸	つりいと	fishing line
	釣鐘	つりがね	hanging bell
	釣り竿	つりざお	fishing rod
	釣り銭	つりセン	change (from shopping, etc.)
	釣り道具	つりドウグ	fishing tackle
	釣り針	つりばり	fishing hook

| 釣り堀 | つりぼり | fishpond |
| 釣る | つる | ***vt***. fish; angle; decoy; allure; entice |

1811

鈍 ⑫ ノ ヽ ㇒ ㇒ 牛 乍 余 金 釒 鈢 鈢 鈍

音	鈍	ドン	dull
熟	鈍角	ドンカク	***math***. obtuse angle
	鈍感	ドンカン	insensible; insensitive; thick-skinned; obtuse
	鈍器	ドンキ	blunt weapon
	鈍痛	ドンツウ	dull pain
訓	鈍い	にぶい	dull; dim; thick; dense
	鈍る	にぶる	***vi***. grow dull/dim

1812

鉛 ⑬ ノ ヽ ㇒ ㇒ 牛 余 金 釒 釢 釢 鉛 鉛

音	鉛	エン	lead (metal)
熟	鉛管	エンカン	lead pipe; plumbing
	鉛直線	エンチョクセン	plumb/vertical line
	鉛筆	エンピツ	pencil
訓	鉛	なまり	lead

1813

鉱 ⑬ ノ ヽ ㇒ ㇒ 牛 余 金 釒 釪 鉱 鉱 鉱

音	鉱	コウ	ore; mineral; mine
熟	鉱業	コウギョウ	the mining industry; mining
	鉱区	コウク	mining region
	鉱山	コウザン	mine
	鉱床	コウショウ	mineral deposit
	鉱石	コウセキ	ore; mineral; crystal
	鉱泉	コウセン	mineral spring/water; spring
	鉱毒	コウドク	mineral/copper poisoning
	鉱夫	コウフ	miner
	鉱物	コウブツ	mineral
	鉱脈	コウミャク	vein of ore/mineral; ore/mineral deposit

1814 鉄 ⑬　ノ ハ ヒ 午 午 金 金 釒 釠 鉞 鉄 鉄

音	鉄	テツ	iron; steel
熟	鉄火	テッカ	red-hot iron; gunfire; swords and guns; cuisine that uses raw tuna and *wasabi*
	鉄管	テッカン	iron pipe/tube
	鉄器	テッキ	ironware; hardware; ironmongery
	鉄橋	テッキョウ	iron bridge
	鉄筋コンクリート	テッキンコンクリート	reinforced concrete
	鉄拳	テッケン	clenched fist
	鉄工	テッコウ	ironworker; blacksmith
	鉄鉱	テッコウ	iron ore
	鉄鋼	テッコウ	steel
	鉄格子	テツゴウシ	iron-barred window
	鉄骨	テッコツ	steel frame
	鉄材	テツザイ	iron material
	鉄索	テッサク	iron cable
	鉄条網	テツジョウモウ	wire entanglements
	鉄製	テッセイ	made of steel/iron
	鉄線	テッセン	steel wire
	鉄則	テッソク	iron rule
	鉄塔	テットウ	steel tower; pylon
	鉄道	テツドウ	railroad; railway
	鉄板	テッパン	hot plate
	鉄板焼	テッパンやき	*teppanyaki* (meat and vegetables grilled on a hot plate)
	鉄瓶	テツビン	iron kettle
	鉄分	テツブン	iron content
	鉄壁	テッペキ	iron wall
	鉄砲	テッポウ	gun; firearms
	鉄砲玉	テッポウだま	bullet; gunshot; bull's-eye; lost person
	鉄面皮	テツメンピ	impudence; brazeness; shamelessness

1815 鉢 ⑬　ノ ハ ヒ 午 午 金 金 釒 釙 鉢 鉢

音	鉢	ハチ （ハツ）	bowl; pot; flower pot

金
長
門
隷
佳
雨
青
非
斉
食

熟 鉢植え　ハチうえ　potted/house plant
　　鉢巻き　ハチまき　headband; hatband; cotton cloth tied around the head

1816

鈴 ⑬　ノ 𠆢 𠆢 𠂉 牟 余 金 釒 釛 鈴 鈴 鈴

音	鈴	リン	bell
		レイ	bell
訓	鈴	すず	bell
	鈴虫	すずむし	bell-ring insect
	鈴蘭	すずラン	lily of the valley

1817

銀 ⑭　𠆢 𠂉 𠂉 牟 余 金 釒 釕 鈤 鈤 鈤 銀

音	銀	ギン	silver; money; banking
熟	銀貨	ギンカ	silver coinage
	銀河	ギンガ	Milky Way
	銀行	ギンコウ	bank
	銀製	ギンセイ	made from silver; silverware
	銀世界	ギンセカイ	silver world; snow-covered scenery
	銀幕	ギンマク	silver screen
¥	銀行界	ギンコウカイ	banking community
	銀行勘定	ギンコウカンジョウ	bank account
	銀行準備金	ギンコウジュンビキン	bank reserves

1818

銃 ⑭　𠆢 𠂉 𠂉 牟 余 金 金' 鈁 鈝 鈝 鉖 銃

音	銃	ジュウ	gun
熟	銃口	ジュウコウ	muzzle of a gun
	銃殺	ジュウサツ	death by shooting; execution by firing squad —*v.* shoot to death
	銃声	ジュウセイ	shot; report of a gun
	銃弾	ジュウダン	bullet
	銃砲	ジュウホウ	firearms

1819

銭 ⑭　ハ　ト　ヒ　牟　釒　金　釒　釒　釒　銕　銭　銭

音	銭	セン	coin
熟	銭湯	セントウ	bathhouse
訓	銭	ぜに	coin; change

1820

銑 ⑭　ハ　ト　ヒ　牟　釒　金　釒　釒　釟　鉒　鉒　銑

| 音 | 銑 | セン | pig iron |
| 熟 | 銑鉄 | センテツ | pig iron |

1821

銅 ⑭　ハ　ト　ヒ　牟　釒　金　釘　釦　釦　銅　銅　銅

音	銅	ドウ	copper
熟	銅貨	ドウカ	copper coin
	銅器	ドウキ	copper utensil; copperware
	銅山	ドウザン	copper mine
	銅像	ドウゾウ	bronze statue
	銅鐸	ドウタク	*dōtaku* (flat bell-like instrument of the Yayoi period)
	銅版	ドウバン	copperplate

1822

銘 ⑭　ハ　ト　ヒ　牟　釒　金　釒　釤　釤　鉻　銘　銘

音	銘	メイ	signature; inscription; name
熟	銘菓	メイカ	quality-brand cakes
	銘記	メイキ	bearing in mind —*v*. bear in mind
	銘酒	メイシュ	fine saké
	銘仙	メイセン	common silk products
	銘木	メイボク	high quality wood
	銘々	メイメイ	each; apiece
¥	銘柄	メイがら	name; issue; brand

金長門隶佳雨青非斉食

1823

鋭 ⑮　ノ　ヒ　ヒ　牟　牟　金　金'　釗'　釟　鈗　鋭

音	鋭	エイ	sharp
熟	鋭角	エイカク	acute angle
	鋭敏	エイビン	sharp-wits; keenness
	鋭利	エイリ	sharp-edged; keen; acute
訓	鋭い	するどい	sharp; acute; keen

1824

鋳 ⑮　ノ　ヒ　ヒ　牟　牟　金　金一　釒一　鋳　鋳　鋳

音	鋳	チュウ	cast
熟	鋳造	チュウゾウ	casting; founding; minting —v. cast; found; mint; coin
訓	鋳る	いる	vt. cast; found; mint
	鋳型	いがた	mold
	鋳物	いもの	casting

1825

鋼 ⑯　ノ　ヒ　ヒ　牟　牟　金　釘　釗　鋼　鋼　鋼

音	鋼	コウ	steel
熟	鋼管	コウカン	steel tubing
	鋼材	コウザイ	steel materials; structural/rolled steel
	鋼鉄	コウテツ	steel
訓	鋼	はがね	steel

1826

錯 ⑯　ノ　ヒ　ヒ　牟　牟　金　金一　釙　錯　錯　錯

音	錯	サク	error; mistake; mix; confuse
熟	錯乱	サクラン	confusion; mix-up —vi. be confused; be mixed-up
	錯覚	サッカク	illusion; hallucination; mistake —vi. have an illusion; hallucinate; make a mistake

1827 錠 ⑯

ハ ケ ヶ 牟 余 金 釦 釦 錠 錠 錠 錠

音	錠	ジョウ	lock
熟	錠剤	ジョウザイ	tablet; pill
	錠前	ジョウまえ	lock

1828 錘 ⑯

ハ ケ ヶ 牟 余 金 針 鈝 鉌 鉌 錘 錘

音	錘	スイ	spindle; weight
訓	錘	つむ	spindle

1829 錬 ⑯

ハ ケ ヶ 牟 余 金 針 釦 鉓 鍊 鍊 錬

音	錬	レン	forge; temper; refine
熟	錬金術	レンキンジュツ	alchemy
	錬成	レンセイ	training —*v*. train
	錬鉄	レンテツ	wrought iron
訓	錬る	ねる	*vi*. forge; temper; refine

1830 録 ⑯

ハ ケ ヶ 牟 余 金 針 鈤 鈩 鈩 録 録

音	録	ロク	record; catalog
熟	録音	ロクオン	sound recording —*v*. make a sound recording
	録画	ロクガ	videotape recording —*v*. record on videotape
訓	*録る	とる	*vt*. record

1831 鍛 ⑰

ハ ヶ 牟 余 金 針 釦 鉈 鋝 鋝 鋝 鍛

音	鍛	タン	forge; temper; train; drill
熟	鍛練	タンレン	forging; temper; training; drilling —*v*. forge; temper; train; drill

訓　鍛える　　きたえる　　**vt**. forge; temper; drill; train; cultivate

1832

鎖 ⑱　　ノ　ム　牟　釒　金　釒'　釒''　釒肖　鎖　鎖　鎖　鎖

音　鎖　　　サ　　　　chain; lock; close

熟　鎖国　　サコク　　national isolation; seclusion —**vi**. close up
　　　　　　　　　　　a country to the outside world

　　鎖骨　　サコツ　　**med**. collarbone; clavicle

訓　鎖　　　くさり　　chain

1833

鎮 ⑱　　ノ　ム　牟　釒　金　釒'　釒''　鎮　鎮　鎮　鎮　鎮

音　鎮　　　チン　　　suppress

熟　鎮圧　　チンアツ　suppression; repression; subjugation
　　　　　　　　　　　—**v**. suppress; repress; subjugate

　　鎮火　　チンカ　　fire extinguishing —**v**. be put out/extinguished

　　鎮座　　チンザ　　enshrinement —**vi**. be enshrined

　　鎮静　　チンセイ　calm; quiet; tranquillity —**v**. become calm;
　　　　　　　　　　　restore quiet; subside; calm

　　鎮静剤　チンセイザイ　tranquilizer

　　鎮痛剤　チンツウザイ　painkiller

訓　鎮まる　しずまる　**vi**. become quiet; calm down; be supressed;
　　　　　　　　　　　be enshrined

　　鎮める　しずめる　**vt**. calm; quiet; still; supress; repress; quell

1834

鏡 ⑲　　ノ　ム　牟　釒　金　釒'　釒''　釒''　鏡　鏡　鏡　鏡

音　鏡　　　キョウ　　mirror; lens; spectacles; mirrorlike

熟　鏡台　　キョウダイ　dressing table; dresser

訓　鏡　　　かがみ　　mirror; looking glass

1835

鐘 ⑳　　ノ　ム　牟　釒　金　釒'　釒''　釒''　鐘　鐘　鐘　鐘

音　鐘　　　ショウ　　hanging bell

| 熟 | 鐘楼 | ショウロウ | belfry |
| 訓 | 鐘 | かね | bell |

1836

鑑 ㉓　丿　仝　牟　金　釦　釸　鈩　鉀　鑑　鑑　鑑　鑑

音	鑑	カン	model; mirror
熟	鑑札	カンサツ	license; certificate
	鑑識	カンシキ	identification; judgment
	鑑賞	カンショウ	appreciation —*v.* appreciate; enjoy
	鑑定	カンテイ	judgment; appraisal; estimation —*v.* judge; appraise; estimate; identify
	鑑別	カンベツ	discrimination; differentiation; judgment —*v.* discriminate; distinguish; differentiate
訓	※鑑み	かんがみ	mirror; model; paragon
	※鑑みる	かんがみる	*vt.* take into consideration

8　長　ながい　long

1837

長 ⑧　丨　厂　厂　E　E　E　長　長

音	長	チョウ	long; far; stretch; head; chief; headman; merit; strong point
熟	長じる	チョウじる	*vi.* grow up; be older; excel; be clever
	長音	チョウオン	long vowel/sound
	長官	チョウカン	director; president; administrator; head; chief
	長期	チョウキ	long period/term
	長距離	チョウキョリ	long distance
	長子	チョウシ	oldest son
	長者	チョウジャ	millionaire
	長寿	チョウジュ	long life; longevity
	長所	チョウショ	merit; strong point; forte
	長女	チョウジョ	oldest daughter
	長身	チョウシン	tall figure; great stature
	長針	チョウシン	the long/minute hand (of a clock)
	長蛇	チョウダ	long (queue)
	長大	チョウダイ	long and stout; huge

787

長短	チョウタン	relative length; merits and demerits
長調	チョウチョウ	major key (in music)
長男	チョウナン	oldest son; heir
長髪	チョウハツ	long hair
長編	チョウヘン	long novel/movie/poem
長方形	チョウホウケイ	*math.* rectangle; oblong
長命	チョウメイ	longevity; long life
長老	チョウロウ	senior; elder

訓

長い	ながい	long; lengthy; lanky
長さ	ながさ	length
長雨	ながあめ	long period of rain
長居	ながい	long stay/visit —*vi.* stay too long; make a long visit
長生き	ながいき	long life; longevity —*vi.* live long; enjoy longevity
長椅子	ながイス	sofa; couch
長靴	ながぐつ	boots
長続き	ながつづき	long lasting —*vi.* last long
長年	ながネン	long time; many years
長引く	ながびく	*vi.* be prolonged/protracted/delayed
長持ち	ながもち	durability; endurance —*vi.* endure; be durable; last long

¥

長期貸付金	チョウキかしつけキン	long-term loans
長期借入金	チョウキかりいれキン	long-term loans repayable
長期金利	チョウキキンリ	long-term rate of interest
長期公債	チョウキコウサイ	long-term government bond
長期信用銀行	チョウキシンヨウギンコウ	long-term credit bank
長期未払金	チョウキみはらいキン	long-term accounts payable

---

8 門 もんがまえ gate

1838

門⑧ 丨 冂 冂 冃 冃ヿ 門 門 門

音	門	モン	gate
熟	門衛	モンエイ	guard; gatekeeper
	門下	モンカ	one's disciple/pupil

門外漢	モンガイカン	outsider; layman
門限	モンゲン	curfew
門戸	モンコ	doorway
門札	モンサツ	name plate
門歯	モンシ	incisor; front teeth
門人	モンジン	pupil; disciple
門前	モンゼン	before the gate
門柱	モンチュウ	gatepost
門弟	モンテイ	disciple; pupil
門灯	モントウ	gate light
門番	モンバン	gatekeeper
門標	モンピョウ	name plate

訓
門	かど	gate; house
門口	かどぐち	front door; entrance
門出	かどで	departure —*v.* depart; set out

1839

閉 ⑪ 丨 冂 冂 冂 冂ˈ 門 門 門 門 閉 閉

音 閉 ヘイ close; shut; confine; end

熟
閉会	ヘイカイ	closing/adjournment (of a meeting) —*v.* close/adjourn a meeting
閉館	ヘイカン	closing (hall/building) —*v.* close (hall/building)
閉口	ヘイコウ	troublesome; confoundment —*vi.* be troubled/confounded by
閉鎖	ヘイサ	closing; closure; lockup —*v.* close; lock up
閉塞	ヘイソク	closing/covering up; blockade —*v.* close/cover up; blockade
閉廷	ヘイテイ	adjournment (of court) —*v.* adjourn court
閉店	ヘイテン	closing a shop (for the day) —*vi.* close the shop
閉幕	ヘイマク	falling of the curtain; end of a play —*vi.* curtain falls; play ends
閉門	ヘイモン	locking up the gate; house arrest (Edo period) —*vi.* lock up the gate; be confined to one's home

訓
閉まる	しまる	*vi.* be shut/closed/locked
閉める	しめる	*vt.* shut; close; lock
閉ざす	とざす	*vt.* close; shut; lock
閉じる	とじる	*vt.* close; shut; lock
閉じ込める	とじこめる	*vt.* shut in; confine
閉じこもる	とじこもる	*vi.* stay indoors; be confined to one's house

金
長
門
隷
佳
雨
青
非
斉
食

1840

開 ⑫

⌉ ⌈ ⌈ ⌈ ⌈ ⌈¹ ⌈⌉ ⌈⌉ ⌈⌉ ⌈⌉ ⌈⌉ 開 開

音	開	カイ	open; begin; civilize; unfold; expand; open up land; develop; reclaim
熟	開運	カイウン	improvement of one's fortune
	開演	カイエン	opening of a performance; raising of the curtain —*vi.* start a performance; raise the curtain
	開化	カイカ	Westernization; becoming civilized —*vi.* become Westernized/civilized
	開花	カイカ	fluorescence; bloom; flourishing —*vi.* flower; bloom; flourish
	開会	カイカイ	opening of a meeting —*v.* open/begin a meeting
	開口	カイコウ	opening; aperture
	開校	カイコウ	opening of a new school —*v.* open a new school
	開港	カイコウ	opening of a port to (foreign trade) —*v.* open a port (to foreign trade)
	開国	カイコク	opening of a country to the world; foundation of a country —*v.* open up a country to the world; found a nation
	開墾	カイコン	reclamation (of waste land) —*v.* reclaim waste land; bring under cultivation
	開催	カイサイ	holding (a meeting/exhibition) —*v.* hold (a meeting); open (an exhibition)
	開始	カイシ	beginning; start; commencement —*v.* begin; start; commence
	開場	カイジョウ	opening (of the doors to a hall, etc.) —*vi.* open; open the doors (to a hall, etc.)
	開設	カイセツ	opening; establishment; setting up —*v.* open; establish; set up
	開戦	カイセン	outbreak of war; commencement of hostilities —*vi.* make/wage war
	開拓	カイタク	reclamation and development; clearing; exploitation —*v.* reclaim; improve; develop; clear; exploit; pioneer
	開通	カイツウ	opening up to traffic —*v.* open up to traffic
	開発	カイハツ	development; exploitation —*v.* develop; open up; exploit
	開票	カイヒョウ	ballot counting —*v.* count votes; open ballot boxes
	開封	カイフウ	unsealing/opening a letter —*v.* unseal/open a letter
	開閉	カイヘイ	opening and shutting —*v.* open and shut
	開放	カイホウ	opening —*v.* open; throw open
	開門	カイモン	opening of a gate —*vi.* open a gate

訓	開く	あく	*vi*. open
	開ける	あける	*vt*. open; begin; bore (a hole, etc.)
	開く	ひらく	*v*. open; solve; start
	開ける	ひらける	*vi*. develop; be open; be civilized
¥	開発銀行	カイハツギンコウ	development bank

1841

間 ⑫　丨 冂 冂 冃 冃 門 門 門 門 門 間 間 間

音	間	カン	interval; between; gap; opportunity
		ケン	between; middle
熟	間一髪	カンイッパツ	hair's breadth
	間隔	カンカク	interval; space; distance
	間隙	カンゲキ	gap; split; discord
	間食	カンショク	eating between meals; snack —*vi*. eat between meals
	間接	カンセツ	indirectness
	間接的	カンセツテキ	indirect
	間断	カンダン	pause; interval
訓	間	あいだ	interval; middle; gap
	間	ま	space; leisure; room; pause; interval; (counter for rooms)
	間口	まぐち	front; facade; width of a building, etc.
	間近	まぢか	nearby; close at hand
	間違う	まちがう	*v*. make a mistake
	間取り	まどり	plan of a house; room arrangement
	間引き	まびき	thinning out of plants
¥	間接税	カンセツゼイ	indirect (consumption) tax
	間接発行	カンセツハッコウ	offer for sale

1842

閑 ⑫　丨 冂 冂 冃 冃 門 門 門 閂 閑 閑 閑

音	閑	カン	quiet; leisure
熟	閑居	カンキョ	secluded residence; quiet life —*vi*. live in seclusion/retirement
	閑散	カンサン	leisure; dullness; slackness; inactivity
	閑寂	カンジャク	quietness; tranquillity
	閑静	カンセイ	quietness; tranquillity
訓	※閑か	しずか	quiet; tranquil; peaceful; leisurely; free

1843

閣 ⑭ 丨 冂 冂 冂 冂' 門 門 門 閂 閃 閉 閣 閣

音	閣	カク	Cabinet; tower
熟	閣議	カクギ	Cabinet meeting/council
	閣僚	カクリョウ	member of the Cabinet
	閣僚理事会 (閣僚理)	カクリョウリジカイ (カクリョウリ)	ministerial/Cabinet committee
	閣下	カッカ	Your Excellency

1844

関 ⑭ 丨 冂 冂 冂' 門 門 門 門 閅 閄 関 関

音	関	カン	barrier; bolt
熟	関する	カンする	*vi*. be related/connected to
	関係	カンケイ	relation; connection; relationship —*vi*. be related/connected; be involved in a relationship
	関西	カンサイ	Kansai district
	関心	カンシン	concern; interest
	関数	カンスウ	*math*. function
	関節	カンセツ	joint of the body
	関知	カンチ	concern —*vi*. be concerned with
	関東	カントウ	Kanto district
	関白	カンパク	*hist*. *Kampaku* (chancellor or chief adviser to the emperor)
	関門	カンモン	gateway; gate
	関与	カンヨ	participation —*vi*. participate
	関連	カンレン	involvement; correlation; connection; reference —*vi*. be connected/associated/correlated
訓	関	せき	checkpoint; barrier
	関所	せきショ	checkpoint; barrier
	関取	せきとり	high-ranking sumo wrestler
	※関わる	かかわる	*vi*. be related to; be connected with; have to do with
¥	関係会社	カンケイガイシャ	associated/affiliated company
	関税	カンゼイ	customs; tariff
	関税障壁	カンゼイショウヘキ	tariff barrier
	関連会社	カンレンガイシャ	affiliate company

1845

閥 ⑭ 丨 厂 厂 厂' 門 門 門 門 閂 閥 閥 閥

音 閥　　バツ　　　　lineage; clique

1846

閲 ⑮ 丨 厂 厂 厂' 門 門 門 門 閂 問 閲 閲

音 閲　　エツ　　　　inspection; review; revision

熟 閲読　　エツドク　　reading; perusal —*v.* read; peruse

閲兵　　エッペイ　　inspection of the troops; parade
—*v.* inspect/review the troops

閲覧　　エツラン　　reading; perusal —*v.* read; persue

閲覧室　エツランシツ reading room

1847

闘 ⑱ 丨 厂 厂 厂' 門 門 門 門 閂 閂 闘 闘

音 闘　　トウ　　　　fight

熟 闘牛　　トウギュウ　bullfight; bullfighting

闘鶏　　トウケイ　　cockfighting

闘士　　トウシ　　　fighter; champion

闘志　　トウシ　　　fight; morale; fighting spirit

闘争　　トウソウ　　struggle; fight; combat —*vi.* fight; put up
a struggle

闘病　　トウビョウ　fight against a disease

訓 闘う　　たたかう　　*vi.* fight; struggle; battle

---

8 隷　れいづくり　servant; slave

1848

隷 ⑯ 一 十 土 圭 圭 隶 隶 隶 隶 隶 隷 隷

音 隷　　レイ　　　　obey; follow; servant; criminal

熟 隷従　　レイジュウ　subordination (to a lord); following orders
—*vi.* be subordinate (to a lord); follow orders

| 隷書 | レイショ | angular-style of writing Chinese characters |
| 隷属 | レイゾク | subordination —*vi*. be subordinate to |

---

8 隹 ふるとり old bird

1849
隻 ⑩ ノ イ イ 疒 什 仹 隹 隹 隼 隻

| 音 | 隻 | セキ | single; (counter for ships) |
| 熟 | 隻手 | セキシュ | one arm |

1850
雇 ⑫ 一 ㇐ ㇈ 戸 戸 戸 雇 雇 雇 雇 雇 雇

音	雇	コ	hire; employ; employment; employee
訓	雇い	やとい	employment; hiring
	雇い人	やといニン	employee
	雇い主	やといぬし	employer
	雇う	やとう	*vt*. employ; engage; hire
¥	雇用	コヨウ	employment —*v*. employ; engage; hire; take on
	雇用者	コヨウシャ	employer

1851
集 ⑫ ノ イ イ 疒 什 仹 隹 隹 隼 隼 集 集

音	集	シュウ	assemble; collect; gather
熟	集荷	シュウカ	cargo collection —*v*. collect cargo
	集会	シュウカイ	meeting; assembly; gathering
	集計	シュウケイ	total; sum; aggregate —*v*. total; sum; collect together
	集結	シュウケツ	collecting things in one place; gathering in one place —*v*. mass; gather; assemble
	集合	シュウゴウ	meeting; gathering; assembly *math*. set —*v*. meet; gather; assemble
	集札	シュウサツ	ticket collection —*v*. collect tickets
	集散	シュウサン	collecting and distribution —*v*. meet and part; collect and distribute
	集積	シュウセキ	accumulation; pile —*v*. accumulate; pile up

集大成	シュウタイセイ	collection; compilation —v. compile (various texts) into one book
集団	シュウダン	group; body
集中	シュウチュウ	concentration —v. center on; concentrate
集配	シュウハイ	collection and delivery —v. collect and deliver
集約	シュウヤク	putting/collecting together —v. put together
集落	シュウラク	village **bio**. colony
集録	シュウロク	compilation of written records —v. compile

訓

集まり	あつまり	meeting; gathering; party; congregation; crowd; attendance
集まる	あつまる	v. gather come; get together; mass; be collected/concentrated
集める	あつめる	vt. gather; get together; collect; accumulate; attract; draw together
集い	つどい	gathering; meeting; get-together
集う	つどう	vi. gather; come; get together; amass

¥

| 集金 | シュウキン | collection of money —v. collect money/bills |
| 集中投資 | シュウチュウトウシ | concentrated investment |

1852

雄 ⑫ 一 ナ ナ ナ 左 右 右 雄 雄 雄 雄

音	雄	ユウ	male; hero; great leader; superiority
熟	雄姿	ユウシ	gallant figure
	雄大	ユウダイ	magnificent; majestic; grand; sublime
	雄飛	ユウヒ	great achievement —vi. do something great
	雄弁	ユウベン	oratory; eloquence
訓	雄	お	male
	雄	おす	male
	雄花	おばな	male flower

1853

雅 ⑬ 一 ー 二 ヲ 牙 牙 邪 邪 邪 雅 雅

音	雅	ガ	elegance
熟	雅楽	ガガク	*gagaku* (Japanese ceremonial court music)
	雅号	ガゴウ	pen name; pseudonym
	雅趣	ガシュ	elegance; tastefulness
訓	※雅やか	みやびやか	elegant; graceful; refined

金長門隷佳雨青非斉食 ●

金長門隷佳雨青非斉食

1854

雌 ⑭　｜　ｆ　ｆ　此　此　此　此′　此″　此″′　此″″　雌

音	雌	シ	female
熟	雌伏	シフク	inactivity; dormancy —*vi.* remain inactive; lie dormant
	雌雄	シユウ	male and female; superior or inferior
訓	雌	め	female
	雌	めす	female
	雌花	めばな	female flower

1855

雑 ⑭　ノ　九　丸　卆　卆　杂　杂′　杂″　杂″′　雑′　雑

音	雑	ザツ	miscellaneous; sloppy; slipshod; messy
		ゾウ	miscellany; various
熟	雑役	ザツエキ	odd jobs; chores
	雑音	ザツオン	noise; static; interference (on radio, etc.)
	雑貨	ザッカ	sundry/miscellaneous goods; general merchandise; sundries
	雑貨屋	ザッカや	general store
	雑学	ザツガク	general knowledge
	雑感	ザッカン	miscellaneous thoughts; casual impressions
	雑記帳	ザッキチョウ	notebook
	雑穀	ザッコク	miscellaneous cereals (excluding rice and wheat)
	雑誌	ザッシ	magazine; journal; periodical
	雑事	ザツジ	household chores; routine work
	雑種	ザッシュ	cross; hybrid; mongrel
	雑食性	ザッショクセイ	omnivorous
	雑然	ザツゼン	untidy; messy; in disorder
	雑草	ザッソウ	weeds
	雑多	ザッタ	miscellaneous
	雑談	ザツダン	chitchat; chat; light conversation; small talk —*vi.* chitchat; chat
	雑踏	ザットウ	congestion; crowd; throng
	雑念	ザツネン	idle thoughts
	雑務	ザツム	odd duties; routine; trivial tasks
	雑用	ザツヨウ	odd business; various chores
	雑木林	ゾウきばやし	growth of trees; copse; coppice

雑巾	ゾウキン	duster; dust/floor cloth
雑炊	ゾウスイ	*zōsui* (porridge of rice and vegetables)
雑煮	ゾウに	*zōni* (soup containing rice cakes)

1856

難 ⑱ 　一　艹　艹　苎　苎　莒　莫　莫　莂　斳　斳　難

音	難	ナン	difficult
熟	難易	ナンイ	hardness; difficulty
	難解	ナンカイ	difficult to understand; unintelligible
	難関	ナンカン	barrier; obstacle; hurdle; difficult situation
	難儀	ナンギ	hardship; difficulty; distress; misery; affliction; trial —*vi*. be in difficulties; have trouble; come to grief
	難行苦行	ナンギョウクギョウ	penance; asceticism; religious austerities
	難局	ナンキョク	difficult situation; crisis; deadlock
	難曲	ナンキョク	challenging piece of music
	難癖	ナンくせ	fault; blemish; faultfinding
	難航	ナンコウ	stormy voyage; rough passage —*vi*. have a difficult sailing/rough passage
	難産	ナンザン	hard labor; complicated birth —*vi*. have a difficult/complicated delivery
	難事	ナンジ	difficult matter; hard task; tough job
	難渋	ナンジュウ	hardship; suffering; distress; misery; sorrow —*vi*. suffer; be in trouble/distress
	難所	ナンショ	dangerous spot; place hard to pass
	難色	ナンショク	disapproval; reluctance; unwillingness
	難船	ナンセン	shipwreck; wreck; ship in distress —*vi*. be shipwrecked; be wrecked
	難題	ナンダイ	unreasonable terms; unfair proposal
	難聴	ナンチョウ	hard of hearing
	難点	ナンテン	crux; difficult point; weakness; fault; flaw
	難無く	ナンなく	without difficulty; with ease
	難破	ナンパ	shipwreck
	難病	ナンビョウ	serious/incurable disease
	難物	ナンブツ	bothersome object/person
	難民	ナンミン	sufferers; refugees
	難問	ナンモン	puzzling question; question that is hard to answer
	難路	ナンロ	hard pass; rough road
訓	難い	かたい	hard; difficult
	難しい	むずかしい	hard; difficult; troublesome; problematic

797

1857

離 ⑱　一　ナ　ナ　卤　卤　卤　离　离　离　斎　離　離

音	離	リ	separate; leave
熟	離縁	リエン	divorce; disowning —v. divorce; disown
	離婚	リコン	divorce —vi. divorce; get a divorce
	離散	リサン	dispersion; scattering —vi. disperse; scatter
	離職	リショク	quitting/losing one's job —vi. quit/lose one's job
	離島	リトウ	outlying island —vi. lie out
	離乳	リニュウ	weaning —vi. wean
	離別	リベツ	separation; divorce —vi. separate; divorce
	離陸	リリク	take-off (of a plane) —vi. take off
訓	離す	はなす	vt. separate; keep apart
	離れる	はなれる	vi. separate; leave
	離れ離れ	はなればなれ	separated; scattered; dispersed

8　雨　あめ／あめかんむり　rain

1858

雨 ⑧　一　厂　闩　币　币　雨　雨　雨

音	雨	ウ	rain
熟	雨季	ウキ	rainy season
	雨後	ウゴ	after the rain
	雨天	ウテン	rainy weather; wet day
	雨量	ウリョウ	rainfall; rain; precipitation
	雨量計	ウリョウケイ	rain gauge
訓	雨	あめ	rain
	雨上がり	あめあがり	after the rain
	雨	あま	(prefix) rain; rainy
	雨合羽	あまガッパ	raincoat
	雨具	あまグ	rainwear
	雨靴	あまぐつ	rain shoes; galoshes
	雨雲	あまぐも	rain cloud
	雨戸	あまど	sliding door; shutter
	雨漏り	あまもり	leak (in the roof)

| 雨宿り | あまやどり | sheltering from the rain —*vi.* take shelter from the rain; get out of the rain |

1859

一 ⼂ 一 一 一 一 一 一 一 一 一

⑪

音	雪	セツ	snow
熟	雪害	セツガイ	snow damage
	雪渓	セッケイ	snow-filled valley
	雪原	セツゲン	snowfield; expanse of snow
	雪辱	セツジョク	revenge; vindication; clearing one's name —*vi.* have revenge; vindicate/clear one's name
	雪中	セッチュウ	in/through the snow
	雪盲	セツモウ	snow blindness
訓	雪	ゆき	snow
	雪男	ゆきおとこ	abominable snowman; yeti
	雪女	ゆきおんな	snow fairy
	雪合戦	ゆきガッセン	snowball fight
	雪達磨	ゆきだるま	snowman
	雪解け	ゆきどけ	thawing; solution of a problem —*v.* thaw; solve a problem
※	雪崩	なだれ	snowslide

1860

一 ⼂ 一 一 一 一 一 一 一 雲 雲 雲

⑫

音	雲	ウン	cloud
熟	雲海	ウンカイ	sea of clouds
	雲泥の差	ウンデイのサ	wide difference
	雲母	ウンモ	mica
	雲量	ウンリョウ	cloudiness; amount of cloud
訓	雲	くも	cloud
	雲行き	くもゆき	sky; weather; circumstances; state of affairs

1861

雰

一 ⼂ 一 一 一 一 一 一 雰 雰 雰 雰

⑫

| 音 | 雰 | フン | fog |
| 熟 | 雰囲気 | フンイキ | atmosphere; ambience |

金
長
門
隶
佳
● 雨
青
非
斉
食

1862

電 ⑬　一　厂　厂　� 〒　雨 雨 雨 雷 雷 電

音	電	デン	lightning; electricity
熟	電圧	デンアツ	voltage; tension; electric pressure
	電化	デンカ	electrification —*v.* electrify; install electricity
	電荷	デンカ	electric charge
	電界	デンカイ	electric field
	電解	デンカイ	electrolysis —*v.* electrolyze
	電気	デンキ	electricity; electric light
	電球	デンキュウ	electric light bulb
	電極	デンキョク	electrode
	電撃	デンゲキ	electric shock
	電源	デンゲン	source of electricity; power/electric source
	電工	デンコウ	electrician
	電光	デンコウ	electric light; lightning
	電子	デンシ	electron
	電子工学	デンシコウガク	electronics
	電磁気	デンジキ	electromagnetism
	電磁石	デンジシャク	electromagnet
	電磁場	デンジば	electromagnetic field
	電車	デンシャ	train
	電信	デンシン	telegraph; telegram; wire; cable
	電信柱	デンシンばしら	telegraph pole
	電線	デンセン	electric wire/cable; telegraph wire
	電送	デンソウ	electrical transmission —*v.* telegraph; wire; cable
	電池	デンチ	battery; electric cell
	電柱	デンチュウ	utility/telephone/telegraph pole
	電灯	デントウ	electric light
	電動	デンドウ	electromotion
	電動機	デンドウキ	electric motor
	電熱	デンネツ	electric heat
	電波	デンパ	electric/radio wave
	電文	デンブン	telegram
	電報	デンポウ	telegram; wire
	電離層	デンリソウ	ionosphere
	電流	デンリュウ	electric current
	電流計	デンリュウケイ	galvanometer
	電力	デンリョク	electric power; electricity

電話	デンワ	telephone
電話局	デンワキョク	telephone office
電話線	デンワセン	telephone wire
電話帳	デンワチョウ	telephone directory
電話番号	デンワバンゴウ	telephone number
訓 ※電	いなずま	flash of lightning

1863

雷 ⑬　一 丨 冂 币 币 雨 雨 雨 雷 雷 雷 雷

音	雷	ライ	thunder
熟	雷雨	ライウ	thunderstorm
	雷雲	ライウン	thunder cloud
	雷撃	ライゲキ	torpedo attack —*v.* torpedo (an enemy ship)
	雷同	ライドウ	agreeing blindly —*vi.* agree without thinking for oneself
	雷名	ライメイ	illustrious name
	雷鳴	ライメイ	thunder
訓	雷	かみなり	thunder

1864

零 ⑬　一 丨 冂 币 币 雨 雨 零 零 零 零 零

音	零	レイ	zero
熟	零下	レイカ	below zero; subzero
	零細	レイサイ	small; meager
	零時	レイジ	12 : 00 (noon or midnight)
	零落	レイラク	reduced circumstances; ruin —*v.* be ruined; fall to a low position; go down in the world
訓	※零す	こぼす	*vt.* spill
	※零れる	こぼれる	*vi.* spill; be split

1865

需 ⑭　一 丨 冂 币 币 雨 雨 雪 雪 需 需 需

音	需	ジュ	demand
¥	需給	ジュキュウ	supply and demand
	需給関係	ジュキュウカンケイ	relation of supply and demand
	需要	ジュヨウ	demand

金長門隶佳
● 雨青非斉食

1866

震 ⑮

一 ア 帀 帀 雨 雨 严 严 霏 霏 震 震

音	震	シン	quake
熟	震央	シンオウ	seismic center; epicenter
	震源地	シンゲンチ	epicenter
	震災	シンサイ	earthquake disaster
	震度	シンド	seismic; intensity
	震動	シンドウ	shock; quake —v. shake; quake
訓	震う	ふるう	*vi.* shiver; tremble; shake; vibrate; quiver; shudder
	震える	ふるえる	*vi.* shiver; tremble; shake; vibrate; quiver; shudder

1867

霊 ⑮

一 ア 帀 帀 雨 雨 雨 雪 雫 霊 霊 霊

音	霊	レイ	spirit; soul
		リョウ	spirit; soul
熟	霊安室	レイアンシツ	morgue
	霊域	レイイキ	sacred ground
	霊園	レイエン	cemetery
	霊界	レイカイ	the spirit world
	霊感	レイカン	inspiration; extra-sensory perception of the supernatural
	霊柩	レイキュウ	coffin; casket
	霊柩車	レイキュウシャ	hearse
	霊験	レイゲン	miracle; wonder-working
	霊魂	レイコン	spirit; soul
	霊山	レイザン	sacred mountain
	霊場	レイジョウ	sacred place; hallowed ground
	霊前	レイゼン	before a spirit
	霊地	レイチ	holy place; hallowed ground
	霊長	レイチョウ	crown of creation; mankind
	霊長類	レイチョウルイ	primates
	霊的	レイテキ	spiritual
	霊媒	レイバイ	spiritualist medium
	霊妙	レイミョウ	miraculous; mysterious
訓	*霊	たま	soul; spirit

1868

霜 ⑰　一　一　一　一　一　一　一　一　一　一　一　霜　霜　霜　霜

音	霜	ソウ	frost; years
熟	霜害	ソウガイ	frost damage
訓	霜	しも	frost
	霜柱	しもばしら	frost/ice columns
	霜焼け	しもやけ	frostbite

1869

霧 ⑲　一　一　一　一　一　一　一　一　一　一　一　霧　霧　霧

音	霧	ム	mist; fog
熟	霧散	ムサン	dissipation; vanishing —*vi.* dissipate; vanish
	霧中	ムチュウ	in the fog
	霧笛	ムテキ	foghorn
訓	霧	きり	fog; mist
	霧雨	きりさめ	misty rain; drizzle

1870

露 ㉑　一　一　一　一　一　一　一　一　一　一　一　霰　霰　露

音	露	ロ	dew; exposure; Russia
		（ロウ）	open; public
熟	露営	ロエイ	camping out —*v.* camp out in the open
	露見	ロケン	exposure; disclosure —*vi.* come to light; be found out
	露光	ロコウ	exposure (in photograpy)
	露骨	ロコツ	frank; conspicuous; open
	露地	ロジ	bare ground
	露出	ロシュツ	exposure (also used for photography) —*v.* expose
	露台	ロダイ	balcony
	露呈	ロテイ	exposure; disclosure —*v.* expose; disclose
	露天	ロテン	open-air; outdoor
	露店	ロテン	street stall; vending booth
	露命	ロメイ	transitory life
訓	露	つゆ	dew

803

露知らず　つゆしらず　completely ignorant
※露　　　　あらわ　　　open; public; frank

---

8 青　おあ／あおへん　blue; green

1871

青 ⑧　一　十　キ　主　青　青　青　青

| 音 | 青 | セイ
（ショウ） | blue; green; young; immature |

熟	青果	セイカ	fruit and vegetables; fresh produce
	青春	セイシュン	youth
	青少年	セイショウネン	young people
	青銅	セイドウ	bronze
	青年	セイネン	youth; young man

訓	青	あお	blue; azure; green
	青い	あおい	blue; azure; green; pale (face)
	青々	あおあお	deep blue; lush green; verdant
	青海原	あおうなばら	wide blue sea
	青写真	あおジャシン	blueprint
	青白い	あおじろい	pale; pallid
	青空	あおぞら	blue sky
	青空市場	あおぞらいちば	open-air market
	青二才	あおニサイ	young and inexperienced fellow
	青葉	あおば	green leaves
	青物	あおもの	greens; vegetables
	青み	あおみ	blueness; greenness
	青む	あおむ	turn blue/green
	青ざめる	あおざめる	turn pale

| ¥ | 青田買い | あおたがい | buying rice before it is reaped *fig.* securing a thing ahead of time; recruitment before the employee graduates from university |

1872

静 ⑭　一　十　主　丰　青　青　青　靑　靗　静　静　静

| 音 | 静 | セイ
（ジョウ） | calm; quiet; peaceful; still |

熟	静脈	ジョウミャク	vein
	静観	セイカン	watching calmly —v. watch calmly; wait and see
	静止	セイシ	standstill; still; at rest; stationary —vi. come to rest/a standstill; be at rest/stationary
	静寂	セイジャク	still; silent; quiet
	静粛	セイシュク	still; silent; quiet
	静聴	セイチョウ	attention; listen quietly —v. pay attention
	静的	セイテキ	static
	静電気	セイデンキ	static electricity
	静物	セイブツ	still life
	静養	セイヨウ	rest; recuperation —vi. rest; recuperate
訓	静	しず	quiet; peaceful; still
	静か	しずか	calm; quiet; peaceful; still
	静まる	しずまる	vi. become quiet; subside; die down
	静める	しずめる	vt. calm; soothe; quell

---

8 非 あらず negative

1873

非 ⑧　ノ　丿　ヲ　ヺ　刲　非　非　非

音	非	ヒ	(prefix) non-; un-; wrong; not
熟	非運	ヒウン	misfortune; bad luck
	非金属	ヒキンゾク	nonmetallic
	非行	ヒコウ	misdeed; misconduct; delinquency
	非業	ヒゴウ	*Bud.* untimely/unnatural death
	非公開	ヒコウカイ	private/closed (meeting); closed-door (session)
	非公式	ヒコウシキ	unofficial; informal
	非公認	ヒコウニン	unauthorized
	非合法	ヒゴウホウ	illegal
	非合理	ヒゴウリ	irrational; unreasonable
	非国民	ヒコクミン	traitor; unpatriotic person
	非才	ヒサイ	lack of ability; incompetence
	非情	ヒジョウ	unfeeling; coldhearted; inanimate
	非常	ヒジョウ	emergency; extraordinary; very; exceeding; extremely
	非常勤	ヒジョウキン	part-time work
	非常口	ヒジョウぐち	emergency exit
	非常時	ヒジョウジ	emergency; crisis

	非常識	ヒジョウシキ	lack of common sense; absurd
	非常手段	ヒジョウシュダン	emergency means
	非戦論	ヒセンロン	pacifism
	非道	ヒドウ	inhuman; unjust; cruel; tyrannical
	非難	ヒナン	blame; reproach —*v.* criticize unfavorably; censure; blame; reproach
	非売品	ヒバイヒン	article not for sale; Not for Sale
	非番	ヒバン	off duty
	非武装	ヒブソウ	demilitarization; unarmed
	非凡	ヒボン	uncommon; rare
	非力	ヒリキ	incapable; powerless; useless; incompetent
	非礼	ヒレイ	impoliteness
訓	非ず	あらず	not; not so
¥	非課税	ヒカゼイ	tax-free; tax exemption

8 斉 せい alike

1874

斉 ⑧ 　 `、一ナ文产产斉斉`

音	斉	セイ	equal
熟	斉唱	セイショウ	unison —*v.* sing in unison

1875

斎 ⑪ 　 `、一ナ文产产斉斉斎斎`

音	斎	サイ	purity; purification; room
熟	斎場	サイジョウ	funeral hall

8 食 see ⇨p.817

9 面 めん face

1876

面 ⑨ 一 ア 了 丙 而 面 面 面 面

音	面	メン	face; mask; surface; aspect; facet; page
熟	面する	メンする	*vi.* face; front; look on
	面会	メンカイ	interview; meeting —*vi.* interview; meet and talk with
	面識	メンシキ	acquaintance
	面積	メンセキ	area
	面接	メンセツ	interview —*vi.* interview; meet and talk with
	面前	メンゼン	in the presence of; before (someone)
	面相	メンソウ	looks; face
	面談	メンダン	interview —*vi.* meet and talk with
	面倒	メンドウ	trouble; difficulty; taking care of
	面倒臭い	メンドウくさい	troublesome; bothersome
	面目	メンボク(メンモク)	honor; face; dignity
	面々	メンメン	each one; all
	面容	メンヨウ	countenance; looks
訓	面	おも	surface; face
	面影	おもかげ	face; visage; image; trace; vestige
	面白い	おもしろい	interesting; amusing
	面長	おもなが	long-faced
	面	おもて	face; surface
	面	つら	surface; face (impolite)
	面当て	つらあて	insinuating/spiteful remark; innuendo

9 革 かくのかわ／つくりのかわ shoe leather

1877

革 ⑨ 一 十 廾 廾 芇 芇 苫 苜 革

音	革	カク	hide; leather; renew
熟	革命	カクメイ	revolution

807

訓	革	かわ	leather; skin
¥	革新	カクシン	reform; renovation; innovation —v. reform; renovate; innovate
	革新的	カクシンテキ	progressive

1878

靴 ⑬　一　十　廾　廿　世　丗　苹　苩　苜　革　靴　靴ˊ　靴

音	靴	カ	shoes
訓	靴	くつ	shoes
	靴下	くつした	socks; stockings

---

9 音　おと　noise

1879

音 ⑨　丶　ー　ナ　立　产　音　音　音

音	音	オン	sound; pronunciation; music
		（イン）	sound; tidings
熟	音域	オンイキ	singing range; register
	音韻	オンイン	phoneme
	音階	オンカイ	the whole series of recognized musical notes; musical scale; gamut
	音楽	オンガク	music
	音感	オンカン	sense of sound/pitch
	音響	オンキョウ	sound; noise
	音曲	オンキョク	music; songs
	音訓	オンクン	Chinese and Japanese readings of kanji
	音質	オンシツ	tonal quality; tonality
	音信	オンシン	correspondence; communication
		（インシン）	
	音声	オンセイ	voice; audio sound
	音声学	オンセイガク	phonetics
	音節	オンセツ	syllable
	音速	オンソク	velocity of sound; sonic speed
	音痴	オンチ	tone deaf
	音程	オンテイ	musical interval; step
	音頭	オンド	leading a song
	音読	オンドク	reading aloud —v. read aloud

音波	オンパ	sound waves
音便	オンビン	euphonic change; euphony
音符	オンプ	musical note
音譜	オンプ	music; musical score
音律	オンリツ	tune; rhythm; pitch
音量	オンリョウ	sound volume; volume

訓 音　おと　sound
音　ね　sound
音色　ねいろ　tonal quality; tonality

1880

韻 ⑲　　一　立　产　音　音　音　音ᵗ　韵ᵗ　韵　韻　韻　韻

音 韻　イン　sound; rhyme
熟 韻文　インブン　verse
韻律　インリツ　meter; rhythm

1881

響 ⑳　ノ　ク　乡　乡ᵀ　乡ᴲ　郷　郷³　郷　郷　響　響　響

音 響　キョウ　sound; reverberate; echo
訓 響く　ひびく　*vi.* sound; resound; be echoed; affect

---

9 頁　おおがい　big shell; page

1882

頂 ⑪　一　丁　厂　厂　厂　而　而　頂　頂　頂　頂

音 頂　チョウ　top of the head; top; peak; summit
熟 頂角　チョウカク　*math.* vertical angle
頂上　チョウジョウ　top; summit; crest; crown; peak
頂戴　チョウダイ　*hon.* please —*v. hon.* receive; get; have; take; eat
頂点　チョウテン　apex; vertex; zenith; climax
訓 頂　いただき　top; summit; peak
頂く　いただく　*vt.* wear a crown; be crowned *hon.* receive; get; be given; eat; drink

1883

項 ⑫

一 丅 工 工 工 圹 邛 項 項 項 項 項

音	項	コウ	clause; term; nape
熟	項目	コウモク	item; clause; provision
訓	※項	うなじ	nape; scruff of the neck

1884

順 ⑫

丿 丿 川 川 川 川 川 川 順 順 順 順 順

音	順	ジュン	submit; order; series
熟	順位	ジュンイ	ranking; order
	順延	ジュンエン	postponement —v. postpone; put off
	順化	ジュンカ	adapting (to climate, etc.)
	順繰り	ジュンぐり	by turns; in turn; one after another; one by one
	順次	ジュンジ	in order; one by one; one after another
	順々	ジュンジュン	by turns; one by one; one after another
	順序	ジュンジョ	order; procedure
	順調	ジュンチョウ	smooth; satisfactory; favorable
	順当	ジュントウ	proper; right
	順応	ジュンノウ	adaptation; adjustment —vi. adapt; adjust; conform
	順番	ジュンバン	order; turn; place
	順風	ジュンプウ	favorable wind
	順法	ジュンポウ	law-abiding
	順列	ジュンレツ	permutation
	順路	ジュンロ	route

1885

頑 ⑬

一 二 テ 元 元 元 刢 珩 頑 頑 頑 頑 頑

音	頑	ガン	hard; obstinate
熟	頑強	ガンキョウ	stubborn; obstinate
	頑健	ガンケン	robust health
	頑固	ガンコ	stubborn; obstinate
	頑張る	ガンばる	vi. try hard; not give up; persist
訓	※頑	かたくな	stubborn; obstinate

1886

頌 ⑬ 　ノ　ハ　今　分　分゛　分゛　分゛　妳　頌　頌　頌　頌

音	頌	ハン	distribute
熟	頌布	ハンプ	distribution; circulation —*v*. distribute; circulate
¥	頌価	ハンカ	paying in installments

1887

預 ⑬ 　ー　フ　ヌ　子　予　予゛　矛゛　矛゛　預　預　預　預

音	預	ヨ	deposit; entrust
熟	預金	ヨキン	deposit; bank account —*v*. deposit money in a bank
訓	預かる	あずかる	*vt*. receive for safekeeping
	預ける	あずける	*vt*. deposit; entrust; hand over for safe-keeping; leave in someone's care
¥	預かり金	あずかりキン	deposit
	預金証書	ヨキンショウショ	certificate of deposit
	預金通帳	ヨキンツウチョウ	bankbook; deposit passbook

1888

領 ⑭ 　ノ　ハ　今　今　令　令゛　令゛　矛゛　領　領　領　領

音	領	リョウ	govern; rule; territory
熟	領域	リョウイキ	domain; territory
	領海	リョウカイ	territorial waters
	領解	リョウカイ	understanding; consent —*v*. understand; consent
	領空	リョウクウ	territorial airspace
	領事	リョウジ	consul
	領事館	リョウジカン	consulate
	領主	リョウシュ	*hist*. feudal lord (Edo period)
	領収書	リョウシュウショ	(written) receipt
	領収証	リョウシュウショウ	receipt; proof of payment
	領地	リョウチ	territory
	領土	リョウド	territory
	領分	リョウブン	territory; domain; sphere of influence
	領有	リョウユウ	possession (of land/territory) —*v*. possess (land/territory)

1889

頭 ⑯ 一 亠 亣 亣 頁 豆 豆 頭 頭 頭 頭 頭

音	頭	ズ	head
		トウ	head; beginning
		（ト）	
熟	頭蓋骨	ズガイコツ	*med*. skull; cranium
	頭巾	ズキン	hood; skullcap; cowl
	頭上	ズジョウ	overhead; above the head
	頭痛	ズツウ	*med*. headache
	頭脳	ズノウ	brain
	頭角	トウカク	top of the head; crown; talent
	頭取	トウどり	president; manager
	頭髪	トウハツ	hair (on the head)
	頭領	トウリョウ	boss
訓	頭	あたま	head; brains; mind; hair; chief; leader
	頭打ち	あたまうち	(highest) limit; peak; ceiling
	頭数	あたまかず	headcount; number of persons
	頭ごなし	あたまごなし	merciless
	頭割り	あたまわり	equal share
	頭	かしら	head; hair; leader
	頭文字	かしらモジ	initial; first letter
¥	頭金	あたまキン	down/initial payment

1890

頼 ⑯ 一 亠 亣 亣 申 束 朿 朿 柿 頼 頼 頼

音	頼	ライ	ask for; request; entrust to
訓	頼む	たのむ	*vt*. ask for; request; entrust to
	頼み込む	たのみこむ	*vt*. earnestly request
	頼もしい	たのもしい	reliable; dependable; promising
	頼る	たよる	*vt*. rely; depend on
	頼り無い	たよりない	unreliable; undependable; vague

1891

頻 ⑰ 丿 ト ﾄ 止 步 步 步 步 步 頻 頻 頻

| 音 | 頻 | ヒン | frequent; repeated |

熟	頻出	ヒンシュツ	frequent appearances —*vi.* appear/occur frequently
	頻度	ヒンド	frequency
	頻発	ヒンパツ	frequency; frequent occurence —*vi.* occur frequently
	頻繁	ヒンパン	over and over; repeatedly; frequently
	頻々	ヒンピン	frequent; repeated

1892
  ` 宀 宀 安 安 客 客 客 客 額 額 額

音	額	ガク	forehead; amount; frame
熟	額縁	ガクぶち	picture frame
	額面	ガクメン	face value
訓	額	ひたい	forehead
¥	額	ガク	amount; sum; volume
	額面金額	ガクメンキンガク	face value; par price
	額面割れ	ガクメンわれ	drop below par

1893
顔 ` ㇒ ㇛ ㇔ 立 产 彦 彦 彦 顔 顔 顔

音	顔	ガン	face; looks
熟	顔色	ガンショク	complexion
	顔面	ガンメン	face
訓	顔	かお	face; looks; honor
	顔色	かおいろ	expression; countenance; color of a person's face
	顔役	かおヤク	boss

1894
  ヽ 丨 冂 日 旦 旱 昂 显 显 显 顕 顕 顕

音	顕	ケン	clear; appear; conspicuous
熟	顕著	ケンチョ	remarkable; conspicuous; striking; obvious
	顕微鏡	ケンビキョウ	microscope
訓	顕す	あらわす	*vt.* clear; appear
	顕れる	あらわれる	*vi.* come out; show itself

1895

題 ⑱ 　｜ 日 旦 早 早 昺 是 昰 昰 題 題 題

音	題	ダイ	title
熟	題する	ダイする	*vi*. entitle
	題材	ダイザイ	subject matter; theme
	題字	ダイジ	title (of a book, etc.)
	題名	ダイメイ	title (of a book, etc.)
	題目	ダイモク	prayer of the Nichiren sect; theme

1896

類 ⑱ 　丶 丷 半 米 米 米 类 类 类 類 類 類

音	類	ルイ	kind; type; genus
熟	類する	ルイする	*vi*. classify
	類火	ルイカ	spreading fire
	類型	ルイケイ	type; pattern
	類語	ルイゴ	*gram*. synonym
	類似	ルイジ	resemblance; similarity —*vi*. resemble; be similar
	類書	ルイショ	books of the same kind
	類焼	ルイショウ	spreading fire —*vi*. spread fire
	類人猿	ルイジンエン	anthropoid; ape
	類推	ルイスイ	analogy —*v*. analogize
	類同	ルイドウ	similar
	類比	ルイヒ	analogy; comparison —*v*. analogize; compare
	類別	ルイベツ	classification —*v*. classify
	類例	ルイレイ	similar example
訓	※類	たぐい	kind; sort; match; equal

1897

願 ⑲ 　一 厂 厂 厈 厇 厈 原 原 原 願 願 願

音	願	ガン	desire; prayer
熟	願書	ガンショ	written application/request
	願望	ガンボウ	desire; wish
訓	願い	ねがい	*vt*. wish; favor; request
	願う	ねがう	pray; wish; request politely

1898

顧 ㉑ 一 ョ 戸 戸 戸 戸 屋 屋 屋 顧 顧 顧

音	顧	コ	look back
熟	顧客	コキャク	customer; patron
	顧問	コモン	advisor; counsellor; consultant; teacher in charge of a club
	顧慮	コリョ	consideration —v. consider; regard
訓	顧みる	かえりみる	vt. look back; review; retrospect

---

9 飛 とぶ flying

1899

飛 ⑨ 乀 乁 乁 飞 飞 飛 飛 飛 飛

音	飛	ヒ	fly; jump
熟	飛語	ヒゴ	groundless rumor
	飛行	ヒコウ	flight; flying; aviation —vi. fly
	飛行士	ヒコウシ	airman; aviator; flier
	飛散	ヒサン	scattering; dispersement —vi. scatter; disperse; fly
	飛沫	ヒマツ ※(しぶき)	splash; spray
	飛躍	ヒヤク	rapid progress; leap; activity; jump —vi. be active; leap; jump
	飛来	ヒライ	by air/airplane —vi. come flying
訓	飛ぶ	とぶ	vi. fly; jump; hurry; progress rapidly
	飛ばす	とばす	vt. fly; spatter; drive fast; skip (pages, etc.); omit
	飛び上がる	とびあがる	vi. fly/jump up; take off
	飛び歩く	とびあるく	vi. run/rush about
	飛石	とびいし	steppingstone
	飛板	とびいた	springboard; diving board
	飛び移る	とびうつる	vi. fly/jump from one place to other
	飛び降りる	とびおりる	vi. jump/leap out
	飛び込む	とびこむ	vi. jump/spring/plung/leap/dive/rush/dash into
	飛び出す	とびだす	vi. spring/bolt out; run away; protrude
	飛び出る	とびでる	vi. protrude; project; fly/jump out; appear suddenly; run/pop out; be exorbitant

9 食 しょく food　　　食　(p.817)

1900

食⑨　ノ　入　今　今　今　今　食　食　食

音 食　ショク　eat; food; meal; appetite
　　　（ジキ）

熟 食塩　ショクエン　table salt
　　食言　ショクゲン　*vi.* go back on one's words; tell lies
　　食後　ショクゴ　after a meal
　　食指　ショクシ　index finger
　　食事　ショクジ　meal; diet —*vi.* eat; dine
　　食傷　ショクショウ　sick and tired; fed up; food poisoning
　　　　　　　　　　　—*vi.* be sick and tired of; get fed up;
　　　　　　　　　　　get food poisoning
　　食前　ショクゼン　before a meal
　　食膳　ショクゼン　dining table
　　食卓　ショクタク　table; dining table
　　食中毒　ショクチュウドク　food poisoning
　　食通　ショクツウ　gourmet
　　食堂　ショクドウ　dining room; eating house; canteen; cafeteria
　　食道　ショクドウ　*med.* gullet; esophagus
　　食費　ショクヒ　food costs/expenses
　　食品　ショクヒン　food
　　食物　ショクモツ　food
　　食用　ショクヨウ　edible
　　食欲　ショクヨク　appetite
　　食料　ショクリョウ　food; provisions
　　食料品　ショクリョウヒン　foodstuff
　　食糧　ショクリョウ　food; provision; staples
　　食間　ショッカン　between meals
　　食器　ショッキ　tableware; dishes, plates and bowls

訓 食う　くう　*vt.* eat (used mainly by men and in some
　　　　　　　　　regional dialects)
　　食らう　くらう　*vt.* eat; drink
　　食べる　たべる　*vt.* eat
　　食べ物　たべもの　food; diet

¥ 食い合い　くいあい　crossing orders
　　食い止める　くいとめる　*vt.* check; curb; prevent

1901

養 ⑮　　ソ　ソ　ヤ　羊　羊　羊　美　羊　羔　养　養　養　養

音	養	ヨウ	foster; bring up; rear; adopt; support; cultivate; develop
熟	養育	ヨウイク	fostering; rearing —v. foster; bring up; near; support
	養育者	ヨウイクシャ	guardian
	養魚	ヨウギョ	fish breeding/farming
	養鶏	ヨウケイ	poultry farming
	養護	ヨウゴ	protection; care —v. protect
	養蚕	ヨウサン	sericulture; silkworm raising/culture
	養子	ヨウシ	adopted child
	養嗣子	ヨウシシ	adopted heir
	養女	ヨウジョ	adopted daughter
	養生	ヨウジョウ	health care —v. take care of one's health
	養殖	ヨウショク	culture; cultivation; raising (marine products) —v. rear; raise; breed; cultivate
	養成	ヨウセイ	training; education; cultivation —v. train; educate; cultivate
	養父	ヨウフ	adoptive/foster father
	養分	ヨウブン	nourishment
	養母	ヨウボ	adoptive/foster mother
	養毛剤	ヨウモウザイ	hair tonic
	養老	ヨウロウ	provision for old age; caring for the aged
	養老金	ヨウロウキン	old-age pension
訓	養う	やしなう	vt. foster; bring up; rear; adopt; support; cultivate; develop

8　食　しょくへん　food

1902

飢 ⑩　　ノ　人　ケ　今　今　今　食　食　食　飢

音	飢	キ	hungry; hunger; famine
熟	飢餓	キガ	starvation; hunger; famine
	飢渇	キカツ	hunger and thirst
	飢饉	キキン	famine; scarcity
訓	飢える	うえる	vi. hunger; starve

817

1903

飲 ⑫ 　ノ　ト　ト　今　今　今　食　食　飲　飲　飲　飲

音	飲	イン	drink
熟	飲酒	インシュ	drinking alcohol
	飲食	インショク	eating and drinking; food and drink —v. eat and drink; take refreshments
	飲用	インヨウ	use for drinking purposes; potable
	飲料	インリョウ	drink; beverage
	飲料水	インリョウスイ	drinking/potable water
訓	飲む	のむ	*vt*. drink; swallow; accept
	飲み物	のみもの	drink

1904

飯 ⑫ 　ノ　ト　ト　今　今　今　食　食　飣　飯　飯　飯

音	飯	ハン	rice; food; meal
熟	飯盒	ハンゴウ	canteen for cooking rice; mess tin
	飯台	ハンダイ	dinner/dining table
	飯場	ハンば	workmen's quarters; construction camp
訓	飯	めし	boiled rice; food; meal

1905

飼 ⑬ 　ト　ト　今　今　今　食　食　飣　飣　飼　飼　飼

音	飼	シ	raise; breed
熟	飼育	シイク	breeding; raising (domestic animals) —v. breed; raise
	飼料	シリョウ	feed; fodder
訓	飼う	かう	*vt*. breed; raise; keep (animals)
	飼主	かいぬし	pet owner; animal keeper

1906

飾 ⑬ 　ト　ト　今　今　今　食　食　飣　飣　飾　飾　飾

音	飾	ショク	decorate
訓	飾り	かざり	ornament; decoration

飾り窓	かざりまど	display/show window
飾り物	かざりもの	ornament; decoration
飾る	かざる	*vt.* decorate; ornament; adorn; display

1907

 飽 ⑬   ⼈ ⼫ ⼹ ⼺ ⼻ ⼼ ⾀ ⾁ ⾂ ⾃ ⾄ 飽

音	飽	ホウ	have enough/grow tired of
熟	飽食	ホウショク	gluttony; engorgement; plenty of food —*vi.* be gluttonous; eat too much
	飽満	ホウマン	satiation —*vi.* be satiated; eat until one is full
	飽和	ホウワ	saturation —*vi.* be saturated
	飽和点	ホウワテン	saturation —*vi.* be saturated
訓	飽く	あく	*vi.* grow tired/have enough of
	飽かす	あかす	*vt.* tire; bore; make (someone) fed up
	飽きる	あきる	*vi.* grow tired/have enough of; get rid of
	飽きっぽい	あきっぽい	easily bored; fickle

1908

餓 ⑮   ⼈ ⼫ ⼹ ⼺ ⼼ ⾀ ⾁ ⾂ ⾃ ⾄ 飰 餓 餓

音	餓	ガ	starve
熟	餓鬼	ガキ	hungry ghost/devil
	餓死	ガシ	starvation —*vi.* starve to death
訓	餓える	うえる	*vi.* starve; go hungry; famish

1909

館 ⑯   ⼈ ⼫ ⼹ ⼺ ⼼ ⾀ 飮 飰 飰 飰 館 館

音	館	カン	mansion; inn; hall
熟	館長	カンチョウ	superintendent; director; librarian; curator
	館内	カンナイ	inside the building; on the premises
訓	※館	たて	palace; mansion; fort
	※館	やかた	mansion; palace; castle

9 首 くび neck

<u>1910</u>

首⑨   、 ゛ ゛ ゛ ゛ ゛ ゛ 首 首

音	首	シュ	head; first; chief
熟	首位	シュイ	first place
	首相	シュショウ	premier; prime minister
	首席	シュセキ	first/top (of the class); chief
	首都	シュト	capital city; metropolis
	首脳	シュノウ	head; leader
	首班	シュハン	head; premier; prime minister
	首尾	シュビ	the result; outcome; beginning and end
	首尾一貫	シュビイッカン	consistent; throughout
	首府	シュフ	capital city
	首謀	シュボウ	ringleader; mastermind
	首領	シュリョウ	leader
訓	首	くび	neck; head
	首飾り	くびかざり	necklace
	首切り	くびきり	dismissal
	首筋	くびすじ	scruff of the neck
¥	首都圏	シュトケン	metropolitan area
	首脳	シュノウ	head; leader
	首脳会議	シュノウカイギ	summit; talks

9 香 かおり perfume

<u>1911</u>

香⑨   一 二 千 禾 禾 禾 香 香 香

音	香	コウ （キョウ）	sweet smell; scent; fragrance
熟	香気	コウキ	fragrance; perfume; aroma
	香水	コウスイ	perfume; fragrance; scent
	香典	コウデン	monetary gift offered in place of incense to a departed soul

香料	コウリョウ	perfume; fragrance; sweet smell
※香港	ホンコン	Hong Kong
訓 香	か	smell; scent; odor; fragrance
香り	かおり	smell; scent; odor; fragrance
香る	かおる	*vi.* smell sweet; be fragrant

10 馬 うま／うまへん horse

1912

馬 ⑩ 　 丨 厂 厂 厂 匡 匡 馬 馬 馬 馬 馬

音	馬	バ	horse
熟	馬鹿	バカ	stupid; silly; foolish *n.* fool; idiot
	馬脚	バキャク	horse's legs *fig.* one's true character
	馬具	バグ	harness; horse gear; trappings
	馬耳東風	バジトウフウ	utter indifference; praying to deaf ears
	馬車	バシャ	coach; carriage; omnibus
	馬術	バジュツ	horsemanship; equestrian skill
	馬上	バジョウ	horseback; mounted
	馬賊	バゾク	mounted bandits
	馬蹄	バテイ	horse's hoof
	馬場	ばば	riding ground; racecourse; race track
	馬力	バリキ	horsepower; energy
訓	馬	うま	horse
	馬面	うまづら	horseface; long face
	馬乗り	うまのり	horse riding; rider; horseman
	馬屋	うまや	stable
	馬	ま	horse
	馬子	まご	wagon driver

1913

騰 ⑳ 　 丿 几 月 月 月 月 朕 朕 朕 朕 騰 騰

音	騰	トウ	rise
熟	騰貴	トウキ	rise/advance/jump (in prices) —*vi.* rise; go up; jump

---

1914

驚 ⑳ 　 一 艹 芍 荀 苟 敬 敬 敬 敬 敬 驚 驚

音	驚	キョウ	surprise; shock
熟	驚異	キョウイ	wonder; miracle; marvel
	驚喜	キョウキ	pleasant surprise —*vi.* be pleasantly surprised

| 驚嘆 | キョウタン | admiration; wonder —*vi*. admire; wonder |

訓 驚かす　おどろかす　*vt*. surprise
驚く　おどろく　*vi*. be surprised

1915

駅 　１ 厂 卩 严 严 馬 馬 馬 馬ﾉ 馬ﾉ 馹 駅 ⑭

音 駅　エキ　post-road stage; train station
熟 駅員　エキイン　station employee
駅長　エキチョウ　station master
駅伝　エキデン　long-distance relay race
駅頭　エキトウ　at or near the train station
駅弁　エキベン　packed lunch sold at railway stations

1916

駆 　１ 厂 卩 严 严 馬 馬 馬 馬ﾉ 馹 馭 駆 ⑭

音 駆　ク　chase; pursue; follow
熟 駆使　クシ　free use —*v*. use freely/as one pleases
駆除　クジョ　extermination; destruction —*v*. exterminate; destroy
駆逐　クチク　expulsion; extermination —*v*. expel; drive away; exterminate
訓 駆ける　かける　*vi*. run; canter; gallop
駆る　かる　*vt*. drive; urge on; prompt; impel
¥ 駆け引き　かけひき　bargaining; tactics

1917

駄 　１ 厂 卩 严 严 馬 馬 馬 馬一 馴 馱 駄 ⑭

音 駄　ダ　load for a horse; petty; unimportant
熟 駄作　ダサク　poor work; shoddy craftmanship
駄目　ダめ　*col*. useless; vain; no good

1918

駐 　１ 厂 卩 严 严 馬 馬 馬ﾞ 馬ﾞ 馴 駐 駐 ⑮

音 駐　チュウ　stay; resident

823

熟	駐在	チュウザイ	residence; stay —*v.* reside; be resident; stay
	駐在所	チュウザイショ	police substation
	駐車	チュウシャ	parking —*vi.* park
	駐車違反	チュウシャイハン	illegal parking —*vi.* be illegally parked
	駐日	チュウニチ	staying in Japan (as an ambassador, etc.)
	駐留	チュウリュウ	stationing —*vi.* stay; be stationed in
	駐留軍	チュウリュウグン	stationary troops

1919

騎 ⑱　ｊ　厂　Ⅱ　Ⅲ　馬　馬　馬ｰ　馬ﾅ　駐ﾒ　騎　騎　騎

音	騎	キ	ride (on a horse)
熟	騎士	キシ	knight
	騎手	キシュ	rider
	騎乗	キジョウ	horse riding
	騎馬	キバ	horse rider; horse-riding
	騎兵	キヘイ	cavalry/mounted soldier

1920

験 ⑱　ｊ　厂　Ⅱ　Ⅲ　馬　馬　馬ﾞ　駖ﾞ　駖ﾟ　験　験　験

音	験	ケン	effect; test; examine
		ゲン	effect
熟	験算	ケンザン	verification of accounts

1921

騒 ⑱　ｊ　厂　Ⅱ　Ⅲ　馬　馬　駅　駅　駱　騒　騒　騒

音	騒	ソウ	make a noise/fuss
熟	騒音	ソウオン	noise
	騒然	ソウゼン	noisy; tumultous
	騒々	ソウゾウ	noisy; clamorous
	騒動	ソウドウ	riot; disturbance
	騒乱	ソウラン	riot; disturbance
訓	騒ぐ	さわぐ	*vi.* clamor

10 骨 ほね／ほねへん bone

1922

骨 ⑩ 　 丶 冂 冂 冂 冂 ,冂 冎 骨 骨 骨 骨

音	骨	コツ	bone; ashes; spirit; looks
熟	骨格	コッカク	framework; skeleton; frame; build; physique
	骨子	コッシ	gist; essential part; main part
	骨髄	コツズイ	bone marrow
	骨折	コッセツ	bone fracture —*v*. fracture a bone
	骨頂	コッチョウ	the height of; the uttermost
	骨肉	コツニク	blood relatives; flesh and blood
訓	骨	ほね	bone; frame; spirit; backbone
	骨折る	ほねおる	*vi*. make efforts; put oneself out
	骨抜き	ほねぬき	boned; filleted; spineless
	骨身	ほねみ	flesh and bones; marrow
	骨休め	ほねやすめ	rest; relaxation —*vi*. rest; relax

1923

髓 ⑲ 　 冂 冂 冂 冂 骨 骨 骨ノ 骨ナ 骨有 骨育 髓 髓

音	髓	ズイ	marrow; pith

10 高 たかい tall; high

1924

高 ⑩ 　 丶 亠 亠 亠 古 冎 高 高 高 高

音	高	コウ	high
熟	高圧	コウアツ	high pressure/tension; coercion; oppression
	高圧的	コウアツテキ	high-handed; coercive; overbearing
	高位	コウイ	high rank; honors
	高遠	コウエン	lofty; noble; exalted
	高音	コウオン	high-pitched tone
	高温	コウオン	high temperature

馬骨
• 高髟
鬼竜

高価	コウカ	expensive; costly; high price
高架	コウカ	overhead; high level; elevated
高額	コウガク	large sum/amount (of money)
高官	コウカン	high official
高貴	コウキ	noble; precious; valuable
高気圧	コウキアツ	high atmospheric pressure
高級	コウキュウ	high-class; seniority
高給	コウキュウ	high salary/pay
高潔	コウケツ	noble/high-mindedness; loftiness; purity
高原	コウゲン	plateau
高山	コウザン	high mountain
高所	コウショ	high ground; broad view
高尚	コウショウ	elegant; high; lofty; noble
高層	コウソウ	altostratus
高速度	コウソクド	high speed
高速道路	コウソクドウロ	expressway; highway; motorway
高低	コウテイ	high and low; uneven; rugged
高度	コウド	altitude; height; high degree
高等	コウトウ	high-grade/class
高等学校	コウトウガッコウ	senior high school
高等裁判所	コウトウ サイバンショ	high court
高熱	コウネツ	high fever/temperature; intense heat
高慢	コウマン	proud; haughty; uppish
高名	コウメイ	fame; repute; renown
高率	コウリツ	high rate/interest rate
高齢	コウレイ	old/great/ripe age

訓
高	たか	amount; quantity; volume
高い	たかい	tall; high; eminent; lofty
高潮	たかしお	flood/high tide; tidal wave
高台	たかダイ	heights; high ground; high, flat area
高々	たかだか	at most; at the best; no more than
高鳴る	たかなる	*vi*. throb; beat
高根の花	たかねのはな	unattainable object; prize beyond one's reach
高飛車	たかビシャ	high-handed; overbearing
高ぶる	たかぶる	*vi*. be highly wrought-up; be excited; be conceited
高まる	たかまる	*vi*. rise; be raised; increase
高める	たかめる	*vt*. raise; lift; promote; elevate

¥
高騰	コウトウ	steep rise in prices —*vi*. soar; skyrocket
高度成長	コウドセイチョウ	high growth
高品位テレビ	コウヒンイテレビ	high-definition television

高値　　　たかね　　　high price
高値引け　たかねびけ　closed higher

10 髟　かみかんむり／かみがしら　long hair

1925

髪 ⑭　丨 广 广 斤 斤 旡 旡 镸 髟 髟 髟 髟 髮 髪

音	髪	ハツ	hair
熟	髪膚	ハップ	hair and skin
訓	髪	かみ	hair
	髪形	かみがた	hairstyle
	髪の毛	かみのけ	hair
	髪結い	かみゆい	hairdressing

10 鬼　おに／きにょう　devil; demon

1926

鬼 ⑩　′ ′ ′ 宀 帀 由 甶 甶 鬼 鬼 鬼

音	鬼	キ	demon; devil
熟	鬼才	キサイ	genius; great talent
	鬼籍	キセキ	*Bud*. death register at a temple
	鬼門	キモン	unlucky quarter; weak point
訓	鬼	おに	ogre; demon; devil
	鬼瓦	おにがわら	ridge-end tile
	鬼婆	おにばば	witch; hag

1927

魂 ⑭　一 二 云 云 云 云′ 云′ 云勹 云勹 云甶 云甶 魂 魂

音	魂	コン	soul; heart; spirit
熟	魂胆	コンタン	intrigue; plot; soul
訓	魂	たましい	soul

827

馬
骨
高
髟
• 鬼
• 竜

1928

魅 ⑮ ⸝ ⸜ 宀 宀 由 鬼 鬼 鬼 鬼 鬼 魅 魅

音	魅	ミ	charm; enchant; fascinate
熟	魅する	ミする	*vt.* charm; enchant; fascinate
	魅了	ミリョウ	charming; captivating; spellbound —*v.* charm; captivating; hold spellbound
	魅力	ミリョク	charm; appeal; fascination
	魅惑	ミワク	charm; fascination; lure —*v.* charm; fascinate; lure

1929

魔 ㉑ 一 广 广 广 广 麻 麻 麻 麻 曆 曆 魔 魔

音	魔	マ	demon; devil; evil spirit
熟	魔王	マオウ	the devil; Satan
	魔境	マキョウ	land of demons; wasteland
	魔手	マシュ	demon hand; evil power
	魔術	マジュツ	magic; sorcery; witchcraft
	魔女	マジョ	witch; sorceress
	魔性	マショウ	diabolical
	魔法	マホウ	magic; sorcery; witchcraft
	魔法使い	マホウつかい	magician; wizard; witch
	魔法瓶	マホウビン	thermos bottle
	魔物	マもの	goblin; demon; devil
	魔力	マリョク	magical power; charm

10 竜 りゅう dragon

1930

竜 ⑩ ⸝ 亠 产 宀 立 产 产 音 音 竜

音	竜	リュウ	dragon
訓	竜	たつ	dragon
	竜巻	たつまき	tornado; waterspout

11 魚 うお fish

1931

 ⑪ ノ ク ク ク 冎 冎 冎 魚 魚 魚 魚

音	魚	ギョ	fish
熟	魚介類	ギョカイルイ	seafood; fishes and shellfish
	魚拓	ギョタク	fish print
	魚雷	ギョライ	torpedo
	魚類	ギョルイ	fishes
訓	魚	うお（さかな）	fish

1932

鮮 ⑰ ノ ク ク ク 冎 冎 魚 魚 鮮 鮮 鮮 鮮

音	鮮	セン	clear; fresh; vivid; Korea
熟	鮮魚	センギョ	fresh fish
	鮮血	センケツ	blood
	鮮度	センド	freshness
	鮮明	センメイ	clear; distinct
訓	鮮やか	あざやか	vivid; clear; bright; colorful

1933

鯨 ⑲ ノ ク ク ク 冎 冎 魚 鮮 鮪 鯨 鯨

音	鯨	ゲイ	whale
訓	鯨	くじら	whale

11 鳥 とり bird

1934

 ⑪ ノ 丶 丫 疒 户 户 自 鳥 鳥 鳥 鳥 鳥

音	鳥	チョウ	bird

魚
● 鳥
● 鹿
麻
黄
黒

熟	鳥瞰図	チョウカンズ	bird's-eye view
	鳥獣	チョウジュウ	birds and beasts
	鳥類	チョウルイ	birds
訓	鳥	とり	bird
	鳥居	とりい	*torii* (gateway to a Shinto Shrine)
	鳥肌	とりはだ	goose flesh

1935

鳴 ⑭ 丶 ㅁ ㅁ ㅁ' ㅁ' ㅁ' ㅁ' ㅁ' ㅁ' 鳴 鳴 鳴

音	鳴	メイ	cry; sing; howl
熟	鳴動	メイドウ	rumbling — *vi.* rumble; move with a loud noise
訓	鳴く	なく	*vi.* cry; sing; howl; chirp
	鳴き声	なきごえ	cry; call; chirping
	鳴る	なる	*vi.* sound; ring
	鳴らす	ならす	*vt.* sound ring

1936

鶏 ⑲ 一 ㄣ ㅁ ㅛ 奚 奚' 奚' 鈏 鷄 鶏 鶏 鶏

音	鶏	ケイ	hen; cock; rooster
熟	鶏舎	ケイシャ	henhouse
	鶏卵	ケイラン	chicken eggs
訓	鶏	にわとり	fowl; chicken

11 鹿 しか deer

1937

麗 ⑲ 一 厂 厈 㐭 㡀 严 严 严 麗 麗 麗 麗

音	麗	レイ	beautiful; pretty; lovely
熟	麗句	レイク	beautiful phrase
	麗質	レイシツ	beauty; charms
	麗人	レイジン	beautiful woman
訓	麗しい	うるわしい	beautiful; pretty; lovely
	※麗か	うららか	beautiful/bright/serene (weather, climate, etc.)

830

11 麻　あさ／あさかんむり　hemp

1938

麻 ⑪　　`　亠　广　广　庐　庐　庲　庲　庲　麻　麻

音	麻	マ	hemp; flax
熟	麻疹	マシン	*med*. measles
	麻酔	マスイ	*med*. anesthesia; anesthetic
	麻酔科	マスイカ	*med*. anesthesiology
	麻痺	マヒ	paralysis —*vi*. be paralysed
	麻薬	マヤク	narcotics
	※麻雀	マージャン	mahjong
訓	麻	あさ	flax; hemp
	麻布	あさぬの	hemp cloth; linen

11 黄　きいろい／き　yellow

1939

黄 ⑪　　一　十　艹　艹　艹　苎　苎　苗　苗　黄　黄

音	黄	コウ	yellow; gold
		オウ	
熟	黄金	オウゴン	gold; money
	黄金時代	オウゴンジダイ	golden age; age of gods
	黄色人種	オウショクジンシュ	yellow race
	黄水	オウスイ	bile; gall
	黄鉄鉱	オウテッコウ	iron pyrite; fool's gold
	黄熱病	オウネツビョウ	*med*. yellow fever
	黄河	コウガ	Yellow River
	黄土	コウド（オウド）	loess; yellow soil
訓	黄	き	yellow
	黄色	きいろ	yellow
	黄身	きみ	yolk
	黄金色	こがねいろ	gold (color)

11 黒　くろい／くろ　black

黒 ⑪　丶　冂　冃　日　甲　甲　里　里　黒　黒　黒

音	黒	コク	black; darkness; bad; wrong
熟	黒人	コクジン	black person
	黒点	コクテン	sunspots; black spots
	黒板	コクバン	blackboard
訓	黒	くろ	black
	黒い	くろい	black; dirty; dark
	黒船	くろふね	*hist*. 'black ships' (term used to refer to all Western ships that visited Japan from 1600 to 1868)
	黒星	くろぼし	black mark; bull's-eye
	黒幕	くろマク	wirepuller; behind-the-scenes man

黙 ⑮　丶　冂　冃　日　甲　甲　里　里　黙　黙　黙　黙

音	黙	モク	silence
熟	黙する	モクする	*vi*. be silent
	黙殺	モクサツ	ignoring —*v*. ignore; take no notice of
	黙視	モクシ	overlooking; conniving —*v*. overlook; connive at
	黙然	モクゼン（モクネン）	silent; mute; tacit
	黙想	モクソウ	meditation; contemplation —*vi*. meditate; contemplate
	黙禱	モクトウ	silent prayer/tribute —*vi*. pray silently
	黙読	モクドク	silent reading —*v*. read silently
	黙認	モクニン	tacit consent —*v*. give tacit consent
	黙秘権	モクヒケン	right to remain silent
	黙々	モクモク	silent; mute; tacit
	黙約	モクヤク	tacit agreement
	黙礼	モクレイ	non-verbal greeting —*vi*. bow silently
訓	黙る	だまる	*vi*. become silent; say nothing
	黙り	だまり	silence; reticence
	※黙す	もだす	*vi*. be silent; not say; leave as it is; ignore

12 歯 は tooth

1942

歯 ⑫ 丨 ト ㅏ � 止 ⺊ 迚 歨 歯 歯 歯

音	歯	シ	tooth; age
熟	歯科	シカ	dentistry
	歯科医	シカイ	dentist
	歯牙	シガ	teeth and tusks
	歯垢	シコウ	plaque
	歯石	シセキ	tartar; plaque
訓	歯	は	tooth; teeth
	歯医者	はイシャ	dentist
	歯車	はぐるま	gear wheel
	歯磨き	はみがき	dentifrice —*vi*. clean one's teeth
	歯向かう	はむかう	*vi*. rise/turn against

1943

齢 ⑰ 丨 ト ㅏ 止 歨 迚 歯 歯 歯 齢 齢 齢

音	齢	レイ	age
訓	※齢	よわい	age

13 鼓 つづみ drum

1944

鼓 ⑬ 一 十 土 吉 声 吉 吉 壴 壴 壴 鼓 鼓

音	鼓	コ	hand drum
熟	鼓笛隊	コテキタイ	drum and fife band
	鼓動	コドウ	beating; pounding; thumping —*vi*. beat; pound; thump
	鼓舞	コブ	encouragement —*v*. encourage; inspire
	鼓膜	コマク	*med*. eardrum
訓	鼓	つづみ	hand drum

14 鼻　はな　nose

1945

鼻 ⑭　　　′　′　′　白　白　鳥　鳥　鼻　畠　畠　鼻　鼻

音	鼻	ビ	nose
熟	鼻炎	ビエン	*med*. nasal inflammation
	鼻音	ビオン	nasal sound
	鼻下	ビカ	under the nose; area between nose and mouth; upper lip
	鼻孔	ビコウ	nostril
訓	鼻	はな	nose
	鼻息	はないき	breathing through the nose; mood; temper
	鼻歌	はなうた	humming
	鼻毛	はなげ	nostril hairs
	鼻声	はなごえ	nasal voice
	鼻先	はなさき	tip of the nose; under one's nose
	鼻白む	はなじろむ	*vi*. look disappointed/bored
	鼻筋	はなすじ	line of the nose
	鼻高々	はなたかだか	proudly; triumphantly
	鼻血	はなぢ	nosebleed *med*. epistasis
	鼻詰まり	はなづまり	nasal congestion
	鼻水	はなみず	nasal mucus; runny nose
	鼻持ちならない	はなもちならない	intolerable; detestable; disgusting; stinking

RADICAL INDEX

RADICAL INDEX

(by radical and kanji number)

1 STROKE

一

一 1
七 2
丁 3
下 4
三 5
上 6
丈 7
万 8
与 9
不 10
且 11
丘 12
世 13
丙 14
両 15

二(二) 31
十(十) 239
才(扌) 853
友(又) 268
互(二) 33
五(二) 32
天(大) 410
戸(戸) 841
甘(甘) 1325
可(口) 314
平(干) 573
正(止) 1128
再(冂) 162
更(口) 321
死(歹) 1133
百(白) 1363
西(西) 1638
亜(二) 35
否(口) 289
更(日) 997

束(木) 1051
求(水) 1155
豆(豆) 1715
表(衣) 1620
事(亅) 30
画(凵) 176
雨(雨) 1858
衷(衣) 1621
面(面) 1876

丨

中 16
巨(匚) 235
半(十) 243
旧(日) 964
甲(田) 1331
申(田) 1332

丶

丸 17
丹 18
主 19

凡(几) 170
勺(勹) 228
以(人) 43
斥(斤) 954
永(水) 1152
州(川) 549
良(艮) 1642
為(灬) 1274

丿

久 20
及 21
屯 22
之 23
乗 24

九(乙) 26
千(十) 240
午(十) 241
升(十) 242
手(手) 847
欠(欠) 1119
毛(毛) 1147
牛(牛) 1289
失(大) 413
生(生) 1327
矢(矢) 1393
先(儿) 145
向(口) 319
年(干) 574
有(月) 1003
朱(木) 1049
気(气) 1150
舌(舌) 1591
系(糸) 1504
受(又) 270
垂(土) 350
重(里) 1802

乙

乙 25
九 26
乾 27

乚

乱 28
乳 29

丸(丶) 17
孔(子) 456
札(木) 1067
礼(礻) 1417

亅

事 30

丁(一) 3
了(亅) 273
予(マ) 275
争(ク) 274

2 STROKES

二

二 31
五 32
互 33
井 34
亜 35
来 36

天(大) 410
仁(亻) 56
干(干) 572
元(儿) 141
夫(大) 411
未(木) 1048
示(示) 1413

亠

亡 37
交 38
京 39
享 40
亭 41

市(巾) 556
玄(玄) 1311
立(立) 1459
充(儿) 144
妄(女) 424
衣(衣) 1619
忘(心) 772
言(言) 1653
卒(十) 245
夜(夕) 406

育(月) 1013
盲(目) 1378
斉(斉) 1874
哀(口) 327
変(夂) 401
帝(巾) 561
恋(心) 784
畜(田) 1339
衰(衣) 1622
高(高) 1924
商(口) 330
率(玄) 1312
産(生) 1328
斎(斉) 1875
蛮(虫) 1609
棄(木) 1065
裏(衣) 1627
豪(豕) 1719
褒(衣) 1629
六(八) 153
文(文) 949
方(方) 957

人

人 42
以 43

内(冂) 160
囚(口) 336

入

介 44
今 45
令 46
会 47
企 48
全 49
余 50
舎 51
倉 52

傘　53
舗　54
合（口）284
命（口）325
念（心）774
金（金）1808
食（食）1900

亻

化　55
仁　56
仏　57
仕　58
仙　59
他　60
代　61
付　62
仮　63
休　64
仰　65
件　66
仲　67
伝　68
任　69
伐　70
伏　71
位　72
何　73
佐　74
作　75
伺　76
似　77
住　78
伸　79
体　80
但　81
低　82
伯　83
伴　84
依　85
価　86
佳　87
供　88
使　89

侍　90
侮　91
併　92
例　93
係　94
侯　95
俊　96
信　97
侵　98
促　99
俗　100
便　101
保　102
個　103
候　104
借　105
修　106
値　107
倒　108
俳　109
倍　110
俵　111
傲　112
俸　113
倫　114
偽　115
偶　116
健　117
側　118
停　119
偵　120
偏　121
偉　122
備　123
傍　124
傾　125
傑　126
催　127
債　128
傷　129
僧　130
働　131
像　132
僕　133

僚　135
億　136
儀　137
儒　138
償　139
優　140

儿

元　141
兄　142
光　143
充　144
先　145
兆　146
克　147
児　148
免　149
売（士）397
完（宀）468
見（見）1643
党（⺌）515

入

入　150
込（辶）675

八

八　151
公　152
六　153
共　154
兵　155
具　156
典　157
興　158
分（刀）180
父（父）1286
穴（穴）1450
呉（口）322
谷（谷）1714
貝（貝）1720
真（目）1385

翁（羽）1571

冂

円　159
内　160
冊　161
再　162

丹（丶）18
丙（一）14
用（用）1329
両（一）15
向（口）319
同（口）320
肉（肉）1010
周（口）324
尚（⺌）514
商（口）330

冖

冗　163
写　164
冠　165
軍（車）1771

冫

冷　166
准　167
凍　168
凝　169
冬（夂）399
兆（儿）146
次（欠）1120

几

凡　170
風　171
冗（一）163
処（夂）398
机（木）1068
肌（月）1021

凵

凶　172
凹　173
出　174
凸　175
画　176
山（山）535
幽（幺）579
歯（歯）1942

刀

刀　177
刃　178
切　179
分　180
初　181
券　182
召（口）279
辺（辶）676
忍（心）771

刂

刈　183
刊　184
刑　185
列　186
判　187
別　188
利　189
刻　190
刷　191
刺　192
制　193
到　194
削　195
前　196
則　197
剣　198
剛　199
剤　200
剖　201

838

剰 202
副 203
割 204
創 205
劇 206

倒（イ）109
側（イ）119
測（氵）1224

力

力 207
加 208
功 209
劣 210
助 211
努 212
励 213
労 214
劾 215
効 216
勅 217
勇 218
勉 219
勘 220
動 221
務 222
勤 223
勝 224
募 225
勧 226
勢 227

協（十）244
脅（月）1019
働（イ）132
幼（幺）578
男（田）1334
勲（灬）1284

勹

勺 228
匁 229
包 230

句（口）315
旬（日）965

匕

北 231
旨 232
化（イ）55
比（比）1146
尼（尸）522
老（老）1576
壱（士）395

匚

区 233
匹 234
巨 235
匠 236
医 237
匿 238
殴（殳）1138
臣（臣）1805
欧（欠）1121

十

十 239
千 240
午 241
升 242
半 243
協 244
卒 245
卓 246
南 247
卑 248
博 249

干（干）572
支（支）932
古（口）278
汁（氵）1157
年（干）574
早（日）966
克（儿）147

辛（辛）1784
直（目）1377
表（衣）1620
単（丷）516
計（言）1658
衷（衣）1621
索（糸）1505
針（金）1809
率（玄）1312
章（立）1460
準（氵）1233

卜

占 250
上（一）6
止（止）1127
外（夕）404
卓（十）246
点（灬）1275
貞（貝）1721
赴（走）1754
掛（扌）896

卩

印 251
却 252
即 253
卵 254
卸 255
御（イ）632
脚（月）1034

巳

危 256
厄（厂）257
犯（犭）1299

厂

厄 257
厚 258
厘 259

原 260
暦（日）980
反（又）267
圧（土）348
歴（止）1132
灰（火）1261
辱（辰）1786

厶

去 261
弁 262
参 263
公（八）152
台（口）280
仏（イ）57
払（扌）855
広（广）581
私（禾）1428
怠（心）777

又

又 264
収 265
266
反 267
友 268
取 269
受 270
叔 271
叙 272
及（丿）21
支（支）932
奴（女）431
皮（皮）1367
度（广）588
隻（隹）1849

了

了 273

ク

争 274
久（丿）20
危（巳）256
色（色）1599
角（角）1650
免（儿）149
急（心）775
負（貝）1722
魚（魚）1931
象（豕）1718

マ

予 275
矛（矛）1392
勇（力）218
柔（木）1057

3 STROKES

口

口 276
右 277
古 278
召 279
台 280
各 281
吉 282
后 283
合 284
名 285
含 286
君 287
告 288
否 289
唇 290
哲 291
唐 292
啓 293
喜 294
善 295

央 412
失 413
奇 414
奉 415
奔 416
契 417
奏 418
奥 419
奨 420
奪 421
奮 422

犬(犬) 1295
因(口) 337
戻(戸) 842
突(穴) 1453
春(日) 971
美(羊) 1566
臭(自) 1588
泰(水) 1156
器(口) 334

女

女 423
妄 424
妥 425
委 426
妻 427
威 428
姿 429
婆 430
奴 431
好 432
如 433
妃 434
妊 435
妨 436
妙 437
姉 438
始 439
姓 440
妹 441
姻 442
娯 443
娠 444

走(走) 1753
幸(干) 575
封(寸) 504

士

士 393
壮 394
壱 395
声 396
売 397

仕(イ) 58
吉(口) 282
志(心) 770
喜(口) 294

夂

処 398
冬 399
麦 400
変 401
夏 402

友(又) 268
各(口) 281
条(木) 1050
愛(心) 790
慶(心) 799
憂(心) 800

夕

夕 403
外 404
多 405
夜 406
夢 407

名(口) 285

大

大 408
太 409
天 410
夫 411

堂 355
堅 356
堕 357
塁 358
塑 359
塗 360
墓 361
塾 362
墨 363
墜 364
懇 365
壁 366
地 367
均 368
坑 369
坂 370
坊 371
坪 372
垣 373
城 374
埋 375
域 376
培 377
堀 378
堪 379
場 380
塚 381
堤 382
塔 383
塀 384
塩 385
塊 386
境 387
増 388
墳 389
壊 390
壌 391
壇 392

去(ム) 261
吐(口) 298
寺(寸) 500
至(至) 1589
社(ネ) 1418
赤(赤) 1751

尚(ツ) 514
知(矢) 1394
衷(衣) 1621
衰(衣) 1622
倉(人) 52
害(宀) 481
宮(宀) 482
営(ツ) 518
鳴(鳥) 1935
中(｜) 16
兄(儿) 142
加(力) 208
占(卜) 250
石(石) 1397
如(女) 433
舌(舌) 1591

口

四 335
囚 336
因 337
回 338
団 339
囲 340
困 341
図 342
固 343
国 344
圏 345
園 346

田(田) 1330
由(田) 1333
曲(曰) 996

土

土 347
圧 348
在 349
垂 350
執 351
報 352
型 353
基 354

吸 296
叫 297
吐 298
吟 299
吹 300
呼 301
味 302
咲 303
唆 304
喝 305
唱 306
唯 307
喚 308
喫 309
嘆 310
嘱 311
噴 312
嚇 313
可 314
句 315
号 316
史 317
司 318
向 319
同 320
吏 321
呉 322
呈 323
周 324
命 325
和 326
哀 327
品 328
員 329
商 330
問 331
喪 332
嗣 333
器 334

虫(虫) 1604
言(言) 1653
谷(谷) 1714
足(足) 1759
舎(人) 51

姫	445	宴	479	守(宀)	466	誉(言)	1654	炭(火)	1267
娘	446	家	480	村(木)	1073			密(宀)	489
婚	447	害	481	耐(而)	1579	**尢**		仙(亻)	59
婦	448	宮	482	討(言)	1663				
婿	449	宰	483	辱(辰)	1786	就	520	**川**	
媒	450	宵	484	奪(大)	421				
嫁	451	容	485	樹(木)	1117	**尸**		川	548
嫌	452	寄	486					州	549
嫡	453	寂	487	**小**			521		
嬢	454	宿	488			尺	522	巡(辶)	677
		密	489	小	511	尼	523	災(火)	1263
安(宀)	464	寒	490	少	512	尽	524	訓(言)	1661
要(西)	1639	富	491	示(示)	1413	局	525	順(頁)	1884
		寛	492	劣(力)	210	尿	526		
子		寝	493	糸(糸)	1503	尾	527	**工**	
		寡	494	系(糸)	1504	居	528		
子	455	察	495	京(亠)	39	屈	529	工	550
孔	456	寧	496	県(目)	1380	届	530	巧	551
字	457	審	497	省(目)	1382	屋	531	左	552
存	458	寮	498	原(厂)	260	展	532	差	553
孝	459					属	533		
学	460	穴(穴)	1450	**ツ**		層	534	功(力)	209
季	461	字(子)	457			履		江(氵)	1160
孤	462	究(穴)	1451	当	513			攻(攵)	934
孫	463	空(穴)	1452	尚	514	戸(戸)	841	紅(糸)	1515
		突(穴)	1453	党	515	刷(刂)	191	貢(貝)	1723
厚(厂)	258	窃(穴)	1454			昼(日)	974	項(頁)	1883
好(女)	432	案(木)	1060	光(儿)	143	尉(寸)	507		
享(亠)	40			肖(月)	1012	殿(殳)	1142	**己**	
		寸		堂(土)	355				
宀				常(巾)	566	**山**		己	554
		寸	499	掌(手)	850			巻	555
安	464	寺	500	賞(貝)	1738	山	535		
宇	465	寿	501			岐	536	紀(糸)	1512
守	466	対	502	**ツ**		岳	537	記(言)	1660
宅	467	専	503			岩	538	起(走)	1755
完	468	封	504	単	516	岸	539	配(酉)	1790
官	469	射	505	巣	517	岬	540	包(勹)	230
実	470	将	506	営	518	峡	541	妃(女)	434
宗	471	尉	507	厳	519	峠	542	忌(心)	769
宙	472	尋	508			島	543	改(攵)	933
定	473	尊	509	労(力)	214	峰	544		
宝	474	導	510	学(子)	460	崎	545	**巾**	
宣	475			栄(木)	1054	崇	546		
客	476	付(亻)	62	挙(手)	849	崩	547	市	556
室	477	団(囗)	339	蛍(虫)	1607			布	557
宜	478			覚(見)	1646	出(凵)	174	帆	558
						幽(幺)	579	希	559

帥 560
帝 561
帰 562
師 563
席 564
帯 565
常 566
帳 567
幅 568
帽 569
幕 570
幣 571

干

干 572
平 573
年 574
幸 575
幹 576
肝(月) 1022
軒(車) 1772
午(十) 241
刊(刂) 184
汗(氵) 1159

幺

幻 577
幼 578
幽 579
幾 580
玄(玄) 1311
糸(糸) 1503
郷(阝) 760

广

広 581
庁 582
序 583
床 584
底 585
店 586
府 587

度 588
庫 589
座 590
庭 591
康 592
庶 593
庸 594
廃 595
廊 596
廉 597
席(巾) 564
麻(麻) 1938
腐(肉) 1011
慶(心) 799
摩(手) 852
応(心) 768
唐(口) 292
磨(石) 1410
魔(鬼) 1929

廴

廷 598
延 599
建 600

廾

弊 601
弁(厶) 262
奔(大) 416
葬(艹) 662
算(竹) 1485
鼻(鼻) 1945

弋

式 602
弐 603
代(亻) 61
武(止) 1129

弓

弓 604

引 605
弔 606
弟 607
弦 608
弧 609
弱 610
強 611
張 612
弾 613

彐

粛 614
君(口) 287
郡(阝) 758
書(曰) 998
雪(雨) 1859
尋(寸) 508
群(羊) 1569

彡

形 615
彩 616
彫 617
彰 618
影 619
参(厶) 263
杉(木) 1072
膨(月) 1043

彳

役 620
往 621
径 622
征 623
彼 624
後 625
待 626
律 627
従 628
徐 629
徒 630
得 631

御 632
循 633
復 634
微 635
徴 636
徳 637
徹 638
行(行) 1613
術(行) 1614
街(行) 1615
衝(行) 1616
衛(行) 1617
衡(行) 1618

艹

芋 639
芝 640
花 641
芸 642
芳 643
英 644
芽 645
苦 646
茎 647
若 648
苗 649
茂 650
荒 651
草 652
荘 653
茶 654
荷 655
華 656
菓 657
菌 658
菜 659
著 660
葬 661
葉 662
落 663
蒸 664
蓄 665
蔵 666
667

薫 668
薪 669
薦 670
薄 671
薬 672
藩 673
藻 674
募(力) 225
墓(土) 361
夢(夕) 407
幕(巾) 570
慕(小) 835
暮(日) 979
繭(糸) 1511

辶

込 675
辺 676
巡 677
迅 678
近 679
迎 680
返 681
述 682
迭 683
迫 684
逆 685
送 686
退 687
追 688
逃 689
迷 690
逝 691
造 692
速 693
逐 694
通 695
逓 696
途 697
透 698
連 699
逸 700
週 701
進 702

伐 (イ) 70
威 (女) 428
栽 (木) 1061
裁 (衣) 1624
載 (車) 1778

戸
戸 841
戻 842
所 843
房 844
扇 845
扉 846
肩 (月) 1014
雇 (隹) 1850

手
手 847
承 848
挙 849
掌 850
撃 851
摩 852
看 (目) 1379

扌
才 853
打 854
払 855
扱 856
抗 857
折 858
択 859
投 860
把 861
抜 862
批 863
扶 864
抑 865
押 866
　 867
　 868

懸 806
窓 (穴) 1455

忄
忙 807
快 808
怪 809
怖 810
性 811
悔 812
恒 813
恨 814
悦 815
悟 816
悩 817
惨 818
情 819
惜 820
悼 821
慌 822
惰 823
愉 824
慨 825
慎 826
慣 827
憎 828
慢 829
憤 830
憶 831
懐 832
憾 833

小
恭 834
慕 835

戈
成 836
我 837
戒 838
戦 839
戯 840

4 STROKES

心
心 766
必 767
応 768
忌 769
志 770
忍 771
忘 772
忠 773
念 774
急 775
思 776
怠 777
怒 778
恩 779
恐 780
恵 781
息 782
恥 783
恋 784
悪 785
患 786
悠 787
悲 788
惑 789
愛 790
意 791
感 792
愚 793
慈 794
愁 795
想 796
態 797
慰 798
慶 799
憂 800
慮 801
憩 802
憲 803
懇 804
懲 805

隅 744
随 745
隊 746
陽 747
隔 748
隠 749
際 750
障 751
隣 752

阝
邦 753
邪 754
邸 755
郊 756
郎 757
郡 758
郭 759
郷 760
都 761
部 762
郵 763

丷
並 764
兼 765
半 (十) 243
前 (刂) 196
美 (羊) 1566
首 (首) 1910
差 (工) 553
益 (皿) 1370
瓶 (瓦) 1324
善 (口) 295
尊 (寸) 509
普 (日) 978
着 (羊) 1567
慈 (心) 794
義 (羊) 1568
養 (食) 1901

逮 703
運 704
過 705
遇 706
遂 707
達 708
遅 709
道 710
遍 711
遊 712
違 713
遠 714
遺 715
遮 716
遭 717
適 718
遺 719
遵 720
選 721
遷 722
還 723
避 724
導 (寸) 510

阝
防 725
阻 726
附 727
限 728
院 729
陥 730
降 731
除 732
陣 733
陛 734
陰 735
険 736
陳 737
陶 738
陪 739
陸 740
隆 741
陵 742
階 743

曜 995
旨(匕) 232
者(耂) 1578
香(香) 1911

曰
曲 996
更 997
書 998
曹 999
最 1000
替 1001
甲(田) 1331
申(田) 1332
由(田) 1333
冒(目) 1384
量(里) 1804

月
月 1002
有 1003
服 1004
朕 1005
朗 1006
望 1007
期 1008
朝 1009
青(青) 1871
前(刂) 196
宵(宀) 484
骨(骨) 1922
豚(豕) 1717
勝(力) 224
謄(言) 1656
騰(馬) 1913

肉
肉 1010
腐 1011

施 958
旅 959
旋 960
族 961
旗 962
防(阝) 725
放(攵) 935
肪(月) 1025
紡(糸) 1521
訪(言) 1667

日
日 963
旧 964
旬 965
早 966
易 967
昆 968
昇 969
昔 970
春 971
是 972
星 973
昼 974
景 975
暑 976
晶 977
普 978
暮 979
暦 980
暫 981
暴 982
曇 983
明 984
映 985
昨 986
昭 987
時 988
暁 989
晴 990
晩 991
暗 992
暇 993
暖 994

整 948
枚(木) 1080
牧(牛) 1291
致(至) 1590
傲(イ) 113
赦(赤) 1752
微(彳) 635
徴(彳) 636
徹(彳) 638
撤(扌) 926

文
文 949
対(寸) 502
斉(斉) 1874
紋(糸) 1522
蚊(虫) 1605
斎(斉) 1875

斗
斗 950
料 951
斜 952
科(禾) 1430

斤
斤 953
斥 954
断 955
新 956
匠(匚) 236
近(辶) 679
折(扌) 860
所(戸) 843
析(木) 1077
祈(ネ) 1419
漸(氵) 1242
質(貝) 1737

方
方 957

揮 914
提 915
搭 916
揚 917
揺 918
携 919
搾 920
摂 921
損 922
搬 923
摘 924
撮 925
撤 926
撲 927
操 928
擁 929
擬 930
擦 931

支
支 932
岐(山) 536
技(扌) 857
枝(木) 1074
肢(月) 1023
鼓(鼓) 1944

攵
改 933
攻 934
放 935
故 936
政 937
敏 938
救 939
教 940
敗 941
敢 942
敬 943
散 944
数 945
敵 946
敷 947

拐 869
拡 870
拒 871
拠 872
拘 873
招 874
拙 875
拓 876
担 877
抽 878
抵 879
拝 880
拍 881
披 882
抱 883
抹 884
括 885
挟 886
拷 887
指 888
持 889
拾 890
挑 891
振 892
捜 893
挿 894
捕 895
掛 896
掘 897
掲 898
控 899
採 900
捨 901
授 902
推 903
据 904
接 905
措 906
掃 907
探 908
排 909
描 910
握 911
援 912
換 913

月

肖 1012
育 1013
肩 1014
肯 1015
胃 1016
背 1017
能 1018
脅 1019
膚 1020
肌 1021
肝 1022
肢 1023
肥 1024
肪 1025
胎 1026
胆 1027
肺 1028
胞 1029
胸 1030
脂 1031
胴 1032
脈 1033
脚 1034
脱 1035
脳 1036
脹 1037
腕 1038
腸 1039
腹 1040
腰 1041
膜 1042
膨 1043
臓 1044
骨(骨)1922
豚(豕)1717

木

木 1045
本 1046
末 1047
未 1048

朱 1049
条 1050
束 1051
果 1052
東 1053
栄 1054
架 1055
査 1056
柔 1057
染 1058
某 1059
案 1060
栽 1061
桑 1062
森 1063
楽 1064
棄 1065
業 1066
札 1067
机 1068
朽 1069
朴 1070
材 1071
杉 1072
村 1073
枝 1074
松 1075
枢 1076
析 1077
杯 1078
板 1079
枚 1080
林 1081
枠 1082
枯 1083
柱 1084
柄 1085
柳 1086
桜 1087
格 1088
核 1089
株 1090
校 1091
根 1092
桟 1093

栓 1094
桃 1095
梅 1096
械 1097
棺 1098
棋 1099
極 1100
検 1101
植 1102
棚 1103
棟 1104
棒 1105
楼 1106
概 1107
構 1108
模 1109
様 1110
横 1111
権 1112
槽 1113
標 1114
機 1115
橋 1116
樹 1117
欄 1118
困(囗)341
床(广)584
相(目)1383
麻(麻)1938
巣(⺍)517
集(隹)1851
禁(示)1416
築(竹)1488

欠

欠 1119
次 1120
欧 1121
欲 1122
款 1123
欺 1124
歌 1125
歓 1126
吹(口)300
炊(火)1265
軟(車)1774
飲(食)1903

止

止 1127
正 1128
武 1129
歩 1130
歳 1131
歴 1132
企(人)48
肯(月)1015
祉(ネ)1420
紫(糸)1507
歯(歯)1942
雌(隹)1854

歹

死 1133
残 1134
殊 1135
殉 1136
殖 1137
列(刂)186

殳

殴 1138
段 1139
殺 1140
殻 1141
殿 1142
没(氵)1167
疫(疒)1348
般(舟)1594
設(言)1666
穀(禾)1441
役(彳)620
投(扌)862

母

母 1143
毎 1144
毒 1145
悔(亻)91
悔(忄)812
海(氵)1184
貫(貝)1725

比

比 1146
批(扌)865
昆(日)968
皆(白)1365

毛

毛 1147
尾(尸)526
耗(耒)1581

氏

氏 1148
民 1149
低(亻)82
底(广)585
邸(阝)755
抵(扌)879

气

気 1150
汽(氵)1162

水

水 1151
永 1152
氷 1153

牛
牛 1289
物 1290
牧 1291
特 1292
犧 1293
犠 1294
件(亻) 66

犬
犬 1295
状 1296
献 1297
獣 1298
伏(亻) 71

犭
犯 1299
狂 1300
狭 1301
狩 1302
独 1303
猫 1304
猛 1305
猟 1306
猶 1307
猿 1308
獄 1309
獲 1310

5 STROKES

玄
玄 1311
率 1312

弦(弓) 608
畜(田) 1339

燥 1272
爆 1273
畑(田) 1337
秋(禾) 1431

灬
為 1274
点 1275
烈 1276
煮 1277
焦 1278
然 1279
無 1280
照 1281
熟 1282
熱 1283
勲 1284
馬(馬) 1912
庶(广) 593
魚(魚) 1931
鳥(鳥) 1934
黒(黒) 1940
蒸(艹) 665
窯(穴) 1458
黙(黒) 1941
薫(艹) 668

四
爵 1285
妥(女) 425
受(又) 270
愛(心) 790

父
父 1286
交(亠) 38

片
片 1287
版 1288

滅 1237
溶 1238
演 1239
漁 1240
漆 1241
漸 1242
潰 1243
滴 1244
漂 1245
漫 1246
漏 1247
潟 1248
潔 1249
潤 1250
潜 1251
潮 1252
澄 1253
激 1254
濁 1255
濃 1256
濯 1257
濫 1258
瀬 1259

染(木) 1058
酒(酉) 1789
婆(女) 430
落(艹) 664
塗(土) 360
薄(艹) 671
藩(艹) 673

火
火 1260
灰 1261
灯 1262
災 1263
炎 1264
炊 1265
炉 1266
炭 1267
焼 1268
煙 1269
煩 1270
燃 1271

派 1192
洋 1193
消 1194
浸 1195
浜 1196
浮 1197
浦 1198
浴 1199
流 1200
涙 1201
浪 1202
液 1203
涯 1204
渇 1205
渓 1206
混 1207
済 1208
渋 1209
淑 1210
渉 1211
深 1212
清 1213
淡 1214
添 1215
涼 1216
温 1217
渦 1218
減 1219
湖 1220
港 1221
滋 1222
湿 1223
測 1224
渡 1225
湯 1226
満 1227
湾 1228
滑 1229
漢 1230
源 1231
溝 1232
準 1233
滞 1234
滝 1235
漠 1236

泉 1154
承(手) 848

氷
求 1155
泰 1156

氵
汁 1157
汚 1158
汗 1159
江 1160
池 1161
汽 1162
決 1163
沢 1164
沖 1165
沈 1166
没 1167
泳 1168
沿 1169
河 1170
泣 1171
況 1172
沼 1173
治 1174
注 1175
泥 1176
波 1177
泊 1178
泌 1179
沸 1180
法 1181
泡 1182
油 1183
海 1184
活 1185
洪 1186
浄 1187
津 1188
洗 1189
浅 1190
洞 1191

玉
玉 1313
璽 1314
宝(宀) 474
国(囗) 344

王
王 1315
珍 1316
珠 1317
班 1318
球 1319
現 1320
理 1321
琴 1322
環 1323
主(丶) 19
全(入) 49
呈(口) 323
狂(犭) 1300
皇(白) 1366
望(月) 1007
聖(耳) 1583

瓦
瓶 1324

甘
甘 1325
甚 1326
某(木) 1059

生
生 1327
産 1328
姓(女) 440
性(忄) 811
星(日) 973
牲(牛) 1292

用
用 1329

田
田 1330
甲 1331
申 1332
由 1333
男 1334
町 1335
界 1336
畑 1337
畝 1338
畜 1339
畔 1340
留 1341
異 1342
略 1343
畳 1344
番 1345
里(里) 1801
画(凵) 176
果(木) 1052
思(心) 776
胃(月) 1016
累(糸) 1508
塁(土) 358
富(宀) 491
蓄(艹) 666
雷(雨) 1863
審(宀) 497
奮(大) 422

疋
疎 1346
疑 1347

疒
疫 1348
疾 1349
症 1350

疲 1351
病 1352
痛 1353
痘 1354
痢 1355
痴 1356
療 1357
癖 1358
癒 1359

癶
発 1360
登 1361

白
白 1362
百 1363
的 1364
皆 1365
皇 1366
伯(亻) 83
迫(辶) 684
拍(扌) 881
泊(氵) 1178
泉(水) 1154
習(羽) 1572
舶(舟) 1596
楽(木) 1064

皮
皮 1367
彼(彳) 624
披(扌) 882
波(氵) 1177
疲(疒) 1351
破(石) 1401
被(ネ) 1631

皿
皿 1368
盆 1369

益 1370
盛 1371
盗 1372
盟 1373
監 1374
盤 1375
血(血) 1611

目
目 1376
直 1377
盲 1378
看 1379
県 1380
盾 1381
省 1382
相 1383
冒 1384
真 1385
眠 1386
眼 1387
眺 1388
睡 1389
督 1390
瞬 1391
見(見) 1643
貝(貝) 1720
具(八) 156
着(羊) 1567

矛
矛 1392
柔(木) 1057
務(力) 222

矢
矢 1393
知 1394
短 1395
矯 1396
医(匚) 237

疾(疒) 1349

石
石 1397
研 1398
砂 1399
砕 1400
破 1401
砲 1402
硬 1403
硝 1404
硫 1405
碁 1406
磁 1407
碑 1408
確 1409
磨 1410
礁 1411
礎 1412
岩(山) 538
拓(扌) 876

示
示 1413
祭 1414
票 1415
禁 1416
宗(宀) 471
斎(斉) 1875
祟(山) 546

ネ
礼 1417
社 1418
祈 1419
祉 1420
祝 1421
神 1422
祖 1423
祥 1424
禍 1425
禅 1426

織 1561
繕 1562
繰 1563

【缶】
缶 1564

【羊】
羊 1565
美 1566
着 1567
義 1568
群 1569
洋(氵) 1193
差(工) 553
祥(ネ) 1424
善(口) 295
詳(言) 1682
養(食) 1901
鮮(魚) 1932

【羽】
羽 1570
翁 1571
習 1572
翌 1573
翼 1574
翻 1575
扇(戸) 845

【老】
老 1576

【耂】
考 1577
者 1578
孝(子) 459
煮(灬) 1277

約 1516
紙 1517
純 1518
納 1519
紛 1520
紡 1521
紋 1522
経 1523
紺 1524
細 1525
終 1526
紹 1527
紳 1528
組 1529
絵 1530
給 1531
結 1532
絞 1532
絶 1534
統 1535
絡 1536
継 1537
続 1538
維 1539
綱 1540
緒 1541
総 1542
綿 1543
網 1544
緑 1545
練 1546
緩 1547
縄 1548
線 1549
締 1550
編 1551
緯 1552
縛 1553
縦 1554
縫 1555
縮 1556
績 1557
繊 1558
     1559
     1560

等 1479
筒 1480
筆 1481
節 1482
箇 1483
管 1484
算 1485
箱 1486
範 1487
築 1488
篤 1489
簡 1490
簿 1491
籍 1492

【米】
米 1493
粋 1494
粉 1495
粗 1496
粘 1497
粒 1498
粧 1499
精 1500
糖 1501
糧 1502
迷(辶) 690
料(斗) 951

【糸】
糸 1503
系 1504
索 1505
素 1506
紫 1507
累 1508
緊 1509
繁 1510
繭 1511
紀 1512
級 1513
糾 1514
紅 1515

容(宀) 485

【立】
立 1459
章 1460
童 1461
端 1462
競 1463
位(イ) 72
辛(辛) 1784
泣(氵) 1171
音(音) 1879
竜(竜) 1930
産(生) 1328
粒(米) 1498
意(心) 791

【罒】
罪 1464
署 1465
置 1466
罰 1467
罷 1468
羅 1469

【旡】
既 1470
概(忄) 825
概(木) 1107

6 STROKES

【竹】
竹 1471
笑 1472
第 1473
笛 1474
符 1475
筋 1476
策 1477
答 1478

福 1427
視(見) 1645

【禾】
私 1428
秀 1429
科 1430
秋 1431
秒 1432
称 1433
租 1434
秩 1435
秘 1436
移 1437
税 1438
程 1439
稚 1440
穀 1441
種 1442
稲 1443
稼 1444
稿 1445
穂 1446
穏 1447
積 1448
穫 1449
愁(心) 795
番(田) 1345
和(口) 326
委(女) 426
利(刂) 189
季(子) 461

【穴】
穴 1450
究 1451
空 1452
突 1453
窃 1454
窓 1455
窒 1456
窮 1457
窯 1458

而
耐 1579
需(雨) 1865

耒
耕 1580
耗 1581

耳
耳 1582
聖 1583
聞 1584
聴 1585
職 1586
取(又) 269
恥(心) 783

自
自 1587
臭 1588
首(首) 1910
息(心) 782
鼻(鼻) 1945

至
至 1589
致 1590
到(刂) 194
室(宀) 477
屋(尸) 530
倒(イ) 109
窒(穴) 1456

舌
舌 1591
活(氵) 1185
話(言) 1684
乱(乚) 28

辞(辛) 1785
舗(八) 54
舎(八) 51
憩(心) 802
括(扌) 885

舟
舟 1592
航 1593
般 1594
船 1595
舶 1596
艇 1597
艦 1598
盤(皿) 1375

色
色 1599
絶(糸) 1534

虍
虐 1600
虚 1601
虞 1602
虜 1603

劇(刂) 206
慮(心) 801
戯(戈) 840
膚(月) 1020

虫
虫 1604
蚊 1605
蚕 1606
蛍 1607
蛇 1608
蛮 1609
融 1610
独(犭) 1303
風(几) 171
触(角) 1652

血
血 1611
衆 1612

行
行 1613
術 1614
街 1615
衝 1616
衛 1617
衡 1618

衣
衣 1619
表 1620
衷 1621
衰 1622
袋 1623
裁 1624
装 1625
裂 1626
裏 1627
製 1628
褒 1629
襲 1630

哀(口) 327
依(イ) 85

衤
被 1631
補 1632
裕 1633
褐 1634
裸 1635
複 1636
襟 1637

初(刀) 181

西
西 1638

要 1639
覆 1640
覇 1641
価(イ) 86

艮
良 1642
根(木) 1092
限(阝) 728
恨(忄) 814
銀(金) 1817
退(辶) 687
眼(目) 1387

聿
建(廴) 600
律(イ) 627
津(氵) 1188
書(日) 998
健(イ) 118
粛(彐) 614
筆(竹) 1481

7 STROKES

見
見 1643
規 1644
視 1645
覚 1646
親 1647
覧 1648
観 1649
寛(宀) 492
現(王) 1320

角
角 1650
解 1651
触 1652

言
言 1653
誉 1654
哲 1655
騰 1656
警 1657
計 1658
訂 1659
記 1660
訓 1661
託 1662
討 1663
許 1664
訟 1665
設 1666
訪 1667
訳 1668
詠 1669
詐 1670
詞 1671
証 1672
詔 1673
診 1674
訴 1675
評 1676
該 1677
詰 1678
誇 1679
試 1680
詩 1681
詳 1682
誠 1683
話 1684
語 1685
誤 1686
誌 1687
説 1688
読 1689
認 1690
誘 1691
謁 1692
課 1693
諸 1694

里

里 1801
重 1802
野 1803
量 1804

厘(厂) 259
埋(土) 375
理(王) 1321
黒(黒) 1940
童(立) 1461
裏(衣) 1627
墨(土) 363
黙(黒) 1941

臣

臣 1805
臨 1806

姫(女) 445
堅(土) 356
監(皿) 1374
緊(糸) 1509
賢(貝) 1740
覧(見) 1648

舛

舞 1807

8 STROKES

金

金 1808
針 1809
釣 1810
鈍 1811
鉛 1812
鉱 1813
鉄 1814
鉢 1815
鈴 1816
銀 1817

輝 1779
輩 1780
輪 1781
輸 1782
轄 1783

庫(广) 589
撃(手) 851
暫(日) 981

辛

辛 1784
辞 1785

宰(宀) 483

辰

辱 1786
農 1787

娠(女) 444
振(扌) 892
震(雨) 1866

酉

酌 1788
酒 1789
配 1790
酔 1791
酢 1792
酬 1793
酪 1794
酵 1795
酷 1796
酸 1797
醜 1798
醸 1799

釆

釈 1800

番(田) 1345

赤

赤 1751
赦 1752

嚇(口) 313

走

走 1753
赴 1754
起 1755
越 1756
超 1757
趣 1758

足

足 1759
距 1760
跡 1761
践 1762
跳 1763
路 1764
踊 1765
踏 1766
躍 1767

促(イ) 99

身

身 1768

射(寸) 505

車

車 1769
軌 1770
軍 1771
軒 1772
転 1773
軟 1774
軽 1775
軸 1776
較 1777
載 1778

逐(辶) 694
塚(土) 381
遂(辶) 707
隊(阝) 746

貝

貝 1720
貞 1721
負 1722
貢 1723
貨 1724
貫 1725
責 1726
貧 1727
賀 1728
貴 1729
貸 1730
買 1731
費 1732
貿 1733
資 1734
賃 1735
賛 1736
質 1737
賞 1738
賓 1739
賢 1740
財 1741
販 1742
貯 1743
賊 1744
賄 1745
賜 1746
賠 1747
賦 1748
購 1749
贈 1750

則(刂) 197
員(口) 329
側(イ) 119
敗(攵) 941
測(氵) 1224
頼(頁) 1890

請 1695
諾 1696
誕 1697
談 1698
調 1699
論 1700
諮 1701
謀 1702
諭 1703
謡 1704
謹 1705
謙 1706
講 1707
謝 1708
識 1709
譜 1710
議 1711
譲 1712
護 1713

獄(犭) 1309

谷

谷 1714

俗(イ) 100
容(宀) 485
浴(氵) 1199
欲(欠) 1122
裕(衤) 1633

豆

豆 1715
豊 1716

頭(頁) 1889
登(癶) 1361
短(矢) 1395

豕

豚 1717
象 1718
豪 1719

家(宀) 480

銃 1818
銭 1819
銑 1820
銅 1821
銘 1822
鋭 1823
鋳 1824
鋼 1825
錯 1826
錠 1827
錘 1828
錬 1829
録 1830
鍛 1831
鎖 1832
鎮 1833
鏡 1834
鐘 1835
鑑 1836

長

長 1837
帳 (巾) 567
張 (弓) 612
脹 (月) 1037
髪 (髟) 1925

門

門 1838
閉 1839
開 1840
間 1841
閑 1842
閣 1843
関 1844
閥 1845
閲 1846
闘 1847
問 (口) 331
聞 (耳) 1584

隶

隷 1848
康 (广) 592
逮 (辶) 703

隹

隻 1849
雇 1850
集 1851
雄 1852
雅 1853
雌 1854
雑 1855
難 1856
離 1857
唯 (口) 307
進 (辶) 702
推 (扌) 903
焦 (灬) 1278

雨

雨 1858
雪 1859
雲 1860
霧 1861
電 1862
雷 1863
零 1864
需 1865
震 1866
霊 1867
霜 1868
霧 1869
露 1870
漏 (氵) 1247
曇 (日) 983

青

青 1871
静 1872

情 (忄) 819
清 (氵) 1213
晴 (日) 990
精 (米) 1500
請 (言) 1695

非

非 1873
扉 (戸) 846
罪 (罒) 1464
俳 (亻) 110
輩 (車) 1780
排 (扌) 909
悲 (心) 788

斉

斉 1874
斎 1875
剤 (刂) 200
済 (氵) 1208

9 STROKES

面

面 1876

革

革 1877
靴 1878

音

音 1879
韻 1880
響 1881
暗 (日) 992

頁

頂 1882
項 1883

順 1884
頑 1885
頌 1886
預 1887
領 1888
頭 1889
頼 1890
頻 1891
額 1892
顔 1893
顕 1894
題 1895
類 1896
願 1897
顧 1898
傾 (亻) 126
煩 (火) 1270
瀬 (氵) 1259

飛

飛 1899

食

食 1900
養 1901

食

飢 1902
飲 1903
飯 1904
飼 1905
飾 1906
飽 1907
餓 1908
館 1909

首

首 1910
道 (辶) 710
導 (寸) 510

香

香 1911

10 STROKES

馬

馬 1912
騰 1913
驚 1914
駅 1915
駆 1916
駄 1917
駐 1918
騎 1919
験 1920
騒 1921
篤 (竹) 1489

骨

骨 1922
髄 1923
滑 (氵) 1229

高

高 1924
稿 (禾) 1445

髟

髪 1925

鬼

鬼 1926
魂 1927
魅 1928
魔 1929
塊 (土) 386
醜 (酉) 1798

竜		12 STROKES
竜	1930	**歯**
滝(氵)	1235	歯 1942
11 STROKES		齢 1943
魚		**13 STROKES**
魚	1931	**鼓**
鮮	1932	鼓 1944
鯨	1933	**14 STROKES**
漁(氵)	1240	**鼻**
鳥		鼻 1945
鳥	1934	
鳴	1935	
鶏	1936	

魚   1931
鮮   1932
鯨   1933
漁(氵) 1240

鳥   1934
鳴   1935
鶏   1936

麗   1937

麻   1938
摩(手) 852
磨(石) 1410
魔(鬼) 1929

黄   1939
横(木) 1111

黒   1940
黙   1941
墨(土) 363

ON/KUN INDEX

ON/KUN INDEX

(by ON/KUN and kanji number)

あ		あさ	朝 1009	あね	姉 438

ア	亜 35	あさ	朝 1009
アイ	哀 327		麻 1938
	愛 790	あざ	字 457
あい	相 1383	あさい	浅 1190
あいだ	間 1841	あざむく	欺 1124
あう	会 47	あざやか	鮮 1932
	合 284	あし	脚 1034
	遭 717		足 1759
あお	青 1871	あじ	味 302
あおい	青 1871	あじわう	味 302
あおぐ	仰 65	あずかる	預 1887
あか	赤 1751	あずける	預 1887
あかい	赤 1751	あせ	汗 1159
あかす	明 984	あせる	焦 1278
	飽 1907	あそぶ	遊 712
あかつき	暁 989	あたい	価 86
あからむ	明 984		値 108
	赤 1751	あたえる	与 9
あからめる	赤 1751	あたたか	暖 994
あかり	明 984		温 1217
あがる	上 6	あたたかい	暖 994
	挙 849		温 1217
	揚 917	あたたまる	暖 994
あかるい	明 984		温 1217
あかるむ	明 984	あたためる	暖 994
あき	秋 1431		温 1217
あきなう	商 330	あたま	頭 1889
あきらか	明 984	あたらしい	新 956
あきる	飽 1907	あたり	辺 676
アク	悪 785	あたる	当 513
	握 911	アツ	圧 348
あく	明 984	あつい	厚 258
	空 1452		暑 976
	開 1840		熱 1283
あくる	明 984	あつかう	扱 856
あける	明 984	あつまる	集 1851
	空 1452	あつめる	集 1851
	開 1840	あてる	充 144
			当 513
あげる	上 6	あと	後 625
	挙 849		跡 1761
	揚 917	あな	穴 1450
		あなどる	侮 91
		あに	兄 142

あね	姉 438
あばく	暴 982
あばれる	暴 982
あびせる	浴 1199
あびる	浴 1199
あぶない	危 256
あぶら	脂 1031
	油 1183
あま	天 410
	尼 522
	雨 1858
あまい	甘 1325
あまえる	甘 1325
あます	余 50
あまやかす	甘 1325
あまる	余 50
あみ	網 1545
あむ	編 1553
あめ	天 410
	雨 1858
あやうい	危 256
あやしい	怪 809
あやしむ	怪 809
あやつる	操 928
あやぶむ	危 256
あやまち	過 705
あやまつ	過 705
あやまる	誤 1686
	謝 1708
あゆむ	歩 1130
あらい	荒 651
	粗 1496
あらう	洗 1189
あらす	荒 651
あらそう	争 274
あらた	新 956
あらたまる	改 933
あらためる	改 933
あらわす	著 661
	現 1320
	表 1620
あらわれる	現 1320
	表 1620
ある	在 349

ある　有 1003
あるく　歩 1130
あれる　荒 651
あわ　泡 1182
あわい　淡 1214
あわす　合 284
あわせる　併 92
あわせる　合 284
あわただしい　慌 822
あわてる　慌 822
あわれ　哀 327
あわれむ　哀 327
アン　安 464
　暗 992
　案 1060
　行 1613

い

イ　以 43
　位 72
　依 85
　偉 123
　医 237
　唯 307
　囲 340
　委 426
　威 428
　尉 507
　違 713
　遺 719
　意 791
　慰 798
　易 967
　胃 1016
　為 1274
　異 1342
　移 1437
　維 1540
　緯 1554
　衣 1619
　井 34
　言 1653
　家 480
い
いい
いう　生 1327
いえ　怒 778
いかす
いかる　域 376
イキ
いき　息 782

いきおい　勢 227
いきどおる　憤 830
いきる　生 1013
イク　育 580
いく　行 1613
いくさ　戦 839
いけ　池 1161
いける　生 1327
いこい　憩 802
いこう　憩 802
いさぎよい　潔 1249
いさむ　勇 218
いし　石 1397
いしずえ　礎 1412
いずみ　泉 1154
いそがしい　忙 775
いそぐ　急 807
いた　板 1079
いたい　痛 1353
いだく　抱 883
いたす　致 1590
いただき　頂 1882
いただく　頂 1882
いたむ　傷 130
　悼 821
　痛 1353
いためる　傷 130
　痛 1353
いたる　至 1589
イチ　一 1
　壱 395
いち　市 556
いちじるしい　著 661
イツ　一 1
　逸 700
いつくしむ　慈 794
いつつ　五 32
いつわる　偽 116
　糸 1503
いとなむ　営 518
いどむ　挑 891
いな　否 289
　稲 1443
いぬ　犬 1295
いね　稲 1443
いのち　命 325
いのる　祈 1419

いま　今 45
いましめる　戒 838
いまわしい　忌 769
いむ　忌 769
いも　芋 639
いもうと　妹 441
いや　嫌 452
いやしい　卑 248
いやしむ　卑 248
いやしめる　卑 248
いる　入 150
　射 505
　居 527
　要 1639
　鋳 1824
いれる　入 150
いろ　色 1599
いろどる　彩 616
いわ　岩 538
いわう　祝 1421
イン　印 251
　員 329
　因 337
　姻 442
　引 605
　院 729
　陰 735
　隠 749
　音 1879
　韻 1880
　飲 1903

う

ウ　右 277
　宇 465
　有 1003
　羽 1570
　雨 1858
うい　初 181
　憂 800
うえ　上 6
うえる　植 1102
　飢 1902
うお　魚 1931
うかがう　伺 76
うかぶ　浮 1197
うかべる　浮 1197

うかる	受	270
うかれる	浮	1197
うく	浮	1197
うけたまわる	承	848
うける	受	270
	請	1695
うごかす	動	221
うごく	動	221
うし	牛	1289
うじ	氏	1148
うしなう	失	413
うしろ	後	625
うず	渦	1218
うすい	薄	671
うすまる	薄	671
うすめる	薄	671
うすらぐ	薄	671
うすれる	薄	671
うた	歌	1125
	謡	1704
うたい	謡	1704
うたう	歌	1125
	謡	1704
うたがう	疑	1347
うち	内	160
うつ	撃	851
	打	854
	討	1663
うつくしい	美	1566
うつす	写	164
	映	985
	移	1437
うったえる	訴	1675
うつる	写	164
	映	985
	移	1437
うつわ	器	334
うで	腕	1038
うとい	疎	1346
うとむ	疎	1346
うながす	促	99
うね	畝	1338
うばう	奪	421
うぶ	産	1328
うま	馬	1912
うまる	埋	375
うまれる	生	1327
	産	1328
うみ	海	1184
うむ	生	1327

うむ	産	1328
うめ	梅	1096
うめる	埋	375
うもれる	埋	375
うやうやしい	恭	834
うやまう	敬	943
うら	浦	1198
	裏	1627
うらなう	占	250
うらむ	恨	814
うらめしい	恨	814
うる	売	397
	得	631
うるおう	潤	1250
うるおす	潤	1250
うるし	漆	1241
うるむ	潤	1250
うるわしい	麗	1937
うれい	愁	795
	憂	800
うれえる	愁	795
	憂	800
うれる	売	397
	熟	1282
うわ	上	6
うわる	植	1102
ウン	運	704
	雲	1860

え

エ	会	47
	依	85
	回	338
	恵	781
え	絵	1530
	柄	1085
	江	1160
エイ	重	1802
	営	518
	影	619
	英	644
	映	985
	栄	1054
	永	1152
	泳	1168
	衛	1617
	詠	1669

エイ	鋭	1823
えがく	描	910
エキ	役	620
	易	967
	液	1203
	疫	1348
	益	1370
	駅	1915
えだ	枝	1074
エツ	悦	815
	謁	1692
	越	1756
	閲	1846
えむ	笑	1472
えらい	偉	123
えらぶ	選	721
えり	襟	1637
える	得	631
	獲	1310
エン	円	159
	園	346
	塩	385
	宴	479
	延	599
	遠	714
	援	912
	沿	1169
	演	1239
	炎	1264
	煙	1269
	猿	1308
	縁	1548
	鉛	1812

お

オ	和	326
	悪	785
	汚	1158
お	小	511
	尾	526
	緒	1542
	雄	1852
おいる	老	1576
オウ	凹	173
	央	412

オウ
奥 419
往 621
応 768
押 868
桜 1087
横 1111
欧 1121
殴 1138
王 1315
皇 1366
翁 1571
黄 1939

おう
追 688
生 1327
負 1722

おうぎ 扇 845
おえる 終 1526
おお 大 408
おおい 多 405
おおいに 大 408
おおう 覆 1640
おおきい 大 408
おおせ 仰 65
おおやけ 公 152
おか 丘 12
おかす 侵 98
　　　犯 1299
　　　冒 1384
おがむ 拝 880
おき 沖 1165
おぎなう 補 1632
おきる 起 1755

オク
億 136
屋 530
憶 831
奥 419

おく 置 1466
おくらす 遅 709
おくる 送 686
　　　贈 1750
おくれる 後 625
　　　　遅 709
おこす 興 158
おこす 起 1755
おごそか 厳 519
おこたる 怠 777
おこなう 行 1613
おこる 興 158
　　　怒 778

おこる 起 1755
おさえる 抑 867
おさえる 押 868
おさない 幼 578
おさまる 修 107
　　　　収 265
　　　　治 1174
　　　　納 1519
おさめる 修 107
　　　　収 265
　　　　治 1174
　　　　納 1519
おしい 惜 820
おしえる 教 940
おしむ 惜 820
おす 押 868
　　推 903
　　雄 1852
おそい 遅 709
おそう 襲 1630
おそれ 虞 1602
おそれる 恐 780
おそろしい 恐 780
おそわる 教 940
おだやか 穏 1447
おちいる 陥 730
おちる 落 664
オツ 乙 25
おっと 夫 411
おと 音 1879
おとうと 弟 607
おどかす 脅 1019
おとこ 男 1334
おとしいれる 陥 730
おとす 落 664
おどす 脅 1019
おとずれる 訪 1667
おどり 踊 1765
おとる 劣 210
おどる 踊 1765
　　　躍 1767
おとろえる 衰 1622
おどろかす 驚 1914
おどろく 驚 1914
おなじ 同 320
おに 鬼 1926
おのおの 各 281
おのれ 己 554
おび 帯 565

おびやかす 脅 1019
おびる 帯 565
おぼえる 覚 1646
おも 主 19
　　面 1876
おもい 重 1802
おもう 思 776
おもて 表 1620
　　　面 1876
おもむき 趣 1758
おもむく 赴 1754
おや 親 1647
およぐ 泳 1168
および 及 21
およぶ 及 21
およぼす 及 21
おり 折 860
おりる 下 4
　　　降 731
おる 折 860
　　織 1561
おれる 折 860
おろか 愚 793
おろし 卸 255
おろす 下 4
　　　降 731
おろす 卸 255
おわる 終 1526
オン
遠 714
恩 779
温 1217
穏 1447
音 1879
おん 御 632
おんな 女 423

か

カ
下 4
化 55
仮 63
何 73
価 86
佳 87
加 208
可 314
夏 402
嫁 451

カ　家 480　寡 494　花 641　荷 655　華 656　菓 657　過 705　暇 993　果 1052　架 1055　歌 1125　河 1170　渦 1218　火 1260　禍 1425　科 1430　稼 1444　箇 1483　課 1724　貨 1878

か　日 963　蚊 1605　香 1911

ガ　画 176　芽 645　我 837　賀 1728　雅 1853　餓 1908

カイ　介 44　会 47　回 338　塊 386　壊 390　階 743　快 808　怪 809　悔 812　懐 832　戒 838　拐 869　改 933　械 1097　海 1184　灰 1261　界 1365　皆　絵 1530

カイ　街 1615　解 1651　開 1840

かい　貝 1720

ガイ　劾 215　外 404　害 481　慨 825　概 1107　涯 1204　街 1615　該 1677

かいこ　蚕 1606

かう　交 38　買 1731　飼 1905

かえす　帰 562　返 681

かえりみる　省 1382　顧 1898

かえる　代 61　変 401　換 913　替 1001　帰 562　返 681

かえる　顔 1893

かお　香 1911

かおり　薫 668

かおる　香 1911

かかえる　抱 883

かかげる　掲 898

かがみ　鏡 1834

かがやく　輝 1779

かかり　係 94

かかる　掛 896

かかる　係 94　懸 806　掛 896

かき　垣 1055

かぎる　限 373

カク　画 728　各 176　嚇 281　客 313　隔 476　郭 748　拡 759　870

カク　格 1088　核 1089　殻 1141　獲 1310　確 1409　穫 1449　覚 1646　角 1650　較 1777　閣 1843　革 1877

かく　書 998　欠 1119

ガク　学 460　岳 537　楽 1064　額 1892

かくす　隠 749

かくれる　隠 749

かげ　影 619　陰 735

かける　懸 806　掛 896　架 1055　欠 1119　駆 1916

かげる　陰 735

かこう　囲 340

かこむ　囲 340

かさ　傘 53　風 171

かさなる　重 1802

かさねる　重 1802

かざる　飾 1906

かしこい　賢 1740

かしら　頭 1889

かす　貸 1730

かず　数 945

かぜ　風 171

かせぐ　稼 1444

かぞえる　数 945

かた　型 353　形 615　方 957　肩 1014　潟 1248　片 1287　固 343

かたい　堅 356

かたい　硬　1403
　　　　難　1856
かたき　敵　946
かたち　形　615
かたな　刀　177
かたまり　塊　386
かたまる　固　343
かたむく　傾　126
かたむける　傾　126
かためる　固　343
かたよる　偏　122
かたらう　語　1685
かたる　語　1685
かたわら　傍　125
カツ　割　204
　　　喝　305
　　　括　885
　　　活　1185
　　　渇　1205
　　　滑　1229
　　　褐　1634
　　　轄　1783
　　　合　284
カッ　且　11
かつ　勝　224
ガッ　合　284
ガツ　月　1002
かつぐ　担　877
かて　糧　1502
かど　角　1650
　　　門　1838
かな　金　1808
かなしい　悲　788
かなしむ　悲　788
かなでる　奏　418
かならず　必　767
かね　金　1808
　　　鐘　1835
かねる　兼　765
かの　彼　624
かぶ　株　1090
かべ　壁　366
かま　窯　1458
かまう　構　1108
かまえる　構　1108
かみ　上　6
　　　神　1422
　　　紙　1517
　　　髪　1925

かみなり　雷　1863
かもす　醸　1799
かよう　通　695
から　唐　292
　　　殻　1141
　　　空　1452
　　　柄　1085
がら　辛　1784
からい　辛　1784
からす　枯　1083
からだ　体　80
からまる　絡　1536
からむ　絡　1536
かり　仮　63
　　　狩　1302
かりる　借　106
かる　刈　183
　　　狩　1302
　　　駆　1916
かるい　軽　1775
かれ　彼　624
かれる　枯　1083
かろやか　軽　1775
かわ　側　119
　　　川　548
　　　河　1170
　　　皮　1367
　　　革　1877
かわかす　乾　27
かわく　乾　27
　　　　渇　1205
かわす　交　38
かわる　代　61
　　　　変　401
　　　　換　913
　　　　替　1001
カン　乾　27
　　　冠　165
　　　刊　184
　　　勘　220
　　　勧　226
　　　喚　308
　　　堪　379
　　　完　468
　　　官　469
　　　寒　490
　　　寛　492
　　　巻　555
　　　干　572
　　　幹　576

カン　還　723
　　　陥　730
　　　患　786
　　　感　792
　　　慣　827
　　　憾　833
　　　換　913
　　　敢　942
　　　肝　1022
　　　棺　1098
　　　款　1123
　　　歓　1126
　　　汗　1159
　　　漢　1230
　　　環　1323
　　　甘　1325
　　　甲　1331
　　　監　1374
　　　看　1379
　　　管　1484
　　　簡　1490
　　　緩　1549
　　　缶　1564
　　　艦　1598
　　　観　1649
　　　貫　1725
　　　鑑　1836
　　　間　1841
　　　閑　1842
　　　関　1844
　　　館　1909
かん　神　1422
　　　丸　17
ガン　元　141
　　　含　286
　　　岩　538
　　　岸　539
　　　眼　1387
　　　頑　1885
　　　顔　1893
　　　願　1897
かんがえる　考　1577
かんばしい　芳　643
かんむり　冠　165

き

キ　企　48

読み	漢字	番号	読み	漢字	番号	読み	漢字	番号	読み	漢字	番号
キ			キク			キュウ			キュウ	球	1319
	危	256	きく	菊	658					究	1451
	喜	294		利	189					窮	1457
	器	334		効	216					級	1513
	基	354		聞	1584					糾	1514
	奇	414		聴	1585					給	1531
	季	461		聞	1584	ギュウ	牛	1289			
	寄	486	きこえる	兆	146	キョ	巨	235			
	岐	536	きざし	兆	146		去	261			
	己	554	きざす	刻	190		居	527			
	希	559	きざむ	岸	539		挙	849			
	帰	562	きし	傷	130		拒	871			
	幾	580	きずく	築	1488		拠	872			
	忌	769	きせる	着	1567		虚	1601			
	揮	914	きそう	競	1463		許	1664			
	旗	962	きた	北	231		距	1760			
	期	1008	きたえる	鍛	1831	ギョ	御	632			
	棄	1065	きたす	来	36		漁	1240			
	机	1068	きたない	汚	1158		魚	1931			
	棋	1099	きたる	来	36	きよい	清	1213			
	機	1115	キチ	吉	282	キョウ	京	39			
	気	1150	キツ	吉	282		享	40			
	汽	1162		喫	309		供	88			
	祈	1419		詰	1678		兄	142			
	既	1470	きぬ	絹	1538		共	154			
	紀	1512	きびしい	厳	519		興	158			
	規	1644	きまる	決	1163		凶	172			
	記	1660	きみ	君	287		協	244			
	貴	1729	きめる	決	1163		叫	297			
	起	1755	きも	肝	1022		境	387			
	軌	1770	キャク	却	252		峡	541			
	輝	1779		客	476		強	611			
	飢	1902		脚	1034		郷	760			
	騎	1919	ギャク	逆	685		恐	780			
き	鬼	1926		虐	1600		恭	834			
	木	1045	キュウ	丘	12		挟	886			
	生	1327		久	20		教	940			
ギ	黄	1939		及	21		脅	1019			
	偽	116		九	26		胸	1030			
	儀	137		休	64		橋	1116			
	宜	478		吸	296		況	1172			
	戯	840		宮	482		狂	1300			
	技	857		弓	604		狭	1301			
	擬	930		急	775		矯	1396			
	欺	1124		救	939		競	1463			
	犠	1294		旧	964		経	1523			
	疑	1347		朽	1069		鏡	1834			
	義	1568		求	1155		響	1881			
	議	1711		泣	1171		香	1911			
きえる	消	1194									

キョウ 驚 1914
ギョウ 仰 65
凝 169
形 615
暁 989
業 1066
行 1613
キョク 局 524
曲 996
極 1100
ギョク 玉 1313
きよまる 清 1213
きよめる 清 1213
きらう 嫌 452
きり 霧 1869
きる 切 179
着 1567
切 179
きれる
きわ 際 750
きわまる 極 1100
窮 1457
きわみ 極 1100
きわめる 極 1100
究 1451
窮 1457
キン 今 45
勤 223
均 368
菌 659
近 679
斤 953
琴 1322
禁 1416
筋 1476
緊 1509
襟 1637
謹 1705
金 1808
ギン 吟 299
銀 1817

【く】

ク 久 20
九 26
供 88
功 209
区 233

ク 口 276
句 315
宮 482
工 550
庫 589
苦 646
紅 1515
貢 1723
駆 1916
具 156
愚 793
グ 悔 812
くいる 空 1452
クウ 食 1900
くう 偶 117
グウ 宮 482
遇 706
隅 744
くき 茎 647
くさ 草 652
くさい 臭 1588
くさらす 腐 1011
くさり 鎖 1832
くさる 腐 1011
くされる 腐 1011
くじら 鯨 1933
くずす 崩 547
くすり 薬 672
くずれる 崩 547
くせ 癖 1358
くだ 管 1484
くだく 砕 1400
くだける 砕 1400
くださる 下 4
くだす 下 4
くだる 下 4
くち 口 276
くちびる 唇 290
くちる 朽 1069
クツ 屈 528
掘 897
靴 1878
くつがえす 覆 1640
くつがえる 覆 1640
くに 国 344
くばる 配 1790
くび 首 1910
くみ 組 1529
くむ 組 1529

くむ 酌 1788
くも 雲 1860
くもる 曇 983
くやしい 悔 812
くやむ 悔 812
くら 倉 52
蔵 667
くらい 位 72
暗 992
くらう 食 1900
くらす 暮 979
くらべる 比 1146
くる 来 36
繰 1563
くるう 狂 1300
くるおしい 狂 1300
くるしい 苦 646
くるしむ 苦 646
くるしめる 苦 646
くるま 車 1769
くれない 紅 1515
くれる 暮 979
くろい 黒 1940
くろ 黒 1940
くわ 桑 1062
くわえる 加 208
くわしい 詳 1682
くわだてる 企 48
くわわる 加 208
クン 君 287
薫 668
勲 1284
訓 1661
郡 758
グン 群 1569
軍 1771

ケ 化 55
仮 63
家 480
華 656
懸 806
気 1150
毛 1147
下 4
け 夏 402
ゲ

【け】

ゲ
外 404
解 1651

ケイ
京 39
係 94
傾 126
兄 142
刑 185
啓 293
型 353
境 387
契 417
形 615
径 622
茎 647
恵 781
慶 799
憩 802
掲 898
携 919
敬 943
景 975
渓 1206
競 1463
系 1504
経 1523
継 1537
蛍 1607
警 1657
計 1658
軽 1775
鶏 1936

ゲイ
芸 642
迎 680
鯨 1933

けがす 汚 1158
けがらわしい 汚 1158
けがれる 汚 1158

ゲキ
劇 206
撃 851
激 1254

けす 消 1194
けずる 削 195

ケツ
傑 127
欠 1119
決 1163
潔 1249
穴 1450
結 1532
血 1611

ゲツ
月 1002

けむい 煙 1269
けむり 煙 1269
けむる 煙 1269
けもの 獣 1298
けわしい 険 736

ケン
件 66
倹 103
健 118
券 182
剣 198
圏 345
堅 356
嫌 452
建 600
遣 715
険 736
兼 765
憲 803
懸 806
肩 1014
検 1101
権 1112
犬 1295
献 1297
県 1380
研 1398
絹 1511
繭 1538
見 1643
謙 1706
賢 1740
軒 1772
間 1841
顕 1894
験 1920

ゲン
元 141
原 260
嫌 452
厳 519
幻 577
弦 608
限 728
減 1219
源 1231
玄 1311
現 1320
眼 1387
言 1653

験 1920

こ

コ
個 104
去 261
古 278
呼 301
固 343
孤 462
己 554
庫 589
弧 609
戸 841
拠 872
故 936
枯 1083
湖 1220
虚 1601
誇 1679
雇 1850
顧 1898
鼓 1944

こ
子 455
小 511
木 1045
粉 1495
黄 1939

ご
五 32
互 33
午 241
呉 322
娯 443
後 625
御 632
悟 816
期 1008
碁 1406
語 1685
誤 1686
護 1713

こい 恋 784
こい 濃 1256
こいしい 恋 784

コウ
交 38
仰 65
侯 95
候 105

コウ

光 143
公 152
興 158
功 209
効 216
厚 258
口 276
后 283
向 319
坑 369
好 432
孔 456
孝 459
岬 540
工 550
巧 551
幸 575
広 581
康 592
後 625
荒 651
降 731
郊 756
恒 813
慌 822
抗 858
拘 873
控 899
攻 934
更 997
肯 1015
格 1088
校 1091
構 1108
江 1160
洪 1186
港 1221
溝 1232
甲 1331
皇 1366
硬 1403
稿 1445
紅 1515
絞 1532
綱 1541
考 1577
耕 1580
耗 1581
航 1593

コウ
行 1613
衡 1618
講 1707
貢 1723
購 1749
酵 1795
鉱 1813
鋼 1825
項 1883
香 1911
高 1924
黄 1939
神 1422

こう
こう 恋 784
請 1695

ゴウ
剛 199
合 284
号 316
強 611
郷 760
拷 887
業 1066
豪 1719

こうむる
こえ 被 1631
声 396
肥 1024

こえる 肥 1024
越 1756
超 1757

こおり 氷 1153
こおる 凍 168
こがす 焦 1278
こがれる 焦 1278
コク
克 147
刻 190
告 288
国 344
石 1397
穀 1441
谷 1714
酷 1796
黒 1940

ゴク
極 1100
獄 1309
こげる 焦 1278
こごえる 凍 168
ここの 九 26
ここのつ 九 26
こころ 心 766

こころざし 志 770
こころざす 志 770
こころみる 試 1680
こころよい 快 808
こす 腰 1041
越 1756
超 1757

こたえ 答 1478
こたえる 答 1478
コツ 骨 1922
こと 事 30
殊 1135
琴 1322
言 1653
異 1342

ことなる 寿 501
ことぶき 断 955
ことわる 粉 1495
こな 好 432
このむ 拒 871
こばむ 細 1525
こまか 細 1525
こまかい 困 341
こまる 込 675
こむ 米 1493
こめ 込 675
こめる 肥 1024
こやし 肥 1024
こやす 歴 980
こよみ 懲 805
こらしめる 凝 169
こらす 懲 805
懲 805
凝 169
こりる 転 1773
こる 転 1773
ころがす 転 1773
ころがる 殺 1140
ころげる 転 1773
ころす 衣 1619
ころぶ 声 396
ころも 怖 810
こわ 壊 390
こわい 壊 390
こわす 今 45
こわれる 困 341
コン 墾 365
婚 447
建 600

志 770

864

コン
- 懇 804
- 恨 814
- 昆 968
- 混 1092
- 献 1207
- 紺 1297
- 金 1524
- 魂 1808

ゴン
- 勤 223
- 厳 519
- 権 1112
- 言 1653

さ

サ
- 佐 74
- 作 75
- 再 162
- 咳 304
- 左 552
- 差 553
- 茶 654
- 査 1056
- 砂 1399
- 詐 1670
- 鎖 1832

ザ
- 座 590

サイ
- 催 128
- 債 129
- 再 162
- 切 179
- 妻 427
- 宰 483
- 彩 616
- 菜 660
- 際 750
- 才 853
- 採 900
- 最 1000
- 栽 1061
- 歳 1131
- 殺 1140
- 済 1208
- 災 1263
- 砕 1400
- 祭 1414
- 細 1525

サイ
- 裁 1624
- 西 1638
- 財 1741
- 載 1778
- 斎 1875
- 剤 200

ザイ
- 在 349
- 材 1071
- 罪 1464
- 財 1741

さいわい — 幸 575

さえぎる — 遮 716

さか
- 坂 370
- 逆 685
- 酒 1789
- 境 387

さかい — 栄 1054

さかえる — 捜 893

さがす — 探 908

さかずき — 杯 1078

さかな — 魚 1931

さからう — 逆 685

さかる — 盛 1371

さがる — 下 4

さかん — 盛 1371

さき
- 先 145
- 崎 545

サク
- 作 75
- 冊 161
- 削 195
- 搾 920
- 昨 986
- 策 1477
- 索 1505
- 酢 1792
- 錯 1826
- 割 204

さく
- 咲 303
- 裂 1626

さくら — 桜 1087

さぐる — 探 908

さけ — 酒 1789

さけぶ — 叫 297

さける
- 避 724
- 裂 1626

さげる
- 下 4
- 提 915

ささえる — 支 932

ささる — 刺 192

さす
- 刺 192
- 差 553
- 指 888
- 挿 894
- 授 902

さずかる — 授 902

さずける — 授 1691

さそう — 誘 473

さだか — 定 473

さだまる — 定 473

さだめる — 定 575

さち — 幸 966

サッ — 早 161

サツ
- 冊 191
- 刷 495
- 察 925
- 撮 931
- 擦 1067
- 札 1140
- 殺 1855

ザツ
- 雑 1801
- 里 1703

さとす — 諭 816

さとる — 悟 1624

さばく — 裁 487

さびしい — 寂 487

さびれる — 寂 487

さま — 様 1110

さます
- 冷 166
- 覚 1646

さまたげる — 妨 436

さむい — 寒 490

さむらい — 侍 90

さめる
- 冷 166
- 覚 1646

さら
- 更 997
- 皿 1368

さる
- 去 261
- 猿 1308

さわ — 沢 1164

さわぐ — 騒 1921

さわる
- 障 751
- 触 1652

サン
- 三 5
- 傘 53
- 参 263
- 山 535
- 惨 818
- 散 944

サン
桟 1093
産 1328
算 1485
蚕 1606
賛 1736
酸 1797

ザン
惨 818
暫 981
残 1134

【し】

シ
仕 58
伺 76
使 89
刺 192
旨 232
史 317
司 318
嗣 333
四 335
士 393
姿 429
姉 438
始 439
子 455
市 556
師 563
志 770
思 776
指 888
支 932
施 958
肢 1023
脂 1031
枝 1074
次 1120
止 1127
死 1133
氏 1148
矢 1393
示 1413
祉 1420
私 1428
糸 1503
紫 1507
紙 1517
自 1587

ジ

シ
至 1589
視 1645
詞 1671
試 1680
誌 1681
諮 1701
資 1734
賜 1746
雌 1854
飼 1905
歯 1942

ジ
事 30
仕 58
似 77
侍 90
児 148
地 367
字 457
寺 500
除 732
慈 794
持 889
時 988
次 1120
治 1174
滋 1222
璽 1314
磁 1407
示 1413
耳 1582
自 1587
辞 1785

じ
路 1764

しあわせ
幸 575

しいたげる
虐 1600

しいる
強 611

しお
塩 385
潮 1252

シキ
式 602
織 1561
色 1599
識 1709

ジキ
直 1377
食 1900

しく
敷 947

ジク
軸 1776

しげる
茂 650

しず
静 1872

しずか
静 1872

しずく
滴 1244

しずまる
鎮 1833
静 1872

しずむ
沈 1166
沈 1166

しずめる
鎮 1833
静 1872
下 4

した
舌 1591
慕 835

したう
従 628

したがう
従 628

したがえる
親 1647

したしい
親 1647

したしむ
滴 1244

したたる
七 2

シチ
質 1737
執 351

シツ
失 413
室 477
湿 1223
漆 1241
疾 1349
質 1737
実 470

ジツ
日 963
十 239

ジッ
品 328

しな
死 1133

しぬ
忍 771

しのばせる
忍 771

しのぶ
芝 640

しばる
縛 1555

しぶ
渋 1209

しぶい
渋 1209

しぶる
渋 1209

しぼる
搾 920
絞 1532

しま
島 543

しまる
絞 1532
締 1552
閉 1839

しみ
染 1058

しみる
染 1058

しめす
湿 1223
示 1413

しめる
占 250
絞 1532

866

しめる	締 1552	ジュ 寿 501	シュツ 出 174
	閉 1839	就 520	ジュツ 述 682
しめる 湿 1223		従 628	術 1614
しも 下 4		授 902	シュン 俊 96
	霜 1868	樹 1865	春 971
シャ 舎 51		シュウ 修 107	瞬 1391
	写 164	収 265	ジュン 准 167
	射 505	周 324	循 633
	遮 716	囚 336	巡 677
	捨 901	執 351	遵 720
	斜 952	宗 471	旬 965
	煮 1277	就 520	殉 1136
	砂 1399	州 549	準 1233
	社 1418	週 701	潤 1250
	者 1578	愁 795	盾 1381
	謝 1708	拾 890	純 1518
	赦 1752	祝 1421	順 1884
	車 1769	秀 1429	ショ 初 181
ジャ 邪 754		秋 1431	処 398
	蛇 1608	終 1526	庶 593
シャク 借 106		習 1572	所 843
	勺 228	臭 1588	暑 976
	尺 521	舟 1592	書 998
	昔 970	衆 1612	署 1465
	爵 1285	襲 1630	緒 1542
	石 1397	酬 1793	諸 1694
	赤 1751	醜 1798	ジョ 助 211
	酌 1778	集 1851	叙 272
	釈 1800	ジュウ 住 78	女 423
ジャク 寂 487		充 144	如 433
	弱 610	十 239	序 583
	若 648	従 628	徐 629
	着 1567	拾 890	除 732
シュ 主 19		柔 1057	ショウ 上 6
	修 107	汁 1157	井 34
	取 269	渋 1209	傷 130
	守 466	獣 1298	償 139
	手 847	縦 1556	勝 224
	朱 1049	重 1802	匠 236
	殊 1135	銃 1818	升 242
	狩 1302	シュク 叔 271	召 279
	珠 1317	宿 488	唱 306
	種 1442	粛 614	商 330
	衆 1612	淑 1210	声 396
	趣 1758	祝 1421	奨 420
	酒 1789	縮 1558	姓 440
	首 1910	ジュク 塾 362	宵 484
ジュ 儒 138		熟 1282	将 506
	受 270		小 511

ショウ

少	512
尚	514
床	584
彰	618
従	628
荘	653
障	751
性	811
承	848
掌	850
抄	859
招	874
政	937
昇	969
星	973
晶	977
昭	987
肖	1012
松	1075
正	1128
沼	1173
消	1194
渉	1211
清	1213
焼	1268
焦	1278
照	1281
生	1327
症	1350
省	1382
相	1383
硝	1404
礁	1411
祥	1424
称	1433
章	1460
笑	1472
粧	1499
精	1500
紹	1527
衝	1616
装	1625
訟	1665
証	1672
詔	1673
詳	1682
象	1718
賞	1738
鐘	1835

ショウ
青	1871

ジョウ
上	6
丈	7
乗	24
冗	163
剰	202
城	374
場	380
壌	391
嬢	454
定	473
常	566
蒸	665
情	819
成	836
条	1050
浄	1187
状	1296
畳	1344
盛	1371
縄	1550
譲	1712
醸	1799
錠	1827
静	1872

ショク
嘱	311
植	1102
殖	1137
織	1561
職	1586
色	1599
触	1652
食	1900
飾	1906

ジョク
辱	1786

しら 白 1362
しらべる 調 1699
しりぞく 退 687
しりぞける 退 687
しる 汁 1157 / 知 1394
しるし 印 1660
しるす 記 251
しろ 代 61 / 城 374 / 白 1362
しろい 白 1362
シン 伸 79 / 信 97

シン

侵	98
唇	290
娠	444
寝	493
審	497
薪	669
進	702
心	766
慎	826
振	892
新	956
森	1063
津	1188
浸	1195
深	1212
申	1332
真	1385
神	1422
紳	1528
親	1647
診	1674
請	1695
身	1768
辛	1784
臣	1805
針	1809
震	1866

ジン

人	42
仁	56
刃	178
尋	508
尽	523
迅	678
陣	733
甚	1326
神	1422
臣	1805

す

ス

主	19
子	455
守	466
数	945
素	1506

す
巣	517
州	549
酢	1792

す〜せ（索引）

ズ
　事 30
　図 342
　豆 1715
　頭 1889

スイ
　出 174
　吹 300
　垂 350
　帥 560
　遂 707
　推 903
　水 1151
　炊 1265
　睡 1389
　穂 1446
　粋 1494
　衰 1622
　酔 1791
　錘 1828
すい
　酸 1797
ズイ
　随 745
　髄 1923
スウ
　崇 546
　数 945
　枢 1076
　吸 296

すう　末 1047
すえ　据 904
すえる　透 698
すかす　姿 429
すがた　杉 1072
すぎ　過 705
すぎる　好 432
すく　透 698
すくう　救 939
すくない　少 512
すぐれる　優 140
すけ　助 211
すける　透 698
すこし　少 512
すごす　過 705
すこやか　健 118
すじ　筋 1476
すず　鈴 1816
すずしい　涼 1216
すすむ　進 702
すずむ　涼 1216
すすめる　勧 226
　　　　　薦 670
　　　　　進 702

すたる　廃 595
すたれる　廃 595
すでに　既 1470
すてる　捨 901
すな　砂 1229
すべる　滑 1535
すべる　統 78
すまう　住 1208
すます　済 1253
すみ　墨 363
　　　隅 744
　　　炭 1267
すみやか　速 693
すむ　住 78
　　　済 1208
　　　澄 1253
する　刷 191
するどい　鋭 1823
すれる　擦 931
すわる　座 590
すわる　据 904
スン　寸 499

せ

セ　世 13
　　施 958
せ　背 1017
　　瀬 1259
　　畝 1338
ゼイ　是 972
セイ　世 13
　　　井 34
　　　制 193
　　　勢 227
　　　声 396
　　　姓 440
　　　婿 449
　　　征 623
　　　逝 691
　　　性 811
　　　情 819
　　　成 836
　　　政 937
　　　整 948
　　　醒 973

セイ
　晴 990
　正 1128
　歳 1131
　清 1213
　牲 1292
　生 1327
　盛 1371
　省 1382
　精 1500
　聖 1583
　製 1628
　西 1638
　誓 1655
　誠 1683
　請 1695
　青 1871
　静 1872
　斉 1874

せい
ゼイ
　背 1017
　税 1438
　説 1688
セキ
　夕 403
　寂 487
　席 564
　惜 820
　斥 954
　昔 970
　析 1077
　石 1397
　積 1448
　籍 1492
　績 1559
　責 1726
　赤 1751
　跡 1761
　隻 1849
　関 1844
　節 1482

せき
セチ
セツ
　切 179
　折 860
　拙 875
　接 905
　摂 921
　殺 1140
　窃 1454
　節 1482
　設 1666
　説 1688
　雪 1859

ゼツ 絶 1534　舌 1591
ぜに 銭 1819
せばまる 狭 1301
せばめる 狭 1301
せまい 狭 1301
せまる 迫 684
せめる 攻 934　責 1726
せる 競 1463
セン 仙 59　先 145　千 240　占 250　宣 475　専 503　川 548　薦 670　選 721　遷 722　戦 839　扇 845　旋 960　染 1058　栓 1094　泉 1154　洗 1189　浅 1190　潜 1251　線 1551　繊 1560　船 1595　践 1762　銭 1819　銑 1820　鮮 1932
ゼン 全 49　前 196　善 295　漸 1242　然 1279　禅 1426　繕 1562

そ

ソ 塑 359　阻 726　想 796　措 906　疎 1346　礎 1412　祖 1423　租 1434　粗 1496　素 1506　組 1529　訴 1675
ソウ 倉 52　僧 131　創 205　双 266　争 274　喪 332　壮 394　奏 418　宗 471　巣 517　層 533　草 652　荘 653　葬 662　藻 674　送 686　遭 717　想 796　捜 893　挿 894　掃 907　操 928　早 966　曹 999　桑 1062　槽 1113　燥 1272　相 1383　窓 1455　総 1543　装 1625　贈 1750　走 1753　霜 1868　騒 1921
そう 沿 1169　添 1215
ゾウ 像 133　増 388　蔵 667　造 692　憎 828　臓 1044　象 1718　贈 1750　雑 1855
そうろう 候 105
そえる 添 1215
ソク 促 99　側 119　則 197　即 253　速 693　息 782　束 1051　測 1224　足 1759
ゾク 俗 100　属 532　族 961　続 1539　賊 1744
そこ 底 585
そこなう 損 922
そこねる 損 922
そそぐ 注 1175
そそのかす 唆 304
そだつ 育 1013
そだてる 育 1013
ソツ 卒 245　率 1312
そと 外 404
そなえる 供 88　備 124
そなわる 備 124
その 園 346
そまる 染 1058
そむく 背 1017
そむける 背 1017
そめる 初 181　染 1058
そら 空 1452
そらす 反 267
そる 反 267
ソン 存 458　孫 463　尊 509　損 922

た

読み	漢字	番号
ソンゾン	村	1073
	存	458
タ	他	60
	多	405
	太	409
	手	847
	田	1330
ダ	堕	357
	妥	425
	惰	823
	打	854
	蛇	1608
	駄	1917
タイ	代	61
	体	80
	台	280
	大	408
	太	409
	対	502
	帯	565
	待	626
	退	687
	逮	703
	隊	746
	怠	777
	態	797
	誉	1001
	胎	1026
	泰	1156
	滞	1234
	耐	1579
	袋	1623
	貸	1730
ダイ	代	61
	内	160
	台	280
	大	408
	弟	607
	第	1473
	題	1895
たいら	平	573
たえる	堪	379
	絶	1534
	耐	1579
たおす	倒	109
たおれる	倒	109
たか	高	1924
たかい	高	1924
たがい	互	33
たかまる	高	1924
たかめる	高	1924
たがやす	耕	1580
たから	宝	474
たき	滝	1235
たきぎ	薪	669
タク	卓	246
	宅	467
	度	588
	択	861
	拓	876
	沢	1164
	濯	1257
	託	1662
たく	炊	1265
ダク	濁	1255
	諾	1696
だく	抱	883
たくみ	巧	551
たくわえる	蓄	666
たけ	丈	7
	岳	537
	竹	1471
たしか	確	1409
たしかめる	確	1409
たす	足	1759
だす	出	174
たすかる	助	211
たすける	助	211
たずさえる	携	919
たずさわる	携	919
たずねる	尋	508
	訪	1667
たたかう	戦	839
	闘	1847
ただし	但	81
ただしい	正	1128
ただす	正	1128
ただちに	直	1377
たたみ	畳	1344
たたむ	畳	1344
ただよう	漂	1245
タツ	達	708
たつ	建	600
	断	955
	立	1459
	絶	1534
	裁	1624
	竜	1930
ダツ	奪	421
	脱	1035
たっとい	尊	509
	貴	1729
たっとぶ	尊	509
	貴	1729
たて	盾	1381
	縦	1556
たてまつる	奉	415
たてる	建	600
	立	1459
たとえる	例	93
たな	棚	1103
たに	谷	1714
たね	種	1442
たのしい	楽	1064
たのしむ	楽	1064
たのむ	頼	1890
たのもしい	頼	1890
たば	束	1051
たび	度	588
	旅	959
たべる	食	1900
たま	弾	613
	玉	1313
	球	1319
	霊	1867
たまご	卵	254
たましい	魂	1927
だまる	黙	1941
たまわる	賜	1746
たみ	民	1149
ためす	試	1680
ためる	矯	1396
たもつ	保	102
たやす	絶	1534
たより	便	101
たよる	頼	1890
たらす	垂	350
たりる	足	1759
たる	足	1759
たれる	垂	350
たわむれる	戯	840
たわら	俵	112
タン	丹	18

タン

反	267
嘆	310
壇	392
単	516
担	877
探	908
胆	1027
淡	1214
炭	1267
短	1395
端	1462
誕	1697
鍛	1831

ダン

団	339
壇	392
弾	613
断	955
暖	994
段	1139
男	1334
談	1698

ち

チ

値	108
地	367
遅	709
恥	783
池	1161
治	1174
痴	1356
知	1394
稚	1440
置	1466
致	1590
質	1737

ち

乳	29
千	240
血	1611

ちいさい	小	511
ちかい	近	679
ちかう	誓	1655
ちがう	違	713
ちがえる	違	713
ちから	力	207
ちぎる	契	417
チク	蓄	666
	逐	694

チク

畜	1339
竹	1471
築	1488

ちち	乳	29
	父	1286
ちぢまる	縮	1558
ちぢむ	縮	1558
ちぢめる	縮	1558
ちぢらす	縮	1558
ちぢれる	縮	1558
チツ	秩	1435
	窒	1456
チャ	茶	654
チャク	嫡	453
	着	1567
チュウ	中	16
	仲	67
	宙	472
	忠	773
	抽	878
	昼	974
	柱	1084
	沖	1165
	注	1175
	虫	1604
	衷	1621
	鋳	1824
	駐	1918
チョ	著	661
	緒	1542
	貯	1743
チョウ	丁	3
	兆	146
	帳	567
	庁	582
	弔	606
	張	612
	彫	617
	徴	636
	懲	805
	挑	891
	朝	1009
	脹	1037
	腸	1039
	潮	1252
	澄	1253
	町	1335
	眺	1388
	聴	1585

チョウ	調	1699
	超	1757
	跳	1763
	重	1802
	釣	1810
	長	1837
	頂	1882
	鳥	1934
チョク	勅	217
	直	1377
ちらかす	散	944
ちらかる	散	944
ちらす	散	944
ちる	散	944
チン	陳	737
	朕	1005
	沈	1166
	珍	1316
	賃	1735
	鎮	1833

つ

ツ	通	695
	都	761
	津	1188
ツイ	墜	364
	対	502
	追	688
ついえる	費	1732
ついやす	費	1732
ツウ	通	695
	痛	1353
つか	塚	381
つかう	使	89
	遣	715
つかえる	仕	58
つかす	尽	523
つかまえる	捕	895
つかまる	捕	895
つからす	疲	1351
つかれる	疲	1351
つかわす	遣	715
つき	月	1002
つぎ	次	1120
つきる	尽	523
つく	付	62

872

読み	漢字	番号
つく	就	520
	突	1453
	着	1567
	接	905
つぐ	次	1120
	継	1537
つくえ	机	1068
つくす	尽	523
つぐなう	償	139
つくる	作	75
	造	692
つくろう	繕	1562
つける	付	62
	就	520
	漬	1243
	着	1567
つげる	告	288
つたう	伝	68
つたえる	伝	68
つたわる	伝	68
つち	土	347
つちかう	培	377
つつ	筒	1480
つづく	続	1539
つづける	続	1539
つつしむ	慎	826
	謹	1705
つつみ	堤	382
つづみ	鼓	1944
つつむ	包	230
つどう	集	1851
つとまる	勤	223
つとめる	努	212
	務	222
	勤	223
つな	綱	1541
つね	常	566
つの	角	1650
つのる	募	225
つばさ	翼	1574
つぶ	粒	1498
つぼ	坪	372
つま	妻	427
つまる	詰	1678
つみ	罪	1464
つむ	摘	924
	積	1448
	詰	1678
	錘	1828
つむ		
つむぐ	紡	1521
つめたい	冷	166
つめる	詰	1678
つもる	積	1448
つゆ	露	1870
つよい	強	611
つよまる	強	611
つよめる	強	611
つら	面	1876
つらなる	連	699
つらぬく	貫	1725
つらねる	連	699
つる	弦	608
	釣	1810
つるぎ	剣	198
つれる	連	699

て

読み	漢字	番号
て	手	847
デイ / テイ	弟	607
	丁	3
	亭	41
	体	80
	低	82
	停	120
	偵	121
	呈	323
	堤	382
	定	473
	帝	561
	底	585
	庭	591
	廷	598
	弟	607
	逓	696
	邸	755
	抵	879
	提	915
	程	1439
	締	1552
	艇	1597
	訂	1659
	貞	1721
デイ / テキ	泥	1176
	適	718
	摘	924
	敵	946
テキ	滴	1244
	的	1364
	笛	1474
テツ	哲	291
	徹	638
	迭	683
	鉄	926
	撤	1814
	寺	500
てらす	照	1281
てる	照	1281
でる	照	174
てれる	照	1281
テン	典	157
	天	410
	展	531
	店	586
	殿	1142
	添	1215
	点	1275
	転	1773
	伝	68
デン	殿	1142
	田	1330
	電	1862

と

読み	漢字	番号
ト	吐	298
	図	342
	土	347
	塗	360
	度	588
	徒	630
	途	697
	都	761
	斗	950
	渡	1225
	登	1361
	頭	1889
	十	239
	戸	841
と	努	212
ド	土	347
	奴	431
	度	588
	怒	778
とい	問	331

トウ
倒 109　凍 168　刀 177　到 194　唐 292　塔 383　冬 399　当 513　党 515　島 543　逃 689　透 698　道 710　陶 738　悼 821　投 862　搭 916　東 1053　桃 1095　棟 1104　湯 1226　灯 1262　痘 1354　登 1361　盗 1372　稲 1443　答 1478　等 1479　筒 1480　糖 1501　納 1519　統 1535　謄 1656　討 1663　読 1689　豆 1715　踏 1766　闘 1847　頭 1889　騰 1913　間 331

とう／ドウ
働 132　動 221　同 320　堂 355　導 510　道 710　胴 1032　洞 1191

ドウ
童 1461　銅 1821

とうげ　峠 542
とうとい　尊 509　貴 1729
とうとぶ　尊 509　貴 1729
とお　十 239
とおい　遠 714
とおす　通 695
とおる　通 695
とかす　溶 1238　解 1651
とき　時 988　匿 238

トク　得 631　徳 637　特 1293　督 1390　篤 1489　読 1689
とく　溶 1238　解 1651　説 1688
とぐ　研 1398
ドク　毒 1145　独 1303　読 1689
とける　溶 1238　解 1651
とげる　遂 707
とこ　常 566　床 584
ところ　所 843
とざす　閉 1839
とし　年 574
とじる　閉 1839
トツ　凸 175　突 1453
とつぐ　嫁 451
とどく　届 529
とどける　届 529
とどこおる　滞 1234
ととのう　整 948　調 1699
ととのえる　整 948　調 1699
となえる　唱 306
となり　隣 752

となる　隣 752
との　殿 1142
どの　殿 1142
とばす　飛 1899
とびら　扉 846
とぶ　跳 1763　飛 1899
とぼしい　乏 23
とまる　止 1127　泊 1178　留 1341
とみ　富 491
とむ　富 491
とむらう　弔 606
とめる　止 1127　泊 1178　留 1341
とも　供 88　共 154　友 268
ともなう　伴 84
とらえる　捕 895
とらわれる　捕 895
とり　鳥 1934　取 269
とる　執 351　捕 895　採 900　撮 925
どろ　泥 1176
トン　屯 22　団 339　豚 1717
とん　問 331
ドン　曇 983　鈍 1811

な

ナ　南 247　納 1519
な　名 285　菜 660
ナイ　内 160
ない　亡 37　無 1280
なえ　苗 649
なおす　治 1174

なおす	直	1377
なおる	直	1174
	治	1377
なか	中	16
	仲	67
ながい	永	1152
	長	1837
ながす	流	1200
なかば	半	243
ながめる	眺	1388
ながれる	流	1200
なく	泣	1171
	鳴	1935
なぐさむ	慰	798
なぐさめる	慰	798
なぐる	殴	1138
なげかわしい	嘆	310
なげく	嘆	310
なげる	投	862
なごむ	和	326
なごやか	和	326
なさけ	情	819
なす	成	836
ナッ	納	1519
なつ	夏	402
なつかしい	懐	832
なつかしむ	懐	832
なつく	懐	832
なつける	懐	832
なな	七	2
ななつ	七	2
ななめ	斜	952
なに	何	73
なの	七	2
なまける	怠	777
なまり	鉛	1812
なみ	並	764
	波	1177
なみだ	涙	1201
なめらか	滑	1229
なやます	悩	817
なやむ	悩	817
ならう	倣	113
	習	1572
ならす	慣	827
	鳴	1935
ならびに	並	764
ならぶ	並	764

ならべる	並	764
なる	成	836
	鳴	1935
なれる	慣	827
なわ	苗	649
	縄	1550
ナン	南	247
	男	1334
	納	1519
	軟	1774
	難	1856
	何	73
なん		

【に】

ニ	二	31
	仁	56
	児	148
	尼	522
	弐	603
	荷	655
にい	新	956
にえる	煮	1277
にがい	苦	646
にがす	逃	689
にがる	苦	646
にぎる	握	911
ニク	肉	1010
にくい	憎	828
にくしみ	憎	828
にくむ	憎	828
にくらしい	憎	828
にげる	逃	689
にごす	濁	1255
にごる	濁	1255
にし	西	1638
にせる	偽	116
ニチ	日	963
になう	担	877
にぶい	鈍	1811
にぶる	鈍	1811
ニャク	若	648
にやす	煮	1277
ニュウ	乳	29
	入	150
	柔	1057
	女	423
ニョ	如	433

ニョウ	女	423
	尿	525
にる	似	77
	煮	1277
にわ	庭	591
にわとり	鶏	1936
ニン	人	42
	任	69
	妊	435
	忍	771
	認	1690

【ぬ】

ぬう	縫	1557
ぬかす	抜	864
ぬかる	抜	864
ぬく	抜	864
ぬぐ	脱	1035
ぬける	抜	864
ぬげる	脱	1035
ぬし	主	19
ぬすむ	盗	1372
ぬの	布	557
ぬま	沼	1173
ぬる	塗	360

【ね】

ね	値	108
	根	1092
	音	1879
ネイ	寧	496
ねがう	願	1897
ねかす	寝	493
ねこ	猫	1304
ネツ	熱	1283
ねばる	粘	1497
ねむい	眠	1386
ねむる	眠	1386
ねる	寝	493
	練	1547
ネン	年	574
	念	774
	燃	1271
	然	1279
	粘	1497
ねんごろ	懇	804

の

読み	漢字	番号
の	野	1803
ノウ	悩	817
	能	1018
	脳	1036
	濃	1256
	納	1519
	農	1787
のがす	逃	689
のがれる	逃	689
のき	軒	1772
のこす	残	1134
のこる	残	1134
のせる	乗	24
	載	1778
のぞく	除	732
のぞむ	望	1007
	臨	1806
のち	後	625
のばす	伸	79
	延	599
のびる	伸	79
	延	599
のべる	延	599
	述	682
のぼす	上	6
のぼせる	上	6
のぼる	上	6
	昇	969
	登	1361
のむ	飲	1903
のる	乗	24
	載	1778

は

読み	漢字	番号
ハ	把	863
	波	1177
	派	1192
	破	1401
	覇	1641
は	刃	178
	葉	663
	端	1462
	羽	1570
	歯	1942
バ	婆	430
	馬	1912
ば	場	380
ハイ	俳	110
	廃	595
	拝	880
	排	909
	敗	941
	背	1017
	肺	1028
	杯	1078
	輩	1780
はい	配	1790
バイ	灰	1261
	倍	111
	培	377
	売	397
	媒	450
	陪	739
	梅	1096
	買	1731
	賠	1747
はいる	入	150
はえ	栄	1054
はえる	映	985
	栄	1054
	生	1327
はか	墓	361
ばかす	化	55
はがね	鋼	1825
はからう	計	1658
はかる	図	342
	測	1224
	計	1658
	諮	1701
	謀	1702
	量	1804
ハク	伯	83
	博	249
	薄	671
	迫	684
	拍	881
	泊	1178
	白	1362
	舶	1596
はく	吐	298
	履	534
	掃	907
バク	博	249
バク	麦	400
	幕	570
	暴	982
	漠	1236
	爆	1273
	縛	1555
はげしい	激	1254
はげます	励	213
はげむ	励	213
ばける	化	55
はこ	箱	1486
はこぶ	運	704
はさまる	挟	886
はさむ	挟	886
はし	橋	1116
	端	1462
はじ	恥	783
はじまる	始	439
はじめ	初	181
はじめて	初	181
はじめる	始	439
はしら	柱	1084
はじらう	恥	783
はしる	走	1753
はじる	恥	783
はずかしい	恥	783
はずかしめる	辱	1786
はずす	外	404
はずむ	弾	613
はずれる	外	404
はた	旗	962
	機	1115
	畑	1337
	端	1462
はだ	肌	1021
はだか	裸	1635
はたけ	畑	1337
はたす	果	1052
はたらく	働	132
ハチ	八	151
	鉢	1815
バチ	罰	1467
ハツ	発	1360
	鉢	1815
	髪	1925
ハッ	法	1181
はつ	初	181
バツ	伐	70
	抜	864

バツ
末 1047
罰 1467
閥 1845

はて 果 1052
はてる 果 1052
はな 花 641
華 656
鼻 1945
はなし 話 1684
はなす 放 935
話 1684
離 1857
はなつ 放 935
はなはだ 甚 1326
はなはだしい 甚 1326
はなやか 華 656
はなれる 放 935
離 1857
はね 羽 1570
はねる 跳 1763
はは 母 1143
はば 幅 568
はばむ 阻 726
はぶく 省 1382
はま 浜 1196
はやい 速 693
早 966
はやし 林 1081
はやす 生 1327
はやまる 早 966
はやめる 速 693
早 966
はら 原 260
腹 1040
はらう 払 855
はらす 晴 990
はり 針 1809
はる 張 612
春 971
はれる 晴 990
ハン 伴 84
凡 170
判 187
半 243
反 267
坂 370
帆 558
藩 673
搬 923

ハン
板 1079
煩 1270
版 1288
犯 1299
班 1318
畔 1340
範 1487
繁 1510
般 1594
販 1742
頒 1886
飯 1904

バン
万 8
伴 84
判 187
晩 991
板 1079
番 1345
盤 1375
蛮 1609

ひ

ヒ
卑 248
否 289
妃 434
彼 624
避 724
悲 788
扉 846
批 865
披 882
肥 1024
比 1146
泌 1179
疲 1351
皮 1367
碑 1408
秘 1436
罷 1468
被 1631
費 1732
非 1873
飛 1899

ひ
日 963
氷 1153
火 1260
灯 1262

ビ
備 124
尾 526
微 635
美 1566
鼻 1945

ひいでる 秀 1429
ひえる 冷 166
ひかえる 控 899
ひがし 東 1053
ひかり 光 143
ひかる 光 143
ひき 匹 234
ひきいる 率 1312
ひく 引 605
弾 613
ひくい 低 82
ひくまる 低 82
ひくめる 低 82
ひける 引 605
ひさしい 久 20
ひそむ 潜 1251
ひたい 額 1892
ひたす 浸 1195
ひだり 左 552
ひたる 浸 1195
ヒツ 匹 234
必 767
泌 1179
筆 1481
ひつじ 羊 1565
ひと 一 1
人 42
等 1479
ひとしい 一 1
ひとつ 独 1303
ひとり 独 1303
ひびく 響 1881
ひま 暇 993
ひめ 姫 445
ひめる 秘 1436
ひや 冷 166
ひやかす 冷 166
ヒャク 百 1363
ビャク 白 1362
ひやす 冷 166
ヒョウ 俵 112
兵 155
拍 881
標 1114
氷 1153

877

読み	漢字	番号
ヒョウ	漂	1245
	票	1415
	表	1620
	評	1676
ビョウ	平	573
	苗	649
	描	910
	猫	1304
	病	1352
	秒	1432
ひら	平	573
ひらく	開	1840
ひらける	開	1840
ひる	干	572
ひる	昼	974
ひるがえす	翻	1575
ひるがえる	翻	1575
ひろい	広	581
ひろう	拾	890
ひろがる	広	581
ひろげる	広	581
ひろまる	広	581
ひろめる	広	581
ヒン	品	328
	浜	1196
	貧	1727
	賓	1739
	頻	1891
ビン	便	101
	敏	938
	瓶	1324
	貧	1727

ふ

読み	漢字	番号
フ	不	10
	付	62
	風	171
	夫	411
	婦	448
	富	491
	布	557
	府	587
	附	727
	怖	810
	扶	866
	敷	947
	普	978
フ	腐	1011
	膚	1020
	歩	1130
	浮	1197
	父	1286
	符	1475
	譜	1710
	負	1722
	賦	1748
	赴	1754
ブ	不	10
	侮	91
	分	180
	奉	415
	部	762
	武	1129
	歩	1130
	無	1280
	舞	1807
フウ	風	171
	夫	411
	富	491
	封	504
ふえ	笛	1474
ふえる	増	388
	殖	1137
ふかい	深	1212
ふかす	更	997
ふかまる	深	1212
ふかめる	深	1212
フク	伏	71
	副	203
	幅	568
	復	634
	服	1004
	腹	1040
	福	1427
	複	1636
	覆	1640
ふく	吹	300
	噴	312
	含	286
ふくむ	含	286
ふくめる	含	286
ふくらむ	膨	1043
ふくれる	膨	1043
ふくろ	袋	1623
ふける	更	997
	老	1576
ふさ	房	844
ふし	節	1482
	伏	71
ふせぐ	防	725
ふせる	伏	71
ふた	二	31
	双	266
	札	1067
ぶた	豚	1717
ふたたび	再	162
ふたつ	二	31
ふち	縁	1548
フツ	払	855
	沸	1180
ブツ	仏	57
	物	1290
ふで	筆	1481
ふとい	太	409
ふところ	懐	832
ふとる	太	409
ふな	舟	1592
	船	1595
ふね	舟	1592
	船	1595
ふまえる	踏	1766
ふみ	文	949
	踏	1766
ふむ	踏	1766
ふやす	増	388
	殖	1137
ふゆ	冬	399
ふる	降	731
	振	892
ふるい	古	278
ふるう	奮	422
	振	892
ふるう	震	1866
ふるえる	震	1866
ふるす	古	278
ふれる	触	1652
フン	分	180
	噴	312
	墳	389
	奮	422
	憤	830
	粉	1495
	紛	1520
	雰	1861
ブン	分	180
	文	949
	聞	1584

878

へ

ベ
辺 676

ヘイ
丙 14 / 併 92 / 兵 155 / 塀 384 / 幣 571 / 平 573 / 弊 601 / 陛 734 / 並 764 / 柄 1085 / 病 1352 / 閉 1839

ベイ
米 1493

ヘキ
壁 366 / 癖 1358

へだたる
隔 748

へだてる
隔 748

ベツ
別 188

べに
紅 1515

へび
蛇 1608

へらす
減 1219

へる
減 1219 / 経 1523

ヘン
偏 122 / 変 401 / 辺 676 / 返 681 / 遍 711 / 片 1287 / 編 1553

ベン
便 101 / 勉 219 / 弁 262

ほ

ホ
舗 54 / 保 102 / 捕 895 / 歩 1130 / 浦 1198 / 補 1632

ほ
帆 558 / 火 1260

ほ
穂 1446

ボ
募 225 / 墓 361 / 慕 835 / 暮 979 / 模 1109 / 母 1143 / 簿 1491

ホウ
倣 113 / 俸 114 / 包 230 / 報 352 / 奉 415 / 宝 474 / 封 504 / 峰 544 / 崩 547 / 芳 643 / 邦 753 / 抱 883 / 放 935 / 方 957 / 胞 1029 / 法 1181 / 泡 1182 / 砲 1402 / 縫 1557 / 褒 1629 / 訪 1667 / 豊 1716 / 飽 1907

ボウ
乏 23 / 亡 37 / 傍 125 / 剖 201 / 坊 371 / 妄 424 / 妨 436 / 帽 569 / 防 725 / 忘 772 / 忙 807 / 房 844 / 暴 982 / 望 1007 / 肪 1043 / 某 1059 / 棒 1105 / 冒 1384 / 紡 1521 / 謀 1702 / 貿 1733

ほうむる
葬 662

ほか
外 404

ほがらか
朗 1006

ホク
北 231

ボク
僕 134 / 墨 363 / 撲 927 / 木 1045 / 朴 1070 / 牧 1291 / 目 1376

ほこ
矛 1392

ほし
星 1679

ほしい
欲 1122

ほす
干 572

ほそい
細 1525

ほそる
細 1525

ほたる
蛍 1607

ホツ
発 1360

ホッ
法 1181

ボッ
坊 371

ボツ
没 1167

ほっする
欲 1122

ほどけ
程 1439

ほとけ
仏 57

ほどこす
施 958

ほね
骨 1922

ほのお
炎 1264

ほまれ
誉 1654

ほめる
褒 1629

ほら
洞 1191

ほり
堀 378

ほる
彫 617 / 掘 897

ほろびる
滅 1237

ほろぼす
滅 1237

ホン
反 267 / 奔 416 / 本 1046 / 翻 1575

ボン
凡 170 / 煩 1270 / 盆 1369

ま

マ　摩 852／磨 1410／魔 1929／麻 1938
ま　目 1376／真 1385／間 1841／馬 1912
マイ　埋 375／妹 441／枚 1080／毎 1144／米 1493／舞 1807
まいる　参 263
まう　舞 1807
まえ　前 196
まかす　任 69
まかす　負 1722
まかせる　任 69
まかなう　賄 1745
まがる　曲 996
まき　巻 555／牧 1291
まぎらす　紛 1520
まぎらわしい　紛 1520
まぎらわす　紛 1520
まぎれる　紛 1520
マク　幕 570／膜 1042
まく　巻 555
まける　負 1722
まげる　曲 996
まご　孫 463
まこと　誠 1683／正 1128
まさる　勝 224
まざる　交 38／混 1207
まじえる　交 38
まじる　交 38／混 1207
まじわる　交 38
ます　升 242／増 388
まずしい　貧 1727

まぜる　交 38／混 1207
また　又 264
またたく　瞬 1391
まち　町 1335／街 1615
マツ　抹 884／末 1047
まつ　待 626／松 1075
まったく　全 49
まつり　祭 1414
まつりごと　政 937
まつる　祭 1414
まと　的 1364
まどう　窓 1455／惑 789
まなこ　眼 1387
まなぶ　学 460
まぬかれる　免 149
まねく　招 874
まぼろし　幻 577
まめ　豆 1715
まもる　守 466
まゆ　繭 1511
まよう　迷 690
まる　丸 17
まるい　丸 17／円 159
まるめる　丸 17
まわす　回 338
まわり　周 324
まわる　回 338
マン　万 8／慢 829／満 1227／漫 1246

み

ミ　味 302／未 1048／魅 1928
み　三 5／実 470／身 1768／見 1643
みえる　見 1643
みがく　磨 1410

みき　幹 576
みぎ　右 277
みことのり　詔 1673
みさお　操 928
みさき　岬 540
みささぎ　陵 742
みじかい　短 1395
みじめ　惨 818
みず　水 1151
みずうみ　湖 1587
みずから　自 586
みせ　店 1643
みせる　見 1232
みぞ　溝 1227
みたす　満 28
みだす　乱 28
みだれる　乱 710
みち　道 510
みちびく　導 1227
みちる　満 489
ミツ　密 5
みつ　三 1723
みつぐ　貢 5
みっつ　三 1690
みとめる　認 1546
みどり　緑 1365
みな　皆 1221
みなと　港 247
みなみ　南 1231
みなもと　源 1798
みにくい　醜 544
みね　峰 470
みのる　実 1582
みみ　耳 482
みや　宮 1033
ミャク　脈 761
みやこ　都 285
ミョウ　名 325／命 437／妙 984／明 1643
みる　見 1674／診 984
ミン　明 1149／民 1386／眠 1386

む

ム	務	222
	夢	407
	武	1129
	無	1280
	矛	1392
	謀	1702
	霧	1869
む	六	153
むい	六	153
むかう	向	319
むかえる	迎	680
むかし	昔	970
むぎ	麦	400
むく	向	319
むくいる	報	352
むける	向	319
むこ	婿	449
むこう	向	319
むし	虫	1604
むす	蒸	665
むずかしい	難	1856
むすぶ	結	1532
むすめ	娘	446
むつ	六	153
むっつ	六	153
むな	胸	1030
	棟	1104
むね	旨	232
	胸	1030
	棟	1104
むら	村	1073
	群	1569
むらさき	紫	1507
むらす	蒸	665
むれ	群	1569
むれる	蒸	665
	群	1569
むろ	室	477

め

め	女	423
	芽	645
	目	1376
	雌	1854

メイ	名	285
	命	325
	迷	690
	明	984
	盟	1373
	銘	1822
	鳴	1935
めぐむ	恵	781
めぐる	巡	677
めし	飯	1904
めす	召	279
	雌	1854
めずらしい	珍	1316
メツ	滅	1237
メン	免	149
	綿	1544
	面	1876

も

モ	茂	650
も	模	1109
	喪	332
モウ	藻	674
	亡	37
	妄	424
	望	1007
	毛	1147
	猛	1305
	盲	1378
	網	1545
	耗	1581
もうける	設	1666
もうす	申	1332
もえる	燃	1271
モク	木	1045
	目	1376
	黙	1941
もぐる	潜	1251
もしくは	若	648
もす	燃	1271
もちいる	用	1329
モツ	物	1290
もつ	持	889
もっとも	最	1000
もっぱら	専	503
もと	下	4
	元	141
	基	354
	本	1046
もとい	基	354
もどす	戻	842
もとめる	求	1155
もどる	戻	842
もの	物	1290
	者	1578
もも	桃	1095
もやす	燃	1271
もよおす	催	128
もらす	漏	1247
もり	守	466
	森	1063
もる	盛	1371
	漏	1247
もれる	漏	1247
モン	問	331
	文	949
	紋	1522
	聞	1584
	門	1838
	匁	229
もんめ	匁	229

や

ヤ	夜	406
	野	1803
や	八	151
	家	480
	屋	530
	矢	1393
ヤク	厄	257
	役	620
	薬	672
	疫	1348
	益	1370
	約	1516
	訳	1668
	躍	1767
やく	焼	1268
やける	焼	1268
やさしい	優	140
	易	967
やしなう	養	1418
やしろ	社	1418
やすい	安	464
やすまる	休	64

や

やすむ 休 64
やすめる 休 64
やっ 八 151
やっつ 八 151
やどう 宿 488
やとう 雇 1850
やどす 宿 488
やどる 宿 488
やなぎ 柳 1086
やぶる 破 1401
やぶれる 敗 941
　　　　破 1401
やま 山 535
やまい 病 1352
やむ 病 1352
やめる 辞 1785
やわらか 柔 1057
　　　　軟 1774
やわらかい 柔 1057
　　　　軟 1774
やわらぐ 和 326
やわらげる 和 326

【ゆ】

ユ 遊 712
　愉 824
　油 1183
　由 1333
　癒 1359
　諭 1703
　輸 1782
　湯 1226
ユイ 唯 307
　　遺 719
　　由 1333
ユウ 優 140
　　勇 218
　　友 268
　　右 277
　　幽 579
　　遊 712
　　郵 763
　　悠 787
　　憂 800
　　有 1003
　　猶 1307
　　由 1333
　　融 1610
　　裕 1633
　　誘 1691
　　雄 1852
ゆう 夕 403
ゆう 結 1532
ゆえ 故 936
ゆか 床 584
ゆき 雪 1859
ゆく 逝 691
　　行 1613
ゆさぶる 揺 918
ゆすぶる 揺 918
ゆする 揺 918
ゆずる 譲 1712
ゆたか 豊 1716
ゆび 指 888
ゆみ 弓 604
ゆめ 夢 407
ゆらぐ 揺 918
ゆる 揺 918
ゆるい 緩 1549
ゆるぐ 揺 918
ゆるす 許 1664
ゆるむ 緩 1549
ゆるめる 緩 1549
ゆるやか 緩 1549
ゆれる 揺 918
ゆわえる 結 1532

【よ】

ヨ 与 9
　余 50
　予 275
　誉 1654
　預 1887
よ 世 13
　代 61
　四 335
　夜 406
よい 善 295
よい 宵 1642
ヨウ 良 484
　　宵 485
　　容 578
　　幼 594
　　庸 663
　　葉 663
　　陽 747
　　揚 917
　　揺 918
　　擁 929
　　曜 995
　　腰 1041
　　様 1110
　　洋 1193
　　溶 1238
　　用 1329
　　窯 1458
　　羊 1565
　　要 1639
　　謡 1704
　　踊 1765
　　養 1901
よう 八 151
よう 酔 1791
ヨク 抑 867
　　欲 1122
　　浴 1199
　　翌 1573
　　翼 1574
よこ 横 1111
よごす 汚 1158
よごれる 汚 1158
よし 由 1333
よせる 寄 486
よそおう 装 1625
よっつ 四 335
よつ 四 335
よぶ 呼 301
よむ 詠 1669
　　読 1689
よめ 嫁 451
よる 因 337
　　寄 486
よる 夜 406
よろこぶ 喜 294
よわい 弱 610
よわまる 弱 610
よわめる 弱 610
よわる 弱 610
よん 四 335

【ら】

ラ 羅 1469

ラ 裸 1635
ライ 来 36
礼 1417
雷 1863
頼 1890
ラク 落 664
楽 1064
絡 1536
酪 1794
ラン 乱 28
卵 254
欄 1118
濫 1258
覧 1648

り

リ 利 189
吏 321
履 534
理 1321
痢 1355
裏 1627
里 1801
離 1857
リキ 力 207
リク 陸 740
リチ 律 627
リツ 律 627
率 1312
立 1459
リャク 略 1343
リュウ 隆 741
柳 1086
流 1200
留 1341
硫 1405
立 1459
粒 1498
竜 1930
リョ 慮 801
旅 959
虜 1603
リョウ 両 15
僚 135
了 273
寮 498
陵 742

リョウ 料 951
涼 1216
漁 1240
猟 1306
療 1357
糧 1502
良 1642
量 1804
霊 1867
領 1888
リョク 力 207
緑 1546
リン 倫 115
厘 259
隣 752
林 1081
輪 1781
臨 1806
鈴 1816

る

ル 流 1200
留 1341
ルイ 塁 358
涙 1201
累 1508
類 1896

れ

レイ 令 46
例 93
冷 166
励 213
戻 842
礼 1417
鈴 1816
隷 1848
零 1864
霊 1867
麗 1937
齢 1943
レキ 暦 980
歴 1132
レツ 列 186
劣 210
烈 1276

レツ 裂 1626
レン 廉 597
連 699
恋 784
練 1547
錬 1829

ろ

ロ 炉 1266
路 1764
露 1870
ロウ 労 214
廊 596
郎 757
朗 1006
楼 1106
浪 1202
漏 1247
糧 1502
老 1576
露 1870
ロク 六 153
緑 1546
録 1830
ロン 論 1700

わ

ワ 和 326
話 1684
わ 我 837
輪 1781
ワイ 賄 1745
わかい 若 648
わかす 沸 1180
わかつ 分 180
わかる 分 180
わかれる 分 180
わかれる 別 188
ワク 惑 789
わく 枠 1082
わく 沸 1180
わけ 訳 1668
わける 分 180
わざ 技 857
わざ 業 1066
わざわい 災 1263

わずらう	患	786
	煩	1270
わずらわす	煩	1270
わすれる	忘	772
わた	綿	1544
わたくし	私	1428
わたす	渡	1225
わたる	渡	1225
わらう	笑	1472
わらべ	童	1461
わり	割	204
わる	割	204
わるい	悪	785
われ	我	837
われる	割	204
ワン	腕	1038
	湾	1228

STROKE INDEX

1
一 1
乙 25

2
七 2
丁 3
九 26
二 31
人 42
入 150
八 151
刀 177
力 207
十 239
又 264
了 273

3
下 4
三 5
上 6
丈 7
万 8
与 9
丸 17
久 20
及 21
亡 37
凡 170
刃 178
勺 228
千 240
口 276
土 347
士 393
夕 403
大 408
女 423
子 455

寸 499
小 511
山 535
川 548
工 550
己 554
干 572
弓 604
才 853

4
不 10
中 16
丹 18
屯 22
乏 23
五 32
互 33
井 34
介 44
今 45
化 55
仁 56
仏 57
元 141
公 152
六 153
円 159
内 160
冗 163
凶 172
切 179
分 180
刈 183
匁 229
区 233
匹 234
午 241
升 242
厄 257
収 265

双 266
反 267
友 268
予 275
太 409
天 410
夫 411
孔 456
少 512
尺 521
幻 577
引 605
弔 606
心 766
戸 841
手 847
支 932
文 949
斗 950
斤 953
方 957
日 963
月 1002
木 1045
欠 1119
止 1127
比 1146
毛 1147
氏 1148
水 1151
火 1260
父 1286
片 1287
牛 1289
犬 1295
王 1315

5
且 11
丘 12
世 13

丙 14
主 19
以 43
令 46
仕 58
仙 59
他 60
代 61
付 62
兄 142
冊 161
写 164
凹 173
出 174
凸 175
刊 184
加 208
功 209
包 230
北 231
巨 235
半 243
占 250
去 261
弁 262
右 277
古 278
召 279
台 280
可 314
句 315
号 316
史 317
司 318
四 335
囚 336
圧 348
処 398
冬 399
外 404
央 412

失 413
奴 431
尼 522
巧 551
左 552
市 556
布 557
平 573
幼 578
広 581
庁 582
込 675
辺 676
必 767
打 854
払 855
斥 954
旧 964
本 1046
末 1047
未 1048
札 1067
正 1128
母 1143
民 1149
永 1152
氷 1153
汁 1157
犯 1299
玄 1311
玉 1313
甘 1325
生 1327
用 1329
田 1330
甲 1331
申 1332
由 1333
白 1362
皮 1367
皿 1368

目 1376
矛 1392
矢 1393
石 1397
示 1413
礼 1417
穴 1450
立 1459

6
両 15
交 38
会 47
企 48
全 49
仮 63
休 64
仰 65
件 66
仲 67
伝 68
任 69
伐 70
伏 71
光 143
充 144
先 145
兆 146
共 154
再 162
刑 185
列 186
劣 210
旨 232
匠 236
印 251
危 256
争 274
各 281
吉 282
后 283

8

漢字: 乳 事 京 享 舎 依 価 佳 供 使 侍 侮 併 例 免 具 典 画 券 刻 刷 刺 制 到 劾 効 協 卓 参 取 受 叔 呼 味 周 命 和 固 国 垂 坪 夜
番号: 29 30 39 40 51 85 86 87 88 89 90 91 92 93 149 156 157 176 182 190 191 192 193 194 215 216 244 245 246 263 269 270 271 301 302 324 325 326 343 344 350 372 406

漢字: 抑 改 攻 更 肖 肝 条 束 材 杉 村 求 汽 決 沢 沖 沈 没 災 状 狂 男 町 社 私 秀 究 系 良 見 角 言 谷 豆 貝 赤 走 足 身 車 辛 里 臣
番号: 867 933 934 997 1012 1022 1050 1051 1071 1072 1073 1155 1162 1163 1164 1165 1166 1167 1263 1296 1300 1334 1335 1418 1428 1429 1451 1504 1642 1643 1650 1653 1714 1715 1720 1751 1753 1759 1768 1769 1784 1801 1805

漢字: 妊 妨 妙 孝 完 寿 対 局 尿 尾 岐 希 序 床 廷 弟 形 役 花 芸 芳 近 迎 返 防 応 忌 志 忍 忘 快 我 戻 技 抗 抄 折 択 投 把 抜 批 扶
番号: 435 436 437 459 468 501 502 524 525 526 536 559 583 584 598 607 615 620 641 642 643 679 680 681 725 753 768 769 770 771 772 808 837 838 842 857 858 859 860 861 862 863 864 865 866

漢字: 伺 似 住 伸 体 但 低 伯 伴 克 児 兵 冷 初 判 別 利 助 努 労 医 却 即 卵 含 君 告 否 吟 吹 呉 呈 囲 困 図 均 坑 坂 坊 壱 声 売 麦 妥
番号: 76 77 78 79 80 81 82 83 84 147 148 155 166 181 187 188 189 211 212 213 214 237 252 253 254 286 287 288 289 299 300 322 323 340 341 342 368 369 370 371 395 396 397 400 425

漢字: 肌 朱 机 朽 朴 次 死 毎 気 汚 汗 江 池 灰 灯 百 竹 米 糸 缶 羊 羽 老 考 耳 自 至 舌 舟 色 虫 血 行 衣 西
番号: 1021 1049 1068 1069 1070 1120 1133 1144 1150 1158 1159 1160 1161 1261 1262 1363 1471 1493 1503 1564 1565 1570 1576 1577 1582 1587 1589 1591 1592 1599 1604 1611 1613 1619 1638

7

漢字: 乱 亜 来 余 位 何 佐 作
番号: 28 35 36 50 72 73 74 75

漢字: 合 名 吸 叫 吐 向 同 更 因 回 団 在 壮 多 好 如 妃 字 存 安 宇 守 宅 当 尽 州 帆 年 式 弐 芋 芝 巡 迅 忙 成 扱 旬 早 曲 有 肉
番号: 284 285 296 297 298 319 320 321 337 338 339 349 367 394 405 424 432 433 434 457 458 464 465 466 467 500 513 523 549 558 574 602 603 639 640 677 678 807 836 856 965 966 996 1003 1010

9

奇	414	迫	684	東	1053	者	1578	乗	24	姿	429	指	888
奉	415	阻	726	枝	1074	表	1620	亭	41	姻	442	持	889
奔	416	附	727	松	1075	金	1808	係	94	孤	462	拾	890
委	426	邪	754	枢	1076	長	1837	侯	95	宣	475	挑	891
妻	427	邸	755	析	1077	門	1838	俊	96	客	476	故	936
姉	438	並	764	杯	1078	雨	1858	信	97	室	477	政	937
始	439	忠	773	板	1079	青	1871	侵	98	専	503	施	958
姓	440	念	774	枚	1080	非	1873	促	99	封	504	春	971
妹	441	怪	809	林	1081	斉	1874	俗	100	単	516	是	972
学	460	怖	810	枠	1082			便	101	峡	530	星	973
季	461	性	811	欧	1121			保	102	峠	541	昼	974
官	469	所	843	武	1129			冠	165	巻	542	映	985
実	470	房	844	歩	1130			風	171	帥	555	昨	986
宗	471	承	848	殴	1138			削	195	帝	560	昭	987
宙	472	押	868	毒	1145			前	196	幽	561	胃	1016
定	473	拐	869	泳	1168			則	197	度	579	背	1017
宝	474	拡	870	沿	1169			勅	217	建	588	胎	1026
宜	478	拒	871	河	1170			勇	218	弧	600	胆	1027
尚	514	拠	872	泣	1171			南	247	後	609	肺	1028
居	527	拘	873	況	1172			卑	248	待	625	胞	1029
屈	528	招	874	沼	1173			卸	255	律	626	栄	1054
届	529	拙	875	治	1174			厚	258	荒	627	架	1055
岳	537	拓	876	注	1175			厘	259	草	651	査	1056
岩	538	担	877	泥	1176			叙	272	荘	652	柔	1057
岸	539	抽	878	波	1177			咲	303	茶	653	染	1058
岬	540	抵	879	泊	1178			哀	327	逆	654	某	1059
幸	575	拝	880	泌	1179			品	328	送	685	枯	1083
底	585	拍	881	沸	1180			型	353	退	686	柱	1084
店	586	披	882	法	1181			垣	373	追	687	柄	1085
府	587	抹	883	泡	1182			城	374	逃	688	柳	1086
延	599	放	884	油	1183			変	401	迷	689	段	1139
弦	608	易	935	炎	1264			契	417	限	690	泉	1154
往	621	昆	967	炊	1265			奏	418	郊	728	海	1184
径	622	昇	968	炉	1266			威	428	郎	756	活	1185
征	623	昔	969	版	1288					急	757	洪	1186
彼	624	明	970	物	1290					思	775	浄	1187
英	644	服	984	牧	1291					怠	776	津	1188
芽	645	肩	1004	的	1364					怒	777	洗	1189
苦	646	肯	1013	直	1377					悔	778	浅	1190
茎	647	肢	1014	盲	1378					恒	812	洞	1191
若	648	肥	1015	知	1394					恨	813	派	1192
苗	649	肪	1024	祈	1419					括	814	洋	1193
茂	650	果	1052	祉	1420					挟	885	炭	1267
述	682			空	1452					拷	886	為	1274
迷	683			突	1453						887	点	1275

牲 1292　軌 1770　娘 446　兼 765　殉 1136　紋 1522
狭 1301　軍 1771　孫 463　恩 779　殺 1140　翁 1571
狩 1302　重 1802　宴 479　恐 780　泰 1156　耕 1580
独 1303　面 1876　家 480　恵 781　消 1194　耗 1581
珍 1316　革 1877　害 481　息 782　浸 1195　致 1590
甚 1326　音 1879　宮 482　恥 783　浜 1196　航 1593
界 1336　飛 1899　宰 483　恋 784　浮 1197　般 1594
畑 1337　食 1900　宵 484　悦 815　浦 1198　蚊 1605
疫 1348　首 1910　容 485　悟 816　浴 1199　蚕 1606
発 1360　香 1911　射 505　悩 817　流 1200　衰 1622
皆 1365　　　　　将 506　恭 834　涙 1201　被 1631

10

皇 1366　　　　党 515　扇 845　浪 1202　記 1660
盆 1369　倉 52　　展 531　挙 849　烈 1276　訓 1661
看 1379　倹 103　島 543　振 892　特 1293　託 1662
県 1380　個 104　峰 544　捜 893　珠 1317　討 1663
盾 1381　候 105　差 553　挿 894　班 1318　貢 1723
省 1382　借 106　帰 562　捕 895　畝 1338　財 1741
相 1383　修 107　師 563　敏 938　畜 1339　起 1755
冒 1384　値 108　席 564　料 951　畔 1340　軒 1772
研 1398　倒 109　帯 565　旅 959　留 1341　辱 1786
砂 1399　俳 110　庫 589　時 988　疾 1349　酌 1788
砕 1400　倍 111　座 590　書 998　症 1350　酒 1789
祝 1421　俵 112　庭 591　朕 1005　疲 1351　配 1790
神 1422　倣 113　弱 610　朗 1006　病 1352　針 1809
祖 1423　俸 114　従 628　能 1018　益 1370　隻 1849
科 1430　倫 115　徐 629　脅 1019　真 1385　飢 1902
秋 1431　准 167　徒 630　胸 1030　眠 1386　馬 1912
秒 1432　凍 168　荷 655　脂 1031　破 1401　骨 1922
窃 1454　剣 198　華 656　胴 1032　砲 1402　高 1924
紀 1512　剛 199　逝 691　脈 1033　祥 1424　鬼 1926
級 1513　剤 200　造 692　案 1060　称 1433　竜 1930
糾 1514　剖 201　速 693　栽 1061　租 1434

11

紅 1515　勉 219　逐 694　桑 1062　秩 1435
約 1516　匿 238　通 695　桜 1087　秘 1436　乾 27
美 1566　原 260　逓 696　格 1088　既 1470　偽 116
耐 1579　唇 290　途 697　核 1089　笑 1472　偶 117
臭 1588　哲 291　透 698　株 1090　粋 1494　健 118
虐 1600　唐 292　連 699　校 1091　粉 1495　側 119
衷 1621　唆 304　院 729　根 1092　索 1505　停 120
要 1639　員 329　陥 730　桟 1093　素 1506　偵 121
計 1658　埋 375　降 731　栓 1094　紙 1517　偏 122
訂 1659　夏 402　除 732　桃 1095　純 1518　剰 202
貞 1721　娯 443　陣 733　梅 1096　納 1519　副 203
負 1722　娠 444　陛 734　残 1134　紛 1520　勘 220
赴 1754　姫 445　郡 758　殊 1135　紡 1521　動 221

務	222	陰	735	脱	1035	粒	1498	黄	1939	弾	613
啓	293	険	736	脳	1036	累	1508	黒	1940	御	632
喝	305	陳	737	械	1097	経	1523	**12**		循	633
唱	306	陶	738	欲	1122	紺	1524	傘	53	復	634
唯	307	陪	739	殻	1141	細	1525	偉	123	葬	662
商	330	陸	740	液	1203	終	1526	備	124	葉	663
問	331	隆	741	涯	1204	紹	1527	傍	125	落	664
執	351	陵	742	渇	1205	紳	1528	割	204	運	704
基	354	郭	759	渓	1206	組	1529	創	205	過	705
堂	355	郷	760	混	1207	習	1572	勤	223	遇	706
域	376	都	761	済	1208	翌	1573	勝	224	遂	707
培	377	部	762	渋	1209	船	1595	募	225	達	708
堀	378	郵	763	淑	1210	舶	1596	博	249	遅	709
婆	430	悪	785	涉	1211	虚	1601	喜	294	道	710
婚	447	患	786	深	1212	蛍	1607	善	295	遍	711
婦	448	悠	787	清	1213	蛇	1608	喚	308	遊	712
寄	486	惨	818	淡	1214	術	1614	喫	309	階	743
寂	487	情	819	添	1215	袋	1623	喪	332	隅	744
宿	488	惜	820	涼	1216	規	1644	圏	345	随	745
密	489	悼	821	猫	1304	視	1645	報	352	隊	746
尉	507	掛	896	猛	1305	許	1664	堅	356	陽	747
巣	517	掘	897	猟	1306	訟	1665	堕	357	悲	788
崎	545	掲	898	率	1312	設	1666	塁	358	惑	789
崇	546	控	899	球	1319	訪	1667	堪	379	慌	822
崩	547	採	900	現	1320	訳	1668	場	380	惰	823
常	566	捨	901	理	1321	豚	1717	塚	381	愉	824
帳	567	授	902	瓶	1324	貨	1724	堤	382	扉	846
康	592	推	903	産	1328	貫	1725	塔	383	掌	850
庶	593	据	904	異	1342	責	1726	塀	384	握	911
庸	594	接	905	略	1343	貧	1727	奥	419	援	912
強	611	措	906	盛	1371	販	1742	婿	449	換	913
張	612	掃	907	盗	1372	赦	1752	媒	450	揮	914
粛	614	探	908	眼	1387	転	1773	寒	490	提	915
彩	616	排	909	眺	1388	軟	1774	富	491	搭	916
彫	617	描	910	祭	1414	酔	1791	尋	508	揚	917
得	631	救	939	票	1415	釈	1800	尊	509	揺	918
菓	657	教	940	移	1437	野	1803	営	518	敢	942
菊	658	敗	941	窓	1455	釣	1810	就	520	敬	943
菌	659	斜	952	窒	1456	閉	1839	属	532	散	944
菜	660	断	955	章	1460	雪	1859	幅	568	景	975
著	661	旋	960	第	1473	斎	1875	帽	569	暑	976
逸	700	族	961	笛	1474	頂	1882	幾	580	晶	977
週	701	曹	999	符	1475	魚	1931	廃	595	普	978
進	702	望	1007	粗	1496	鳥	1934	廊	596	暁	989
逮	703	脚	1034	粘	1497	麻	1938			晴	990

漢字	番号	漢字	番号	漢字	番号	漢字	番号	漢字	番号	漢字	番号
試	1680	源	1231	嫁	451	費	1732	短	1395	晩	991
詩	1681	溝	1232	嫌	452	貿	1733	硬	1403	最	1000
詳	1682	準	1233	寛	492	貯	1743	硝	1404	替	1001
誠	1683	滞	1234	寝	493	越	1756	硫	1405	期	1008
話	1684	滝	1235	幕	570	超	1757	税	1438	朝	1009
豊	1716	漠	1236	幹	576	距	1760	程	1439	脹	1037
資	1734	滅	1237	廉	597	軽	1775	童	1461	腕	1038
賃	1735	溶	1238	微	635	軸	1776	筋	1476	森	1063
賊	1744	煙	1269	蒸	665	酢	1792	策	1477	棺	1098
賄	1745	煩	1270	蓄	666	量	1804	答	1478	棋	1099
跡	1761	照	1281	違	713	鈍	1811	等	1479	極	1100
践	1762	献	1297	遠	714	開	1840	筒	1480	検	1101
跳	1763	猿	1308	遣	715	間	1841	筆	1481	植	1102
路	1764	痴	1356	隔	748	閑	1842	粧	1499	棚	1103
較	1777	盟	1373	愛	790	雇	1850	紫	1507	棟	1104
載	1778	睡	1389	意	791	集	1851	絵	1530	棒	1105
辞	1785	督	1390	感	792	雄	1852	給	1531	款	1123
農	1787	碁	1406	愚	793	雲	1860	結	1532	欺	1124
酬	1793	禁	1416	慈	794	雰	1861	絞	1532	殖	1137
酪	1794	禍	1425	愁	795	項	1883	絶	1534	温	1217
鉛	1812	禅	1426	想	796	順	1884	統	1535	渦	1218
鉱	1813	福	1427	慨	825	飲	1903	絡	1536	減	1219
鉄	1814	稚	1440	慎	826	飯	1904	着	1567	湖	1220
鉢	1815	罪	1464	戦	839	歯	1942	蛮	1609	港	1221
鈴	1816	署	1465	携	919			衆	1612	滋	1222
雅	1853	置	1466	搾	920	**13**		街	1615	湿	1223
電	1862	節	1482	摂	921	傾	126	裁	1624	測	1224
雷	1863	継	1537	損	922	傑	127	装	1625	渡	1225
零	1864	絹	1538	搬	923	催	128	裂	1626	湯	1226
靴	1878	続	1539	数	945	債	129	補	1632	満	1227
頑	1885	義	1568	新	956	傷	130	裕	1633	湾	1228
頒	1886	群	1569	暗	992	僧	131	覚	1646	焼	1268
預	1887	聖	1583	暇	993	働	132	詠	1669	煮	1277
飼	1905	艇	1597	暖	994	勧	226	詐	1670	焦	1278
飾	1906	虜	1602	腸	1039	勢	227	詞	1671	然	1279
飽	1907	膚	1603	腹	1040	嘆	310	証	1672	無	1280
鼓	1944	裏	1627	腰	1041	嗣	333	詔	1673	猶	1307
14		褐	1634	楽	1064	園	346	診	1674	琴	1322
像	133	裸	1635	棄	1065	塑	359	訴	1675	畳	1344
僕	134	解	1651	業	1066	塗	360	評	1676	番	1345
僚	135	触	1652	楼	1106	墓	361	象	1718	疎	1346
塾	362	誉	1654	歳	1131	塩	385	賀	1728	痛	1353
墨	363	該	1677	殿	1142	塊	386	貴	1729	痘	1354
境	387	詰	1678	滑	1229	夢	407	貸	1730	痢	1355
		誇	1679	漢	1230	奨	420	買	1731	登	1361

増	388	碑	1408	需	1865	敵	946	談	1698	隣	752
奪	421	穀	1441	静	1872	敷	947	調	1699	憩	802
嫡	453	種	1442	領	1888	暫	981	論	1700	憲	803
寡	494	稲	1443	駅	1915	暴	982	賛	1736	憶	831
察	495	端	1462	駆	1916	膚	1020	質	1737	懐	832
寧	496	罰	1467	駄	1917	横	1111	賞	1738	憾	833
層	533	箇	1483	髮	1925	権	1112	賓	1739	操	928
彰	618	管	1484	魂	1927	槽	1113	賜	1746	擁	929
徴	636	算	1485	鳴	1935	標	1114	賠	1747	整	948
徳	637	精	1500	鼻	1945	歓	1126	賦	1748	曇	983
遮	716	維	1540			潟	1248	趣	1758	膨	1043
遭	717	綱	1541	**15**		潔	1249	踏	1766	機	1115
適	718	緒	1542	舗	54	潤	1250	輝	1779	橋	1116
隠	749	総	1543	億	136	潜	1251	輩	1780	樹	1117
際	750	綿	1544	儀	137	潮	1252	輪	1781	激	1254
障	751	網	1545	劇	206	澄	1253	舞	1807	濁	1255
態	797	緑	1546	嘱	311	熟	1282	鋭	1823	濃	1256
慣	827	練	1547	噴	312	熱	1283	鋳	1824	燃	1271
憎	828	聞	1584	器	334	勲	1284	閲	1846	獣	1298
慢	829	製	1628	墜	364	監	1374	震	1866	獲	1310
慕	835	複	1636	墳	389	盤	1375	霊	1867	磨	1410
摘	924	誓	1655	審	497	確	1409	養	1901	穏	1447
旗	962	語	1685	寮	498	稼	1444	餓	1908	積	1448
暮	979	誤	1686	導	510	稿	1445	駐	1918	築	1488
曆	980	誌	1687	履	534	穂	1446	魅	1928	篤	1489
腐	1011	説	1688	幣	571	窮	1457	默	1941	糖	1501
膜	1042	読	1689	弊	601	窯	1458			繁	1510
概	1107	認	1690	影	619	罷	1468	**16**		緯	1554
構	1108	誘	1691	徹	638	箱	1486	儒	138	縛	1555
模	1109	豪	1719	蔵	667	範	1487	興	158	縦	1556
様	1110	踊	1765	遺	719	緊	1509	凝	169	縫	1557
歌	1125	酵	1795	遵	720	縁	1548	墾	365	融	1610
歷	1132	酷	1796	選	721	緩	1549	壁	366	衛	1617
演	1239	酸	1797	遷	722	縄	1550	壊	390	衡	1618
漁	1240	銀	1817	慰	798	線	1551	壌	391	親	1647
漆	1241	銃	1818	慶	799	締	1552	壇	392	諮	1701
漸	1242	銭	1819	憂	800	編	1553	奮	422	謀	1702
漬	1243	銑	1820	慮	801	衝	1616	嬢	454	諭	1703
滴	1244	銅	1821	憤	830	褒	1629	薫	668	謡	1704
漂	1245	銘	1822	戯	840	謁	1692	薪	669	賢	1740
漫	1246	閣	1843	撃	851	課	1693	薦	670	輸	1782
漏	1247	関	1844	摩	852	諸	1694	薄	671	鋼	1825
獄	1309	閥	1845	撮	925	請	1695	薬	672	錯	1826
疑	1347	雌	1854	撤	926	諾	1696	還	723	錠	1827
磁	1407	雑	1855	撲	927	誕	1697	避	724	錘	1828

錬	1829	礁	1411	**18**		臨	1806	簿	1491	護	1713
録	1830	縮	1558			鎖	1832	繰	1563	醸	1799
隷	1848	績	1559	藩	673	鎮	1833	覇	1641	鐘	1835
頭	1889	繊	1560	懲	805	闘	1847	警	1657	響	1881
頼	1890	翼	1574	曜	995	難	1856	識	1709	騰	1913
館	1909	聴	1585	濫	1258	離	1857	譜	1710	**21**	
17		覧	1648	癖	1358	額	1892	鏡	1834		
償	139	膳	1656	癒	1359	顔	1893	霧	1869	艦	1598
優	140	謹	1705	瞬	1391	顕	1894	韻	1880	躍	1767
嚇	313	謙	1706	礎	1412	題	1895	願	1897	露	1870
厳	519	講	1707	穫	1449	類	1896	髄	1923	顧	1898
懇	804	謝	1708	簡	1490	騎	1919	鯨	1933	魔	1929
擬	930	購	1749	糧	1502	験	1920	鶏	1936	**22**	
擦	931	轄	1783	繭	1511	騒	1921	麗	1937		
濯	1257	醜	1798	織	1561	**19**		**20**		襲	1630
燥	1272	鍛	1831	繕	1562					驚	1914
爵	1285	霜	1868	翻	1575	藻	674	懸	806	**23**	
犠	1294	頻	1891	職	1586	臓	1044	欄	1118		
環	1323	鮮	1932	襟	1637	瀬	1259	競	1463	鑑	1836
療	1357	齢	1943	覆	1640	爆	1273	籍	1492		
矯	1396			観	1649	璽	1314	議	1711		
				贈	1750	羅	1469	譲	1712		

（新装版）常用漢英熟語辞典
Kodansha's Essential Kanji Dictionary

2002年5月　第1刷発行
2005年6月　第5刷発行

印刷・製本所　凸版印刷株式会社

編　者　講談社インターナショナル株式会社
発行者　畑野文夫
発行所　講談社インターナショナル株式会社
〒112-8652　東京都文京区音羽1-17-14
電話　03-3944-6493（編集部）
　　　03-3944-6492（営業部・業務部）
ホームページ　www.kodansha-intl.com

落丁本・乱丁本は購入書店名を明記のうえ、小社業務部宛にお送りください。送料小社負担にてお取替えします。本書の無断複写（コピー）、転載は著作権法の例外を除き、禁じられています。

定価はカバーに表示してあります。

© 講談社インターナショナル株式会社 2002
Printed in Japan
ISBN 4-7700-2891-1

RADICAL CHART

1	一 1	丨 17	丶 19	丿 22	乙 24	乚 25	亅 26
2	二 28	亠 31	人 33	𠆢 37	亻 42	儿 77	入 82	八 83
冂 88	冖 93	冫 94	几 95	凵 97	刀 100	刂 105	力 116	勹 125
匕 126	匚 127	十 128	卜 134	卩 134	㔾 136	厂 136	厶 139	又 141
了 146	勹 147	マ 147	3	口 149	囗 173	土 179	士 195	夂 198
夕 201	大 205	女 215	子 224	宀 228	寸 244	小 249	𭕄 251	灬 253
尢 255	尸 256	山 260	川 263	工 264	己 266	巾 267	干 273	幺 276
广 278	廴 283	廾 285	弋 285	弓 286	彐 290	彡 291	彳 292	艹 301
辶 313	阝 338	阝 348	䒑 351	忄 370	扌 389	犭 572	氵 516
4	心 353	小 379	戈 379	戶 383	手 385	支 417	攵 418	文 427
斗 429	斤 430	方 433	日 436	曰 450	月 453	月(肉) 458	木 468	欠 496
止 499	歹 502	殳 505	毋 507	比 508	毛 509	氏 509	气 511	水 512
火 553	灬 558	灬 565	父 566	片 566	牛 567	犬 571	王 578	衤 623